*The Routledge Encyclopedia of Film Theory* is an international reference work representing the essential ideas and concepts at the centre of film theory from the beginning of the twentieth century to the beginning of the twenty-first.

When first encountering film theory, students are often confronted with a dense, interlocking set of texts full of arcane terminology, inexact formulations, sliding definitions, and abstract generalities. *The Routledge Encyclopedia of Film Theory* challenges these first impressions by aiming to make film theory accessible and open to new readers.

Edward Branigan and Warren Buckland have commissioned over 50 scholars from around the globe to address the difficult formulations and propositions in each theory by reducing these difficult formulations to straightforward propositions.

The result is a highly accessible volume that clearly defines, and analyses step by step, many of the fundamental concepts in film theory, ranging from familiar concepts such as apparatus, gaze, genre, and identification to less well-known and understood, but equally important, concepts such as Alain Badiou's inaesthetics, Gilles Deleuze's time-image, and Jean-Luc Nancy's evidence.

*The Routledge Encyclopedia of Film Theory* is an ideal reference book for undergraduates of film studies, as well as graduate students new to the discipline. Additional resources are available via www.routledge.com/9780415781800.

**Edward Branigan** is Professor Emeritus in the Department of Film and Media Studies at the University of California, Santa Barbara. He is the author of *Projecting a Camera: Language-Games in Film Theory* (2006), *Narrative Comprehension and Film* (1992), and *Point of View in the Cinema: A Theory of Narration and Subjectivity in Classical Film* (1984). With Charles Wolfe, he is the general editor of the American Film Institute Film Readers series.

**Warren Buckland** is Reader in Film Studies at Oxford Brookes University. His areas of research include film theory (*Film Theory: Rational Reconstructions*, 2012, and *The Cognitive Semiotics of Film*, 2000) and film narratology (*Puzzle Films: Complex Storytelling in Contemporary Cinema*, 2009, and *Hollywood Puzzle Films*, 2014). He is editor of the quarterly journal the *New Review of Film and Television Studies*.

'*The Routledge Encyclopedia of Film Theory* is an astonishing achievement. Comprehensive – organized around no fewer than 83 distinct concepts – and authored by recognized specialists, it is sure to establish itself as a great teaching resource. Entries are concise and informative, written in clear language, which makes them especially helpful to students coming to film theory for the first time and seeking a user-friendly, but focused guide. The editors are to be highly commended for the way they cross-list entries and map the connections between them.'

Thomas Elsaesser, *Professor Emeritus, University of Amsterdam*

'Branigan and Buckland's *Encyclopedia of Film Theory* is an extraordinary accomplishment. The entries present with clarity and order concepts from the entire history of film theory, often revealing surprising connections and filiations among ideas and authors. In the crowded field of theory overviews, this will be the essential reference work for many years to come for both beginning and advanced researchers.'

D. N. Rodowick, *Glen A. Lloyd Distinguished Service Professor in Cinema and Media Studies, University of Chicago*

'*The Routledge Encyclopedia of Film Theory* is both a wonderful map and intriguing maze. The encyclopedia retraces the history of film theory through more than eighty entries. Each reconstructs a debate, but also offers an up-dated perspective. My advice to the reader: (1) investigate your question; (2) then proceed randomly, as if you were surfing the Internet; (3) make connections be as strange as possible; (4) challenge the path from light to dark suggested by Branigan in the Epilogue, and disrupt it by finding new ways to make film live. Above all, savour the reading: it brings to light important chapters in the history of thought, and rediscovers what we thought we knew and what we think now.'

Francesco Casetti, *Professor, Film Studies Program, Yale University*

# THE ROUTLEDGE
# ENCYCLOPEDIA
# OF FILM THEORY

*Edited by*
*Edward Branigan and Warren Buckland*

Routledge
Taylor & Francis Group

LONDON AND NEW YORK

# CONTENTS

# LIST OF CONTRIBUTORS

**Richard Allen**
*Professor and Chair of Cinema Studies, Department of Cinema Studies,*
*   Tisch School of the Arts, New York University*
Identification, theory of

**Dudley Andrew**
*Professor of Film and Comparative Literature, Yale University*
Ontology of the photographic image

**Henry Bacon**
*Professor of Film and Television Studies, University of Helsinki, Finland*
Representation

**Brian Bergen-Aurand**
*Assistant Professor of English and Film, Nanyang Technological University, Singapore*
Ethics; Queer theory/queer cinema

**Marcelline Block**
*PhD candidate, Princeton University*
Fantasy and spectatorship; Gaze theory

**Peter J. Bloom**
*Associate Professor, Department of Film and Media Studies, University of California, Santa Barbara*
Sound theory; Voice

**Edward Branigan**
*Professor Emeritus, Department of Film and Media Studies, University of California, Santa Barbara*
Apparatus theory (Plato)

**William Brown**
*Senior Lecturer in Film, University of Roehampton, London*
Digital cinema; Minor cinema; Movement-image; Time-image

**Warren Buckland**
*Reader in Film Studies, Oxford Brookes University*
Attraction; Auteur theory; Contemporary film theory; Interface; Semiotics of film; Structural/
   materialist film

**Colin Burnett**
*Assistant Professor in the Film and Media Studies Program, Washington University, St. Louis*
Perspectivism versus realism

**Catherine Constable**
*Associate Professor in the Department of Film and Television Studies, University of Warwick*
Postmodern cinema

**Sean Cubitt**
*Professor of Film and Television, Goldsmiths, University of London*
Ideology, cinema and; Suture

**Chris Dzialo**
*Program Administrator of the Global Centers for Health and Development at the Annenberg Norman Lear Center, University of Southern California*
Reception theory

**Ruggero Eugeni**
*Professor of Media Semiotics, Università Cattolica del Sacro Cuore, Milano*
Enunciation, film and; Rhetoric, film and

**Pete Falconer**
*Lecturer in Film, University of Bristol*
Genre theory

**Martin Flanagan**
*Independent Scholar*
Dialogism

**Scott Higgins**
*Associate Professor of Film Studies, Wesleyan University*
Art, film as

**Laurent Jullier**
*IRCAV, Sorbonne Nouvelle, Paris; IECA, Université de Lorraine, Nancy*
Illusion; Specificity, medium II

**Russell J.A. Kilbourn**
*Associate Professor, English and Film Studies, Wilfrid Laurier University, Waterloo, Ontario*
Memory and film

**Angelos Koutsourakis**
*Postdoctoral Research Fellow, Centre for Modernism Studies, University of New South Wales*
Brecht and film; Symptomatic reading

**Allan Langdale**
*Independent Scholar*
Attention

**Martin Lefebvre**
*Professor and Concordia University Research Chair in Film Studies, Concordia University*
Symbol and analogon (Mitry)

**Kevin McDonald**
*Adjunct Instructor, Department of Communication Studies, California State University, Northridge*
Anglo-American film theory

**Laura McMahon**
*College Lecturer in French, Gonville and Caius College, Cambridge*
Evidence (Nancy)

**Stephen Mamber**
*Professor, University of California, Los Angeles*
Cinematic movement

**Laura U. Marks**
*Dena Wosk University Professor, School for the Contemporary Arts, Simon Fraser University*
Pixel/cut/vector

**Adrian Martin**
*Professor of Film Studies, Goethe University, Frankfurt*
*Mise en scène*

**Allen Meek**
*Senior Lecturer, Massey University, New Zealand*
Trauma and cinema

**John Mullarkey**
*Professor of Film and Television Studies, School of Performance and Screen Studies, Kingston University, London*
Inaesthetics

**Ted Nannicelli**
*Lecturer in Film and Television Studies, School of English, Media Studies and Art History, University of Queensland, Australia*
Formalist theories of film

**Karla Oeler**
*Associate Professor, Department of Film and Media Studies, Emory University*
Poetic cinema

**Diana Pozo**
*PhD Candidate in Film and Media Studies, University of California, Santa Barbara*
Feminist film theory, core concepts; Feminist film theory, history of

**Brian Price**
*Associate Professor of Film and Visual Studies, University of Toronto*
Concept; Specificity, medium I

**Christian Quendler**
*Associate Professor, Department of American Studies, University of Innsbruck*
Apparatus theory (Baudry); Blending and film theory; Camera

**Daniel Reynolds**
*Assistant Professor, Department of Film and Media Studies, Emory University*
Cognitive film theory; Gaming and film theory

**Richard Rushton**
*Senior Lecturer in Film, Lancaster University*
Counter-cinema; Imaginary signifier

**Anne Rutherford**
*Senior Lecturer, Cinema Studies, School of Humanities and Communication Arts, University of Western Sydney*
Mimetic innervation

**Bhaskar Sarkar**
*Associate Professor, Department of Film and Media Studies, University of California, Santa Barbara*
Third World cinema

**Jeff Scheible**
*Banting Postdoctoral Fellow, Concordia University*
Depth of field; Long take

**Philipp Schmerheim**
*University Lecturer, Faculty of Linguistics and Literary Studies, University of Bremen, Germany, and Adjunct Lecturer at the Department of Philosophy, University of Amsterdam*
Scepticism

**Robert Sinnerbrink**
*Senior Lecturer in Philosophy, Macquarie University, Sydney*
Film-philosophy

**David Sorfa**
*Senior Lecturer in Film Studies, University of Edinburgh*
Phenomenology and film

**Jane Stadler**
*Associate Professor, School of English, Media Studies and Art History, University of Queensland*
Affect, film and; Emotion, film and

**Melinda Szaloky**
*Independent Scholar*
Close-up

**Paul Taberham**
*PhD student, University of Kent*
Seeing/perceiving

**Eleftheria Thanouli**
*Assistant Professor in Film Theory, Aristotle University of Thessaloniki*
Diegesis; Narration

**Temenuga Trifonova**
*Associate Professor of Cinema and Media Studies, York University, Toronto*
European film theory; Redemption (Kracauer)

**Yuri Tsivian**
*William Colvin Professor, University of Chicago*
Montage theory I (Hollywood continuity); Montage theory II (Soviet avant-garde)

**Malcolm Turvey**
*Teaches at Sarah Lawrence College*
Classical film theory; Modernism versus realism

**Margrethe Bruun Vaage**
*Lecturer, University of Kent*
Imagined observer hypothesis; Point of view

**Hunter Vaughan**
*Assistant Professor, Oakland University*
Film fable (Rancière); 'Ordinary man of cinema' (Schefer)

**Liz Watkins**
*Lecturer, University of Leeds*
Excess, cinematic

**Charles Wolfe**
*Professor, Department of Film and Media Studies, University of California, Santa Barbara*
Documentary theory

**James Zborowski**
*Lecturer in Film and Television Studies, University of Hull*
Classic realist text

# LIST OF ENTRIES A–Z

# ACKNOWLEDGEMENTS

The editors greatly appreciate the diligence of the contributors to this encyclopedia. Their talent is evident on every page. We have also been exceptionally well served by the editorial and production staff at Routledge: Natalie Foster, Publisher, has guided and encouraged us throughout, along with the hard-working crew of Daniel Bourner, Avril Ehrlich, Hamish Ironside, Sheni Kruger, Asha Pearse, Fintan Power, and Andrew Watts. Thomas Felder deserves special thanks for generating the cluster map that appears on the cover using Gephi open source software.

Edward Branigan wishes to especially thank his co-editor, Warren Buckland, for inviting him to participate in this enterprise. Warren's friendship has been as invaluable as his insight and intelligence. Always, and in all ways, Edward is grateful to his sons, Alex, Evan, Liam, and Nicholas, for their loving support.

Warren Buckland wishes to thank Edward Branigan for patiently developing this project with him over a five-year period, which began with the conjuring of a list of entries in an Oxford pub in the summer of 2009.

Warren's dedication is to his brother, Jason. Edward dedicates this book to his parents, Evelyn and Henry Odell, as well as to those who fought at Khe Sanh and Lang Vei, in Vietnam, while he was nearby. Those wishing to know more might start with the books *Valley of Decision: The Siege of Khe Sanh* by John Prados and Ray W. Stubbe and *A Patch of Ground: Khe Sanh Remembered* by Michael Archer.

Edward Branigan
Warren Buckland
July 2013

# INTRODUCTION (I)

## The rationale behind the encyclopedia

*Warren Buckland*

The difference between a novice and a professional researcher is that the novice sees research simply as an exercise in information gathering. Too many students in the humanities just gather information when writing. A more fundamental activity in the humanities is the pursuit of understanding. In their discussion of intellectual virtues, R.C. Roberts and W.J. Wood locate 'understanding' in the practice of reading – the need to turn students into careful, critical readers. Commenting on Locke's *Of the Conduct of the Understanding*, they argue that excellent reading

> is digestion, critical assessment, and systematic assimilation of what is read to a coherent view of things ... knowledge is not just a collection of facts; [the good reader] critically insists on good reasons for affirming what he affirms and denying what he denies. He does not just seek support for his prejudices but is open to learning, willing to take a critical look at his own preexisting views. Insofar as tutoring can teach these things in the course of a curriculum of reading, it is not just skill purveyance, but an education, a nurturing in the intellectual virtues.
>
> (Roberts and Wood 2007, 123)

When first encountering film theory, students are confronted with and confounded by a dense, interlocking set of texts full of arcane terminology, inexact formulations, sliding definitions, and abstract generalities (I give an example below). Students find it difficult to assimilate film theory concepts into their pre-existing understanding. Our aim in this *Routledge Encyclopedia of Film Theory* is to guide novice readers through the dense, interlocking concepts that form the core education in film theory. Our guidance, which is aimed at facilitating the novice's reading of film theory, involves a threefold process:

(1) to make explicit the implicit assumptions and presuppositions behind each film theory by defining and contextualizing the theory's terminology;
(2) to rewrite and clarify the inexact and variant formulations; and
(3) to avoid abstract generalities.

The major technique the editors encouraged contributors to employ throughout the encyclopedia was to avoid making broad, sweeping summaries of huge amounts of information. Novice readers are unable to grasp the generalities necessarily found in sweeping and schematic summaries. Instead, the editors asked contributors to anchor and re-anchor their discussion in a few well-known (canonical) texts. To a major extent, each entry is grounded in a comprehensive discussion of just *one* or *two* pieces of work (essays, books), followed by a short critique or development of that work, usually found in another essay or book (in one instance we asked an author, Adrian Martin, to summarize his own canonical text; see the entry on MISE EN SCÈNE). Edward Branigan mentions in his Introduction that the focus of this encyclopedia on specific essays and books results in an assessment of 'a concept within a specific moment of its use, at a moment when a specific argument is being aggressively generated to serve a project'. These essays and books were therefore chosen carefully, since in many cases they represent an entire tradition of thought: they are parts that stand in for the whole, a rhetorical move based on the recognition that the whole cannot be adequately represented. The exceptions to this technique are a series of 'survey entries' that act to provide context for the entries that examine specific concepts (I discuss these survey entries at the end of this Introduction).

A second technique we employed to make film theory accessible was to ask contributors to forthrightly address the difficult formulations and propositions in a theory, and to reduce these difficult formulations to straightforward propositions. While not proposing to reduce film theory to the 'basic' or 'elementary' statements of logical positivism, we none-theless asked contributors to avoid making vague metaphysical statements. This is a demanding task and can only be carried out by experts who already know the theories well. Many writers make film theory unnecessarily complex because they do not under-stand it adequately (a little knowledge of something large can be a dangerous thing). We therefore chose scholars who were sufficiently versed in the film theory concepts they undertook to clarify.

A third technique involved contributors discussing their selected texts in some detail using ordinary vocabulary and short sentences. Schopenhauer said that 'an obscure or bad style means a dull and confused brain'. We went back to basics, offering our contributors advice from Strunk and White's influential *The Elements of Style*: 'Use definite, specific, and concrete language'; 'use the active voice'; 'omit needless words'; 'do not construct awkward adverbs' – plus advice from Gowers's equally influential *Complete Plain Words*: 'Be simple, be short, be human'; 'be correct'; 'choose the precise word'.

For example, my entry on CONTEMPORARY FILM THEORY was limited to commentary on a single but influential 15-page essay by Stephen Heath ('On Screen, in Frame: Film and Ideology'), followed by an outline of critiques Heath received (from David Rodowick, David Bordwell, and Noël Carroll). By offering a careful summary and clarification of Heath's seminal essay, the entry presents to the novice reader the core information relating to contemporary film theory, defines the necessary terms and concepts using definite, specific, and concrete language, and untangles Heath's difficult propositions to better understand contemporary film theory's agenda. Students can then use this explica-tion to read and understand other seminal essays and critiques of contemporary film theory.

Of course, no reference book written by over 50 authors will be completely uniform in its language and style; nonetheless, authors generally followed and interpreted the same advice in their own way. A few did query the advice of Strunk and White, and Gowers, arguing that some concepts are complex for they exceed our common sense understanding. And I encountered difficulties in adhering to this advice when writing a particularly demanding entry devoted to Slavoj Žižek's concept of the 'interface'. But Strunk, White, and Gowers served as a useful point on the horizon to aim at when writing such difficult entries.

The encyclopedia contains 83 entries on the essential ideas and concepts at the centre of film theory from the beginning of the twentieth century to the beginning of the twenty-first. These ideas and concepts constitute the core knowledge of film theory: familiar concepts such as apparatus, classic realist text, diegesis, enunciation, gaze, genre, ideology, and identification, combined with less well-known but, in our opinion, equally important concepts such as pixel/cut/vector, mimetic innervation, Alain Badiou's concept of inaesthetics, and Jean-Luc Nancy's concept of evidence. A few entries are, unfortunately, missing because some authors were unable to deliver, and we were not able to re-commission those entries without delaying the publication of the encyclopedia further.

Each entry, limited to the explication of a few key texts, as mentioned above, is a mini-essay ranging from 2,000 to 4,000 words. Because the entries are narrowly focused, most contributors have included a list of further reading. Most entries are cross-referenced (with the cross-referenced terms in SMALL CAPS) – for concepts are not isolated chunks of knowledge and information, but are interrelated in a web of knowledge. That web has become increasingly complex, technical, and specialized, with film scholars working in great depth on narrowly focused issues. We represent this web (along with additional concepts and names that appear within the entries) in a cluster map on the book's cover. (The cluster map can be viewed in full at www.routledge.com/9780415781800.) The large names and circles represent  the actual 83 entries in the encyclopedia, and the lines between them represent conceptual links. The smaller circles and names, and their fainter lines, represent secondary concepts (found within the entries) and their conceptual links – to each other and to the main concepts. This map is not, therefore, a general map of film theory *per se*, but of film theory as represented in this particular encyclopedia (with thanks to Thomas Felder for generating the map).

This encyclopedia attempts to overcome two problems that hinder students' comprehension of film theory as an academic discipline: it is becoming less accessible and more fragmented. This volume is designed to be a reference book for undergraduates in film studies as well as for graduate students new to the discipline. One of the volume's strongest selling points is an ability to present a notoriously arcane discipline in straightforward, non-mystifying terms.

This is where the encyclopedia overcomes the weaknesses of similar books. *The Critical Dictionary of Film and Television Theory* (edited by Roberta Pearson and Philip Simpson, 2000) is at times difficult to read. It is a useful and informative handbook for scholars *already familiar* with film theory but, for this reason, it may put off the novice coming to film theory for the first time. *Cinema Studies: The Key Concepts* (Susan Hayward, 2006) is much broader (it is not limited to film theory, but includes film studies concepts). It is aimed at an undergraduate audience, but is well known for being uneven. Some entries – such as 'feminist film theory' – are clear and detailed. Others, such as the one on 'subjective camera', are too short to be of use to students. Other entries are dense and uninviting. For example, the discussion of 'suture' opens with a feminist polemic (the entry could have ended on this). It then begins the discussion of suture with the following sentence:

> Lacan used the term *suture* to signify the relationship between the conscious and the unconscious which, in turn, he perceived as an uneasy conjunction between what he terms the Imaginary and the Symbolic orders—two orders which, after infancy, are always co-present.
>
> (Hayward 2006, 355)

This opening sentence is too long, complex and dense; it tries to say everything at once by piling on the concepts instead of explaining them. The opening, and the entry as a whole, accumulates a series of words and elliptical phrases without really defining the main concept. This accumulation of words simply circles around the main concept and ends up alienating the novice reader, for it does not relate and map out each facet of this complex idea. In subsequent paragraphs, the entry continues to pile on the concepts (mirror phase, pre-Oedipal, pure *jouissance*, narcissism, Oedipus complex, and the Other), offering only cursory definitions, before quickly moving on to the next set of concepts. (This indirect, roundabout activity – defining concepts in passing as if to rush towards something else that is more important though never reached – is a fundamental problem that we have tried to avoid.)

The entry ends the way it began (355–6):

> The Symbolic now becomes the Other (which Lacan signifies with a capital 'O'). The subject represents itself in the field of the Other (language)—capital 'O' because the Law of the Father. To this first sense of fragmentation comes another, felt by the fact that the subject can never fully be represented in speech since speech cannot reflect the unconscious (the repressed, unspeakable desire for the mother or the father). The subject, in representing itself, can only do so at the cost of division (conscious/unconscious; self/Other). The difference for the two sexes is of course the degree of division or fragmentation.

This is a jumble of concepts that requires unpacking and more careful exposition. The author reifies, isolates, and decontextualizes the concepts; she gives the impression of randomly plucking them out of the air, especially fragments such as: 'capital "O" because the Law of the Father' and 'the unconscious (the repressed, unspeakable desire for the mother or the father)'. In fact, this entry on 'suture' reads like a first draft, a series of notes hastily jotted down. We have endeavoured to avoid such a writing style by using the techniques mentioned above: employing straightforward, clear language, and grounding the discussion in a few specific texts. Sean Cubitt's entry on SUTURE follows these guidelines and offers an alternative account of this notoriously difficult concept.

The majority of entries in this encyclopedia conform to the threefold format spelled out above, and limit their discussion to one or two canonical film theory texts. But in a number of entries – most notably ANGLO-AMERICAN FILM THEORY, APPARATUS THEORY (PLATO), BLENDING, CONCEPT, EUROPEAN FILM THEORY, FEMINIST FILM THEORY (both entries: CORE CONCEPTS and HISTORY OF), ILLUSION, MONTAGE (I and II), SPECIFICITY II, and THIRD WORLD CINEMA – the authors have provided a broader overview of the concept and, at times, have developed the concepts in new directions. These entries are meant to contextualize the more narrowly focused entries (the majority of the encyclopedia), thereby complementing them. Edward Branigan's Introduction also offers a broad, comprehensive presentation, analysis, and development of film theory from the perspective of the philosophy of Ludwig Wittgenstein.

## Works cited

Gowers, Ernest. 1987. *The Complete Plain Words*. 3rd edition. Harmondsworth: Penguin.
Hayward, Susan. 2006. *Cinema Studies: The Key Concepts*. 3rd edition. London: Routledge.

Pearson, Roberta, and Philip Simpson, eds. 2000. *The Critical Dictionary of Film and Television Theory*. London: Routledge.

Roberts, Robert C., and W. Jay Wood. 2007. *Intellectual Virtues: An Essay in Regulative Epistemology*. Oxford: Clarendon Press.

Strunk, William, and E.B. White. 1999. *The Elements of Style*. 4th edition. London: Longman.

# INTRODUCTION (II)

## Concept and theory

*Edward Branigan*

### List of sections in this essay

Concepts have no ontology
Film as language
Language is theory-laden
Unobservables
Our craving for generality
Radial concepts
Concepts are always intermediate
Relativism and relational-ism
Future film theories
Concept and theory as practices of language
Notes

> We feel as if we had to *see right into* phenomena: yet our investigation is directed not towards *phenomena*, but rather, as one might say, towards the '*possibilities*' of phenomena. What that means is that we call to mind the *kinds of statement* that we make about phenomena ... Our inquiry is therefore a grammatical one.[1]
>
> Ludwig Wittgenstein

> Indeed, when we look into ourselves as we do philosophy, we often get to see just such a [mental] picture. Virtually a pictorial representation of our grammar. Not facts; but, as it were, illustrated turns of speech.[2]
>
> Ludwig Wittgenstein

> To understand a concept, it is necessary to grasp not merely the meanings of the terms used to express it, but also the range of things that can be done with it ... [T]here can be no histories of concepts as such; there can only be histories of their uses in argument.[3]
>
> Quentin Skinner

### Concepts have no ontology

Wittgenstein asserts that philosophical investigations must be 'grammatical,' that is, based on analysing our use of language within specific contexts, interpretive communities, and pragmatic environments. We select certain language-games in daily life from among many ways of talking and taking a measure of our world. Each language-game makes use of a distinctive grammar or conceptual scheme to achieve a goal. Wittgenstein's target is the operation of ordinary language – weighing the various kinds of concepts and linked statements that are available for characterizing phenomena. He does not seek to develop an invented, more exacting language that relies on a specialized vocabulary. The language-games we need – tangled though they may be – are already in front of us.

Similarly, I believe that an investigation of film-theoretical discourse must focus on the linguistic and figurative design of concepts and arguments that align with specific social and institutional practices. Theoretical concepts are created out of ordinary language-games that bring into play rules and norms for talking about contexts of use. Which theoretical language-game is in force on a particular occasion? There is no single, timeless language, logic, or calculus that can anchor a concept apart from the possibilities of changing goals and usage.

This amounts to saying that a theoretical concept has no final, singular essence.[4] A concept is an instrument employed to take action. Though it may appear static and noun-like or even super-noun-like, a concept should be seen as a gerund – a verbal noun with the features of tense, voice, and the ability to act upon objects. To understand a concept, one must understand its actions within arguments aimed at objects.

For example, the word 'death' can be made to move from a simple name for a bodily state to a film theory concept that functions as a compact argument holding together incompatible claims, making of inanimate cinema something paradoxically (once, or once again) alive (see the epilogue on pp. 494–504). A second example: when the word 'camera' appears in a description, it typically refers not to a physical camera with a weight and serial number, but instead functions as a disguised *compression* of many ideas that point towards human perception and mobility: eye, vision, attention, scanning, seeing a scene, envisioning. The camera-concept may be pushed still further into consciousness through methods derived from phenomenology and psychoanalysis.[5] (*See* BLENDING AND FILM THEORY; CAMERA; CINEMATIC MOVEMENT; APPARATUS THEORY [BAUDRY].) It is as if the camera has come alive. A theoretical concept is thus shorthand for some process that is guiding us and actively working over things on our behalf (as a camera might): selecting, eliding, blending, bending, and making things appear in a new light, fit to a new goal not yet reached.

A network of concepts can do even more, as shown in the entries EUROPEAN FILM THEORY and REDEMPTION (KRACAUER). Consider as an illustration how the idea of 'postmodernism' may be made to emerge under a dense, descriptive weave of familiar debates involving such terms as auteurism, allusionism, pastiche, nostalgia, utopianism, reflexivity, and late capitalism. A conceptual network works to create the contours of a meta-object – in this case, 'postmodernism' or a 'postmodern camera'. Concepts and arguments do not just lie out there on an ideal stage in front of us, called forth by objects, but instead act to comprise the very stuff we conceptualize as an object.[6] Thus a film theory implicitly incorporates an image of its readers who are also the spectators it imagines for films along with the social realities and attitudes that define these persons, including such traits as gender identity, sexual orientation, class, race, ethnicity, national origin, and personhood.[7] As Catherine Constable notes in her entry on POSTMODERN CINEMA: '[I]t is vital to acknowledge that we are within the systems that we analyse, utilizing the concepts and discourses that they provide.' Through living in a particular world we learn pertinent ways to talk to ourselves and to others about things deemed significant.

The present essay aims to survey key issues bearing on the general nature of a concept for students new to film theory, while also pointing towards more advanced material. What is a concept and what does it do? This encyclopedia examines various concepts that film theorists have fashioned to live by. The goal is not to offer definitions as in a dictionary or to review a lengthy series of modifications of a given concept, but rather to assess a concept within a specific moment of its use, at a moment when a specific argument is being aggressively generated to serve a project. A theoretical concept – even one that begins as merely a technical term (as in the entry LONG TAKE) – is designed to knit together diverse strands of an argument, refute opposing claims, and become a cutting edge to carry on future debates and actions.

There are, of course, ways to conceptualize concepts other than through the methods of rhetoric and language (*see* CONCEPT). I have elsewhere sketched a range of these approaches when theorizing film theories, including a series of language-based approaches.[8] In what follows, however, I will continue to explore language manipulation as a source for the invention of concepts. It will be seen later that this approach leads not to an arbitrary or uncertain relativism where only words are real, but to a 'relational-ism' that is firmly anchored in a community's activities and values.

## Film as language

I have been contending that film theory creates images in our mind, not of films or facts of films but of 'illustrated turns of speech' from available language-games about our present experience of films, and ultimately about our present experience of ourselves in a given world (cf. epigraph above). Moreover, films themselves may be directly connected to language. This is not an accident. It will therefore be useful in what follows to briefly outline four general classes of such theories, though I will not rehearse details of the many attempts to delineate a filmic language.[9]

Semiotics provides an example of an objective approach to mapping patterns on the screen onto a visual language. Works by Sergei Eisenstein, Christian Metz, and Umberto Eco explore how concrete imagery becomes meaningful because it is symbolic of a world and hence systematic in ways that viewers can learn.[10] Film may also be said to map straight onto the disciplinary language of philosophy (*see* FILM-PHILOSOPHY).

Communication theories explored by Francesco Casetti are an example of an inter-objective approach that focuses on connecting elements of a social space where film acts as a medium of exchange between authors and viewers. Messages and impressions circulate according to strictures governing such elements as intentions of agents, institutional codes, craft norms, union rules, capital formation, and resources of technology.

A third set of language approaches is oriented towards examining subjective regularities among psychic states, e.g. cognitive (*see* COGNITIVE FILM THEORY), emotional, dream, and/or unconscious states of a viewer. Lacan, for example, argues that the unconscious is structured like a language.

Finally, there is a class of inter-subjective approaches that focus on a community's cultural matrix. How do spectators make meaning out of a film's depiction of problems and values? What shared metaphors and prevailing heuristics anchor thought?[11] Which ordinary protocols do spectators employ to generate a mental picturing of relevant grammars (cf. Wittgenstein epigraph)? This class of approaches is pursued by David Bordwell, Robert

Stam, and David Black,[12] as well as by such writers in other fields as George Lakoff, Mark Johnson, and Roland Barthes in his later works. Bryan Vescio, drawing firmly on a tradition of scholarship derived from Wittgenstein, asserts that in an inter-subjective context there is no important distinction between image and word, perceiving and reading: film is a series of visual and aural metaphors endlessly paraphrasable.[13]

My interest in the present essay lies in situating a language of film, along with a language of concept formation about film, within the latter, inter-subjective framework. This raises the question: is there something about film or the world outside of film that completely escapes language and thus theory? Can something be known – or somehow felt – that in principle is wholly inexpressible, and thus communicable only to oneself, or not even to oneself?[14]

## Language is theory-laden

Paul Churchland believes that theoretical language is implicit in *all perceptual judgements*, i.e. every observation of the world is already theory-laden. Here is his argument:

(1) Any judgment consists in the application of *concepts* (e.g., *a* is *F*).
(2) Any concept is a node in a *network* of concepts [i.e. a node in the network of general beliefs and assumptions in which it is embedded] whose connecting threads are sentences, and its meaning or semantic identity is determined by its peculiar place in that network ...
(3) Any network of concepts is a *theory*, minimally, a theory as to some of the classes into which nature divides itself, and some of the relations that hold between them.
(4) Therefore, any judgment presupposes a theory.
(5) Therefore, any *observation* judgment presupposes a theory.

The theory-ladenness of observation terms thus emerges as a consequence [not primarily, nor even perhaps at all, from the typical etiology (causal matrix) of its observational application or experimental context, nor from observation terms] having some special [status], but simply as a consequence of their being meaningful terms at all.[15]

Is a theory, then, made up of a sequence of generalizations – i.e. covering laws using a network of concepts – where each generalization ranges over a set of (at least potential) observational particulars?[16] If so, perhaps one might liken a theory to a physical landscape, where a theory would be a promontory offering a view of, say, a valley. How much will one see from the overlook? The analogy I propose is meant to capture the idea that a theory is a 'detached' and 'distant' view of something while other parts of the landscape are blocked from view.

Note that in this analogy the person who has the view from a promontory is nevertheless also *part of* the chosen landscape. To put it a bit more technically: in acquiring a theoretical view, the view has been *projected from* the very particulars we are *part of* and viewing. Isn't it the person, not the promontory, who has the view? To put it still another way: explanation or generalization is always in a specific language-landscape and hence in a linguistic practice. In the analogy, this means: having access to the skills and equipment necessary for going on a particular hike, finding a path, having a destination, and being aware of (one's desire for) the aesthetics of viewing.

Furthermore, each member of a community constructs a theory – a theoretical model – of a *Self* to live by that functions to orient him or her in a world and predict behaviour in relation to the movements of *Others*. What one comes to know about oneself and one's position in a world – including issues of gender, class, and race – is thus relevant to the working of film on a spectator and the place of film in a theory. (For this reason, many entries in the encyclopedia pursue the impact of social and cultural realities on theorists and theories of film.)[17] The interpretation and evaluation of films by critics, too, emerges from a landscape shaped by a community. Craft and social practices impart a sense of how things are properly, or indelicately, said and done.

For someone new to the landscape – a curious and motivated student – learning one's way around a given theory will require more than a single hike and a view from one promontory. To begin to feel the landscape intuitively, bodily, one must cross and re-cross the same point from many *different* directions and then start again with another point, crossing and re-crossing, in effect mentally constructing many actual and possible journeys.[18]

Of course, my analogy of theory-construction to a physical landscape and to a sense of an autobiographical self may or may not allow for radical disjunctures, earthquakes, floods, voids, black holes, etc., that redraw boundaries within a landscape or psyche. Startling and seemingly unpredictable events may appear as conjectured by chaos theory, parallel distributed processing, connectionist cognitive architecture, emergent behaviour, the unconscious, and so forth.[19] These sorts of events raise the issue of a theory's relationship to what cannot be observed, either because one's sightline on a landscape is partially blocked or because something completely unknown is said to be moving below one's feet.

## Unobservables

A theory and its concepts must deal with unobservables: that which cannot be directly seen, yet is implicated in the nature of the objects posited by the concepts. Minimally, a theory makes generalizations over sets of particulars, but such generalizations themselves cannot be *seen* in the same way as one or several particulars; nor can *relationships* that exist or are postulated among particulars be seen in the same way as the particulars. Furthermore, concepts are typically designed to cover unseen particulars that may have existed in the past or may exist in the future. Clearly, unobservables – much like hypotheses derived from inferences about observed data – come in many shapes, colours, and degrees of invisibility.

In James Cameron's *Avatar* (2009), take, for example, the fictional planet Polyphemus, which is reminiscent of the name of a particular Cyclops that plays a role in the real, though mythic, journey story of Odysseus. Polyphemus has a moon, Pandora, which is the setting for various journeys of the characters of *Avatar*. The name Pandora has mythic resonance, though also referring obliquely to real human situations (Pandora's Box). Earth has a moon that is believed to have been created through a cataclysmic collision between a proto-Earth and a hypothesized planetary body, Theia, who was a Greek goddess, the mother of Selene, the Moon goddess, and, through overtones of 'brightness' in Theia's full name, perhaps connects to the general 'illumination' provided by 'theoria'/theory. Though Theia in the form of a likely planetary body was obliterated, there is recent physical evidence for its existence based on chemistry, which is based on subatomic particles (e.g. protons for which there is strong evidence), which, in turn, are based on quarks (less evidence because never seen), which may or may not be based on still smaller particles (never seen) called preons, but whose name actually is merely a generic descriptor covering a wide number of *different theories* that attempt to explain gaps in physical experiments by postulating new sorts of matter and force particles, some of which entities, or perhaps as yet untheorized relatives of which, may exist.

Isn't there a more or less continuous set of links joining the above fictional things to hypothetical, possible, likely, or real objects and processes?[20] There would seem to be a series of gradations and intermediate cases lying between the qualities of nominal fictions and non-fictions, unobservables and observables.[21]

Where on the spectrum of unobservables–observables should a theory's concepts be fitted? Warren Buckland relies on a semiotic theory to model a goal for the concepts of film theory:

> Film semiotics does not conceive 'film' to be a pre-given, unproblematic entity. Instead, it defines film's specificity – its uniqueness in terms of its underlying reality, rather than its immediately perceptible qualities. The role of theory is to make visible this invisible reality by constructing a model of it. Like other semiotic studies, film semiotics adopted the two-tier semiotic hierarchy (between manifest/ latent levels of reality) and formulated hypotheses describing that underlying reality.
>
> ... A theory is a system of inter-related hypotheses, or tentative assumptions, about the unobservable nature of reality (a reality assumed to be a regular, economical, cohesive structure underlying a chaotic, heterogeneous, observable phenomenon).[22]

In this approach, observable surface phenomena are chaotic while an underlying, hidden reality is organized and regular. A theory's concepts must be formulated to highlight the logical principles that rule a deep reality. In an exceptional book, *Film Theory: Rational Reconstructions*, Buckland uses this approach to dissect the claims of nine film theories.[23] His method exposes the unique array of concepts and techniques used by each theory to create regularities – first, within each theoretical argument, and, second, inside each theoretical model that is built to explicate the supposed deep nature of film. In addition, Buckland considers several strategies for analysing films, including the approach of the present essay based on an inter-subjective framework.[24]

Note that the two-tier semiotic model composed of manifest/latent levels of reality can be strengthened in some film theories by arguing that certain aesthetic devices attempt to reverse the two levels in order to create an illusion of a continuous, unproblematic perceptual reality on the screen. It has been claimed that classical Hollywood cinema seeks to create a 'transparency' effect (as if a spectator were seeing the world through the film screen become window) and that one of its favoured techniques is so-called 'invisible' editing. The result is that the world appears to be smoothly presented and perfectly real to a spectator while a deeper reality of filmmaking that should have been revealed is instead obscured – remaining unseen, constructed, riven by psychic and political forces, chaotic, contingent, resistant, and heterogeneous.[25]

For David Bordwell, too many film-theoretical concepts have been directed at entities too far down in the depths. He has famously voiced this complaint in several books.

> This is not to complain about theorizing, in which I've often indulged myself. It is to suggest that the theoretical concepts that guide our inquiries should be treated as hypotheses, delicate enough to respond to fluctuations in the material but crisp enough to be corrigible. Ideas guide our observations, but observations challenge our ideas. We put questions to the material, and often we must stand corrected. Most theories on offer in film studies, however, are not hypothesis driven. They are simply bodies of doctrine (usually not as complex as their baroque presentations make them appear) concerning how society works (usually to the misery of its members) or how the mind works (usually to the unhappiness of its owner). Most of these theories have slender empirical support, but they are immune to testing or refutation because they tend to be vague, equivocal, truistic, or all three at once. They are incorrigible.[26]

Bordwell's worry is that many theoretical concepts originate from top-down doctrines too far removed from testing for possible relevance. An allied worry is that a concept will be overgeneralized until it is left vacuous and incorrigible.

## Our craving for generality

We yearn to see film at a single glance, to hold it tightly in view, to sum it up with concepts, to fashion a completely general theory. Wittgenstein warns against 'our craving for generality', which, he claims, stems from 'particular philosophical confusions' and leads to the creation of defective concepts.

> If we say thinking is essentially operating with signs, the first question you might ask is: 'What are signs?'—Instead of giving any kind of general answer to this question, I shall propose to you to look closely at particular cases which we should call 'operating with signs' ... We [will] see that we can build up the complicated forms [of language-games, of operating with signs] from the primitive ones by gradually adding new forms.
>
>   Now what makes it difficult for us to take this line of investigation is our craving for generality.
>
>   This craving for generality [results from] particular philosophical confusions. There is—
>
> (a)   The tendency to look for something in common to all the entities which we commonly subsume under a general term ... The idea of a general concept being a common property of its particular instances connects up with other primitive, too simple, ideas of the structure of language. It is comparable to the idea that *properties* are *ingredients* of the things which have the properties; e.g. that beauty is an ingredient of all beautiful things as alcohol is of beer and wine, and that we therefore could have pure beauty, unadulterated by anything that is beautiful.
> (b)   There is a tendency rooted in our usual forms of expression, to think that the man who has learnt to understand a general term, say, the term 'leaf,' has

thereby come to possess a kind of general picture of a leaf, as opposed to pictures of particular leaves ... [W]e are inclined to think that the general idea of a leaf is something like a visual image ['some kind of general image'], but one which only contains what is common to all leaves ... This again is connected with the idea that the meaning of a word is an image, or a thing correlated to the word. (This roughly means, we are looking at words as though they all were proper names, and we then confuse the bearer of a name with the meaning of the name.)

(c) [There is a philosophical] confusion between ... a state of a hypothetical mental mechanism, and ... a state of consciousness ...

(d) Our craving for generality has another main source: our preoccupation with the method of science. I mean the method of reducing the explanation of natural phenomena to the smallest possible number of primitive natural laws; and, in mathematics, of unifying the treatment of different topics by using a generalization ... This tendency is the real source of metaphysics, and leads the philosopher into complete darkness.[27]

To summarize Wittgenstein's four sources of 'our craving for generality', one might say:

- that for a 'family resemblance' concept there is no general answer as to its essence ((a) above; to be discussed in the next section);
- that an image in mind (or on the screen?!) may be mistakenly seen as some kind of general picture-concept or perfect concept that covers all relevant particulars – say, a perfect Idea of 'cat' that covers all possible cats – including all that can be said about a vivid and captivating image or the proper uses of a word or description ((b); but for a different view, *see* INAESTHETICS);
- that from introspection and conscious thought – i.e. from the tyranny of working memory – we may mistakenly generalize how thought and concept formation proceed ((c)); and
- that the analytical method of logical dissection and reduction of phenomena in the search for deep realities may yield an empty generalization, especially in metaphysics ((d); cf. the misplaced faith in properties-as-ingredients (a)).

All four sources of our craving for generality assume a too simple view of language as a stable picture of reality without considering the enormous variety of uses that we make of language and its devices, corresponding to the multiplicities of tasks in our environment.[28] One way to avoid overgeneralized claims[29] is to treat a concept as an open array of applications without an essence and then to evaluate separately each instance of its use.

## Radial concepts

Film theory acts to place films in a world – in a 'form of life'[30] – by rationalizing a way of talking about films using a specified network of concepts. Some of these concepts, however, are chameleon-like and possess a diversity of meanings open to subtle, adaptive, contingent, and even mysterious shifts. That is, some concepts appear to be complete and general only because they have been overgeneralized. This special type of word open to contingency is composed of a series of linked, distinct meanings and is called 'radial' by George Lakoff and a 'family resemblance' concept by Wittgenstein (as in (*a*) above).[31] At the largest scale, a film theory, I believe, exhibits this same type of radial structure as it attempts to hold together a set of radial concepts, including radial concepts describing sensory qualities on the screen, e.g. colour, movement, and depth.[32] Thus a film theory may not be as tightly unified and non-contradictory as its ambitions may proclaim.

Here are some prominent radial concepts for film: shot, frame, image, camera, motion, motion picture, medium, editing, montage, style, sound, realism, performance, auteur, voice, motivation, intention, causation, point of view, spectatorship, fiction, narrative, and narration.[33]

Figure 1 shows two graphic representations of a film theory – or equally of a single concept – analysed into its radial components and dispersed over many systems producing a (partially motivated) *heterarchy* – i.e. an open network of relations and links – rather than a hierarchy of surface/depth based on first principles.[34] In this representation, a film theory is depicted as a complicated language-game made up of many scattered concepts, each with radial extensions. Notice that the mobility – the radial nature – of a concept is not represented as a progressive, incremental evolution towards a final state because no objective standard exists by which to measure such a 'continuity'.

If a concept may contain incompatible, radial elements or produce applications at different scales while remaining open to unpredictable changes, and also be employed – knowingly or unknowingly – with conflicting senses in an argument as well as sliding along the axis of unobservables–observables, how might one discover and anchor its meaning in a particular context and instance?

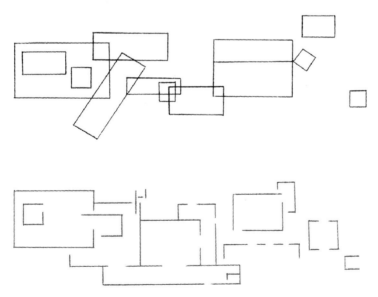

*Figure 1* Radial meaning in a concept or in a film theory. Two graphic versions of an image schema for the notion of 'radial meaning', either in a concept of a film theory or in the film theory as a whole, where each of the individual boxes frames a single category of meaning based on a container schema, while the set of boxes taken as a whole represents a single lexical entry (a set of related meanings) for a polysemous word as well as represents the resulting composite film theory.

## Concepts are always intermediate

A concept can always be anchored by situating it between at least two adjacent concepts that seek to squeeze it out of existence. That is, a concept must fight for and justify the space it takes up in a particular grammar or network of concepts. Imagine the network as a crowded sphere where even concepts on the surface will always have relationships with neighbours.

Intermediate positions exist at various scales of description. David Bordwell and Noël Carroll, for example, situate a group of methodologies – 'middle-level research' and 'piecemeal theorizing' – in between a large set of film and literary theories they call Grand Theory and another set referred to as empiricist approaches.[35] Christian Metz's semiotic methodology exists between theories of the natural expressivity of objects and theories of an individual's expressivity. At a smaller scale, a single theory may be located between two others: Jean Mitry's film theory between the theories of Sergei Eisenstein and André Bazin; Jean-Louis Comolli's theory between Jean-Louis Baudry and Jean Mitry/Jean-Patrick Lebel.

At a still smaller scale, a given concept in a theory finds a place among its neighbours. The reason is that concepts are crafted to work within a specific field of language, i.e. inside a semantic network that constructs a sea of ordered differences. For example, Rudolf Arnheim struggles to define the 'partial illusion' of art that must exist between the illusion of no illusion – an absolute realism – and complete delusion, which has no contact with reality. He also posits a $2\frac{1}{2}$-dimensional spatial effect for film as opposed to 2-dimensional and 3-dimensional effects achieved by other arts.[36] Another example: Vsevolod Pudovkin labours to define the exact qualities of an 'invisible observer' who can be taken to motivate the editing of a scene but who must not be too powerful with too many special abilities besides invisibility (because although special abilities would lead to an explanation of many types of editing, these abilities would provide little explanatory power since almost anything could be justified as being consistent with various extraordinary, god-like abilities assigned to an invisible observer); nor must the invisible observer be too weak (which would cover fewer cases of editing with greater explanatory power but which would restrict the range of acceptable editing schemes due to the invisible observer's greater limitations).[37] Thus Pudovkin must carefully adjust the powers granted to his theoretical, invisible observer: not too strong, not too weak (*see* IMAGINED OBSERVER HYPOTHESIS).

The important point here is that a theoretical concept should be understood and measured according to its differential position within a network of concepts at various scales of analysis.[38] If a concept were like an image on screen, then what should be tested is the placement of frame lines: where are the limits of a concept and what area is just beyond a border, felt and expressible perhaps, but unseen? Extending this analogy, one might say that the conceptual network of a theory *functions as a medium* (like film) transferring the force of an argument (theme/moral) – or, if you wish: transferring the will of an author – onto the particulars of a world – or, if you wish: onto the will of a reader living such a world.

Does a network of concepts imply that there exist only endless differences – that only differences matter? If concepts are constructed and embedded within semantic networks, is there a danger of rampant relativism? – with the result that, as Turner/Mick Jagger remarks in *Performance* (Donald Cammell and Nicolas Roeg, 1970): 'Nothing is true. Everything is permitted.' What might ground a language-game?

## Relativism and relational-ism

Relativism does have treacherous shoals (*see* PERSPECTIVISM VERSUS REALISM). A more moderate approach would be to focus on what might be called 'relational-ism'.[39] Here both a concept and its object are defined by relationships to proximate things or to things that may reasonably become proximate, including certain dispositional properties. These related things cannot be *all* things or all possible or imaginable things, but only important or likely things. And judging the degree of importance of objects crucially involves our present desires and values in a world, and their expression in argument.

Relational-ism does not lead to a relativism where every judgement is arbitrary and anything counts. Since some values termed 'contingent universals'[40] are cross-cultural and may have biological aspects, one cannot rule out very broad agreements about some of the values that guide our concepts and descriptions. Language does not rely only on language, on itself, but is situated in a world.

Another danger of relativism besides arbitrariness that needs to be qualified has to do with 'openness', i.e. the claim that nothing is ever certain or definite in language or in a network of concepts or in a context because something new can always be added, stretched, or imagined. Wittgenstein:

> But does one have to take the words 'colour' and 'length' [and 'number'] in just *this* way? – Well, we'll just have to explain them. Explain, then, by means of other words! And what about the last explanation in this chain? (Don't say: 'There isn't a "last" explanation.' That is just as if you were to say: 'There isn't a last house in this road; one can always build an additional one.')[41]

The world changes, and also our desire for how the world ought to be changes. We use languages that are at hand – what other ones are there? – to fashion and re-fashion objects and their descriptions for our purposes. Theoretical discourse endeavours to act as an interface for these changes because one of its functions is to explain the consequences of present effects and hence to point towards the future. How, then, might future film theories be characterized from the perspective of a moderate relational-ism?

## Future film theories

From an inter-subjective perspective, it is not images on a screen that make of film a language. Rather, images become a language *when we respond and talk and marvel* about our experiences in watching film. I believe that one of the aims of film theory should be to explore the concepts we have embraced about film; that is, to explore the cognitive and emotive fields that assign intelligibility and pertinence to the images we care about through networks of concepts. Images acquire a 'being' – a status in our language – because they are of a piece with those circumstances and concerns that we diligently seek to express about our lives. In this sense, a 'concept' is an attempt to formalize the basis for a feeling or idea that we may have had about something in a film, something felt or believed about our world through film.

Thus a key problem for future film theories will be to examine how spectators *focus on, handle, and manage* in language their many experiences with film. That is, *which networks* of concepts, metaphors, scenarios, judgement heuristics, folk theories, abduction, schemata, routines, models, and procedures/templates for conducting an analysis will be used by a spectator to formulate the values found in a film? I do not believe that spectators are 'placed' or 'positioned' by signs, codes, or even by 'cues on the screen', but instead that spectators re-find themselves continuously through the languages they adopt to communicate and use concepts – consciously or non-consciously – in the process of reiterating to themselves and others what is important for their lives.

Film theories of the future should be aimed at interpreting the expression of human cognition and emotion. These theories will be characterized by at least six features, as follows:

- Future theories will not attempt to define the absolute and final, logical nature of a concept, but will instead study the intricate applications of radial concepts (see Figure 1) together with the *grammar(s)* by which an ensemble of words acquires a purpose. The conceptual structure of a theory – including that of the present essay – should be evaluated relative to (i) concepts that are nearby; (ii) arguments using the concepts; and (iii) criteria for employing arguments to achieve goals.
- Future theories will not seek a set of universal or logical propositions about film, but will produce *inter-subjective descriptions* tied to social practices, concerns, values, attractions, and a community consensus about the past and present boundaries of the film medium and its uses. The issue will be which (grammatical) rules and concepts to design in order to conduct inquiry and promote relevant value.
- Future theories will be *fragmentary*,[42] incomplete, and responsive to ongoing changes in our daily lives and favoured language-games. Wittgenstein argues that philosophy is not a science (cf. part (*d*) of the quotation on p. xxviii).[43] This idea applied to the philosophy of film would mean that the goal is not to produce new knowledge (as a science), but instead to concentrate on the evaluation, interpretation, and understanding of what is presently known about us and our lives through film. This does not mean that the results of scientific endeavour, say, of cognitive science, cannot be employed within film theories.
- Future theories will recognize the *figurative nature* of theorizing, i.e. recognize that high-level abstractions within a theory are often metaphorical projections or displacements based on bodily experiences and embodied concepts. This means that a film theorist is directly implicated in his or her discourse. Wittgenstein:

  > Perhaps what is inexpressible (what I find mysterious and am not able to express) is the background against which whatever I could express has its meaning.
  >     Working in philosophy ... is really more a working on oneself. On one's own interpretation. On one's way of seeing things. (And what one expects of them.)[44]

  Working on and against one's unique background is vital in working out a theory of the many demands that frame both theorist and film in an environment.
- Future theories will not analyse film as if it were composed of simpler and simpler constituents that could be exposed by a microscope, dissected, and then arranged into a rigid hierarchy, as if to explain film were a matter of penetrating a surface to discover the most basic and essential elements hidden within levels of the depths, finally to be grounded by the lowest level, its essence. [Recall in part (*a*) of the quotation above Wittgenstein's warning about the mistaken idea that properties of a thing are its

ingredients.] Further, one might ask, in what situation would a person be speaking about film *it*self, of film – all film – being just itself unseen, unheard, idealized apart from any thought or use of it? This would be as if film could take on a perfect, crystalline structure analogous to Gilles Deleuze's time-image. What question would such a person be seeking to answer by invoking film's make-believe being when being only itself?

Furthermore, a dissective analysis fosters a misguided drive to see a greater number of visible details on screen, and closer, as if all differences in an image matter for all purposes. Instead, film should be analysed for the many ways it spreads outwards in a *radial fashion* by connecting and jumping to parts in new systems and grammars in order to make a provisional network or heterarchy.[45] As a paradigm, think here of the self-organizing, non-linear, distributed and connectionist neural networks posited within contemporary theories of mind. Thus interpretation of films within a variety of community contexts is vital. It is certainly a business – 'Interpretation, Inc.', according to Bordwell[46] – but only because interpretation has been established and incorporated by a community faced with the business of life.

- Future theories will take seriously André Bazin's claims in his essay 'For an Impure Cinema'[47] and – pushing Bazin a bit further – will be inclined to give up the search for a medium of film or a specificity of film.[48] Instead, the notion of a medium would be based on a consensus about those properties we have selected from a group of materials that presently interest us as well as the present ideas we have about how these properties may be used to clarify our experience of film. The properties chosen may be discarded in future and new ones for the 'same' object found. Thus the idea of 'film' is itself mutable.

Clarifying one's vocabulary and language(-games) may amount to specifying more exactly the object seen under a description, and the value assigned. Accordingly, there will be no Theory specific to film. Instead, there will be only the messy, *impure*, and adaptive ordinary languages that we struggle to fit to present contingencies. In looking around, we find an appropriate way of looking for the occasion, not a metaphysical platform. This makes film theory, like language, historical and anthropological (see the epilogue on pp. 494–504).

## Concept and theory as practices of language

If Wittgenstein is correct that the essence of things already lies open to view and to change, and is not evanescent or shrouded in darkness beneath a surface,[49] then certainly the film screen is a sight, and its philosophy lies in front of us plainly. No matter that films may be fiction: could we talk even hypothetically about things that are not meaningful to us, that do not resonate, that do not occasion thought, that do not arise from anxieties and plans?[50] And talk about films we must: as Béla Balázs declares, 'No art has ever grown great without theory', especially, he argues, the art of film with its ability to concentrate attention and provoke a dialogue with what is palpable, the physiognomy of a world (*see* CLOSE-UP).[51]

Furthermore, aren't the many ordinary words that we employ about our world, including theorizing the films seen in our world, already to a degree conceptual? Perhaps there is less difference than might be imagined between a formal, theoretical concept and an ordinary word that we employ often and rely upon for description.

In deploying terms and concepts to do film theory, one speaks, writes, and does things with words under specified norms of description. One need only recall attending film and media conferences where images are offered merely as illustration and talk is the only currency. Images, dialogue, and the soundtrack would seem to remain mute until we have given them voice, however informally, by framing them with rhetorical devices through ordinary practices of language. An image on screen does not dictate what can be said in its name. Therefore the two questions to ask about a concept are: what is its value to an argument and what values does it promote, i.e. to what is it true?

This encyclopedia aims to illuminate concepts and their patterns of reasoning when thinking about how we are thinking about film experience. Which conceptual forms have we adopted in making intelligible our experience? The diversity of these concepts reveals a history of tireless competition among theoretical languages struggling over the nature of film and its value.

## Notes

My thanks to Warren Buckland, Jeff Scheible, and Melinda Szaloky for astute observations on this essay.

1 Ludwig Wittgenstein, *Philosophical Investigations*, translated by G.E.M. Anscombe, P.M.S. Hacker, and Joachim Schulte (Oxford: Wiley-Blackwell, rev. 4th edn, 2009), § 90 (Wittgenstein's emphases). There are several fine introductions to Wittgenstein's ideas, e.g. A.C. Grayling, *Wittgenstein: A Very Short Introduction* (Oxford: Oxford University Press, 2001). A more advanced introduction is Severin Schroeder, *Wittgenstein: The Way out of the Fly-Bottle* (Cambridge: Polity Press, 2006). Another place to begin is with Wittgenstein's *The Blue and Brown Books* (Oxford: Blackwell Publishing, 2nd edn, 1969). O.K. Bouwsma's works offer many lucid applications of Wittgenstein's methods to a variety of philosophical topics; see *Toward a New Sensibility: Essays of O.K. Bouwsma*, edited by J.L. Craft and Ronald E. Hustwit (Lincoln: University of Nebraska Press, 1982) and *Philosophical Essays* (Lincoln: University of Nebraska Press, 1965). Highly useful is Hans-Johann Glock's *A Wittgenstein Dictionary* (Oxford: Blackwell, 1996). G.P. Baker and P.M.S. Hacker have written an important four-volume study, "An Analytical Commentary on the *Philosophical Investigations*." Each volume is in two parts comprising "Essays" and "Exegesis." All are Blackwell Publishing (Oxford). Hacker is the sole author of volumes 3 and 4. Vol. 1, *Wittgenstein: Understanding and Meaning* (2nd ed. rev. by Hacker, 2005); vol. 2, *Wittgenstein: Rules, Grammar and Necessity* (2nd ed. rev. by Hacker, 2009); vol. 3, *Wittgenstein: Meaning and Mind* (1993); vol. 4, *Wittgenstein: Mind and Will* (1996).

2 Wittgenstein, *Philosophical Investigations*, § 295; cf. §§ 367–74. No doubt Wittgenstein's notion of mental pictures that illustrate 'turns of speech' (and hold us captive?) may also illustrate 'parts of speech'; cf. §§ 1, 17, 23, 27. For applications of the latter idea to film theory and criticism, see Edward Branigan, 'Of Prepositions: Lost and Found', *The Velvet Light Trap* 64 (Fall 2009): 95–8. Note that what is at stake with such a mental picture is not that we have a false idea of what a thing is, but that the picture prompts or directs us how to (properly) *interact* with the thing.

3 Quentin Skinner, 'A Reply to My Critics', in *Meaning and Context: Quentin Skinner and His Critics*, edited by James Tully (Princeton, NJ: Princeton University Press, 1989), 283. Duncan Ivison discusses Skinner's approach to 'the new history' in *The Self at Liberty: Political Argument and the Arts of Government* (Ithaca, NY: Cornell University Press, 1997), 11–23.

4 To discover the deep 'essence' of a thing means to identify the permanent relationships among underlying, simple components that are both necessary and sufficient for the thing's existence. But for Wittgenstein, there is no seeing into a thing's depths. There are only places that have been prepared in evolving languages where concepts may be consigned and then shifted according to occasion. *Philosophical Investigations*, §§ 31, 49, 257.

5 For example, Christian Metz begins to fill the interval between camera and mind as follows:

> All vision consists of a double movement: projective (the 'sweeping' searchlight) and introjective: consciousness as a sensitive recording surface (as a screen) ... The

technology of photography carefully conforms to this (banal) phantasy accompanying perception ... During the performance [of a film] the spectator is the searchlight ... duplicating the projector, which itself duplicates the camera, and he is also the sensitive surface duplicating the screen, which itself duplicates the filmstrip ... When I say that 'I see' the film, I mean thereby a unique mixture of two contrary currents: the film is what I receive, and it is also what I release ... Releasing it, I am the projector, receiving it, I am the screen; in both these figures together, I am the camera, which points and yet which records.

Metz argues that seeing a film is not merely a matter of perception, but is inextricably bound to preference and memory. In watching film, there is always the hope (or fear) of recognizing our self misrecognizing our self. 'The Imaginary Signifier', in *The Imaginary Signifier: Psychoanalysis and the Cinema*, translated by Celia Britton, Annwyl Williams, Ben Brewster, and Alfred Guzzetti (Bloomington: Indiana University Press, 1982), 50–1. *See* IMAGINARY SIGNIFIER. See also Metz's comments in 'Story/Discourse (A Note on Two Kinds of Voyeurism)', in *The Imaginary Signifier*, esp. 91–4.

Considering digital technology, one may dissolve the 'camera and mind' relationship into a remarkably coherent 'posthumanist perspective on cinema'. See William Brown, 'Man Without a Movie Camera – Movies without Men: Towards a Posthumanist Cinema?', in *Film Theory and Contemporary Hollywood Movies*, edited by Warren Buckland (London and New York: Routledge, 2009), 66–85.

6 A constructed, but evolving, conceptual network that creates its object suggests that the so-called 'specificity' of film – the idea that some thing or special something about all films makes film unique – amounts merely to a temporary platform or outpost devised by a theorist to enable his or her speech acts about effects he or she deems important. The material of a thing does not determine its significant forms, effects, or ends; and conversely, these latter are not tied to a single material manifestation. Many film specificity theorists rely implicitly on Plato's reasoning about the notion of an object's 'function' in order to select among material properties, or imagine dispositional properties, of film. According to H.S. Thayer (p. 33):

> In Western philosophy the use of functional language, encouraged and stimulated by Plato's theory of function, has been a favourite *genre* of metaphysics. We have seen [as a consequence] how metaphysical and evaluative issues will proliferate ... What were once empirically informative statements get strait-jacketed into definitional truths of little or questionable usefulness. Bad metaphysics thrives on semantic confusion.
>
> 'Plato: The Theory and Language of Function', in *Plato's* Republic: *Interpretation and Criticism*, edited by Alexander Sesonske (Belmont, CA: Wadsworth Publishing, 1966), 21–39 (Thayer's emphasis).

For some of the arguments of film specificity theorists, see SPECIFICITY, MEDIUM I AND II as well as CLASSICAL FILM THEORY.

7 For some entries in this encyclopedia that explicitly incorporate social realities into film theory, see note 17 below.

8 On ways of theorizing film theories, see Edward Branigan, 'Teaching Film Theory', in *Teaching Film*, edited by Lucy Fischer and Patrice Petro (New York: The Modern Language Association of America, 2012), 26–39. Many present-day conceptualizations of the nature of a 'concept' (though not the present essay) owe allegiance to Plato's formulation; cf. Alexander Sesonske, 'Knowing and Saying: The Structure of Plato's *Meno*', in *Plato's* Meno: *Text and Criticism*, edited by Alexander Sesonske and Noel Fleming (Belmont, CA: Wadsworth Publishing Co., 1965), 84–96.

9 For a more extensive discussion and application of the four-part grid objective/inter-objective/ subjective/inter-subjective, see Edward Branigan, 'If-then-Else: Memory and the Path Not Taken', in *Transmedia Frictions: The Digital, the Arts, and the Humanities*, edited by Marsha Kinder and Tara McPherson (Berkeley: University of California Press, forthcoming).

10 One sort of objective approach to film language has been proposed by the linguist John A. Bateman, 'Towards a *Grande Paradigmatique* of Film: Christian Metz Reloaded', *Semiotica* 167 (Nov. 2007): 13–64.

11 I examine how metaphor and rhetoric arrange concepts in the early film theory of Noël Burch in 'To Zero and beyond: Noël Burch's *Theory of Film Practice*', in *Defining Cinema*, edited by Peter Lehman (New Brunswick, NJ: Rutgers University Press, 1997), 149–68.

12 A few inter-subjective approaches: David Bordwell, *Making Meaning: Inference and Rhetoric in the Interpretation of Cinema* (Cambridge, MA: Harvard University Press, 1989); Robert Stam, *Subversive Pleasures: Bakhtin, Cultural Criticism, and Film* (Baltimore, MD: Johns Hopkins University Press, 1992); David A. Black, *Law in Film: Resonance and Representation* (Chicago: University of Illinois Press, 1999) and '*Homo Confabulans*: A Study in Film, Narrative, and Compensation', *Literature and Psychology* 47 (3) (2001): 25–37.

13 Bryan Vescio, 'Reading in the Dark: Cognitivism, Film Theory, and Radical Interpretation', *Style* 35 (4) (Winter 2001): 572–91. For another inter-subjective approach to language and film, see Jan Simons, '"Enunciation": From Code to Interpretation', in *The Film Spectator: From Sign to Mind*, edited by Warren Buckland (Amsterdam: Amsterdam University Press, 1995), 192–206.

14 In case one is tempted to imagine a *private* sort of language, accessible only to oneself, Wittgenstein offers one of the most important philosophical arguments of the twentieth century to debunk the very idea of a private language; *Philosophical Investigations*, §§ 243–315.

15 Paul M. Churchland, *A Neurocomputational Perspective: The Nature of Mind and the Structure of Science* (Cambridge, MA: The MIT Press, 1992), 271 (Churchland's emphases).

16 According to Noël Carroll:

> [L]et anything count as film theorizing, so long as it involves the production of generalizations or general explanations or general taxonomies and concepts about film practice … This view of film theorizing conflicts sharply with certain of the most traditional preconceptions of film theory.
>
> 'Prospects for Film Theory: A Personal Assessment', in *Post-theory: Reconstructing Film Studies*, edited by David Bordwell and Noël Carroll (Madison: University of Wisconsin Press, 1996), 39.

My view of 'generalizations' is that they provide either a starting point or a conclusion, nothing more. The most important part of a theory lies in the vast middle where arguments and assumptions are made and concepts are deployed, that is, where a generalization is being elaborated or justified and where grounds exist for changing the generalization.

17 For some of the entries in this encyclopedia that explore interconnections among film, gender, class, and/or race, see the following: AFFECT, FILM AND; DIALOGISM; ETHICS; EXCESS, CINEMATIC; FANTASY AND SPECTATORSHIP; FEMINIST FILM THEORY, CORE CONCEPTS; FEMINIST FILM THEORY, HISTORY OF; GAZE THEORY; QUEER THEORY/QUEER CINEMA; RECEPTION THEORY; THIRD WORLD CINEMA.

18 Wittgenstein used geographical metaphors when describing how one works with philosophy, language, and conceptual frameworks as well as how one teaches philosophy through crossing and re-crossing points in a landscape from various directions. See Edward Kanterian, *Ludwig Wittgenstein* (London: Reaktion Books, 2007), 170–2. Cf. Wittgenstein's 'Preface' to *Philosophical Investigations*.

19 On unpredictability, see, e.g., Paul Cilliers, *Complexity and Postmodernism: Understanding Complex Systems* (London and New York: Routledge, 1998).

20 Here is a schematic version of the more or less continuous set of links joining the fictional, partly fictional, and non-fictional entities discussed in the text beginning with the film *Avatar*:

> Polyphemus (fictional planet of *Avatar* and name of Cyclops) — polymorphous — morphing — changeable — journey of change through quest — quest to become worthy of a mate through change — (Cyclops as humanoids, Na'vi humanoids living on the moon of Polyphemus in *Avatar*, Jake as disabled-human-turned-avatar-turned-Na'vi, actors as avatars in a human story about humanoids, hybrids, and identity changes) — journey narrative to Polyphemus's moon Pandora — goddesses Pandora and Theia (Theia's daughter Moon, Theia as hypothetical planetary body in collision with proto-Earth creating Earth's moon) — Theia/theoria/theory of this colli-sion — evidence for the collision — chemistry, protons, quarks — hypothetical preons — preon particles as merely an arbitrary name for a particular class of speculative theories.

21 The same sort of mixed cases between fiction and non-fiction, unobservable and observable, can be found in (any?) film. Consider the following sequence of questions about the fictional film *Carlos* (Olivier Assayas, 2010), which concerns the real terrorist Carlos the Jackal.

Did the real Carlos utter certain exact words heard in the film to a certain depicted real person? Likely not. Did the real Carlos utter something to someone whose actions were then the effect of some such words as depicted in the film? More likely. To what degree does the actor portraying Carlos physically resemble the real Carlos and to what degree do the clothes worn by the actor resemble those that might have been worn by the real Carlos? Is the music heard on the soundtrack appropriate to the period and place being depicted and might it have been heard by the real Carlos? Or, instead, is the music appropriate symbolically to some other aspect of Carlos's history? What is the effect of the film on our understanding of Carlos the Jackal and his actions?

Another way of putting these issues about the relation of fiction and history is to ask whether representations must always be of the same type and one-to-one, never more fluid. Do we think of some meanings as moving along a too-narrow bridge: signifier to signified, sign to referent, word to denotation, stimulus to response, idea to an-object-in-reality? Might instead some representations be more expansive, context-sensitive, figurative, affective, and designed to fit along a scale between fiction and non-fiction – a scale that responds to differing criteria in effect for a historical fit, thus making multiple the ways for assembling a match and being understood? A fiction does not mark out a closed and limited region of sense apart from the everyday experience of using a language. Imagine, for example, one of the middle boxes in Figure 1 to be a 'fiction' – a counterfactual proposition – then the preceding and subsequent boxes may be interpreted as representing a set of *conditions* and associative links that work to tie the fiction to a reality (or else render it a *false* fiction under specified conditions). As an example, consider how the encyclopedia entry on the method of cooking the mythical (fictional and nominal) bird the phoenix also makes eminent, nonfictional sense: Allen S. Weiss, 'Cryptogastronomy', in *Curiosity and Method: Ten Years of Cabinet Magazine* (New York: Cabinet Books, 2012), 72–5. For fictions within fictions, the links to reality simply multiply, as in *Certified Copy* (Abbas Kiarostami, 2010) and Gillian Flynn's novel *Gone Girl* (2012).

22 Warren Buckland, 'Film Semiotics', in *A Companion to Film Theory*, edited by Toby Miller and Robert Stam (Oxford: Blackwell Publishing, 1999), 88.

23 Warren Buckland, *Film Theory: Rational Reconstructions* (London and New York: Routledge, 2012). See Kevin McDonald's review of Buckland's book in the online journal *Alphaville* : http://www.alphavillejournal.com/Issue%204/HTML/ReviewMcDonald.html (accessed 9 January 2013).

24 On types of strategies for analysing films, see, e.g., Buckland, *Film Theory*, 168–9.

25 On transparency effects in film and theory, see, e.g., Mary Ann Doane, 'Ideology and the Practice of Sound Editing and Mixing', in *Film Sound: Theory and Practice*, edited by Elisabeth Weis and John Belton (New York: Columbia University Press, 1985), 54–62; Doane, 'The Object of Theory', in *Rites of Realism: Essays on Corporeal Cinema*, edited by Ivone Margulies (Durham, NC: Duke University Press, 2002), 80–9. Cf. the concentration on inauthentic or mystified everyday experience in the entry EUROPEAN FILM THEORY. By contrast, see Rick Altman's reliance on, and defence of, the everyday in constructing a theory of genre in the entry GENRE THEORY.

26 David Bordwell, *Figures Traced in Light: On Cinematic Staging* (Berkeley: University of California Press, 2005), 266. For an informal introduction to Bordwell's approach, see Bordwell, 'Never the Twain Shall Meet', *Film Comment* 47 (3) (May/June 2011): 38–41. For more battles over the nature of concepts in film theory, see *Post-theory: Reconstructing Film Studies*, edited by David Bordwell and Noël Carroll (Madison: University of Wisconsin Press, 1996); *Film Theory and Philosophy*, edited by Richard Allen and Murray Smith (Oxford: Clarendon Press, 1997); *Reinventing Film Studies*, edited by Christine Gledhill and Linda Williams (London: Arnold, 2000). The debate continues unabated: D.N. Rodowick, 'An Elegy for Theory', and Malcolm Turvey, 'Theory, Philosophy, and Film Studies: A Response to D.N. Rodowick's "An Elegy for Theory"', *October* 122 (Fall 2007): 91–120. Kendall Walton discusses some of the key issues in the relationship between theory construction and aesthetics in 'Aesthetics – What? Why? and Wherefore?', *Journal of Aesthetics and Art Criticism* 65 (2) (Spring 2007): 147–61.

27 Wittgenstein, *The Blue Book*, 16–18 (Wittgenstein's emphases); cf. 19–20, 23, 27, 35, 55.

28 On the enormous variety of language, see Wittgenstein, *Philosophical Investigations*, §§ 1–88. It would seem that one may indulge a craving for generality in two main directions. Film's presence may be sliced up by abstracting downwards to a hyponym – to a figure of speech that might be

called a 'dissociating synecdoche' – as in the reductive characterization of film as 'moving shadows' or other versions of light, depth, motion, and movement often mentioned lightly by film theorists but pursued quite earnestly in certain realist film theories relying on physical causation and photographicity. Alternatively, one may abstract upwards to one or more classificatory terms to an often surprising hypernym – to a figure of speech that might be called a 'transcendent synecdoche' – as in Garrett Stewart's claim that 'cinema exists in the interval between two absences', which interval presumably amounts to a still more transcendent Presence of Generalized Absence; see the epilogue on pp. 494–504.

29 I list fifteen common, though nearly vacuous, theoretical propositions about film in *Projecting a Camera: Language-Games in Film Theory* (London and New York: Routledge, 2006), 194. In lectures based on ideas from the present essay, I have offered examples (and not solely from the usual suspects) of how film theorists have over-reached through overgeneralization by falling into one or more of the four philosophical confusions *(a)* to *(d)* discussed by Wittgenstein in the text above. Here ... I will forebear offering examples.

30 'Form of life' is Wittgenstein's term. See Glock, *Wittgenstein Dictionary*, 124–9.

31 On radial concepts, see especially George Lakoff, *Women, Fire, and Dangerous Things: What Categories Reveal about the Mind* (Chicago, IL: University of Chicago Press, 1987), chap. 6 'Radial Categories', 91–114, and 146–7, 290, 346–8, 537–40, passim. For a summary of Lakoff's approach, see pp. 153–4, 334–7. Lakoff emphasizes that radial meanings are neither predictable from a core meaning (because as a whole they fail to have relevant common properties or a collective essence), nor the result of a series of arbitrary conventions, but something *in between* – a *partially motivated convention* based on living within a community and sharing a way of life. See also George Lakoff and Mark Johnson, *Metaphors We Live By* (Chicago, IL: University of Chicago Press, 2003, with new afterword), chap. 18 'Some Consequences for Theories of Conceptual Structure', 106–14. On family resemblance concepts, see Glock, *Wittgenstein Dictionary*, 120–4. Wittgenstein points out that, especially in 'ethics or aesthetics', a concept must have a family of meanings (Wittgenstein, *Philosophical Investigations*, § 77). He also advances the very striking claim that a formal proposition has no essence but is a family resemblance concept: §§ 108, 114, 134.

32 I discuss in depth how the sensory quality of movement is systematically coloured into a radial series of metaphors and abstractions in *Projecting a Camera*; see index entry 'motion/movement, abstract/nonphysical kinds of'.

33 On radial concepts in film theories, see Branigan, *Projecting a Camera*. I discuss, for example, fifteen major classes of meaning for the word 'frame' together with numerous sub-classes, 102–15, along with one special type of framing, 'suture', which devolves into six major types, 133–45. See also Branigan, 'Teaching Film Theory', 30–2. See the entries SUTURE; MONTAGE THEORY I AND II. For detailed studies of two (radial) concepts that have been applied to film, see Anneleen Masschelein, *The Unconcept: The Freudian Uncanny in Late-Twentieth-Century Theory* (Albany, NY: State University of New York Press, 2011) and *Ostrannenie: On 'Strangeness' and the Moving Image – The History, Reception, and Relevance of a Concept*, edited by Annie van den Oever (Amsterdam: Amsterdam University Press, 2010).

34 The first of the two diagrams of a heterarchy in Figure 1 comes from Figure 4.1 in Branigan, *Projecting a Camera*, 122. Both diagrams of Figure 1 depict a wide range of film phenomena; see *Projecting a Camera*, index entry 'figure 4.1, interpretations of'. The diagrams of Figure 1 also depict a version of Wittgenstein's 'family resemblance' concept; for some technical details of this comparison, see *Projecting a Camera*, chapter 4, note 61. On the notions of 'partial motivation' and 'family resemblance', see note 31 above. By way of contrast, two forms of a hierarchical arrangement of elements (in the context of film narration) are diagrammed in Branigan, *Narrative Comprehension and Film* (London and New York: Routledge, 1992), 114.

35 On the intermediate status of 'middle-level research' and 'piecemeal theorizing', see David Bordwell, 'Contemporary Film Studies and the Vicissitudes of Grand Theory', and Noël Carroll, 'Prospects for Film Theory: A Personal Assessment', in *Post-theory*, 3–68.

36 Rudolf Arnheim, *Film as Art* (Berkeley: University of California Press, 1957), 12, 24–9, 59.

37 Vsevolod Pudovkin, *Selected Essays*, edited by by Richard Taylor, translated by Richard Taylor and Evgeni Filippov (London: Seagull Books, 2006), 'The Film Script (The Theory of the Script)', Part Three: The Methods for Processing the Material, 56–64. The most sophisticated (radial!) descendant of Pudovkin's invisible observer is George M. Wilson's film spectator, who views a

fictional showing from an unoccupied, indeterminate visual perspective: *Seeing Fictions in Film: The Epistemology of Movies* (Oxford: Oxford University Press, 2011). Note that concepts incorporating 'invisibility' illustrate generally how concepts are tied to various degrees of 'unobservables'. Consider, for example, concepts about invisible observers, invisible editing, fictions (that make invisible the real world), the concealed logic of plot structure and style, the genesis of image qualities, and the provenance of camera movements.

38 I examine a large number of concepts that are positioned midway between two others while making use of four middle-level approaches to film theory lying between realism and relativism in *Projecting a Camera*; see the two index entries 'middle-level (i.e. theoretical concepts as positioned between opposites)' and 'middle-level approaches to film theory'. One of Wittgenstein's key analytical techniques involves the search for 'intermediate cases'. I mention more than two dozen of his techniques in *Projecting a Camera*; see index entry 'Wittgenstein, techniques of analysis'.

39 I am using the notion of 'relational-ism' (with hyphen) loosely without deciding among specific doctrines of relationalism (no hyphen), relationism, speculative realism as well as, for example, an object-oriented ontology, as in Graham Harman's *The Quadruple Object* (Alresford: John Hunt Publishing, 2011). Cf. Meinard Kuhlmann, 'What Is Real?', *Scientific American* 309 (2) (August 2013): 40–7.

40 On 'contingent universals', see especially David Bordwell's essay 'Convention, Construction, and Cinematic Vision', reprinted from *Post-theory* with a new 'Afterword' in *Poetics of Cinema* (London and New York: Routledge, 2008), 57–82. For an informal introduction to the important notion of 'contingency', I recommend the encyclopedia entries on 'Contingency' by William Safire (68–71) and what lies within and without a number of diagrams in 'Time (Diagrammed)' by Daniel Rosenberg (399–405) in *Curiosity and Method*. Notice that from a *cultural* standpoint the contingent event depicted in the 'Contingency' entry has much valuable information in it about the forms of a form of life that is not specifically American and not hypothetical. Cf. note 21 above.

41 Wittgenstein, *Philosophical Investigations*, § 29 (Wittgenstein's emphasis). See also Wittgenstein, *On Certainty*, edited by G.E.M. Anscombe and G.H. von Wright, translated by Denis Paul and G.E.M. Anscombe (New York: Harper & Row, 1969).

42 On the idea that film may require a multiplicity of partial theories, see Stephen Hawking and Leonard Mlodinow, 'The (Elusive) Theory of Everything', *Scientific American* 303 (4) (October 2010): 68–71 ('Physicists have long sought to find one final theory that would unify all of physics. Instead they may have to settle for several.').

43 For Wittgenstein's view of the nature of philosophy, see note 49 below.

44 Ludwig Wittgenstein, *Culture and Value*, edited by G.H. Von Wright, translated by Peter Winch (Chicago, IL: University of Chicago Press, 1980), 16. Embracing theoretical concepts is about more than external objects. Drawing on Wittgenstein's unpublished work, P.M.S. Hacker elaborates on Wittgenstein's comment in the text above that working in philosophy is working on oneself:

> It leads one to abandon certain combinations of words as senseless, and that involves a kind of resignation, not of intellect but of feeling. For [as Wittgenstein notes] it can be as difficult not to use an expression as to hold back tears ... hence Wittgenstein's daunting remark that every philosophical error is the mark of a character failing.
> *Wittgenstein's Place in Twentieth-Century Analytic Philosophy*
> (Oxford: Blackwell Publishers, 1996), 112.

For Metz:

> Psychoanalysis does not illuminate only the film, but also the conditions of desire of whoever makes himself its theoretician. Interwoven into every analytical undertaking is the thread of a self-analysis.
> 'The Imaginary Signifier', 79.

On embodiment and the figurative nature of theorizing, see, e.g., George Lakoff and Mark Johnson, *Philosophy in the Flesh: The Embodied Mind and Its Challenge to Western Thought* (New York: Basic Books, 1999). Roland Barthes reaches a similar conclusion from a very different perspective in *The Pleasure of the Text*, translated by Richard Miller (New York: Hill and Wang, 1975).

45 Since a radial analysis or heterarchy emphasizes our abilities to form clusters of knowledge by crafting (family) resemblances, it will lead theorists towards constructing what Wittgenstein refers

to as an 'overview' (*Übersicht*) or a 'perspicuous representation' (*übersichtliche Darstellung*) – a visual description or figure – that depicts not an a priori truth, but a 'form of life'. The method is more like passe-partout than photoengraving. See Glock, *Wittgenstein Dictionary*, 'Overview', 278–83. Here's a thought question: is it possible for some images in a film to function as 'concepts' for the film, offering an overview or perspicuous representation of the arguments of the film? Cf. note 2 above.

46 Bordwell, *Making Meaning*, 21–9.

47 André Bazin, 'For an Impure Cinema: In Defence of Adaptation', in *What Is Cinema?*, translated by Timothy Barnard (Montreal: Caboose, 2009), 107–37; also translated as 'In Defense of Mixed Cinema' by Hugh Gray in *What Is Cinema?* [vol. I] (Berkeley: University of California Press, 1967), 53–75. Dudley Andrew argues that: 'In effect there are two Bazins: the one of "L'Onto-logie de l'image photographique" founding a history of cinema's realism – from Stroheim through Renoir to neorealism – and the one of "Pour un cinéma impur", bolstering a modernist cinema.' *What Cinema Is! Bazin's* Quest *and Its Charge* (Oxford: Wiley-Blackwell, 2010), 110. *See* ONTOLOGY OF THE PHOTOGRAPHIC IMAGE.

48 On film specificity, see note 6 above.

49 Wittgenstein, *Philosophical Investigations*, §§ 89, 92, 106–33, 436. It is not that an object is viewed as being only a sensuous surface and essentially 'hollow' or that we cannot know whether the depths are 'empty' (which ideas lead towards such theoretical permutations as phenomenalism, idealism, solipsism, nominalism, nihilism, illusion, and scepticism), but rather that the mental picture itself of surface/depth or a palimpsest is rejected as a guide for thought about phenomena. What is hidden for Wittgenstein lies not in the depths but in one's language and memory concerning forms of life, thus requiring only 'reminders' of what makes sense to bring it forth (§§ 89, 127, 129, 140), like opening a drawer to re-collect some objects (cf. §§ 193, 194). In this connection, isn't it true that objects have normally been arranged in a drawer to form a provisional picture of their significance or non-significance? See generally Stanley Cavell, 'The World as Things: Collecting Thoughts on Collecting', in *Cavell on Film*, edited by William Rothman (Albany, NY: State University of New York Press, 2005), 241–79.

Related to mysterious depths are cinema's supposed evanescent qualities: an apparently fleeting, shadowy, elusive, even ghostly flow on screen that seems to carry the nature of cinema just beyond our grasp towards an elsewhere, even though in the same moment cinema is acknowledged to be a machine at work. Compare three grammatically different norms of description of a machine – physical, philosophical (ideal mode), and modal (where the latter is seemingly able to produce 'shadow' movements) distinguished by Wittgenstein (§§ 193, 194) – with various descriptions of film as a spectral machine (see, e.g., the entries APPARATUS THEORY [BAUDRY] and APPARATUS THEORY [PLATO]). Do claims about a spectral film machine depend on a slippage among norms of description?

50 On the notion of fiction, see note 21 above.

51 Béla Balázs, *Béla Balázs: Early Film Theory* – Visible Man *and* The Spirit of Film, edited by Erica Carter, translated by Rodney Livingstone (New York: Berghahn Books, 2010), 3.

# AFFECT, FILM AND

The term 'affect' was not widely used in cinema studies until the 1990s, when it emerged in research at the intersection of film and philosophy. This overview will begin by establishing how Linda Williams's important essay 'Film Bodies: Gender, Genre and Excess' (1991) conceptualizes the affective impact of film on the bodies of audience members. It will then examine changing approaches to affect, with particular attention to cognitivist accounts and to phenomenological film theorist Vivian Sobchack's noteworthy intervention in the field.

## Affect

Although Williams uses the term 'sensational' rather than 'affective', in context both terms describe felt bodily responses and sensory reactions to cinema. Affect refers to sensations, feelings, and bodily states including visceral reactions, physiological arousal, and reflex responses to stimuli, such as flinching at startling sounds or movements. While affect is an essential component of emotion (for instance, blushing is a tell-tale sign of embarrassment), emotion is a broader category of feeling that also involves desire, imagination, and complex forms of cognition (*see* EMOTION, FILM AND).

Williams was not the first researcher to take affect seriously. Philosophers dating back to Plato and Aristotle have debated the instructive and negative influence of passionate responses to poetry, art, music, and theatre. Later, in *Carnal Thoughts*, Sobchack traced studies of film and affect to Soviet filmmaker Sergei Eisenstein's 'interest in the somatic effects of the cinema' in the 1920s and to film theorist Siegfried Kracauer's fascination in the 1940s with film's capacity to 'stimulate us physiologically and sensually' (2004, 55). Until recently few film scholars followed these thinkers in tackling the importance of affect. Instead, approaches such as Marxist ideological criticism, semiotics, structuralism, and psychoanalysis dominated film theory until the 1990s. In particular, Laura Mulvey's 'Visual Pleasure and Narrative Cinema' (1975) (*see* GAZE THEORY) and Deleuze's account of masochism (1971) inform Williams's essay. While psychoanalytic film theory engaged with notions of desire and pleasure, it did not focus specifically on affect. Consequently, part of Williams's challenge was to test how psychoanalysis could help explain how audiences engage with affective screen texts.

## Linda Williams's 'Film Bodies'

'Film Bodies' commences by describing affective responses to what Williams terms 'body genres' – such as melodrama, horror, and pornography – that provoke strong visceral reactions, inducing 'a physical jolt' (Williams 1991, 2). Drawing on commentary from fans and critics, Williams's article describes these genres as 'excessive', 'gross', 'unseemly' movies, referring to them as 'tear jerkers', 'fear jerkers', and 'jerk-off films' that provoke heated 'arousal' and elicit sensations including 'sobs of anguish', prickling eyes and constricting throats, or hairs on the nape of the neck 'bristling' frightfully. The language used to describe these genres and responses prompts Williams to examine cultural judgements about affect and its relationship to gender. Negative judgements about genres associated with an excess of sensation derive from a gendered hierarchy of value based on the mind/body split of Cartesian dualism – the idea that human ontology is grounded in cognition, as proposed by philosopher Descartes in his famous adage 'I think, therefore I am'. Williams points out that 'the bodies of women figured on the screen have functioned traditionally as the primary *embodiments* of pleasure, fear, and pain' in pornography, horror, and melodrama (1991, 4), thereby cementing presumptions aligning femininity with affect. While complicating gender biases associating women with embodiment rather than rationality, Williams's choice of words nevertheless betrays the assumption that films have the capacity to wrest or 'jerk' reactions from the spectator's body in ways that leave little room for resistance or critical interpretation. Later in the article Williams goes on to state that '[t]he rhetoric of violence of the jerk suggests the extent to which viewers feel too directly, too viscerally manipulated by the text' (5). This suggests a lack of volition in affective responses, which renders them a suspect yet powerful and intriguing aspect of the film experience.

Williams's central thesis is that there is value in analysing film affect, even in disparaged 'body genres' such as pornography, horror, and 'women's films' or 'weepies':

> sex, violence, and emotion are fundamental elements of the sensational effects of these three types of films ... by thinking comparatively about all three 'gross' and sensational film body genres we might be able to get beyond the mere fact of sensation to explore its system and structure as well as its effect on the bodies of spectators.
>
> (Williams 1991, 3)

Underpinning Williams's work is a concern with gender that typifies feminist psychoanalytic film criticism. Yet, she is also concerned with the cultural position of certain genres in relation to their visceral qualities. The label 'low cultural status' is often applied to films with exaggerated affective qualities due to the devaluation of emotion and bodily sensation by comparison with critical distance and aesthetic and intellectual engagement. The success of these genres is based on their abilities to arouse affective or bodily responses that mirror, to a certain extent, those of screen characters: 'what may especially mark these body genres as low is the perception that the body of the spectator is caught up in an almost involuntary mimicry of the emotion or sensation of the body on the screen' (Williams 1991, 4).

## Psychoanalysis

Williams contends that the attraction of body genres and their denigration as low cultural texts hinge on the sense in which, in psychoanalytic terms, 'we are all perverts' (Williams 1991, 6). She states that audience members are understood to derive perverse pleasure from feelings of masochistic powerlessness or sadistic, voyeuristic empowerment and the fantasies and affective stimulation films offer. Strongly affective films and the perverse pleasures they afford are distinguished by 'an apparent lack of proper esthetic distance, a sense of over-involvement in sensation and emotion' (5).

Williams establishes perversion as 'a category of cultural analysis' crucial to understanding genres based on affect and desire (6). She argues that affective responses to body genres function to address problems in our culture, sexualities, and identities (9), and concludes that: 'The deployment of sex, violence, and emotion is thus in no way gratuitous and in no way strictly limited to each of these genres; it is instead a cultural form of problem solving' (9), a cultural form that operates in relation to gender fantasies. This does not just involve mimicry of bodies on screen, but a more complex negotiation of changing ideas and feelings about gender and sexuality expressed through the physical release of tension in visceral narratives (11–12).

Williams is not alone in using psychoanalysis to theorize cinematic viscerality. The assumption of a strong relationship between gender, sexuality, and the unconscious disturbances and pleasures offered by narrative film is a defining feature of psychoanalytic criticism. Following Deleuze, Steven Shaviro argues in *The Cinematic Body* that 'film moves and affects the spectator precisely to the extent that it lures him or her into an excessive intimacy' (1993, 54). Shaviro views the dynamics of spectatorship as 'masochistic, mimetic, tactile, and corporeal' (1993, 56). Similarly, in *The New-Brutality Film: Race and Affect in Contemporary Hollywood Cinema*, Paul Gormley argues that sensational, violent films are 'concerned with the dynamics of sadism and masochism in the viewing experience' (2005, 192–3). These authors rely on accounts of psychosexual perversion to explain the affective impact of screen violence. Like Williams, Shaviro and Gormley assume perversions govern visual pleasure rather than adopting a holistic approach to affect that recognizes cognitive, evaluative aspects as well as its basis in sensation.

'Film Bodies' remains significant for its role in problematizing mimetic understandings of how audiences respond to screen characters' expressions of affect, and for complicating psychoanalytic assumptions about the gendered pleasures of cinema by shifting the focus from unconscious fantasy and its ideological implications to physical sensation. This work legitimated the study of bodily reactions in disparaged genres, identifying their cultural significance.

Williams's article was published at a turning point when scholars began to question psychoanalysis and to search for alternative understandings of spectatorship. Cognitivist and phenomenological accounts of affect have since gathered credence, placing unconscious fantasies and fears as secondary to affective experiences of the audiovisual, kinetic qualities of cinema.

## Cognitivism

Psychoanalysis remained a dominant approach until Noël Carroll's *Mystifying Movies* (1988) and *The Philosophy of Horror, or, Paradoxes of the Heart* (1990) and Murray Smith's *Engaging Characters* (1995), which were among the first extended cognitivist studies of film affect. These cognitivists explore how empathic engagement – 'feeling with' screen characters – invokes the affective dimension of emotion (*see* IDENTIFICATION, THEORY OF; IMAGINED OBSERVER HYPOTHESIS).

Smith's influential account discerns three distinct components of empathy: affective mimicry, autonomic reactions, and emotional simulation. Affective mimicry involves mirroring a character's feelings via 'perceptual registering and reflexive simulation of the emotion of another person', 'involuntary neuromuscular response', or 'kinaesthetic mimicry' (Smith 1995, 99). For instance, close-ups of faces can cue empathy by prompting spectators to mimic a character's expression; however, close-ups can also prompt a contrasting reaction such as perceiving someone's rage and responding with fear. Autonomic reactions are involuntary: spectators relate to screen characters partly by experiencing coinciding responses to stimuli common to the screen world and the cinematic environment when, for instance, reacting to an unexpected loud noise (102). Emotional simulation comes closest to the lay definition of empathy. It involves simulating feelings by forming hypotheses about how one might respond to a situation. Spectators imaginatively project themselves into a character's situation to the extent that they empathically share the character's affective responses.

More recent research, such as Carl Plantinga's cognitive-perceptual theory of spectatorship in *Moving Viewers*, concedes some ground to psychoanalysis by acknowledging unconscious responses that 'bypass conscious inference-making', while contending that the audience's feelings about films and film characters are predominantly conscious and rational (2009, 8). Plantinga understands affective responses to cinema in relation to cognitive psychology, mirror neurons, and the paradigm scenarios, cultural scripts, or schemata through which members of a society learn affective and emotive responsiveness.

## Phenomenology

Phenomenology is another philosophical strand of film theory that developed parallel to cognitivism (see PHENOMENOLOGY AND FILM). Differences in emphasis between these approaches are evident in their language use. Distinct from cognitivists' concern with the rationality of 'empathic reactions', 'cognitive-perceptual processes', and 'autonomic responses', phenomenologists' fascination with 'carnality', 'embodiment', and 'the sensorium' evinces their interest in the role of the body in film experience. Although cognitivism has a tendency to focus on aesthetic cues and intellectual responses in ways that abstract the affective dimensions of cinematic experience, many goals of cognitivism and phenomenology are complementary (see Hanich 2010; Plantinga 2009).

Instead of seeking the unconscious cause of pleasure or discomfort, or attempting to categorize and rationalize audience responses, phenomenology describes the experience of watching, listening, and responding to film, then considers what the effects or cultural implications of these reactions might be. Building primarily on philosopher Maurice Merleau-Ponty's work, a number of film theorists have used phenomenology to analyse affect in relation to screen aesthetics and character engagement. Sobchack's groundbreaking study *Address of the Eye* (1992) came to define the field, and by the new millennium phenomenology was emerging as an alternative to cognitivist and psychoanalytic interpretations of film affect. Sobchack positions her phenomenological methodology in relation to Williams's 'Film Bodies', but eschews psychoanalysis in favour of a holistic account of embodied perception.

Sobchack's work has led to an explosion of research on affective responses to cinema that seeks to redress the oversights of established film scholarship, with its focus on visual pleasure grounded in ideology and psychosexual theory. For instance, in *The Skin of the Film* (2000) and *Touch* (2002), Laura Marks examines how screen texts evoke affect through the tactile qualities of vision and sound. Marks discusses 'haptic perception', explaining that the tactile impression of indistinct, unfocused images or sounds prompts audiences to grasp for sensory meaning rather than intellectualizing what they see and hear. She suggests the texture of haptic imagery touches the viewer's body in a direct, affective manner instead of just working through characterization or through acts of categorization and narrative interpretation (Marks 2000, 164). Such work demonstrates that film can elicit responses that may include but also exceed identification with or reactions to protagonists' affective displays.

Marks's account of hapticity informed Sobchack's second volume on phenomenology, *Carnal Thoughts: Embodiment and Moving Image Culture* (2004). This body of work provides the foundation from which researchers have developed phenomenological approaches to the moving image, including Jennifer Barker's sensuous approach to the cinematic experience, *The Tactile Eye* (2009), and Julian Hanich's account of genre, aesthetics, and affect in *Cinematic Emotion in Horror Films and Thrillers* (2010).

In *Carnal Thoughts* Sobchack asks 'what it means to say that movies "touch us"' (2004, 1). Using phenomenology to focus on bodily experience and perception, she sets out to make conscious meaning out of affective, sensory responses to cinema. Indeed, the most significant contribution of phenomenology to understandings of film and affect is the emphasis on sensory engagement and the physical body. We know and access screen texts in and through our bodies, hence Sobchack seeks to understand 'the embodied structures that allow for more than a merely cognitive or rudimentary knee-jerk cinematic sensibility and attempts to demonstrate how cinematic intelligibility, meaning, and value emerge carnally through our senses' (8). The body, she contends, 'grounds and mediates' the affective experience of film, yet she also notes that affect is culturally and contextually inflected (60). This reconceptualization of cinematic identification suggests audiences do more than identify with characters and the affect they display; they also draw on personal and cultural experience as they respond to cinematic elements including velocity, spatiality, and tactility.

Phenomenology has the capacity to offer fresh insights into films eliciting strong affective responses. In bypassing traditional ways of understanding, phenomenology facilitates a reassessment of how we make sense of cinema, and a revaluation of film, affect, and the embodied role of the spectator. Theories of affect are becoming increasingly important in response to technological advances that are extending the sensory, experiential dimensions of 3D film, television, and digital games.

JANE STADLER

## Works cited

Barker, Jennifer. 2009. *The Tactile Eye: Touch and the Cinematic Experience*. Berkeley: University of California Press.

Carroll, Noël. 1988. *Mystifying Movies: Fads and Fallacies in Contemporary Film Theory*. New York: Columbia University Press.

——. 1990. *The Philosophy of Horror, or, Paradoxes of the Heart*. New York: Routledge.

Deleuze, Gilles. 1971. *Masochism: An Interpretation of Coldness and Cruelty*. Translated by Jean McNeil. New York: Braziller.

Descartes, René. 1984. 'First Meditation: Meditations on First Philosophy'. In *The Philosophical Writings of Descartes*, vol. 2, translated by J. Cottingham, R. Stoothoff, and D. Murdoch. Cambridge: Cambridge University Press.

Gormley, Paul. 2005. *The New-Brutality Film: Race and Affect in Contemporary Hollywood Cinema*. Bristol: Intellect.

Hanich, Julian. 2010. *Cinematic Emotion in Horror Films and Thrillers: The Aesthetic Paradox of Pleasurable Fear*. New York: Routledge.

Marks, Laura U. 2000. *The Skin of the Film: Intercultural Cinema, Embodiment and the Senses*. Durham, NC: Duke University Press.

——. 2002. *Touch: Sensuous Theory and Multisensory Media*. Minneapolis: University of Minnesota Press.

Mulvey, Laura. 1975. 'Visual Pleasure and Narrative Cinema'. *Screen* 16 (3): 6–18.

Plantinga, Carl. 2009. *Moving Viewers: American Film and the Spectator's Experience*. Berkeley: University of California Press.

Shaviro, Steven. 1993. *The Cinematic Body*. Minneapolis: University of Minnesota Press.

Smith, Murray. 1995. *Engaging Characters: Fiction, Emotion and the Cinema*. Oxford: Clarendon Press.

Sobchack, Vivian. 1992. *Address of the Eye: A Phenomenology of Film Experience*. Princeton, NJ: Princeton University Press.

——. 2004. *Carnal Thoughts: Embodiment and Moving Image Culture*. Berkeley: University of California Press.

Williams, Linda. 1991. 'Film Bodies: Gender, Genre and Excess'. *Film Quarterly* 44 (4): 2–13.

# ANGLO-AMERICAN FILM THEORY

## Overview

There is a long history in both Britain and the United States of serious interest regarding the significance of moving images. Important forerunners, including Vachel Lindsay, Hugo Münsterberg, and Rudolf Arnheim, established film as a proper object of study. Their cumulative efforts paved the way for later critics interested both in the specificity of the cinematic medium and in exploring broader questions concerning the nature of representation, changing notions of the modern subject, and the sociological effects of new, technologically mediated forms of popular culture. Though these writers helped to set the stage for more in-depth theoretical research, their work did not lead to a distinct scholarly endeavour or field of inquiry.

Instead, what was later recognized as 'Anglo-American film theory' was largely an *ex nihilo* creation of the 1970s – one that did not so much share a set of clear intellectual or philosophical principles as a common political and institutional context. As film theory expanded rapidly over the next two decades, its fortunes were closely tied to the entirely new discipline of film studies. Theory benefited from being part of this uniquely interdisciplinary endeavour – opportunistically drawing on neighbouring fields such as art history, comparative literature, and literary criticism. However, it was also limited due to the fact that the field's still embryonic infrastructure was dependent on practical considerations, such as the emergence of new scholarly journals and the nominal availability of films for research purposes.

As a result of these factors, film theory has been a largely *ad hoc*, hybrid formation vexed by several uneven and conflicting developments. In the most glaring example of this, Anglo-American film theory rose to prominence by aligning itself with a number of French thinkers known for their work within semiotics, psychoanalysis, and Marxism (*see* CONTEMPORARY FILM THEORY). As much as these affiliations allowed the new discipline to distinguish its critical virtues from other disciplines, and establish legitimacy by grounding itself in 'serious' theory, they also engendered a fundamental rift with what would subsequently be constructed as 'classical' film theory (*see* ART, FILM AS; CLASSICAL FILM THEORY).

The rapport with contemporaneous European influences furthermore insulated film theory from pertinent debates regarding popular culture and dismissed potential allies ranging from Herbert Marcuse, Norman O. Brown, Gregory Bateson, and Marshall McLuhan. Even as theory found its place within the academy, these rifts and missed opportunities engendered intense debates and eventual divisions. Although film theory ultimately succeeded in establishing itself as a distinct field within the humanities, it was simultaneously marred by a combustible blend of bravado and idiosyncrasy, a number of contentious methodological and jurisdictional debates, and by recurrent feuds that threatened to overshadow its larger contributions.

## Prelude to political modernism

In the 1960s the New Left, along with a growing counterculture, had a significant impact across college campuses just as the first wave of the post-Second World War 'Baby Boom' began to matriculate in record-setting numbers. The New Left emerged as an earlier generation of liberals collapsed under the acute pressures of McCarthyism and anti-communist paranoia. Specific groups such as the Students for Democratic Society reinvigorated the Left by initiating a new wave of student activism and social protest that soon dovetailed with broader efforts such as the Civil Rights Movement, Black Power, and anti-war movements (Gitlin 1993). The sharp rise in political consciousness coincided with an expanding and amorphous counterculture that had taken root in the previous decade. Widely identified with the Beats and their various artistic endeavours, the counterculture more broadly encouraged experimentation with new forms of knowledge (*vis-à-vis*, for example, existentialism, Buddhism, and drugs) and a predilection for youthful rebellion (often linked to new forms of popular culture such as rock 'n' roll and sexual freedom).

As a corollary to these developments, 'film culture' began to expand on campuses and throughout major metropolitan areas (Zryd 2008). Film societies, made possible by the wider availability of 16mm prints and speciality distributors keen on catering to the youth market, exposed students to a wide array of European and International New Wave cinemas. While introducing important formal and stylistic innovations, this encounter was equally significant for the way in which it amplified the angst and oppositional sensibilities already incumbent in many students. In the case of select figures such as Jean-Luc Godard, there was also the suggestion that cinematic experimentation was a primer for more radical forms of political engagement. To some degree, campus film societies were following the success of various grass-roots groups that began to flourish in New York, San Francisco, and Los Angeles over the course of the 1950s. Distribution companies like Cinema 16, Film-Makers Cooperative, Art in Cinema, and Canyon Cinema were vital for encouraging the production, distribution, exhibition, and criticism of new and experimental forms of cinema. Like their counterparts in the New Left, these groups were guided by a cadre of luminaries devoted to proselytizing a new generation and to cultivating a more participatory approach to filmmaking (James 2002). This new vanguard and the rising tide of film culture not only recalled earlier efforts to democratize the film medium (i.e. the Film and Photo Leagues of the 1930s) but also echoed the Parisian salons of the 1920s where filmmaking, criticism, and theory all coalesced as part of an exuberance shared by connoisseurs and dilettantes alike (Abel 1988).

The correspondence between New Left student movements and grass-roots film organizations is especially clear in the work of groups like the Newsreel collective. Formed in 1967, the group was committed to moving beyond either simply participating in the intensifying conflicts of the era or objectively recording them. Newsreel instead subscribed to a revolutionary politics in which theory and practice were necessarily synthesized. And it was believed that filmmaking was an ideal vehicle for carrying out this principle (Nichols 1980). Events in France, culminating in the uprisings known simply as May 1968, both paralleled and then accelerated these ideas. *Cahiers du cinéma* and the newly formed *Ciné-thique* were closely engaged in these events, and both journals stridently debated the relationship between film and politics (Harvey 1980). These debates, in turn, spawned a number of theoretically based groups devoted to a more militant style of filmmaking. The groups aligned themselves with the more doctrinaire Soviet practitioners of the 1920s (taking as their namesakes Vertov and Medvedkin) and thus renounced any common heritage with the more aesthete, and ostensibly bourgeois, French avant-garde. While the combination of politics and filmmaking had been fermenting for at least a decade, it was in many ways these developments in France that finalized the launch of what D.N. Rodowick (1994) later identified as 'political modernism'. That is, at their core these groups believed political analysis and aesthetic practice must be joined together to effect radical social change, and that theory was a fundamental component within this performative discourse and its larger rhetorical strategies.

## *Screen* memories

For many, the British journal *Screen* stands as the quintessential locus of Anglo-American film theory. Though primarily associated with the theoretical positions it advanced throughout the 1970s, the journal was in fact the result of a long gestation under the auspices of the British Film Institute and the Society for Education in Film and Television where it was originally conceived to take the place of *Screen Education* and other publications focused mainly on pedagogical concerns.[1] It was ultimately because of these circumstances that *Screen* began its formative period with a large degree of financial support and intellectual independence (Bolas 2009, 266).[2] With the arrival of new editor Sam Rohdie, the journal exploited these advantages and began to articulate a more pronounced theoretical agenda. This was immediately evident in 1971 with the publication of Comolli and Narboni's 'Cinema/Ideology/Criticism' (*see* IDEOLOGY, CINEMA AND) and then, shortly thereafter, with an entire issue devoted to translating and publishing debates among Soviet artists and filmmakers. This signalled a clear alignment with the more politicized rhetoric that had been brewing in the US and France as well as the editorial policies that had emerged at the *New Left Review* under Perry Anderson (Buckland 2008, 530–1). *Screen* went on to further establish itself as a trailblazer in a broader shift towards theory with regular contributions by Peter Wollen, Colin MacCabe, Stephen Heath, and Ben Brewster (who also translated several key texts and served as editor between 1974 and 1976).[3]

The work of *Screen*'s contributors directly engaged with contemporaneous French thinkers flourishing in a period of vibrant intellectual development. This diverse milieu included several individuals (e.g. Claude Lévi-Strauss, Gérard Genette, and Christian Metz) working within a model of structuralist linguistics founded by Ferdinand de Saussure. It also included Jacques Lacan, the leading figure in an iconoclastic 'return' to Freudian psychoanalysis, Louis Althusser, who initiated a new wave of interest in ideology and Marxist theory, and Roland Barthes, whose *Mythologies* paved the way for a more sophisticated model of cultural analysis. (This particular group – Saussure, Lacan, Althusser, and Barthes – would later be disparagingly lumped together as 'SLAB theory'.) As *Screen* found success with its new, and at times polemical, devotion to theory, similar developments were under way in the US, where the journal *Jump-Cut* was founded in 1974, the UW-Milwaukee's Center for Twentieth Century Studies in 1976 and 1978 held two major conferences featuring leading figures from both France and the UK, and a first wave of scholarly publications devoted to theory began to appear (e.g. Andrew 1976; Nichols 1976).

This turn to theory, both at *Screen* and across the burgeoning discipline more generally, was part of a much larger zeitgeist that would later be labelled 'French Theory'. Often considered the starting point for this broader development, the 1966 Johns Hopkins conference, 'The Languages of Criticism and the Sciences of Man: The Structural Controversy', featured many of the key figures that later shaped Anglo-American film theory. The conference not only introduced these thinkers to an English-speaking audience, but whetted the intellectual appetite of the New Left generation – directing students to complex theoretical material that might supplement both their oppositional temperament and their political endeavours (Cusset 2008). The flood of French Theory was further expedited by the arrival of several academic journals devoted to translating and analysing this work. Among the most notable of these were *Diacritics* (established in 1971), *Sub-Stance* (est. 1971), *Critical Inquiry* (est. 1974), and *October* (est. 1976).

While the influx of theory enjoyed a large degree of success, it is also important to note that it was never part of a clearly defined or homogeneous project. Individual theorists rarely came to any kind of consensus and the nature of the academy actually encouraged undue competition among them and their advocates. As factionalism took root, perplexing schisms and general confusion loomed on the horizon. For example, whereas film theorists gravitated to Althusser and Lacan, literary theorists were pulled in very different theoretical directions. One particular group pursued deconstruction and the work of Jacques Derrida, who had posed something of a separate controversy for the way he blurred the line between structuralism and post-structuralism. Though Derrida was an important voice within the broader milieu of French Theory, it is difficult to say why he (and others ranging from Michel Foucault and Jean Baudrillard to Julia Kristeva and Luce Irigaray) were never allotted the same central role that had been reserved for the likes of Althusser and Lacan.

The overall success and incongruity of theory's uptake are also evident in one of the most important and representative strands within Anglo-American film theory. In 1975, *Screen* published Laura Mulvey's 'Visual Pleasure and Narrative Cinema', a galvanizing feminist critique of how patriarchy structures Hollywood's prevailing system of representation. Feminist critique certainly fit within *Screen*'s larger agenda and several female scholars – Claire Johnston, Diana Matias, and Christine Gledhill – were involved in the journal leading up to Mulvey's piece. Nonetheless, the journal's primary focus on semiology and psychoanalysis meant that feminist issues were something of a secondary concern. The 'Visual Pleasure' essay, which was soon followed by the inaugural publication of *Camera Obscura: A Journal of Feminism and Film Theory* in 1976, was a clear turning point, even though the larger impact of feminist film theory was part of a long-term academic development that would not be fully manifested until the following decade as a subsequent wave of important scholars – Kaja Silverman, Mary Ann Doane, Teresa De Lauretis, and Constance Penley among many others – began to publish regularly.

In some respects, as Mulvey's prominence grew over this period her essay became synonymous with film theory as a whole. This not only skirted the various disputes within *Screen* itself, but also elided the specificity of her claims whereby theory was appropriated as a 'political weapon' in the service of developing a radical counter-cinema. More often than not, subsequent feminist theory deviated from Mulvey's call to action by pursuing substantial engagements with psychoanalysis on its own terms, while also returning to earlier paradigms such as authorship and genre in order to reclaim overlooked female directors and the 'woman's film'. Mulvey's provocative rhetoric also prompted an intense questioning of the male gaze and various attempts by other under-represented groups to outflank her position (*see* GAZE THEORY). This eventually both diluted the main thrust of her argument and undercut the aims of a strictly feminist agenda within film theory. What's more, the success of feminist film theorists often coincided with more convoluted and increasingly incendiary debates that were part of an ongoing fracturing of the discipline. By the end of the 1980s, certain factions were leaving for the more welcoming environment of emerging fields such as media studies and cultural studies. Meanwhile, within film studies there was a steadily growing antipathy for theory that was about to explode into a full-scale onslaught.

## The backlash

Although film theory had enjoyed a great deal of success, it also had its detractors. Noël Carroll, for instance, initiated a caustic debate with his scathing 1982 review of Stephen Heath's *Questions of Cinema* (Carroll 1982). Carroll subsequently expanded the attack into a book-length interrogation of contemporary film theory (Carroll 1988). David Bordwell meanwhile noted his scepticism on a number of occasions, most explicitly in his critique of the 'symptomatic interpretations' supported by theory (Bordwell 1989) (*see* SYMPTOMATIC READING). In 1996, Bordwell and Carroll jointly edited the collection *Post-theory: Reconstructing Film Studies*. Featuring introductions by both editors, their earlier reservations culminated in a full-scale indictment against the theoretical manoeuvres that held sway throughout the 1970s and 1980s. They criticized the penchant for unnecessary jargon and indicated a general dismay at the speed and vigour with which theory had gained acceptance within the academy. To counter what they termed 'Grand Theory', both scholars made the case for a more modest form of theorizing based on evidence, arguments, and implications rather than doctrinaire abstractions. To this end, Bordwell advocated a more formalist-oriented approach he labelled 'historical poetics', while Carroll encouraged the adoption of more empirically based models provided by either cognitive psychology or analytic philosophy.

Despite their interest in opening new avenues of research, there were some flaws in their position. The most problematic was that Bordwell and Carroll gave undue credence to the notion that theory had either reached some kind of totalized apotheosis or that it had been universally accepted. In point of fact, film theory had been embattled from its outset as dissenting views – typically supported by competing journals – vigorously questioned the merits of *Screen* and its ilk (Altman 1985). Of course, even *Screen* had its share of internal discord. It suffered a succession of quarrelsome resignations, was the target of bureaucratic admonishment, and its acolytes had been labelled intellectual terrorists by at least one critic, and all before the journal had finished its first decade.[4]

The larger problem with the *Post-theory* account was its unwillingness to engage in a genuine debate with the theoretical positions it was wont to reject. In the end, Bordwell and Carroll may have simply added to the overall morass of the situation, exacerbating the proclivity for interpersonal animosity and petulant bickering that was already par for the course in many humanities departments. Another problem was that their objections coincided with the rightward political thrust under way in both the US and UK. By the end of the 1980s the backlash that had been directed most pointedly at feminism began to expand to multiculturalism, political correctness, and any other vestige of the New Left. The critique put forward by Bordwell and Carroll only reinforced the then entrenched anti-intellectualism and the distrust of academics ignited by scandalous revelations of past indiscretions that culminated in the infamous 1996 Sokal Affair.[5] On the one hand, these developments dovetailed with larger shifts within higher education whereby universities were forced to cut many of the resources that had been instrumental in film theory's formation. On the other hand, the backlash against theory managed to intensify the fault lines in an already heterogeneous and relatively unstable field, creating a much more antagonistic and cynical atmosphere.

## Current issues

Despite much lamenting about the state of theory, high-level, theoretically engaged scholarship has continued more or less unabated. It is also true, however, that many of the new directions within film studies (e.g. the historical turn to early cinema and the emergence of new media), while still in dialogue with various theoretical discourses, have contributed to a qualitative shift away from the canonical debates and terminology to which an earlier generation had been beholden. This underlying shift is evident even in many of the more theoretically oriented works. For example, recent accounts devoted to Walter Benjamin, André Bazin, and Gilles Deleuze (who for various reasons had been overlooked or misunderstood by previous scholars) combine the utmost theoretical sophistication with dynamic new perspectives. At the same time, this work suggests a fundamentally inward turn: theory is mobilized as part of an established set of disciplinary protocols and is more strictly utilized for the purpose of enhancing or expanding the field as such. In some respects, this shift is a mark of the discipline's overall maturation and its acceptance as a legitimate area of study. Having established this merit, it now has the luxury of focusing primarily on the issues and mechanics necessary for its internal functioning instead of its broader relationship to the world outside the academy.

There are, of course, several potential problems with this new situation. There is the threat that the radical politics and grass-roots practices that were such crucial assets in film theory's formation will be diminished or forgotten. Also, the system of global capitalism that partly initiated the political opposition of the 1960s has grown all the more dominant. This means that higher learning is increasingly subservient to the market and its contradictory demands. Intellectual endeavours, such as film theory, now run the risk of extinction unless they can be rationalized within the university and the larger economic system that it supports and maintains.

KEVIN MCDONALD

## Notes

1 According to Terry Bolas (2009), *Screen* debuted in 1969 as a replacement for the Society for Education in Film and Television's two existing publications: *Screen Education* (published bimonthly since 1959) and the *Screen Education Yearbook*. Despite the detailed account provided by Bolas, there is still some confusion surrounding these journals. *Screen* begins in 1969 numbered as volume 10, ostensibly continuing the numbering that had been initiated with *Screen Education*. *Screen Education* then re-emerged as a notes section in the back of *Screen* in 1971, only to resume its status as a separate publication between 1974 and 1982.

2 The Birmingham Centre for Contemporary Cultural Studies, for instance, was not as well funded as *Screen*. The centre was unable to pursue questions concerning cinema mainly because it lacked necessary resources such as screening facilities and 16mm projectors.
3 For a more detailed account, see Rosen (1977 and 2008).
4 These criticisms are discussed and quoted by Bolas (2009, 279).
5 The Sokal Affair refers to Alan Sokal, a physicist who submitted a pseudo-scientific article to the journal *Social Text* with the intent of ridiculing 'high theory'. The publication of the article set off a minor scandal that emboldened many critics of the university system and the humanities in particular. See Cusset (2008, 5–7).

## Works cited

Abel, Richard, ed. 1988. *French Film Theory and Criticism: A History/Anthology, 1907–1939*, Volume 1. Princeton, NJ: Princeton University Press.

Altman, Charles F. 1985. 'Psychoanalysis and Cinema: The Imaginary Discourse'. In *Movies and Methods*, Volume 2, edited by Bill Nichols, 517–31. Berkeley: University of California Press.

Andrew, Dudley. 1976. *The Major Film Theories: An Introduction*. London: Oxford University Press.

Bolas, Terry. 2009. *Screen Education: From Film Appreciation to Media Studies*. Bristol: Intellect.

Bordwell, David. 1989. *Making Meaning: Inference and Rhetoric in the Interpretation of Cinema*. Cambridge, MA: Harvard University Press.

Bordwell, David, and Noël Carroll, eds. 1996. *Post-theory: Reconstructing Film Studies*. Madison: University of Wisconsin Press.

Buckland, Warren. 2008. 'Film and Media Studies Pedagogy'. In *The Oxford Handbook of Film and Media Studies*, edited by Robert Kolker, 527–56. New York: Oxford University Press.

Carroll, Noël. 1982. 'Address to the Heathen'. *October* 23: 89–163.

——. 1988. *Mystifying Movies: Fads and Fallacies in Contemporary Film Theory*. New York: Columbia University Press.

Comolli, Jean-Luc, and Jean Narboni. 1971. 'Cinema/Ideology/Criticism'. Translated by Susan Bennett. *Screen* 12 (1): 27–38.

Cusset, François. 2008. *French Theory: How Foucault, Derrida, Deleuze, and Co. Transformed the Intellectual Life of the United States*. Translated by Jeff Fort. Minneapolis: University of Minnesota Press.

Gitlin, Todd. 1993. *The Sixties: Years of Hope, Days of Rage*. New York: Bantam.

Harvey, Sylvia. 1980. *May '68 and Film Culture*. London: BFI Publishing.

James, David E. 2002. '"The Movies Are a Revolution": Film and the Counterculture'. In *Imagine Nation: The American Counterculture of the 1960s and '70s*, edited by Peter Braunstein and Michael William Doyle, 275–304. New York: Routledge.

Mulvey, Laura. 1975. 'Visual Pleasure and Narrative Cinema'. *Screen* 16 (3): 6–18.

Nichols, Bill, ed. 1976. *Movies and Methods*, vol. 1. Berkeley: University of California Press.

——. 1980. *Newsreel: Documentary Filmmaking on the American Left*. New York: Arno Press.

Rodowick, D.N. 1994. *The Crisis of Political Modernism: Criticism and Ideology in Contemporary Film Theory*. 2nd edition. Berkeley: University of California Press.

Rosen, Philip. 1977. 'Screen and the Marxist Project in Film Criticism'. *Quarterly Review of Film Studies* 2 (3): 273–87.

——.2008. '*Screen* and 1970s Film Theory'. In *Inventing Film Studies*, edited by Lee Grieveson and Haidee Wasson, 264–97. Durham, NC: Duke University Press.

Zryd, Michael. 2008. 'Experimental Film and the Development of Film Study in America'. In *Inventing Film Studies*, edited by Lee Grieveson and Haidee Wasson, 182–216. Durham, NC: Duke University Press.

# APPARATUS THEORY (BAUDRY)

In the 1970s Jean-Louis Baudry published two essays that became founding texts of apparatus theory. The first article, 'Effets idéologiques produits par l'appareil de base', was published in *Cinéthique* 7/8 in 1970 (translation: Baudry 1986a); the second, 'Le dispositif: approches métapsychologiques de l'impression de réalité', appeared five years later in *Communications* (translation: Baudry 1986b).

In the first, 'Ideological Effects of the Basic Cinematographic Apparatus', Baudry sets out to analyse cinema as a specific mode of production. Reflections on the cinematic apparatus, Baudry argues, should not be limited to semiotic and aesthetic frameworks but 'integrated into a general theory of the ideology of cinema' (1986a, 296). He extends the question of how social relations are encoded as artistic and symbolic expression to an inquiry into the ways the medium of film itself (i.e. the technological conditions of these expressions) predisposes certain orders of social thought and relations.

In 'The Apparatus: Metapsychological Approaches to the Impression of Reality in the Cinema', Baudry shifts the focus towards uncovering connections between the cinematic apparatus and the optical models Sigmund Freud and Jacques Lacan used to describe the organization and development of the human psyche. Since Plato, Baudry observes, optical metaphors have been a privileged means to expose epistemological and psychological conditions of human understanding. Seizing on 'term for term' (1986b, 300) resemblances between these models and cinema, Baudry outlines a theory of cinema's intricate relationship with structures of truth and desire.

Taken together, both essays orchestrate a critique of media that challenges the view of technology as ideologically neutral. The doctrine of technological neutrality holds that ideology is merely a 'content' that can be dropped into any form or apparatus as, say, wine fills a glass. Baudry attacks this notion by showing how the cinematic apparatus is invested with desire and premised on social values and assumptions.[1] Thus Baudry's reflections on the apparatus combine, in fact, two kinds of dispositional theories. One investigates the instrumental role of technology in the organization of social systems and institutions; the other examines cinema's deep connections with the basic psychical apparatus. In the former, the cinematic apparatus mediates between the material of the medium and the social; in the latter, it serves as a node between the neural and the mental or, by extension, the body and the mind. Another way of describing this twofold alignment of the apparatus is to say that in realizing our desires it forges a link to our intrinsic drive structure, whereas in producing truth it establishes a network within our body of knowledge and belief. This makes the cinematic apparatus a privileged site for analysing the interdependence of truth and desire, or knowledge and ideology (*see* CONTEMPORARY FILM THEORY; IDEOLOGY,

CINEMA AND). Baudry's terminology acknowledges these different dimensions of the apparatus by distinguishing between a kind of sub- and superstructure: 'l'appareil de base', the mechanisms performed in recording, editing, and projecting a film, and the 'dispositif', the arrangement of the screening situation that informs the viewer.

For Baudry the cinematic apparatus is conceived of as a juncture in a network of psycho-social relations. Its heuristic value as a node or threshold is that it allows us to conceptualize relations that cut across dualistic or binary structures such as body and mind, subject and object, technology and culture, or conscious and unconscious.[2] Apparatus theory generates a powerful model that can align a host of different theoretical frameworks.

## The cinematic apparatus as ideology

Apparatus theory aims at disclosing the processes that transform 'objective reality' into the finished product of a film. When the transformational processes elude the viewer, the apparatus seems to have performed a kind of magic; or, in the terminology of Louis Althusser (1971), it generates an ideological effect. Ideological effects merely project the illusion of transparency – permitting insight and an effect of knowledge – by manipulating our relation to the represented object.[3] For instance, by inviting us to identify with a perspective implied in a representation, the represented world appears as the seamless continuation or extension of our 'real world' experience. In this sense, cinema's power of illusion results not so much from the imitation of an authentic reality ('what we see') as from the simulation of a 'realistic' perception or point of view ('how we see').

Baudry outlines three moments of transformation, which he links to the operations of the camera, projector, and screen. The camera mediates between *découpage*, the breakdown of scenes based on a written scenario, and *montage*, the editing of the camera's recording. While the former draws on language as the signifying raw material, the latter operates in the visual regime of the image. Projector and screen frame the transformations of the film from a material product into a performative event, a transformation that is connected to cinema's economy of exchange and use values (correlating the price of admission – a measure of labour and capital – with the pleasure of the experience).

The ideological effect of the cinematic apparatus is that it conveys continuity and equivalence where there is discontinuity and disparity. While the impression of reality on the screen seems to return the light absorbed by the camera, it actually involves a number of exchanges across domains that are irreducible to one another (see levels 1 and 2 in Figure 2). Whereas the effect of knowledge is attained through dissection and differentiation, ideology works to efface differences and contradictions. Baudry illustrates this by drawing attention to homologous relations between narrative continuity and the cinematic image (levels 3 and 5). The film projection negates the differences between individual frames. By turning these differences into relations, film projection creates an illusion of continuous movement and time. Both narratives and moving images involve transformations where integral elements are displaced (replaced) by their relations: narratives entangle places, characters, and events into a network of relations; moving images turn segments of time and space into vectors of motion and time. Moving images evolve from a technical level (level 6), of which the viewer is largely unaware unless the projector breaks down; narratives can be described as the semiotic result of editing (level 4). While moving images establish relations on pre-conscious, material and technical levels, narrative relations pertain to consciousness and assigned meaning.

| Levels of signification | Degrees of cognitive accessibility | Relations of continuity | Units constructed |
|---|---|---|---|
| 1 | Conscious | Impression of reality | World-view, ideology |
| 2 | to | Meaning | Identity (identification) |
| 3 | | Coherent order of experience | Narration (discourse) |
| 4 | preconscious | Continuity editing | Spatio-temporal orientation |
| 5 | to | Continuous projection (persistence of vision) | Conscious stream of imagistic impressions |
| 6 | unconscious | Individual images: disparity, discontinuity, materiality | Pre-conscious, unconscious, neural |

*Figure 2* Baudry's network of homologies.

Since continuity is a common feature of technological and semiotic levels (i.e. each level replaces the one below by installing a new form of continuity), the term offers a conceptual bridge with which to speculate about the ideological biases of films predisposed by the apparatus. One inference, often applied to the critical analysis of continuity editing in classical Hollywood cinema, maintains that the ideological effect is most powerful when cinematic and narrative continuity affirm each other (see Bellour 1975). We may illustrate this by a comparison with medieval paintings, where unities of time and space are often subordinated to unities of meaning, for example when the same story space features an important character on a larger scale than others and/or at several moments. In such paintings, the representations of the social order clash with perceptual impressions of reality (level 1). Similarly, the spatio-temporal orientation does not create a homogeneous diegetic space (level 4). In cinema, however, continuity editing can create the illusion of a continuous story space. Social hierarchies among characters and values may be represented effectively in ways that conform to standards of perceptual realism. According to Baudry, the ideological effect of such techniques is that symbolic and social orders appear simply as perceptual orders of time and space. Baudry does not advocate a causal model of technological determinism. But how can we qualify the relationship between cinematic and narrative continuity? Baudry describes it as an '"organic" unity' (1986a, 295) using a chemical metaphor: 'the "subject" is put forth, liberated (in the sense that a chemical reaction liberates a substance)' (1986a, 291).

His model of interrelation draws on organic chemistry, which since its inception in the nineteenth century has become a popular frame of reference for rethinking dualistic structures. Organic chemistry challenged the dualist theory of earlier electrochemical approaches, which regarded electricity as the basic principle of organization and interactions. Positively and negatively charged compounds are not only attracted to each other but they can also switch partners. This elementary model of mechanical combination and exchange was revised by discoveries in organic chemistry. Scientists were able to synthesize organic substances from seemingly inorganic compounds, and they showed how substances of the same elementary composition and molecular weight can have different properties. Thus, a key insight of organic chemistry was that a compositional analysis of elements alone cannot account for the properties of a substance, as these properties also depend on arrangement and structure (or what chemists today refer to as constitution, configuration, and conformation).

The importance of organization and arrangement as constructive forces informs Baudry's view of art history, which is not simply the contingent product of a technological and artistic evolution (i.e. the effect of material conditions and a mechanical principle). Rather, for him cinema is the result of a positive feedback mechanism and the organic chain reactions between technological constraints and an organizational principle that is driven by the 'the wish to construct a simulation machine capable of offering the subject perceptions which are really representations mistaken for perceptions' (1986b, 315).

## The cinematic apparatus as psychical apparatus

Where does the desire for this confusion of perceptions and representations come from? Following Althusser, Baudry bases his ideological critique of the cinematic apparatus on Lacan's psychoanalytical model of subjectivity, where this confusion is central to psychogenesis, i.e. to the development and structure of the psychical apparatus. The transcendental subject, i.e. the implicit position of view in the 'artificial perspective', which since the Renaissance has dominated Western ideology of art, is compared with Lacan's theory of identity formation in what he termed the mirror-stage. Between the age of six months and eighteen months children develop a unified image of their body and a sense of self by proxy with their mirror images, i.e. they position themselves by intuiting the positionality of their mirrored image. For Baudry the cinematic apparatus involves a similar process of identification by situating the viewer at the imaginary centre of the projection of its perceptions. This primary process of identification, which empowers the viewer with attributes of the camera and projector, is complemented by a secondary process of identification: the viewer's empathic relation with characters on the screen (see IMAGINARY SIGNIFIER).

The psychoanalytic framework of apparatus theory supports Baudry's materialist rebuttal of the tradition of idealist film theories, which he in particular identifies with François Cohen-Séat and André Bazin (see ONTOLOGY OF THE PHOTOGRAPHIC IMAGE). While he invokes Marx as a reminder that 'there is often a truth hidden from or in idealism that belongs to materialism' (1986b, 302), he cites Freud to remind us that the work of philosophy and rational discourse rests upon the thrust and imperatives of the unconscious; just as Plato's cave allegory can be read as a reconfiguration that serves to rationalize and disguise the maternal womb.

Baudry adds a further analogy to his series of homologies. He compares the discrete and discontinuous images that feed the projector to the discontinuous and fragmentary characteristics of the unconscious, which are evident in dreams, hysterical discourse, or slips of the tongue, but tend to be suppressed on higher levels of consciousness and signification. Transformations of the apparatus are not merely changes in modality like transcriptions or adaptations, but the reconstruction of a 'mechanical model ... of a system of writing constituted by a material base and a countersystem (ideology, idealism) which uses this system while also concealing it' (1986a, 291). Baudry's analogy to the psychoanalytical model of the unconscious runs transversal to the homologies discussed thus far (see Figure 2). Theorizing relations across homologous levels, it accounts for the link between the cinema's technological base and its ideological disposition. Psychoanalysis thereby serves as a model of semiosis that accounts for the emergence of meaning as a transformation from no-sense to non-sense to sense.

As this analogy between cinema and psyche represents a kind of master paradigm promising insights into hidden layers and modes of production, Baudry's theory depends on the conclusiveness of this analogy (Carroll 1988; Buckland 1989). How do we know whether this analogy is a correct interpretation of symptoms and not itself the construction of a fantasy? Put in psychoanalytical terms, if it were merely the construction of a theorist or spectator, it would undercut the 'intersubjective' engagement with the film. An unduly programmatic application that maps cinema and psyche too closely would merely reproduce a given body of knowledge but fail to reach a particular film's truth. Yet, the validity and scope of an interpretation depend on the question of the symptomatic, what kind of evidence is recognized or omitted in the elaboration or the analogy. (Charles Altman discusses these problems in applying psychoanalytic theory under the headings of 'incomplete', 'programmatic', and 'imaginary' discourses of analogy [Altman 1985].)

Baudry seems to be aware of this problem when he phrases his boldest theses cautiously as questions. As a thorough analyst, he reviews a long history of optical models of the mind before he wonders whether this conspicuous obsession supports a reversed reading of the model: namely, explaining the cinematic apparatus as a reconstruction of the psychical apparatus. Reading the mind-as-optical-apparatus analogy in the opposite way raises important questions about the status of the model in both film theory and psychoanalysis. If cinema performs and perfects what in philosophy and psychoanalysis has been described in terms of projection and mirroring, does that mean cinema becomes its own psychoanalytical model? As Altman observed, the operations performed by the cinematic apparatus are themselves based on an imaginary unity between cinema and optical models in psychoanalysis. This caveat invites historical and aesthetic differentiations that include the status of the soundtrack, other forms of cinema and media, and the impact of alternative viewing situations.

Since the application of optical models of the psyche to the study of cinema implies also the transference of psychoanalytic methods and heuristics, we may ask how the discipline of film studies will benefit. As Baudry observes, Freud uses optical metaphors to describe the relation between the physical and psychical apparatus. Mental items, Freud points out (1953, 611), 'must never be regarded as localized in organic elements of the nervous system but rather, as one might say, *between* them, where resistances and facilitations [*Bahnungen*] provide the corresponding correlates. Everything that can be an object of our internal perception is *virtual*, like the image produced in a telescope by the passage of light-rays.'[4]

While Freud repeatedly lamented the imperfection of the optical analogy as it shows 'our complete ignorance of the *dynamic* nature of the mental processes' (1964, 97), Baudry welcomes this conceptual gap because he sees in it a great potential for cinema to elaborate the basic optical model (which is, of course, different from closing the gap). Like Freud's theory of the unconscious, the notion of a cinematic apparatus thereby becomes a way of rethinking problems of body–mind dualism and its socio-political and philosophical ramifications.

How are the pathways that shape theories of identity and sexual difference prefigured in a politics of the body? Again, Freud's *Interpretation of Dreams* can serve as a blueprint: 'It is highly probable that all complicated machinery and apparatus occurring in dreams stand for the genitals (and as a rule male ones)' (1953, 356). As a vehicle of desire, the cinematic apparatus, like Lacan's mirror, serves as an imaginary site for the origins of sexual identity. While feminist critics like Mary Ann Doane and Joan Copjec proposed female versions of such an anthropomorphic apparatus, Constance Penley (1989), in her critique of Baudry's apparatus as a 'bachelor machine' argued for a theory that retains the question of sexual difference as an open play of fantasy (*Phantasie*) (*see* FANTASY AND SPECTATORSHIP).

In a more general sense, the cinematic apparatus can be conceived as a virtual space where synaptic links are mapped onto semantic ones. Gilles Deleuze's formula 'the brain is the screen' implies this juncture or superimposition of perceptual and material facts. While cinema has been invoked as the paradigmatic medium, the model may be extended to other technologies of virtualization (e.g. new media) and to cultural techniques utilizing different strategies of identity formation. Systems theory has offered perhaps the most abstract model, where the mind's censoring mechanism aimed at establishing continuity and identity translates to principles of self-reference, self-organization, and autopoiesis.[5]

CHRISTIAN QUENDLER

## Notes

1 Jean-Louis Comolli emphasized this point in his essays 'Machines of the Visible' (1980) and 'Technique and Ideology: Camera, Perspective, Depth of Field' (1986).
2 In this methodological regard, Baudry's apparatus comes close to Michel Foucault's use of the term, which he developed around the same time. For a philosophical genealogy of Foucault's notion of the *dispositif* see Agamben (2009).
3 Althusser defines ideology as 'a "representation" of the imaginary relationship of individuals to the real conditions of existence' (1971, 109).
4 Freud continues the analogy as follows: 'But we are justified in assuming the existence of the systems (which are not in any way psychical entities themselves and can never be accessible to our psychical perception) like the lenses of the telescope, which cast the image. And, if we pursue this analogy, we may compare the censorship between two systems to the refraction which takes place when a ray of light passes into a new medium' (1953, 611).
5 For a discussion of Freud's optical model of mind in media theory, see Thomas Elsaesser (2009).

## Works cited

Agamben, Giorgio. 2009. *What Is an Apparatus? And Other Essays*. Stanford, CA: Stanford University Press.

Althusser, Louis. 1971 [1970]. 'Ideology and Ideological State Apparatuses (Notes towards an Investigation)'. In *Lenin and Philosophy, and Other Essays*, translated by Ben Brewster, 85–126. London: New Left Books.

Altman, Charles F. [Rick]. 1985 [1977]. 'Psychoanalysis and Cinema: The Imaginary Discourse'. In *Movies and Methods: An Anthology*, vol. II, edited by Bill Nichols, 517–31. Berkeley: University of California Press.

Baudry, Jean-Louis. 1986a [1970]. 'Ideological Effects of the Basic Cinematographic Apparatus'. In *Narrative, Apparatus, Ideology*, edited by Philip Rosen, 286–98. New York: Columbia University Press.

——. 1986b [1975]. 'The Apparatus: Metapsychological Approaches to the Impression of Reality in Cinema'. In *Narrative, Apparatus, Ideology*, edited by Philip Rosen, 299–318. New York: Columbia University Press.

Bellour, Raymond. 1975 [1973]. 'The Obvious and the Code'. *Screen* 15 (4): 7–17.

Buckland, Warren. 1989. 'Critique of Poor Reason'. *Screen* 30 (4): 80–103.

Carroll, Noël. 1988. *Mystifying Movies: Fads and Fallacies in Contemporary Film Theory*. New York: Columbia University Press.

Comolli, Jean-Louis. 1980 [1971]. 'Machines of the Visible'. In *The Cinematic Apparatus*, edited by Teresa de Lauretis and Stephen Heath, 121–43. London: Macmillan.

——. 1986 [1972]. 'Technique and Ideology: Camera, Perspective, Depth of Field'. In *Narrative, Apparatus, Ideology*, edited by Philip Rosen, 421–43. New York: Columbia University Press.

Elsaesser, Thomas. 2009. 'Freud as Media Theorist: Mystic Writing-Pads and the Matter of Memory'. *Screen* 50 (1): 100–13.

Freud, Sigmund. 1953 [1901]. *The Interpretation of Dreams*. In *The Standard Edition of the Complete Psychological Works of Sigmund Freud*, vol. 5, edited and translated by James Strachey. London: Hogarth Press.

——. 1964 [1939]. *Moses and Monotheism: An Outline of Psycho-Analysis*. In *The Standard Edition of the Complete Psychological Works of Sigmund Freud*, vol. 23, edited and translated by James Strachey. London: Hogarth Press.

Penley, Constance. 1989 [1985]. 'Feminism, Film Theory, and the Bachelor Machines'. In *The Future of an Illusion: Film, Feminism, and Psychoanalysis*, 56–80. Minneapolis: University of Minnesota Press.

## Further reading

Metz, Christian. 1982 [1977]. *The Imaginary Signifier: Psychoanalysis and Cinema*. Bloomington: Indiana University Press.

# APPARATUS THEORY (PLATO)

## Plato's cave apparatus

Plato's cave story concerning appearance and reality in *Book VII* of *Republic* has been an enduring allegory within Western philosophy. It continues to influence issues in epistemology and aesthetics. How do we know whether the way something looks is what it truly is? Could it be that the world of our daily activities is not at all what it seems – that we are held tightly in a robotic trance by many compelling illusions and simulacra? Is art itself one of these deceptions? More fundamentally, how can we be certain that we truly know what we think we know? Might having a feeling also sometimes be a delusion?

It is no surprise to find that film theorists have wrestled with these problems, since films confront spectators with strong impressions delivered artificially from screens. Although ordinarily we have no difficulty in perceiving the filmic world as a constructed fiction, we may nonetheless recognize and value elements in it that we believe to be quite real – personality types, situations, ideas, actions, possibilities, delights, felt fantasies, hopes, metaphors. A fiction is not simply a lie or necessarily *false*: one needs to know how to interpret and relate to it, i.e. how to re-tell a story by connecting it to life. In addition, we sometimes seem to *enter* a fiction. Thus Plato's story about fictions within fictions and a quest for knowledge may be relevant to our encounters with the fictions of literature and film.

Filmmakers have portrayed variants of Plato's cave problem in such films as the following: *The Matrix*, *The Thirteenth Floor*, *Welt am Draht* (*World on a Wire*), *Dark City*, *The Village*, *The Truman Show*, *Pleasantville*, *Abre los ojos* (*Open Your Eyes*), *Vanilla Sky*, *Total Recall* (1990; 2012), *Blade Runner*, *The Sixth Sense*, *Jacob's Ladder*, *Donnie Darko*, *Papurika* (*Paprika*), *Fight Club*, *La doppia ora* (*The Double Hour*), *Zelig*, *Il conformista* (*The Conformist*), *La double vie de Véronique* (*The Double Life of Veronique*), *Mulholland Dr.*, *Lost Highway*, and *L'année dernière à Marienbad* (*Last Year at Marienbad*). In these depictions a special physical apparatus or mental barrier is usually present to enforce a separation between the real and delusion or between the real and fantasy. Manipulations of narrative point of view operate to place the spectator in a series of uncertain relationships to the real and the aberrant within a story world. Jean-Luc Godard goes one step further: in the orgy scene of *Sauve qui peut (la vie)* (*Every Man for Himself*), the oppressive mechanism at work, constructed by a character, is a perverse double of the 'filmic apparatus' that stands as a parable for filmmaking in general or at least Godard's view of commercial filmmaking.

Theorists of the 1970s argued that every film determines a spectator's experience through concealed devices that act to create (punishing) illusions. This led to a profoundly sceptical attitude towards imagery, underpinned by the adoption of critical methods derived from semiotics, psychoanalysis, and Marxism. In what follows I will analyse the substance of Plato's cave story as well as its use of a distinctive narration and rhetorical strategy in order to reveal how the procedures selected to tell the story are intimately connected to what is being told, i.e. to what we are to finally understand. I will show in detail which features of Plato's story have been recruited to justify and defend a set of film theories that first arose in the 1970s and remain vital today (Rosen 1977; 1986; 2008; Stam *et al.* 1992). More generally, the deep issues of epistemology that are raised through a series of metaphors in the cave story – and are raised whenever one uses rhetorical devices to persuade – remain fundamental to philosophy and continue to be reworked in various ways by contemporary film theorists.

## Three analogies

At least three basic analogies are involved, built one upon the other. Plato's cave parable is said to be *like* a certain thing or process, '*x*'. Next, and one level higher, the 'cave-as-*x*-ness' is said to be *like* film; and, finally, 'film-as-cave-as-*x*-ness' is said to be *like* the operation of a spectator's psyche. Figure 3 is a diagram of this logic, where the first box on each level is the subject or signifier about which something (shown in the second box on that level) is predicated or signified. That is, an entity/subject is selected on each level and then something is asserted about it – predicated of it.

It should be mentioned that film theorists have been highly selective about what they have appropriated from the cave parable, i.e. '*x*' on the bottom level. Commentators on Plato have detected a wide range of additional matters that may relate to strong or weak analogies set in motion by the parable. The following are some of these matters leading to (what I will call) 'shadow metaphors' that I will, nevertheless, set aside for the purposes of the present entry since they have been ignored by film theorists: the tyranny of 'custom'; the tyranny of the body (cf. Plato's *Phaedo* 82e–83a); the city; politics; the philosophical life; the soul; birth and death; master/slave impulses within every person; Socrates's 'descent' to the 'subnatural'; and 'the recovery of the body'. Must all allegories be constructed

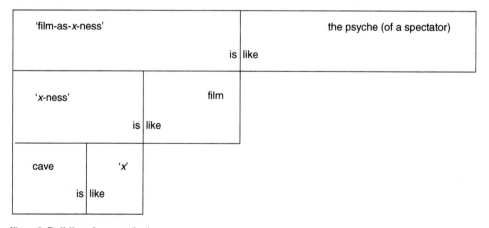

*Figure 3* Building three analogies.

to serve merely a single meaning, especially keeping in mind the 'ironical or esoteric side of Socrates's presentation' (Rosen 2005, 269–84)? Let's first turn to the details of the cave story and to Socrates's presentation of it.

## Prisoners of the cave

I will begin at the bottom level by trying to specify some of the meanings of Plato's story that have been attractive to film theorists, i.e. the value(s) of 'x' that will eventually be mapped into new realms to characterize a spectator's engagement with film. Plato imagines a number of prisoners held in a cave for their entire lives, their bodies chained.[1] The prisoners are unable to move, unable to turn their heads, able only to perceive what is in front of them. The prisoners do not even know that they *have* heads that could move. Behind the prisoners on an inclined slope is a low wall beneath which some persons are hiding. Let us call these persons 'artists'. Still higher up in the cave is a bonfire. Notice that the 'higher up' one moves, the more 'real' things become. This metaphor of ascendancy will continue throughout the story. It is a way of thinking about spatial orientation that remains entrenched within conceptual structure today (Lakoff and Johnson 1980).

Light from the bonfire illuminates the cave rock in front of the prisoners, making it a kind of 'screen'. The artists are busy thrusting puppets into the light above the barrier wall and chattering among themselves. But since the prisoners know nothing except what is projected on the cave wall in front of them, and don't know they possess heads that could turn, the sounds and images they perceive can only be attributed to the cave wall, not to any source behind them. The prisoners cannot conceive of any sort of world that exists 'behind or beyond'; nor is there a 'front' to contrast with a 'back'. Thus, for example, from the perspective of the prisoners, the sounds being heard are not 'echoes' from elsewhere originating from other persons, not even a form of 'ventriloquism'. (The implications here concerning the audible have been developed into certain theories about a film's sound track [Branigan 2010].) The shadows of puppets in front of the prisoners are not 'shadows' or 'puppets', for there can be no notion of 'light' from elsewhere, only a 'glow' from the wall; and the cave wall is not the 'wall of a cave' (it *is* the world). In short, what the prisoners see and hear on the wall is the entirety of their world – simply, directly, and absolutely; there can be no thought or evidence of anything other or different.

The account of the cave locale being offered by Plato through the character of Socrates – who is relating the story to Glaucon, Plato's older brother – contains descriptions (puppets, bonfire, shadows …) that only *we*, not the prisoners, can understand, and, moreover, the descriptions are being framed through a view – familiar to us today from novels and films – of an omniscient narrator hovering over the action, maintaining a degree of suspense without prematurely exposing 'secrets' and 'outcomes', managing the flow of information while orchestrating the developing viewpoints of two nondiegetic character-narrators (Socrates, Glaucon) as well as presenting the direct experiences of several diegetic characters, principally involving a conflict between an escaped prisoner and someone aiding him against his will and a conflict between the prisoner and his fellow prisoners.

Plato systematically strips away (and does not replace) the embodied language of spatial orientation – front and back, side to side, on and off, up and down (cf. Lakoff and Johnson 1980) – as well as strips away metaphors available to the prisoners based on spatial orientation and proximity, as if language itself were something ephemeral and an artifice. Plato then asks us to imagine such an impoverished state. What words are left to describe it? What descriptions could be offered of (proximate) causation?

After hearing the details of this opening scene accompanied by its back story, Glaucon remarks, 'It is a strange picture and a strange sort of prisoners.' Socrates replies, 'Like ourselves.'

## Art

I believe that Plato's argument – carefully filtered through the narrational levels mentioned above (from Plato's omniscient narration to Socrates to Glaucon to a prisoner to an artist-helper, and to other prisoners) – is that the prisoners are at least six steps removed from a true reality. Alternatively, one might say that there are six different levels of showing, or different ways in which the same 'thing' or 'object' may show itself or appear, since a beholder/prisoner in the cave forms (1) an idea or mental image of, let us suppose, cat-ness based on (identical to?) (2) a shadow cast on the wall of the cave being only (3) a copy of a cat-puppet casting the shadow being only (4) a copy of an artist's idea or mental image of cat-ness when the puppet was fabricated being only (5) an idealization of an actual (particular) living cat being only (6) a copy of the 'invariant form' for all cats being (7) a reflection of the Idea of the Good/Idea of the True/God's 'vision' for Cat-ness, which is the absolute real source of cat in an Ideal of a stable, perfectly rational order. The 'invariant form' (i.e. 6) for all cats is the defining principle of the class containing all actual and particular cats, including past and future cats, by which finally any specific cat can be recognized 'to be' a cat. An absolute Form, unlike an actual cat or a human, does not die. When one knows the Form of a cat, one knows all possible cats. Hence all art lacks a true being, for how can a false appearance – a shadow cat on a cave wall of a puppet cat – have a real existence rather than being merely an imperfect, ephemeral copy of a copy of a copy, etc., of the real?

For Plato art is an illusion, a systematic deception in which each copy/imitation from a higher level to a lower level, and finally reaching the prisoners, loses something of reality by being composed of new, substitute materials and effects. For example, comparing a puppet to its shadow on the cave wall, one finds that the shadow is composed of quite different materials (partly illuminated, wet rock) from the puppet (clay, cloth, wood ...) and the shadow has a different colour, larger size, and moves faster (since it covers a greater distance on the cave wall in the same amount of time than the puppet). One finds also that the puppet's volume has been replaced by a flat area on the wall. For Plato artists systematically create counterfeit materials and delusions, stirring the emotions in bad faith and in false directions, making what is real indistinct and unknowable.[2]

## Reality

The prisoners, however, are quite firmly attached to their illusions and pleasures. Socrates argues that if a prisoner were to be released from his chains, he would be able to move his body only with enormous pain and would be blinded by light from the bonfire. Notice that the 'pain' is what is real, not the contentment formerly felt by the prisoner. Nevertheless, the prisoner would seek to return immediately to his chains and the familiar shadows upon the cave wall. Everything else in the cave, Glaucon agrees, would seem 'not nearly so real'. To free the prisoner, Socrates states, would require some person (a guilty artist? a teacher? or perhaps a 'philosophy'?) to 'drag him away forcibly'.

But Plato does not have Socrates create an explicit character in the story world who will forcibly drag a prisoner out of the cave. Instead, Glaucon and the reader are invited only to *imagine* a series of events that might transpire, were a prisoner to be dragged away. The story no longer moves forward, but instead is converted into a hypothetical series of tableaux. We are thus drawn deeper into the levels of the story since we must now begin to narrate/imagine it *for ourselves* and reflect upon possible consequences of possible actions. As Plato hides behind Socrates, Socrates now attempts to hide behind us. As a result, the different realities that will soon be found to lie outside the cave, along with the 'real' when it finally appears, will be somewhat more distant and tentative for us because in weighing hypotheses about these next stages of the prisoner's story (his escape), we are seemingly alone in our search – searching our selves for answers, speculating about outcomes. Plato seems to be saying that just such a solitary journey will be necessary, with no guarantee of success, if one wishes to learn and know things for oneself about what is real.

Prompted by Socrates, we expect that more agony would await the prisoner outside the cave. Adjustment to this upper world would be extremely painful and slow, proceeding in a series of steps analogous to the levels of existence in the cave. First, the former prisoner would be able to discern shadows and presumably hear echoes; then he would be able to see images reflected in water – and here, interestingly, Plato makes a distinction between 'divine' natural shadows and reflections as opposed to those shadows in the cave that come from mere man-made objects and tricks (lowly 'fictions'? appearances of appearances? but, one may ask, how are the different types of 'shadows' to be distinguished?; *VII* 532b–c). Next, the former prisoner would see the real objects being reflected (copied/imitated) on the surface of the water; then he would perceive (by looking still 'higher') the night sky by light of the moon and stars; and, finally, he would be able to face the sun – the real bonfire, the First Cause that truly lights the world, causes the seasons, and brings life.

At this point the prisoner would be able to understand that each of the preceding 'levels of reality', inside and outside of the cave, was a measured delusion produced through, Socrates says, the employment on each level of an 'alien medium' (*VII* 516b). Whether we have noticed or not, the world displays itself by way of a series of alien (alienating?) media. Socrates is suggesting that sensation does not exist 'in itself', but only in contexts that have been framed and determined through a *succession of media*.

Plato is proposing that the aim of a philosophical theory is to reveal entities and processes that cannot be detected through the senses and sensations, but must instead be discovered through the (higher) intellect. Accordingly, one theory about the general nature of theoretical inquiry is that it must aim to elucidate the hidden principles controlling the appearance of phenomena. What we are able to sense are only surfaces transmitted through unreliable media. In this view, 'practice' is much further from reality and truth than is *theory*.

## Education

Socrates now prompts us to wonder whether the prisoner might decide to educate and free the captives in the cave. It's a natural question since any well-formed 'journey narrative' should end in a 'return' in order to measure the value of the journey. However, in returning to the cave, Socrates asserts that, 'coming suddenly out of the sunlight, his eyes would be filled with darkness'. The prisoner is horrified to learn that his former abilities in the cave environment are now sadly diminished. He can no longer properly compete with the other prisoners for the prizes they award each other, specifically, prizes for

> those persons who are the quickest to recognize a shadow and best remember ones already seen [*mise-en-scène?*]; those who know which elements belong together in what order [narrative causality?]; those who have the keenest memory for a continuous movement of shadows [camera movement?], and finally, those who are the most successful in anticipating what will appear next [editing?].
>
> (cf. *VII* 516c–d)

These prizes would seem to have clear analogues in film form. But for Plato, and the returned prisoner, the prizes are meaningless – what some film scholars today would term 'empty formalism'.

Worse, the returned prisoner is ridiculed by the other prisoners. He is told that leaving the cave left his "sight ruined" and filled with illusions, and that if he dared attempt to free them, "they would kill him". Plato ends the story with this final statement by Socrates, which is an allusion to the fate of his teacher, Socrates, who sought only to educate his fellow Athenians, but who was forced to drink poison.

## Lessons from the cave

Here are a few crucial lessons, warnings, and open questions from the cave story.

1. Can we trust our senses? The cave in *Book VII*, of course, is a startling instance of the failure of our senses. The opening of *Book I* (to be discussed in the next section) presents a more subtle warning about our senses.
2. What is real about reality? Suppose, for example, someone told you that the room in which you presently sit is only a 'reflection' from another place/dimension that you cannot see because no matter in which direction you turn, you see only what is being projected 'in front of' you.
3. Can everything that is true, real, meaningful, just, beautiful, or good be discovered through the intellect – disclosed through a meticulous and correct logic?
4. What logic or methodology is appropriate in fashioning a theory of the real (or a theory of film/film narrative as a real object about the real)? Plato's approach in the cave story is to analytically subdivide and to drastically reduce what a person can know and speak about, beginning with the senses; then he applies this simplification through a series of analogies in order to slowly rebuild, level by level, towards much more complicated issues of epistemology. Is higher cognition therefore a trajectory, a sum of parts, or at least a leaping from level to level? How many levels (or platforms) can be said to exist in the world? And, more basically, what defines a *level?* That is, what is its purpose? Is a level a methodological convenience? Is it, for example, like the subheadings of an essay?
5. What is it possible to know? Are there 'connections' (leakages) among the 'levels of reality' or 'levels of narration'? What kinds of inferences are possible from our sense data and from our analogies? Perhaps analogies are merely likenesses like shadows! Consider the danger of forming analogies in the case where the prisoners attempt to

create a theoretical *abstraction* from a procession of, say, different shadow-cats appearing on the cave wall, i.e. when the prisoners attempt to find the important likenesses among the shadow-cats so as to form a generalized idea of 'shadow-cat'. The resultant abstraction may serve to define the essence of a 'shadow-cat', but it will be hopelessly wrong about *cats*, not to mention being wrong about a concept like 'justice', which begins as an invisible abstraction made impossibly visible ('the shadows of justice', *VII* 517d–e). The ancient subtitle of *Republic* was 'On Justice', which was an acknowledgement of Plato's interest in the nature and construction of theoretical abstractions.

6. Is the search for knowledge dangerous? Recall the fate of Socrates.

## Framing the cave: lessons from Plato's rhetoric

I have been exploring the fine-grain of the cave story because its implications resonate to far more complicated and quite general issues that underlie the construction of film theories. Intertwined with the details of the story, I have been analysing aspects of Plato's telling of the story. For example, I have considered the rhetoric of layered analogies and metaphors; Plato's position as a certain kind of narrator (floating and effaced omniscience, suspense, and disclosure); the special linguistic methods employed by both Plato and Socrates (above, as in the conversion of narrative into tableaux[3]); and the notion of levels of narration – possibilities for restricted points of view – that parallel and track the physical and mental barriers marking the well-ordered levels of reality in the cave story that become successive alienating media platforms. We have also seen theory being developed incrementally through dialogue and counterpoint, where deliberation and contemplation are to supplant intuitive practice. This process of theory construction is meant to forestall being swayed by received ideas, emotion, mere sensation, and 'empty formalism'.

I would like to continue analysing Plato's rhetorical design by briefly considering the beginning of *Book I*, which is one of the delicate ways Plato frames the cave story to come in *Book VII*. Socrates is narrating in the first person:

> I went down to the Piraeus yesterday with Glaucon, the son of Ariston. I wanted to say a prayer to the goddess, and I was also curious to see how they would manage the festival, since they were holding it for the first time. I thought the procession of the local residents was a fine one and that the one conducted by the Thracians was no less outstanding. After we had said our prayer and seen the procession, we started back towards Athens. Polemarchus saw us from a distance as we were setting off for home and told his slave to run and ask us to wait for him. The slave caught hold of my cloak from behind: Polemarchus wants you to wait, he said. I turned around and asked where Polemarchus was. He's coming up behind you, he said, please wait for him. And Glaucon replied: All right, we will.
>
> Just then [!] Polemarchus caught up with us. Adeimantus, Glaucon's brother, was with him and so were Niceratus, the son of Nicias, and some others, all of whom were apparently on their way from the procession.
>
> Polemarchus said: It looks to me, Socrates, as if you two are starting off for Athens.
>
> It looks the way it is, then, I said.

At first glance, Socrates's opening narration seems perfectly straightforward and the dialogue transparent, even a bit boring and undramatic. But on closer inspection, we see that Socrates is offering judgements about the festival events that he had seen while also making judgements about how events that had happened 'yesterday' should be told to us, that is, keeping in mind what *will* happen in the story. For example, Polemarchus's speech concerning Socrates's return to Athens echoes the very language Socrates has already employed in telling us about the return to Athens. The repetition is important, as we shall see.

On leaving the festival, there are several small surprises for Socrates, who explains how he was forced to make additional judgements based on hurried *inferences* to understand what appeared to happen. Is Polemarchus's motive apparent? No, it is not, and Socrates will not tell us about it until later. Had Polemarchus been to the festival? 'Apparently', Socrates says. Where on the road was Polemarchus? Nearby, but not seen by Socrates. Already in *Republic*, it seems, appearance alone is not enough for firm judgement. But, then, apparently, only sometimes it is not enough, as Socrates informs us of his response to an assessment by Polemarchus: 'It looks the way it is, then, I said.'

Note that we as readers already well know the truth of Socrates's rejoinder to Polemarchus since Plato has provided us with split narrative perspectives: (1) now and yesterday; (2) Socrates and Polemarchus, whose quasi-perspective begins with a statement that Socrates could not have known at the time, and perhaps infers even now, 'Polemarchus saw us from a distance ... '. Socrates has been established as the authoritative narrating voice and we have no reason to doubt his inferences, but, like the Socrates of 'yesterday', we cannot discern the full extent of what Polemarchus has in mind.

On a larger scale, we see that the interrupted opening journey ('down'!) to Piraeus and now back (up) to Athens is matched by an (intermittently remembered) closing journey at the end of *Republic* of one thousand years. *Republic* is the story of these two interrupted journeys. As W.K.C. Guthrie notes: 'Essentially ... the *Republic* is not a piece of political theory but an allegory of the individual human spirit, the *psyche*' (1975, 561; Guthrie's emphasis). If there is to be doubt about Socrates's narration of events, it will lie in the uncertainty of the journey of one thousand years, that is, lie in the greater story of the human psyche of which the journey from the cave (up) towards awareness is already a part – though not yet told – of who Socrates is.

## Another lesson: subjectivity

Film theorists of the 1970s posed questions about cinema similar to the ones listed above: 'what's real about film?' In addition, they asked a powerful new sort of question in the spirit of Plato: 'what's real about *oneself?*' When we look into ourselves, don't we simply see a kind of abbreviated 'screen'? How well can we see into our own mental 'cave'? Could it be, for example, that our conscious thoughts are merely a projection/reflection from elsewhere in our psyche, from a place(s) we cannot access that is significantly different in its processes and goals – that involves disguised impulses emerging from a nonconscious level?

The question becomes: of what are thoughts really made? And, further, what theoretical scenario will allow us to escape and achieve the requisite 'distance' to know ourselves – to narrate a story about ourselves to ourselves? Many film theorists assert that only by glimpsing our true selves – including a range of dim anxieties, ambivalences, unresolved reactions to events, repressions – will we be able to understand why and how we value the films we see.

Plato says explicitly that a prisoner cannot see any part of himself or of his companions, including shadows on the cave wall of himself or others. As a consequence, Plato emphasizes that a prisoner cannot talk about him*self*, only about the shadows on the wall. Film theorists of the 1970s have been able to expand Plato's allegory, in effect, by pausing the cave story at that moment when the escaped prisoner looks at reflections in water. What would happen if the prisoner were to see an image of himself in the water – i.e. not just an image of an inanimate object near the water – and so be led to contemplate the 'shadow(s)' of his own nature?

This image of a self in the water evokes the centrality that some film theories have placed upon Lacan's mirror stage in the development of personal identity. Further, if the prisoner were to see a second image in the water, say, of a woman, would this not raise problematic issues about gender identity, sexual difference, and self-versus-other? That is, would seeing himself together with an Other bring forth mnemonic traces of disturbances related to such enforced (cave-like) mental conditions as daytime fantasies, sleep, childhood, infancy, and the womb?

## A cautious scepticism

For Plato the brilliant sun at the end of the ascent from the cave to reality is merely the beginning. The sun itself stands for additional unseen realities in an elegant, teleological universe – realms existing, as it were, in a rational order 'beyond' the sun. But is Plato confident that he can accurately describe human life with its many hidden realms? Does his parable point the way? Through the character of Socrates, he says, 'Heaven knows whether it is true; but this, at any rate, is how it appears to me' (*VII* 517b). Plato remains cautious about his own parable and well aware of how it 'appears'. The notion of what 'may appear' is exactly the problem![4]

In a variety of ways, 1970s film theories were riven by suspicions about film and its effects. The antidote to deep scepticism lay in still deeper theory (*see* ANGLO-AMERICAN FILM THEORY; EUROPEAN FILM THEORY; SCEPTICISM). The hope was that by utilizing theory to expose the specific properties and operations of the medium of film, the medium would become less 'alien' or 'alienating', returning to its spectators at least some measure of control. With knowledge would come the ability to better project a suitable reality.

## 1970s film theory

What analogies to film may be developed from the cave? There are four distinct kinds of 'light' in the parable: the artificial 'glow' from the cave wall, the bonfire, the night sky (the moon and stars, including their 'mathematical movements'), and the sun. These would seem to match four different states of mind and associated methodologies discussed by Plato and might have applications to the viewing of film.[5] Nevertheless, this and other analogies have not been pursued by film theorists. The exception is a dominant strand of 1970s film theory that extracted certain aspects from the story in order to fit its epistemological claims and aesthetic goals (*see* APPARATUS THEORY [BAUDRY]; SYMPTOMATIC READING; see also the epilogue on pp. 494–504).

Figure 4 is a diagram with seven distinct columns representing seven topics that may each be divided into three parts corresponding to three parts of Plato's cave story, omitting other elements of the story. The diagram is designed merely to be suggestive about possible ways of applying Plato's parable in the context of 1970s film theory.

| STATE OF WORLD | PLATO'S CAVE | COMPUTER | FILM | PSYCHE | LANGUAGE | SOCIETY |
|---|---|---|---|---|---|---|
| ILLUSION<br>False continuity, unity, and coherence | Moving shadows on cave wall | User interface (the virtual machine, e.g., Windows 8) | Moving shadows on screen; continuous screen motion; plot continuity | Ego; consciousness; sense of self; unified person-personality; Freud's 'secondary process', 'misrecognition' | Sentences; thoughts; images, ideas, sense; signified, referent | Marx's 'superstructure', 'false consciousness', 'alienation', 'commodity fetishism' |
| MECHANISM OF PRODUCTION<br>Apparatus | Fire | Hexadecimal arithmetical operations | Film projector; linear perspective; invisible continuity editing | Superego, conscience; censorship; the preconscious | Materials of signifiers; signifiers; processes of myth-making | Dialectical laws; exploitation of labour; capital markets; class struggle |
| HIDDEN REALITY<br>Material discontinuity, heterogeneity | Puppets | Silicon chips, electrons | Discontinuous, photographic frames; written script; studio financing | Id; the unconscious; dread, desire, ambivalence, repression; Freud's 'primary process', 'split subject'; instincts; drives | Types of signs; codes; cultural conventions; ideologies; 'methodologies' | Economic base; profit; surplus value; patriarchy |

*Figure 4* Plato's world.

The type of large-scale scheme depicted in Figure 4 allows a theorist to contrive new descriptions of film using metaphors that are conceptual *blends* – controlled over-generalizations – among the columns (*see* BLENDING AND FILM THEORY). For example, it might be claimed that a film's narrative discourse harbours an innate 'excess/surplus/trace/residue' projected from some unknown psychic 'region'; or, it might be claimed that, despite efforts at 'repressing' a particular ideology, 'symptoms' within the narrative allow subversive or taboo ideas to appear – to return 'against the grain'. These claims are somewhat at odds with the idea that the specific nature of the filmic apparatus works to 'position' or 'suture' a spectator in place as a prisoner, determining his or her responses while stealthily communicating the ideology of those who wield the technology (*see* SUTURE).

On the other hand, perhaps there are special aesthetic techniques that can overcome these sorts of suturing processes and other invisibly produced effects of the apparatus in order to break the spell binding a spectator. For instance, the moment in Plato's story when the escaped prisoner first uncovers the concealed technology – the puppets and bonfire – might be analogized to the aesthetic technique of 'self-reflexivity', which reminds a viewer that what is being seen is only a film and/or displays a film being critical of itself. But still, is such a device effective? Has a prisoner truly escaped by seeing the apparatus, even an apparatus framing itself? One might instead claim that no escape is necessary since a viewer already knows that he or she is merely watching a film … but, then, does a film have no connection at all to reality, to what is not literally present? In spite of the fiction, don't we recognize its significance? Aren't we to a degree always complicit in its operations?

The above issues will turn on whether a theorist accepts the outlines of Plato's cave story and, if so, which elements are taken from the story as a guide to epistemological issues. A film theorist will interpret the elements in order to build analogies to the film medium and mind. A reader of the theory will determine whether the assembled model properly situates his or her film experiences within, apparently, a world of appearance and belief.

EDWARD BRANIGAN

## Notes

1 Strictly, Plato's cave parable in *Republic, Book VII* 514–18, written about 380 BC, concerns the problem of 'education', not the nature of art (514a1–2). (So is a 'classroom' a cave? Interestingly, the word 'education' also lies in the etymology of 'encyclopedia' …) Nonetheless, the cave parable about education is frequently interpreted as a vivid depiction of Plato's views on art, which are made explicit in *Republic X* 595–608b. For a more extensive treatment of the relationships among art, imitation, and existence, see Plato's *Sophist*. For significant passages bearing on the cave parable, see *Republic V* 472b–80; *VI* 507–11c; *VII* 532–34a; *X* 596–98c.

One should be aware that Plato's sources in Greek life and religious practice provide a very different background for the notion of the cave than the circumstances of a modern reader. Is Franz Kafka's short story 'The Burrow' a modern revision of the cave parable? Two important philosophical revisions of the cave are Descartes's 'evil genius' in *Meditations on First Philosophy* and John Searle's 'Chinese Room' argument. Alain Badiou (2012), in his sublime and wondrous 'hyper-translation' of *Republic*, replaces the cave with 'an enormous movie theater'. For more on Badiou's embrace of Plato, *see* INAESTHETICS.

2 Plato excludes artists from entering the Republic in *Republic X* 605b, 607–8a. His views on art, however, are quite complex (Asmis 1992; Janaway 1995).

3 See also note 4 below.

4 Plato does not employ the present tense or the historical present tense in narrating the cave story, i.e. where past events are made to appear in the present, as in the following: 'the prisoner *was now* outside the cave and while *walking* forward *notices* shadows and then *sees* images *being* reflected

in water'. Instead, Plato avoids a simple 'telling of the story' by continually reframing the action using modal verbs to create a subjunctive conditional mood: 'Now imagine what would happen if ...' *Republic VII* 516e2. Plato is aware that his own cave allegory is a form of conjecture and imperfect 'picture-thinking' that he asserts is the lowest of four general states of the soul/mind, even though the allegory as told by his character Socrates, presumably, is meant to (imperfectly) depict all four states (*VI* 509d–511e). Very roughly, the four states are: copies, appearances, and illusions; contact with tangible particulars; methods and abstractions; and, finally, unconditional principles, unities, and ideals (Nettleship 1966).

Plato has arranged the allegory in such a way that the objects encountered at each of the four stages provide an absolute *limit* on one's clarity of mind in that state. This is a strong claim where the *essence* of objects – the exact and underlying state of affairs in effect at a given stage – prescribes the mode of *existence* of the objects, ruling our thought about them. This, in turn, raises the problem of how it is possible to know that there is a higher stage and how one could come to know the means of escaping one stage for the next (*Republic VI* 511a, e). For example, we as readers know that the objects casting reflections in water outside the cave are real things (not puppets as in the cave), but how and when does the prisoner come to know this fact? The idea that the prisoner merely 'looks up' (or whatever) from the water to see the real things (apparently) casting the reflections must itself be a condensed analogy for a certain method of education (involving, say, concepts of causality) that reliably can guide a person from reflections in water to an acquaintance with objects casting reflections as well as guide a person to knowledge of other objects *capable of* casting reflections. Ultimately, there must be a collection of educational methods able to lead a person from sensations in the cave to knowledge of the sun.

One might wonder what method of education is proper for studying film and media. Further, how do individual film theories proceed to 'educate' a reader? Some film theories, similar to Plato's approach, begin by establishing an ontology (an essence) for film, i.e. what film *is*, what its limits are – the sort of *presence* a presumed filmic apparatus permits – and then derive from this ontology an epistemology and aesthetics (an existence) for film, even deriving principles that underlie the history of film. A closely related question that is seldom raised concerns the nature of the 'apparatus' or 'medium' responsible for generating a given philosophy or film theory in the first place. What essential rhetorical processes and mental systems project (the apparatus of) a theory?

5 See note 4 above.

# Works cited

Asmis, Elizabeth. 1992. 'Plato on Poetic Creativity'. In *The Cambridge Companion to Plato*, edited by Richard Kraut, 338–64. Cambridge: Cambridge University Press.

Badiou, Alain. 2012. *Plato's* Republic: *A Dialogue in 16 Chapters*. Translated by Susan Spitzer. New York: Columbia University Press.

Branigan, Edward. 2010. 'Soundtrack in Mind'. *Projections* 4 (1): 41–67. [Plato's influence on a class of film sound theories known as 'nonidentity' theories.]

Guthrie, W.K.C. 1975. *A History of Greek Philosophy*, vol. IV, 'Plato, the Man and His Dialogues: Earlier Period'. Cambridge: Cambridge University Press. [A masterful study of *Republic*.]

Janaway, Christopher. 1995. *Images of Excellence: Plato's Critique of the Arts*. Oxford: Clarendon Press.

Lakoff, George, and Mark Johnson. 1980 [2003 Afterword]. 'Orientational Metaphors'. In *Metaphors We Live By*, 14–21. Chicago, IL: University of Chicago Press.

Nettleship, Richard Lewis. 1966. 'The Four Stages of Intelligence'. In *Plato's* Republic: *Interpretation and Criticism*, edited by Alexander Sesonske, 103–15. Belmont, CA: Wadsworth Publishing.

Plato. 1941. *The Republic of Plato*. Translated by Francis MacDonald Cornford. London: Oxford University Press. [The text of the present entry mainly quotes from this translation. Thirteen other noteworthy translations of *Republic*, which were consulted, are by R.E. Allen (2006); G.M.A. Grube (2nd edn, 1992); Edith Hamilton and Huntington Cairns, editors (1963); Raymond Larson (1979); Louise Ropes Loomis (1942); W.H.D. Rouse (1956); Joe Sachs (2007); Richard W. Sterling and William C. Scott (1985); Allan Bloom (1968); Benjamin Jowett (1999, Barnes & Noble edition);

Desmond Lee (rev. of 2nd edn, 1987); C.D.C. Reeve (2004); Robin Waterfield (1993). The last five offer excellent commentary and summaries of *Republic*.]

——. 1997. *Plato: Complete Works*. Edited by John M. Cooper. Indianapolis, IN: Hackett Publishing. [The quotation in the above section 'Framing the cave: lessons from Plato's rhetoric' is taken from this book, which for *Republic* uses the translation of G.M.A. Grube, as revised by C.D.C. Reeve.]

Rosen, Philip. 1977. '*Screen* and the Marxist Project in Film Criticism'. *Quarterly Review of Film Studies* 2 (3): 273–87.

——, ed. 1986. *Narrative, Apparatus, Ideology*. New York: Columbia University Press.

——. 2008. '*Screen* and 1970s Film Theory'. In *Inventing Film Studies*, edited by Lee Grieveson and Haidee Wasson, 264–97. Durham, NC: Duke University Press.

Rosen, Stanley. 2005. *Plato's* Republic: *A Study*. New Haven, CT: Yale University Press. [An erudite, finely balanced, and comprehensive commentary on *Republic*.]

Stam, Robert, Robert Burgoyne, and Sandy Flitterman-Lewis. 1992. *New Vocabularies in Film Semiotics: Structuralism, Post-structuralism and Beyond*. London and New York: Routledge. [See esp. parts II and IV: 'Cine-semiology' and 'Psychoanalysis'.]

## Further reading

Allen, Richard. 1995. *Projecting Illusion: Film Spectatorship and the Impression of Reality*. Cambridge: Cambridge University Press.

Altman, Charles F. [Rick]. 1985. 'Psychoanalysis and Cinema: The Imaginary Discourse' [orig. 1977]. In *Movies and Methods: An Anthology*, vol. II, edited by Bill Nichols, 517–31. Berkeley: University of California Press. [Cinema evaluated as a psychic apparatus and problems raised by arguments based on analogies.]

Annas, Julia. 2009. *Plato*. New York: Sterling Publishing. [An excellent, brief overview of Plato's philosophy.]

Baudry, Jean-Louis. 1986. 'Ideological Effects of the Basic Cinematographic Apparatus' [orig. 1970] and 'The Apparatus: Metapsychological Approaches to the Impression of Reality in Cinema' [orig. 1975]. In *Narrative, Apparatus, Ideology*, edited by Philip Rosen, 286–318. New York: Columbia University Press. [Both essays invoke Plato, especially the second.]

Branigan, Edward. Forthcoming. 'If-then-else: Memory and the Path Not Taken'. In *Transmedia Frictions: The Digital, the Arts, and the Humanities*, edited by Marsha Kinder and Tara McPherson. Berkeley: University of California Press. [Plato's cave and aviary as models for media memory.]

Cha, Theresa Hak Kyung, ed. 1980. *Apparatus*. New York: Tanam Press.

de Lauretis, Teresa, and Stephen Heath, eds. 1980. *The Cinematic Apparatus*. New York: St. Martin's Press.

Elsaesser, Thomas, and Malte Hagener. 2010. *Film Theory: An Introduction through the Senses*. New York and London: Routledge. [Apparatus theory is discussed in various contexts along with intricate analogies among cinema, mind, and body.]

Falzon, Christopher. 2002. 'Plato's Picture Show – The Theory of Knowledge'. In Falzon, *Philosophy Goes to the Movies: An Introduction to Philosophy*, 17–48. London and New York: Routledge.

Ferrari, G.R.F., ed. 2007. *The Cambridge Companion to Plato's* Republic. Cambridge: Cambridge University Press.

Greene, Brian. 2011. 'Black Holes and Holograms: The Holographic Multiverse' and 'Universes, Computers, and Mathematical Reality: The Simulated and the Ultimate Multiverses'. In Greene, *The Hidden Reality: Parallel Universes and the Deep Laws of the Cosmos*, 238–306. New York: Alfred A. Knopf. [A leading contemporary physicist discusses serious, recent work in which Plato's ideas are reversed: two-dimensional reality on a 'cave wall' is what is real, while our lived, three-dimensional reality is a profound illusion; moreover, we may ourselves be simulations living in a cave of simulations!]

Penley, Constance. 1989. 'Feminism, Film Theory, and the Bachelor Machines' [orig. 1985]. In Penley, *The Future of an Illusion: Film, Feminism, and Psychoanalysis*, 56–80. Minneapolis: University of Minnesota Press. [An evaluation of 'apparatus theory' in the context of feminism.]

# ART, FILM AS

Early theorists often sought to define and defend cinema as an art. They developed aesthetic theories of film in order to come to grips with the medium and to gain for it respect and prestige among the arts. Rudolf Arnheim's book *Film as Art* exemplifies this tradition. Originally published as *Film als Kunst* in 1932, and revised in English in 1957, *Film as Art* argues that silent cinema constituted a true art form, which was threatened and weakened by the coming of sound and colour (*see* SOUND THEORY). Arnheim offers an essentialist theory of cinema; he first tries to identify the essence, or specific and unique qualities, of the medium and then argues that artistic cinema must exploit these qualities. The following summary uses *Film as Art* to illuminate the assumptions and concepts of early aesthetic film theories.

## Essentialism and materialtheorie

Cinema's essence, for Arnheim, lies in its ability to transform images into meaningful and significant *forms*. This approach is influenced by Gotthold Ephraim Lessing's 1766 book *Laocoön* (1969). Lessing claimed that the physical medium of each art form determined its unique province and purpose: painting best represented bodies in space, while poetry should be reserved for actions rendered in time (1969, 91). Likewise, Arnheim argued that film art depended on particular material limitations that distinguished it from other arts. To this he added the claim that those material limitations must also distinguish film from simple reproduction. He writes that 'art begins where mechanical reproduction leaves off, where the conditions of representation serve in some way to mold the object' (57). If cinema were simply an automatic means of duplicating the world, then it could not count as art. Arnheim set out to show that cinema, like painting, entailed choices about *how* to represent the world, and this gave artists the power to creatively 'mould' images.

Arnheim uses the term 'materialtheorie' to encapsulate his view that 'artistic and scientific descriptions of reality are cast in molds that derive not so much from the subject matter itself as from the properties of the medium – or *Material* – employed' (1957, 2). *Film as Art* systematically analyses aspects of cinema that block exact reproduction, for these must constitute the medium's specificity.

The book is divided into two parts: the first lays out Arnheim's taxonomy of ways that film diverges from mechanical reproduction; the second describes (and prescribes) how these divergences can be used artfully. As a summary, Arnheim condenses his argument into a list of twenty 'characteristics of the film medium' and a set of 'applications' for each trait (1957, 127–33). For instance, his first characteristic is that 'every object must be photographed from one particular vantage point' that facilitates the following alternatives: 'a) View that shows the shape of an object most characteristically; b) View that conveys a particular conception of the object (e.g. worm's-eye-view, indicating weight and forceful-ness); c) View that attracts the spectator's attention by being unusual; d) Surprise effect due to the concealment of the back side (Chaplin sobbing; no! [he's] mixing a cocktail!)' (127, 128). Thus Arnheim catalogues areas where film itself diverges from normal perception, including the depiction of a three-dimensional image in two dimensions, the isolation of vision from other bodily sensations, and the presence of frame lines. In each kind of divergence, Arnheim finds expressive possibilities. This logic led him infamously to count qualities like silence and black-and-white reproduction among film's essential generative characteristics, locking his aesthetics to obsolete technological traits.

## Art and the spectator

Arnheim grounded his theory in the concepts of Gestalt psychology, which had been developed by Max Wertheimer and Wolfgang Kohler, his teachers at the University of Berlin. Gestalt's universal principles of visual perception and cognition underwrite most of Arnheim's aesthetic doctrine, granting the theory scope and elevating cinema as an exemplary art. Gestalt psychologists understood perception as a creative act in which the mind organizes the material of the world. This gave Arnheim insight into the creative work of the artist. Art translates the stuff of the world into the materials of its medium in much the way that the act of perception creatively transforms raw sensory input into patterns the mind can grasp. The basic rules of perception (the striving for balance, simplicity, clarity, continuity, expressiveness, and others) should then inform successful art. In this model, art becomes an exalted form of perception. Artists do not strictly derive their works from reality, but shape an equivalent that is sharp, clean, and meaningful because it conforms to the medium's essence and hence its special capabilities. Art functions as an exercise for viewers, helping them to appreciate and focus their perceptual powers as they work through the artist's specific materials to unlock an expressive representation.

Arnheim supported his claims with detailed descriptions of film form. He is particularly attuned to the way composition, lighting, and the absence of sound served storytelling. His best-known example of the power of camera placement reveals how his approach wove together Gestalt concepts with aesthetic judgements and beliefs about the function of art. Arnheim cites the opening of *The Immigrant* (1917) in which Charlie Chaplin, back to camera, bends over a ship's railing so that 'everyone thinks the poor devil is paying his toll to the sea', only for him to turn around and reveal 'that he has hooked a large fish with his walking stick' (Arnheim 1957, 36). The moment is compelling, partly because it draws attention to the limits of cinema's vantage point. The viewer accepts the hypothesis that Chaplin is seasick because of the seeming completeness of the initial view. Upon the reveal, however, Arnheim's spectator becomes aware both of Chaplin's deception and of the camera placement: 'The idea underlying the scene is no longer "a man is doing such and such a thing, for example, he is fishing or being sick," but "a man is doing this and that *and* at the same time the spectator is watching him from a particular station point"' (36). Arnheim is fond of sight gags, which depend on a 'Gestalt switch' (Koch 1990, 173). Having grasped the image as a whole, the viewer is required by Chaplin to construct an alternative Gestalt, which has the salutary effect of highlighting the very capacity of film to select views. A moment of expressive framing leads the viewer back to an essential quality of the medium: the choice of a single vantage point on an object. For Arnheim this formal awareness was not self-conscious, much less reflexive; it was a tool to solicit the viewer to experience content for a particular purpose.

Film art depends not just on the moulding of a representation, but also on the viewer's acknowledgement *of* that moulding: 'It is no longer merely a matter of realizing "there stands a policeman"; but rather of realizing "how he is standing"' (Arnheim 1957, 43). Popular filmmakers like Chaplin gave Arnheim hope that cinema might train viewers to develop formal awareness. In his preface to the revised edition of *Film as Art* Arnheim signalled a social mission for his theory by pointing out the strong bond between artistic form and culture:

> Shape and colour, sound and words are the means by which man defines the nature and intention of his life. In a functioning culture, his ideas reverberate from his buildings, statues, songs, and plays. But a population constantly exposed to chaotic sights and sounds is gravely handicapped in finding its way. When the eyes and ears are prevented from perceiving meaningful order, they can only react to the brutal signals of immediate satisfaction.
>
> (Arnheim 1957, 6–7)

Sharp, meaningful forms, viewers who discern order in artworks, and artists who discover the innate order of things were for Arnheim culturally important. One senses in his work the belief that thoughtful form could be a bulwark against the fascist bombast that he fled in the early 1930s.

## Aesthetic judgement

Like most essentialist theorists, Arnheim aimed his abstractions towards practical evaluation of works of art. Good works were by definition essentially cinematic in that they used the peculiarities of the medium to achieve something beyond mere reproduction. But it wasn't enough for a filmmaker to lay stress on the materials of his craft. For Arnheim artistic films depart from reproduction in significant and meaningful ways. Above all, he values cleverness and subtlety: films that experiment with novel stylistics to achieve meaning without revealing the hand of the director. Consider, for instance, his criticism of a scene in G.W. Pabst's *Diary of a Lost Girl* (1929) in which two lovers are seen to kiss first from inside a pharmacy, with a glass door beyond them, and then from the street, in silhouette through that door. Arnheim finds the shot change 'wholly superficial and decorative'. He explains: 'It signifies nothing. And things which have no significance have no place in a work of art' (Arnheim 1957, 50). The shot might be stronger, Arnheim conjectures, if Pabst had offered sufficient motivation within the story world, such as a character 'looking through the door and watching the scene from the outside'. Yet the real test of artistic validity would be for the shot change not simply to function as 'a clever visual interpretation' but to achieve 'symbolic depth' (81, 121). This vision of significance achieved in a motivated fashion, of meaning that appears to emerge without drawing attention to the device, found its highest expression, for Arnheim, in Chaplin's work. Chaplin's dining on an old boot in *The Goldrush* (1925), for instance, exemplifies how a film artist can forcefully embody an abstract concept (the contrast between rich and poor) in concrete terms *without* breaking from the story world.

36

Materialtheorie, which emphasizes artistic purism and formal awareness, anticipates Clement Greenberg's modernist arguments for medium specificity (O'Brian 1986). Yet, Arnheim's watchwords of subtlety and motivation, his dislike of overt artifice and 'interfering with reality', and his overriding concern that art 'interprets and molds material without doing violence to it' placed him in an ambivalent position with regard to modernism (Arnheim 1957, 81, 121). Far from endorsing abstraction, *Film as Art* repeatedly returns to meaningful significance as the sole purpose of visual distortion. Filmmakers must resist reproduction, but, Arnheim warns, 'the character of the objects represented should not thereby be destroyed but rather strengthened, concentrated, and interpreted' (35). From this perspective, black-and-white cinematography clarifies faces, turning them into 'stylized expressive masks', and the absence of sound shapes, interprets, and concentrates gesture (68, 109). Arnheim's rejection of imitation, which may well have derived from his Gestalt background, resembles aesthetic modernism, but the goal for him was always a sharper and clearer expression of meaning, not its questioning and dissolution (Koch 1990, 170–3). Bound on one hand to notice form but on the other to seek meanings justified through narrative, Arnheim, and his ideal spectator, are aesthetically aware connoisseurs of an art that rewards contemplation with significance.

## Criticism of essentialism

Arnheim's position has been roundly criticized for its narrowness. Just four years after the publication of *Film als Kunst*, Walter Benjamin fired a shot across the bow of Arnheim's brand of aesthetic theory in his essay 'The Work of Art in the Age of Mechanical Reproduction' (1969). For Benjamin questions of whether photography and film counted among the arts were 'futile' and 'ill-considered' because they had fundamentally changed the very nature of art (1969, 227). Where Arnheim hoped for a spectator who could contemplate film as one might a painting, Benjamin concluded that cinema delivered a 'shock effect' to a distracted subject (239) (*see* MIMETIC INNERVATION). Arnheim's definition of art had little relevance to the modern perceiver. Though he cites Arnheim's discussion of performance as evidence for his own argument, Benjamin's rejection of traditional aesthetics and rallying call for political criticism closed off the avenues traversed by *Film als Kunst*.

Theorists who continued to labour in the field of film aesthetics had more specific objections. André Bazin, though he didn't single out Arnheim by name, criticized the elevation of silent cinema as essentially artistic because it ignored filmmakers who put their 'faith in reality' and who emphasized film's power to reproduce images of the world (Bazin 1967, 26–8) (*see* ONTOLOGY OF THE PHOTOGRAPHIC IMAGE). Writing in 1972, V.F. Perkins was more pointed in his rejection. He characterized Arnheim as a dogmatic theorist who laid unwarranted demands upon filmmakers. In Perkins's view, Arnheim reified silent cinema because he was defending the new medium according to standards from the graphic arts. For Perkins, these were the wrong standards because they prevented Arnheim from granting 'the recorded action a place in the critical scheme or [allowing] it any artistic status' (Perkins 1972, 17). Perkins rebuked silent film theorists like Arnheim for offering a 'false definition of the medium' and celebrating a kind of cinema that 'is a fossil when it is not a myth' (11, 17).

Noël Carroll offers the most detailed dismantling of Arnheim's theory in his book *Philosophical Problems of Classical Film Theory* (1988). Writing from the perspective of analytical philosophy, Carroll uncovers logical errors in Arnheim's reasoning and rejects essentialism. Carroll isolates and challenges three 'philosophically suspect presuppositions' that drive *Film as Art*. Arnheim's definition of art as necessarily expressive is too narrow, as is his claim that art must diverge from reproduction. Further, Carroll sees little reason to suppose that 'each art form has a specific area of invention defined primarily by the limitations of the specific medium' (1988, 91). Beyond the obvious historical shortcomings of Arnheim's refusal to admit sound, colour, and widescreen into cinema's artistic arsenal, Carroll uncovers key assumptions at the base of his model that few theorists or historians of art would support. None of these criticisms really diminish Arnheim's achievement, fully realized with *Art and Visual Perception* and subsequent works, which was to account for art's power by interrogating the perception of form. By the time of Carroll's critique, however, the turn in media theory encouraged by Benjamin had come to pass. Questions of film as art had given way to cinema as ideology, desire, and identity.

## The legacy of film as art

Essentialist aesthetic arguments were historically important in gaining legitimacy for cinema as an art form. Even Carroll concedes that Arnheim performed a valuable service when he 'defeated the philosophical prejudices that confronted the nascent art of film' (1988, 90). Arnheim's theory as a whole may be indefensible, but *Film as Art*'s legacy survives in the methods and questions of formal analysis. Scholars seeking to understand film's constructive principles by analysing the choices available to filmmakers and the purposes that film style can serve are working in furrows that Arnheim first helped to plough. David Bordwell, the most articulate practitioner in this tradition, terms this approach the 'poetics of cinema'. Taking his cue from Russian Formalism as well as aesthetic theorists like Arnheim and Bazin, Bordwell characterizes poetics in part as reconstructing a filmmaker's creative situation (as opposed to the more narrow view of a filmmaker's 'intention'), and explaining how fine-grained formal choices guide viewer perception and experience (Bordwell 2008, 28, 47).

When dealing with the particulars of film form, *Film as Art* models a kind of poetics. Arnheim analyses formal choices by posing hypothetical alternatives, as when he suggests a variety of framings for a shot of a prisoner leaving his jail in Abram Room's *Ghost That Never Returns* (1929), to throw light on the particular power of a filmmaker's preference (Arnheim 1957, 46–8). He also poses the task of filmmaking as a weighing of various solutions to artistic problems, for example when he discusses the means for depicting conversations, concluding that in the case of Jacques Feyder's *Les Nouveaux Messieurs* (1929), where a woman's face is shadowed by a man's in the foreground, 'one seems to see more by seeing less' (56). Similarly, 'indirect representation' could make events sharper and more vivid by seeking visual equivalents for sound. In finding novel translations of events, or 'robbing the real' as Arnheim puts it, film can deliver an expressive charge with startling concreteness (111). Arnheim's commitment to materialtheorie engendered an outstanding grasp of film style and led him to speculate convincingly about filmmakers' choices, and connect form to perceptual effects. Aesthetic theorists hardened these observations into law. Yet, if we bracket such essentializing off from insights about film form, aesthetic theories like *Film as Art* emerge as precise and insightful treatises on the formal possibilities of silent narrative cinema.

SCOTT HIGGINS

## Works cited

Arnheim, Rudolf. 1957. *Film as Art*. Berkeley: University of California Press.

Bazin, André. 1967. *What Is Cinema?* Vol. 1. Berkeley: University of California Press.

Benjamin, Walter. 1969. *Illuminations*. New York: Schocken Books.

Bordwell, David. 2008. *Poetics of Cinema*. New York: Routledge.

Carroll, Noël. 1988. *Philosophical Problems of Classical Film Theory*. Princeton, NJ: Princeton University Press.

Koch, Gertrud. 1990. 'Rudolf Arnheim: The Materialist of Aesthetic Illusion'. *New German Critique* 51: 164–78.

Lessing, G.E. 1969 [1766]. *Laocoön: An Essay upon the Limits of Poetry and Painting*. New York: Noonday Press.

O'Brian, John, ed. 1986. *Clement Greenberg: The Collected Essays and Criticism*. Chicago, IL: University of Chicago Press.

Perkins, V.F. 1972. *Film as Film*. Harmondsworth: Penguin Books.

## Further reading

Andrew, Dudley. 1976. *The Major Film Theories*. London: Oxford University Press.

Dalle Vacche, Angela, ed. 2003. *The Visual Turn: Classical Film Theory and Art*. New Brunswick, NJ: Rutgers University Press.

Higgins, Scott, ed. 2011. *Arnheim for Film and Media Studies*. New York: Routledge.

# ATTENTION

When Hugo Münsterberg wrote *The Photoplay: A Psychological Study* in 1916, he was well known in America as a Harvard professor and the principal champion of the discipline known as applied psychology. Indeed, Münsterberg is often credited with being the progenitor of that particular field. *The Photoplay* was not the first time Münsterberg had written on the arts. In 1905, for example, he published a book called *Principles of Art Education*, in 1909 an article called 'The Problem of Beauty', and throughout his career other writings that dealt with aesthetics and art. In each case Münsterberg's evaluations of art, or the spectator's psychological interaction with art, were informed by his broader theories from applied psychology. Nowhere is this more evident than in his key concept 'attention'. In his 1913 volume *Psychology and Industrial Efficiency* he wrote:

> The problem of attention, indeed, seems to stand quite in the center of the field of industrial efficiency. This conviction has grown upon me in my observations of industrial life. The peculiar kind of attention decides more than any other mental trait for which economic activity the individual is adapted.
>
> (Münsterberg 1913, 136)

Attention governed all acts of perception and it became a vital concept in his evaluation of the film medium. Münsterberg subdivided the phenomenon into two parts, voluntary and involuntary attention. When doing psychological testing for streetcar drivers – which he did for the Boston Railway Company – the attentiveness of the prospective employees was measured in terms of not just the quality of their momentary attentiveness but also how it remained sharp after a long shift of work. Both voluntary (i.e. 'paying attention') and involuntary attention (i.e. good reflexes, perceiving motion in the periphery of vision) were crucial physiological and mental components of the ideal worker (Münsterberg 1913, 63–82). However, when viewing a work of art, while we may voluntarily go to the museum or stage play, according to Münsterberg, we must eventually give up our volition and allow the work of art, including the film, to take over the guidance of our perceptions. We cede volition to the work of art, which then directs our attentions through various artistic means. In the film the technical element that most exemplified this directing of attention was the close-up. He writes: 'The close-up has objectified in our world of perception our mental act of attention and by it has furnished art with a means which far transcends the power of any theater stage' (Münsterberg 1916, 87). Notice particularly the word 'objectified', which suggests that a subjective/mental process or act has taken tangible form on the screen – has been reproduced – through the apparatus of film. The close-up focused attention on a single object, making it come to the centre of consciousness and making it more vivid for the spectator – a concept borne out in some contemporary experiments on cognitive vividness and creativity (Pearson *et al.* 2011) – whether it be a face expressing emotion, the menacing knife of a murderer, or an eloquently gesturing hand. The close-up accurately mirrored/objectified the act of attending to something with our eyes and mind. At the same time, while we focus our attention on something, peripheral things become less distinct and less important to our consciousness. The close shot made the object photographed more vivid by having it as the only thing in the (filmic) visual field, cutting out all other ancillary objects that might distract from the dramatization being offered by the object itself.

Cognitive science has demonstrated that our mental engagement with things is hierarchically organized. Our brains tend not to work if they don't have to. If I see a picture of a lion, it is manifestly different from seeing a lion. If I see a real lion, depending on the context, which I also determine perceptually, my brain might have to do a lot of work and it will likely receive a shot of adrenaline in order to facilitate both the mental and other physiological demands that may momentarily be placed on me (escape! fight! scream!). If I see a picture of a lion, I no less accurately identify the thing as a lion, or, rather, a picture of a lion. And because it is a picture and I know it is a picture, I also know, intuitively, that I need not engage my mind with excessive work. It poses no threat. A picture allows one, cognitively speaking, to merely perceive without many distractions or demands. Only those distractions crucial to the object's place in the narrative world of the film need occupy my consciousness, with whatever specialized or personal association I may supply from my biography or individual mental world.

In *The Photoplay* some of the most engaging observations are made in the trio of chapters entitled 'Attention', 'Memory', and 'Imagination'. (*See* MEMORY AND FILM.) Münsterberg contends that part of the incomparable effectiveness of film as an artistic medium derives from the ease with which it can parallel the operations of the human mind. Just as one can remember things from the past ('Memory') in a split second as the images and sounds from the past are generated in the mind, so too can the film bring us, with the rapidity of an edit, to the images of earlier times in a flashback. Similarly, we can imagine things ('Imagination') in the future and here also the film's spatio-temporal flexibility can keep pace with the elasticity and tempo of mental operations. Münsterberg notes the film's superiority to the live theatre stage in these regards, where the stage actor must recall the past or imagine the future in a soliloquy in which words alone fail to match the eloquence of film's compelling visuality. The awkward and time-consuming changing of the stage's backdrops seem maladroit and clunky compared to film's ability to make rapid alternations in place and time. In these chapters Münsterberg seems, at times, to be on the verge of claiming – though he is ultimately unable to – that the film can be seen to provide perceptions that are superior to the mind's memories or imaginings. No memory or imagined thing can be as vivid as the perception of that actual thing or vivid image of that thing. In this regard, film provides an actual perception for what in the mind is merely a thought. In other words, when the film presents a flashback or an imagined place and time, it presents it as a powerful visual and auditory perception marked as different from but paradoxically related to a mental event. The spectator actually sees and hears something. No thought can claim to be so vivid and have the spatio-temporal comprehensiveness that film provides, even in the silent version Münsterberg was dealing with in 1916. Film thus provides for the spectator a sort of super-cognitivity in relation to these things – pasts, futures, fantasies – which in the mind are things that one can never actually perceive since sensory perception is always in the here and now. In this sense, there is another element of vivaciousness, linking the etymology of vividness more closely to another one of film's chimerical qualities: the complete lack of presence of objects yet at the same conveying an enhanced presence of those same objects.

## Vividness

Theories of contemporary cognitive psychology confirm in indirect ways some of Münsterberg's important concepts. In cognitive psychology's Availability-Valence Hypothesis, 'availability refers to the ease with which an association can be accessed from memory' (Kisielius and Sternthal 1986, 418–31). The more vivid the perceptual experience of an object, the greater the availability valence will be, thus making it easier for the mind to recall and re-form the image of the thing in imagination. Many factors come into play, but it seems nonetheless valid to claim that the pasts, futures, and fantasies that film offers as convincing perceptions (and as prompts for the spectator's own imagination) obtain a vivacity far in excess of any mental image that offers itself to thought alone imagining an event that *did not happen*, i.e. was fictional. It is thus this super-cognitivity in relation to these alternative spatio-temporal realms that might be seen to contribute to the transcendental spectator generated by the incomparable vivacity provided/facilitated by the filmic apparatus. Could it be, too, that contemporary film images, imbued as they are with vivid colours, monumental size, and advanced and rich sonic environments, supply perceptions to viewers that, in being so extraordinarily vivacious, make more dramatic impacts as perceptions and thus are more easily accessed than perceptions of mundane ordinary life?

There is thus a rhetorical dimension to vividness and the Availability-Valence Hypothesis in the sense that a more vivid image, more easily remembered or re-imagined – or re-imagined with greater frequency – could potentially be more persuasive or have more psychological and emotional impact on the viewer. It comes as no surprise that cognitive psychologists who do research on these issues are often interested in the efficacy of advertising, as was Hugo Münsterberg, who was the first to propose how psychology could be applied to more efficient and effective marketing and product promotion (Münsterberg 1918/1924, 105, 106, 128, 161).

Merely twenty years after Münsterberg's book on film came out, Walter Benjamin wrote in 1936 his landmark essay on film, 'The Work of Art in the Age of Mechanical Reproduction' (Benjamin 1969). In it he developed the key concept of 'aura' (*see* MIMETIC INNERVATION). Both Benjamin's aura and Münsterberg's involuntary attention posit a certain type of spectator, one who has either given up volition and agency or who seems to be a passive entity upon which objects of art 'work'. For Münsterberg this was merely an account of the aesthetic experience parsed by a psychologist's eye for the dynamics of perception accompanying a series of mental acts. For Benjamin the aura of the work of art was a potentially enslaving aesthetic experience that had been abused by fascism to sway the masses into obedience and social ignorance. For Benjamin, however, the film, unlike painting and sculpture (Botticelli's *Primavera* or Michelangelo's *David*), was an art form essentially free of auratic qualities, being not a unique work of art produced by the creative hand of an individual but, rather, a mechanically reproduced work that did not have the unique and authentic auratic presence that defined the perception of works of art. Thus, for Benjamin, the film was an art form that was viewed by the spectator in a state of 'distraction' rather than 'concentration' (absorption). This meant that viewers were liberated from the mesmerizing and controlling aura that characterized their relationship with unique, non-mechanically produced, works of art. Benjamin and Münsterberg, then, at least in terms of how they analyse the spectator's relation to the medium of film, offer conflicting views. While Münsterberg sees the giving up of voluntary attention to the medium as bringing about the incomparable dramatic and artistic effects of the film, Benjamin believes that the film, as a mechanically reproduced medium, cannot fascinate the spectator's attention in the same way as an original work of art. The ways in which Münsterberg's voluntary and involuntary attention and Benjamin's distraction and concentration interplay reveal much about the lenses – psychology and politics – through which the two address the cinema and the nature of the cinematic spectator that they theorize.

ALLAN LANGDALE

## Works cited

Benjamin, Walter. 1969. 'The Work of Art in the Age of Mechanical Reproduction'. In *Illuminations*, translated by Harry Zohn, edited by Hannah Arendt, 217–52. New York: Harcourt Brace & World, Inc.

Kisielius, Jolita and Brian Sternthal. 1986. 'Examining the Vividness Controversy: An Availability-Valence Interpretation'. *Journal of Consumer Research* 12 (4): 418–31.

Münsterberg, Hugo. 1913. *Psychology and Industrial Efficiency*. Boston, MA: Houghton Mifflin.

——1916. *The Photoplay: A Psychological Study and Other Writings on Film*. Edited by Allan Langdale. New York: Routledge, 2002.

——1918/1924. *Business Psychology*. Chicago, IL: La Salle Extension University.

Pearson, Joel, Rosanne L. Rademaker, and Frank Tong. 2011. 'Evaluating the Mind's Eye: The Metacognition of Visual Imagery'. *Psychological Science* 22 (12): 1535–42.

## Further reading

Andrew, Dudley. 1976. 'Hugo Münsterberg'. In *The Major Film Theories: An Introduction*, 14–26. London/Oxford/New York: Oxford University Press.

Carroll, Noël. 1988. 'Film/Mind Analogies: The Case of Hugo Münsterberg'. *Journal of Aesthetics and Art Criticism* 46 (4): 489–99.

D'Anguiulli, Amedeo, and Adam Reeves. 2007. 'The Relationship between Self-Reported Vividness and Latency during Mental Size Scaling of Everyday Items: Phenomenological Evidence of Different Types of Imagery'. *American Journal of Psychology* 120 (4): 521–51.

Fredericksen, Donald Laurence. 1977. *The Aesthetic of Isolation in Film Theory: Hugo Münsterberg*. New York: Arno Press.

Hale, Matthew, Jr. 1980. *Human Science and Social Order: Hugo Münsterberg and the Origins of Applied Psychology*. Philadelphia, PA: Temple University Press.

Keller, Phyllis. 1979. Chapter in *States of Belonging: German-American Intellectuals and the First World War*. Cambridge, MA, and London: Harvard University Press.

Landy, Frank J. 1992. 'Hugo Münsterberg: Victim or Visionary?'. *Journal of Applied Psychology* 77 (6): 787–802.

Langdale, Allan. 2002. 'Introduction'. In Hugo Münsterberg, *The Photoplay: A Psychological Study and Other Writings on Film*. New York: Routledge.

Moskowitz, Merle. 1977. 'Hugo Münsterberg: A Study in the History of Applied Psychology'. *American Psychologist* 32 (10): 824–42.

Nyyssonen, Pasi. 1998. 'Film Theory at the Turning Point of Modernity'. *Film-Philosophy: Electronic Salon* 17: http://www.film-philosophy.com/vol2–1998/n31nyyssonen (accessed 1 December 2012).

Spillmann, Jutta and Lothar. 1993. 'The Rise and Fall of Hugo Münsterberg'. *Journal of the History of the Behavioral Sciences* 29 (4): 322–38.

Wicclair, Mark. 1978. 'Film Theory and Hugo Münsterberg's "The Film, a Psychological Study"'. *Journal of Aesthetic Education* 12 (3): 33–50.

# ATTRACTION

Tom Gunning's essay 'The Cinema of Attraction: Early Cinema, Its Spectator, and the Avant-Garde' (1986; subsequently published under the title 'The Cinema of Attractions' in 1990) is an influential, theoretically informed essay on early film history. It attempts to understand and explain – rather than simply describe – the specific qualities of early cinema (the first ten or eleven years of film history, from 1895 to around 1906).

Gunning identifies the origin of the term 'attraction' in the work of Sergei Eisenstein:

> In his search for the 'unit of impression' of theatrical art, the foundation of an analysis which would undermine realistic representational theater, Eisenstein hit upon the term 'attraction'. An attraction aggressively subjected the spectator to 'sensual or psychological impact' [Eisenstein]. According to Eisenstein, theater should consist of a montage of such attractions, creating a relation to the spectator entirely different from the absorption in 'illusory imitativeness' [Eisenstein].
>
> (Gunning 1986, 66)

Eisenstein is precise about the spectator effect an attraction should create: an attraction employs shock as an aesthetic and political strategy, an assault on the senses that also changes the audience's political consciousness (*see* MONTAGE THEORY II [SOVIET AVANT-GARDE]). In fact, his theory is premised on the attraction's impact: one cannot separate out an attraction and its impact on the spectator. This in turn became the principle behind his montage theory, in which the juxtaposition of two attractions creates a third meaning, which is not contained in the attractions themselves but is actively constructed by the spectator (who is nonetheless strongly guided by the film).

The origin of the term 'attraction' does not end with Eisenstein. Gunning reminds us that Eisenstein in turn borrowed it from the circus – from the fairground attraction, the mass form of entertainment that delivers a sensual and psychological impact (1986, 66). In general terms, for Gunning the attraction refers to a cultural mode of experience specific to the turn of the twentieth century. An attraction is non-illusionistic, non-deceptive, and non-voyeuristic. Instead, it declares its intentions; it is exhibitionistic and aims to astonish rather than deceive.

The term 'attraction' therefore means an act of display, an act of showing and exhibiting. Gunning implies that displaying, showing, and exhibiting are film's specific qualities, and that early cinema exploits this specific quality of film. Although Gunning discusses the attraction in cinema before 1906, he argues that showing, displaying, and exhibiting are film's specific qualities, and that early cinema is special because it exploits this specific quality of film in an unadulterated form – these specific qualities become the dominant trait in most films prior to 1906.

Gunning uses the concept of the attraction to explore the relation between early cinema and the avant-garde (or avant-gardes – French impressionism, German expressionism, Soviet montage, surrealism, and the American avant-garde), and to identify a break in cinema production from 1906, after which narrative began to dominate. Narrative cinema does not simply replace the cinema of attractions, but absorbs it, as can be seen in prolonged action sequences in contemporary blockbusters, or other moments of spectacle, such as song and dance sequences in musicals, or, more generally, in cinema's tendency to fetishize women, to put women on display for the male gaze. Rather than set up a relation of opposition between early and narrative cinema, Gunning establishes a relation of inclusion (before 1906 early cinema existed by itself; thereafter it becomes a subset of narrative cinema).

If early cinema can be defined as a cinema of attractions, then it is the 'exhibitionist confrontation rather than diegetic absorption' offered by both early cinema and the avant-garde that links the two together: 'I believe that it was precisely the exhibitionist quality of turn of the century popular art that made it attractive to the avant-garde' (Gunning 1986, 66).

## André Gaudreault

Gunning initially introduced the concept of attraction in collaboration with André Gaudreault, in their joint conference paper in 1985 'Le cinéma des premiers temps: un défi à l'histoire du cinéma?' (English translation: Gaudreault and Gunning 2006). Developing the concept of attraction from Eisenstein, the authors distinguished monstrative attractions (1895–1908) from the system of narrative integration (1909–14) – where the term 'monstration' similarly means the act of showing (Gaudreault and Gunning 2006, 373).

More recently, Gaudreault has redefined the concept of 'attraction' in *Film and Attraction* (2011). Much of the book is concerned with bringing into question the activities performed by film historians, including the quest to identify who invented cinema, the search for the 'first' time a technique was used, periodization (dividing up the history of cinema into distinct periods), the significance of naming those periods, and the importance of using precise terminology to name one's object of study. He continues to identify a decisive break between early cinema and narrative cinema, but emphasizes that the break is so decisive that we cannot even call the early period 'cinema' (and therefore there is no need to call it 'early' either). Instead, he comes up with the unwieldy (but nonetheless precise) term kine-attractography, which he opposes to cinema, an institutionalized practice premised on narration:

> in the case of kine-attractography, which dominated the world of animated pictures until about 1908–10, we have not yet entered the history of cinema. For the simple reason that 'cinema' – cinema as we generally understand it today – was not a late-nineteenth-century invention. The emergence of cinema, in the sense we understand the term today, dates instead from the 1910s.
>
> (Gaudreault 2011, 4)

## Critique of Gunning

One of the key issues in evaluating the concept of attraction is whether Gunning over-extends its applicability. All research makes generalizations and relies on implicit assumptions, but such generalizations and assumptions need to be critically evaluated. Can early cinema, the avant-gardes, as well as Vaudeville, circuses and fairgrounds, and contemporary Hollywood blockbusters, really be discussed under the same concept? Is not the concept of attraction being stretched too far? This raises two issues:

(1) the uneasy relation between early (pre-classical) cinema and post-classical narrative cinema;
(2) the thorny cultural generalization that early cinema and the avant-garde 'expressed' the visual experience of modernity.

I shall address (1) below. In relation to (2), I shall defer to David Bordwell's commentary on several of Gunning's essays. Bordwell first summarizes how Gunning presents a cultural explanation of the cinema of attractions, and then expresses his concerns:

> Tom Gunning suggests that many tactics of the 'cinema of attractions' reflect culturally determined modes of experience at the turn of the century. He adduces examples of an 'aesthetics of astonishment' – locomotives hurtling to the viewer, early audiences' wonder at magical transformations, the charm of the very illusion of motion. The attraction, Gunning claims, at once epitomizes the fragmentation of modern experience and responds to alienation under capitalism. It reflects the atomized environment of urban experience and the new culture of consumption; like an advertisement, the movie's isolated gag or trick tries to grab attention.
> (Bordwell 1997, 144)

> The more exactly Gunning ties modernity to this phase of stylistic history, though, the more problematic the case seems to become.
> (Ibid.)

Bordwell then criticizes Gunning's claims that not all early films express modernity, for the concept of attraction loses its explanatory power and becomes merely contingent. Bordwell's critique implies that Gunning artificially inflated the importance of attractions in early cinema as a way to justify his primary research issue – his investigation of the influence of early cinema on the avant-garde. Other theoretically informed film historians then presented counter-evidence (especially Charles Musser [1994] on Porter and Alison McMahan [2002] on Alice Guy Blaché), which diminishes the concept's power.

In a long endnote, Bordwell also responds to Gunning's claim that he does not see attractions as a causal consequence of modernity (Bordwell 1997, 301–2, note 100); instead, he simply identifies a rich 'congruence' (Gunning's word) between modernity and early cinema. Gunning is choosing his words carefully, because 'congruence' simply suggests 'similarity', or 'analogy' between early films and modernity, rather than causality. Gunning is trying to avoid theorizing early films as a mere effect of a more general cause (modernity) while still attempting to articulate the relationship between early films and their cultural-historical context.

In relation to issue (1), Gunning argues that 'recent spectacle cinema has reaffirmed its roots in stimulus and carnival rides, in what might be called the Spielberg-Lucas-Coppola cinema of [special] effects' (1986, 70) – or 'tamed attractions', as he writes in the next sentence. The attractions are tamed because they have lost their political shock value, leaving only an aesthetic shock. If the attraction loses its political shock value, can it still be considered an attraction? The link between attraction and political shock value remains indeterminate in Gunning's essay. We do not discover if the political shock value is a necessary condition for the definition of an attraction. Moreover, can we really claim that special effects in contemporary cinema are non-illusionistic, that they are not co-opted into the ideology of realism and credibility?

Linda Williams also emphasizes the differences between early and post-classical cinema of attractions: 'The point of invoking the term "attractions" ... is not to argue that contemporary postmodern American cinema has reverted to the *same* attractions of early cinema. While there is certainly an affinity between the two, this new regime entails entirely different spectatorial disciplines and engages viewers in entirely different social experiences' (Williams 2000, 356).

Gunning uses the concept of attraction to revise what previous film historians have written about early cinema. To give just one concrete example: *The Gay Shoe Clerk*, made by Edwin M. Porter for the Edison Film Company in 1903. The Edison catalogue describes the film in the following way:

> Interior of shoe-store. Young lady and chaperon enter. While a fresh young clerk is trying a pair of high-heeled slippers on the young lady, the chaperon seats herself and gets interested in a paper. The scene changes to a close view, showing the lady's foot and the clerk's hands tying the slipper. Her dress is slightly raised, showing a shapely ankle, and the clerk's hands begin to tremble, making it difficult for him to tie the slipper. The picture returns to the previous scene. The clerk makes rapid progress with his fair customer, and while he is in the act of kissing her the chaperon looks up and proceeds to beat the clerk with an umbrella. Then she takes the young lady by the arm, and leads her from the store.
>
> (IMDb.com)

For standard film historians, the close-up of the woman's ankle signifies Porter's attempt to develop a narrative scene. But Gunning argues that the close-up is an attraction because its function is to display a woman's ankle. In his turn, Gunning has been criticized for mis-classifying the data. According to Charles Musser, for example, Gunning mis-labels the close-up in *The Gay Shoe Clerk* wholly as an attraction. Musser argues that the close-up is an attraction integrated into 'a quite complex narrative unfolding' because it maintains the illusion of the fourth wall, and sets up different spaces of awareness between the lovers and the chaperone (1994, 210).

In sum, Gunning's concept of the cinema of attractions is formulated in tentative language (such as 'congruence') and is based on indeterminate assumptions (especially the indeterminacy of the link between early cinema and modernity and the link between an attraction and political shock value). Nonetheless it is generally recognized as an original idea that had a significant impact on the re-conceptualization and re-periodization of early cinema. This is evident from the *The Cinema of Attractions Reloaded* (Strauven 2006), a 450-page volume offering a comprehensive overview of the origins of the concept of the 'attraction' and its extension and application to both early and post-classical cinema.

WARREN BUCKLAND

## Works cited

Bordwell, David. 1997. *On the History of Film Style*. Cambridge, MA: Harvard University Press.

Gaudreault, André. 2011. *Film and Attraction: From Kinematography to Cinema*. Translated by Timothy Barnard, foreword by Rick Altman. Urbana: University of Illinois Press.

Gaudreault, André, and Tom Gunning. 2006. 'Early Cinema as a Challenge to Film History'. In *The Cinema of Attractions Reloaded*, edited by Wanda Srauven, 365–80. Amsterdam: Amsterdam University Press.

Gunning, Tom. 1986. 'The Cinema of Attraction: Early Cinema, Its Spectator, and the Avant-Garde'. *Wide Angle* 8 (3/4): 63–70.

——1990. 'The Cinema of Attractions: Early Cinema, Its Spectator, and the Avant-Garde'. In *Early Cinema: Space, Frame, Narrative*, edited by Thomas Elsaesser, 56–62. London: British Film Institute.

McMahan, Alison. 2002. *Alice Guy Blaché: Lost Visionary of the Cinema*. New York: Continuum.

Musser, Charles. 1994. 'Rethinking Early Cinema: Cinema of Attractions and Narrativity'. *Yale Journal of Criticism* 7 (2): 203–32.

Strauven, Wanda, ed. 2006. *The Cinema of Attractions Reloaded*. Amsterdam: Amsterdam University Press.

Williams, Linda. 2000. 'Discipline and Fun: *Psycho* and Postmodern Cinema'. In *Reinventing Film Studies*, edited by Christine Gledhill and Linda Williams, 351–78. London: Arnold.

## Further reading

Buckland, Warren. 2012. *Film Theory: Rational Reconstructions*, chapter 7. Abingdon: Routledge.

# AUTEUR THEORY

The popular perception of Hollywood cinema is that it consists of a mass of impersonal films lacking artistry. The auteur critic attempts to 'save' a handful of Hollywood directors from oblivion, which assumes that seeing a film with a recognized name attached confers added value upon that film. Films we now take for granted as auteur 'masterpieces' – John Ford's *The Searchers* (1956); Alfred Hitchcock's *Rear Window* (1954) and *Vertigo* (1958); Fritz Lang's *The Woman in the Window* (1944) and *The Big Heat* (1953) – were, in the 1950s, initially classified as anonymous genre movies. Auteur criticism is evaluative criticism that transformed the critical climate towards popular American cinema, for it promoted the serious study of Hollywood films: it analysed Hollywood films with the same care and attention that critics used to praise European art films.

Traditional auteur criticism, developed in the journal *Cahiers du cinéma* in the 1950–60s (see Hillier 1985; 1986) and by Andrew Sarris (1962; 1968), privileged the director's individual subjectivity: their intuition, spontaneous creativity, and personal expression. The distinctive properties that define an auteurist's films are thought to be located in a purely personal or subjective vision, ineffable 'sensibility', or obscure 'interior' meaning. Auteur critics also value the unity of style and themes that a director is able to impose on his or her films. That is, the auteur critic seeks to identify throughout the same director's corpus (whatever the genres involved) a pattern of thematic preoccupations and similarities in visual style. One of the most important aspects of an auteur analysis therefore involves analysing an individual film's style and themes within the context of a director's entire output. (Some auteur critics reserve the term *metteur en scène* for a director who only maintains consistency in style across their films.)

## Andrew Sarris

For Andrew Sarris, the auteur theory is based on three premises: technical competence; personal style; and, most importantly, interior meaning. He defined interior meaning as 'the tension between a director's personality and his material' (1962, 7). He adds that interior meaning:

> is not quite the vision of the world a director projects nor quite his attitude toward life. It is ambiguous, in any literary sense, because it is imbedded in the stuff of cinema and cannot be rendered in noncinematic terms. Truffaut called it the temperature of the director on the set, and that is a close approximation of its

professional aspect. Dare I come out and say what I think it to be is an élan of the soul?

(Sarris 1962, 7)

For Sarris, soul 'is that intangible difference between one personality and another' (7). The term 'interior meaning' is based on Kierkegaard's discussion of shadowgraphs and inner pictures in *Either/Or*, a discussion Sarris quotes as the epigraph to his 1962 essay. Kierkegaard argues that the 'inner picture [is] too delicately drawn to be outwardly visible, woven as it is of the tenderest moods of the soul' (quoted in Sarris 1962, 1). Interior meaning therefore refers to indirect meanings, like an implicit theme.

## Peter Wollen's auteur-structuralism

In Chapter 2 of his canonical book *Signs and Meaning in the Cinema* (1972) Peter Wollen attempted to place auteur criticism on a firm theoretical grounding, one that dismisses intangible concepts such as 'soul' and 'ineffable sensibility', and instead establishes the fundamental logic underlying a director's corpus of films. He attempted to achieve this by incorporating structuralism into auteur criticism.

Structuralists replace individual expression, personal psychology, and subjective vision with an emphasis on rational knowledge – an impersonal system of underlying codes and structures. They replace individual free will with general causes that determine the meaning of individual utterances, artworks, or films. When speaking or when making a film, the individual simply actualizes one possible combination of codes from the underlying system. His or her consciousness does not spontaneously create, for consciousness is determined and controlled by underlying structures: 'the apparent arbitrariness of the mind, its supposedly spontaneous flow of inspiration, and its seemingly uncontrolled inventiveness imply the existence of laws operating at a deeper level' (Lévi-Strauss 1970, 10). The primary aim of structuralism (and its close ally, semiotics) is to study this underlying system. In terms of recounting a myth, Lévi-Strauss indicated that the individual may not even realize the significance of the stories they tell, for the meaning of a story or a sentence exists prior to its utterance, in the underlying system of codes from which it is generated.

What are the implications of structuralism for auteur criticism? The structuralist method of analysis entails deciphering – that is, abstracting or disengaging – from the experience of an auteur's films an underlying, elementary latent structure that confers upon the films their shape and identity. This assumes that an auteur's films are unified, that they all manifest the same latent structure.

The structural approach to auteur criticism only focuses on theme. Wollen sees the stylistic approach by itself as superficial; for him, auteurs are distinguishable in terms of the thematic deep structures at the centre of their films. Style is not rigorously coded in the same way as the deep thematic level. In this, he is influenced by the structural methods of Lévi-Strauss: 'Myths, as Lévi-Strauss has pointed out, exist independently of style, the syntax of the sentence or musical sound, euphony or cacophony' (Wollen 1972, 105). For Wollen, an auteur's films share the same deep underlying structure, in contrast to the mere *metteur en scène*, who only controls the style of their films (78).

Structuralism orders themes into their invariant basic components, and works out the logical relations between those features, which are ultimately reducible to binary oppositions. What this means is that each basic component receives its meaning via an opposition to another term – raw/cooked, male/female, East/West, consonant/vowel. Binary oppositions are a form of absolute ordering: they divide up thematic units into two mutually exclusive terms.

For Lévi-Strauss, mythical thought is rigorously organized into binary oppositions. Identifying from a structuralist perspective the invariant thematic components of a director's films involves isolating their small number of basic themes, organizing them into binary oppositions, and identifying their different combinations. Such a study does not presuppose that film is like natural language (or, indeed, myth).

Wollen attempts to make auteur studies rigorous by following this three-step process: he isolates a director's ultimate themes, reduces them to binary oppositions, and identifies their different combinations. One assumption in Wollen's structural auteur theory is that auteurs create their own specific universe – their own system of beliefs, thinking, and behaviour – by combining several binary themes in distinct ways. Ultimately, it is this system of binary oppositions, expressing a certain set of beliefs and way of thinking, that becomes the object of analysis for auteur structuralists.

## Wollen on John Ford

As case studies, Wollen identified binary oppositions in the films of Howard Hawks and John Ford. Here we shall focus on his study of Ford.

After discussing Hawks in some detail, primarily from a traditional thematic perspective, Wollen shifts his attention to Ford's heroes, whom he analyses in structuralist terms by focusing on binary oppositions:

> The most relevant are garden versus wilderness, ploughshare versus sabre, settler versus nomad, European versus Indian, civilised versus savage, book versus gun, married versus unmarried, East versus West.
>
> (Wollen 1972, 94)

Wollen points out (94) that each binary opposition can in turn be subdivided into other binary oppositions:

> These antinomies can often be broken down further. The East, for instance, can be defined either as Boston or Washington and, in *The Last Hurrah*, Boston itself is broken down into the antipodes of Irish immigrants versus Plymouth Club, themselves bundles of such differential elements as Celtic versus Anglo-Saxon, poor versus rich, Catholic versus Protestant, Democrat versus Republican, and so on.

In the terms of formal logic, this process involves a successive 'division by dichotomy'. Each successive sub-division operates at a different level of generality, and uses different criteria to divide up the terms. In Wollen's example, the division by dichotomy begins with general terms, using the criterion of geographical location (East versus West), gradually moves towards more specific terms based on class and ethnic origins (Irish immigrants versus Plymouth Club), before becoming (in this example) more general again, with a division based on religion (Catholic versus Protestant) and American politics (Democrat versus Republican).

'Wilderness versus garden' is, according to Wollen, the 'master antinomy in Ford's films' (96) – and, in fact, one of the master antinomies of American culture, structuring its founding myth. A second related antinomy is that between nomad (living in the wilderness) and settler (in the cultivated garden) (97). Both pairs feed into the quest for the Promised Land, a major theme in Ford's films. In terms of heroes who rule in this new land, Wollen divides them into another binary opposition: rational legal authority versus charismatic authority. Wollen therefore identifies three binary oppositions dominant in Ford:

- wilderness/garden
- nomad/settler
- rational legal authority/charismatic authority.

He gives three examples, focusing on the heroes in *The Searchers*, *The Man Who Shot Liberty Valence*, and *My Darling Clementine*.

## The Searchers

Wilderness (nomad) versus garden (settler):

> Ethan Edwards [John Wayne] ... remains a nomad throughout the film. At the start, he rides in from the desert to enter the log-house; at the end, with perfect symmetry, he leaves the house again to return to the desert, to vagrancy. In many respects, he is similar to Scar; he is a wanderer, a savage, outside the law: he scalps his enemy. But, like the homesteaders, of course, he is a European, the mortal foe of the Indian. Thus Edwards is ambiguous; the antinomies invade the personality of the protagonist himself.
>
> (Wollen 1972, 96)

This combination of binary oppositions embedded in Ethan Edwards makes him a complex, contradictory character.

Rational legal authority/charismatic authority: 'In *The Searchers* ... the two kinds of authority remain separated' (101). That is, Edwards remains the charismatic authority figure who exists outside the law. In sum, Edwards embodies the values of the nomad, wilderness, and charismatic authority.

## The Man Who Shot Liberty Valence

Wilderness versus garden: 'the image of the cactus rose ... encapsulates the antinomy between desert and garden which pervades the whole film' (Wollen 1972, 96). In particular, Tom Doniphon (John Wayne) builds a log cabin and garden – but a garden full of cacti, not yet a real garden. However, before it can reach that stage, Doniphon burns it down when he realizes he will be unable to settle down. He never makes the full transition out of the wilderness.

Rational legal authority/charismatic authority:

> Ransom Stoddart [James Stewart] represents rational legal authority, Tom Doniphon represents charismatic authority. Doniphon abandons his charisma and cedes it, under what amount to false pretences, to Stoddart. In this way

charismatic and rational-legal authority are combined in the person of Stoddart and stability thus assured.

(Wollen 1972, 101)

By killing Liberty Valance in cold blood, Tom Doniphon is unable to make the transition to legal–rational authority. That place is taken by the lawyer Stoddart, who embodies it along with charismatic authority, for it is believed that he killed Valance in self-defence. Doniphon embodies the same three binary values as Edwards in *The Searchers*: nomad, wilderness, charismatic authority, while Stoddard embodies the two opposite terms – settler, garden – and dissolves the third opposition by embodying both terms: charismatic authority and rational legal authority.

### My Darling Clementine

Wilderness versus garden: Wyatt Earp (Henry Fonda) visits the barber, 'who civilizes the unkempt' (Wollen 1972, 96). The barber sprays Earp's hair with honeysuckle, an artificial perfume. The barbershop scene marks Earp's transition 'from wandering cowboy, nomadic, savage, bent on personal revenge, unmarried, to married man, settled, civilized, the sheriff who administers the law' (96). For Wollen, Earp's progress 'is an uncomplicated passage from nature to culture, from the wilderness left in the past to the garden anticipated in the future' (96).

Rational legal authority/charismatic authority: these two types of authority 'are combined naturally in Wyatt Earp' (101). According to Wollen, therefore, Earp begins like Edwards and Doniphon by embodying nomad/wilderness/charismatic authority, but transforms into the three opposite terms as the film progresses. Bill Nichols disputes Wollen's reading of *My Darling Clementine*, and offers an alternative structural analysis (discussed below).

As *My Darling Clementine* shows, Ford's system is not static; neither is each western the same: 'different pairs are foregrounded in different movies' (94), or the opposite terms in the same pairs are foregrounded in different movies. In his later films, such as *Cheyenne Autumn*, Ford's attitude towards his themes underwent a reversal: 'in *Cheyenne Autumn* it is the Europeans who are savage, the victims [Indians] who are heroes' (96).

In a controversial move, Wollen uses his structural method to carry out the auteur critic's traditional activity of evaluating directors. He finds Ford's films to be more complex than Hawks's because of 'the richness of the shifting relations between antinomies in Ford's work' (102). In Hawks, by contrast, one does not encounter a development and transformation of thematic structure; instead, the basic themes remain the same throughout his career. For Wollen, 'shifting relations' therefore names a valuable characteristic of the auteur film.

In summary, Wollen's version of the auteur theory posits the existence of a specific, objective thematic structure underlying all the films of the same auteur but not found in the films of other auteurs. The coherence of a director's film is not attributable to his or her subjectivity or 'soul', but to an underlying thematic structure.

### Critique

Wollen's controversial structuralist theory of the auteur has attracted a great deal of attention and criticism. He was criticized for downplaying logical relations beyond the binary opposition and for not taking into account an auteur's film style. In terms of the first point of criticism, a director's underlying thematic structure could be categorized more precisely in terms of numerous overlapping, finely graded categories, rather than a few mutually exclusive binary categories. In terms of the second point of criticism, Sam Rohdie noted that film style should be incorporated into a deep thematic study, otherwise one ignores film's specificity: 'There is nothing in Wollen's argument specific to the medium of the movies or the way in which Ford and Hawks handle that medium ... If structuralism is *the* key to cinematic understanding it needs to be used on various levels specific to the medium' (Rohdie 1969, 68–9). Raymond Durgnat (1982, 305) echoed this sentiment: 'You can't perform a Lévi-Straussian analysis of Ford *qua* Ford until you can perform a structural analysis on his images.'

Wollen's auteur structuralism brings order to the 'chaotic' auteur criticism, but at the cost of almost losing sight of the director in favour of impersonal underlying structures – which help us perceive at least one type of basic logical process (the binary opposition) at the root of the films analysed. Wollen's chapter is nonetheless significant for completely transforming the terms of debate in auteur criticism.

WARREN BUCKLAND

## Works cited

Durgnat, Raymond. 1982. 'From Signs to Meaning in the Cinema'. *Film Reader* 5: 300–23.

Hillier, Jim, ed. 1985. *Cahiers du cinéma. The 1950s: Neo-realism, Hollywood, New Wave.* Cambridge, MA: Harvard University Press.

——. 1986. *Cahiers du cinéma. The 1960s: New Wave, New Cinema, Reevaluating Hollywood.* Cambridge, MA: Harvard University Press.

Lévi-Strauss, Claude. 1970. *The Raw and the Cooked: Introduction to a Science of Mythology, 1.* Translated by John and Doreen Weightman. London: Jonathan Cape.

Rohdie, Sam. 1969. '[Review of] Signs and Meaning in the Cinema'. *New Left Review* 55: 66–70.

Sarris, Andrew. 1962. 'Notes on the Auteur Theory in 1962'. *Film Culture* 27: 1–8.

——. 1968. *The American Cinema: Directors and Directions 1929–1968.* New York: Dutton.

Wollen, Peter. 1972 [1969]. *Signs and Meaning in the Cinema.* Revised edition. London: Secker and Warburg/British Film Institute.

## Further reading

Buckland, Warren. 2012. *Film Theory: Rational Reconstructions*, chapter 1. Abingdon: Routledge.

Caughie, John, ed. 1981. *Theories of Authorship: A Reader.* London: BFI.

Elsaesser, Thomas. 2012. *The Persistence of Hollywood.* New York: Routledge.

# BLENDING AND FILM THEORY

In his introduction to *Film Theory* Robert Stam (2000, 2 and 22) draws attention to the power of conceptual metaphors such as 'cine-eye', 'window-to-the-world', 'camera pen', 'film language', and the 'film dream'. He also approaches the history of film theory by investigating the etymologies of the original names given to cinema. For instance, moving image technologies were understood as ways of recording life or looking at life ('Biograph' and 'Animatograph' vs. 'Vitascope' and 'Bioscope'), highlighting the temporal dimension during which light 'writes' ('Chronophotography') or the movement it allows us to see ('Kinetoscope'). While Stam reviews early and proto-cinematic neologisms as compact conceptual antecedents of later film theories,[1] these metaphoric projections are also instructive in understanding the general cognitive and rhetorical operations that support our notions of cinema. Coming to terms with cinema means arriving at theoretical concepts and filmic techniques that match the visions, expectations, and desires we invest and invent anew in cinema.

In the following, I will discuss Gilles Fauconnier and Mark Turner's (2002) model of conceptual integration or blending as a meta-theoretical framework for studying inferential structures in theorizing about cinema. Turner and Fauconnier envision blending theory as a cognitive rhetorical theory that combines classical rhetoric and neuroscientific insights. They are particularly indebted to cognitive linguistics and theories of metaphor that view language, metaphorical thinking, and analogy as being rooted in our bodily experience, following George Lakoff and Mark Johnson's conviction that 'our conceptual systems draw largely upon the commonalities of our bodies and the environments we live in' (1999, 6).

Fauconnier and Turner propose a model of how mental spaces are manipulated in making human-scale projections in what they call double-scope blending: 'Through double-scope blending, we pull what is alien to us … into our own native sphere, and thereby comprehend, manage and organize it. That which is foreign becomes a second nature. Exotic expanses become familiar human-scale terrain' (Turner 2008, 22). While the names 'Biograph', 'Animatograph', 'Vitascope', and 'Bioscope' conceptualize cinema as familiar and personal techniques of writing and seeing, the invocations of 'life' convey the promise that movie-goers will gain insight into something that is vitally close to them yet seems impossible to fully grasp. Note the different senses of life that are suggested in these names: the lived life (*vita*), a life-endowing spirit (*anima*), and what may be understood as a combination of both (*bio*).

Film, like media in general, can be understood as an instrument that extends the scope of our senses and facilitates increasingly complex mental operations. Yet media also offers ways of understanding ourselves by blending vague notions of the self with those of the self as a user and beneficiary of technology (Turner 2008, 25). Inquiries into the ways we think about ourselves in terms of cinema may look at blends that deal with:

(1)  film as an instrument of recording, a material medium that holds in place what cannot be held in mind and thereby supports various kinds of complex mental operations, ranging from measuring to memorializing;
(2)  film as a model for understanding phenomena and processes to which we have no direct access; and
(3)  filmic notions of self and subjectivity.

## Film as instrument

The first area of inquiry deals with the material base of cinema as a technology of sensory display. The cognitive anthropologist Edwin Hutchins introduced the term 'material anchors' for perceived patterns in physical structures that 'enable more complex reasoning processes than would be possible otherwise' (2005, 1562). Perceiving a line of people as a queue, recognizing constellations by projecting figures onto celestial bodies, or reading watches, compasses, sundials, and gauges are all conceptual blends that draw on physical structures. These material anchors increase the stability of conceptual representations.[2] By holding information in place (and discarding much else), they release the mind or make room for new kinds of mental operations. Cognition in this sense appears to be distributed between mind and the material world.

Walter Benjamin's idea of the 'optical unconscious' draws on this kind of interaction by relating the viewer's experience to specific features ('material anchors') of cinema's photographic base. In 'The Work of Art in the Age of Its Technological Reproducibility' he uses this metaphor to describe effects of film and cinematic techniques, such as the close-up or slow and accelerated motion, that reveal hidden or unseen phenomena, shedding light on 'entirely new structures of matter' (Benjamin 2002, 117).

In Fauconnier and Turner's model of conceptual integration the blend 'optical unconscious' can be schematized as emerging from cross-mapping elements between two conceptual input spaces: the physical regime of optics and the psychological domain of the unconscious (see Figure 5). The links between input spaces, which in this case are largely established through disanalogies (visible and manifest vs. hidden and latent; physical vs. mental), are captured by a generic space (something like 'filmic reception' or 'perception of cinematic images') that describes the shared structure of the input spaces. The emergent structure of the blend arises from selectively projecting elements of both input spaces into a blended space. The blend develops in three ways, which Fauconnier and Turner refer to as composition, completion, and elaboration (2002, 42–4). Composition creates new relations that were not available in either of the input spaces: the unconscious becomes manifest, physical phenomena become mental events. Completion draws on a vast amount of background knowledge. In making sense of the blend we bring in familiar and related frames. Elaboration can support this process of comprehension by imaginatively modifying the blend as we 'run' through its network, consciously and non-consciously.

Benjamin corroborates the relations between the optical and the unconscious (completion) by situating a 'mechanical camera' and the 'organic eye' within the respective scenarios of communication and perception (elaboration) (on communicative and perceptual frames, *see* CAMERA). By running the blend within a frame of perception, he stresses the disanalogy

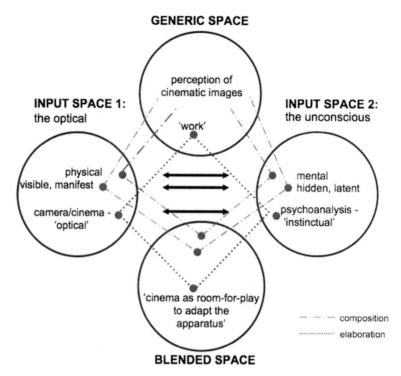

*Figure 5* Conceptual blend of the notion of an 'optical unconscious'.

between camera and eye: 'Clearly, it is another nature which speaks to camera as compared to the eye. "Other" above all in the sense that a space informed by human consciousness gives way to space informed by the unconscious' (Benjamin 2002, 117). However, when he addresses the communicative or transactional frame, Benjamin promotes an analogy between the 'work performed' (generic space) by a 'camera' (input space 1) and the work of 'psychoanalysis' (input space 2): 'It is through the camera that we first discover the optical unconscious, just as we discover the instinctual unconscious through psychoanalysis.'

Since psychoanalysis can refer to both a therapeutic practice of doctors as well as a place where patients engage in dialogue disentangled from the social constraints of everyday life, this double meaning may serve as a convenient guide for Benjamin's elaboration of the social and political function. What complements the notion of film as an analytical technique of discovery of one's place in the world is the idea of cinema as an institutional place, a social 'room for play' (*Spielraum*) of coming to terms with the demands posed by modern technology (Hansen 2004). Benjamin uses play in an anthropological sense of a joyful activity of experimentation and exploration. By playing, we can try out or learn new things and we may also experience other aspects of ourselves. For him film lies in a long tradition of cultural technology which has its origins in play, 'where, by an unconscious ruse, human beings first began to distance themselves from nature' (Benjamin 2002, 207). In this sense film can help us in a playful manner to adapt to an increasingly technological culture: '*The function of film is to train human beings in the apperceptions and reactions needed to deal with a vast apparatus whose role in their lives is expanding almost daily'* (108; original emphasis). Still other elaborations of the blend may bring out new possible relations between memory and media, as Miriam Hansen observes: 'The memory mobilized by the optical unconscious differs from any other form of premeditated, discursive remembering or reminiscing; it belongs to the side of Proust's *mémoire involuntair* or the Surrealist's exercises in "profane illumination" (and thus by implication to the realm of psychoanalysis)' (Hansen 1991, 110). The optical unconscious in this reading becomes emblematic of a modernist approach to artistic invention and intentionality. Jürgen Habermas drew attention to its philosophical ramifications. The optical unconscious invites us to rethink our notions of subject–object relations: 'a whole field of surprising correspondences between animate and inanimate nature is opened up, wherein even *things* encounter us in the structures of frail intersubjectivity' (Habermas 1979, 79; see also Stafford 2007).

## Film as model

From such conceptions of film as an instrument of scientific, critical, and aesthetic technique implementing cognitive operations through technological management, it is only a short step to appropriating these mechanisms of manipulation as conceptual inputs for film theoretical models. For example, Benjamin draws attention to intricate connections between the optical unconscious and the instinctual unconscious. In this blend the 'diverse aspects of reality captured by film [that] lie outside only the *normal* spectrum of sense impression' are mapped across impressions of reality encountered in psychosis, hallucinations, and dreams (2002, 118). This rationale of blending apparent analogous relations between the cinema and the mind within a generic framework of psychoanalytic diagnoses became an influential method in apparatus theory of the 1970s (*see* APPARATUS THEORY [BAUDRY]). Since psychoanalysis is interested in symbolic transpositions from non-representational and pre-conceptual domains (e.g. bodily impulses and emotions), its film theoretical application promises either an alternative to or an extension of purely linguistic or semiotic theories of cinema (*see* SEMIOTICS OF FILM).

Film history is replete with the double-scope blending of cinematic mechanisms with what appear to be cognitively impenetrable domains. Long after physiological theories that sought to explain the perception of continuous movement in imagery or the phenomenon of apparent motion by a delay in retinal processing had been rejected, this mechanism that became known as 'the persistence of vision' remained powerful in popular imagination and film theories (Anderson and Anderson 1980; 1993; Nichols and Lederman 1980). Frederick A. Talbot's *Moving Pictures: How They Are Made and Worked* (1912, 4) offers an early example:

> The eye is in itself a wonderful camera. The imprint of an object is received upon a nervous membrane which is called retina. This is connected with the brain, where the actual conception of the impression is formed, by the optic nerve. The picture therefore is photographed in the eye and transmitted from that point to the brain. Now a certain period of time must elapse in the conveyance of this picture from the retina along the optic nerve to the brain, in the same manner that an electric current flowing through a wire, or water passing through a pipe, must take a certain amount of time to travel from one point to another, although the movement may be so rapid that the time occupied on the journey is reduced

to an infinitesimal point and might be considered instantaneous. When the picture reaches the brain a further length of time is required to bring about its construction, for the brain is something like a photographic plate, and the picture requires developing. In this respect the brain is somewhat sluggish, for when it has formulated the picture imprinted on the eye, it will retain that picture even after the reality has disappeared from sight.

In this elaborate description organic and mental processes are blended with mechanical and electric events. Talbot's illustrations are filled with many compressions of time and space. They orchestrate the notion of delay, which is a key notion in this model because it enables the construction and fusion from which a mental motion picture arises. Persistence of vision and the cinematic apparatus constructs a model for understanding the multiplicity of so-called backstage processes of cognition (itself a metaphor that invokes a theatrical medium of display to refer to what is unknown or 'speculative', but nevertheless visually staged).

## Self as cinema

In a sense, Talbot's recourse to the apparatus seems to replace the homunculus we encounter in Descartes's 'Discourse on Optics'. The conceptual functions are indeed similar. While homunculi stand in for unknown cognitive operations, machines embody them through imaginative blends. What makes them so powerful as representational models is that they break down the vast complex of human subjectivity into cognitively manageable packages and thereby promise insight into what we identify as characteristics of human consciousness. Thomas Elsaesser and Malte Hagener's *Film Theory: An Introduction through the Senses* (2010) points in this direction. Films synthesize basic sensory modalities (such as sight, sound, taste, smell, touch as well as our perception as a mobile body) into a unified cinematic experience. Films serve as a medium that directs and manages attention (they 'point' and 'remember'). Films create their own internal relations generating 'organic' or autopoietic systems. They offer us diverse perspectives and facilitate alternative interpretations. Finally, when we are engrossed in watching movies, we can forget ourselves as if we were sleeping, or we can become aware that we are dreaming and desiring. In refracting all these dimensions of consciousness, cinema may instill the suspicion that the self too is a composite, the (temporary, convenient, strategic) blend of an expansive network. It is in this assumption that the network model of blending theory seems to converge with Deleuze's conception of the *dispositif* and the idea of 'machinic thinking' (Deleuze 1992).

CHRISTIAN QUENDLER

## Notes

1 See Stam (2000, 22): "'Biograph' and "animatographe" emphasize the recording of life itself (a strong current, later, in the writings of Bazin and Kracauer). "Vitascope" and "Bioscope" emphasize *looking* at life, and thus shift emphasis from recording life to the spectator and scopophilia (the desire to look), a concern of 1970s psychoanalytic theorists. "Chronophotographe" stresses the writing of time (and light) and thus anticipates Deleuze's (Bergsonian) emphasis of the "time image," while "Kinetoscope," again anticipating Deleuze, stresses the visual observation of movement.'

2 It is important to note that Hutchins reserves the term 'material anchor' for non-representational phenomena. In contrast to symbols, which denote an arbitrary relation to things, 'the material structure only provides a perceptual identity of the physical form as distinct from other physical forms' (2005, 1572).

## Works cited

Anderson, Barbara, and Joseph Anderson. 1980. 'Motion Perception in Motion Pictures'. In *The Cinematic Apparatus*, edited by Teresa de Lauretis and Stephen Heath, 76–95. New York: St. Martin's Press.

——. 1993. 'The Myth of Persistence of Vision Revisited'. *Journal of Film and Video* 45 (1): 3–12.

Benjamin, Walter. 2002. 'The Work of Art in the Age of Its Technological Reproducibility' [second version, orig. 1936]. In *Selected Writings*, vol. 3, edited by Howard Eiland and Michael W. Jennings, 101–33. Cambridge, MA: Harvard University Press.

Deleuze, Gilles. 1992. 'What Is a Dispositif?'. In *Michel Foucault, Philosopher*, edited by T.J. Armstrong, 159–68. New York: Routledge.

Descartes, René. 1637. *Discourse on method, optics, geometry and meteorology*. Trans. and ed. Paul J. Olscamp. Indianapolis: Hackett, 2001.

Elsaesser, Thomas, and Malte Hagener. 2010. *Film Theory: An Introduction through the Senses*. New York: Routledge.

Fauconnier, Gilles, and Mark Turner. 2002. *The Way We Think: Conceptual Blending and the Mind's Hidden Complexities*. New York: Basic Books.

Habermas, Jürgen. 1979. 'Consciousness-Raising or Redemptive Criticism: The Contemporaneity of Walter Benjamin'. *New German Critique* 17: 30–59.

Hansen, Miriam. 1991. *Babel & Babylon: Spectatorship in American Silent Film*. Cambridge, MA: Harvard University Press.

——. 2004. 'Room-for-Play: Benjamin's Gamble with Cinema'. *Canadian Journal of Film Studies* 13 (1): 2–27.

Hutchins, Edwin. 2005. 'Material Anchors for Conceptual Blends'. *Journal of Pragmatics* 37 (10): 1555–77.

Lakoff, George, and Mark Johnson. 1999. *Philosophy in the Flesh: The Embodied Mind and Its Challenge to Western Thought*. New York: Basic Books.

Nichols, Bill, and Susan J. Lederman. 1980. 'Flicker and Motion in Film'. In *The Cinematic Apparatus*, edited by Teresa de Lauretis and Stephen Heath, 96–105. New York: St. Martin's Press.

Stafford, Barbara Maria. 2007. *Echo Objects: The Cognitive Work of Images*. Chicago, IL: University of Chicago Press.

Stam, Robert. 2000. *Film Theory: An Introduction*. Malden, MA: Blackwell Publishers.

Talbot, Frederick A. 1912. *Moving Pictures: How They Are Made and Worked*. Philadelphia, PA: Lippincott.

Turner, Mark. 2008. 'What Are We? The Convergence of Self and Communications Technology'. In *Integration and Ubiquity: Towards a Philosophy of Telecommunications Convergence*, edited by Kristóf Nyíri, 21–8. Vienna: Passagen.

## Further reading

Chow, Kenny K.N., and Harrell, D. Fox. 2009. 'Material-Based Imagination: Embodied Cognition'. In *Animated Images*. UC Irvine: Digital Arts and Culture. Retrieved from: http://escholarship.org/uc/item/6fn5291r.

Gunning, Tom. 2003. 'The Exterior as *Intérieur*: Benjamin's Optical Detective'. *boundary 2* 30 (1): 105–30.

Krauss, Rosalind E. 1993. *The Optical Unconscious*. Cambridge, MA: MIT Press.

Manovich, Lev. 2001. *The Language of New Media*. Cambridge, MA: MIT Press.

Quendler, Christian. 2012. 'The Conceptual Integration of Intermediality: Literary and Cinematic Camera-Eye Narratives'. In *Blending and the Study of Narrative*, edited by Ralf Schneider and Marcus Hartner, 211–39. Berlin: de Gruyter.

Ryder, Robert G. 2007. 'Walter Benjamin's Shell-Shock: Sounding the Acoustical Unconscious'. *New Review of Film and Television Studies* 5 (2): 135–55.

Welchman, Alistair. 1997. 'Machinic Thinking'. In *Deleuze and Philosophy: The Difference Engineer*, edited by Keith Ansell Pearson, 211–29. London: Routledge.

# BRECHT AND FILM

## Brecht's political aesthetic

Widely known for his call for a politicized art, the modernist playwright, theatre theorist, and practitioner Bertolt Brecht exercised a major influence in contemporary film theory and practice (*see* CONTEMPORARY FILM THEORY). Brecht's radicalism resided in his conviction that the political implications of a play do not rest on the reproduction of political subject-matter. He suggested that changes in social and historical reality demand new modes of representation that are not keen on reproducing reality as one experiences it in everyday life, but instead expose the contradictions of reality. As a Marxist, he argued that people tend to regard as 'natural' aspects of social life that are historical and thus changeable. Brecht advocated formal abstraction that would guarantee a distance between reality and representation, so as to politicize aspects of social life that one considers as unquestionable. To achieve this he proposed the *Verfremdungseffekt* (translated as 'making the familiar strange'), which aims at preventing the actor and the audience empathizing with the characters on stage. The actor should not 'become' the character, while the director should point to the fictionality of the material, so as to prevent the audience's empathetic identi-fication with the story and arouse their critical reflection (Brecht 1964, 57). Brecht's aim was to go beyond the Aristotelian/conventional dramatic structure, so as to change the language of the medium and make the audience question the world beyond the limits of the drama.

Embedded in his will to change the established theatre language was an interest in revealing that the reproduction of the experiential aspect of reality fails to grasp the 'real' processes and historical developments. Viewed from this standpoint, Brecht's aes-thetics intended to analyse the reality that one experiences with one's direct senses into its social/historical laws. The ultimate aim was that the audience would question the por-trayed reality and the established tropes one uses to make sense of the drama. This politi-cized aesthetic introduced the idea that social relationships and history cannot be simply perceived dramatically. Drama presupposes processes that can be understood in terms of subjects and individuals, whereas capitalism valorizes processes that take place at the level of the masses (Brecht 1974, 40). Consequently, one of the aims of Brecht's *Verfremdungseffekt* is the demonstration of the individual's dependence on social and historical processes. Unlike naturalist theatre, Brecht's theatre is anti-heroic, in the sense that character is not a given but a nexus, the product of political circumstances.

## Brecht and film

Brecht as a modernist was fascinated by the film as medium. He wrote many film articles, and he was practically involved in filmmaking. Having co-directed the short film *Mysteries of a Hairdresser's Shop* (Brecht, Engel, 1923) and the famous *Kuhle Wampe or Who Owns the World?* (Brecht, Dudow, Ottwalt, 1932), he was convinced that film has the potential to offer representations of reality that could encourage critical reflection on the part of the audience. One of the aspects of the medium that he considered to be revolutionary was its ability to do away with character psychology and show the individual as representative of his/her social role, given that it prioritizes actions over characters. 'In fact the film demands external action and not introspective psychology. Capitalism has an impact on this by provoking, organizing, and mechanizing certain needs on a mass scale, revolutionizing everything' (Brecht 2001, 171).

By valorizing actions over characters, cinema could become a means of teaching historical awareness and revealing that social reality is not natural but subject to change. To achieve this, filmmakers should adopt an external point of view that de-individuates the narrative and focuses on the historical processes and their changeability. 'The external point of view is proper to cinema and it makes it important. For the cinema the principles of non-Aristotelian drama (a type of drama not depending on empathy, mimesis) are immediately acceptable' (2001, 171).

On this basis, Brecht distinguished between the reproductive and the constructive use of the medium. The former paradigm is keen on reproducing the empirical reality, whereas the latter is more interested in showing that what appears as 'real' is subject to transformation, because reality is socially constructed. As such, a constructive use of the medium presupposed the presentation of a familiar reality in such a way that it would appear strange and changeable. The key principle of the constructive method is montage, a term he employs in his theatre writings too. Montage stresses representational discontinuity and serves the role of isolating moments that can reveal aspects of social reality which are not necessarily visible (Mueller 1989, 483). Brecht's understanding of montage as a radical formal structure was very influential in the post-1968 film theory.

## Colin MacCabe and Stephen Heath

Brecht's penchant for montage sequences that lead to a collision of antithetical materials and negate the smoothness of the narrative is consonant with his view that reality can only be understood by means of experimentation and not through reduplication. Realism for Brecht stands for a film practice that takes things apart and analyses them so as to show their changeability. During the 1970s, in the wake of the popularity of Althusserian Marxism, many critics writing for the British journal *Screen* employed Brecht's writings to envisage an oppositional cinema (*see* CLASSIC REALIST TEXT). The main figures of Brechtian criticism were Colin MacCabe and Stephen Heath, who espoused Brecht's theory and employed an anti-realist approach towards the film as medium. The core of their argument was that radical cinema should go beyond the understanding of cinema as a reflecting medium.

Both critics opposed the school of thought inaugurated by André Bazin, whose writings on cinema argued that, unlike other arts, film's dependence on the photographic image offers a more genuine image of reality to the audience (*see* ONTOLOGY OF THE PHOTOGRAPHIC

IMAGE). Bazin advocated certain formal realist principles, such as the long take and deep focus, on the grounds of their ability to incorporate aspects of reality that did not serve dramaturgical purposes (*see* LONG TAKE). For Bazin, this type of cinema gave the audience a more direct access to reality than a type of cinema based on montage sequences (Bazin 1971, 13). The popularity of Brecht's call for a constructive realism led MacCabe and Heath to oppose Bazin's theory as a critical appeal for reproductive realism.

This anti-realist rhetoric is evidenced in MacCabe's essay 'Realism and the Cinema: Notes on Some Brechtian Theses', published in *Screen* in 1974. MacCabe puts forward the conjecture that the narrative in the classic realist novel – whose structure can be used to describe the classical film narrative – does not go beyond the phenomenological manifestation of social reality. As such, reality appears as something which simply exists and not as subject to changeability (MacCabe 1974, 12). The classic realist text denies its own status as writing and unconsciously reproduces the Western ideology of the visible. By not questioning the means of its own production, the classic realist narrative structure offers an illusion of 'knowledge' to the audience, which is nothing but the reconfirmation of certain oppressive social structures.

MacCabe's evaluation of classic realism's characteristics aims at investigating the possibility for a subversive filmmaking practice based upon Brecht's theory. The question that radical cinema needs to address is that of the position of the audience towards the material. In this way, revolutionary objects start by questioning the spectator's role as a viewing subject. This change in the subject and object relations can be achieved by a narrative structure that does not provide 'ready-made' knowledge but creates diegetic gaps and questions that encourage the audience's productivity (25). Consequently, the productive participation of the audience depends on the presentation of sets of contradictions that stimulate questions about the fictional material as well as the reality outside the cinematic world.

It is crucial here to elucidate that MacCabe's mistrust of realism is mainly a critique of the conventional narrative structure and not of realism *per se*. At one point, MacCabe identifies strategies of subversion even in Italian neorealist objects, such as Rossellini's *Germany Year Zero* (1948). As he proposes, Rossellini's film does not offer one-dimensional messages; 'the story simply provides a framework for various scenes' (MacCabe 1974, 19). Furthermore, Rossellini's film avoids the narrative closure of the classic realist text and, by pointing to unresolved historical contradictions, he implies that it is through social mobilization that change can take place. Later on, and here one can observe his hostility to Bazin, MacCabe suggests that, despite the progressive elements in Rossellini's films, his employment of the camera is conservative, because the camera is used as a transparent tool and not as something which is part of the film's productive process (21). The core of his argument is that filmmakers interested in politicizing the medium need to investigate the contradictory ways of representing reality, by experimenting with the possibilities of the camera. The latter point is a direct reference to Brecht's idea that one cannot produce for a medium without changing it.

While MacCabe rightly points out the lack of the contradiction principle in classic realism, his discussion does not succeed in demonstrating the connection between experimentation and political effects. Brecht as a Marxist thought that narrative and formal structures are directly interwoven with the material conditions of society. Thus, the Aristotelian/classical narrative structure, which is the basis of the Western understanding of realism, fails to show social reality and history as subject to processes of perpetual transitions. His emphasis on experimentation aimed at viewing things from a distance so as to minimize dramatic development in favour of historically contextualized situations, something that MacCabe does not highlight.

Stephen Heath's essay 'Lessons from Brecht' (Heath 1974), which was published in the same *Screen* volume, is perhaps the most detailed piece of scholarship of the time exploring the productive effects that Brecht's theory may have in filmmaking practice. Heath proceeds to identify Brechtian elements in contemporary cinema using references to Freudian psychology and Althusserian Marxism. For Heath, the task of a Brechtian film practice is to challenge the ideology of the subject, by questioning the very materials of representation, such as 'the invisible camera eye' (104) and mainstream cinema's fixity of the spectator in a position of passivity.

Subsequently, radical cinema shall negate 'the structure of separation' (106) which one can identify in the Aristotelian/classical narrative structure. To clarify this point, Heath resorts to Freud and suggests that the structure of representation in classical cinema is a fetishist structure; the spectator assumes an imaginary sense of unity and identity, by being placed in a fixed/non-productive position, which makes him/her simply reconfirm the projected material on screen. Heath compares this process with Freud's discussion of sexual fetishism, which has its origins in the male subject's discovery of the sexual difference with its female counterpart (107). Man fetishizes the female genitalia in fear that he might end up lacking a phallus (like women), and it is through this process that he acquires a pseudo-sense of unity and identity (107).

Heath invites the reader to think of the photographic image – which is the essence of the cinema according to Bazin – as fetishist because it places the subject in a position of 'specularity' (107). While film-viewing is a social activity, the audience's role is restricted to the passive consumption of images leading to the reproduction of attitudes and behavioural patterns, which portray the existing social reality as normal. Heath's comparison reconciles Brecht's Marxist thinking with Freudian psychology to explain that the major issue that political cinema has to face is the role of the subject. Capitalism reproduces itself because it places the subject in a position of non-production, something which is perpetuated by the cinematic institution (107). Mainstream cinema treats the audience as voyeurs; thus, radical cinema needs to challenge this, by assigning a more productive role to the audience (*see* COUNTER-CINEMA).

For Heath, political cinema must question 'the fetishistic facet' of the photographic image by 'literalizing' the medium (108). This is a direct reference to Brecht's concept of 'literalization of the theatre' (Brecht 1964, 44) which prioritized the changing of the institution of theatre over its storytelling function. Brecht's aim was to encourage a reading attitude in the auditorium, which would prevent the audience from being completely absorbed by dramatic action. Heath argues that cinema can accomplish this by employing an aesthetics of interruptibility, which gives the audience the ability to be inside and outside the film. Interruptibility can be achieved by way of montage sequences that disrupt the narrative flow and give the audience the chance to step out of the story and reflect on it (Heath 1974, 125). By abandoning organic unity, such an aesthetics endorses a reading attitude which opposes dominant cinema's commitment to providing a perfect illusion of reality. In this formulation, Heath seems clearly influenced by the anti-realist rhetoric of the time. His understanding of montage as a formal element that can make representation more complex is in direct opposition with Bazin's valorization of continuity editing.

Heath's exploration of the ways that film culture can benefit from Brecht incorporates references to Althusserian Marxism, so as to show how a social apparatus like the cinema can reproduce capitalism as a natural rather than a historical reality (114, 124). He explains that radical cinema can reveal the contradictions of capitalism by questioning classical narrative's organic unity. On this basis, one can understand montage as 'a principle of contradiction' (122), simply because it defies unity and challenges the relationship between the film and the viewing subject. Story development is minimized in favour of a loose sequence of episodes that present conflicts rather than coherent dramatic actions and force the audience to respond in a productive way.

## Criticisms of 1970s Brechtian film theory

Certainly, the aforementioned essays have stimulated thinking regarding Brecht's link with radical film practice. However, one can take issue with the critics' tendency to over-emphasize theory over filmmaking practice. Despite Brecht's interest in form, it seems that, in MacCabe's and Heath's essays, discussions of formal experimentation were simply the means for the reproduction of late Marxist and Freudian axioms.

Dana Polan has criticized the ways Brecht was employed by the 1970s film theory, arguing that their discussions failed to clarify how formal abstraction/experimentation could change the audience's perception of the historically formed reality. Polan concludes that film theory needs to be more open to the possibility that Brecht's theory can be operative in films that manipulate familiar aspects of the dominant cinema. His argument is predicated on the basis that defamiliarization can only be fruitful if something familiar is rendered strange (Polan 1974).

The validity of the anti-realist trend has also been called into question, since films were classified as political on the grounds of certain stylistic traits, such as montage, which were assumed to be transhistorically radical. Sylvia Harvey has criticized the 'anti-realist theorists of the 1970s', because they tended to assume that certain objects were viewed as radical 'on the basis of stylistic properties alone, rather than on the basis of the tripartite relationship between textual properties, contemporary social reality and historically informed readers' (Harvey 1982, 51). The core of Brecht's theory is that forms are changeable and historically defined. In the course of time, certain formal elements become de-radicalized, whereas others require reassessment. Currently, Hollywood employs montage sequences not to engage the audience politically, but to increase the pleasures of narrative consumption (King 2000, 105).

On the other hand, contemporary films by the Dardenne brothers and Béla Tarr, which follow long-take Bazinian aesthetics, challenge our habitual viewing of films in a more effective way. The prerequisite for making the familiar strange is to understand the historicity of both the term 'familiar' and 'defamiliarization'. Nonetheless, MacCabe's and Heath's essays are historically important, because they have invited us to think of film as a productive rather than a reflective medium, pointing to the fact that realism in film is a set of conventions, rather than the authentic reproduction of social reality. Brecht's call for a film practice that reveals the social processes behind the events is pertinent in the current historical circumstances, but film theory needs to rethink his writings in ways that can deal with the different historical conditions.

ANGELOS KOUTSOURAKIS

## Works cited

Bazin, André. 1971. *What Is Cinema?* Vol. 1. Edited and translated by Hugh Gray. Berkeley: University of California Press.

Brecht, Bertolt. 1964. *Brecht on Theatre: The Development of an Aesthetic.* Edited and translated by John Willet. London: Methuen.

——. 1974. 'Against Georg Lukács'. *New Left Review* 84: 39–53.

——. 2001. *Bertolt Brecht: On Film and Radio.* Edited and translated by Marc Silberman. London: Methuen.

Harvey, Sylvia. 1982. 'Whose Brecht? Memories for the Eighties'. *Screen* 23 (1): 45–59.

Heath, Stephen. 1974. 'Lessons from Brecht'. *Screen* 15 (2): 103–28.

King, Geoff. 2000. *Spectacular Narratives: Hollywood in the Age of the Blockbuster.* New York: I.B. Tauris.

MacCabe, Colin. 1974. 'Realism and the Cinema: Notes on Some Brechtian Theses'. *Screen* 15 (2): 7–27.

Mueller, Roswitha. 1989. *Bertolt Brecht and the Theory of Media.* Lincoln: University of Nebraska Press.

Polan, Dana B. 1974. 'Brecht and the Politics of Self-Reflexive Cinema'. *Jump Cut* 1: http://www.ejumpcut.org/archive/onlinessays/JC17folder/BrechtPolan.html.

## Further reading

Heath, Stephen. 1975. 'From Brecht to Film: Theses Problems (On *History Lessons* and *Dear Summer Sister*)'. *Screen* 16 (4): 34–45.

Lellis, George. 1982. *Bertolt Brecht, Cahiers du Cinéma and Contemporary Film Theory.* Ann Arbor: University of Michigan Research Press.

Rodowick, D.N. 1988. *The Crisis of Political Modernism: Criticism and Ideology in Contemporary Film Theory.* Urbana: University of Illinois Press.

Silberman, Marc. 1987. 'The Politics of Representation: Brecht and the Media'. *Theatre Journal* 39 (4): 448–60.

——. 2009. 'Brecht, Realism and the Media'. In *Realism and the Audiovisual Media*, edited by Lúcia Nagib and Cecília Mello, 31–46. New York: Palgrave Macmillan.

Walsh, Martin. 1981. *The Brechtian Aspect of Radical Cinema.* Edited by Keith Griffiths. London: BFI.

# CAMERA

The idea of a camera is fundamental to film studies. It is central to theories of film as art, language, and medium. It informs communicative, psychoanalytical, and cognitive approaches to film theory. The manifold contexts in which the camera appears have generated a variety of, sometimes contradictory, senses for the term. Thus reflections on ideas about the camera can turn into inquiries about the basic tenets and assumptions of a given film theory. In *Projecting a Camera: Language-Games in Film Theory* (2006), Edward Branigan proposes to understand the camera as a linguistic and rhetorical construct, whose meaning depends on the sense shared by an interpretive community and its particular investment in cinema. In the third chapter of his book, 'What Is a Camera?', Branigan places his own meta-communicative approach at the end of a list of seven major camera conceptions in the history of film theory. In what follows I will discuss Branigan's eight distinct meanings of 'camera' in relation to their film theoretical perspectives and contexts of use (see Figure 6). I will review Branigan's meta-theoretical posture as a response to, and a continuation of, the tendency to understand a camera increasingly in figurative terms connected to our desire for cinema.

## Art

In the context of art criticism, the camera plays an ambivalent if not paradoxical role. While many critics refer to the camera as a recording device that distinguishes film from other forms of art, the camera itself does not qualify film as art (Carroll 1996; Danto 1999). Placed at the intersection of art and technology, the instrumental value of the camera in film theories oscillates between recording device and means of expression. Is the camera more like a pen and a brush or is it better understood as a kind of writing or painting? Is it simply a machine that captures impressions of light or does its mechanism already gear towards an expressive form?

To what extent a mechanical recording may be expressive (let alone meaningful) was a question that dominated early theories of film as art. In the 1920s, the French filmmakers and critics Louis Delluc (2004) and Jean Epstein (1988) proposed the impressionist notion of *photogénie* as a possible solution to this problem. Delluc and Epstein appropriated the term from still photography to describe an intrinsic quality of the moving image that is generated by the camera's transformative power to poeticize life. If only for a brief moment, Epstein argued, the camera lets us glimpse the inner nature of things. The idea of photogeny not only projects human characteristics of perception onto the camera (e.g. an anthropomorphic world-view or a sense of the ephemeral, pre-conceptual, and inexplicable

| Major conceptions of the camera | Theory of narrative meaning: how are present entities related to absent ones? | One favoured camera technique | One major value of narrativity for society | One major principle for the writing of a history of narrative |
|---|---|---|---|---|
| 1 Camera as origin of a sensory display (a machine) | Illusion (e.g. of depth) | Kinetic depth | Hallucinatory involvement | Edison, Griffith (vs. Lumière, Méliès) |
| 2 Camera as sensory (or material) form | Defamiliarization | Unmotivated camera | Art as social and political tool | Pressure from an avant-garde |
| 3 Camera as recorder of the pro-filmic (an act of pointing) | Casual: the physics of light rays<br>**Bazinian theory** | Deep focus (objective camera) | Reproduction of visible, unobtrusive reality | Lumière (vs. Méliès) |
| 4 Camera as agent for a post-filmic viewing situation | Perceiver sees a as he or she *would see b* (subjunctive conditional) | Lateral depth of field | Reproduction of human perception at work | Renoir, Welles; neorealism |
| 5 Camera as expressive of bodily and mental states | Intention | Subjective camera | Celebration of the individual and the inner world | The auteur |
| 6 Camera as channel for communication | Casual: signal of transmission | Personification of the camera (= narrator's presence objectified) | Information (and information about information = reflexivity) | Art cinema |
| 7 Camera as phantasy | Unconscious mechanisms | Visualization of dream-thought (representability) | Visual pleasure and the dynamic of the repressed | Classical cinema |
| 8 Camera as semantic label or reading hypothesis | Symbol | | The world as narrative text | Types of reference: filmic and non-filmic codes; reading procedures |

*Figure 6* Branigan's comparison of eight conceptions of the camera.

aspects of experience); it also presents the camera as the filmmaker's counterpart. The transformative virtue of the camera is only fully realized when it converges with the film-maker's vision. On the one hand, the camera acquires a sense of autonomy and agency, a realm of chance and technological contingency that lies beyond the filmmaker's plans. On the other hand, the camera is symbiotically joined to the filmmaker.

# Language

Vsevolod Pudovkin criticized Delluc's notion of photogeny as vague symbolism that obscures traditional notions of taste and beauty. For him photogeny is not 'the merging of the photographic image with the "genius" of cinema', but rather results from correctly applying principles of montage (2006a, 5). His critique also marks a historical shift from aesthetic to semiotic theories of film. The former is concerned with aesthetic possibilities of cinematic expression and, for example, the attainment of sublime experience; the latter examines the conditions of a film language. In the first case the camera transforms reality into a sensory form that shows new or unseen aspects of reality. For avant-garde film-makers the camera becomes a means of defamiliarization that points to an alternative way of seeing or towards the 'otherness' of human perception. In the second case, the camera enacts compositional rules of montage and manufacture. For Pudovkin, the camera serves as a deictic device that manages the viewer's attention; it guides the viewer through time and space in the order, and to the effect, intended by the filmmaker. While 'the camera lens is the viewer's eye' (2006b, 16), it is the filmmaker who sees the viewer through.

The camera not only points to a pro-filmic event; it also presents this event within a specific narrative or argumentative frame. As a rhetorical interface between filmmaker and viewer, it marks the position of an ideal observer, whose perception is the synthetic product premeditated by the filmmaker's observations. As this position is extended to the post-filmic viewing situation, the camera comes to include aspects of cinematography and editing as two additional forms of attention management. Camera movement and editing are now being theorized by analogy to eye movements and shifts in attention. Similarly, the act of synthesizing perception into observation becomes an analogy for montage and cinematic exposition.

## Medium

While theorists following Pudovkin highlighted the importance of editing, André Bazin advocated the long take (see LONG TAKE). Like Pudovkin, Bazin's notion of camera combines a pro-filmic and a post-filmic sense, which he views in a dialectic that reconciles the possibilities of the filmic medium with the perceptual constraints of human vision. In a pro-filmic sense, it is above all the technique of deep focus, which by extending depth of field charges and involves the viewer's searching gaze (see DEPTH OF FIELD). The paramount directive of a post-filmic camera is to amplify the illusion of an extended off-screen reality. Rather than 'analyzing the dramatic field' by cutting up space and time, Bazin favours a continual reframing by camera movement, lightning, sound, etc. (1967, 34).

Using as an illustration Jean Renoir's *The Rules of the Game* (1939), Bazin compares his model of a camera to an invisible guest and an omniscient narrator. The camera thus comes to signify a narrative stance that is at once bound and unbound to the diegetic world: 'it is a way of seeing which, while free of all contingency, is at the same time limited by the concrete qualities of vision: its continuity in time and its vanishing point in space. It is like the eye of God, in the proper sense of the word, if God could be satisfied with a single eye' (Bazin 1973, 88).

## Perception and communication

The tendency towards expansive, figurative understandings of a camera in relation to a centre for experience is a characteristic of many camera conceptions in film theory. It accounts for the instrumental function of the camera to operate on behalf of humans and the human disposition of embodied thinking (Lakoff and Johnson 1999). As an extension of the body and mind, we can think of the camera as a vehicle that stands in for processes of perception and communication (McLuhan 1964; Luhmann 2000). Analogous to the twofold operations of the camera as proflimic act of pointing and post-filmic act of presenting (or what, for narrative films, André Gaudreault [2009] called acts of monstration and narration), the camera interfaces perception and communication along with their corresponding frames of interpretation.

A perceptual frame of interpretation invites the audience to contemplate a film as an imaginary experience. The movie theatre offers a 'safe' place to participate imaginatively in alternative and impossible worlds. We are free to invest these worlds with imaginative licence and to identify with characters on the screen or with the way in which they are presented to us. To the extent that films are produced *for* a public, they engage us in a social practice of communication. Even if there is no necessity to continue the communication (there may be silence, a caustic review, or fan mail), its communicative frame asks us to decode a message. The double function of the camera as a vehicle of perception and communication creates a paradox: the filmic image is simultaneously the product of a perceptual and a communicative act.

This paradox can be resolved by privileging the frame of either communication or perception. As Branigan points out, if the mode of presentation is seen as filtered or refracted by a communicative frame, then a camera takes on 'authorial forms of address: overt commentary, indignation, irony, melancholy, ambiguity, paradox, playfulness, lyricism, enigmatic presentations, unreliability, and so on' (2006, 84). Conversely, psychoanalytic approaches anchor the camera in a perceptual or experiential frame in order to uncover scenarios of fantasy and desire as the deeper motives of cinematic exchanges. The subject and mode of presentation organized by a camera are analysed as a cultural imaginary: a mirror where unconscious processes inform meanings shared with the symbolic order of the social world.

## Conceptual metaphor

Communicative and psychoanalytic approaches employ the word camera as a heuristic concept in the interpretive process of identifying conscious intentions or unconscious desires. The camera in these approaches serves as a construct that seeks to align audio-visual sensation either with an intentional rationale or with scenarios of unconscious fantasy. To the extent that the camera accounts for all or almost all the filmic evidence, it becomes a global tool of interpretation supporting top-down processes of understanding. In order to better account for the cognitive mobility of viewers, cognitive approaches to film studies have complemented such global notions with bottom-up models of understanding that operate with local or distributed conceptions of a camera. Viewers continually re-interpret a 'camera' by placing it within different mental models aligning it with the world of characters, invisible observers, or disembodied agencies that transgress the rules of time and space and the limits of human vision (Bordwell 1991; Branigan 1992).

Integrating this insight into his definition of a camera, Branigan proposes to regard a camera as 'part of a mental procedure employed by a spectator to solve interpretive problems' (2006, 90). A camera in this sense is a 'convenient label' to identify a textual effect that frames the interpretive process itself: 'how we see objects *under descriptions* and how *interpretations* are made' (2006, 21; original emphasis). This meta-theoretical approach allows us to review different camera conceptions in relation to specific frames of interpretation and to highlight the aesthetic and textual effects that support these frames. Accordingly, the idea of a camera as the source of sensory display can be understood in reference to an aesthetic frame of defamiliarization, rhetorical principles of composition, media-specific possibilities, and communicative or psychoanalytic frameworks. Put differently, the idea of a camera as a 'reading hypothesis' helps to address pertinent visual features and attempts to make sense of various dichotomies, such as: matter vs. form, mechanic vs. organic, unmotivated vs. motivated, pro-filmic vs. post-filmic, diegetic vs. non-diegetic, conscious intention vs. unconscious desire.

The idea of the camera as a conceptual metaphor can help to integrate – or, at least, to reflect upon – different approaches to theorizing a camera. The single word 'camera' does not have a single meaning but changes and adapts its signification according to its contexts of use. As a key term in film and media studies, the term 'camera' is charged with theoretical presuppositions, convictions, and the desire to persuade (Branigan 2006, 201–2, 217–18, 222–4). Thus, approaching the camera as a conceptual metaphor offers a critical perspective on the way mental models of the camera differ across theories and change over time. As Branigan observes: 'Today the camera seems to be neither a machine nor an invisible witness recording facts of the world but, rather, an aspect of a collective subjectivity – a name for how we ourselves are talking and thinking about cinema at a particular time for a particular purpose ... As a collective subjectivity, the camera's status fluctuates in the twilight area between material object and interpretive subject, between world and language' (2006, 96). Branigan's meta-theoretical camera conception adds another distinction to the dichotomies listed in the previous paragraph: it becomes the conceptual interface between our ways of interpreting filmic evidence and our understanding of cinema altogether. In this sense, Branigan's definition of a camera continues the metonymical extension we can observe in early theories of film, where the mechanism of the camera comes to define cinema as such. Yet, instead of understanding cinema as an art form, the cinematic field is thereby expanded to the cultural habitus created by all kinds of film genres and institutions.

CHRISTIAN QUENDLER

## Works cited

Bazin, André. 1967 [1958]. 'The Evolution of the Language of Cinema'. In *What Is Cinema?*, vol. I, translated by Hugh Gray, 23–40. Berkeley: University of California Press.

——. 1973 [1971]. *Jean Renoir*. Translated by W.W. Halsey II and William H. Simon. New York: Simon and Schuster.

Bordwell, David. 1991 [1977]. 'Camera Movement and Cinematic Space'. In *Explorations in Film Theory: Selected Essays from Ciné-tracts*, edited by Ron Burnett, 229–36. Bloomington: Indiana University Press.

Branigan, Edward. 1992. *Narrative Comprehension and Film*. New York: Routledge.

——. 2006. *Projecting a Camera: Language-Games in Film Theory*. London: Routledge.

Carroll, Noël. 1996. 'Defining the Moving Image'. In *Theorizing the Moving Image*, 49–74. Cambridge: Cambridge University Press.

Danto, Arthur. 1999. 'The Moving Pictures'. In *Philosophizing Art: Selected Essays*, 205–32. Berkeley: University of California Press.

Delluc, Louis. 2004 [1920]. 'Photogénie'. In *Film Theory: Critical Concepts in Media and Cultural Studies*, edited by K.J. Shepherdson, Philip Simpson, and Andrew Utterson, 49–51. New York: Routledge.

Epstein, Jean. 2004 [1924]. 'On Certain Characteristics of *Photogénie*'. In *Film Theory: Critical Concepts in Media and Cultural Studies*, edited by K.J. Shepherdson, Philip Simpson, and Andrew Utterson, 52–6. New York: Routledge.

Gaudreault, André. 2009 [1988]. *From Plato to Lumière: Narration and Monstration in Literature and Cinema*. Toronto: University of Toronto Press.

Lakoff, George, and Mark Johnson. 1999. *Philosophy in the Flesh: The Embodied Mind and Its Challenge to Western Thought*. New York: Basic Books.

Luhmann, Niklas. 2000. *Art as a Social System*. Stanford, CA: Stanford University Press.

McLuhan, Marshall. 1964. *Understanding Media: The Extensions of Man*. New York: McGraw-Hill.

Pudovkin, Vsevolod. 2006a [1925]. 'Photogeny'. In *Vsevolod Pudovkin: Selected Essays*, edited by Richard Taylor, 4–13. London: Seagull Books.

——. 2006b. 'The Montage of a Scientific Film'. In *Vsevolod Pudovkin: Selected Essays*, edited by Richard Taylor, 15–18. London: Seagull Books.

## Further reading

Quendler, Christian. 2011. 'Rethinking the Camera Eye: *Dispositif* and Subjectivity'. *New Review of Film and Television Studies* 9 (4): 395–414.

Silverman, Kaja. 1993. 'What Is a Camera? or: History in the Field of Vision'. *Discourse* 15: 3–56.

Sobchack, Vivian. 1982. 'Toward Inhabited Space: The Semiotic Structure of Camera Movement in the Cinema'. *Semiotica* 41: 317–35.

Turvey, Malcolm. 1999. 'Can the Camera See? Mimesis in *Man with a Movie Camera*'. *October* 89: 25–50.

# CINEMATIC MOVEMENT

For most of its history, cinematic movement has been closely equated with camera movement. Conceived of as an activity of an actual camera, it has been looked at generally as a significant aspect of directorial style (*see* CAMERA). This has led to great appreciation and close analysis of sublime cinema artists like F.W. Murnau, Max Ophuls, and Stanley Kubrick, and also to some misunderstanding of what constitutes camera movement. If we were looking at this subject thirty years ago or more, we would probably concentrate upon defining tracking shots, crane shots, Steadicams, and the like – something of a technological survey. As theory has evolved, however, we are now more likely to see movement as an issue in relation to the spectator rather than to the technology. How do we 'read' and understand movement? Leading the way in this reconceptualization of movement have been David Bordwell and Edward Branigan, both of whom have frequently addressed camera movement issues, especially as they relate to narrative concerns. Most particularly, we will consider Bordwell's article 'Camera Movement and Cinematic Space' (1977) and Branigan's chapter 'A Camera-in-the-Text' in *Projecting a Camera: Language-Games in Film Theory* (2006). We will also look at some of the ways camera movement has 'spilled over' into film history and film criticism.

Bordwell, Staiger, and Thompson's *The Classical Hollywood Cinema* mentions camera movement among 'all the systems of space, time, and causality actually manifested' in film, and from fairly early in cinema history an awareness of camera movement as an area for expressivity was clearly evident (1985, 12). While noting, for example, that by the early 1930s 'there was no doubt that camera movement had become a significant instance of virtuosity', Bordwell also observes that particularly celebrated camera movements such as those in Mamoulian's *Applause* and Vidor's *Hallelujah* were not isolated occurrences but 'extensions of common practice' (Bordwell *et al.* 1985, 307).

Even earlier, camera movement could be identified as a characteristic of directorial virtuosity. According to Jean Mitry: 'It was only from 1924 onward that the camera really began to move – around rather than with the characters of the drama (first appearing in Murnau's *The Last Laugh*)' (Mitry 2000, 184). Mitry, though, also looks back to Griffith's *Intolerance* (1916) for its 'amazing track forward' and finds important instances of moving camera in Vidor's *The Crowd* (1928) and Lang's *Woman on the Moon* (1929).

Whether, as Mitry says, 'camera movement should be justified – physically, dramatically, or psychologically' has been a continual thread throughout the examination of camera movement (2000, 185). Max Ophuls, surely one of the greatest directors to extensively utilize camera movement, has sometimes been accused of using the device either excessively or for its own sake. Branigan, too, will look at this question of how camera movement can be considered motivated by narrative concerns.

Generally, we can say that camera movement has been one of the key sites of discussion in debates about the desirability of noticeability (or invisibility) in film style. Even directors celebrated for the use of movement have spoken against overly apparent use of movement, as for example the director Rouben Mamoulian in 1932, two years after *Applause*: '[Camera movement] focuses the attention of the audience on the mechanical rather than upon the story, and confuses instead of clarifies the issue. Unjustified movement is a sign of directorial weakness, rather than strength' (in Bordwell *et al.* 1985, 109). Here too, 'justification' for movement is put forth as a concern. It is a relatively modern position to see camera movement as potentially an activity which can be celebrated as worthwhile in its own right, for stylistic expressivity or independent exploration, rather than as a hidden element in service of other ostensibly more significant narrative and cinematic agendas.

## Bordwell's 'Camera Movement and Cinematic Space'

Bordwell's essay 'Camera Movement and Cinematic Space' seeks to develop what he calls a 'perceptual approach', situating his investigation here in the realm of how we 'read' camera movement. The essay's principal contribution is in linking the idea of camera movement to considerations of cinematic space. 'Representing space, depicting an absent space, seems fundamental to camera movement as ordinarily used.' By asserting this, Bordwell starts his inquiry into 'how camera movement asks to be read perceptually' (1977, 20).

One intriguing direction Bordwell takes is to attempt to separate the appearance of camera movement from the probable actual event of a camera having moved. He sees the need to do this as a way to stress how we perceive movement and its significance, rather than simply to identify that movement has taken place. Animated films are a 'supreme example' he provides where it may appear movement has taken place without the camera actually moving, as is the case with many instances of back projection. As Bordwell says, 'the movement of the camera during production does not guarantee that a perceptible camera movement will appear on the screen', so his concern is to shift to looking for what he calls the 'perceptual cues which determine a "camera movement effect"'. By doing so, he seeks to get beyond what he sees as overly loose theoretical ideas about camera movement, which he assesses as 'not derived from a unified critical theory, but rather ... from a mixture of technical jargon and actual parlance' (1977, 20–1).

Rejecting the idea of needing to situate ourselves theoretically in an actual space where camera movement occurs (what he calls the 'profilmic event model'), he instead argues in favour of what he identifies as a 'constricted but effective range of visual cues for subjective movement' which camera movement presents. In other words, he shifts attention to 'the impression of subject movement' rather than looking at the actual circumstance of camera movement. The cues he locates are best explained in terms of Gestalt psychology, of how depth is perceived and movement experienced. As he says, 'camera movement could be described as a system of perceptual relationships' (1977, 21–2).

Where this perceptual orientation leads is to seeing camera movement in terms of the spectator's position, rather than the ostensible position of the camera. This shifts concern to what Bordwell identifies as 'represented space', how space looks to us as the result of our perceiving movement, how we read it, or how we read it in a particular manner.

One intriguing direction in which this takes Bordwell is to look at instances of how spaces might be misread, as in cases where off-screen space becomes ambiguous as a result of perceived movement. ('Obviously, offscreen space plays a considerable role in camera movement'.) He employs examples of camera movement from Murnau's *Sunrise* and Leger/Murphy's *Ballet mécanique* to explore the circumstances in which 'it is possible to establish a scenographic space which, in one way or another, becomes difficult to read', or cases where camera movement leads to 'the creation of inconsistent subject positions' (Bordwell 1977, 24).

These problematic instances lead Bordwell to locate 'camera movement's impression of reality' as having been undermined at the level of narrative, issues which Branigan will take up with considerable interest. Bordwell concludes with a most appropriate reference to Michael Snow's films, whose works he says 'point toward ways of making problematic the sheerly perceptual features of camera movement' (1977, 25).

## Branigan's 'A Camera-in-the-Text'

Edward Branigan's *Projecting a Camera: Language-Games in Film Theory* includes extensive discussion of camera movement, particularly in chapter 2 ('A Camera-in-the-Text') and chapter 5 ('When Is a Camera?'). We will focus upon the plenitude of movement ideas in chapter 2, which in many ways develop from and significantly extend Bordwell's arguments.

One of Branigan's great contributions is to foreground the idea of narrative motivation in relation to camera movement. In considering the amount of plot or screen time consumed by camera movement, Branigan lists seven narrative functions by which movement can be said to be motivated, such as 'follows or discovers a glance', 'establishes scenographic space', and 'reveals character subjectivity' (2006, 26). This then allows for, of course, all other camera movements not fulfilling any of these functions to be unmotivated. The provocative result of this way of looking at camera movement is his argument that motivated camera movements are invisible, while unmotivated movements are not.

While not explicitly stated at this point, Branigan is working in a region which links Bordwell, Noël Burch, and Mitry, all of whom have been concerned with the degree of awareness and motivation of shots. Invisibility of style is one of the key characteristics of classical Hollywood cinema (if not the key characteristic), and camera movement itself would seem to run counter to this goal. The simple rule would be that a still camera is not noticed, while a moving camera is, but, by making this an issue of narrative motivation, both Bordwell and Branigan explain the problem more completely: many forms of movement, if not motivated, run counter to the effect of invisibility. This is the kind of important discovery (and argument) that makes looking at camera movement an important theoretical issue and not simply a matter of visual style.

If motivated camera movements are the province of classical style, then unmotivated movements are the province of art and experimental cinema. Here Branigan is closely aligned with Bordwell, who, as we noted, reached essentially this same conclusion. Branigan provides a nice offering of the usual suspects (Godard, Resnais, Dreyer, Straub and Huillet, and Snow again) and a few surprises (von Trier, Cuarón, Ken Jacobs) in indicating the wide range of aesthetic uses for unmotivated camera movement (2006, 27).

After time, narrative causality is the next area where Branigan sees a way of measuring the motivation of a camera movement, here, too, taking a key Bordwell concern regarding classical Hollywood cinema. Camera movement can be seen as supporting causality if any of the basic elements of classical narrative (Branigan provides eight) are supported by a stylistic activity such as movement. Branigan again links to Bordwell by seeing narrative as a cognitive activity, a process which must be looked at with regard to how a spectator processes sensory data such as movement in terms of its relation to narrative causality (2006, 32).

Relating camera movement to the scale of a shot is Branigan's third approach to exploring motivation. By arguing for general patterns of shot scale in classical style (from establishing shots to close-ups, with points in between), Branigan is able to identify the tendency to see extensive use of camera movement as upsetting this customary scheme. Like Bordwell, he looks to such sources as an industrial discourse (a cinematography textbook) to find a great dislike for unmotivated camera movement. ('Movement purely for the sake of movement is an abuse of an otherwise forceful technique', Herb Lightman, quoted in Branigan 2006, 35.) Branigan correctly sees here, and in the work of Jean Mitry, a claim that unmotivated camera work is not aesthetically pleasing, a position well worth exposing.

The force of this argument, for which Branigan also finds support in Noël Burch, is what ultimately can lift camera movement to a worthy position in film theory – it can be accounted for both in relation to narrative and outside of it. In this way, camera movement can be a principal means by which we see the shift from classical cinema, with its emphasis upon linkage and causality, to the alternative practices of unmotivated and 'post-wandered' movement.

An essential aspect of camera movement, and an inevitable area of concern if one is thinking of narrative structure, is to consider issues of anthropomorphism, subjectivity, and point of view. A tempting way to formalize this matter would be to ask how camera movement might be associated with the physical activities of a character within a narrative. Does rapidly moving a handheld camera approximate a character running? Can a wavering camera convey drunkenness? Rather than see this simplistic one-to-one relationship as a potential solution, Branigan is able to tackle these questions as important additional areas for consideration. Regarding anthropomorphism, for instance, he asserts that 'there is no necessary connection between a camera's degree of motivation ... and its degree of anthropomorphism' (2006, 39). The suggestion of 'ghostly' cameras or the presence of impossible camera movements through a wall or a keyhole (both clearly non-anthropomorphic) makes it clear that an association between a moving camera and a physical body is but one option among many.

Expanding considerably upon the list that Mitry provides of types of camera movement, Branigan, in exploring camera movement as an issue of space, provides a list of thirteen kinds of movement 'that produce "motion" on the screen'. Calling this list 'tentative', and also putting quotes around motion, he comes to ask which of these 'count as a "camera movement"' (2006, 57). Branigan's careful hesitancy here is also in keeping with Bordwell. The idea is that listing types of physical movements of a camera can only be a limited description, neither a necessary starting point for theoretical investigation nor an end in itself, but only one of a set of partial explanations and mental pictures out of which a spectator or critic fashions a story about a 'camera' (being) in-the-text.

Some of the items on Branigan's list are common to Mitry's as well – the expected tracking shots, zooms, and so on. Like Bordwell, he has a place for unusual forms of movement such as rear projection and special effects, the argument once more being that it is the effect or appearance of movement which is more of concern than whether an actual physical camera had to move. Branigan even incorporates ideas of mental or psychic movements produced by the spectator in response to static shots (following Žižek's psychoanalytic theory) and sees the spectator's eye movements in a deep focus shot as significant as well. These continue to be useful distinctions, as they enable Branigan to develop a more complete and nuanced view of what constitutes camera movement than would a simple listing of circumstances when a camera 'actually' moves. As with Bordwell, this elevates his ideas on camera movement to a theoretical level of considerable substance and subtlety, a far preferable alternative to what Branigan labels as 'restrictive definitions'. Branigan's second chapter, which we have been discussing, goes finally in a similar direction to Bordwell's article, by raising perceptual issues, particularly questions of attention which emphasize the role of the spectator in experiencing moving camera effects (*see* ATTENTION). As he says, 'I believe it is significant that psychologists who study the processes of *attention* – through which our awareness of things undergoes a change – have recourse to the metaphors of *zoom lenses, moving spotlights*, and *close-ups* in explaining what attention is and does' (2006, 61; italics in original). Branigan sees a 'large gap' remaining between camera movement and attention, but expresses his 'belief that one of the goals of film theory should be to bridge this gap'. Speaking like a true Bordwellian, he argues for concepts that 'show not just the different ways a piece of equipment can move, but how a camera *registers* with us' (2006, 62; italics in original).

This argument is supported by the provocative idea he introduced earlier of the 'post-wandered' camera, instances where 'a wandering has taken place and is inferred after the fact' (2006, 60). Basically, in these cases, the spectator is able to infer that 'wandering movement' has already occurred, so, in effect, we see movement after it has been completed. So, like Bordwell, and drawing upon Žižek, Branigan finds in 1960s European art cinema advanced ideas of camera movement which stress the role of the spectator regarding the narrative circumstances of experiencing camera movement, even when no movement is visible on the screen.

Although it appears in a (considerable) footnote, Branigan makes an observation which no introductory examination of cinematic movement can ignore: 'A major theme in film theory has involved the study of the nature and effects of the so-called "long take," often accompanied by a lengthy camera movement' (2006, 234). Long takes, like deep focus, have been seen as an alternative to montage, but while deep-focus shots are generally static, long takes, as Branigan says, usually employ camera movement. (There are exceptions to deep focus shots being static, as in the *Citizen Kane* shot of young Kane playing in the snow as a boy.) Two feature-length films based on a single take are almost continuously in motion, Figgis's *Timecode* and Sukorov's *Russian Ark*, both 'early' examples (2000 and 2002 respectively) of digital cinema's ability to extend celluloid experiments like Hitchcock's *Rope* (1948) into a new age (*see* LONG TAKE). Indeed, camera movement can be seen as having been accelerated by the use of handheld cameras in the documentary arena, principally in *cinéma vérité* of the early 1960s. Together with the Steadicam (introduced 1976), an invention which allowed for smooth movements not tied to tracks or cranes (employed to great effect, for example, in Kubrick's *The Shining*), camera movement has become much more extensively employed than in the days of heavy celluloid-dependent technology. The theoretical implications of these new technologies upon cinematic movement (if we can still call it that in a digital age) await a new generation of media theorists.

STEPHEN MAMBER

## Works cited

Bordwell, David. 1977. 'Camera Movement and Cinematic Space'. *Ciné-Tracts* 1 (2): 19–25: http://dl.lib.brown.edu/cinetracts/CT02.pdf (accessed 15 March 2011).

Bordwell, David, Janet Staiger, and Kristin Thompson. 1985. *The Classical Hollywood Cinema: Film Style and Mode of Production to 1960*. New York: Columbia University Press.

Branigan, Edward. 2006. *Projecting a Camera: Language-Games in Film Theory*. New York, Routledge.

Mitry, Jean. 2000. *The Aesthetics and Psychology of Cinema*. Translated by Christopher King. Bloomington: Indiana University Press.

# CLASSIC REALIST TEXT

Colin MacCabe presented his notion of the 'classic realist text' in his 'Realism and the Cinema: Notes on Some Brechtian Theses', published in *Screen* in 1974 (MacCabe 1974). 'Realism and the Cinema' was a controversial and influential article from a period when film studies was seeking to establish itself as an academic discipline in the UK and USA. *Screen* was one of the key sites of this struggle, and hosted fierce debates concerning fundamental intellectual, pedagogical, and political issues. Its Winter 1975/6 issue included an article by four editorial board members registering resistance to 'the recent use of psychoanalysis in *Screen*' (Buscombe *et al.* 1975, 119), which used MacCabe's article to exemplify the problems they wished to highlight. Two issues later, the same individuals published their statement 'Why We Have Resigned from the Board of *Screen*' (Buscombe *et al.* 1976). Two specific criticisms they offered were of the use of 'psychoanalysis as sciences' and of the fact that, on the pages of *Screen*, 'all forms of realism are simply collapsed into one general expression of bourgeois ideology which seems to have dominated in an unchanged form since the beginning of the 19th century' (ibid., 108). Both charges are extremely pertinent to an analysis of 'realism and the cinema'.

After a half-page introduction, MacCabe proceeds swiftly to the task of defining 'The Classic Realist Text' (1974, 7). He invites the reader to consider 'the use of inverted commas within the classic realist novel' (ibid.) – that is, the way characters' direct speech is usually signalled. Such passages of speech, he suggests, 'may cause … a certain confusion vis-à-vis what is really the case' (ibid.), due to characters disagreeing, being deceived or duplicitous, and so on. However, 'this difficulty is abolished', MacCabe claims, by the 'prose that surrounds them' (ibid.). This leads to a preliminary definition: 'In the classical realist novel the narrative prose functions as a metalanguage that can state all the truths in the object language – those words held in inverted commas – and can also explain the relation of this object language to the real' (ibid.). He then attempts to illustrate his definition's validity with a passage from George Eliot's *Middlemarch* (1872).

Next, MacCabe turns his attention to film, asking 'does this definition carry over into films where it is certainly less evident where to locate the dominant discourse?' (1974, 10). Unsurprisingly, he answers affirmatively:

> The narrative prose achieves its position of dominance because it is in the position of knowledge and this function of knowledge is taken up in the cinema by the narration of events … The camera shows us what happens – it tells the truth against which we can measure the discourses [of a film's characters].
>
> (Ibid.)

Following these brief discussions of literature and film, MacCabe offers 'two essential features of the classic realist text':

1 [It] cannot deal with the real as contradictory.
2 In a reciprocal movement [it] ensures the position of the subject in a relation of dominant specularity.

(Ibid., 12)

Let us return first to MacCabe's discussion of 'the classic realist novel', and proceed from there. It should be immediately clear that MacCabe's assertions concerning how 'narrative prose' functions falsify through oversimplification. As Bordwell points out, the relationship between literary texts' fictional narrators and the fictional worlds they narrate can possess many dimensions that preclude a straightforward relationship between the two. Perhaps the most famous of such effects is unreliable first person narration. A second fatal weakness of the proposed distinction is that it fails to account for one of literary narration's most pervasive features from the nineteenth century onwards: free indirect style, which colours the 'narrative prose' with the thoughts and feelings of characters, mingling (at least) two perspectives without clearly distinguishing between them (Bordwell 1985, 19). As Bordwell pithily concludes, in MacCabe's account, '[n]arration comes down to typography' (20).

When MacCabe turns his attention to film, his distinctions are, again, crude: we have the 'characters' discourses' on the one hand and the 'camera' on the other, and nothing else. But 'all materials of cinema function narrationally – not only the camera but speech, gesture, written language, music, color, optical processes, lighting, costume, even offscreen space and offscreen sound' (Bordwell 1985, 20). The 'surface properties' and 'physical marks' (ibid.) MacCabe fixes upon are not an adequate basis for analysis of the complex functioning of novels or films.

In a book-length account of the complexities of filmic point of view, George Wilson takes particular exception to MacCabe's undifferentiated attribution of omniscient narration to such a large number of texts (1986, 194–5). This objection is of relevance to the argument MacCabe advances in relation to his single filmic case study: *Klute* (Pakula, 1971). The end of this film shows Klute (Donald Sutherland) and Bree (Jane Fonda) about to move out of Bree's now-empty apartment. On the soundtrack we hear Bree talking to her psychiatrist. 'Her own estimation of the situation is that it most probably won't work', MacCabe tells us, before adding: 'but the reality of the image ensures us that this is the way it will really be' (1974, 11). What is 'this'? The images we see do not substantiate MacCabe's earlier assertion that 'what [Bree] really wants to do is to settle down in the mid-West with John Klute ... and have a family' (ibid.). Bordwell suggests that '[t]he narration is as conventional as MacCabe suggests, but the convention employed is not that of definite closure but that of ambiguity: *Klute* is "open-ended" in a way characteristic of those American genre films influenced by the European art cinema of the 1960s and 1970s' (1985, 20). MacCabe appears to have chosen an example which constitutes a particularly obvious challenge to his model; *Klute* ostentatiously eschews omniscience with regard to its characters' futures.

As a framework for detailed analysis, MacCabe's model is irredeemable. Its weaknesses become glaringly obvious the moment one brings it into proximity with case studies. It is worthwhile to continue our explication of MacCabe's article, however, because his two-part definition of the classic realist text as (i) unable to deal with the real as contradictory and (ii) placing the subject 'in a relation of dominant specularity' is followed by a lengthy theoretical discussion which at least helps us to understand why he would wish to propose such a model.

## Brecht

One important and clearly signalled source of such ideas is Bertolt Brecht, the twentieth century's most famous theorist of aesthetic distance (*see* BRECHT AND FILM). Brecht's notion of the 'Aristotelian play' (1964, 79) overlaps with MacCabe's classic realist text. As an alternative and remedy, Brecht offered his epic theatre, which employs techniques that break with mimesis in order to prompt the audience to not accept the 'naturalness' of the story shown, but instead imagine alternative sets of circumstances and events which would produce different outcomes. 'In short, the spectator is given the chance to criticize human behaviour from a social point of view' (86).

Murray Smith has noted that Brecht's dismissal of mimesis rests upon the premise that '[h]aving an emotional response of the empathetic type deadens our rational and critical faculties' (1996, 132). However, this idea is contradicted by recent work in cognitive science and philosophy, which demonstrates that 'emotion is integrated with perception, attention, and cognition, not implacably opposed to any of them' (133). We might also note that it is perfectly possible to adopt the kind of perspective Brecht proposes above in relation to an 'Aristotelian' artwork. As Smith pointedly asks, 'how critical is the spectator who can only be constructed as such by an estranging text?' (139).

MacCabe's use of the terms 'the real' and 'the subject' in his definition of the classic realist text points in another direction: psychoanalysis. Smith suggests that 'Realism and the Cinema' (along with Stephen Heath's 'Lessons from Brecht', published in the same issue of *Screen*) 'form[ed] an important bridge between Brecht, Althusser, and the psychoanalytic semiotics that was to dominate *Screen* and film theory in general for a decade or more' (1996, 136) (*see* CONTEMPORARY FILM THEORY).

It is during MacCabe's engagement with the writings of filmmaker and theorist Sergei Eisenstein that what is fundamentally at stake in 'Realism and the Cinema' emerges most clearly. MacCabe upbraids Eisenstein for his account of montage, which 'leaves both subject and object unchallenged', thus betraying a naive belief in 'a set of identities [which exist] in the world' (1974, 14). By contrast, what MacCabe wants to emphasize is that these 'identities rest in … discourses' (ibid.). The classic realist text, according to MacCabe, not only misrepresents the real by effacing its own constructedness and, at the same time, the constructedness of the real itself; it allows the perceiving subject ('in a reciprocal movement') to misrecognize itself as a whole, already-achieved thing.

The idea that reality is, to use a familiar phrase, 'discursively constructed' is one that can be held by individuals with a wide range of epistemological positions, but MacCabe's particular, Lacanian gloss on this idea renders his account vulnerable from quarters beyond those of literary and film studies already noted. As Stuart Hall observed in an article reviewing the work of *Screen* at the end of the 1970s: '"Screen theory" is … a very ambitious theoretical construct indeed – for it aims to account for how biological individuals become social subjects, *and* for how those subjects are fixed in positions of knowledge in relation to language and representation, *and* for how they are interpellated in specific ideological discourses' (1980, 159, original italics). Before he embarks upon his article's main passage of engagement with Lacanian theory, MacCabe appeals to 'the scientific concepts offered to us by psychoanalysis' (1974, 17). As the authors of 'Psychoanalysis and Film' would point out on the pages of *Screen* the following year, many of the articles in the journal, including 'Realism and the Cinema', in the course of their 'appeal to science', make '[c]ontroversial intellectual choices ... appear unproblematic', when it ought rather to be 'incumbent' upon them to 'be as explicit as possible about [their] choices' (Buscombe *et al.* 1975, 121). And this, Buscombe *et al.* argued, is before we even reach the subjects of 'the intellectual status of psychoanalysis and the obscurity with which it is often presented' and 'the question of the usefulness of the attempts to apply it to the cinema' (124).

The penultimate subsection of MacCabe's article is entitled 'A possible category: the revolutionary text' (1974, 21). MacCabe cites *Tout Va Bien* (Godard, Gorin, 1972) as one candidate for this category. He expands upon this idea in his later article 'The Politics of Separation', which discusses the film in more detail (MacCabe 1975/6). Kristin Thompson, in her article 'Sawing through the Bough: *Tout Va Bien* as a Brechtian Film', originally published in 1976, makes critical observations regarding 'The Politics of Separation' which are also of relevance to MacCabe's approach in 'Realism and the Cinema'.

Echoing Bordwell's critique of MacCabe's focus upon 'surface properties' and 'physical marks' in 'Realism and the Cinema', Thompson notes that MacCabe's 'scheme' in 'The Politics of Separation' 'does not include narrative, causality, or any other *functional* categories' (1988, 111, original italics). Thompson's neoformalist approach, by contrast, treats surface properties such as camera movements or dialogue as *devices* capable of fulfilling a range of *functions*. These functions in turn together comprise *systems* (narrative being one, very important, system). Such an approach does greater justice to a text's 'deep' organization (its compositional principles) than does MacCabe's focus on 'metalanguage versus object language' or 'camera versus characters' utterances'.

In place of MacCabe's concept of the 'classic realist text', to which a film like *Tout Va Bien* might provide an alternative by ensuring that 'the narrative is in no way privileged as against the characters' (1974, 24) and thus abstaining from the production of a metalanguage, Thompson offers the idea of the 'classical Hollywood cinema', in which the 'stylistic elements [are] fused to the narrative by a thoroughgoing compositional motivation ... the continuity system render[s] spatial and temporal relations clear [and] unambiguous characters provide the wellspring for the narrative events' (1988, 113). *Tout Va Bien* deviates from this model, according to Thompson, by separating those elements which the classical film is careful to fuse. For example, the Godard–Gorin film systematically interrupts the narrative flow, and uses editing that is 'argumentative' (116) rather than subordinated to narrative, space, and time.

Thompson is more parsimonious in her approach to the viewer than is MacCabe. Rather than his ahistorical psychoanalytic subject, under the thrall of the classic realist text, Thompson's spectator is one who activates the textual cues that his/her existing viewing of historically specific filmic modes has made available, with the result that a film like *Tout Va Bien* may make a spectator who generally encounters classical films 'come to see how filmic conventions have been used in the past, and how they may be used in new ways' (128). (Thompson is careful to stress, however, that there is no 'guarantee' of it producing 'this response – or any other' [ibid.].)

The model of the classical Hollywood cinema sketched in 'Sawing through the Bough' is a precursor to the 'classical Hollywood' paradigm/historical mode that Bordwell *et al.* (1985) would consolidate at great length later. Their book *The Classical Hollywood Cinema* (which has generated a wide range of critiques) remains the most thorough formalist account of the mode of filmmaking that – still – represents a 'dominant' mode and an international baseline, and teaches its spectators a certain set of viewing skills which they may misrecognize, along with the object those skills are applied to, as 'transparent'. As such, their model possesses significant points of overlap with MacCabe's, upon which it is an immeasurable improvement.

JAMES ZBOROWSKI

## Works cited

Bordwell, David. 1985. *Narration in the Fiction Film*. London: Methuen.

Bordwell, David, Janet Staiger, and Kristin Thompson. 1985. *The Classical Hollywood Cinema: Film Style and Mode of Production to 1960*. London: Routledge.

Brecht, Bertolt. 1964. *Brecht on Theatre: The Development of an Aesthetic*. Translated by John Willett. London: Methuen.

Buscombe, Edward, Christine Gledhill, Alan Lovell, and Christopher Williams. 1975. 'Statement: Psychoanalysis and Film'. *Screen* 16 (4): 119–30.

———. 1976. 'Why We Have Resigned from the Board of *Screen*'. *Screen* 17 (3): 106–9.

Hall, Stuart. 1980. 'Recent Developments in Theories of Language and Ideology: A Critical Note'. In *Culture, Media, Language: Working Papers in Cultural Studies, 1972–9*, edited by Stuart Hall, 157–62. London: Hutchinson.

Heath, Stephen. 1974. 'Lessons from Brecht'. *Screen* 15 (2): 103–28.

MacCabe, Colin. 1974. 'Realism and the Cinema: Notes on Some Brechtian Theses'. *Screen* 15 (2): 7–27.

———. 1975/6. 'The Politics of Separation'. *Screen* 16 (4): 46–57.

Smith, Murray. 1996. 'The Logic and Legacy of Brechtianism'. In *Post-theory: Reconstructing Film Studies*, edited by David Bordwell and Noël Carroll, 130–48. Wisconsin: University of Wisconsin Press.

Thompson, Kristin. 1988. 'Sawing through the Bough: *Tout Va Bien* as a Brechtian Film'. In *Breaking the Glass Armor: Neoformalist Film Analysis*, 110–31. Princeton, NJ: Princeton University Press.

Wilson, George M. 1986. *Narration in Light: Studies in Cinematic Point of View*. Baltimore, MD: Johns Hopkins University Press.

## Further reading

Bordwell, David. 1996. 'Contemporary Film Studies and the Vicissitudes of Grand Theory'. In *Post-theory: Reconstructing Film Studies*, edited by David Bordwell and Noël Carroll, 3–36. Wisconsin: University of Wisconsin Press.

Britton, Andrew. 2009. *Britton on Film: The Complete Film Criticism of Andrew Britton*. Edited by Barry Keith Grant. Detroit, MI: Wayne State University Press.

Carroll, Noël. 1988. *Mystifying Movies: Fads and Fallacies in Contemporary Film Theory*. New York: Columbia University Press.

# CLASSICAL FILM THEORY

Classical film theory can be defined as film theory produced before the emergence of semiotic and psychoanalytical theories of film in the 1970s. Although differing in many respects, classical film theorists shared a concern with identifying cinema's most important capacities; explaining their value; and exploring the stylistic techniques that best exploit them. The French film theorist and filmmaker Jean Epstein, for example, argued in the 1920s that the reproduction of movement is cinema's most significant ability; that its importance lies in revealing the mobility of reality; and that the best techniques for realizing it are the close-up as well as slow and fast motion (Abel 1988). Moreover, many classical film theorists identified the powers they conceived of as essential to the cinema, i.e. ones a film must exploit in order to be cinematic, as well as specific to it, i.e. ones that no other medium possesses, or possesses to the same degree. Epstein claimed that *photogénie*, a moment of pure cinema, occurs only when a 'mobile aspect of the world' is reproduced on film, and he believed that the cinema alone can reveal the mobility of reality (Abel 1988, 315).

Due in part to the prescriptiveness of medium-essentialism and medium-specificity, film theorists ostensibly rejected classical film theory in the 1970s and 1980s (although in practice they continued to rely on many of its premises). Under the sway of anti-essentialism (the belief that nothing has an essence), semiotic and psychoanalytical film theorists devoted themselves to exposing the ways in which cinema putatively reinforces or resists dominant ideologies rather than identifying 'the cinematic' and its value. But even theorists with no such philosophical qualms about essentialism turned away from classical film theory. In his landmark *Philosophical Problems of Classical Film Theory* (1988), Noël Carroll, who has proposed an essential definition of the moving image, contested almost all the theoretical arguments of Rudolf Arnheim, André Bazin, and Victor Perkins, three major classical film theorists.[1] Recently, however, a new generation of film theorists has revisited the work of Arnheim and others in an attempt to resurrect and build on their claims. After examining Arnheim's film theory as well as Carroll's critique of it, I will show how a contemporary film theorist, Berys Gaut, has advanced a neo-Arnheimian, medium-specific theory of film art, one that tries to deflect some of Carroll's criticisms of Arnheim.

## Arnheim's *Film as Art*

Although first published in the early sound era, *Film as Art* (1957) is a defence of silent cinema as art.[2] Arnheim and other film theorists of his generation saw their primary task as demonstrating that silent cinema can be art because many theorists and critics of art in the nineteenth and early twentieth centuries denied that a photographic medium such as film can be art (*see* ART, FILM AS). Photography can only mechanically reproduce reality, they argued, and because they also believed that art must consist of more than the automatic duplication of reality, they asserted that photography was not art, extending this argument to cinema after it emerged in the mid-1890s. At best, they suggested, film is a mechanical reproduction of another art, namely, theatre. All the art in cinema, in other words, takes place in front of the camera in the acting and staging of a story, as in theatre. Film has nothing artistic to contribute; it is merely a recording or transmission medium, much like a phonograph, which records or transmits a pre-existing musical work but is not itself an artistic medium.

There are three components to Arnheim's theory of film art. First, like most other film theorists of the period, Arnheim accepts the premise that mechanical reproduction is not art but rejects the conclusion that cinema automatically copies reality or theatre. 'It is worth while to refute thoroughly and systematically the charge that photography and film are only mechanical reproductions and that they therefore have no connection with art', he states at the beginning of *Film as Art*, and he goes on to explore cinema's various limitations as a medium of mechanical duplication (Arnheim 1957, 9). As Carroll has pointed out, Arnheim's conception of mechanical reproduction is somewhat inconsistent (Carroll 1988, 31). Usually, however, when Arnheim claims that film fails at mechanical recording, he means that the way something appears to the viewer when filmed diverges from the way it would appear to an observer in reality. 'The basic elements of the film medium will be examined separately and compared with the corresponding characteristics of what we perceive "in reality"', he states. 'It will be seen how fundamentally different the two kinds of image are' (Arnheim 1957, 9). For example, Arnheim argues that the frame of a shot imposes a limitation on what can be seen by the viewer that 'in the actual range of human vision ... simply does not exist'. This is because our eyes, heads, and bodies are 'mobile'. Hence, 'the field of vision is in practice unlimited and infinite'. We can move our eyes, heads, and bodies to see what is at any one moment out of sight, beyond the periphery of our vision. 'It is otherwise with the film or photograph', for the frame of a still shot prevents us from seeing what lies beyond the edge of the frame (17). Hence, cinema fails at mechanical reproduction because the frame of a shot restricts what we can see, and no such restriction obtains in normal visual experience. Arnheim makes similar claims about editing and the absence of depth, colour, and sound in silent film. All, for Arnheim, ensure that 'the images we receive of the physical world differ from those on the movie screen' and thereby 'refute the assertion that film is nothing but the feeble mechanical reproduction of real life' (34).

However, cinema's various limitations as a medium of mechanical reproduction do not, in and of themselves, entail that it is art. 'Film ... is a medium that may, but need not, be used to produce artistic results' (8), Arnheim acknowledges, which brings us to the other two components of his theory. 'In order that the film artist may create a work of art', he states, 'it is important that he consciously stress the peculiarities of his medium. This, however, should be done in such a manner that the character of the objects represented should not thereby be destroyed but rather strengthened, concentrated, and interpreted' (35). The filmmaker must use cinema's failures at mechanical duplication to 'shape and interpret' reality for the viewer (109). Moreover, these failures must be specific to film ('the peculiarities of his medium'). Here, we encounter both Arnheim's medium-essentialism, his belief that in order to create a work of art the filmmaker must exploit its limitations as a medium of mechanical reproduction, and his medium-specificity, his view that these limitations must be peculiar to it. For the sceptic about film art might grant that cinema does not merely copy reality yet maintain that it contributes nothing artistic to a film because all the artistry – the shaping and interpreting of reality – occurs in front of the camera in the acting or staging. Hence, Arnheim insists that, for something to be a work of film art, it must employ a feature specific to cinema for an artistic purpose. For instance, he cites as an example of film art the scene at the beginning of Charlie Chaplin's *The Immigrant* (1917) when, due to the fact that he is filmed from behind, the Tramp appears to be bending over the side of a boat and vomiting, like the other seasick passengers (Arnheim 1957, 36). However, when he turns around to face the camera, the viewer discovers he has been happily fishing. Here, the artistic effect is only partially due to Chaplin's acting, which is a theatrical technique. Additionally, through the technique of framing – which, as we have seen, for Arnheim prevents cinema from mechanically reproducing reality – the camera is being used to 'shape and interpret' the subject for the viewer, leading him or her to make a false inference about it by restricting the viewer's knowledge of what the Tramp is really doing for a moment or two. Moreover, for Arnheim, this technique is specific to film as no other medium possesses mobile framing.

Due to his animus against mechanical reproduction, Arnheim was hostile to the introduction of synchronized sound in the late 1920s. He saw it as a step towards what he called the 'complete film', i.e. a film that perfectly replicates reality in all its colour, three-dimensionality, and sound. The complete film, he believed, could not be art because it merely mechanically reproduces reality and hence offers the artist no medium-specific limitations on mechanical duplication for shaping and interpreting reality for the viewer. Hence, he was pessimistic about the future of film art, and worried that cinema was 'on its way to the victory of wax museum ideals over creative art' (154).

## Carroll's *Philosophical Problems of Classical Film Theory*

Carroll (1988) criticizes all three components of Arnheim's theory. As we have seen, Arnheim believed that only a medium's divergences from mechanical reproduction can be used by an artist to shape and interpret reality and thereby create art. But Carroll points out that mechanical duplication can also perform this function when a filmmaker employs it to express feelings of detachment and 'matter-of-factness' (78), as Andy Warhol arguably does in films such as *Empire* (1964). Nor is it necessary for an artist to manipulate the appearance of reality in order to create art, according to Carroll, as many artists, especially of a realist persuasion, have aimed to copy reality as accurately as possible. The realist film theorist and critic André Bazin, for instance, argued that in the silent era, while some filmmakers, such as Sergei Eisenstein and Abel Gance, 'put their faith in the image', by which he meant 'everything that the representation on the screen adds to the object there represented', others, primarily Erich von Stroheim, F.W. Murnau, and Robert Flaherty, 'evaluated [the image] not according to what it adds to reality but what it reveals of it' (Bazin 1967, 26, 28) (*see* MODERNISM VERSUS REALISM; ONTOLOGY OF THE PHOTOGRAPHIC IMAGE). For Bazin, their films were just as much examples of 'cinematographic art' as those of Eisenstein and Gance (28). Moreover, some artworks do not represent reality and consist merely of formal play, for example Hans Richter's abstract film *Rhythm 21* (1921), while others are comprised of real events that the artist plays no role in shaping or interpreting, such as the sounds of the audience in John Cage's *4'33"* (1952).

It is Carroll's criticism of Arnheim's medium-essentialism and medium-specificity, however, that has probably had the biggest impact as it can also be applied to the work of many other classical film theorists. A major problem with Arnheim's insistence that the filmmaker must exploit cinema's specific limitations as a medium of mechanical reproduction in order to create film art, Carroll suggests, is that it 'seems to urge us to sacrifice excellence on principle', whereas 'excellence is ... always the overriding consideration in deciding whether a particular practice or development is acceptable in art' (85). Carroll's point is that there are many films that achieve artistic excellence using the mechanical recording of non-cinematic techniques, such as Chaplin's. Chaplin was a gifted mime, and the fact that he recorded his mimes in his films is a major reason they are celebrated as art, but miming is not peculiar to film. Conversely, a film that employs cinema's medium-specific failures at mechanical duplication to shape and interpret reality need not be a work of art. Television commercials often exploit such failures to make products seem appealing, but this does not mean they are artworks. Artistic value, in other words, does not correlate with the exploitation by the artist of the features deemed to be specific to a medium. Carroll's basic point is that a physical medium has no normative consequences for the art form that employs it. As he puts it, 'the physical medium does not select a unique purpose, or even a delimited range of purposes, for an art form' (Carroll 1996, 28).

## Gaut's *A Philosophy of Cinematic Art*

Gaut (2010) argues that there is 'something important and correct' about Arnheim's claim that 'film can be an art because of the divergences between film and reality, where these divergences are used for artistic ends'. However, in 'Arnheim's hands', this claim 'goes astray' because it leads to the view that sound cinema is artistically inferior to silent film. Gaut therefore sets out to 'disentangle what is correct about Arnheim's claim' (36). He agrees with Arnheim that cinema's divergences from mechanical reproduction make it an artistic medium. However, he thinks these divergences include not only failures to automatically record reality, as Arnheim argued, but also 'presentational capacities'. Editing, for example, is a presentational capacity 'rather than a limitation' because it enables film to do something that cannot be done in reality, namely to 'flip from one represented point of time or space to another point instantaneously' (37). Moreover, such divergences must be capable of being varied in order to be used for artistic purposes. For example, in the cinema, unlike in reality, we watch moving images projected onto a screen. But the fact that the beam of light from the projector is a fixed divergence, i.e. it cannot be varied in the way that framing or sound volume can be, means it is not artistically relevant.

These refinements allow Gaut to resist one of the most contentious ramifications of Arnheim's theory: that the closer a medium comes to reproducing reality, the fewer the divergences it affords for artistic creation and therefore the more artistically inferior it is. Gaut argues that, because there exist variable presentational capacities, both sound and colour can be used artistically, as when Hitchcock uses the colour green to express romantic renewal in *Vertigo* (1958), or Kane's voice echoes through the 'resounding emptiness of Xanadu' in order to express his loneliness in *Citizen Kane* (1941) (41). Arnheim's animosity towards sound and colour is therefore unwarranted. Indeed, Gaut suggests, if and when what Arnheim calls a 'complete' film becomes possible, it would still be a work of art as long as it could have been filmed differently. Gaut's neo-Arnheimian theory therefore deflects at least some of Carroll's criticisms of Arnheim as it allows that films in which cinema's presentational capacities are used to reproduce reality as accurately as possible can be art. Thus, it is the 'plasticity of the cinematic recording medium, the fact that it can record its subject matter in a number of ways', rather than its failure to mechanically reproduce reality, as Arnheim thought, that enables it to be art (43).

In addition, Gaut defends several versions of medium-specificity, including the claim that 'for a medium to constitute an art form it must instantiate artistic properties that are distinct from those that are instantiated by other media' (287). It is this version of medium-specificity, he suggests, that Arnheim invoked in claiming that film must diverge from the mechanical recording of reality in specific ways in order to be art. Digital cinema, for example, is not just a new medium but a new art form, according to Gaut, because 'distinct artistic properties and values are achievable in digital cinema' that are not possible using celluloid film, such as the creation of photorealistic content using computer software. This is in contrast to new media such as the acetate safety stock which replaced nitrate stock in the early 1950s and which, Gaut suggests, did not give rise to a new art form because 'nothing artistically interesting and distinctive can be accomplished in acetate film that cannot be accomplished in nitrate film, and vice versa' (305). This does not mean Arnheim was correct to claim that a filmmaker must employ medium-specific features of cinema in order to create art, only that film does possess such features and is therefore an art form, thereby once again deflecting some of Carroll's criticisms. Whether or not it is persuasive, Gaut's attempt to build and improve on Arnheim's film theory demonstrates that classical film theory continues to offer rich resources for theorists of cinema in both its digital and celluloid forms.[3]

MALCOLM TURVEY

## Notes

1 According to Carroll in his essay 'Defining the Moving Image' (Carroll 1996), something is a moving image if it is a detached display; if it has, unlike paintings and other still images, the potential to impart the impression of movement, a potential that need not be realized, as in films of photographs; if its exhibition or performance is generated mechanically by a template, as opposed to the performance of a play, which is generated by an interpretation of the play; if its performance cannot be considered an artwork in its own right, unlike the performance of a play; and finally, if it is two-dimensional.

2 *Film als Kunst* (*Film as Art*), first published in 1932 in German, appeared in English under the title *Film* the following year. In 1957 Arnheim republished *Film as Art* in English in a condensed form (along with some essays he had written on film later in the 1930s), and it is this abridged version of *Film as Art* with which most English-language scholars are acquainted today.

3 One problem with Gaut's argument is that if the only criterion for a new art form is a medium's capacity to instantiate distinct artistic properties, then the replacement of black and white by colour film, or silent by sound film, or the academy ratio by widescreen processes would all have constituted new art forms. Gaut's definition of an art form, in other words, seems much too wide (Turvey forthcoming).

## Works cited

Abel, Richard, ed. 1988. *French Film Theory and Criticism: A History/Anthology, Volume 1: 1907–1929.* Princeton, NJ: Princeton University Press.

Arnheim, Rudolf. 1957. *Film as Art.* Berkeley: University of California Press.

Bazin, André. 1967. *What Is Cinema?* Vol. 1. Berkeley: University of California Press.
Carroll, Noël. 1988. *Philosophical Problems of Classical Film Theory*. Princeton, NJ: Princeton University Press.
———. 1996. *Theorizing the Moving Image*. Cambridge: Cambridge University Press.
Gaut, Berys. 2010. *A Philosophy of Cinematic Art*. Cambridge: Cambridge University Press.
Turvey, Malcolm. Forthcoming. 'Review of Berys Gaut's *A Philosophy of Cinematic Art*'. *Mind: A Quarterly Review of Philosophy*.

## Further reading

Higgins, Scott, ed. 2011. *Arnheim for Film and Media Studies*. New York: Routledge.

# CLOSE-UP

## Béla Balázs and the close-up

Béla Balázs's writings on the close-up are considered to be his most valuable and original contributions to film theory. One of the most recognizable units of cinematic discourse, the close-up marks, in Mary Ann Doane's words, 'the emergence of film as a discourse, as an art' (2003, 90, 91). Writing in the mid-1920s, Balázs was among the first theorists to argue that cinema is a nascent art given its capacity to reveal something fundamentally new about humanity. It is primarily through the close-up, 'film's true terrain' (2010, [VM], 38), that the camera shows us an unseen – since routinely overlooked and unnoticed – sphere of experience, that of 'the face of things, the mimicry of nature, and the microdynamics of physiognomy' (Balázs 1970, 197). Through the close-up of the human face and the face of things, the 'magnifying glass' of the film camera is able to visualize what is non-spatial and sub-conscious, namely, 'feelings, emotions, moods, intentions, and thoughts' (1970, 61).

Balázs argues that while words are mere translations and distorting abstractions of primal and non-rational human experiences, the language of silent film offers a 'visual corollary of human souls immediately made flesh' (2010, [VM], 10). The clairvoyant optic of the close-up externalizes intangible 'inner experiences', making silent cinema the artistic expression par excellence of the emerging popular visual culture of 'the *embodied human being*' (2010, [VM], 11; original emphasis).

In this entry I will take my cue from Balázs in examining the close-up as a cinematic technique endowed with an aesthetic mission and significance, but, at the same time, firmly situated in a social and cultural context, in line with Balázs's Marxian historical materialist world-view. Balázs's ideas of the close-up stand out in film theory by virtue of their originality, their contemporary air, and their poetic poignancy. I will situate Balázs's conception of the close-up – especially of the silent film close-up – within a philosophical discourse that supports Gilles Deleuze's insight that '[c]inema's concepts are not given in cinema' (Deleuze 1989, 280). The close-up will be tied to ideas developed by Immanuel Kant, Johann Wolfgang von Goethe, Karl Marx, and Henri Bergson. It will also be related to the work of Pierre Bourdieu. Erica Carter's essay on Balázs's film theory (Carter 2010) provides valuable historical and cultural background. Through this 'polyphonic' interplay of voices I will attempt to do justice to Balázs's notion of the synaesthetic potential of the close-up. In particular, I will examine Balázs's seminal and much-discussed ideas of anthropomorphism, physiognomy, and the human face as self-contained entity.

## The close-up as aesthetic reflection

Balázs considers the close-up as the pre-eminent technique of aesthetic clairvoyance. In this, he follows an intricate philosophical logic, one that makes aesthetics a privileged domain where the divisive dichotomies of Western thought may be reconciled (object vs. subject, outside vs. inside, immanent vs. transcendent), and where the true nature of subjectivity is revealed. 'Beauty', Balázs observes, 'is a subjective experience of human consciousness brought about by objective reality' (1970, 33). Erica Carter explains that in Balázs's thought the Romantic heritage with its emphasis on subjective experience is fertilized, and complemented, by phenomenological approaches to consciousness, and by a Central-European utopian Marxism or 'everyday utopianism', which finds the imaginary, the supernatural, and the irrational (marvellous or uncanny) firmly rooted in the familiar objective reality of the here and now (Carter 2010, xviii–xxxiv). The result of this mixture is a fascinating 'enchanted' naturalism, manifest in the close-up's anthropomorphic, physiognomic animation of concrete objects as well as in its method of getting to the truth, which compounds an almost naturalistic 'sharp observation of detail' with a profoundly poetic, intuitive perception that involves the 'the heart not the eye' (Balázs 2010, [VM], 39; 1970, 56).

It is, moreover, important to note here that in Balázs's writing a binary-structured language is constantly at odds with the aesthetic goal to transcend fundamental dichotomies. Consider, for example, the following expressions: 'the deepest layers of the soul', hidden aspects of 'inner' experiences, and 'what is *really* happening *under* the surface of appearances' (Balázs 2010, [VM], 21; 1970, 40, 56; emphasis added). Parallel to this, Balázs advances a stunning argument for the flattening of dichotomies and the conflation of the traditionally incommensurable dimensions of inner and outer, surface and depth, through his idea of 'visible man' as presented in the '*surface art*' of cinema (Balázs 2010, [VM], 19; emphasis added).

The clairvoyance or truth-revealing potential of the cinematic close-up is clearly what Balázs values above all. For him the 'deep gaze' of the close-up 'unmask[s] every sign of fakery' and shows 'what is *really* happening under the surface of appearances' (Balázs 2010, [VM], 27–8; 1970, 56; emphasis added). The close-up is considered to be a 'magnifying glass', the 'art of emphasis', a 'mute pointing' to significant detail (Balázs 2010, [VM], 38, 39, 40). Moreover, since 'time as well as space can be dislocated by cutting in extreme close-ups', the close-up emerges as a device capable of slowing down, indeed suspending, narrative time in order to allow for a closer scrutiny of what is being presented – in a time and space apart (Balázs 2010, [VM], 39). Mary Ann Doane describes this effect of the close-up as the creation of a 'temporality of contemplation' (2003, 97).

By suspending details from everyday space and time and making them stand out as a separate reality, the close-up invites thoughtful contemplation, which for the Romantic modernist Balázs is a moment of pure aesthetic reflection (Szaloky 2005, 39). In a Kantian spirit, Balázs grapples through the close-up with the mind's unalterable *habit* to attach symbolic meaning to the world as a part of perception (Balázs 2010, [VM], 56). In Balázs's elegant paraphrase: 'Our normal situation is that we perceive the objects around us only vaguely, paying heed to them only through the fog of habitual generalizations and schematic conceptions. We look out mainly for the possible benefits they could bring or the damage they might inflict' (Balázs 2010, [VM], 60). In historical materialist terms, this normal situation is identified with the perceptual logic of capitalist abstraction and alienation. Thus, for Balázs, the aesthetic pursuit – here through the close-up – is designed to re-attune perception to its revolutionary, consciousness-altering potential (Szaloky 2005, 39–40).

The close-up performs aesthetic de-familiarization (as Doane confirmed in 2003, 107) when it 'strips the veil of our imperceptiveness and insensitivity', allowing the familiar to appear strange, 'unaccustomed, mysterious, *unnatural*', or simply to appear to our selective awareness (Balázs 2010, [VM], 61). Whether this new experience can ever be that of 'pure objectivity', of things as they are 'when we are not present', or whether it must always remain subjectively biased and directed is an undecided quandary in Balázs's film theory (Balázs 2010, [SoF], 159; [VM], 61). In fact, it may not amount to a quandary at all, but simply be a matter of emphasis, that is, as to which objective and subjective constituents of consciousness are put in relief. The function of the close-up is to make the subjective objective, that is, to reveal the transcendental dimension of the soul (of pure consciousness or intentionality) within the extensive, visible world of objects organized according to a narrative film logic. As Balázs succinctly puts it (Balázs 1970, 60): 'When the film close-up ... shows us the face of objects, it still shows us man, for what makes objects expressive are the human expressions projected on to them. The objects only reflect our own selves ... The close-ups of the film are the creative instruments of this mighty visual anthropomorphism.'

## The close-up, anthropomorphism, and physiognomy

Anthropomorphism and the close-up are inseparable for Balázs, who states that '*all objects* ... are necessarily symbolic' and all 'make a physiognomical impression on us' (Balázs 2010, [VM], 56). This is so because, in a Kantian spirit, the physiognomical is 'a necessary category of our perception' on a par with space and time, and 'can never be eliminated from the world of our experience' (Balázs 2010, [VM], 56). (Carter [2010, xxv] cites William James's phenomenology as the immediate source of Balázs's notion of a symbolic perception.) Anthropomorphism and physiognomy are, thus, synonymous for Balázs. Remarkably, the close-up's physiognomic look presents a peculiar sort of anthropomorphism. Since, as Carter observes, Balázs applies the physiognomic to the 'entirety of the diegetic, and indeed the object world', objects acquire a face, a soul, and even a look – a '*living physiognomy*' – which is turned back towards the human observer (Carter 2010, xxvi; original emphasis). For example, landscape as physiognomy 'gazes out at us, as if emerging from the chaotic lines of a picture puzzle' (Balázs 2010, [VM], 53). The strange, at times uncanny, autonomy and 'life' that objects acquire through physiognomic presentation is enhanced by the *silence* and the two-dimensionality of the image, which for Balázs allow humans and objects to appear 'almost homogeneous' in cinema (Balázs 2010, [VM], 23; 1970, 58). The close-up's anthropomorphism, paradoxically, flattens the distinction between animate and inanimate, object and subject, to produce a pervasive holism.

Carter is thus able to argue that Balázs's notion of physiognomy is quite distinct from the essentialist, and racist, 'pseudoscience' that Johan Kaspar Lavater championed. For Balázs, Carter explains, physiognomy is a 'mode of aesthetic as opposed to crudely empirical knowing', inspired by Goethe's, rather than Lavater's, thinking (Carter 2010, xxvi). Goethe's belief that forms are but a 'fleeting presence within the perpetual flux of natural or organic life' appears to poignantly come to life in the strangely animated objects presented in close-up isolation in cinema (Carter 2010, xxvii).

## The close-up as child's-eye-view

Carter notes that Balázs discusses the 'vitality and significance', the '*living physiognomy*' that objects possess when in close-up in connection with a child's imaginative view and understanding of the world (Carter 2010, xxvi). Further, Carter associates the close-up with the temporal organization and logic of the fairy tale, which in her view serves as a key source for Balázs's conception of the close-up as 'a magical space in which relations of time and space are transformed and boundaries are broken' (xxxi). The fairy tale – which was a source of inspiration generally in Central-European Romanticism – and the close-up are also connected through their shared 'utopian social aspirations' (xxxi). In fact, Balázs's keen interest in the fairy tale's 'suffusion of the object world with subjective affect' is already evident in his 1910 libretto to Béla Bartók's *Bluebeard's Castle*, which in Carter's view can be read as an 'allegorical prefiguring of *Visible Man*'s account of the close-up in film' (xxxi).

Balázs finds an important model of the close-up's clairvoyance in *children's* perceptual-cognitive engagement with the world: '*Children see the world in close-up*' (Balázs 2010, [VM], 62; original emphasis). Artistic sensibility at its best is akin to that of children for Balázs, even though it is the film director's poetic sensibility that guides the selection and emphasis of the essential microcosmic detail – or the foregrounding of its *absence* (!), as in the case of a noticeably withheld close-up (Balázs 1970, 57–8). It is during a time of suspended play that the pensive gaze of children, and the aesthetic perception of the close-up, explore unnoticed nooks and crannies, savouring 'the little moments of life' (Balázs 2010, [VM], 62). The child's-eye-view constitutes the prototypical physiognomic engagement with the world. 'Children have no difficulty understanding … physiognomies. This is because they do not yet judge things purely as tools, means to an end, useful objects not to be dwelt on. They regard each thing as an autonomous living being with a soul and face of its own. Indeed, children are like artists, who likewise want to depict objects, not make use of them' (Balázs 2010, [VM], 46).

Children's affinity for physiognomic perception may also be explained by 'the closer perspective' that 'little people' have on the world (Balázs 2010, [VM], 62). Children are imagined here to still possess an *existential* closeness to objects. Art seeks to recapture this immediate substantial reality with which adults have lost touch. A child's experience is assumed to be less distancing and ocular-centric and more immediate and immersive than that of adults. It is 'the heart not the eye', feelings and intuitions, rather than views, which guide the child's-eye-view as manifest in the close-up (Balázs 1970, 56).

## The close-up as synaesthetic sensibility and Deleuze's movement-image

The immersive perception of the 'heart' conveyed in the close-up intermingles the senses, including the experience of inner and outer, whose form is respectively time and space (as per Kant, a major influence on Balázs). In other words, the result is a complex synaesthesia, which entails the interchangeability not only of, say, vision and audition but also of space and time, the extensive and the disembodied, the physical and the mental. The silence – that is, the non-verbal nature – of the close-up allows for the foregrounding, so to speak, of a visibly registered and played-out 'polyphony', which Balázs associates both with facial features and the soul. Facial features, Balázs insists, are 'no mere optical matter' – just as music 'is not just an acoustic matter' but 'a separate sphere of the soul'

(2010, [VM], 24). Isolated in close-up, facial features take us out of space (of our consciousness of space) and into 'another dimension', a mental one, that of 'physiognomy' (1970, 61). Carter astutely observes, moreover, that for Balázs also sound can 'traverse the boundaries between interior and exterior' (Carter 2010, xxviii). It is through the 'sound close-up' that the director will lead our ears as 'he led our eyes in the silent film' (Balázs 2010, [SoF], 185). Further, I would add, Balázs envisions the extension of the close-up to the colour film, which through its use will be able to 'reproduce even the most subtle movement of colour' (Balázs 2010, [SoF], 179).

Significantly, the permeability between traditionally incommensurable dimensions – especially inside and outside, time and space, mental and physical – which is brought to life in the film close-up is not only a phenomenological and aesthetic construct but also supported by historical materialistic logic. The *embodied human being* that is resurrected as 'visible man' in silent cinema literally wears his heart on his sleeve, so to speak, a heart that is imbued with culture, and embodied in unconscious, spontaneous, and often minuscule facial movements and gestures, which are magnified and accentuated in close-up (Balázs 2010, [VM], 11, 10; original emphasis). 'The fathers' thoughts become the nervous sensitivity, the taste and instinct of the children', Balázs writes. 'Conscious knowledge turns into instinctive sensibility: *it is materialized as culture in the body*' (Balázs 2010, [VM], 13; original emphasis). Far from being philosophically naïve (as some have suggested), Balázs's provocative insistence that in cinema 'the body becomes unmediated spirit, spirit rendered visible', is a thoroughly contemporary idea, which resurfaces, most notably, in Pierre Bourdieu's influential concept of the *habitus* (Szaloky 2009, 47; Carter 2010, xxv).

For Balázs, cinema – which he considers as a *'surface art'* – renders dualistic thinking obsolete by showing 'live' and in close-up essential and physically present, yet normally unseen or overlooked, micro-movements of transformations between traditional binary opposites (Balázs 2010, [VM], 19; original emphasis). At stake is the 'vivisection of a heartbeat', the 'direct transformation of spirit into body', the 'very instant in which the general is transformed into the particular' as captured and shown in a series of close-ups (Balázs 2010, [VM], 31, 13; 1970, 55). It is no coincidence that in his recapitulation of Henri Bergson's definition of the movement-image, Deleuze quotes almost verbatim Balázs's description of cinema as a two-dimensional *'surface art'*, where 'whatever is inside is outside', with 'nothing "behind" the image surface, and no "hidden" meaning' (Balázs 2010, [VM], 19, 20; original emphasis). Balázs, as well as Deleuze, owes a substantial debt to Bergson, who, according to Deleuze, equates image, movement, and matter (Deleuze 1986, 59) (*see* MOVEMENT-IMAGE). 'You may say that my body is matter or that it is an image', Bergson writes, anticipating Balázs's flattening of matter and form, substance and physical presence into the expressive surface of the moving image (59).

## The close-up, mental time, and the soulful human face

The human face is for Balázs the ultimate surface that conflates moving matter *and* image. Photographed in close-up, the face takes us out of space and places us in a mental dimension. Deleuze credits Balázs for realizing that the close-up, in general, abstracts its object *'from all spatio-temporal co-ordinates'* and raises it 'to the state of Entity' (1986, 96; original emphasis). In Balázs's words, when we are shown no space (as in close-up) that would allow us to measure the time, 'the time becomes simply immeasurable'. An image that is no longer bound by space is 'also not bound by time. In this psychological dimension of the close-up, the image becomes concept and can be transformed like thought itself' (Balázs 2010, [SoF], 134). Similarly, when the close-up isolates a face, 'we do not perceive space … A dimension of another order opens up', again, that of physiognomy (Deleuze 1986, 96).

Carter examines Balázs's Bergsonian understanding of temporality in terms of 'pure duration' (*durée*), which compounds present and past into a temporal synthesis, similar to the experience of a melody (Carter 2010, xxxiii–xxxiv). Duration is the temporality of mental movements, and a close-up of the uncontrolled, not consciously manipulated micro-movements of the face authentically presents the dynamism of relations that for Balázs is uniquely human. 'In a sort of physiognomic chord a variety of feelings, passions and thoughts are synthesized in a play of the features as an adequate expression of the multiplicity of the human soul' (Balázs 1970, 64).

The face speaks best through a silent soliloquy for Balázs, who professes that 'no statement is as utterly revealing as a facial expression' (Balázs 2010, [VM], 37). For this reason, Balázs fastens on the most eloquent faces in silent cinema. The performances of Asta Nielsen, Lilian Gish, and Sessue Hayakawa epitomize the soulful facial expressivity that Balázs finds so revealing. It is, however, the face of Greta Garbo that in Balázs's eyes conveys the *Zeitgeist*, the atmosphere of the historical moment of his writing. Balázs reads into Garbo's 'brooding glance' – which 'comes from afar' and 'looks into an endless distance' – a boundless longing for an elsewhere, away from the 'unclean' world of the present day. Behind a variety of facial expressions, Balázs claims, Garbo's face preserves a fixed and unchanged mien, that of a permanent exile, one who is always 'in a distant land' no matter where he or she may be (1970, 286). Significantly, Garbo's visage possesses a 'strange sort of beauty', one that bears the stamp of suffering, loneliness, and *estrangement* (Balázs 1970, 286, 287; Szaloky 2006, 202–3). For Balázs beauty expresses the essence of the human soul. It appears to us in exemplary fashion when animated in physiognomic detail by the close-up.

MELINDA SZALOKY

## Works cited

Balázs, Béla. 1970. *Theory of the Film: Character and Growth of a New Art*. Translated by Edith Bone. New York: Denver Publications.

——. 2010. *Béla Balázs: Early Film Theory*. Visible Man [VM] and *The Spirit of Film* [SoF]. Edited by Erica Carter, translated by Rodney Livingstone. New York, Oxford: Berghahn Books.

Carter, Erica. 2010. 'Introduction'. In *Béla Balázs: Early Film Theory Theory. Visible Man and The Spirit of Film*, edited by Erica Carter, translated by Rodney Livingstone. New York, Oxford: Berghahn Books.

Deleuze, Gilles. 1986. *Cinema 1: The Movement-Image*. Translated by Hugh Tomlinson and Barbara Habberjam. Minneapolis: University of Minnesota Press.

——. 1989. *Cinema 2: The Time-Image*. Translated by Hugh Tomlinson and Robert Galeta. Minneapolis: University of Minnesota Press.

Doane, Mary Ann. 2003. 'The Close-up: Scale and Detail in the Cinema'. *Differences* 14(3): 89–111.

Szaloky, Melinda. 2005. 'Making New Sense of Film Theory through Kant: A Novel Teaching Approach'. *New Review of Film and Television Studies* 3 (1) (May): 33–58.

——. 2006. '"As You Desire Me": Reading the "Divine Garbo" through Movement, Silence, and the Sublime'. *Film History* 18 (2): 196–208.

——. 2009. 'Transcendental Reflections on Cinema and the Aesthetic between Kant and Deleuze'. Doctoral dissertation, University of California, Los Angeles.

# COGNITIVE FILM THEORY

There is no consensus – nor might there ever be – about what cognition is, how it works, or the scope of what it does, even among scholars who have dedicated their lives to its study. Likewise, film theory means many things to many people and can seem to mean *any*thing to some. Yet looking at one of these diffuse entities through the perspective of the other can bring both into new kinds of visibility. When David Bordwell (1989) writes of 'the cognitivist perspective' on film, he is referring to a disciplinary orientation as well as to an analytic 'frame of reference' (11). The cognitive perspective, as Bordwell develops it, is an attitude of inquiry that allows for not one but variable frames of reference from different, if not radically different, perspectives and at different scales of analysis. This entry discusses how essays by Bordwell and by Noël Carroll construct such movable conceptual frames and shows how some more recent ideas about cognition can help us to think about the utility of the idea of *the* cognitive perspective rather than that of a cognitive perspective.

## Framing and reframing

Stephen Heath (1976) points out the complexity of artistic, and particularly of cinematic, frames, which can be at once like the end of a screen and the beginning of a window: they establish the limits of a depiction while also implying that the depicted world extends beyond what we can see from our own vantage point (cf. 80–2). When we talk about a scholarly 'frame of reference', as Bordwell does here, we most often mean something more like a window, or an organizing filter through which to observe and by way of which to formulate assessments about data or phenomena or texts. We view large amounts of data by visually representing the patterns we find in it; we read Beckett through Foucault. By doing the latter, we construct a frame called 'Foucault' and use it to view and filter what we see, or what we think to say we see, in Beckett.

In constructing what he presents as *the* cognitivist frame of reference, Bordwell favours computationalist and representationalist forms of cognitive theory. These approaches model cognition as rule-based manipulation of more-or-less abstract symbols, images, or words in the mind. Bordwell also allows for a degree of flexibility in his cognitivist framework, a versatile but not limitless range of ways of thinking about cognition as it pertains to film. Thus, the methodology that Bordwell constructs has, like a mobile film camera, an advantageous capacity to reposition itself and reframe its subjects. It creates a tool for meaning-making, as does a picture; it establishes a perspective, like a window; but it also provides a movable, adjustable, and representational resource for developing new approaches to the relationship between cinema and mind.

Bordwell excuses himself, unnecessarily, for contributing to 'that grim genre of academic writing wherein author A summarizes theoretical assertions made by Authors B, C, D, and so on, embellishing each with occasional commentary' (Bordwell 1989, 11). To the contrary, 'A Case for Cognitivism' does not merely recount and compare work in cognitive theory; the essay builds a powerful platform from which to reconsider film and film theory. Bordwell compares the history of film theory to E.H. Gombrich's rendering of the history of visual art as 'a process whereby vivid images or metaphors are disseminated, recast, filled in, mapped onto diverse phenomena, and elaborated to fit specific institutional purposes' (29–30). This process of disseminating and revising vivid mental images is critical for Bordwell because, from a *cognitive* standpoint, this is how theories of film are constructed and evaluated, whether or not the theories are cognitive theories of film. Bordwell thereby compares a history of the *theory* of film to a history of art itself, and the reciprocal comparison of film to the history of art theory would hold as well. The concern here is with ways of looking, interpreting, and deciding via 'schemata and heuristics that novices learn by ostension and that experts apply through imitation and extrapolation' in thinking about both media and media theory (29).

The cognitivist perspective that Bordwell promotes relies on disputed phenomena, such as mental representations or images in what is often called 'the mind's eye'. Among the theorists that Bordwell discusses, these representations take a number of forms that can be materially and epistemically different things, though they are united by a shared emphasis on the relationship between the body and events and objects in the world external to the body. In more recent works, Mark Johnson and Paul Churchland elaborate on what can be considered representations, arguing that the mind's eye is a dualistic concept that unnecessarily fractures models of the mind into representing and observing *parts* when it is more realistic to think of the mind as a complex function of the *whole* organism or brain. Johnson (2007), informed by almost two decades of empirical research conducted after the publication of 'A Case for Cognitivism', denies that we manipulate 'mental entities that have the remarkable capacity to be "about" external things'. To Johnson, the closest things we have to mental representations are:

1. Patterns of sensorimotor neural activation … [which are] recurring patterns of neural activation with … structural features of the organism's environment …
2. Conceptual structures … not abstract, internal entities, [but] selective discriminations from the ongoing, continuous flow of our experience …
3. External structures of symbolic interaction [such as] linguistic signs and symbols …
4. Theoretical models [that] help us explain natural and human phenomena.
   (Johnson 2007, 134)

Johnson argues that there is no mind's eye in the sense of a theatre of symbol generation and manipulation that is instantiated wholly in the 'internal' mind. He cautions against turning from 'speaking of a "representation in the brain" … to speaking of a "representation in the mind"'. The former is a tenable way of talking about physical structure in the body, while the latter 'comes loaded with dualistic metaphysical and epistemological baggage that it ultimately cannot carry' (146). Churchland, likewise, asserts that the brain functions – that, in fact, the function of the brain is – to take 'a picture' of the landscape or configuration of the abstract universals, the temporal invariants, and the enduring symmetries that structure the objective universe of its experience ... [This produces maps that] constitute the 'conceptual frameworks' so familiar to the philosophical tradition, and so vital to any creature's comprehension of the world in which it lives ... However ... these frameworks are not families of predicate-like elements.

(Churchland 2012, vi–viii)

Both Churchland and Johnson allow for varieties of representational relationships (including indexical, i.e., causally related ones in a physical sense) between the brain and the 'external' world, but both are opposed to what Bordwell calls a 'kind of propositional syntax that underlies inference-making' (Bordwell 1989, 23). Although Bordwell's discussion largely favours just this kind of symbolic/propositional understanding of cognitive processes, the tent he erects is big enough to accommodate ideas from both Johnson and Churchland. This cognitivist tent has a large frame; it allows for any number of ways of describing cognition, excluding only theories that ignore or deny the central role of cognitive activity in film spectatorship.

Bordwell concludes by stressing the 'general unity of this perspective and its various levels and directions of inquiry', while acknowledging that he has 'played down many differences and disputes' and 'neglected significant critiques' (32–3). The task of the essay is not to design an airtight research paradigm for cognitive film theory, but rather to articulate a set of values largely common to the various kinds of cognitive theories so as to point towards the possibilities for cognitive film theory. In particular, it values certain kinds of observation and evidence – and, for that matter, it is distinguished from much critical theory by valuing empirical evidence from films. Bordwell's goal is to propose ways of looking at the mind, in the context of the environment, that facilitate new ways of looking at film in the context of the mind.

## Cinema's causal power

The philosopher and cognitive theorist Noël Carroll (1996) is interested in the ability of Hollywood-style filmmaking to provoke the 'widespread engagement and intense engagement' of audiences (80). Carroll diverges, as does Bordwell, from the 'illusionist medium' approach common to much contemporary theory, favouring instead a close examination of cinematic form. The power he finds in movies is not derived from an illusion of reality or any kind of deception of the audience, but rather lies in the ways spectatorial faculties are engaged and stimulated by film form. In short, this power is about what film does, rather than about an essentialist notion of what it *is*, e.g. an illusion.

Carroll opens the essay with an account of the history of the film-as-realism argument, recounting first André Bazin's metaphysical take on the essential reality of the cinematic image and then the claims of some contemporary theorists that film has no literal connection to reality but rather produces an illusory 'reality effect'. This preoccupation with realism across theoretical paradigms, Carroll argues, is ultimately tied up with a desire to explain the power of the medium, particularly in the popular and commercial spheres. How, he asks, did the moving picture become 'the dominant art form of the twentieth century?' (78). Carroll thus roots his essay in an historical debate and in a tradition of scholarship while simultaneously revising the terms of the discussion. Realism is reframed as power, but as a power to stimulate the mind rather than as a power to deceive it.

Carroll finds that this power stems from three principal capacities of Hollywood-style film: pictorial representation, variable framing, and erotetic narrative. Each of these capacities addresses 'the cognitive faculties of the audience' (92). Pictorial recognition results from encountering

> a very special kind of symbol … Psychological evidence strongly supports the contention that we learn to recognize what a picture stands for as soon as we have become able to recognize the objects, or kinds of objects, that serve as the models for that picture.
>
> (Carroll 1996, 80)

Recognizing a picture of a thing is not the same as recognizing the thing itself, as Bazin might have said, but the tasks are so bound up in one another as to be inseparable. In this, pictorial media differ from other media, such as the written word, which do not enjoy the instant recognizability that the image has, even in somewhat ideographic languages (81–3). Likewise, movies 'are easier to follow than plays', writes Carroll (84), due largely to film's variable framing, or its ability to 'scale', 'bracket', and 'index' the attention of the viewer. Carroll returns here to some basic psychological distinctions established by Hugo Münsterberg and Rudolf Arnheim in early theory, as well as to their methodological device of thinking about film form by opposing it to one of its predecessors, theatrical form (*see* ATTENTION; MEMORY AND FILM; ART, FILM AS).

Erotetic narrative is narrative based on an ongoing series of questions being posed and answered from one shot, scene, sequence, or act of the film to the next. Later scenes in erotetic narratives 'answer' questions posed in earlier scenes, or they provide material for formulating possible answers to questions prompted or suggested earlier, so that

> the narrative structure is … fundamentally a system of internally generated questions that the movie goes on to answer … [The key scenes] either raise questions or answer them, or perform related functions including sustaining questions already raised, or incompletely answering a previous question, or answering one question but then introducing a new one.
>
> (Carroll 1996, 89)

Movies thus unfold in constant dialogue with the minds of their viewers, who recognize their pictures, are guided by their framings and camera movements, and who ask questions and assess answers as prompted by the unfolding of the film.

Carroll writes (92) that, by focusing on the relationships between films and such cognitive capacities,

> we will be in the best position to find the features of movies that account for their phenomenally widespread effectiveness; since cognitive capacities, at the level discussed, seem the most plausible candidate for what mass-movie audiences have in common … [If] we can suggest the ways in which movies are designed to engage and excite cognitive and perceptual structures, we will have our best initial approximation of their generic power.

'Phenomenally' is used here to mean 'impressively' or 'overwhelmingly', but it might as well mean 'sensorially'. When Gerald Edelman (2004) refers to the 'phenomenal gift of consciousness', he specifies that he means both the significance of the human 'gift' of being conscious and the phenomenal character of consciousness itself. Film's address and stimulation of the cognitive faculties are likewise phenomenal both in the sense of creating the cultural phenomenon of Hollywood's global dominance and in the sense of creating a widespread experience of sensory stimulation and thereby contributing, in near-identical ways, to countless spectators' conscious phenomenal states and preconscious and conscious cognitive processes.

## Structures and frames

Bordwell looks at structures of the mind, establishing a frame of reference for what film might do, while Carroll looks at structures of film, extrapolating towards what the mind might do. Carroll restricts himself to a particular kind of film; Bordwell restricts himself to a particular kind of model of the mind. Within these constraints, Bordwell and Carroll arrive at seemingly complementary conclusions, initiating a line of theoretical inquiry that remains robust and productive decades later. Plantinga (2002) offers a concise summary and discussion of cognitivist film scholarship up to that point, describing the cognitive approach as a general set of 'tendencies' drawing on 'hybrid [methodologies]' and united by a commitment to 'clarity of exposition and argument and to the relevance of empirical evidence and the standards of science (where appropriate)' (20–1). The continued development and diversification of the cognitivist approach in the decade since Plantinga's essay are a testament to the importance of discovering 'things along the way' (Bordwell 1989, 33) or of establishing frames of reference with the expectation that we will never stop refining and repositioning them.

In 'thinking about important and intriguing models' (33), in assuming that 'empirical science may help solve traditional philosophical problems' (15), and in suggesting that we study cinema partly in terms of the 'mental representations ... in the mind's eye' (27), Bordwell's cognitivism seems to suggest not only that the mind responds to the erotetic narratives, the variable framing, and the sensuous representation of cinema, as Carroll argues, but also that the mind is itself somewhat like – or is at least profoundly resonant with – the cinema of Carroll's model. This is an old comparison being made on new, and sturdier, ground. The 'power of movies' may thus be neither a power over minds, nor an undermining of minds' own power, but rather a power *with*, and dependent upon, minds. It is a power expressed not through illusion nor through symbolic abstraction, but through material interaction, through intimate collaboration.

DANIEL REYNOLDS

## Works cited

Bordwell, David. 1989. 'A Case for Cognitivism'. *Iris* 9: 11–40.
Carroll, Noël. 1996. 'The Power of Movies'. In *Theorizing the Moving Image*, 78–93. Cambridge: Cambridge University Press.
Churchland, Paul. 2012. *Plato's Camera*. Cambridge, MA: MIT Press.
Edelman, Gerald. 2004. *Wider Than the Sky*. New Haven, CT: Yale University Press.
Heath, Stephen. 1976. 'Narrative Space'. *Screen* 17 (3): 68–112.

Johnson, Mark. 2007. *The Meaning of the Body*. Chicago, IL: University of Chicago Press.

Plantinga, Carl. 2002. 'Cognitive Film Theory: An Insider's Appraisal'. *Cinémas* 12 (2): 15–37.

## Further reading

Anderson, Joseph D. 1996. *The Reality of Illusion: An Ecological Approach to Cognitive Film Theory*. Carbondale: Southern Illinois University Press.

Bordwell, David. 1990. 'A Case for Cognitivism: Further Reflections'. *Iris* 11: 107–12.

Dudai, Yadin. 2008. 'Enslaving Central Executives: Toward a Brain Theory of Cinema'. *Projections* 2 (2): 21–42.

Gombrich, E.H. 2000. *Art and Illusion*. Princeton, NJ: Princeton University Press.

Grodal, Torben. 2009. *Embodied Visions: Evolution, Emotion, Culture, and Film*. Oxford: Oxford University Press.

Vescio, Bryan. 2001. 'Reading in the Dark: Cognitivism, Film Theory, and Radical Interpretation'. *Style* 35 (4): 572–91.

# CONCEPT

Film theory is to be distinguished from the practice of criticism and historical research insofar as it concerns itself with the creation of concepts. The concept informs both interpretive work and historical research, but it is in no sense identical to those practices. Before defining the concept directly, however, I would like to give an example of how the concept – as that which emerges in the work of film theory – might contribute to the practice of interpretation. Doing so will enable us consider more clearly the relation of a concept to any given film, even if it means making use of a concept before we properly understand what a concept is. What such a distinction will allow us to overcome, for instance, is the translation of a concept into what David Bordwell rather notoriously described as a 'semantic field', which he defines as a conceptual structure that 'organizes potential meanings in relation to one another' (Bordwell 1989, 107). In particular, what Bordwell worried over, it seems, in a book that played no small role in the denigration of theory in the decade that followed its release, was the use of a concept derived externally from the film in order to organize the signs generated *by any given film* strictly – if not identically – in the likeness of the signs implied by the concept itself, and irrespective of whatever else it is that the film shows. But as we will see, a concept can never truly function in this way; it never operates as a heuristic device, since the only thing that theory demands of, or evokes in, the work of art is a necessarily partial and mutually informing relation. That relation, it will be shown, is better described in terms of friendship and interference rather than dominance, containment, or identity (however mistaken that identity is said to be).

## Interpretation: *Panic Room*

Let us begin, then, with an interpretation of David Fincher's *Panic Room* (2002) that makes use of the concept of the index, especially as it has come to be understood in light of André Bazin's 'Ontology of the Photographic Image': as an image that features the object that stood before the camera in a relation of counterfactual dependence (*see* ONTOLOGY OF THE PHOTOGRAPHIC IMAGE). If the image is in a relation of counterfactual dependence to the object it features, then the absence of the image of that object would stem from an absence of that object before a camera. In other words, the existence of the image attests to the reality of the object, which is itself necessary to the production of the image itself. What Fincher's film shows us is how, in a surveillance society such as ours, it is no longer only the surface of the world that stands before us in a state of absolute exposure; rather, the electronic eye now has the capacity to see through durable material forms, forever eroding a distinction between inside and outside, which is understood in related terms as both a question of privacy and also as the defining distinction of the theretofore inalienable sub-ject: if I no longer have an 'inside' (private, distinct), then there will be no more 'me'. To make this claim, I point to a long, uninterrupted travelling shot that not only spans the home of the family under siege but is also seen to pass directly through unbroken walls and the seemingly solid mass of an ordinary chair – a moment, that is to say, when the indexical character of the image comes into question. The virtuosity of Fincher's camera movement attracts our fascination – it *secures* our attention – precisely for the ways in which we are asked to consider the material difficulties of moving a camera up, down, and across space despite the risks of running into every manner of material obstacle along the way. Such a reading depends on the belief that what the image shows was caused by the material pre-sence of what appears in the image and, hence, before a camera. The successful take is one in which the human negotiates the precarious surface of space through care and dexterity, which is an important expression of our ability to manage a mutual relation between technology and world that depends entirely on our own thoughtfulness. The camera is assumed to be an index of the human that moves as it records, in equally indexical terms, what stands before it. In the absence of an obviously animated image – which would be better understood as an iconic rather than as an indexical sign – we have no reason to believe that the space we see in the image was not in fact materially present before a camera. The risk of failure thus feels palpable to us at every turn. Until, that is, we witness the camera move through the unbroken wood of a chair in one uninterrupted movement. At this moment, we begin to doubt the indexical character of the image even though the spatial coordinates of the image otherwise compel us to believe that the objects in the image are also what *caused* the image. Our doubts likely extend to the human we imagine to be moving the camera in a cooperative and careful relation with technology. Citing this moment in which I now have to understand an animated, digitally produced image as one that merely *appears* indexical – understood as an expression of a counterfactual dependence between a really existing object and its appearance on film – I will go on to argue that the camera can do more than merely expose the surface of the world: it is now capable of penetrating the theretofore resistant material surface of the world itself. And it does so as an expression of technology that has overcome the limits of both matter and the human – what might once have been indexed in a cooperative relationship by the film.

My reading of camera movement, here, is motivated by a concept that comes into contact with a literal content – this film which tells a story about surveillance in the home – which then yields a figurative content, which I take to be a philosophical claim about privacy (also a concept) and the human subject that is not identical to the concept of the index; it is merely related to it. My idea, which is also a concept, overlaps – but does not replicate – the concept of the index. In this sense, we can say that the film is itself involved in the articulation of a concept, even if it also does more than that.

## What is a concept?

We need, then, to ask two related questions. First, what is a concept? And second, how will we describe the relation of a concept to film if it is not identical to what the film does in its entirety? A related concern will bring us to a third question, still; namely, to what extent does any instance of film merely serve as an illustration of someone else's concept? In what way do concepts refer to one another? These questions should help us to clarify the kind of work that any theory of film does, or can be expected to do.

In answer to the first question, consider Martin Heidegger's definition of the concept in his lectures on 'Basic Concepts'. If a concept is 'basic', then, as Heidegger there argues, it is the ground of something (Heidegger 1998). If it is the ground of something, it will be tempting to think of the concept as something that can be either true or false, as that which provides access to the understanding, which would be nothing less than the ordering of all possible phenomena in accordance with a metaphysical essence. It is tempting to do so precisely because we typically regard 'ground' as something firm, something foundational – which is to say, unshakeable in its truth. We should, however, resist that temptation. With this complication in mind, Heidegger defined concepts as 'representations in which we bring before ourselves an object or entire regions of objects in general' (1998, 1). A concept is representational because what it stands in for, in nearly every case, is something that cannot otherwise be seen, or at least something that has yet to be seen *as such*, even if the things (people, objects, and ideas) that now appear gathered before us have always been potentially seeable or recordable by a camera. One takes recourse to concepts and the practice of concept formation when the order of the visible appears to us by rote, such that we barely notice it, or else in cases where the relations or objects are either too large or too small to be detected without some form of representational act of imagining. And as Heidegger points out, this newly imagined object or relationship between objects is something that has to be understood as generalizable.

Perhaps the most difficult aspect of understanding the nature of what a concept is involves making sense of how a concept is something that is both singular and general; singular, insofar as it is decidedly different from other concepts – other possible relations that may very well involve some partial aspect of any other concept – and general, since it must also describe something that can contain more than one instance. Or as Gilles Deleuze and Felix Guattari suggest, a concept is both absolute *and* relative: 'As whole it [the concept] is absolute, but insofar as it is fragmentary it is relative' (Deleuze and Guattari 1994, 21). In other words, a concept is complete in itself and generalizable, but only in relation to what that concept describes. What the concept describes or effects is never a totality that admits of no rival, or friend, insofar as friend merely comes to describe a relation of commonality rather than identity. What I share with my friend is a series of things in common, but never all things.

The concept of the index provides a very useful example of the seemingly paradoxical character of the structure of a concept. If we understand the index in contrast to Bazin and in a manner closer to the way it was formulated by Charles Sanders Peirce, as a deictic shifter – that is, as a manner of pointing, which is indicated in linguistic terms by words such as 'here', 'there', or 'that' – then what is singular, in each case of indexical representation, is whatever is indicated by the shifter. If I say 'there' and point to Lake Michigan, that lake – Lake Michigan – is what remains singular because infinitely interchangeable. I can also say 'there' and refer, this time, to Lake Ontario. The same would be true of the concept of the index for film – the camera, only slightly more literally, points to an object, which is what the camera shows us, having been pointed at something, which can also be said to leave its trace on film in a relation of counterfactual dependence. The index is what happens every time, but what it shows will always involve some difference and will include things that bear no important relation to the concept. This is true even if what is indexed in both instances can be related to each other in different terms – here, as two lakes. It is the trope of pointing that remains, not the object indicated in any instance. That a piece of furniture in *Panic Room* might make reference – by virtue of its style, age, and national origin – to another historical period with which the film might be said to be engaging in allegorical terms nevertheless contributes nothing in particular towards the satisfaction of the basic conditions of the concept of the index. Put otherwise, a concept never explains or describes everything that is visible in the image at the same time. Thus, if I rely on the concept of the index to elaborate my response to *Panic Room*, i.e. by creating a new concept of the image as something that can now see 'inside' of things, then I am not concerned to account for every possible signifier or logic that the film can also be said to contain.

For this reason, we must insist that a concept is a restrictive form, insofar as it does not intend to explain all of the film, and despite the fact that it is also constitutive of visibility; that is, it is what makes *seeing in this way* possible, even as we can still see in other ways. This is why the representational dimension of the concept has been a source of consternation among film theorists and produced at least two problems. The first concerns the moment in which the concept is conflated with the category; the second problem follows from this and has to do with the ways in which 'representation' describes a mental, rather than an apparent, perceivable form. As an example of the first problem, consider the concept of *film noir* as Paul Schrader articulated it in his 1971 essay 'Notes on Film Noir' (reprinted in Schrader 1990). There, Schrader isolates seven stylistic criteria of film noir – a list of stylistic elements that characterize a film as an instance of film noir. The seven 'necessary' elements include: scenes lit for night, a marked preference for oblique and vertical lines over horizontal ones, actors and settings lit in a non-hierarchical manner, compositional tension over and above physical conflict, a near 'Freudian attachment to water, romantic narration, and a complex chronology' (Schrader 1990, 84–5). As genre theorists have long been aware, the appearance of all seven of these elements might be a sufficient condition for membership of the category of *film noir*, but those conditions can never constitute a totality, lest we assume, counter-intuitively, that each film that meets those criteria is identical to every other instance. 'Category' is to be understood as what comes by way of the many instances that come to visibility through the concept and are collected as general, but only when general is an absolute expression of identity; when every instance – when every film – is gathered under a category expressly as one that is, paradoxically, the same as every other.

This is where the genre theorist typically protests. A film may very well meet these seven criteria, but in all likelihood the film will also do many other things. For instance, one could easily identify these seven aspects of style in Raoul Walsh's *Pursued* (1947), but we might also find it difficult to not notice that it also bears the iconography of the western. Thus, if we want to say that *Pursued* is a *film noir*, and only a *film noir*, then we will be guided by a weak understanding of the concept as that which collects instances in a relation of absolute identity rather than in a relation of mere resemblance or shared partiality. A category proceeds on the basis of an identical relation. There would otherwise be no need of something called 'categorical distinction', which implies absolute difference as a condition of belonging. By contrast, a concept remains singular even as it accumulates instances for the sake of generalization. If the concept allows us to collect instances and to see something on the basis of a shared partiality, then my concept cannot exhaust the work that nevertheless confirms that concept's viability.

## The risk of Idealism

The only way for us to understand the concept as a form of representation that allows us to see what we see, in entirety – in a relation of absolute identity – is if we regard representation as something strictly mental. In the various expressions of Idealism in the history of philosophy, from Plato through Kant and on through film theory, the concept is a mental image that constitutes the visibility of objects and the world. Within an Idealist framework, epistemology and ontology, thought and being, are thus correlated. What we know and what we see are inseparable from who we are and from what *is*, in total. If thinking and being are correlated, then we will not be able to see, think, or be in a way that does not relate to the concept, or image, that makes seeing possible to begin with. In an Idealist tradition, the realm of the visible is decided, in total, by the concept.

One potential – but in no sense confirmed – example of an Idealist understanding of the concept can be found in Gilles Deleuze's *Cinema 1* (*see* MOVEMENT-IMAGE), most notably around the concept of 'liquid perception'. For Deleuze, liquid perception comes to describe the movement from subjectivity to objectivity, as introduced by the philosopher Henri Bergson, and does so by way of images of water that come to broker a particular relation between subjectivity and objectivity. Deleuze characterizes Bergson's distinction this way: '*a subjective perception is one in which the images vary in relation to a central and privileged image; an objective perception is one where, as in things, all the images vary in relation to one another, on all their facets and in all their parts*' (Deleuze 1986, 76; emphasis in the original). While Bergson's conception of subjective perception depends on a central and privileged image that is in no sense metaphysically determined – indeed, it owes its existence strictly to the movement of the body in time as a mode of accumulative recognition – Deleuze's invocation of the image and metaphor of 'liquid', as a way of characterizing the essence of perception, allows the concept to function just as any mental representation would; that is, as an image that makes the visible forms in the phenomenal world appear in and as a result of our perception. The mental image described by Deleuze gives way to a material fact. The image of water is the 'perfect environment in which movement can be abstracted from the thing moved, or mobility from movement itself' (1986, 77). Perception is like water since it moves with what it moves and also without what it moves. For Deleuze, water is a redistributive force, insofar as it rearranges objects in motion, just as any fresh perceptual act will likewise gather objects in a new relation of visibility. Seen thus, Deleuze unsurprisingly turns to films that feature aquatic themes and images of river, sea, and the people and objects that get pushed around in and by water. Thus, what the film *shows* is to be understood as evidence of what the mind *does*. It is a phenomenal portrait of the mental image that makes seeing, in a redistributive fashion, possible. It is a visible image of what is said to contribute to the overcoming of subjectivity by objectivity, which moves us from successive views of the same object to an objective field constituted by the simultaneous presentation of every object that was previously seen only in terms of relations of succession or superimposition. Regard Deleuze's reading of the ending of Jean Vigo's *L'Atalante*:

> If there is any reconciliation between land and sea, this takes place in the father Jules, but only because he knows how to impose spontaneously on the land the same law as the sea: his cabin contains the most extraordinary fetishes, partial objects, souvenirs and scrap; however, he does not make them a memory, but a pure mosaic of present states, down to the old record which works again.
>
> (Deleuze 1986, 78)

If the souvenirs were understood in terms of memory, they would be related to subjectivity – to a series of different images of the same thing, which would remain visible to us, potentially, but only in superimposition or some other means of subjective depiction – strategies that one finds throughout the beginning of Vigo's film. The image of water, which gives rise to the concept of liquid perception and is featured throughout *L'Atalante*, comes instead to describe the shift from subjectivity to objectivity, where the numerous objects of subjective reflection are re-ordered in an ever-present unfolding of a relation of simultaneity rather than subjective succession, hence the 'pure mosaic of present states'. Thought, in other words, gives way to world and does so by way of an image on film that is said to correlate directly to an image *in* and *of* the mind.

The risk that follows from Deleuze's concept stems from his understanding of representation as a mental image; representation not as an instance of standing for something – which is what allows concepts to retain their singularity even as they point to something more general – but as that which is constitutive of the act of seeing itself. For this reason, it is important to retain the image merely as a representation in its more properly pictorial sense, as that which stands for something that cannot otherwise be seen, rather than as that which makes seeing possible. If we understand representation in strictly mental terms, then we will only ever be able to describe, in metaphysical terms, the entire field of the visible. An especially unhelpful and often unintentional by-product of a metaphysical conception of representation – of the generation of the concept itself – involves the application of the contained aspects of 'liquid perception', or its like, to images of water wherever they appear in an exegetical fashion – where the work of the theorist as disciple is reduced to the accumulation and repetition of identical cases where the creation of concepts ought to involve innovation, partiality, and above all else the establishment of difference within continuity or generality. The trouble with such instances of undifferentiated application is that the examples – continually repeated as same – come to mimic the metaphysical potential of pictorial representations of mental representations insofar as they accumulate and spread identical cases that could never really be so.

## Theory as interference

However, if we understand the concept as a mode of representation that implies a relation of *standing for*, then we will be more capable of seeing what remains singular and thus also outside of any given concept. In this respect, if we merely take note of the way that related iterations of the same concepts are described in surveys of film theory – such as we find in Andrew (1984) and Casetti (1999) – we can see that concepts can only be described in terms of likeness rather than identity, as that which exists in a relation that depends on difference just as much as it does on similarity. Otherwise, concepts would never be 'testable' against each other, including the concepts put forward by a filmmaker in a film. The concept thus preserves its partial character, which is crucial if we are going to understand a concept as a contingent articulation of a partial realm of the visible rather than as a necessary – or metaphysically determined – concept of visibility, *tout court*. This is ultimately the way that Deleuze himself understood the concept, even if his own concepts flirt rather strenuously with a sense of metaphysical determination. At the end of *Cinema 2*, Deleuze concludes that

> philosophical theory is itself a practice, just as much as its object. It is no more abstract than its object. It is a practice of concepts, and it must be judged in the

light of the other practices with which it interferes. A theory of cinema is not 'about' cinema, but about the concepts that cinema gives rise to and which are themselves related to other concepts corresponding to other practices, the practice of concepts in general having no privilege over others, any more.

(Deleuze 1989, 280)

If a concept interferes with other concepts, then the relation between film and theory, as Deleuze suggests, has to be understood in terms of equality not identity. Rather, both theory (as a practice of writing) and film (as relation of image and sound) interfere with one another. If one concept interferes with another, then what it prevents is a relation of absolute identity between the concept of the film and the concept of film theory. Interference, moreover, is not the same as refutation or negation. If the concept of a film and the concept of film theory – or two related concepts of film theory – interfere with one another, they do so because they share something in common, just not everything in common – which is what prevents the concept from 'working', which here implies accumulating as same and mimicking a mental and metaphysical function of representation.

My interpretation of *Panic Room* proceeds on the basis of a concept that the film also shares in a partial way, insofar as its own discourse about the digital passes through a concept of the index. My own concept, which is a result of interpretive work that I have done with the concept of the index and then with what Fincher adds as a discourse of the digital, can also be said to interfere with the concept or concepts that animate that film. After all, what I am arguing for there is an idea of how the camera, in allowing us to now see in and through things, comes to express technology's 'successful' eradication of the human, which is marked by the instability of the index. Call my concept 'the digital inside'. Of course, the idea represented by this particular relation between people and objects cannot reasonably stand as a total interpretation of the work, even though it is interpretive work that brought me to my concept – with, above, and in partial respect to what the film shows. If we expect a film theoretical concept to meet, in a relation of absolute correspondence, all of the signs at work in a film, then what we are involved in is neither theory nor interpretation, but an act of fundamentalism, which refuses difference in any relation of continuity.

BRIAN PRICE

## Works cited

Andrew, Dudley. 1984. *Concepts in Film Theory*. New York: Oxford University Press.

Bordwell, David. 1989. *Making Meaning: Inference and Rhetoric in the Interpretation of Cinema*. Cambridge, MA: Harvard University Press.

Casetti, Francesco. 1999. *Theories of Cinema, 1945–1995*. Translated by Francesca Chiostri and Elizabeth Gard Bartolini-Salimbeni, with Thomas Kelso. Austin: University of Texas Press.

Deleuze, Gilles. 1986. *Cinema 1: The Movement-Image*. Translated by Hugh Tomlinson and Barbara Hammerjam. Minneapolis: University of Minnesota Press.

——. 1989. *Cinema 2: The Time-Image*. Translated by Hugh Tomlinson and Robert Galeta. Minneapolis: University of Minnesota Press.

Deleuze, Gilles, and Félix Guattari. 1994. *What Is Philosophy?* Translated by Hugh Tomlinson and Graham Burchell. New York: Columbia University Press.

Heidegger, Martin. 1998. *Basic Concepts*. Translated by Gary E. Aylesworth. Bloomington: Indiana University Press.

Schrader, Paul. 1990. *Schrader on Schrader & Other Writings*. Edited by Kevin Jackson. London: Faber and Faber.

## Further reading

Adorno, Theodor. 1973. *Negative Dialectics*. Translated by E.B. Ashton. London and New York: Routledge.

Brinkema, Eugenie. 2007. 'e.g., Dogtooth'. *World Picture* 7 (Autumn): http://www.worldpicture-journal.com/WP_7/Brinkema.html.

Kant, Immanuel. 1999. *The Critique of Pure Reason*. Edited and translated by Paul Guyer. Cambridge: Cambridge University Press.

Zarzosa, Agustin. 2012. 'The Case and Its Modes: Instance, Allusion, Example, Illustration, and Exception'. *Angelaki* 17 (1) (March): 41–55.

# CONTEMPORARY FILM THEORY

Contemporary film theorists of the 1970s, such as Stephen Heath, Colin MacCabe, Jean-Louis Baudry, and Christian Metz, applied semiotics, psychoanalysis, and Marxism to the study of film. With these theories they uncovered how mainstream Western cinema contributes to capitalist exploitation. Contemporary film theorists also opposed mainstream cinema by promoting politically militant avant-garde filmmaking.

Stephen Heath's essay 'On Screen, in Frame: Film and Ideology' (1976) is a manifesto for contemporary film theory – it outlines in abstract theoretical terms how to uncover capitalist values in mainstream cinema, and spells out what a political avant-garde film should achieve. Heath carried out his agenda by analysing ideology. The following summary explores the agenda of contemporary film theory through Heath's important but difficult essay.

## Ideology

In the nineteenth century, Marx and Engels (*The German Ideology* [1970]) defined ideology as a process that conceals the contradictions inherent in capitalism. Capitalism exploits and alienates the working class, and the purpose of ideology is to conceal that process of exploitation. Marx and Engels therefore defined ideology negatively, as mistaken ideas that distort thought, leading to false consciousness. In the twentieth century, Gramsci and Lenin developed a positive theory, which defines ideology as necessary because it forms an individual's consciousness. Yet, this positive definition downplays ideology's function: to conceal the contradictions of capitalism from individuals.

Louis Althusser combined the two theories by developing a positive theory (of ideology in general) plus a negative theory (of particular ideologies). Althusser's most famous formulations – 'Ideology represents the imaginary relationship of individuals to their real conditions of existence' (1971, 162) and 'Ideology interpellates individuals as subjects' (1971, 170) – support the negative definition of ideology. The first quotation sets up an opposition between the 'imaginary' and the 'real'. It suggests the real exists outside the imaginary, that the imaginary is false, distorted thought. The second quotation indicates that individuals exist before and outside of ideology. Ideology therefore works to impose a distorted form of subjectivity on them – a distorted sense of self, a false self-image.

But Althusser also argued that the imaginary relation is constant, or universal; we cannot escape it: 'ideology is eternal' (1971, 175). This means we always adopt an ideological subject position. In Althusser's terms, 'individuals are always-already subjects' (1971, 176). This positive sense of imaginary derives from the psychoanalyst Jacques Lacan (1977, chapter 1). For Lacan, our access to reality is always mediated through the imaginary. The imaginary is constant because it forms the basis of our relation to the world: as soon as we wake, we always and only see the world from our own perspective.

In summary, ideology in Althusser's formulation is both enabling (positive) and limiting (negative): it enables individuals to function in society, but it also prescribes how they should act and think. For Althusser, the only escape from the imaginary and ideology, and from our own perspective, is through science, or what he calls theoretical practice.

## Stephen Heath's 'On Screen, in Frame'

Heath and other contemporary film theorists used Althusser to identify film as a particular practice of ideology, and therefore discuss it from a negative perspective. This means they used theory to expose mainstream cinema's process of ideological concealment. Heath examined the way cinema's own ideology, the impression of reality, is produced. For him, the crucial issue is the way ideology in the cinema affects the consciousness or subjectivity of the individual. Heath and other contemporary film theorists preferred to talk about the way ideology in the cinema affects 'the subject'.

We can now identify the problems Heath addresses: his essay examines 'the articulation of film and ideology on the figure of the subject' (Heath 1976, 261). This is the clearest statement of Heath's agenda, the way film and ideology work together to conceal contradictions from the film spectator's consciousness. This process of concealment creates an illusion of unity in the subject's consciousness, a unified subject position. For Heath, the purpose of a political avant-garde cinema must be to challenge the illusion of a coherent subjectivity that ideology sets up. Avant-garde cinema aims to dissolve ideology and its coherent subject effects.

As its title indicates, Heath's essay privileges the screen and frame. The screen is only discussed briefly. It is the support of the image: 'The screen is the projection of the film frame which it holds and grounds' (258). Heath then devotes three pages to the frame, gradually transforming it from an intuitive to a theoretical concept. He lists the various meanings of the term 'frame' in film studies, and compares the film frame to painting's frame, and to theatre. He initially discovers four fairly conventional meanings: (i) physically, the frame is a single transparent photograph printed on the strip of film; (ii) it also names the boundary of the photographic image projected onto the screen; (iii) the term is also used to talk about the passage of the film through the projector (the image is in or out of frame, just as it is in or out of focus); (iv) it additionally refers to the activity of filming, of framing a scene (it names the camera's viewpoint) (258). But towards the end of his discussion of the frame, he adds more theoretical definitions: (v) 'frame, framing, is the very basis of disposition – German *Einstellung*: adjustment, centring, framing, moral attitude, the correct position' (260). He also links up the frame to the rhetorical figure of metaphor: (vi) 'the frame itself is the constant metaphor' (260). Metaphor involves the transfer of meaning from one object to another. For Heath, the frame transfers the spectator's vision from the film theatre to the film's fictional world, or diegesis.

The fiction film creates a representation – the film's diegesis, an alternative fictional world, an imaginary scene. The camera's frame (at the time of filming) and the frame projected on screen at the cinema both function simultaneously to position the spectator at the correct distance in front of that diegesis. But, for Heath, this alignment of spectator and fictional world involves more framing: (vii) 'Analysis … must trace the windowing identity of subject and camera, the setting of the gaze to accompany the play of "point of view" between characters in the diegetic space of the film (always the drama of the eye) which organizes the images in the coherence of the fiction' (260). In other words, some camera framings are aligned to the characters' point of view in the fictional world. No longer is diegesis as a whole simply being framed, but, inside that diegesis, certain frames represent the look of characters. These point-of-view framings located inside the diegesis help to centre the spectator's eye within that diegesis. As an aside, we can note that Heath's metaphor of 'window' ('the windowing identity of subject and camera') is useful in discussing ideology, for the window offers a 'perspective' that one is not really aware of (it is transparent, invisible). Ideology works in the same way, for it also offers a 'perspective' that is not easy to change. Both window and ideology orientate individuals onto a scene, giving them the impression that their perspective on that scene is natural and inevitable.

Heath introduces one final meaning of frame – (viii) as narrative: 'Narrative, that is, may be seen as a decisive instance of framing in film' (261). A narrative is like a frame in that it 'contains' an embedded moral (ideological) lesson involving a character seeking a goal and overcoming obstacles. Both narrative and frame therefore contain the subject in relation to the film's diegesis.

Two other concepts Heath develops in his essay include: the semiotic concept of film as a specific signifying practice, and the psychoanalytic concept of suture. To define film as a signifying practice means that it does not simply represent and replicate pre-existent meanings; it is a practice or process that manufactures or produces meanings. Practice is a mediator between individuals and the material world; it is a process that guides humans in transforming matter into products. Marxism identifies three forms of practice: economic, political, and ideological. Economic practice produces, from raw materials, machinery, and a workforce, the material conditions of subsistence. Political practice produces and organizes social relations between different social groups. In capitalism, political practice produces the antagonistic relation between the middle class and the working class. Ideological practice is a practice of representation that produces a subjectivity for individuals. Ideological practices therefore manufacture subject positions, which play an active, determining role in the successful functioning of ideology. These subject positions, in turn, ensure that individuals play their role in reproducing economic and political practices.

Suture is crucial to Heath, because it names the subject's relation to film and ideology. The manufacture of subject positions is not a one-time, static process. The subject position is not complete, but is an ongoing process. It is this ongoing process of positioning that Heath calls suture (*see* SUTURE).

In summary, Heath's essay emerges from a real problem at the core of Marxism – exposing the role of ideology in concealing the contradictions of capitalism – and from the need to develop a political avant-garde practice that challenges ideology.

## Criticisms of contemporary film theory

Within the specific context of film theory in the 1970s, Heath's essay is well-formed, significant, and innovative in the way it deploys the semiotic concept of a specific signifying practice, the Marxist concept of ideology, plus the psychoanalytic concepts of the imaginary and suture to analyse 'the articulation of film and ideology on the figure of the subject' (Heath 1976 261).

Heath's agenda has been criticized from different theoretical perspectives. D.N. Rodowick, in many respects sympathetic to Heath's political agenda, finds his theory too formalist: 'To the extent that the destiny of the subject is decided "in the text" it can be none other than a formal problem' (Rodowick 1988, 208). In other words, the problem Heath identifies and his solution are worked out only in terms of an aesthetic text (the unity/disunity of a formal subject position), not in terms of political practices. The text, whether mainstream or avant-garde, is conceived as the sole factor in the determination of the film spectator's consciousness. This is a problem with the scope of Heath's theory. The beginnings of theory building necessarily involve the simplification of the problems in order to make them manageable. But the progress of a theory is dependent on its ability to expand and take account of new phenomena. What we witness in 'On Screen, in Frame' is an *initial* attempt to theorize subject positioning from the perspectives of semiotics, Marxism, and psychoanalysis. This is where the value of Heath's essay lies in the history of film theory. Once we move beyond the essay's immediate time frame, we can perceive (as Rodowick does) its limitations, including its formalism.

A more fundamental critique emerged from cognitive film theory in the 1980s. Cognitive film theorists such as David Bordwell (1985) rejected the reliability of Heath's theoretical statements. The Marxist agenda of exposing the role of ideology in concealing contradictions, and the need to develop a revolutionary practice, are not Bordwell's concern. The problems Bordwell addresses lie elsewhere. For cognitivists, consciousness is not a mere superstructure on top of a hidden, repressed unconscious. Instead, it is the basis of identity. Bordwell therefore argues that film theorists should begin with cognitive explanations of film phenomena, and should move on to psychoanalytic explanations only if the cognitive account is found wanting: 'The theory I advance attends to the perceptual and cognitive aspects of film viewing. While I do not deny the usefulness of psychoanalytic approaches to the spectator, I see no reason to claim for the unconscious any activities which can be explained on other grounds' (1985, 30). In analysing the way spectators comprehend films, Bordwell argues that they do not passively take up a subject position and absorb the film's finalized, pre-constituted meaning; instead, films (even classical narrative films) are fragmentary, and spectators are actively involved in constructing their meaning. At the same time, he argues that spectators are not free agents who can construct a film's meaning in any way they wish. Instead, they process the fragmented film guided by schemata – norms and principles in the mind that organize the film into a coherent mental representation. (See Bordwell [1985, chapters 3 and 4] for a detailed outline of his cognitive theory of filmic comprehension.) Much of Bordwell's work involves applying his cognitive theory to distinct historical periods of filmmaking, resulting in what he calls an historical poetics of cinema.

But the most devastating critique of Heath's theory emerged from analytic philosophy. Noël Carroll (1982) wrote a 74-page acerbic review of Heath's *Questions of Cinema* (1981), in which 'On Screen, in Frame' is reprinted. Carroll does not attempt to understand Heath's work on its own terms. His intervention is far more polemical: he wants to demonstrate that Heath's theory is fundamentally flawed and should be discarded.

One effect of Carroll's review, and subsequent book (Carroll 1988), was that film studies bifurcated, with contemporary film theorists deepening their theories of subjectivity, merging film into cultural studies, while an alliance between analytic philosophy and cognitive theory took on board Carroll's critique of Heath and developed Bordwell's alternative theory. 'On one side', writes Dudley Andrew, 'stood a politicized cultural studies and, on the other, the more formalist cognitive film theory (including historical poetics [and analytic philosophy]). While the former profits from sliding away from the medium to examine whatever it finds of interest around it, the latter resolutely holds onto the specificity of film' (Andrew 2009, 906). Heath's concept of film as a specific signifying practice is valuable for representing a brief, historical moment in film theory when these two (now bifurcated) positions found a temporary balance, for Heath offered a politicized theory of film that remains grounded in the semiotic study of filmic specificity.

WARREN BUCKLAND

## Works cited

Althusser, Louis. 1971. *Lenin and Philosophy and Other Essays*. Translated by Ben Brewster. New York: Monthly Review Press.

Andrew, Dudley. 2009. 'The Core and the Flow of Film Studies'. *Critical Inquiry* 35 (4): 879–917.

Bordwell, David. 1985. *Narration in the Fiction Film*. Madison: University of Wisconsin Press.

Carroll, Noël. 1982. 'Address to the Heathen'. *October* 23: 89–163.

——. 1988. *Mystifying Movies: Fad and Fallacies in Contemporary Film Theory*. New York: Columbia University Press.

Heath, Stephen. 1976. 'On Screen, in Frame: Film and Ideology'. *Quarterly Review of Film Studies* 1 (3): 251–65.

——. 1981. *Questions of Cinema*. London: Macmillan.

Lacan, Jacques. 1977. *Ecrits: A Selection*. Translated by Alan Sheridan. London: Tavistock.

Marx, Karl, and Frederick Engels. 1970. *The German Ideology*. Edited by C.J. Arthur. London: Lawrence and Wishart.

Rodowick, D.N. 1988. *The Crisis of Political Modernism: Criticism and Ideology in Contemporary Film Theory*. Urbana: University of Illinois Press.

## Further reading

Casetti, Francesco. 1999. *Theories of Cinema, 1945–1995*. Austin: University of Texas Press.

MacCabe, Colin. 1985. *Theoretical Essays: Film, Linguistics, Literature*. Manchester: Manchester University Press.

Rosen, Philip, ed. 1986. *Narrative, Apparatus, Ideology*. New York: Columbia University Press.

# COUNTER-CINEMA

Counter-cinema refers to filmmaking that opposes the dominance of the commercial cinema associated with Hollywood. Why would a counter-cinema be considered desirable or necessary? Much of the desire for a counter-cinema – and the notion of a counter-cinema is locatable as a historical moment of the early to mid-1970s – was the result of a political dissatisfaction with commercial cinema. Inspired to a large extent by Marxist philosophies – especially the kinds of theorizations put in place by German playwright Bertolt Brecht (*see* BRECHT AND FILM) and French political philosopher Louis Althusser – proponents of counter-cinema wanted films and filmmaking to be part of the dismantling of capitalism (*see* CONTEMPORARY FILM THEORY; IDEOLOGY, CINEMA AND). Insofar as Hollywood and commercial filmmaking more generally were (and are) driven by economic imperatives born out of a capitalist economic framework, then a counter-cinema could offer another way of making films which would, in their turn, be part of a differently structured way of ordering the socio-political world.

The most evocative formulation of counter-cinema was that of British film scholar Peter Wollen in an article on 'Godard and Counter Cinema: *Vent d'Est*' first published in 1972 (Wollen 1985). There, Wollen makes explicit the opposition between commercial Hollywood cinema, on the one hand, and a proposed counter-cinema, which he identifies with the contemporary films of Jean-Luc Godard, on the other. (Wollen himself would go on to make films, most significantly *Penthesilea* [1974] and *Riddles of the Sphinx* [1977], both co-directed with Laura Mulvey.) A series of seven categories are fleshed out in the article according to a division between commercial cinema and counter-cinema. Wollen sets out these categories schematically and here they will be approached one by one.

## Narrative transitivity v. narrative intransitivity

A transitive verb is one which is linked to a direct object ('she *kicks* him') and so too can narrative transitivity be described as a narrative that works towards an object. In working towards an object the narratives in commercial films are structured in very particular ways. First, events follow one another according to a chain of causation, that is, according to a logic of cause and effect. Second, Wollen argues that the links between cause and effect are usually psychologically motivated. That is, characters in these films do things 'for a reason'. Finally, these motivations, causes, and effects are built around an overall narrative structure which begins with the establishment of an equilibrium, followed by a disturbance of that equilibrium – a narrative's 'conflict' – which will be worked out and resolved by the restoration of equilibrium.

An intransitive verb is one that is not directly linked with an object ('she *sings*'). Wollen argues that Godard's films of the 1960s had begun to explore notions of narrative intransitivity. The links between causes and effects, for example, were thrown into question by the use of chapter divisions which separated the events of a narrative in such a way as to stifle any causal connection between them. By the time of *Vent d'Est* in 1970, all traces of connection between incidents had been more or less erased. 'The basic story', states Wollen, 'does not have any recognizable sequence, but is more like series of intermittent flashes' (Wollen 1985, 502). Such strategies break any possibility of establishing psychological motivations, clear character reasoning, or clear links between narrative causes and effects. 'The constructive principle of the film is rhetorical, rather than narrative' (502).

Why might a filmmaker want to adopt such strategies? Wollen claims that Godard's films use anti-narrative strategies in order to 'disrupt the emotional spell of the narrative' (502). The 'spell' cast over spectators by the narratives of commercial films goes hand in hand with the ideological manipulations which underpin a capitalist society. Counter-cinema aims to break this spell, and it can do so first of all, Wollen argues, by cutting its ties with narrative form.

## Identification v. estrangement

In commercial cinema, identification takes place with the people in films. These people might be characters in a dramatic story or they might be stars, for Wollen contends that a spectator's identification with a star might easily override her/his identification with a character. He asserts, in addition, that 'identification can only take place in a situation of suspended disbelief' (Wollen 1985, 502). Wollen is thus taking the term 'identification' in its very strong sense, for identifying with a character or star must entail, for Wollen, a strong sense of the erasure of the spectator's own identity and a belief that they *are* the character or star with whom they are identifying (*see* IDENTIFICATION, THEORY OF).

The task for counter-cinema is to bring about 'the breakdown of identification' (502). Estrangement means just that: the breaking of identification, the severing of emotional involvement so that the spectator is distanced from the people and situations on screen. If spectators no longer truly 'believe' in the characters or stars they see on screen and thus no longer identify with them, then the ideological spell cast by identification will be broken.

Wollen outlines three ways that estrangement can be invoked. First, a film can promote the breakage between the soundtrack and the image-track, resulting, for example, in the 'non-matching of voice to character' (502). Second, a film can introduce 'real people' into the narrative. Wollen discusses an episode in *Vent d'Est* in which one of the characters is shown having his make-up applied so that the disjunction between his 'fictional character' and his 'real person' is amplified. Finally, Wollen claims that a character's direct address to the audience – that is, when a character speaks directly to the camera – offers another way of stifling identification.

Wollen admits that his advocacy of estrangement is indebted to Bertolt Brecht's theories of the alienation-effect so that the strategies he describes here go hand in hand with those of narrative intransitivity: they break the spell of the spectator's being 'caught up in' a story and the plight of its characters and instead push the spectator to ask questions about what is being portrayed. Wollen states that: 'It is impossible to maintain "motivational" coherence, when characters themselves are incoherent, fissured, interrupted, multiple and self-critical' (503). Instead, the spectator will ask questions of what they have seen – 'What is this film for?', 'Why did that happen?', 'What is going to happen next?' (503) – rather than merely 'going along with it'.

## Transparency v. foregrounding

To be transparent means to be easy to see through, to be clear and obvious. Commercial films typically aim for transparency. Wollen makes the connection between transparency and the notion of looking through a window so that, to a certain extent, he relies on an analogy between the cinema screen and its possibilities of offering a transparent window on the world. Insofar as the cinema (and photography before it) offer such a window on the world, it follows in the footsteps of the discovery of perspective in Renaissance painting. Along with this Wollen is keen to stress the role of language in offering transparency. 'From the seventeenth century onwards', he argues, 'language was increasingly seen as an instrument which should efface itself in the performance of its task' (503).

Rather than transparency, a counter-cinema should offer *foregrounding*. Instead of showing a window on the world, a counter-cinema intends to declare: *this is a film* (see MODERNISM VERSUS REALISM). Such a strategy builds on the notion of estrangement by blocking the audience's suspension of disbelief. In other words, if the goal of transparency is one of making the spectator believe s/he is looking through a window on the world, then by foregrounding the processes of production a counter-cinema shatters that belief.

Wollen emphasizes that Godard advocated foregrounding from his earliest films. With *Vent d'Est* he breaks new ground, especially in his decision to deliberately scratch the surface of the film. In doing this, Godard's work comes close to the work of North American avant-garde filmmakers whose techniques of altering the surface of the film strip are made central to the film itself. But Wollen hesitates to take this comparison too far, for what is central for Godard are not the scratches themselves, but the relation between what the image represents and the scratches which block or alter that representation. Godard is making explicit his attempts to break down the supposed transparency of cinematic representation. Rather than seeing cinema as a mode of representation, Godard instead wants to demonstrate that cinema can be a mode of writing or image building (cf. Rodowick 1994, 1–41; Wollen 1972).

## Single diegesis v. multiple diegesis

'In Hollywood films', Wollen declares, 'everything shown belongs to the same world' (1985, 504). Hollywood films show us only one version of events, and those events are typically contained within a single story with the unities of space and time strictly adhered to. If there is a double level of diegesis – a film within a film, a play within a film, a dream within a film, or a framing narrative – then these will be very clearly divided from the main narrative. In short, commercial films follow the classical tenets of dramatic unity.

Counter-cinema aims to undo dramatic unity. Wollen argues that Godard begins to make full use of this possibility in *Weekend* (1967) inasmuch as characters and figures from different historical epochs are overlaid and intermingled with one another. A multiple diegesis aims to place a number of different stories and worlds alongside one another in ways that are disruptive and jarring rather than being clearly signalled and easy to understand. One of the most successful ways Godard achieves this multiplicity, claims Wollen, is by offering many layers of images and sounds, often in ways that do not match up, so that one sound will block another or where one stream of images will not be directly related to another. What this adds up to is that 'Godard systematically explores the areas of misunderstanding' (505). Again, this production of misunderstanding is aimed at blocking the spell cast by commercial cinema so that the spectator will instead be urged to ask questions of what s/he is seeing and hearing.

## Closure v. aperture

As has already been pointed out, commercial Hollywood films typically aim for closure and resolution, a formula of equilibrium followed by disequilibrium then concluding with a restoration of equilibrium. A counter-cinema resists this urge towards closure and instead aims for openness.

Wollen stresses Godard's penchant for quotation and allusion insofar as many of his films invoke other films and filmmakers or poets, painters, writers, philosophers, and historical figures. It is this multiplicity of voices, none of which achieves a determinate priority and none of which is encompassed by an overarching whole, which constitutes a genuine openness of the filmic text (cf. Wollen 1972, 155–74). For Godard it is not simply a matter of leaving the ending of a film open; rather, it is a matter of opening up the whole filmic text into multiple layers, each of which heads off in its own direction. This openness runs counter to the dominant mode of narrative closure in commercial cinema.

## Pleasure v. unpleasure

Perhaps the most contentious aspect of Wollen's argument is that a counter-cinema should aim for *unpleasure*. If commercial films are built on the sale of pleasure, then one way to counter this is to offer a resistance to pleasure. Wollen argues that 'Cinema is conceived of as a drug that lulls and mollifies the militancy of the masses, by bribing them with pleasurable dreams, thus distracting them from the stern tasks which are their true destiny' (1985, 506). He thus claims that in *Vent d'Est* Godard tries to undo the fantasies associated with pleasure so that those fantasies are turned back on the audience as unpleasurable. Consider, for example, that if a film ends with the happy marriage of the leading man and woman, and if an audience finds this pleasurable, then this is also an articulation of the ways that the dominant ideology affirms heterosexual marriage as pleasurable. What Godard tries to do in *Vent d'Est* – and what a counter-cinema should aspire to – is to break the link between pleasure and the ideology that underpins that pleasure. What this necessitates therefore is a sense of unpleasure.

## Fiction v. reality

If the commercial fiction cinema tries to create diegetic worlds which exist alongside the real world – fictional facsimiles of the real world – then a counter-cinema aims to bring us face to face with reality. Wollen explains this division primarily in terms of *acting*. To 'act' is to automatically 'put on an act', to fictionalize, so that what Godard aspires to is a reduction to zero of the processes of acting. For this reason, Godard includes many sequences of interviews in his films in an attempt to uncover a pure form of speaking, while in *Vent d'Est*, Wollen writes, 'there is almost no dialogue at all' (1985, 508). If the commercial cinema aims for fictionalization, then a counter-cinema aims fairly and squarely at reality.

Against all of the forms of lying and deception which are promoted by commercial cinema, Wollen cautions that 'cinema cannot show the truth' (509). A too-simplistic opposition between commercial cinema as false and counter-cinema as true is quite simply not possible. There is no way that 'a counter-cinema can have an absolute existence'. Rather, Wollen contends, '[i]t can only exist in relation to the rest of cinema' (509). Therefore, if there is an opposition between commercial cinema and counter-cinema, this opposition is not one of an absolute wrong opposed to an absolute right. Rather, it is a struggle by counter-cinema against the prevailing ideological tendencies of the commercial cinema.

Wollen's article and associated writings of the early 1970s offer a formidable programme of oppositions between commercial Hollywood cinema and a potential counter-cinema (cf. Wollen 1982 [orig. 1975]). As a way of defining a political cinema, however, its major problem lay in its advocacy of unpleasure. A different mode of questioning the politics of cinema was put in place by another British film scholar, Richard Dyer, in an important article on 'Entertainment and Utopia' published in 1977 (Dyer 1985). Dyer complicates what in Wollen's article might be seen as an all-too simplistic dismissal of Hollywood films as straightforward vehicles for ideological manipulation. In a manner as systematic as Wollen's, Dyer charts the relationships between 'entertainment forms' and their 'emotional signification' in a series of eight categories. His analysis demonstrates that the kind of opposition between Hollywood and counter-cinema sought by Wollen might not be automatically as politically progressive as he had hoped. Rather, Dyer takes seriously the political possibilities opened up by Hollywood films with a focus on Hollywood musicals. What is most at stake in the films Dyer discusses is their potential for providing pleasure and the political consequences of this. Dyer certainly considers the political shortcomings offered by these openly capitalist forms of entertainment ('At our worst sense of it, entertainment provides alternatives *to* capitalism which will be provided *by* capitalism'; Dyer 1985, 229), yet he also, like Wollen, invokes Brecht insofar as the Hollywood musical might provide ways in which to 'organise the enjoyment of changing reality' (232). Debates over the political stakes of pleasure in the cinema and alternatives to the dominance of Hollywood of the kind provided by 'counter-cinema' continue to this day.

RICHARD RUSHTON

## Works cited

Dyer, R. 1985. 'Entertainment and Utopia'. In *Movies and Methods*, vol. II, edited by B. Nichols, 220–32. Berkeley: University of California Press.

Rodowick, D.N. 1994. *The Crisis of Political Modernism: Criticism and Ideology in Contemporary Film Theory*. 2nd edition. Urbana: University of Illinois Press.

Wollen, P. 1972. *Signs and Meaning in the Cinema*. 3rd edition. London: Secker and Warburg.

——. 1982. 'The Two Avant-Gardes'. In *Readings and Writings: Semiotic Counter Strategies*, 92–104. London: Verso.

——. 1985. 'Godard and Counter Cinema: *Vent d'Est*'. In *Movies and Methods*, vol. II, edited by B. Nichols, 500–9. Berkeley: University of California Press.

# DEPTH OF FIELD

The term *depth of field* refers to the degree to which deep space is represented in deep focus in the cinematic image. An image with 'shallow' depth of field presents a relatively limited amount of space in focus, while an image with a greater depth of field contains more spatial planes in sharp focus. Throughout the history of film theory, writers have discussed the significance of depth of field and the phenomenon of being able to cinematically represent space in depth. Depth of field therefore serves as an instructive lens through which to review multiple movements of film theory and the different sets of priorities and ways of talking about cinema found in each. Significant attention is paid to cinematic depth whether one reads the classical film theories of Rudolf Arnheim and Hugo Münsterberg or the realist film theory advanced by André Bazin, the apparatus theory of Jean-Louis Comolli or the 'post-theory' framework endorsed by David Bordwell and Noël Carroll.

To understand the place of depth of field in film theory, it would be necessary to review all these movements and figures, but this entry will focus only on the last two so as to give a sense of, first, what we might take to be the most conceptually charged nexus in this conversation (found in Comolli) and, second, a more recent direction this conversation has taken (with Bordwell). Considering Bordwell's remarks on the matter will demonstrate film studies' continuing interest in depth of field. Perhaps more than any other single technique or concept, depth of field serves as a particularly useful topic with which to consider the evolving history and very status of film theory. Many theories operate under the implicit belief that film is fundamentally a visual medium, and thus a close, dissective analysis of depth of field would seem to provide a way of seeing into imagery itself, of seeing film's essence.

Technically speaking, depth of field is controlled by multiple facets of cinematography, such as the distance between the photographer and the subject, the focal length of the camera lens, the format size of the camera's image sensor, the lens aperture, and lighting. When discussing depth of field, however, film theorists tend to focus less on such technical properties and more on the philosophical and aesthetic stakes of being able to represent the everyday phenomenon of depth perception in an otherwise two-dimensional cinematic image. For example, depth was a crucial aspect of cinematic ontology for Arnheim when he set out to demonstrate that film was distinct from reality and therefore an art. He claims in *Film as Art* that the 'effect of film is neither absolutely two-dimensional nor absolutely three-dimensional, but something in between. Film pictures are at once plane and solid' (1957, 12). For Arnheim the fact that film reduces depth – avoiding a simple mechanical reproduction of the world, while not reducing it to a pure, painterly flatness – is the very condition that allows film to become a unique art (*see* ART, FILM AS).

In his writings on cinema, André Bazin champions depth of field as a 'dialectical step forward in the history of film language' (1967, 35). Bazin praises directors such as Jean Renoir and Orson Welles for their virtuoso abilities to choreograph the cinematic image like a 'dramatic checkerboard', filling up shots in depth with multiple layers of detail, action, and meaning (34). Such visual orchestration in depth aligns with Bazin's belief that cinema realizes its fullest potential when drawing minimal attention to its own techniques (think by contrast of the close-up and how, through its magnification, it calls attention to the camera's powers), allowing the viewer the freedom to take in all the 'ambiguities of reality' we see in our fields of vision in everyday life.

## Depth of field in Comolli's 'Technique and Ideology'

It was Bazin's colleague at the film journal *Cahiers du cinéma*, Jean-Louis Comolli, who launched the most extended theoretical argument about depth of field, intended to be part of an article published in six instalments in the pages of *Cahiers du cinéma* in 1971 and 1972, though he only wrote the first five. It is not until part 4 that he begins discussing depth of field in detail, and it is this and the third part preceding it that are the most widely translated, reprinted, and remembered parts of the article.

Comolli, like many French film theorists and critics of the post-1968 period, was significantly influenced by a convergence of post-structuralist, semiotic, psychoanalytical, and Marxist theories (*see* CONTEMPORARY FILM THEORY). These intellectual movements found common ground in their critique of, and profound scepticism towards, the ways in which a wide range of institutions – what Louis Althusser (1971), one of the writers cited by Comolli, refers to as 'state apparatuses' – disseminate knowledge through social formations and cultural practices, which through their very structures manipulate and shape our thought. Central to this critique is the notion that apparatuses – including the cinema – pervade everyday life and are easily taken for granted. They become, as another prominent French critic of the time, Roland Barthes (1973), would say, 'naturalized' (Comolli mobilizes this term with some frequency as well). And so Comolli, building on previous discussions of depth of field by film theorists whom he refers to as 'idealist', such as Bazin and Jean Mitry, argues that depth of field has been naturalized within accounts of film history. He reminds his readers that the technique is not outside ideology (Comolli 1986, 423). Although standard accounts of film history would have us believe that camera technologies evolved towards a state of perfection that allowed filmmakers by the 1940s to produce impressive depth effects, Comolli argues that this technical capacity has in fact been produced to serve ideological purposes, in line with a history of representational practices that pre-date cinema, and which seek to reproduce (the illusion of) 'normal vision' and Renaissance perspective. This argument hinges on the notion that earlier, idealist ruminations on depth of field aligned skilful uses of depth of field with a realist aesthetic, whereby cinema achieves a more perfect way of mimicking a normal way of seeing the world. Technology in idealist theory is assumed to be neutral, rather than a socially constructed set of instruments. As Comolli writes: 'Contrary to what the technicians seem to believe, the restoration of movement and depth are not the effect of the camera, but the camera is the effect – the solution – to the problem of their restoration' (434).

An instructive index of Comolli's critique of ideological assumptions can be found by visually skimming his writing. One will notice an extensive use of quotation marks. There are 210 pairs of quotation marks in the fifteen pages of parts 3 and 4. In the same pages, however, there are only two dozen footnotes. This is because the vast majority of Comolli's quotation marks are not references but *scare quotes*, around terms such as 'histories of cinema', 'births', 'first times', 'origin', 'cinema', and 'notion'. Consider the opening paragraph of part 3, where he sets forth his project (Comolli 1986, 422–423):

> I will now try to apply along two main axes the general principles for the conditions of a materialist approach to the history of cinema. Firstly, what it is that drives all current 'histories of the cinema' ... to go on endlessly and systematically cataloguing the long series of 'first times,' that chain of 'inaugurations' of technical devices and stylistic figures by this or that film. They adopt the empirical object 'cinema' without troubling to construct its theory, and proceed to exhaust themselves in an obsessive re-marking of its proliferation of 'births' ... ; in other words, they seek to establish its 'origin,' what can only prove to be dispersed. This should of course seriously shake the very notion of an 'origin', but these histories hasten to slide over and confine the damage by making the dispersal itself the justification for their basic eclecticism.

The four sentences in this introductory paragraph contain seven pairs of scare quotes – an indication that Comolli intends to radically revise familiar concepts. His extensive use of these punctuation marks provides a sense of his larger intellectual position: he wants his readers to doubt and complicate the naturalness of the language used to describe cinema, especially in teleological accounts of film history and criticism that posit single films or filmmakers as being the first to develop a given technique. He is sceptical of such claims, because, after all, techniques such as close-ups or depth of field that describe degrees of scale in the cinema are relative and have varying shades of denotations and connotations in different contexts. (He asserts that the close-up is an 'operational index' in practice and a 'false abstraction' in theory; 429.) In response to Mitry, he writes: 'What must we ultimately understand by "the closeup as we know it"? The least one can say is that "we" don't "know" a single variety, but a thousand, an infinite number' (427). Because of the relative nature of terms like close-up and depth of field, Comolli wants to question film historians' very impulse to identify first appearances of cinematic techniques in their accounts: hence his quotation marks around words such as 'first times', 'inaugurations', 'births', and 'origin.'

In conducting a surface reading of Comolli's text, a reader might be surprised that, in a work purportedly focusing on depth of field, part 3 primarily focuses on discourses and histories of the close-up. Such a move serves to remind the reader that depth of field is only one of several possible examples that could have been provided as part of a larger critique of the ideological biases in film historiography. In Comolli's words, 'this study designated depth of field as one of the scenes for an operational analysis of the connections between cinematic technique and its economic and ideological determinations' (423). It is also a way for us to realize that, for Comolli, knowledge production is fundamentally relative and impossible to disentangle from broader concerns and connected practices: in order for Comolli to even begin talking about depth of field, he must first consider various conversations – and the conditions and norms that allow conversations – about art history, ideology, the philosophy of history, and the close-up.

While Comolli certainly helps us think about problems of historiography and the instability of the language we use to talk about cinema, reading his article too literally a contemporary reader might find that his rhetoric overcompensates for the naturalized discourse of film history that he criticizes. Are there really, for example, an infinite variety of close-ups or depths of field, as Comolli would have us think? A more measured writer, such as David Bordwell, suggests that while we could delineate a variety of practices of staging in depth, many of which would challenge the standard accounts that find endless 'firsts' in the films of Griffith, Renoir, or Welles, it would be more productive to consider a finite typology. Moreover, Bordwell reminds us that the specific research questions we pose from the outset shape the answers we give.

## 'Staging in depth' in Bordwell's *History of Film Style*

In the concluding and most extensive chapter of his book *On the History of Film Style*, which focuses on 'staging in depth', Bordwell is overwhelmingly critical of what he refers to as Comolli's 'empirical inaccuracies', 'conceptual shortcomings', and 'sweeping general-izations', dismissing his contributions as 'vague' and 'oddly capricious' (1998, 160, 161). To understand this dismissal of Comolli, one must understand Bordwell's intellectual position. The co-author of one of the most widely read introductory film studies textbooks, *Film Art*, he is a proponent of what he refers to as 'fine-grained' approaches to film studies that use concrete films as case studies to examine specific 'problems' in light of films' visual details as well as the decisions filmmakers make and the contexts in which they make them. In addition, he and Noël Carroll co-edited a collection published in 1996 entitled *Post-theory: Reconstructing Film Studies*, where they launch a fiery critique against applications of critical theories in film studies. They suggest that many film scholars employ a top-down method that begins with theoretical ideas about ideology, difference, representation, or identity, and then proceed to plug a given film or group of films into an already conceptualized argument. They contend that this method teaches us hardly anything specific or original about the films being studied. Bordwell proposes that concrete, 'fine-grained' work be based on 'middle-level' research and a 'problem/solution model'.

The title of Bordwell's 123-page final chapter – 'Exceptionally Exact Perceptions: On Staging in Depth' – is instructive to consider both for understanding Bordwell's approach and for comparing it with Comolli's. Importantly, Bordwell's language itself is 'exception-ally exact' in discussing 'staging in depth' rather than 'depth of field'. In doing so, he carefully reframes the issue so as to make filmmakers central to the debate (since a human must be responsible for 'staging'). Thus Bordwell will not be talking about an array of ideologies inscribed in technologies, but rather about a long history of the ways in which filmmakers have choreographed planes of the cinematic image to achieve different artistic effects. The chapter is accompanied by 265 film frames and includes a broad range of references to theorists, historians, and filmmakers to help construct this history. While the phrase 'exceptionally exact perceptions' would seem to apply to Bordwell's own scholarly methodology, it is also a direct reference to one filmmaker, the early Soviet director Lev Kuleshov, and his often-neglected 1929 remarks about cinematic depth, lens optics, and the filmmaker's ability to shape an audience's attention.

Kuleshov points out that in film, as opposed to theatre, members of the audience see the action before them through the perspective of the camera lens. Bordwell identifies Kuleshov's remarks as an example of an important conversation about depth that has been abandoned in the shadows of more widely circulated theories by Bazin and Comolli. Indeed, Bordwell productively situates the phenomenon of staging in depth within world cinema, realigning it from its strong scholarly ties with French theory and criticism. The Kuleshov reference in his chapter title signals that Bordwell is interested in sketching an alternative account of depth of field in his effort to provide a corrective account to those that have dominated film history and theory. While Comolli reveals the ideological biases and technological determinism in earlier accounts, Bordwell reintroduces the teleology Comolli finds problematic and ultimately concludes that one 'surprising consequence' of examining film history 'is to rehabilitate the idea of progress', the idea that filmmakers 'inherit' and improve upon a 'body of techniques' (Bordwell 1998, 268).

One might contrast Comolli's extensive use of scare quotes that are often not derived from any particular source to Bordwell's direct citation in his own title that avoids quotation marks and simply adopts Kuleshov – at least in his title. If Comolli is sceptical of a generalized discourse that does not have a precise location, Bordwell confidently affirms his own authority by appropriating the exact language of others without quotation. Reading Bordwell alongside Comolli helps situate the place of depth of field in film theory as at once important and contested, raising difficult questions about the triangulated relationships among technology, vision, and knowledge and about the sets of theoretical beliefs we inscribe when writing film historiography.

JEFF SCHEIBLE

## Works cited

Althusser, Louis. 1971. 'Ideology and Ideological State Apparatuses'. In *Lenin and Philosophy and Other Essays*, translated by Ben Brewster, 127–85. New York: Monthly Review Press.

Arnheim, Rudolf. 1957. *Film as Art*. Berkeley: University of California Press.

Barthes, Roland. 1973. 'Myth Today'. In *Mythologies*, translated by Annette Lavers, 109–59. London: Paladin.

Bazin, André. 1967. 'The Evolution of the Language of Cinema'. In *What Is Cinema?*, vol. 1, translated by Hugh Gray, 23–40. Berkeley: University of California Press.

Bordwell, David. 1998. 'Exceptionally Exact Perceptions: On Staging in Depth'. In *On the History of Film Style*, 158–272. Cambridge, MA: Harvard University Press.

Bordwell, David, and Noël Carroll, eds. 1996. *Post-theory: Reconstructing Film Studies*. Madison: University of Wisconsin Press.

Comolli, Jean-Louis. 1986. 'Technique and Ideology: Camera, Perspective, Depth of Field [Parts 3 and 4]'. translated by Diana Matias. In *Narrative, Apparatus, Ideology: A Film Theory Reader*, edited by Philip Rosen, 421–43. New York: Columbia University Press.

## Further reading

Bazin, André. 1997. *Bazin at Work: Major Essays and Reviews from the Forties and Fifties*. Edited by Bert Cadullo, translated by Alain Piette and Bert Cadullo. New York: Routledge.

Bonitzer, Pascal. 1999. *Le champ aveugle: Essais sur le réalisme au cinema*. Paris: Cahiers du Cinéma Livres.

Bordwell, David. 2005. *Figures Traced in Light: On Cinematic Staging*. Berkeley: University of California Press.

Branigan, Edward. 2006. *Projecting a Camera: Language-Games in Film Theory*. New York: Routledge.

Burch, Nöel. 1979. *To the Distant Observer: Form and Meaning in Japanese Cinema*. Berkeley: University of California Press.

Carroll, Noël. 1990. 'Buster Keaton, *The General*, and Visible Intelligibility'. In *Close Viewings: An Anthology of New Film Criticism*, edited by Peter Lehman, 125–40. Tallahassee: Florida State University Press.

Comolli, Jean-Louis. 1971–2. 'Technique et ideologie: camera, perspective, profondeur de champ', parts 1–5. *Cahiers du cinéma*.

Harpole, Charles. 1978. *Gradients of Depth in the Cinema Image*. New York: Arno Press.

Heath, Stephen. 1976. 'Narrative Space'. *Screen* 17 (3): 68–112.

Koch, Gertrud. 1985. 'Exchanging the Gaze: Revisioning Feminist Film Theory'. *New German Critique* 34 (Winter): 139–53.

Kracauer, Siegfried. 1997. *Theory of Film: The Redemption of Physical Reality*. Princeton, NJ: Princeton University Press.

Kuleshov, Lev. 1974. *Kuleshov on Film: Writings*. Translated and edited by Ronald Levaco. Berkeley: University of California Press.

Mitry, Jean. 2000. *The Aesthetics and Psychology of the Cinema*. Translated by Christopher King. Bloomington: Indiana University Press.

Münsterberg, Hugo. 1916. *The Photoplay: A Psychological Study*. New York: D. Appleton and Company.

Ogle, Patrick L. 1972. 'Technological and Aesthetic Influences upon the Development of Deep Focus Cinematography in the United States'. *Screen* 13 (1): 45–72.

Turvey, Gerry. 2004. 'Panoramas, Parades and the Picturesque: The Aesthetics of British Actuality Films, 1895–1901'. *Film History* 16 (1): 9–27.

Williams, Christopher. 1972. 'The Deep Focus Question: Some Comments on Patrick Ogle's Article'. *Screen* 13 (1): 73–9.

Wölfflin, Heinrich. 1950. *Principles of Art History: The Problem of the Development of Style in Later Art*. New York: Courier Dover Publications.

# DIALOGISM

The 1980s saw Mikhail Bakhtin (1895–1975) enjoy a period of fresh recognition as a literary thinker, as opposed to being known simply as the major theorist of carnival (see Bakhtin 1984). This was aided by the introduction of his work to the theoretical mainstream via two articles by Julia Kristeva (1973; 1980) and a book by Tzvetan Todorov (1984). With the publication of *Subversive Pleasures* in 1989, Robert Stam became another important interpreter of Bakhtinian thought, this time with special reference to the field of film studies. Stam declared it necessary to remedy the 'slighting' (1989, 17) of certain dimensions of Bakthin's thought and bring them to bear, in all of their 'transdisciplinary' promise, upon film theory.

The work of the so-called 'Bakhtin Circle' (which encompassed collaborators like V.N. Voloshinov [1986] and P.N. Medvedev, who were notable scholars in their own right) harbours many important concepts, but it is dialogism that Stam (1989, 12) identifies as the one which '"horizontally" embraces and comprehends' several others that unfold against its semantic backdrop. It is thus frequently prioritized among Bakhtin's concepts (see Holquist 2002). Dialogic theory proposes that every communicative act, every instance of speech (whether everyday or artistic in form), takes place in *an exchange of meaning*. Every communication is socially framed, involves more than one participating 'voice', and trails a history of prior usage. Understanding texts as utterances produced (or 'spoken') by an industry, culture, or time period involves becoming conscious of such factors.

As the reference to 'transdisciplinarity' suggests, Stam sees Bakhtin as a developer of concepts that challenge and cross borders. *Subversive Pleasures* brings a Bakhtinian 'translinguistic' perspective to cinema, and its approach follows the tactic of some 1980s re-evaluations that had productively cast Bakhtin as a thinker of language. Bakhtin is thus introduced to a heavily theorized field – language and cinema – which has concerned scholars since 'some of the earliest theorists of the cinema' (Stam 1989, 27). Surprisingly, Bakhtin never discussed films in his own writing (Stam 1989, 16; Flanagan 2009, 20–1). Stam uses his book to make a case for the general suitability of a Bakhtinian way of understanding textual communication and, at the same time, derive a film studies-friendly version of dialogism from the concept's diffuse Bakhtinian sources.

Stam sets up the first chapter of his book to accomplish several things. These include: the establishment of the points where Bakhtin differs from theories of language that held sway during his time (the Russian Formalists and Saussure; *see* FORMALIST THEORIES OF FILM); opening out the term ('utterance') that most keenly illustrates Bakhtin's insistence upon the always social and communicative nature of the linguistic act; and presenting the argument that a Bakhtinian view of discourse helps to overcome the deficiencies of a Saussure-inspired 'filmolinguistics'. This last tendency is represented in Stam's discussion by the work of Christian Metz (1974) (*see* SEMIOTICS OF FILM).

The fine detail of Stam's reading of dialogism begins to emerge in his introduction. Alluding to Bakhtin's preference to endorse the novel as the literary form most open to social voices (particularly in writings from the 1920s and 1930s; see Bakhtin 1994), Stam interestingly notes one feature of dialogism above all others: its propensity to 'accrete ... meanings and connotations' without ever losing the concern for 'the relation between the utterance and other utterances' that is the nucleus of the term through all of its revisions and extensions (Stam 1989, 13, 189). Similar statements about the dialogic concept itself attracting new meanings as its use proliferates are often found in presentations of Bakhtin's work. The real significance of Stam's early stress on the 'relation between utterances' is that it supports the notion that texts become involved in a network of meaning. Although dialogic effects are not limited to situations where verbal dialogue takes place, Bakhtin frequently draws upon images of conversations between speakers and the exchange of positions. The way that context adds meaning to one's words is highly relevant: every utterance 'has its "others"' (Stam 1989, 13).

In chapter 1, Stam develops the role of the utterance, guiding it out of the work of Bakhtin and Voloshinov, and applying it to questions of filmic meaning. Aware of both the semiotics proposed by Saussure, and then-current attempts in their Soviet context to divorce artistic expression from everyday speech and channel it into a separate, poetic realm (cf. Russian formalism), Bakhtin/Voloshinov attempted to unify the sign and its internal and contextual social values into 'utterance'. For them, this term denoted the material act of communication: living speech, as opposed to the abstracted linguistic specimen of Saussurean linguistics. Stam takes up this idea and contrasts it with the attitudes to language found in those other theoretical camps. For instance, he noted that Bakhtin did not, like the Formalists, reserve the artistic word for aesthetic uses and contexts, for any word/utterance is socially meaningful and also capable of being part of a cultural discourse (36). With this attitude, Bakhtin calls into question unhelpful 'dyads' or binaries cherished by the Formalists, such as 'form' and 'content' (36); all types of cultural discourse are subject to the same echoes of 'prior speakings', and each previous context remains ready to be recalled and play a role in any language event (36).

Dropping hints at the relevance of dialogism's two-way model to studies of film audiences (see also Flanagan 2009, 48–52), Stam wants to convince his reader that Bakhtin's concept has a natural place in our thinking around cinema. Stam first takes care to outline the theoretical model of film language that Bakhtinian notions can expand upon, or even supersede. He evaluates the contribution of Christian Metz in his 'filmolinguistic' phase as significant on two major counts: the emphasis on the importance of narrative (film organizes signifying elements into *discourses*); and his attention to the cinematic signifier (Stam 1989, 39), whereby Metz engages with filmic specificity in a manner of which the Formalists would approve. Stam views the Bakhtinian utterance as capable of going beyond the *énoncé* ('statement') of Metz's linguistic model, encompassing narrative dimensions (for instance, in its sense of 'prior speakings', where genre and intertextual relations might become involved), and managing to integrate signification with the material world of 'history and struggle' (40). This is how the utterance becomes exposed to other discourses, revealing the power structures that underlie language use, but also where it becomes a meaningful part of human experience; whereas structuralism is 'value free' (20), Stam contends that translinguistics makes questions of 'value' central. Seeking to demonstrate

Bakhtin's claim that 'every utterance ... has a specific form of an author (and addressee)' (2006, 146) – that is, is always organized around an expected response – Stam looks at how point of view (POV) operates in Griffith's *The Birth of a Nation* (1915). This involves discerning the 'voice' or accent behind shots attributed to the perspective of black sexual aggressor Gus (Walter Long). A standard reading of Gus's POV shot would suggest that it aligns the audience with him, giving us access to what he feels; however, Stam's view is that the shot anticipates and calls for a spectatorial response that supports the film's central ideological direction (the justification of 'ambient racism' and celebration of the Ku Klux Klan). Instead of aligning the viewer with Gus, the shot reiterates prejudices and sympathies already assumed in the viewer by Griffith (Stam 1989, 41), a reading that comes to light when we comprehend the cinematic unit as utterance, as opposed to Metz's *énoncé*. A few paragraphs later, Stam notes that Bakhtinian concepts equip us to restore 'rights' to a reader/spectator 'framed' in such a presumptuous way by the text: 'Individual shots and entire films might be seen on one level as utterances with their own rhetoric, their own persuasive or provocative relation to an assumed interlocutor' (42). Yet this power has limits, as Stam continues: 'Although fiction films are constructed as persuasive machines designed to produce specific impressions and emotions, they are not all-powerful; they may be read differently, and even subversively, by different audiences' (42). Here, Stam captures both why a dialogic approach transcends pure 'ahistorical' (or 'value free') semiotics and is simultaneously obliged to retain the premise of signs and their ambiguity. Indeed, he has argued elsewhere that a notion of differential readings is difficult without a basis in ideology, which requires the sign relation (see Stam 2000, 244–6).

Viewers foster their own distinctive 'dialogical angle' (Stam 1989, 43) on the film's semiotic material, producing not only a response that exceeds or differs from that solicited by the forces behind the text, but also one which becomes part of a dialogic series of unique meanings. The fact that the viewer experiences a 'multiplicity' of semantic positions may sound fragmenting and alienating, but the viewer also joins a community around the film, about which a diversity of 'cultural orientation[s] and political aspirations' are activated (43). This burgeoning multiplicity of spectatorial angles and readings offsets the reductive 'myth of the single spectator' (43), a legacy of earlier film theory arguments (see also Flanagan 2009, 25–9, 32–4). Stam proposes that the film text itself is able to draw upon an equally numerous and open-ended array of signifying 'tracks', layers, and discourses to produce meanings and represent contending values and social voices (Stam 1989, 45–6). Here, another aspect of specificity of the sound film is registered by Stam; that is, the ability to 'context' the spoken word and thus modify its authority, by giving the spectator access to visual factors that may ironize, complicate, or augment it. This is illustrated in an analysis of how visual conventions used in the non-fiction current affairs show *ABC News Nightline* (1981–2005) enhance the authority of its presenter, Ted Koppel, giving him an advantage in his conversations with ostensibly more powerful public figures (Stam 1989, 46–7). Stam thus identifies influential dialogic relations occurring *between* the strategies and techniques of moving image productions as well as playing out between viewer and text. The film utterance is encrusted with these sorts of 'subtle contextualising factors' (46). It might be said that such factors develop individual signifying moments or shots into a discourse that resists the 'finalization' (Bakhtin 1994, 426) of ultimate meaning. The film event is always 'incontrovertibly social' (Stam 1989, 44), because as an utterance it is always positioned, always addressed to someone. Being social, it also always exceeds the limited, Saussurean view of how signification evolves into meaning.

Testing his model of dialogism in a more concentrated film analysis, chapter 6 ('From Dialogism to *Zelig*') sees Stam examine the 1983 Woody Allen mock-documentary. His analysis notes many features in the text that benefit from a Bakhtinian reading. These include: the 'quoting' of various genres and stock footage that expands the film's range of 'voices'; the mischief the film makes with the objective, evidentiary basis of the historical documentary; and the serious theme of the splintering of Jewish identity under repeated persecution, as comically rendered by Allen in the motif of chameleonism. Stam develops the latter point into a comparison between the hapless Leonard Zelig (Allen) – whose chronic tendency to 'blend in' with the people and social backgrounds around him can only be allayed by therapeutic intervention – and the fragmented cinematic subject as described by classical film theory (Stam 1989, 209–10), before rounding off his study of the film with an extended discussion of the significance of the Zelig character for a social reading of the co-existence of race cultures in America (210–17). Stam's summation of the film notes a more positive, 'utopian' (217) angle to Leonard Zelig, whereby his chameleon-like lack of core self can be interpreted as an openness to the influence of the other. This is a fittingly dialogic observation about a text that, with carnivalesque zeal, breaks down 'the frontiers of self as well as the frontiers of genre' (218).

Bakhtin refers to another key concept, the 'chronotope', as the textual material or 'ground ... [for] the representability of events' (1994, 250). He explains that chronotopes arise from the fusion of temporal and spatial markers in texts, and thus have something to show us about the intrinsic connectedness of time and space. Stam notes the chronotope's significance for 'understanding the ways in which spatiotemporal structures in the novel evoke the existence of a life/world independent of the text and its representations' (Stam 1989, 41). However, in *Subversive Pleasures*, he does not make full use of the device's specifically filmic potential for helping to understand relations between texts and their reception. Michael Holquist (2002, 113) argues that the chronotope is able to serve as a 'lens' which can make visible the spatio-temporal strategies encoded in distinct genres, and scholars have contributed interesting work drawing on this capacity; examples include Vice (1997, 210–17) on the road film and Massood (2003) on the urban 'hood' film. Yet, the term still seems to offer more. In the essay where the concept is introduced, Bakhtin suggestively notes that the chronotope throws a kind of bridge between the worlds of the real and the represented (1994, 253–4), thus attesting to its significance to the broader discussion of dialogical dynamics in film reception. In my own work (Flanagan 2009), I have addressed this dimension of the chronotope with regard to 'event' action films that take distinctive chronotopic forms (such as *Speed*, Jan de Bont, 1994; *Die Hard 4.0*, Len Wiseman, 2007), focusing upon extra-textual phenomena and discourses involved in their circulation. Some of these discourses are 'official' (marketing, the provision of 'mask-dropping' DVD features), some revolve around or originate with fans but are sanctioned by studios (social media contact with filmmakers, message boards), and others are broadly 'critical' but bring into play fan knowledge/competences (review websites like www.aint-it-cool-news.com). All manifest in attitudes to narrative, and can be understood as tokens of a shifting compact between consumers and a nervous industry at a time when new ways of receiving and using film texts seem capable of evading or overwhelming traditional studio methods for their commercial control and exploitation. In this way, a new sense of how audiences and media institutions talk to each other – and recognize each other's power – emerges. As Bakhtin notes, the embedding of time/space values into narrative representation is crucial to the success of the communication. This is explored in close discussion of aesthetic strategies like computer-generated imagery (CGI), and how digital methods are accepted or critiqued by audiences in relation to previous aesthetic norms and standards (Flanagan 2009, 160–78).

In summarizing the key contribution of Bakhtinian dialogics to film theory, it is essential to note that Saussure's work – and the filmolinguistics that it inspired – see unity and neutrality in language, whereas the Bakhtin Circle finds relativity and ideological specificity. Dialogism proposes that literary (cinematic) and social values are engaged in productive and unfinished conflict and conversation, a relation that sees each shape the other. Filmic 'utterances', even those designed to be mass products, can therefore be seen as aimed towards specific addressees and marked by local values. Their meaning is refreshed in every exchange with a viewer.

MARTIN FLANAGAN

## Works cited

Bakhtin, Mikhail Mikhailovich. 1984. *Rabelais and His World*. Translated by Helene Iswolsky. Bloomington: Indiana University Press.

———. 1994. *The Dialogic Imagination*. Edited by Michael Holquist, translated by Caryl Emerson and Michael Holquist. Austin: University of Texas Press.

———. 2006. *Speech Genres and Other Late Essays*. Edited by Caryl Emerson and Michael Holquist, translated by Vern W. McGee. Austin: University of Texas Press.

Flanagan, Martin. 2009. *Bakhtin and the Movies: New Ways of Understanding Hollywood Film*. Basingstoke: Palgrave Macmillan.

Holquist, Michael. 2002. *Dialogism: Bakhtin and His World*. 2nd edition. London and New York: Routledge.

Kristeva, Julia. 1973. 'The Ruin of a Poetics'. In *Russian Formalism: A Collection of Articles and Texts in Translation*, edited by Stephen Bann and John E. Bowlt, 102–19. New York: Barnes & Noble.

———. 1980. 'Word, Dialogue and Novel'. In *Desire in Language: A Semiotic Approach to Literature and Art*, edited by Leon S. Roudiez, 64–91. New York: Columbia University Press.

Massood, Paula J. 2003. 'City Spaces and City Times: Bakhtin's Chronotope and Recent African-American Films'. In *Screening the City*, edited by Mark Shiel and Tony Fitzmaurice, 200–15. London: Verso.

Metz, Christian. 1974. *Language and Cinema*. Translated by Donna Jean Umiker-Sebeok. The Hague: Mouton.

Stam, Robert. 1989. *Subversive Pleasures: Bakhtin, Cultural Criticism and Film*. Baltimore, MD: Johns Hopkins University Press.

———. 2000. *Film Theory: An Introduction*. Oxford: Blackwell.

Todorov, Tzvetan. 1984. *Mikhail Bakhtin: The Dialogical Principle (Theory and History of Literature, Volume 13)*. Translated by Wlad Godzich. Minneapolis: Minnesota University Press.

Vice, Sue. 1997. *Introducing Bakhtin*. Manchester: Manchester University Press.

Voloshinov, Valentin Nikaelovich. 1986. *Marxism and the Philosophy of Language*. Translated by Ladislav Matejka and I.R. Titunik. Cambridge, MA: Harvard University Press.

## Further reading

Palmer, R. Barton. 1989. 'Bakhtinian Translinguistics and Film Criticism: The Dialogical Image?'. In *The Cinematic Text: Methods and Approaches*, edited by R. Barton Palner, 303–41. New York: AMS Press.

Sierek, Karl. 2011. 'Beyond Subjectivity: Bakhtin's Dialogism and the Moving Image'. In *Subjectivity in Film: Filmic Representation and the Spectator's Experience*, edited by Dominique Chateau, 135–46. Amsterdam: Amsterdam University Press.

# DIEGESIS

The term diegesis derives from the Greek word διήγησις, which was used by Greek philosophers, such as Plato and Aristotle, to signify the act of 'telling' a story as opposed to μίμησις (mimesis), the act of 'showing' a story. This modal distinction in the process of communicating a story to an audience cast a shadow on the ways in which film theorists attempted to conceptualize the storytelling function in the cinema, but the meaning of diegesis in film narratology is far from being unequivocal. To begin to trace the history of this term in the writings on the cinema, it is essential to have a close look at Étienne Souriau's article 'The Structure of the Filmic Universe and the Vocabulary of Filmology', which first appeared in *Revue International de Filmologie* in 1951.

As a pioneer of what he calls 'Filmology', Souriau seeks to lay the ground for a science of the cinema, which requires a very specific language for studying the cinematic phenomena. This language, consisting of a scientific terminology, is essential for posing the right questions, conducting reliable research, and formulating concrete observations regarding the 'filmic universe'. With the term 'filmic universe', Souriau designates an ensemble of beings, things, events, and phenomena that inhabit a spatio-temporal frame (Souriau 1951, 231). Every film, he claims, poses its own filmic universe, which is merely a variation of the more general category of the 'filmic universe' that encompasses all the types of films, despite their generic differences. According to Souriau, this overarching universe constitutes the very object of study of filmology and it should be analysed with minute precision using clear and scientifically rigorous terms.

The structure of the filmic universe comprises seven levels of existence: the afilmic reality, the pro-filmic reality, the filmographic realities, the filmophanic realities, the diegesis, the spectatorial facts, and the creatorial level (234–40). Souriau defines *afilmic* reality as the external reality, the real world, which exists outside the filmic realm but functions as a frame of reference for the filmic universe. The *pro-filmic* reality is the part of the real world which is placed in front of the cinematic camera and acquires a physical and organic relation to the film. In the next step, the *filmographic* level, we enter the world of the film but we address it merely as a physical object, i.e. as the celluloid that bears certain technical qualities. In other words, the filmographic includes all the techniques, such as editing, colouring, and superimposing, that exist at the level of the film as a material object. On the other hand, the *filmophanic* (or screen) reality is the reality that unfolds on the screen during the projection time in front of an audience. The filmophanic level is at the threshold between the film as a concrete physical material and the film as representation, which is then fully developed within what Souriau describes as *diegesis*. The diegesis is the imaginary world proposed by the film and encompasses 'everything which concerns the film to the extent that it represents something' (237). Finally, Souriau identifies the role of both the spectator and the creator of the film, attributing to each a separate level. The *spectatorial events* include the cognition, the reception, as well as the effects of the film on the audience after the screening. At the other end stands the *creatorial level*, which departs from the film itself back into the external reality where we can trace the intentions, fulfilled or not, of a certain creator who functions as a point of reference for the film itself.

From this filmic cosmology, it was Souriau's concept of diegesis which became the most influential among narratologists, not only within film studies but in literary theory as well. Yet, as we dig into the genealogy of this term, it is worth mentioning that the maternity of the modern use of diegesis is, in fact, attributed to Anne Souriau, Étienne Souriau's daughter, who was a member of his research group in aesthetics at the Institute of Filmology at the University of Paris. In the aforementioned article, Étienne Souriau acknowledges the contribution of his students to his vocabulary of filmology, without spe- cifying his daughter's input (231). However, when Anne Souriau wrote the 'diegesis' entry for the *Vocabulaire d'esthétique*, a collective volume initially edited by Étienne Souriau and completed posthumously by herself, she claims full rights for the coinage of the term (Souriau and Souriau 1990, 581). Here, I would like to discuss in further detail the sig- nificance of diegesis as it was developed by the Souriaus, combining Étienne Souriau's earlier piece with his daughter's entry in the *Vocabulaire*.

Étienne Souriau concentrated almost exclusively on the cinema, seeking to establish the principles of an independent scientific field – hence the broad and aspiring terms, such as filmic universe, vocabulary, and filmology. In this context, the definition of diegesis was bound to remain sketchy or even tautological. Souriau notes that the diegesis consists of the diegetic facts, i.e. the events that are related to the story and are presented at the fil- mophanic level (Souriau 1951, 237). Instead of insisting on the meaning of diegesis, how- ever, he prefers to employ the term 'diegetic' to define the two main dimensions of the frame: space and time. 'Diegetic space' is the space where the events of the story take place, while 'diegetic time' is the time in which those events unfold. In both cases, the viewer depends on what appears strictly on the screen (the filmophanic) in order to *infer* the diegetic, which is reconstructed in the mind (233). For instance, a switch from an estab- lishing shot to a close-up of a building is a change in space at the filmophanic level but not in the diegesis. Similarly, a flashback or a slow-motion constitutes a change in the order or the duration of the filmophanic time but not the time of the diegesis. It is the mental activity of the viewer which deciphers the various functions of the filmic elements in order to construct a coherent diegesis.

In Anne Souriau's work, the meaning of diegesis is explored through examples drawn not only from films but also from other arts, given the scope of a vocabulary on aesthetics. According to Souriau, the diegesis is the world that is *represented* as well as *implied* in a film. In other words, the film creates a story world both by means of representation as well as by implication. As she writes, 'the diegetic elements that are not directly manifested in the work could be inferred by reasoning, as long as they are sufficiently and virtually present in there' (Souriau and Souriau 1990, 582). Thus, the diegesis becomes *virtually* contained in the work of art; it is a potential existence (*existence en puissance*) compared to the actual work (*existence en acte*) (583). What is striking about Souriau's account is her concluding argument that multiple films can have the *same diegesis*, despite the logical problems that such a pro- position entails. The fact that she elaborated on, or rather expanded, her father's initial definition so much as to give precedence to what is implied over what is actually seen on the screen resulted in this provocative statement, which is not further developed in the *Vocabulary* and nor has it been addressed by other theorists.

In summary, in the early 1950s Étienne Souriau and a group of researchers at the Institute of Filmology in Paris worked collaboratively in order to establish the systematic study of the cinema and to formulate the concepts which would be apt for analysing the filmic universe. At this initial stage, the term 'diegesis' was coined in order to signify the story world of the film in, admittedly, broad terms.

## Contemporary approaches to diegesis

In his article 'Diegesis and Authorship', published in *Iris* in 1986, Edward Branigan proposes a more nuanced approach to diegesis. He begins by examining the relationship between 'diegesis' and 'narration' through a series of equivocations that arose from the use of these terms in the works of various theorists, such as Christian Metz (1974), Noël Burch (1979), and Bill Nichols (1981). Amid a number of problematic assumptions, he singles out the blurry distinction between narration and narrative, the confusion between diegesis and non-narrative aspects, and, above all, the recourse to semiotic concepts such as denotation, connotation, and referent (Branigan 1986, 37–40). Instead, Branigan suggests we regard the narration as 'the overall regulation and distribution of knowledge in a text' (38), which can be scaled into at least two broad levels: the diegetic and the non-diegetic. The distinction between these two levels is not an entirely objective one to make; rather, it is the spectator who can interpret the sensory data either as a part of the story world (diegetic) or as an external intervention (non-diegetic). As he writes, 'it is therefore better to limit the meaning of diegesis to the spectator's judgements about a specific large-scale pattern of diverse textual elements, including elements which must be inferred' (40; emphasis in the original). Like Souriau, Branigan emphasizes the role of the spectator in the construction of diegesis, but he advances the argument insofar as he specifies the delicate interactions between the spectator and the filmic narration. Thus, through a series of examples of how the viewer might interpret the filmic elements (objects, editing, camera movement) he expands the notion of diegesis to include three different levels of significance: (a) the objects of perception that surround the character; (b) the methods that characters, as well as other potential observers within the story world, use to experience those objects; and (c) the methods, not available to characters, that spectators use to experience objects (44). Therefore, Branigan claims that 'diegetic' is not merely a characteristic attributed to an object/character of the story but is also a method of experiencing the story either through the characters' perception or through other non-diegetic agents.

Furthermore, in the process of revisioning a number of fundamental concepts in film narratology, such as diegesis, narration, expression, and authorship, Branigan praises David Bordwell's theory of narration (*see* NARRATION), and he refers briefly to its three key components, namely plot, story, and style. However, he refrains from examining the relation of these three terms with diegesis, leaving one wondering whether there is any pertinence among them. Perhaps, we could infer that the plot is more heterogeneous than the diegesis, since it contains non-diegetic passages as well, but the relation between diegesis and what Bordwell calls 'story' is harder to explain. A head-on treatment of these questions is found in Gérard Genette's 'Introduction' to *Narrative Discourse Revisited* (1988). Even though literature is his main focus, Genette is highly critical of the story/plot distinction, readily dismissing it as belonging to the 'prehistory of narratology' (Genette 1988, 14).

Instead, he takes us back to Souriau, observing that the diegesis is not merely a train of events (a story) but rather 'the universe in which the story takes place' (17). In this sense, diegesis appears as a broader concept than the story, even though the vagueness of the term 'universe' still persists.

Genette's most interesting insight, though, regards the Greek origin of the word diegesis, which has been rather misleading. Genette calls attention to the crucial difference between diegesis, which comes from ancient Greek, and *diégèse*, which is Souriau's modern application. The diegesis signifies a mode of representation that consists exclusively of 'telling' without any dramatic elements, such as dialogue. Evidently, when we employ the term *diégèse* to signify the universe of the story, we mean something totally different. This key distinction between the two concepts is almost impossible to maintain as we translate *diégèse* into diegesis in English, but Genette's point is well-taken. In fact, it is André Gaudreault's binary narration/monstration that comes closest to conceptualizing the pair diegesis/mimesis for the cinema, although, again, a complete correspondence is not attainable (Gaudreault 1990).

Furthermore, I would like to refer once more to Branigan's work and particularly his book *Narrative Comprehension and Film* (1992). where the definition of diegesis appears to be more settled. As he writes, 'the diegesis, then, is the implied spatial, temporal and causal system of a character – a collection of sense data which is represented as being at least potentially accessible to a character' (Branigan 1992, 35). In this lucid, if dense, definition I would like to highlight the words 'implied', 'causal', and 'potentially' in order to point out Branigan's relation to the Souriau legacy. First of all, a film presents on the screen a fragment of the diegesis, while the greater part of it is implied. Anne Souriau had underlined the power of implication in a work of art, but the fragment that does indeed appear in the work could not possibly be the same in another work. Hence, the impossibility of two films sharing the same diegesis. Second, Branigan adds the parameter of causality, which constitutes the third axis, alongside time and space, of narration. Issues of causality, however, were absent from the early definitions of diegesis. Finally, in the adverb 'potentially' Branigan implies the crucial contribution of the spectator, whose judgement determines, sometimes provisionally and sometimes more definitively, whether an element is or could be part of a character's world.

In conclusion, even though Souriau's vision of filmology as a science has not fully materialized, the introduction of diegesis to the film vocabulary has been highly successful. As the studies in narratology progress and films experiment with new ways of telling their stories on the screen, the concept of diegesis is open for several future revisions.

ELEFTHERIA THANOULI

## Works cited

Branigan, Edward. 1986. 'Diegesis and Authorship in Film'. *Iris* 58 (7): 37–54.

——. 1992. *Narrative Comprehension and Film*. London and New York: Routledge.

Burch, Noël. 1979. *To the Distant Observer: Form and Meaning in the Japanese Cinema*. Berkeley: University of California Press.

Gaudreault, André. 1990. 'Film, Narrative, Narration: The Cinema of the Lumiére Brothers'. In *Early Cinema: Space, Frame, Narrative*, edited by Thomas Elsaesser, 68–75. London: BFI Publishing.

Genette, Gérard. 1988. *Narrative Discourse Revisited*. Ithaca, NY: Cornell University Press.

Metz, Christian. 1974. *Film Language: A Semiotics of the Cinema*. New York: Oxford University Press.

Nichols, Bill. 1981. *Ideology and the Image: Social Representation in the Cinema and Other Media*. Bloomington: Indiana University Press.

Souriau, Étienne. 1951. 'La structure de l'univers filmique et le vocabulaire de la filmologie'. *Revue international de Filmologie* 7–8: 231–40.

Souriau, Etienne, and Anne Souriau, ed. 1990. *Vocabulaire d'esthétique*. Paris: Presses Universitaires de France.

## Further reading

Chatman, Seymour. 1978. *Story and Discourse: Narrative Structure in Fiction and Film*. Ithaca, NY: Cornell University Press.

Genette, Gérard. 1980. *Narrative Discourse*. Ithaca, NY: Cornell University Press.

Souriau, Étienne. 1953. 'Les grands caractères de l'univers filmique'. In *L'univers filmique*, edited by Étienne Souriau, 11–31. Paris: Flammarion.

# DIGITAL CINEMA

In this entry we shall look at the changes brought about by digital technology to film production, distribution, and exhibition, before examining how film theory has endeavoured to map some of these changes, particularly through discussions of work by Stephen Prince and Stuart Minnis.

## What is digital cinema?

Digital technology, or the use of electronic hardware and software, has irreversibly changed the face of film culture and, necessarily along with it, film studies. Computers are now involved in every stage of film production and post-production, as well as distribution and exhibition. Perhaps the most salient example of digital technology's effect upon cinema is the now-commonplace presence of computer-generated imagery (CGI), or digital special effects, in mainstream films, particularly (though not uniquely) in action blockbusters.

Not only are digital special effects, in the form of explosions, monsters, and scenery, in abundant evidence in films such as the *Lord of the Rings* trilogy (2001–3), but there are also countless *invisible* effects created through the use of the digital intermediary (DI), which sees even films shot on traditional formats such as 35mm digitized for post-production purposes, whether or not they are then reprinted on 35mm for theatrical release. Through the DI, unwanted details can be removed from images, such as the graffiti from the streets of Montmartre in French blockbuster *Amélie* (Jean-Pierre Jeunet, 2001); other details can be added (creating huge crowds where only a few extras had previously featured); and yet other details can simply be changed (fixing a dark sky to a bright blue sky, for example).

As the example of *Amélie* should make clear, the use of digital special effects is not limited to Hollywood productions. Digital special effects have also found their way into various mainstream cinemas from across the globe – including Russia (*Night Watch*, Timur Bekmambetov, 2004), South Korea (*The Host*, Joon-ho Bong, 2006), China (*Red Cliff*, John Woo, 2008), and many more.

Not only are digital special effects globally visible, then, but the globalized nature of computer culture and the dispersed spread of software skills have fed back into Hollywood in such a way that its business is no longer organized around a geographical place in California; instead 'Hollywood' films now involve lengthy post-production processes that take place in locations as diverse as New Zealand (Peter Jackson's Weta Digital), the UK (Framestore), and India (see Govil 2005).

While digital effects are present at, commercially speaking, the highest end of the film industry across the globe, computer technologies have pervaded all other areas of moving-image production and consumption – again, pan-globally, as opposed to in any single geographical location. The development of digital cameras, for example, has led to the creation of low-budget cinemas, some of which have achieved noteworthy international critical and commercial success. Prominent examples include the Dogme 95 movement that originated in Denmark (even though the use of digital cameras is in fact forbidden in the original Dogme manifesto signed by Lars von Trier and Thomas Vinterberg) and the work of such digital 'auteurs' as China's Jia Zhangke and Iran's Abbas Kiarostami, and certain members of the so-called 'mumblecore' movement in the USA. These examples do not begin to include work by film and video artists, some of whom, such as John and James Whitney, were also pioneers of CGI, which has also found its way into uniquely computer generated films such as *Toy Story* (1995).

Furthermore, digital technology has also transformed the nature of film distribution and exhibition. If it was by 1986 that home video sales had surpassed theatrical releases in terms of revenue for Hollywood (Schatz 1993, 25), then the development of DVD and, now, Blu-Ray technologies for home viewing have not involved a slowing down of this process. Furthermore, the internet has proven a viable platform through which to release certain types of film, particularly those that help to advertise mainstream commercial products, such as trailers and music videos, and libraries of films that are also available on DVD and other formats.

Projects such as *Dr Horrible's Sing-Along Blog* (Joss Whedon, 2008) and *Film Socialisme* (Jean-Luc Godard, 2010), both of which were first released on the internet, further suggest that this platform might yet prove a viable medium for first-run film distribution and exhibition, even if downloads and streaming sites have already been put to efficient use as 'ancillary markets' for theatrical releases. In addition, the number of digital projectors in cinemas, particularly in connection with the latest round of films in 3D, has, since 2003 if not before, been on the rise.

Finally, websites like YouTube together with the development of cheap cameras, which can often feature on other devices such as mobile phones, have transformed the nature of contemporary film culture, such that digital technology has not just greatly affected professional filmmaking at every level, but has also given amateur filmmaking an outlet and an opportunity, in terms of viewing figures if not revenues, to compete with major cinema releases.

## Digital cinema and film theory

If the above is the tip of the digital iceberg, then we can easily see how the 'D-word' has now 'become an inescapable element of moving image technology' (Enticknap 2005, 202). As Stephen Prince says in his landmark 'True Lies: Perceptual Realism, Digital Images, and Film Theory,' '[t]he rapid nature of these changes is creating problems for film theory' (1996, 27). We shall turn our attention to Prince's essay now.

Following a brief introduction concerning the use of digital special effects in mainstream (American) cinema, Prince's primary concern is how theories of realism are affected by the advent of photorealistic CGI. Prince is one of various scholars to have pointed out that CGI challenges the indexicality of photographic images. That is to say, if photographs are traces, or indices, of real objects that were in front of the camera lens at the time of the photo's being taken, then we cannot say the same of CGI. Work by Roland Barthes and André Bazin on the realism of photography, a realism based on the indexical relationship between the image and what was before the camera at the time of exposure, had long been influential in explaining the 'power' of cinematic images (*see* ONTOLOGY OF THE PHOTO-GRAPHIC IMAGE). However, as Prince points out, once what we see on screen is not a representation of something that physically was before the camera, but a photorealistic simulation of something that does not exist and perhaps never has existed, then those images have a different ontology to indexical, photographic images.

Prince takes some time to consider the major concerns in making digital images look like photographic images. Being simulations, the digital elements of a film image have no solidity, and so careful programming must be employed to make sure both that the digital elements do not 'blend' into each other when they meet, and that they cast shadows. That is, animators must make the images seem as solid as possible, so that digital dinosaurs neither collide (or rather that they bump off each other when they do collide) nor seem divorced from the space into which they are inserted. Similarly, motion can be added via digital painting to images, but motion blur is also useful for greater fidelity to photographic realism – because digital dinosaurs can otherwise seem too crisp when moving.

And yet, asks Prince, if we talk of the realism of CGI, what kind of realism is this? For while theorists like Barthes and Bazin have spoken of indexicality as a basis for realism, there have also been various film scholars, particularly those working in semiotics and film in the 1970s (e.g. Jean-Louis Baudry and Colin McCabe), who have argued that cinematic realism is an *effect*; that is, photographic films are not realistic *per se*, but their perceived realism is the product of a set of discourses that do not reflect, but produce their own, reality (*see* APPARATUS THEORY [BAUDRY]; CLASSIC REALIST TEXT).

Prince then argues that when digital imagery convincingly interacts with real life foo-tage, there is a perceptual realism to the digital elements of the image. That is, the digital elements of the image correspond to natural human perception – even if, as in *Jurassic Park* (Steven Spielberg, 1993), dinosaurs have no real world referent because dinosaurs have long since been extinct (unless the Loch Ness monster exists and is a dinosaur). Because these elements correspond to our everyday perception in terms of light, colour, texture, movement, and sound, perceptual realism can bypass the problems of indexicality, not least because those digital elements are often also embedded in traditional photographic images.

Prince discusses how, at time of writing, convincing movement and texture were still hard and perhaps prohibitively expensive to achieve, such that realistic but digital humans were not (and, arguably, still are not) possible for digital animators. Part of this challenge is not simply that solidity and movement must be realistic, but that the digital creatures must be 'expressive of mood and affect' as well (Prince 1996, 33). Nonetheless, the perceptual realism of *Jurassic Park*'s dinosaurs remains convincing, therefore troubling traditional conceptions of realism. For it is not a matter now of cinematic realism being either a question of indexicality (as per Barthes and Bazin) or a product of a certain film style (as per Baudry and MacCabe). Rather, cinema in the digital age is unquestionably *both*.

While there have long since been methods for manipulating aspects of the photographic image, such as flashing film prior to development in order to produce lighting effects, digital technology gives filmmakers significantly more *control* over images. Indeed, neither the camera nor the pro-filmic event (an event that literally takes place before a camera) is now necessary in order to create a credible yet synthetic reality.

The perceptual realism of this synthetic reality illustrates how cinematic realism for viewers is, and has arguably always been, an interplay between realistic (including indexical) elements and stylistic conventions (which are not 'realistic' precisely because stylized/stylistic). Because in the contemporary age the digital elements of films are most commonly cued to correspond to our experience of the real world, cinematic realism is not a topic to be dismissed from film studies in an age of CGI, Prince concludes. But if we are properly to understand what digital images are, how viewers see them, and how these relate to how viewers see at all, then, says Prince, more and ongoing work must be done in film theory to achieve this.

## Digital cinema: the instrumentalist approach

Stuart Minnis's essay 'Digitalization and the Instrumentalist Approach to the Photographic Image' appeared in Anglo-French film journal *Iris* in 1998 as part of a special issue on film theory and the digital image, *Iris* being one of several journals, including *Wide Angle* and *Convergence*, to run such an issue at around that time. In his essay, Minnis perhaps goes some way to furthering Prince's cause by proposing the relevance of the instrumentalist approach to understanding images.

Like Prince, Minnis seeks to trouble the 'naïve' approach to photographic realism. While admitting that photographic images do in some senses record 'reality', he observes, after analytic film theorist Carl Plantinga, that pictures never function in isolation and that they work in conjunction with other discourses, particularly when being considered as 'evidence' of a fact. To this end, Minnis proposes a 'middle ground' between the 'naïve' and the sceptical approach (which suggests that images are *solely* constructs), which he terms the instrumentalist approach: 'instrumentalism is a variety of pragmatism stressing that the truth of an idea of practice is determined by its utility in solving a given problem' (1998, 52).

Cinema, for Minnis, is an invention. One might conclude that, as an invention, cinema is arbitrary and historically contingent; that is, only certain circumstances allowed it to come into being. However, not all inventions are arbitrary, cinema, or at least the human ability to understand images, being one of them. Cinema is a medium, yes, but this does not make the conventions of cinema arbitrary; they in fact use and respond to natural human perception (and, according to some research, the perceptual abilities of certain other species as well).

Admitting a long history of 'faked' documentary photographs, Minnis applies his instrumentalist approach to digital images. There might well be digital images that are re-touched and therefore 'fake', but these do not necessarily mean that we must dismiss all digital images as fake. Instead, viewers should and perhaps do understand images according to the context in which they see them. That is, once again, images are not seen in isolation. Instead we can, to use one of Minnis's examples, understand that a doctored but personal image of a regular Joe finishing first in the New York marathon is precisely that, doctored, and that it does not threaten our faith in all images as a result.

On the level of journalistic reportage, there is perhaps more at stake in believing manipulated images, because our relationship with newspapers is, for example, based on trust that we are receiving reliable evidence. But, not least because we trust some newspapers more than we trust others (the *Washington Post* is not the same as the *National Inquirer*), this relationship is similarly based on context, here the newspaper itself, and not on the photograph alone.

In conclusion, then, Minnis proposes that the question of context is far more important than trying to reach a hard and fast conclusion concerning the veracity or reliability of *all photographs*. And in this sense, by in effect proposing a case-by-case approach to analyzing digital images, Minnis goes some way to putting in place the methodology for analysis that Prince was seeking in his earlier article.

Indeed, in light of various audience responses to James Cameron's digital extravaganza *Avatar* (2009), we might find evidence to prove that Minnis is correct. Following screenings of the film, certain viewers have expressed dissatisfaction that the fictional world of Pandora is more beautiful than the real world, which is disappointing in comparison. The implication may be that the film has a powerful grip on its audience members, but their 'depression' after seeing the film is not based upon believing the film to be real, but quite the opposite: that it is *not* real. While some might express concerns that these audiences are impressionable and/or that they do not recognize the beauty of the real world, it would seem that, in the light of the most cutting edge contemporary special effects, we have not yet all gone insane in believing to be real what is patently fictional, even if those fictional images conform in relief and detail to perceptual realism.

WILLIAM BROWN

## Works cited

Enticknap, Leo. 2005. *Moving Image Technology: From Zoetrope to Digital*. London and New York: Wallflower.

Govil, Nitin. 2005. 'Hollywood's Effects, Bollywood's FX'. In *Contracting out Hollywood: Runaway Productions and Foreign Location Shootings*, edited by Greg Elmer and Mike Gasher, 92–116. Lanham, MD: Rowman & Littlefield.

Minnis, Stuart. 1998. 'Digitalization and the Instrumentalist Approach to the Photographic Image.' *Iris: A Journal of Theory on Image and Sound/Revue de théorie de l'image et du son* 25: 49–59.

Prince, Stephen. 1996. 'True Lies: Perceptual Realism, Digital Images, and Film Theory.' *Film Quarterly* 49 (3): 27–37.

Schatz, Thomas. 1993. 'The New Hollywood'. In *Film Theory Goes to the Movies*, edited by Jim Collins, Hilary Radner, and Ava Preacher Collins, 8–36. London: Routledge.

## Further reading

Bolter, Jay David, and Richard Grusin. 2000. *Remediation: Understanding New Media*. Cambridge, MA: MIT Press.

Brind, Susan, Ray McKenzie, and Damian Sutton, eds. 2007. *The State of the Real: Aesthetics in the Digital Age*. London and New York: I.B. Tauris.

Bukatman, Scott. 1993. *Terminal Identity: The Virtual Subject in Post-modern Science Fiction*. Durham, NC: Duke University Press.

——. 2003. *Matters of Gravity: Special Effects and Supermen in the 20th Century*. Durham, NC: Duke University Press.

Cubitt, Sean. 2004. *The Cinema Effect*. Cambridge, MA: MIT Press.

Darley, Andrew. 2000. *Visual Digital Culture: Surface Play and Spectacle in New Media Genres*. London and New York: Routledge.

Elsaesser, Thomas, and Kay Hoffmann, eds. 1998. *Cinema Futures: Cain, Abel, or Cable? Cinema Futures in the Digital Age*. Amsterdam: Amsterdam University Press.

Everett, Anna, and John T. Caldwell, eds. 2003. *New Media: Theories and Practices of Digitextuality*. London and New York: Routledge.

Hanson, Matt. 2004. *The End of Celluloid: Film Futures in the Digital Age*. Mies: RotoVision.

Harries, Dan, ed. 2004. *The New Media Book*. London: BFI.

Keane, Stephen. 2007. *CineTech: Film, Convergence and New Media*. Basingstoke: Palgrave Macmillan.

Manovich, Lev. 2001. *The Language of New Media*. Cambridge, MA: MIT Press.

Mulvey, Laura. 2006. *Death 24x a Second*. London: Reaktion.

Ndalianis, Angela. 2004. *Neo-Baroque Aesthetics and Contemporary Entertainment*. Cambridge, MA: MIT Press.

North, Dan. 2008. *Performing Illusions: Cinema, Special Effects and the Virtual Actor*. London and New York: Wallflower.

Pierson, Michele. 2002. *Special Effects: Still in Search of Wonder*. New York: Columbia University Press.

Rodowick, D.N. 2007. *The Virtual Life of Film*. Cambridge, MA: Harvard University Press.

Rombes, Nicholas. 2009. *Cinema in the Digital Age*. London: Wallflower.

Shaw, Jeffrey, and Peter Weibel, eds. *Future Cinema: The Cinematic Imaginary after Film*. Cambridge, MA: MIT Press.

Sobchack, Vivian, ed. 2000. *Meta-morphing: Visual Transformation and the Culture of Quick Change*. Minneapolis: University of Minnesota Press.

Stewart, Garrett. 2007. *Framed Time: Toward a Postfilmic Cinema*. Chicago, IL: University of Chicago Press.

Strauven, Wanda, ed. 2006. *The Cinema of Attractions Reloaded*. Amsterdam: University of Amsterdam Press.

Willis, Holly. 2005. *New Digital Cinema: Reinventing the Moving Image*. London and New York: Wallflower.

Wood, Aylish. 2007. *Digital Encounters*. London and New York: Routledge.

# DOCUMENTARY THEORY

Theoretical speculation concerning the defining principles, formal contours, and social value of documentary cinema dates back at least to the late 1920s, when lively dialogue opened up among filmmakers and critics about the concept of documentary as a genre. John Grierson's much-cited description of documentary cinema as 'the creative treatment of actuality' was but one of a cluster of similarly worded phrases then in circulation, designed to escape the constraints of thinking of documentary as simply the capacity of the medium to produce photographic evidence mechanically (see Rotha 1939, 68). Prevailing notions of documentary as a genre were capacious enough to encompass the use of emblematic stories, dramatic re-enactments, and abstract or impressionistic montages, among other formal strategies. Writings by Grierson, Dziga Vertov, Paul Rotha, Joris Ivens and others, moreover, explicitly linked documentary practices to larger social and political purposes.

Heightened interest in the efficacy and ethics of political propaganda during the Second World War also fuelled debates about the ideological import of documentary films among state officials, social scientists, and social critics. In the 1960s the availability of new mobile recording technologies raised fresh questions concerning appropriate documentary techniques, centered in part on varied interpretations of the concept of *cinéma vérité*, allegedly a more 'truthful' documentary approach. Questions of genre boundaries, evidential authority, ideological significance, and aesthetic and ethical practices have only multiplied over the past three decades, during which time documentary studies has emerged as a vibrant academic field, invigorated by the proliferation of new documentary formats and forms.

The writings of Bill Nichols have been central to these contemporary developments. Historical in scope, conceptual in design, Nichols's sustained effort to map a typology of documentary modes of representation has been especially influential. In his 1976 essay 'Documentary Theory and Practice', Nichols challenged the commonplace notion of documentary as a 'window on reality', lamented a lack of theoretical rigour in documentary criticism, and argued that an adequate definition of documentary required that films so labelled be 'examined as a genre with conventions and audience expectations, like any other' (36). An expanded version of this essay, exploring principles of documentary exposition, served as a pivotal chapter in Nichols's first book, *Ideology and the Image: Social Representation in the Cinema and Other Media*, published in 1981.

Two years later, Nichols (1983) introduced a more comprehensive guide, dividing documentary films into four categories based on their characteristic 'voice', in an expansive sense of that term. Drawing on refinements made to the categories by Julianne Burton (1990), Nichols then offered a richly illustrated elaboration of this four-part typology in his

1991 book *Representing Reality: Issues and Concepts in Documentary*, a foundational text in contemporary documentary studies. Here he labelled the four categories 'documentary modes of representation', foregrounding one of his key assumptions: documentary films do not simply present reality to the viewer but symbolically represent it, in ways that coalesce into legible, historically variable conventions. The choices made by documentary filmmakers are not arbitrary, but are shaped by common understandings of appropriate representational modes. In later writings, Nichols has expanded this typology, adding two additional categories to the original four, in response to new documentary cinema, as well as to new documentary scholarship. Below I offer an analytical summary of Nichols's concept of documentary modes and consider two critiques, assessing their relation to Nichols's revising of his original categories.

## Bill Nichols's 'documentary modes of representation'

Nichols's typology of documentary modes is designed to provide a set of conceptual tools and language to explain the governing principles that guide the practices of documentary filmmakers and shape the expectations of film viewers. In accord with his prior interest in documentary exposition, in *Representing Reality* Nichols focuses centrally on questions of rhetoric, aligning documentary with what he labels 'discourses of sobriety' (1991, 3–4). He proceeds inductively, attending closely to the formal structure of a wide swath of films, grouping them according to the ways they advance claims about the world. In the second chapter of *Representing Reality*, Nichols names and analyses four such documentary modes. *Expository* documentaries address viewers directly, typically through the spoken word, mounting arguments about aspects of the historical world. *Observational* documentaries purport to depict everyday life, with minimum intrusion by the filmmaking process, conveying a sense of unmediated access to local ways of experiencing the world. *Interactive* documentaries stage encounters between the filmmaker as participant-observer and witnesses who testify to past or present states of affairs. *Reflexive* documentaries comment on their own processes of representing a subject, with the construction of knowledge itself now among the topics of documentary inquiry.

Nichols emphasizes that these four modes are not hermetic but flexible and permeable categories. While most documentaries are organized around a dominant mode, no single organizing principle governs all of a film's structural features. Furthermore, elements of one mode may bear close affiliation with those in other categories. An interview format, for example, is common to expository, interactive, and reflexive documentaries, yet functions differently in each case, given variations in the hierarchies of authority found in each mode. Likewise, assertions of narrative causality recur throughout documentary, but take the shape of problem-solving in the expository mode, of lived experience in the observational mode, and of segmented testimony in the interactive mode. In a reflexive documentary, causal stories may be subject to interrogation or exposure as artifice. Nichols's four-part typology is thus relational, serving as an analytical grid that enables close comparative study of particular works, including those that border or straddle different categories. The typology provides a way of examining how competing documentary principles are organized in particular films.

Nichols's typology is also historical, in three important respects. First, Nichols presupposes the existence of a world prior to and apart from symbolic representations of it, one in which historical forces are always and already at work. The phrase to which Nichols frequently returns when explaining the referential field of documentary images and sounds is the 'historical world'. In a later chapter of *Representing Reality* he asserts: 'As the referent of documentary, history is always what stands outside the text' (1991, 142). Note that in this conception of documentary, the referent is not a specific object, place, or person, but rather the historical relations that obtain among many different things. Informed by a Marxist concept of ideology, Nichols's theory of documentary posits a critical role for the analyst, who must attend to the ways documentaries potentially conceal or reveal aspects of the historical world. A drive for knowledge fuels all documentary practices, carrying with it ideological potentialities and force. Deep knowledge of historical relations is thus a benchmark against which documentaries can and should be evaluated.

Second, Nichols's documentary modes are historically contingent, emerging from specific social, political, and cultural contexts, and coalescing into intelligible conventions. The authority of these conventions is reinforced by the institutions in which documentaries are produced, distributed, viewed, and discussed. Nichols's categories thus give a name to the conventional ways of representing reality that have gained prominence in different historical periods.

Third, Nichols's typology is historiographical, structured as a trajectory of dominant practices, the chronology of which is explained. Employing a framework drawn from Russian formalism, Nichols proposes that as the conventions of a given mode become overexposed, a sense of artifice takes over and the mode loses persuasive force. A new documentary mode then arises in dialectical response to the deficiencies of its predecessor, providing a fresh sense of realism as the conventions of that predecessor begin 'to frost the window onto reality' (1991, 32).

Nichols's commitment to categories that are pliable and historically contingent is reflected in his subsequent revising of the typology. In *Blurred Boundaries: Questions of Meaning in Contemporary Culture*, published in 1994, he introduces a fifth documentary mode of representation: the *performative*. Performative documentaries, he argues, cohere not through unities but expressive and evocative affinities. In such a context, expressive elements are freed from subordination to logic, reason, or cogent argumentation. Like the reflexive mode, from which it springs, the performative mode reflects back on its own representational strategies. But performative documentaries take a still more radical step, making the viewer the primary referent rather than the historical world. Addressing the viewer affectively and subjectively, performative documentaries do not assume that there is a single, stable position from which to comprehend this world. For Nichols, this constitutes an epistemological shift in documentary cinema, leaving the work of explanation to the viewer, and hence calling into question the ground upon which shared knowledge of the world can be secured. While performative documentaries retain a referential claim to the historical world, they also 'address the challenge of giving meaning to historical events' (Nichols 1994, 98).

If the performative mode radically alters expectations concerning documentary as a genre, Nichols nonetheless proceeds to outline a genealogy for the mode, tracing its roots both to experimental practices by silent-era Soviet filmmakers and to early expository documentaries that were 'as much poetic as argumentative' (1994, 102). This then provides a framework for his broader reconsideration of early documentary history, a line of inquiry Nichols pursues in detail in his 2001 essay 'Documentary Film and the Modernist Avant-Garde'. In *Introduction to Documentary*, also published in 2001, Nichols recasts his typology once again, adding a sixth category: the *poetic* mode. Originally treated as simply a stylistic variant of the expository mode, poetic conventions for Nichols now stand apart as the first historically dominant way of representing reality in documentary form. At least by name, the poetic mode suggests how, from early on, documentary representation in various guises has bordered on or transitioned into various fictional modes. In its most recent arrangement, then, Nichols's topology has six categories (with the 'interactive' mode renamed 'participatory'), the historical span of which is bookended by two newly conceived modes, neither of which conforms closely to Nichols's initial tenet that a constitutive element of documentary as a genre was the mounting of arguments about the historical world.

## Documentary theory and history:
## Nichols's typology critiqued

Widely embraced by documentary scholars for its heuristic value, Nichols's typology has enabled close study of the comparative rhetorical structure, style, and communicative function of documentaries of many different types. Substantive questions have been raised, however, about the scope and logic of the typology's historical scaffolding. In a thoughtful and largely supportive reading, for example, Carl Plantinga in *Rhetoric and Representation in Nonfiction Film* (1997) takes issue with the 'built-in teleology' of Nichols's four-part typology, contending that it strongly favours the final, reflexive mode. Nichols notes in *Representing Reality* that his chronology may create the impression of evolutionary development, yet cautions against reading the typology this way, stressing that modes cross time periods, overlap, and interact. Acknowledging Nichols's caveat, Plantinga nonetheless argues that the progressive implications of the typology are powerfully reinforced by Nichols's evaluative commentary, which suggests that earlier modes are naive, and that the reflexive mode is most capable of registering the complexities – or, in Nichols's terms, the 'magnitudes' – of the historical world. Writing in advance of Nichols's 2001 revisions, Plantinga also contends that the typology greatly oversimplifies documentary history, ignoring the range of early documentary types and reducing the first poetic documentaries to a subset of the expository mode, for which they are ill-suited.

Stella Bruzzi, in *New Documentary: A Critical Introduction* (2000), offers a related but more astringent critique of Nichols's historical approach. Deeming the genealogy of documentary the 'first issue of documentary theorization', Bruzzi faults Nichols's typology for imposing 'a false chronological development onto what is essentially a theoretical paradigm', the rigidity of which undermines his claim that the categories are flexible and permeable. The result is 'the creation of a central canon of films that is deeply exclusive and conservative' (2). Furthermore, the progressive implications of Nichols's typology, Bruzzi claims, are Darwinian in their logic. Documentary history follows an evolutionary path, 'determined by the endless quest for better and more authentic ways of representing reality', as if moving towards a utopian future in which 'documentary will miraculously be able to collapse the difference between reality and representation altogether' (2). The effect is not simply a necessary streamlining of categories for the purposes of clarity, but a more fundamental misreading of the emergence and development of documentary, and of the newer forms the genre has taken.

The evolutionary implications of Nichols's chronology are unmistakable, as Nichols himself concedes. Considered simply in terms of breadth of coverage, moreover, his explanatory commentary in *Representing Reality* favours the interactive and reflexive modes by a wide margin. In this regard, the initial typology appears constructed on a narrow historical base, with Nichols's commentary on the expository and observational modes supporting richer, more detailed analyses of contemporary documentary forms. Nichols's recent work on early documentary and the modernist avant-garde, however, serves to remedy this imbalance, as does his treatment of the poetic register as its own distinct mode. In *Introduction to Documentary*, moreover, his analysis of the strengths and limitations of all six modes is even-handed, with commentaries equitably apportioned. Nichols also now explicitly states that no mode is inherently superior to another. Still, it is clear that he continues to find analytical value in the mapping of documentary history according to the succession of chronologically dominant modes. In both *Blurred Boundaries* and *Introduction to Documentary*, for example, he presents a schematic history of documentary as a linear trajectory, rather than, say, charting some of the complex affiliations among modes he elsewhere describes.

Bruzzi's characterizations of Nichols's chronology as 'Darwinian' and 'utopian' are misleading, however. According to Nichols's model, each new mode brings with it evident deficiencies or gaps, as well as opportunities. Despite the progressive aspects of his historical survey, he does not view the reflexive or performative modes as free of drawbacks. He makes a distinction, for example, between reflexive techniques that are 'consciousness-raising' – on the model of early feminist documentaries, whose role in the emergence of the reflexive mode he finds crucial – and those whose reflexive loop is so tight that it 'squeezes this social element out' (Nichols 1991, 67). He also cautions that 'social subjectivity will lie beyond the horizon of any text that affirms the personal visions and subjective experience of individual, poetic consciousness and little more', a problem highlighted in 'the absence of a specifically political frame within which performative documentary might be received' (Nichols 1994, 106).

Bruzzi seems to acknowledge as much when she later contrasts Nichols's 'latent wariness' of the performative mode with her own more positive account (Bruzzi 2000, 154). Such wariness reflects Nichols's sustained commitment to the historical world as a benchmark against which documentary representations must be assessed. Given his evaluative framework, documentaries whose conventions are deemed most realistic by contemporaneous viewers would seem to be prime candidates for ideological critique, and those of the critic's own moment especially. Far from positing a utopian future in which representation and reality are collapsed, Nichols advises a reader to 'take with a grain of salt any claims that a new mode advances the art of cinema and captures aspects of the world never before possible' (2001, 101).

Nichols's expansion and revision of his original four-part typology demonstrates an ongoing responsiveness to developments in documentary cinema and criticism, as well as the inductive and generative aspects of his initial approach. He may have framed his typology too narrowly at the outset by making exposition and argument the bases for a more general theory of documentary representation. At the very least, exposition and argument have proven an inadequate ground for charting documentary history, early to late, as suggested by Nichols's introduction of the new categories. His adjustments, however, have added range, complexity, and balance to the typology's original design.

In 1993, Michael Renov registered 'measured opposition' to Nichols's alignment of documentary with discourses of 'sobriety', in that this 'presumed a rationalist foundation for documentary rather than one that issues from an encounter of the creative imagination with the historical world' (Renov 1993, 194–6). In counterpoint, Renov proposed his own typology of documentary poetics, based on 'desires' or 'impulsions' (1993b, 22) – 'unconscious, delirious, fantastic, or ecstatic elements' (1993a, 194) – that also fuel documentary discourse. As Renov has also pointed out, Nichols in *Blurred Boundaries* offers his own complementary response to the taxonomic approach of *Representing Reality*, 'exploring the outer limits of current practices and its altered epistemic underpinnings' (Renov 1999, 318). I would add that Nichols's subsequent investigations of the relation between poetic documentaries and the modernist avant-garde present a more comprehensive and fertile framework for rethinking the history of documentary cinema as a dynamic social construct. In light of the early documentary experiments he now foregrounds, Nichols's performative mode may signal less a radical shift in documentary epistemology than a reactivation and reconfiguration of a primary tension in documentary between poetics and rhetoric, affinities and unities, ambiguities and certainties, and boundaries that blur and boundaries that bind.

CHARLES WOLFE

## Works cited

Bruzzi, Stella. 2000. *New Documentary: A Critical Introduction*. London and New York: Routledge.

Burton, Julianne. 1990. *The Social Documentary in Latin America*. Pittsburgh, PA: University of Pittsburgh Press.

Nichols, Bill. 1976. 'Documentary Theory and Practice'. *Screen* 17 (4): 34–48.

——. 1981. *Ideology and the Image: Social Representation in the Cinema and Other Media*. Bloomington: Indiana University Press.

——. 1983. 'The Voice of Documentary'. *Film Quarterly* 36 (3): 17–30.

——. 1991. *Representing Reality: Issues and Concepts in Documentary*. Bloomington: Indiana University Press.

——. 1994. *Blurred Boundaries: Questions of Meaning in Contemporary Culture*. Bloomington: Indiana University Press.

——. 2001. 'Documentary Film and the Modernist Avant-Garde'. *Critical Inquiry* 27: 580–610.

——. 2001. *Introduction to Documentary*. Bloomington: Indiana University Press.

Plantinga, Carl R. 1997. *Rhetoric and Representation in Nonfiction Film*. Cambridge: Cambridge University Press.

Renov, Michael. 1993a. 'Introduction: The Truth about Non-Fiction'. In *Theorizing Documentary*, edited by Renov, 1–11, 193–8. New York and London: Routledge.

——. 1993b. 'Towards a Poetics of Documentary'. In *Theorizing Documentary*, edited by Renov, 12–36, 198–204. New York and London: Routledge.

——. 1999. 'Documentary Horizons: An Afterword'. In *Collecting Visible Evidence*, edited by Jane M. Gaines and Renov, 313–26. Minneapolis: University of Minnesota Press.

Rotha, Paul. 1939. *Documentary Film*. London: Faber & Faber.

## Further reading

Barnouw, Erik. 1993. *Documentary Film: A History of Non-fiction Film*. Oxford: Oxford University Press.

Branigan, Edward. 1992. *Narrative Comprehension and Film*. London and New York: Routledge.

Carroll, Noël. 1996. 'Nonfiction Film and Postmodernist Skepticism'. In *Post-theory: Reconstructing Film Studies*, edited by David Bordwell and Noël Carroll, 283–306. Madison: University of Wisconsin Press.

Corner, John. 2006. 'Bill Nichols'. In *Encyclopedia of Documentary Films*, vol. 2, edited by Ian Aitken, 994–7. New York and London: Routledge.

Gaines, Jane, and Michael Renov, eds. 1999. *Collecting Visible Evidence*. Minneapolis: University of Minnesota Press.

Nichols, Bill. 2008. 'Documentary Reenactment and the Fantasmatic Subject'. *Critical Inquiry* 35: 72–89.

Plantinga, Carl. 2009. 'Documentary'. In *The Routledge Companion to Philosophy and Film*, edited by Paisley Livingston and Carl Plantinga, 491–504. London and New York: Routledge.

Renov, Michael. 2004. *The Subject of Documentary*. Minneapolis: University of Minnesota Press.

Waldman, Diane, and Janet Walker, eds. 1999. *Feminism and Documentary*. Minneapolis: University of Minnesota Press.

Winston, Brian. 1995. *Claiming the Real: The Documentary Film Revisited*. London: British Film Institute.

# EMOTION, FILM AND

Emotion is a crucial component of the film experience: it explicitly underpins genres such as comedy, tragedy, and horror, and it anchors the spectator to the screen through engagement with characters and the issues they confront. Emotion is also an indicator of value: emotional responses tell us something about the ethical, ideological, or aesthetic worth we perceive in a film, its narrative, and the people and events it represents. Indeed, Murray Smith argues that emotional engagement with characters is the main way film influences viewers' beliefs, values, and ideologies. Smith's essay 'Altered States: Character and Emotional Response in the Cinema' (1994) details emotion's centrality to film reception. The following summary examines how Smith systematically develops an account of cinematic emotion. It then situates his influential work in relation to other perspectives, including those of Noël Carroll and Carl Plantinga.

The study of film and emotion can be traced back to Hugo Münsterberg's 1916 book *The Film: A Psychological Study* (republished 1970), which identifies 'picturing emotions' as a core feature of filmmaking (see Plantinga 2009, 5). Subsequently, psychoanalytic film scholars have suggested spectators experience perverse pleasures including masochism, sadism, and voyeurism because of unconscious drives or repressed psychosexual fears and desires that govern our feelings in ways we do not fully apprehend. Other theorists have argued film is part of an institutional apparatus in which the pleasures of spectatorship secure assent for dominant ideologies. More recently, researchers critical of Cartesian dualism – an assumed division between mind and body that privileges cognition and suggests emotion interferes with rationality – have identified a close relationship between thinking and feeling. Contemporary scholars are developing sophisticated accounts of emotional engagement with film and are examining how responses to fictional characters and narratives differ from, yet have continuities with, emotional responses to actual people and events. Starting with Carroll's *Philosophy of Horror* (1990), cognitive film theorists have analysed emotion's constituent parts and processes, examined how emotions are cued by narrative and aesthetic elements including music and characterization, and investigated emotion's influence on interpretation.

## Emotion

Philosopher Justin Oakley understands emotional states as 'complex phenomena involving dynamically related elements of cognition, desire and affect' (1992, 2). This view has considerable support in film studies and is advocated by Carroll (1999, 21), Smith (1994, 42), and Plantinga (2009, 6). Without including all three elements it is difficult to distinguish between emotional states and other experiences like feeling lethargic or being in a good mood, or to distinguish between different emotions. For example, the affect (physiological feeling) that accompanies excitement might be expressed in ways that resemble anxiety and create similar effects such as surging adrenaline, but excitement and anxiety are linked to different cognitions (thoughts and other mental acts), which in turn relate to different intentions and desires (where desire is the goal- or action-oriented dimension of emotion). This connection between cognition and emotion does not mean emotions can't be irrational. Rather, it recognizes that mental acts like imagining or believing are central to emotions such as jealousy; similarly, evaluations of right and wrong are core aspects of guilt and shame. Affect is also grounded in cognitive judgements. Bodily reactions such as nausea and the recoil response of disgust, or the tears accompanying grief, reflect judgements that the object of disgust is bad or impure and that grief arises from the loss of something or someone greatly valued.

Philosopher Ronald de Sousa builds on the argument that emotions have cognitive, rational components to contend emotions are socially constructed, learned responses to situations, contextualized in narrative understandings of actions and events. In *The Rationality of Emotion*, de Sousa claims our emotional vocabulary is learned 'first from our daily life as small children and later reinforced by the stories, art, and culture to which we are exposed' (1987, 182). Narrative film is one of the arts from which we learn an emotional repertoire. There are, however, differences between emotional responses to fiction and reality.

The centrality of cognition to emotion is sometimes used to suggest we do not experience actual emotional responses to fictional narratives because emotions rely on belief. For example, fear is based on the belief that a threat exists and since film audiences know they are watching recorded performances of fictional events, they do not believe characters in a monster movie are in danger. Consequently, some scholars have argued spectators do not really feel fear; they feel 'make-believe emotions' (Walton 2006) or their response is 'quasi-emotional' (Currie 1990). This position reduces complex cognitive processes to a simplistic account of belief and makes a mockery of the experiences of horror film fans. Rather than supporting this view, Smith suggests that, in emotional responses to fiction, the cognitive component of emotion is frequently imaginative, instead of being directly belief oriented.

## Murray Smith's 'Altered States: Character and Emotional Response in the Cinema'

Smith works from the premise that spectators' reactions to screen characters are governed by imaginative acts that are closely bound up with emotional responses. He argues that, in order to understand identification with screen characters, we need to break emotional and imaginative engagement down into more precisely defined terms, processes, and components. In doing so, Smith challenges assumptions that emotion indicates irrationality, that imagination means visualizing images, and that identification connotes a loss of identity or sharing identical feelings.

Smith identifies sympathy and empathy, loosely defined as 'feeling for' and 'feeling with', as two ways spectators engage emotionally with characters. He uses the terms 'central imagining' (imagining from the inside of a character's experience) and 'acentral imagining' (imagining from the outside) to complicate reductive understandings of identification as vicarious experience of a character's thoughts and feelings (Smith 1994, 35). In terms of the relationship between imagination and emotional responses to characters, Smith regards 'acentral imagining as cognate with sympathy, while central imagining is a type of empathy' (53).

Smith positions his work in relation to other approaches, critiquing psychoanalytic film theory's claims that aesthetic cues such as camera position often lead spectators to adopt the viewing position of a heterosexual male and become aligned with his desires. This implies that spectators centrally imagine a narrative scenario, become subsumed within the protagonist's ideology and subject position, and respond emotionally as if they were that character. By contrast, Smith supports cognitive film theorists who believe films typically invite acentral imagining. In this view, we do not imagine that we are a character in the story, nor do we necessarily feel what characters feel: 'Rather, we comprehend the character and the situation and react emotionally (if we react at all) to the thought of the character in that situation (as opposed to the thought of ourselves as the character in that situation)' (39).

Smith is generally in agreement with cognitivists such as Carroll, who argues that sympathetic emotional engagement with screen characters relies primarily on acentral imagining. However, he qualifies and builds on such work by introducing the concept of empathy and its subcategories, 'emotional simulation', 'affective mimicry', and 'autonomic reactions' (*see* AFFECT, FILM AND). Smith contends: 'One of the key mechanisms for arriving at the kind of acentral assessments Carroll posits may be a form of imaginative "simulation" of the mental states of characters, that is, a form of central imagining' (39). Since empathy only foregrounds one of the three components of emotion, affect, we will concentrate on sympathy, which is the focus of Smith's article.

Sympathy, Smith writes, is an aspect of identification that involves three levels of imaginative engagement with characters: recognition, alignment, and allegiance. On the most obvious level, Smith proposes that spectators identify representations and performances as characters (a process he refers to as recognition). He goes on to say:

> Spectators are also provided with visual and aural information more or less congruent with that available to characters and so are placed in a certain structure of alignment with characters. In addition, spectators evaluate characters on the basis of the values they embody and hence form more-or-less sympathetic or antipathetic allegiances with them.
>
> (Smith 1994, 35)

Alignment refers to how spectators are positioned in relation to screen characters. Alignment provides access to what characters know and feel through point-of-view shots, subjective imagery, and sound, especially interior monologues and music. As Smith says: 'Perceptual alignment – optical POV and its aural equivalent – is regarded as simply one resource of the narration in controlling alignment' (41). Contrary to psychoanalytic theory, he is quick to point out that optical alignment does not necessarily cause identification.

Allegiance has connotations of choosing allies and 'pertains to the moral and ideological evaluation of characters by the spectator' (41). It operates in relation to narrative content and context, and it depends upon the spectator having 'access to the character's state of mind, understanding the context of the character's actions, and having morally evaluated the character on the basis of this knowledge. Evaluation, in this sense, has both cognitive and affective dimensions' (41). More than just experiencing fellow feeling, allegiance entails judging and responding emotionally to a character's traits and behaviour 'without replicating the emotions of the character' (42).

Smith develops his ideas in an analysis of the textual cues and narrative conventions that facilitate identification in Hitchcock's *The Man Who Knew Too Much* (1956). Smith's interpretation of this film demonstrates that character engagement is plural and multi-faceted, enabling 'a kind of imaginative mobility that has been almost entirely obscured by the stress on "subjection" (ideological determination) in contemporary theory' (49). This means subjective imagery and other cinematic techniques can invite the audience 'to "identify" informationally with a character from whom we are simultaneously emotionally alienated' (49).

Smith distances his work from models 'in which the spectator is conceptualized as the passive subject of the structuring power of the text' (40). The three aspects of sympathetic engagement Smith elucidates do indicate that, to some extent, the spectator's viewing position in relation to screen characters is influenced by the position of the camera and other techniques, but in other respects character engagement depends on the narrative context and on factors such as spectators' personal experiences and ethical judgements.

## Other perspectives

Like Smith, Carroll is committed to an active model of spectatorship. However, Carroll gives more ground to the idea that mechanisms of emotional identification (which he terms 'assimilation') can steer audience interpretation. For Carroll, emotions are analogous to 'searchlights' that 'manage our attention, guiding both what we look at and what we look for' (1999, 28). He makes the important point that in fiction films salient details are foregrounded for the audience by the narrative structure, editing, lighting, the reactions of surrounding characters, music, performance, cinematography and so forth, and hence the audience's emotional reactions are guided or 'prefocused' by the film (30), perhaps to a greater degree than Smith allows.

Plantinga builds on research by both Smith and Carroll by examining emotion more broadly than in relation to character engagement or identification. He reclaims elements of psychoanalysis, co-opts ideas from cognitive psychology, and draws on recent neuropsychological work on mirror neurons to expand understandings of the film experience. Plantinga develops what he calls a 'cognitive-perceptual' approach to the study of emotions, arguing that emotions are states involving perceptual appraisal and mental construals as well as physiological arousal and action tendencies (2009, 55). In this view cognition and emotion are both sensory, embodied processes that not only entail conscious interpretation but are also influenced by cultural context, social convention, unconscious and automatic elements of the film experience. Plantinga goes further than Smith in attempting to bridge the gap between psychoanalytic and cognitive approaches to film, reframing psychoanalytic concepts such as 'desire', 'pleasure', and 'fantasy' and incorporating them within an expansive model of conscious, rational, and emotive processes of film comprehension.

The important point to emerge from the accounts of emotion and character engagement discussed here is that spectators identify with select aspects of screen characters' experience instead of being totally subsumed. We do not have to feel what characters feel or agree with their actions or opinions in order to imaginatively identify with their situations or their aspirations, as Smith's work shows. Rather than taking on a character's subjectivity wholesale when we watch a film, different cinematic techniques invite a shifting intersubjective experience in which we share in the optical, affective, motivational, evaluative, or epistemic perspective of particular characters (or of the film itself, and its implied narrator) at various points in the narrative (see Stadler 2008).

Attention to the ethical, evaluative dimension of emotion, and careful analysis of emotion's component processes, are distinctive features of Smith's work. Smith's analysis of the structure of cinematic emotion does much to reveal how engaging with a character doesn't simply mean identifying with heroes, feeling badly for victims, and becoming influenced by a protagonist's moral perspective when the camera shoots from their point of view. His nuanced examination of character engagement extends the argument that 'emotions proper have both a cognitive component and an affective component' (Smith 1994, 42) by detailing the significance of affect, and the rich variety of forms cognition can take. In examining different types of affective reactions and expanding understandings of the cognitive component of emotion to include ethical evaluation and acts of imagination, Smith makes an important contribution to cognitive film theory's accounts of spectatorial response. Moreover, his model of emotion overturns the 'antinomy between reason and the emotions' (42). In other words, the integrated model of emotion developed by Smith and other cognitive film theorists critiques the Cartesian mind/body dichotomy. By extension, it also undermines assumptions that reason, which was traditionally considered a masculine attribute, is superior and opposed to emotion, which was denigrated as feminine. Arguing for the significance of emotion within and beyond the cinema and asserting the interlinked nature of cognition, affect, and their mutual influence on the desire to act therefore constitute a theoretical perspective that has ethical, political, and cultural implications.

JANE STADLER

## Works cited

Carroll, Noël. 1990. *The Philosophy of Horror, or, Paradoxes of the Heart*. New York: Routledge.

——. 1999. 'Film, Emotion and Genre'. In *Passionate Views: Film, Cognition and Emotion*, edited by Carl Plantinga and Greg M. Smith, 21–47. Baltimore, MD: Johns Hopkins University Press.

Currie, Gregory. 1990. *The Nature of Fiction*. Cambridge: Cambridge University Press.

De Sousa, Ronald. 1987. *The Rationality of Emotion*. Cambridge, MA: Massachusetts Institute of Technology Press.

Münsterberg, Hugo. 1970. *The Film: A Psychological Study. The Silent Photoplay in 1916*. New York: Dover.

Oakley, Justin. 1992. *Morality and the Emotions*. London: Routledge.

Plantinga, Carl. 2009. *Moving Viewers: American Film and the Spectator's Experience*. Berkeley: University of California Press.

Smith, Murray. 1994. 'Altered States: Character and Emotional Response in the Cinema'. *Cinema Journal* 33 (4): 34–56.

Stadler, Jane. 2008. *Pulling Focus: Intersubjective Experience, Narrative Film and Ethics*. New York: Continuum.

Walton, Kendall. 2006. 'Fearing Fictions'. In *Philosophy of Film and Motion Pictures*, edited by Noël Carroll and Jinhee Choi, 234–46. Malden, MA: Blackwell.

## Further reading

Grodal, Torben. 2009. *Embodied Visions: Evolution, Emotion, Culture and Film*. New York: Oxford University Press.

Hanich, Julian. 2010. *Cinematic Emotion in Horror Films and Thrillers: The Aesthetic Paradox of Pleasurable Fear*. New York: Routledge.

Smith, Murray. 1995. *Engaging Characters: Fiction, Emotion and the Cinema*. Oxford: Clarendon Press.

Tan, Ed S. 1996. *Emotion and the Structure of Narrative Film: Film as an Emotion Machine*. Translated by Barbara Fasting. Mahwah, NJ: L. Erlbaum Associates.

# ENUNCIATION, FILM AND

Since the 1970s some scholars have applied the concept of enunciation, originally devised by Emile Benveniste for verbal language, to film. The starting point of the debate is Christian Metz's essay 'Story/Discourse (a Note on Two Kinds of Voyeurism)' (1975), in which Metz connects Benveniste's linguistic categories with concepts derived from psychoanalysis. Yet, the ensuing debate focused on the linguistic and semiotic dimension of the concept, either to propose an original conception of filmic enunciation or to deny the possibility of using it within the field of film studies. This entry examines the seminal essay by Metz, recaps the following discussion, and sketches recent developments in the debate.

## Enunciation

The French linguist Emile Benveniste proposed the concept of enunciation in a series of essays written between 1946 and 1970. Enunciation is the act of producing verbal utterances. Enunciation can also be defined as the act of appropriation and use of linguistic signs. In particular, there are three categories of signs which find their referential meaning only within utterances: the personal pronouns of the first and second person (me, you); pronouns and adverbs of time and space, which refer to the 'here' and 'now' of the enunciation (this, that, yesterday, tomorrow, etc.); and the system of tenses (present perfect, future). Once set, these signs fulfil two functions: on the one hand, they inscribe subjects and conditions of enunciation within the utterance, and therefore they are 'marks'; on the other hand, they refer to the context of enunciation and are therefore 'deictics' (from the Greek verb *deiknumi*, which means 'to indicate').

Benveniste generally refers to situations of face-to-face dialogue, but in a 1959 essay he reflects on written statements; in this regard he discovers two possibilities. In some cases, written utterances simulate face-to-face dialogue: correspondingly Benveniste speaks of discursive enunciation, or simply *discourse*. In other cases, written utterances use repertories of signs avoiding any reference to the situation of enunciation – it is third person language – and verbal tenses which refer to a past isolated from the present of the enunciation. In these cases, 'no one speaks here: the events seem to narrate themselves' (1971, 208). Benveniste calls this historical enunciation, or *history*.

## Christian Metz's 'Story/Discourse (a Note on Two Kinds of Voyeurism)'

Christian Metz revisited Benveniste's distinction between story and discourse in his 1975 essay, originally written for a collection in honour of Benveniste and then published in the book *The Imaginary Signifier*.

157

'I'm at the cinema. The images of a Hollywood film unfold in front of me. It doesn't even have to be Hollywood: the images of any film based on narration and representation ... the kind of film which is the industry's business to produce' (Metz 1982, 91). In these opening lines of the essay, Metz defines the object of his discourse: the situation of fiction film watching. He believes that this situation is not 'natural'; rather, it is constructed by the Cinema Institution within the cultural and ideological context of our society. Furthermore, this construction consists in the production of a particular regime of desire for movie watching. The essay inquires into the specific characteristics of such a regime of desire, and does so primarily by mobilizing tools from psychoanalysis.

Metz recovers Freud's analysis of voyeurism and exhibitionism as reciprocally mirrored perversions (especially as conducted in the 1915 essay 'Triebe und Triebschicksale'): the exhibitionist takes his or her pleasure in showing him/herself, while a voyeur's pleasure comes from watching someone else, and the pleasure of both requires the awareness of the active presence of the partner. However, this framework does not apply perfectly to the situation of fiction film watching, which is complicated by a split: 'The film is exhibitionist, and at the same time it is not ... The film knows that it is being watched, and yet does not know ... The one who knows is the cinema, the *institution* ... the one who doesn't want to know is the film, the *text*' (1982, 93–5). Indeed, film exhibitionism is subjected to a dynamic of disavowal: it is part of its cinematographic nature, but it has to be denied within its textual manifestation. The 'regime of desire' of the fiction film spectator derives from the particular kind of voyeuristic pleasure implied by such a situation: 'for this mode of voyeurism ... the mechanism of satisfaction relies on my awareness that the object I am watching is unaware of being watched' (95).

Metz connects this description of the film watching situation with a description of the corresponding internal logic of the fiction film text. In this regard, he borrows Benveniste's distinction between 'history' and 'discourse': 'In Emile Benveniste's terms, the traditional film is presented as story, and not as discourse. And yet, it is a discourse, if we refer it back to the film-maker's intention, the influence he wields over the general public, etc.; but the basic characteristics of this kind of discourse, and the very principle of its effectiveness as discourse, is precisely that it obliterates all traces of enunciation, and masquerades as story' (91). Such internal logic of the film text is produced by the particular system of voyeuristic pleasure sketched above: '[The] fundamental disavowal [governing spectator's pleasure] is what has guided the whole of classical cinema into the paths of "story", relentlessly erasing its discursive basis, and making it (at best) a beautiful closed object which must remain unaware of the pleasure it gives us' (94). It is for this reason that in the fiction film (as the essay ends up) 'It is the "story" which exhibits itself, the story which reigns supreme' (97).

## The debate on film enunciation

Some authors have criticized Metz's positions, and have radically denied the option to apply the linguistic concept of enunciation to film studies; on the contrary, others scholars have developed the idea of film enunciation, even without fully sharing Metz's ideas.

Within the first group, we find David Bordwell and Noël Carroll. The two thinkers share the idea that the language of cinema does not have deictic features similar to those of verbal language. They deny both that the film possesses a repertoire of forms comparable to the persons and tenses of verbal language, and that the film carries an activity comparable to that of verbal enunciation – and therefore they deny the fact that any 'subjects' of the enunciation should be found in the film. Any attempt to shift linguistic deictics to film language – for instance by personifying the film itself – 'is just a bit of perfectly arbitrary word play that has nothing determinate to do with grammatical personhood' (Carroll 1988, 154).

Bordwell focuses on both the roots and the consequences of the shift of the linguistic concept of enunciation to cinema studies. The roots are detected in Metz's seminal essay. 'Metz does not so much borrow from Benveniste as rewrite him, and not for the better' (Bordwell 1985, 23). Indeed, the French theorist (i) turns abstract instances such as 'films' and 'institution' into personal subjects; (ii) overlaps the concept of enunciation and that of discourse, and (iii) transforms enunciation as a verbal activity into an optical activity (based on showing and watching actions).

There were two consequences of this approach, both negative. On the one hand, the pairs of concepts enunciation/utterance and history/discourse have produced different and not mutually comparable views and definitions among film scholars. On the other hand, these studies arbitrarily privileged a few film techniques: camera work and editing in particular.

In contrast, among the scholars who have taken up and developed a theory of film enunciation, the most comprehensive and influential work was Francesco Casetti's *Inside the Gaze* (1991; originally published in 1986). Casetti borrows from Metz the project of a theory intended as an account of the fiction film watching situation. Moreover, like Metz, he thinks that the key feature of this situation is the constitution of the spectator as a subject. Finally, Casetti shares the idea with Metz that the spectator's subjectivity is understandable in terms of visual enunciation, that is, as the result of a network of relationships between a subject who shows, a subject who is shown and a subject who watches.

The main point of detachment from Metz concerns the Italian theorist's belief that the constitution of the spectator's subjectivity is due to the use of certain formal configurations of cinema language. Furthermore, these linguistic forms combine both story and discourse features. Finally, from a methodological point of view, Casetti excludes psychoanalytic tools; rather, he builds a semiotic theory as a deductive device, and draws up a formal framework from which it should be possible to account for a number of variants empirically found.

According to Casetti, each filmic utterance implies an instance of origin, or 'enunciator', and an instance of destination, or 'enunciatee'. The presence of two instances is constant and implicit, but it can be made explicit by various kinds of marks, and even figurativized by the characters who tell a story (narrators) or listen to it (narratees).

Enunciator, enunciatee and characters are differently arranged in the four major types of shot, already identified by classical film grammar: the objective, or nobody's, shot – described as 'I, the enunciator, and You, the enunciatee, look at Him, the character or the scene'; the interpellation (for example, the character looking into the camera), where 'He and I look at You'; the subjective shot, where 'You and He look at what I show you'; and finally the unreal objective shot (with spectacular view, unusual angles, or elaborated camera movements), described as 'I show Him to You'.

## From film enunciation to film experience

Metz's essay 'The Impersonal Enunciation or the Site of Film' (originally published in 1987 and translated into English in 1991) critically summarizes the debate and sets the ground for a deep rethinking of the concept.

The intent of the essay is metatheoretical: Metz still does not inquire what the situation of fiction film watching is; rather, he asks how a film enunciation theory can properly account for this situation. Indeed, the French scholar identifies three risks of a theory of enunciation: 'anthropomorphism, artificial use of linguistic concepts, and transformation of communication into enunciation ( = "real", extra-textual relationships)' (1991a, 758). The first risk to avoid is the idea that the film situation is comparable to a face-to-face dialogue between the film and its viewer: the two entities have different statutes, and the interaction is asymmetric because the viewer cannot speak with the film. In other words, the film makes an enunciation statement without interaction (1991b, 200). The theory must therefore avoid configuring the two subjects in anthropomorphic terms: 'If what is meant is the physical inscription of enunciation, using things' names would be more appropriate. I would suggest "source (or origin) of the enunciation" and "enunciative target (or destination)"' (1991a, 748).

The second risk is that the theory sees in the film text an effective reference to the real context of the vision. Against a 'deictic' theory of enunciation, Metz proposes a 'reflective' one: 'Enunciation is the semiologic act by which some parts of a text talk to us about this text as an act' (1991a, 754). 'Cinematic enunciation is always enunciation on the film. Reflexive, rather than deictic, it does not give us any information about the outside of the text, but about a text that carries in itself its source and its destination' (762).

Finally, the last risk is that the theory sees the different forms of film enunciation as a rigidly fixed repertory (i.e. a 'grammar'): 'cinema does not have a closed list of enunciative signs, but it uses any sign … in an enunciative manner' (754–5). Indeed, voices on, off and over, intertitles, windows and mirrors within the diegetic world, subjective and objective shot etc. should be analysed for their enunciative value.

Metz's essay made it possible to reset, restart, and recast the debate on film enunciation. In his concluding remarks, the scholar refers to two possible 'stages' of enunciation: 'a textual stage (the "markers"; source and target), and a personal stage (imaginary author and spectator, enunciator and addressee; this is the level of attributions: the marker is ascribed to someone)' (768). Metz's theoretical approach is exclusively interested in the textual stage, probably because of the fear of coming back to an anthropomorphic conception of enunciation. Nonetheless, the subsequent reflection developed a further reflection on what Metz calls the 'personal' stage. In these cases, the aim of the theory is still to account for the film watching situation; however, the main object of study is not the film text any more: rather, scholars focus on the film experience itself, seen in its cognitive and affective dimensions, as a culturally embedded and a bodily situated phenomenon.

On the basis of this 'experiential turn', the main issues addressed by the debate on film enunciation return in two respects. On the one hand, the theory analyses the different ways in which the spectator constructs a representation of the enunciator and defines its degree of reliability from ethic, aesthetic, referential points of view (see, for instance, Odin 2000). On the other hand, the theory describes how, within the sensory motor dimension of his/her experience, the film viewer adopts a system of spatial and temporal orientation designed and driven by the audiovisual materials. In some cases, this orientation system is radically different from the actual situation of the film viewer: indeed, this should be called the 'historical' mode of orientation; in other cases, there is a partial overlap between the two systems – what should be called the 'discursive' mode of orientation (see suggestions in Buckland 2000, 52–76).

RUGGERO EUGENI

## Works cited

Benveniste, Emile. 1971. *Problems in General Linguistics*. Translated by Mary Elizabeth Meek. Coral Gables: University of Miami Press.

Bordwell, David. 1985. *Narration in the Fiction Film*. Madison: University of Wisconsin Press.

Buckland, Warren. 2000. *The Cognitive Semiotics of Film*. Cambridge: Cambridge University Press.

Carroll, Noël. 1988. *Mystifying Movies: Fad and Fallacies in Contemporary Film Theory*. New York: Columbia University Press.

Casetti, Francesco. 1991. *Inside the Gaze: The Fiction Film and Its Spectator*. Bloomington: Indiana University Press.

Metz, Christian. 1982. 'Story/Discourse (a Note on Two Kinds of Voyeurism)'. In *The Imaginary Signifier: Psychoanalysis and the Cinema*, translated by Celia Britton and Annwyl Williams, 91–8. Bloomington: Indiana University Press.

——. 1991a. 'The Impersonal Enunciation, or the Site of Film (in the Margin of Recent Works on Enunciation in Cinema)'. *New Literary History* 22: 747–72.

——. 1991b. *L'Enonciation impersonelle ou le Site du Film*. Paris: Klincksieck.

Odin, Roger. 2000. *De la fiction*. Brussels: De Boeck & Larcier.

## Further reading

Buckland, Warren, ed. 1995. *The Film Spectator: From Sign to Mind*. Amsterdam: Amsterdam University Press.

Casetti, Francesco. 1999. *Theories of Cinema, 1945–1995*. Austin: University of Texas Press.

Marie, Michel, and Marc Vernet, eds. 1990. *Christian Metz et la théorie du cinéma*. Paris: Klincksieck.

Stam, Robert, Robert Burgoyne, and Sandy Flitterman-Lewis. 1992. *New Vocabularies in Film Semiotics: Structuralism, Post-structuralism and Beyond*. London and New York: Routledge.

# ETHICS

'What is the good of film experience?' Siegfried Kracauer closes his 1960 *Theory of Film: The Redemption of Physical Reality* by addressing this question – the question of film ethics. According to Kracauer, the modern world has resulted in a culture of 'abstraction' that removes us from the particularity of physical reality. The loss of common beliefs and the increasing prestige of science reduce the particulars of the world to a system of themes. The good of film experience, argues Kracauer, is that its specific images of physical reality come from the outside to contest our institutions and abstractions. It testifies to more than our themes contain:

> In acquainting us with the world we live in, the cinema exhibits phenomena whose appearance in the witness stand is of particular consequence. It brings us face to face with the things we dread. And it often challenges us to confront the real-life events it shows with the ideas we commonly entertain about them.
>
> (Kracauer 1960, 304–5)

The good of film experience is that it calls us to question our self-assuredness. It leads us from surface particulars to something beyond surfaces, to something beyond that interrupts the certainty of our comprehension and self-satisfaction.

As basic as the question of film ethics is, surprisingly it has been little articulated in the history of film studies. Outside a few instances, such as the concluding chapter of Kracauer's book, the question of film ethics has garnered little attention. Certainly, questions of religion, morality, societal norms, and redemption have been important since the birth of cinema. Likewise, questions of film politics and cinematic authenticity have been central to many debates within film studies. Film theory has always been concerned with questions of ontology and epistemology. Even before the first motion pictures, theorists asked such questions as 'what is cinema?' and 'how do I understand it?'. Yet, until recently, few theorists have inquired into the specific complexities of film ethics.

## The encounter

To be clear, the question of film ethics is always the question of an encounter between the self and the other. In the cinema, this encounter plays out: (1) between filmmaker and subjects or characters; (2) between subjects or characters themselves; (3) between the subject or characters and the rest of the world; and (4) between the film and film-goers.

Previously, theorists have addressed these encounters through political, phenomenological, psychoanalytical, cognitive, and analytical approaches. However, in such instances, questions of ethics have been determined either by outside rules or codes or by a return to the self as the centre of the moral universe, not by the immediate encounter with the other. Additionally, this determination has been made possible by seeing the other as 'different from' me, as a different version of me or an alter-ego rather than 'irreducibly different', unique and incomparable. The turn towards the question of film ethics challenges the totalitarian and authoritarian foundations of these assumptions and approaches.

Although the key thinkers to influence contemporary questions of film ethics include Michel Foucault, Jacques Derrida, Jacques Lacan, Slavoj Žižek, Alain Badiou, and a number of feminist and queer theorists, the most significant voice in the debate has been Emmanuel Levinas. It is the specific turn towards the primacy of the singularity of the other that makes Levinasian ethical inquiry unique. For Levinas (1969), ethics is 'an optics' (23), a 'calling into question of my spontaneity by the presence of the Other' (43), and 'a non-allergic relation with alterity' (47). It is a way of looking at the world that is embodied and visible but also beyond the embodied and visible that opens systems and selves to critique as I 'encounter the indiscreet face of the Other that calls me into question' (171). Ethics immediately arises through encountering the other; therefore, it cannot be based on prior rules and cannot be used to found a system of law. Furthermore, ethics is a provocation to respond to an encounter with exteriority rather than return to self-assuredness.

This description of the *encounter* (sometimes referred to as the *face-to-face*) and of *responsibility* engendered through this encounter have led recent theorists – Renov (2004), Cooper (2006; 2007), Aaron (2007), Girgus (2010), and Downing and Saxton (2010) – to explore specifically the intersection of film specificity and ethics.

## Sarah Cooper's *Selfless Cinema?*

The first book significantly dedicated to the question of film ethics in this uniquely Levinasian sense is Sarah Cooper's *Selfless Cinema? Ethics and French Documentary* (2006). Traditionally, we think of ethics in terms of comparisons between like terms. We ask about goodness, fairness, and equality in terms of recognition between ourselves and others. In her book, Cooper (following Levinas) inverts the traditional question and asks what it might mean to maintain the separation between self and other, *not* to see the face of the other as my own but to value and valorize separation from the filmed subject. She asks after responsibility towards the other rather than recognition between the self and the other. What might it mean to ask after the other first, without expecting reciprocity? What might it mean to ask how I am responsible for the other? And what might this mean in terms of the cinema and the separation the cinematic apparatus creates but cannot thematize?

Cooper establishes two paths for analysing the ethics of filmic separation, specifically as we experience it through documentary. First, when I look at documentary, I look through the eyes of another, through the camera, at an other. This double look challenges the reduction of those I see to their own image or an image of myself. Second, when I experience cinematic time, I experience a time separate from my own. The experience of cinematic time is the experience of what Levinas calls 'fecundity', the time that comes before me and remains after me. 'Fecund time' (Cooper 2006, 26) is neither the time of the film-goer nor the time of the image, but is the relation between the two, linking them 'asymmetrically, disjunctively in a space and time common to neither' (25), maintaining a separation their relation makes possible. This tension between relation and separation is crucial for film ethics.

Building on the encounter of film *and* ethics, Cooper argues that within documentary film, as well as in the wider realm of all cinema, subjects of films 'might be seen to resist reduction to the vision of the film-maker who fashions them' and aligns this irreducibility 'with the asymmetrical relation to the Other' (5) we see in Levinas's 'ethics of responsibility'. Addressing the vision of the filmmaker – the ethics and politics attached to filmmaker presence or absence within the filmic space and time – Cooper redefines how we currently understand documentary when some images 'not only escape the control of the film-maker who fashions them but also the spectator' (6). Some images, because they provoke us to see film in the light of other films, compel an 'interfilmic mode of viewing' (8) that resists 'the reflective mechanism that would refer one back to oneself or one's own world' (8). This excess escapes the filmmaker and the viewer, separating them from the filmed subjects. When what we see exceeds what we expect, the limitations of filmmaking, the inability of films to completely thematize and totalize the world, disturb us with the encounter of the face and skin of the other. When such encounters occur in the cinema, argues Cooper, ethics 'ruptures the being of documentary film' (12). The separation that arises from these interfilmic encounters interrupts and disturbs the cinema by calling into question its spontaneity and authority, its ability to capture and re-present the other. In this way, ethical and cinematic disturbances run parallel.

Cooper further pursues these two paths through the rest of the book. Chapter 2 investigates Jean Rouch's ethnographies and their attentive positioning of the subject of vision to create an ethical space within a colonial framework. Chapter 3 analyses Chris Marker's profound calling into question of the filmmaker's control in order to elevate the ethical priority of the other over the self. Chapter 4 highlights Raymond Depardon's almost-still images from within institutions, images that resist thematization by creating a conditional rather than future tense: images of what *could* happen rather than what *will* happen to me. Chapter 5 focuses on Agnès Varda's dissident, incomplete self-portraiture that reiterates the primacy of the other over the self in the constitution of the filmmaker's vision.

In the Marker chapter especially, Cooper is able to connect these two paths regarding film ethics by showing how his films play hide and seek with the vision of the filmmaker. Through a close study of *San Soleil* (1982), with detours through *La Jetée* (1962) and *Level 5* (1996), Cooper draws out Marker's connection between camera operator absence/presence and the implications of fecund time, showing how the two lines collaborate. For Cooper, *San Soleil*'s juxtaposition of supposed masculine images and memories with female voice-over, deployment of strategic close-ups of a man's face and a woman's face, reliance upon complex and de-contextualizing montage, and use of shots from where the camera operator has never been, displace the self of the operator and viewer. According to Cooper, such composition of separation 'calls us to bear witness to the existence of a subjectivity that could never have come into being, or be sustained in the future, without the others it filmed' (61), interrupting the themes of the images and the film-goers. This separation that resists thematization (in documentary and other filmic modes) compels us 'to view in a manner otherwise than being bound to the symmetry of self–other relations' (92), and *not* to see the face of the other as our own.

## Separating film and ethics

As much as Cooper demonstrates the intersections between film and ethics, though, she also cautions against reducing either one to the other. Even here, separation is what makes the encounter possible because the encounter displaces the ground beneath cinema, the filmmaker, the filmed subject, the film-goer, and the ethics of responsibility for 'the ethical traverses the filmic but shatters an exact mirroring of the terms of Levinasian ethical debate and discussion of cinema in general or documentary in particular, since neither can contain the other' (Cooper 2006, 12). The key to film ethics is the relation founded on separation. Cooper does film *and* philosophy as she uses ethics to question film and film to question ethics. Not just using one to illustrate the other, Cooper's approach is a dialogue between film and ethics where ethics alters our understanding of film and film alters our understanding of ethics. Rather than give examples of an under-examined Levinasian ethics or prioritize ethics to give us the barest of plot summaries, character analyses, or shot generalizations (especially regarding close-ups of faces), Cooper stages an encounter between film and ethics.

## Criticisms of film ethics

Film ethics, and Cooper's intervention into film ethics, are open to at least three challenges: filmic, Levinasian, and post-Levinasian. The first questions Cooper's emphasis on separation in the encounter; the second echoes objections found in Levinas's own iconoclastic writings; and the third arises from rebuttals of the 'beyond' or 'excess' in Levinasian ethics.

First, although Cooper emphasizes the meaning of the separation of looking and *not* seeing the face of the other as my own, film ethics also has to ask after the proximity of looking and seeing the face of the other as my own. Film ethics must address responsibility *and* recognition if cinema, ethics, and politics are to be connected. Judith Butler (2004) and Susan Sontag (2004) raise this question in their work on trauma, mourning, and regard. Levinas (1991) himself also raises this question in his explorations of 'non-indifference', 'the relation of saying and the said', and 'the relation between separation and proximity'. Extending Cooper, then, film ethics might ask how viewers encounter films between the proximity of sound and images and the separation created by their origins.

Second, like all commentators on Levinas and aesthetics, Cooper acknowledges Levinas's early iconoclastic writing, where he describes the aesthetic encounter as a violent freezing of relations rather than an opening towards ethics. For many, these early writings block considerations of a positive Levinasian film ethics. For example, in 'Reality and Its Shadow', Levinas (1989 [1948], 139) writes:

> We can then understand that time, apparently introduced into images by the non-plastic arts such as music, literature, theatre and cinema, does not shatter the fixity of images ... Such a fixity is wholly different from that of dialectic. By its reflection in a narrative, being has a non-dialectical fixity, stop dialectics and time.

The work of art – especially the image – bewitches us and traps us in irresponsibility. In several later essays and interviews, Levinas alters this stance to address the difference between complete and incomplete works of art, where 'incomplete' art has the potential to escape this fixity. When he addresses artists such as Jean-Michel Atlan, Sacha Sosno, and Charles Lapicque, Levinas admits to the ethical possibility of an aesthetic encounter that does not completely fix separation. Questions of film ethics need to engage with this full range of ethical inquiry into aesthetics.

Third, for some thinkers, such as Alain Badiou (2001) and Slavoj Žižek (2006), no current revision of Levinas will rehabilitate what they see as an ethics of 'excess' or 'beyond'. For Badiou, Levinasian ethics invokes an 'ethical ideology' which blocks access to 'the truth', the true course of philosophy. For Žižek, Levinas's ethics fails to be ethical because it remains transcendent and beyond human experience, where ethics should be located. Such critiques raise valid points for the future of studies into the intersection of film and ethics. Cooper's work addresses the question of the good of the film experience in a way that puts film and ethics in sustained conversation. The next steps are to further engage in discussions of the separation and proximity of ethical specificity and filmic specificity without reducing either to the same.

BRIAN BERGEN-AURAND

## Works cited

Aaron, M. 2007. *Spectatorship: The Power of Looking On.* London: Wallflower Press.
Badiou, A. 2001. *Ethics: An Essay on the Understanding of Evil.* Translated by Peter Hallward. London: Verso.
Butler, J. 2004. *Precarious Life: The Powers of Mourning and Violence.* London: Verso.
Cooper, S. 2006. *Selfless Cinema? Ethics and French Documentary.* London: Legenda.
——, ed. 2007. 'The Occluded Relation: Levinas and Cinema'. *Film-Philosophy* 11 (2) (special issue).
Downing, L., and L. Saxton. 2010. *Film and Ethics: Foreclosed Encounters.* London: Routledge.
Girgus, S.B. 2010. *Levinas and the Cinema of Redemption: Time, Ethics, and the Feminine.* New York: Columbia University Press.
Kracauer, S. 1960. *Theory of Film: The Redemption of Physical Reality.* Princeton, NJ: Princeton University Press.
Levinas, E. 1989 [1948]. 'Reality and Its Shadow'. In *The Levinas Reader*, edited by Sean Hand, 129–43. Oxford: Blackwell.
——. 1969. *Totality and Infinity: An Essay on Interiority.* Pittsburgh, PA: Duquesne University Press.
——. 1991. *Entre Nous: On Thinking-of-the-Other.* New York: Columbia University Press
Renov, M. 2004. *The Subject of Documentary.* Minneapolis: University of Minnesota Press.
Sontag, S. 2004. *Regarding the Pain of Others.* New York: Picador.
Žižek, S. 2006. 'Neighbors and Other Monsters: A Plea for Ethical Violence'. In *The Neighbor: Three Inquiries in Political Theology.* Chicago, IL: University of Chicago Press.

## Further reading

Drabinski, J.E. 2008. *Godard between Identity and Difference.* New York: Continuum.
Mai, J. 2010. *Jean-Pierre and Luc Dardenne.* Urbana: University of Illinois Press.
Stadler, J. 2008. *Pulling Focus: Intersubjective Experience, Narrative Film, and Ethics.* London: Continuum.
Wheatley, C. 2009. *Michael Haneke's Cinema: The Ethic of the Image.* London: Berghahn Books.
Zylinska, J. 2005. *The Ethics of Cultural Studies.* London: Continuum.

# EUROPEAN FILM THEORY

## An attempt at a definition

The various theoretical positions that constitute 'European film theory', also described by David Bordwell as 'SLAB theory' (Saussure–Lacan–Althusser–Barthes), share a common philosophical heritage: Husserl's phenomenology and the post-Husserlian and Heideggerian phenomenological tradition, including hermeneutics, structuralism, and post-structuralism (see Ian Aitken's *European Film Theory and Cinema: A Critical Introduction*).[1] European film theory is particularly indebted to the existential phenomenology of Heidegger, Sartre, and Merleau-Ponty, who viewed everyday experience as essentially inauthentic or mystified (e.g. Heidegger's notion of 'throwness' or 'facticity') and for whom the concept of 'intentionality', central to Husserl's eidetic phenomenology, came to reflect a greater awareness of the situatedness of consciousness within the world than that allowed by Husserl's transcendentalism and cognitivism.

European film theory is distinguished by its historicism (the belief that conditions of intelligibility are shaped by language, culture, and history), political commitment (the belief that conditions of intelligibility are contingent and therefore subject to change), self-reflexivity (a preoccupation with the question of what 'theory' is), and scepticism (scepticism about the power of concepts – and thus the power of theory – to tell us anything about reality or cinema and, at the same time, a secret *hope* that cinema can bypass conceptual under-standing and that theory need not be 'theoretical' in the scientific sense of the term) (Trifonova 2008, xv). Dudley Andrew draws attention to the speculative or self-reflexive aspect of Continental theory, in which 'meaning, significance, and value are never thought to be discovered, intuited, or otherwise attained naturally. Everything results from a mechanics of work: the work of ideology, the work of the psyche ... and the work of technology' (Andrew 1984, 15).

From the perspective of Anglo-American analytic theory, Continental theory's scepticism – reflected in concepts such as 'construction', 'alienation', 'subject-positioning', 'misrecognition', and 'suture' (*see* CONTEMPORARY FILM THEORY; SUTURE) – always occupies a *secondary* position with respect to the *untroubled belief* that infuses analytic theory, which focuses on *primary* processes such as perception, cognition, recognition, and concentration. The reason for this is that while the analytic tradition considers philosophy and film theory autonomous disciplines engaged primarily in conceptual analysis, Continental film theory is premised on the understanding that circulating, extra-filmic discourses – culture, ideology, society, sub- and unconscious drives, history, and technology – decisively shape film meaning.

## European film theory's resistance to the rationalizing forces of modernity/postmodernity

Continental theory is rooted in the philosophies of life (Schopenhauer, Freud, Nietzsche, Bergson) that emerged in the nineteenth and early twentieth century in response to the increasing ascendancy of scientific thought. The concept of 'life' is essential to Continental theory, from Epstein's '*photogénie*' (cinema's ability to capture the soul of things, to make the inanimate animate) and Eisenstein's 'montage of attractions' (predicated on a dialectical view of life), through Balázs's 'physiognomic poetics', Benjamin's 'aura' (the Romantic notion of nature awake and 'returning our gaze'), Bazin's and Kracauer's 'redemptive' film theories, to the filmmaker Tarkovsky's 'imprinted time' (the 'living duration' of film shots) and Deleuze's 'time-image'. Continental theory tends to promote non-cognitive and irrationalist forms of expression as a *resistance* to the rationalizing forces of modernity and postmodernity. Indeed, many of the concepts it privileges appear to be *aestheticized* symptoms of a range of mental illnesses: *affective flattening* (cf. 'de-dramatization' and 'dead time' in neorealist theory, or Deleuze's emphasis on 'any-moment-whatever' and 'any-space-whatever'); *avolition* (cf. the weakening of character and narrative motivation in realist film and theory); *dissociation* (cf. the privileging of defamiliarization as a way of reestablishing a more intimate connection to an underlying reality); *fragmentation* (cf. the privileging of 'episodic' over 'dramatic' narratives); *temporal deregulation or drift* (cf. Tarkovsky's 'sculpting in time'); *spatial dislocation* (cf. Kracauer's notion of 'the solidarity of spaces' foregrounding the interconnectedness of disconnected spaces/phenomena); *paranoid fears of one's mind or memory being invaded* (cf. Benjamin's notion of the optical unconscious as a repository of collective memory pervading individual memory); and *dissociative fugues* (cf. Kracauer's notion of 'distraction').

Epstein's revelationist aesthetic and Balázs's anthropomorphic theory are both informed by animistic beliefs, translating into the realm of the aesthetic the symptoms of various types of delusional and anxiety disorders characterized by the inability to distinguish the living from the non-living. Benjamin's work on photography and cinema betrays a similar dependence on the appropriation of the language of madness and mental illness. For him the radical potential of photography and cinema is exemplified by those aspects – involuntary memory, absent-mindedness, arbitrariness, indeterminacy, distraction, derealization, shock, and the uncanny – that resist the standardization of life in the industrialized age by encouraging non-rational responses to reality. In Kracauer's *Theory of Film* affective states commonly perceived as symptomatic of madness or mental illness – detachment from reality, ennui, melancholy, distraction, and disinterestedness/apathy – are posited as necessary to film's 'redemption of physical reality'. Similarly, Deleuze emphasizes the overturning of filmic logic, insisting on the constitutive indiscernibility of reality, fantasy and dream, past, present and future.

## Challenges to European film theory

Starting in the early 1980s European film theory began to be criticized for its 'penchant for Platonizing' (Carroll 1988, 226–7), its social constructivism, its overdependence on psychoanalytical and literary theory models, its use of argument as bricolage, and its scorn for the methods of empirical research (Bordwell 1996, 18–23). Since then, European film theory has been 'reconstructed' by history (Bordwell's 'historical poetics of film'), science

(Bordwell and Carroll's call to make film theory conform to scientific models of theorizing), and philosophy (Allen and Turvey's Wittgenstein-inspired attempt to subject the presumed association of theory with science to a philosophical critique) (Rodowick 2010, 23–38). European film theory has been found at fault for (1) betraying the Enlightenment project by misinterpreting the events in France of 1968 as proof of the power of ideological structures and institutions rather than as evidence of the potential of the masses to reshape history and escape ideological false consciousness; (2) overestimating the constructed nature of subjectivity and refusing to acknowledge the importance of agency, thereby denying cinema any political significance; (3) offering abstract and over-generalized analyses of the institutions of cinema and the film spectator, instead of analysing specific audiences in their historical and social context; (4) focusing on gender and class differences to the exclusion of other forms of difference (race, ethnicity, postcolonial struggles); (5) exaggerating the power of mainstream cinema to induce misrecognition, from which the viewer can be liberated only by the self-reflexive strategies of the avant-garde; (6) overestimating the constitutive power of language and automatically rejecting realism as a potential oppositional practice; (7) trying to legitimize itself as a metanarrative of emancipation; and (8) positioning the spectator exclusively as the subject of enunciation or else as a voyeur (Metz) rather than as the addressee of an impossible, ethical demand (Levinas) (see Robert Lapsley and Michael Westlake's *Film Theory: An Introduction* [2006]).

Cognitivist analyses of the narrative comprehension of film and of the spectator's mental and emotional processes have incorporated research from perceptual and cognitive psychology, evolutionary psychology, cognitive philosophy, narratology, and neuroscience (e.g. Richard Rushton and Garry Bettinson's *What Is Film Theory? An Introduction to Contemporary Debates* [2010]). Propounding mid-level theorizing that uses the methods of scientific inquiry (e.g. falsifying theories like psychoanalysis and semiotics), cognitivists (e.g. Bordwell, Carroll, Branigan, Smith, Grodal, and Anderson) challenged European film theory's basic premises: identification, illusionism, and subject positioning. The three main premises of cognitivism – the natural understanding thesis, the rational problem-solving thesis, and the commonsense interpretation thesis – have been, in turn, criticized by Daniel Frampton, among others. Taking issue with Carroll's critique of the illusion theory, the pretend theory, and the 'thought' theory of emotional response to fiction, Frampton propounds a phenomenological critique of the claim that film comprehension takes place at a rational level rather than being perceptually intuitive (Daniel Frampton's *Filmosophy* [2006]).

## Contemporary directions in European film theory

Contemporary European film theory is doubly ungrounded, marked by metacritical debates about *the status of theory* and the role philosophy has to play in the reinvention of film theory, and by debates *about the status of film* in an era when film as a physical object might be disappearing. There are three main strands in recent Continental theory: (1) a return to earlier ontological theories of film in response to the emergence of the digital, i.e. a *historicization of theory*; (2) a turn to ethics, as evidenced by a number of recent publications on Levinas and cinema; and (3) a re-evaluation of the status of film theory in relation to philosophy and science. Each of these strands will now be considered.

The digital has prompted a critical revival of theorists like Bazin, Kracauer, Epstein, Balázs and Arnheim, and a renewed interest in the relationship between film and photography reflected in the return to questions of medium specificity and indexicality (e.g.

David Campany's *Photography and Cinema* [2008] and *The Cinematic* [2007], and Karen Beckman and Jean Ma's edited collection *Still Moving: Between Cinema and Photography* [2008]). In 'What's the Point of an Index?' Gunning argues that indexicality cannot be divorced from iconicity (Gunning 2008, 23–41); in *The Virtual Life of Film* Rodowick challenges Gunning's reduction of indexicality to perceptual realism, insisting that photography and film provide a spatial record of duration, whereas the technological criteria of digital images' perceptual realism 'wrongly assume … that the primary powers of photography are spatial semblance' (Rodowick 2007, 103–5). Theoretical discussions of indexicality have been shifting away from a strictly semiotic analysis to a phenomenological analysis of the index in terms of *affect:* Thierry de Duve urges us to consider the psychological response produced by the photograph's illogical temporality, rather than the semiotics of the index (de Duve 2007) and in *The Emergence of Cinematic Time: Modernity, Contingency, the Archive* Mary Ann Doane understands the index no longer in terms of the deeply historical relationship to reality that photography was said to guarantee by virtue of its automatism, but in terms of the affective response produced by *both* analogue and digital images.

The 'ethical turn', which could be related to the revival of Bazin's ethically flavoured ontological theory, or else could be seen as continuing the legacy of Continental theory's critique of epistemology as an ethical critique of modernity (Allen and Smith 1997, 1–35), can be tentatively traced back to the late 1990s. Since then there has been a special edition of *Film-Philosophy* on Levinas and cinema (2007) and a series of books on ethics and cinema, drawing on Levinas, Derrida, Deleuze, and Lacan. In *The Virtual Life of Film* Rodowick (2007) discusses an 'ethics of time' in relation to Barthes's reflections on death and photography. Several of the essays in his *Afterimages of Gilles Deleuze's Film Philosophy* (2010) are similarly dedicated to ethics and cinema. In *Levinas and the Cinema of Redemption: Time, Ethics and the Feminine*, Sam Girgus discusses films that 'enact the struggle to achieve ethical transcendence by subordinating the self to the greater responsibility for the other, primarily as delineated in Levinas's ethical philosophy' (Girgus 2010, 5). In *Film and Ethics: Foreclosed Encounters* Lisa Downing and Libby Saxton explore 'the ways in which postwar continental philosophy (Levinas, Derrida, Foucault, Lacan, Žižek) helps us to conceptualize the phenomenology of cinema along ethical lines' (Downing and Saxton 2010, 14). Drawing on Lacanian psychoanalysis, in *Out of Time: Desire in Atemporal Cinema*, Todd McGowan (2011) demonstrates that atemporal cinema – which, he argues, arose in response to the digital era and constitutes a new atemporal ethics embodying Levinas's idea of time as opening the subject to alterity – unfolds according to the logic of the death drive rather than that of the pleasure principle.[2]

Malcolm Turvey's 'Theory, Philosophy, and Film Studies: A Response to D.N. Rodowick's "An Elegy for Theory"' (2010) sums up the major points of the debate between Continental and analytical philosophers about the role philosophy has to play in film theory. According to Rodowick, 'analytic philosophy has produced a disjunction between philosophy's ancient concern for balancing epistemological inquiry with ethical evaluation' (2010, 27). He calls for a philosophy of film that would acknowledge the irreducible difference between philosophy and science: 'science tests its hypotheses against external phenomena [whereas] philosophy admits only to internal or self-investigation. This is less a question of truth and error than judgements concerning the "rightness" of a proposition tested against prior experience and knowledge' (28). Rodowick concludes that 'it is important … to find and retain in theory the distant echo of its connection to philosophy, or to *theoria*, as restoring an ethical dimension to epistemological self-examination' (29), something he sees accomplished in Deleuze's and Cavell's philosophy of film. In response, Turvey argues that epistemological and ethical commitments do not seem of use to film theory since they 'typically *underdetermine* theories' (41). For Turvey, (analytic) philosophy should 'serve as a model for film theorizing' (42) as well as fulfilling a propaedeutic role, helping us 'clarify and therefore better understand the concepts, particularly the psychological concepts, we employ in theorizing about and studying film' (42).

Ultimately, the critique of European film theory refuses to acknowledge the irreducible difference between the human and the natural sciences: a special mode of understanding, *verstehen*, which tries to grasp the world from an individual's (participatory) viewpoint, rather than from an impersonal (scientific or positivist) viewpoint, is essential in the human sciences. Continental theory rejects the use of both analytic and inductive procedures, while recognizing that such procedures are necessary in the natural sciences to compensate for the lack of a tacit antecedent understanding. Analytic theory, on the other hand, insists that analytic and inductive procedures reveal universally shared mental functions, a form of 'technical competence' construed as analogous to 'antecedent understanding'. Thus, Continental and analytic theory start from two very different concepts of 'understanding'. While cognitivists assume the existence of a very basic level of cognition, a form of understanding not concealed by, or distorted into, some kind of false consciousness, Continental theory borrows the notion of 'understanding' from Dilthey, Gadamer, and Heidegger, who reject the reduction of understanding to mere perception or cognition, to universally shared and unchanging mental functions or skills, and instead emphasize the pragmatism and situatedness of understanding.

The theoretical areas that have flourished since the late 1980s are indicative of the continued historicization of theory (cinema of attractions, audience research; Richard Rushton and Garry Bettinson's *What Is Film Theory? An Introduction to Contemporary Debates* [2010]) and of the importance of Continental theory's phenomenological roots. Challenging the historicization of film theory on the basis of geography and language, Thomas Elsaesser and Malte Hagener's *Film Theory: An Introduction through the Senses* (2010) reorganizes film theory around the question of the relationship between cinema, perception, and the human body. This approach to film theory, they argue, attempts to bridge the divide between formalist and realist theories, between theories of authorship and reception, between photographic and post-filmic cinema, and between European film theory and Anglo-American film theory.

TEMENUGA TRIFONOVA

## Notes

1 Aitken traces the intuitionist modernist and realist tradition (which he defines in terms of irrationalism, intuitive insight, artistic autonomy, and indeterminate expression, distinguishing it from the post-Saussurian tradition) back to the philosophical lineage encompassing German idealist philosophy, romanticism, phenomenology, and the Frankfurt School.
2 For a more general account of the above issues, see Jerrold Levinson, ed., *Aesthetics and Ethics: Essays at the Intersection* (Cambridge: Cambridge University Press, 1998).

## Works cited

Aitken, Ian. 2001. *European Film Theory and Cinema: A Critical Introduction*. Bloomington: Indiana University Press.

Allen, Richard, and Murray Smith. 1997. 'Introduction: Film Theory and Philosophy'. In *Film Theory and Philosophy*, 1–35. Oxford: Oxford University Press.

Andrew, Dudley. 1984. *Concepts in Film Theory*. Oxford: Oxford University Press.

Beckman, Karen, and Jean Ma, ed. 2008. *Still Moving: Between Cinema and Photography*. Durham, NC: Duke University Press.

Bordwell, David. 1996. 'Contemporary Film Studies and the Vicissitudes of Grand Theory'. In *Post-theory: Reconstructing Film Studies*, edited by David Bordwell and Noël Carroll, 18–23. Madison: University of Wisconsin Press.

Campany, David. 2007. *The Cinematic*. Cambridge, MA: MIT Press.

——. 2008. *Photography and Cinema*. London: Reaktion Books.

Carroll, Noël. 1988. *Mystifying Movies: Fads and Fallacies in Contemporary Film Theory*. New York: Columbia University Press, 226–7.

de Duve, Thierry. 2007. 'Time Exposure and Snapshot: The Photograph as Paradox'. In *The Cinematic*, edited by David Campany, 52–62. Cambridge, MA: MIT Press.

Doane, Mary Ann. 2002. *The Emergence of Cinematic Time: Modernity, Contingency, the Archive*. Cambridge, MA: Harvard University Press.

Downing, Lisa, and Libby Saxton. 2010. *Film and Ethics: Foreclosed Encounters*. New York: Routledge.

Elsaesser, Thomas, and Malte Hagener. 2010. *Film Theory: An Introduction through the Senses*. London: Routledge.

Frampton, Daniel. 2006. *Filmosophy*. London: Wallflower Press.

Girgus, Sam. 2010. *Levinas and the Cinema of Redemption: Time, Ethics and the Feminine*. New York: Columbia University Press.

Gunning, Tom. 2008. 'What's the Point of an Index? Or, Faking Photographs'. In *Still Moving: Between Cinema and Photography*, edited by Karen Beckman and Jean Ma, 23–41. Durham, NC: Duke University Press.

Lapsley, Robert, and Michael Westlake. 2006. *Film Theory: An Introduction*. 2nd edition. Manchester: Manchester University Press.

Levinson, Jerrold, ed. *Aesthetics and Ethics: Essays at the Intersection*. Cambridge: Cambridge University Press.

McGowan, Todd. 2011. *Out of Time: Desire in Atemporal Cinema*. Minneapolis: University of Minnesota Press.

Rodowick, D.N. 2007. *The Virtual Life of Film*. Cambridge, MA: Harvard University Press.

——. 2010. 'An Elegy for Theory'. In *The Film Theory Reader: Debates and Arguments*, edited by Marc Fursteneau, 23–38. New York: Routledge.

——, ed. 2010. *Afterimages of Gilles Deleuze's Film Philosophy*. Minneapolis: University of Minnesota Press.

Rushton, Richard, and Garry Bettinson. 2010. *What Is Film Theory? An Introduction to Contemporary Debates*. Maidenhead: Open University Press.

Trifonova, Temenuga. 2008. 'Introduction: That Perpetually Obscure Object of Theory'. In *European Film Theory*, edited by Temenuga Trifonova, i–xv. New York: Routledge.

Turvey, Malcolm. 2010. 'Theory, Philosophy, and Film Studies: A Response to D.N. Rodowick's "An Elegy for Theory"'. In *The Film Theory Reader: Debates and Arguments*, edited by Marc Fursteneau, 38–47. New York: Routledge.

# EVIDENCE (NANCY)

The work of contemporary French philosopher Jean-Luc Nancy traverses the fields of politics, deconstruction, phenomenology, aesthetics and the arts, exploring such wide-ranging issues as existence, identity, the body, community, justice and the 'deconstruction of Christianity'. Nancy's most sustained engagement with cinema can be found in *The Evidence of Film* (2001), a text which focuses ostensibly on the work of the Iranian filmmaker Abbas Kiarostami, while raising a number of broader philosophical questions about cinema. What follows here outlines some of the key propositions of *The Evidence of Film*, with a particular focus on the central motif of evidence. This summary then turns to a short essay by Laura Mulvey on the Iranian New Wave, in order to explore the potentially problematic relation between Nancy's philosophical reflections on cinema and a politics of the image.

Nancy offers no systematic theory of film in *The Evidence of Film*. He seeks rather to outline, through a series of philosophical and often poetic reflections, cinema's own specific mode of presenting the world and its particular form of access to the real. Nancy's view of cinema marks a clear shift away from a conception of the filmic image as a projection of reality or as a representation of a world outside itself. Such a conception is shaped, as Nancy notes, by a Platonic logic of mimesis, underwritten by a suspicion of the image as mere copy of the Idea (2001, 46). Nancy considers the cinematic image rather as that which presents, takes part in and makes manifest the world. Film is 'a matter of opening the seeing to a real, toward which the look carries itself and which, in turn, the look allows to be carried back to itself' (18; translation modified). The real is defined here as 'that which resists, precisely, being absorbed in any vision ("visions of the world", representations, imaginations)' (18). This model of cinema's relation to the real is what Ian James has described as Nancy's 'non-representational realism' (James 2007, 68).

Nancy's emphasis upon the real appears at times to evoke the revelatory potential of cinema theorized variously by Dziga Vertov, Siegfried Kracauer and André Bazin. However, Nancy's realism is not one which views film as a photographic reproduction maintaining an indexical relation to the pro-filmic reality that it represents. Such a realism would remain locked within a logic of immediacy and a metaphysics of presence that Nancy seeks to deconstruct throughout his philosophical writings. For Nancy, the filmic image is made manifest in a form of 'coming-to-presence', a mode of simultaneous presentation and withdrawal. Nancy considers film's 'opening' to the real, then, as irreducible to either a Platonic theory of mimesis or a Bazinian faith in indexicality (*see* ONTOLOGY OF THE PHOTOGRAPHIC IMAGE). Film's participation in the world ruptures the separation implied by the mimetic copy, yet the simultaneous withdrawal of the image interrupts the metaphysics of presence governing any investment in indexicality.

Nancy articulates this specific philosophical understanding of the relation between cinema and world through the motif of *evidence*, in a section of the text devoted to a discussion of this term. He glosses the term as follows:

> Evidence refers to what is obvious, what makes sense, what is striking and, by the same token, opens and gives a chance and an opportunity to meaning. Its truth is something that grips and does not have to correspond to any given criteria. Nor does evidence work as unconcealment, for it always keeps a secret or an essential reserve: its very light is reserved, and its provenance.
>
> (Nancy 2001, 42)

The filmic image makes manifest the world, exposing that which is obvious while simultaneously holding something in reserve. Nancy's formulation of this relation between image and world draws implicitly on Martin Heidegger's understanding of the artwork as *aletheia* (simultaneous revelation and concealment). Yet Nancy implicitly invokes another philosophical context here too: Edmund Husserl's phenomenological model of evidence. For Husserl, evidence relates to 'originary' or 'pure' intuition of the givenness of the phenomenal world (James 2007, 71–2); following Descartes (to whom Nancy directly refers in his discussion of evidence), Husserlian evidence is that which resists all possible doubt. Yet in the passage cited above, Nancy appears to recast the term evidence: evidence is that which 'opens and gives a chance and an opportunity to meaning [*sens*]'. 'Sense' (*sens*) is a privileged term in Nancy's philosophical lexicon: 'sense' is always already manifest in the world and makes meaning possible; it is prior to yet in excess of signification. Far from being synonymous with proof or apodicticity, the evidence of film thus engenders the possibility of meaning; it marks an opening to sense.

Nancy thus decouples the term evidence from its Husserlian association with intuition and self-presence, strategically marking a divergence from this particular phenomenological context (James 2007, 72). Yet the term evidence also signals a distance from Jacques Derrida (who has influenced Nancy's thought considerably), as Nancy seeks here to 'maintain an insistence upon the presentation of an image as a relation to worldly existence' (James 2007, 73). *The Evidence of Film* offers a re-consideration of the place of the real in cinema in the aftermath of deconstruction's unease with concepts of realism, presence and truth. Emphasizing a coming-to-presence of the image in more affirmative terms than a Derridean caution might allow, Nancy's figure of evidence ushers in an ontology of cinema extricated from a logic of representation yet opened to a realm of worldly presentation. Evidence acts here as a privileged figure of what Derrida, in another context, has called Nancy's 'post-deconstructive realism' (Derrida 2005, 46).

Nancy develops and clarifies the notion of evidence through recourse to its etymological roots. The Latin term *evidentia* stems from *videre* (to see), glossed here as meaning 'what is seen from afar' (2001, 42). Notions of distance, distinction or what Nancy calls 'spatial removal' are important: 'Something is *seen distinctly* from far away because it detaches itself, it separates … ' (42; original emphasis). This language of distinction, detachment and separation, deployed here in the context of cinema, connects with Nancy's broader reflections on the image elsewhere. In *The Ground of the Image*, the image is 'distinct' in that it marks a simultaneous contact with and separation from the world – a relation to worldly presentation which resists categorization in terms of a dichotomy of truth and appearance (2005, 1–9). Here in *The Evidence of Film*, Nancy uses a lexicon with precise resonance in this cinematographic context: the distinction of the image becomes the matter of 'a cut, a framing' (*une découpe, un cadrage*) (2001, 42). Through editing and framing, cinema thus affirms and foregrounds the ontological distinction – the detachment, the cut – of the image.

Nancy presents Kiarostami's filmmaking as an exemplification of the philosophical framework that he outlines here, drawing attention to certain techniques which predominantly shape Kiarostami's films: lengthy, contemplative takes; emphatic framing (through open doors, car windows); the patient, observational gaze. Such a gaze is described by Nancy as 'respectful' and 'just' in that it affirms both the distinction of the image and what Nancy sees as the ontological spacing of the world. Here film does justice to worldly presentation via the evidence of its images: 'Evidence is what presents itself at the right distance, or else, that in front of which one finds the right distance, the proximity that lets the relation take place, and that opens to continuity' (2001, 70). This argument is foregrounded in Nancy's discussion of Kiarostami's *Life and Nothing More* (1991), a film which explores the aftermath of the Manjil-Rudbar earthquake in Iran in 1990. For Nancy, the 'respectful' distance adopted by the film in relation to this cataclysmic event renders justice to the continuation of existence in its aftermath. Nancy reads this aesthetics and ethics of justice in terms of a relay between film, existence and world: 'if [life] continues while exposing itself to the evidence of images, it is because it renders justice to the world, to itself' (2001, 72).

Nancy thus deploys the motif of evidence in order to explore relations between film, justice, distinction, spacing and the real, and draws on the work of Kiarostami to exemplify these relations. In a parenthetical paragraph at the end of the section on evidence, Nancy suggests that his philosophical reflections ought not to be dissociated from a recognition of the daily social, political and practical contexts of contemporary Iran in which Kiarostami's films remain embedded (2001, 46). Yet, Nancy simultaneously acknowledges his position as a (Western) viewer who finds it difficult to grasp the films' encoded references to certain aspects of Iranian life. Aside from a very brief example of the enigmatic actions of a group of soldiers in *Taste of Cherry* (1997), Nancy does not dwell on this point about the political dimension of Kiarostami's films. Presented parenthetically, the issue of politics appears almost as an afterthought, indicating an oversight at the heart of Nancy's reflection on Kiarostami and a possible failure to engage with the politics of the cinematic image more broadly.

In her 'Afterword' to *The New Iranian Cinema*, Mulvey acknowledges the attention that Western cinephiles, critics and theorists have devoted to the New Iranian Cinema and to Kiarostami's work in particular. She notes the risks of a critical appropriation of such new cinemas 'without adequate understanding of the circumstances under which they have been produced and then circulated abroad' (Mulvey 2006, 255). Mulvey draws on an essay by Azadeh Farahmand in the same volume, which charts the ways in which the production, distribution and exhibition contexts of post-revolutionary Iranian cinema are determined by issues of censorship, foreign funding, the international film festival market and a complex 'web of global economic and political relations' (Farahmand 2006, 93). Emphasizing the importance of these insights, Mulvey argues for a 'relocation' of new cinemas such as the Iranian New Wave 'within their cultural, political and production contexts' (Mulvey 2006, 256). Such acts of 'relocation' add to the '"texture"' of understanding, so that films that travel abroad can begin to convey more explicit meanings and resonate beyond the appeal of the exotic' (257).

Mulvey's argument does not address Nancy's reading of Kiarostami in particular, nor is his reading referenced at any point in *The New Iranian Cinema*. Yet it is clear that Nancy's philosophical abstraction of Kiarostami's cinema from its particular contexts of production and circulation risks enacting the move against which Mulvey cautions here. Nancy's philosophical privileging of Kiarostami is indicative of the way in which Kiarostami's films 'travel' well and garner considerable critical success abroad (particularly in France). Yet, as Farahmand argues, Kiarostami's access to the international market relies on a significant degree of self-censorship, as his films generally avoid any direct political and social criticism of the Iranian state. In particular, in the films shot in Iran, Kiarostami uses predominantly male or child actors, thereby eliding the issue of repressive restrictions on representations of women in post-revolutionary Iranian cinema. (However, the more recent films featuring Iranian women, such as *Ten* (2002) and *Shirin* (2008), suggest a shift towards a more inclusive approach.) Mulvey invokes Farahmand's critique that Kiarostami's films tend to display a 'political escapism' which facilitates his international marketability (Mulvey 2006, 255) (an escapism and a marketability further demonstrated by recent transnational productions *Certified Copy* (2010) and *Like Someone In Love* (2012)). Nancy steers clear of such issues in his text, failing in particular to address the political complexity of the place of women in post-revolutionary Iranian cinema and society. If Kiarostami's films suggest 'political escapism', the same might be said of Nancy's philosophically focused reflections on evidence, justice, and the real.

However, the interpretative approaches of Nancy and Mulvey may not be entirely incompatible. For, once Mulvey has acknowledged the importance of engaging with the specific politics of film production, distribution and exhibition, she goes on to argue for the value of continuing to read film in aesthetic, theoretical and philosophical terms. She asserts that the Iranian New Wave has 'renewed and re-articulated' particular questions about 'ways of seeing' and about 'the construction of the visible' (2006, 257–8). Referring to Kiarostami in particular, she suggests that his work raises the question of the nature of cinema itself through an exploration of the relation between illusion and reality. Kiarostami's work enacts what Mulvey describes here as a '"what is cinema?" approach to filmmaking' which 'affects the spectator's relation to the screen' (2006, 260). Her view clearly resonates with Nancy's interpretation of Kiarostami as a filmmaker who poses questions about looking and subtly interrogates the ontology of the filmic image.

Thus the readings of cinema offered by Nancy and Mulvey are not necessarily mutually exclusive. Rather, Mulvey argues that film theory ought to be philosophically and aesthetically orientated towards a consideration of the ontology of the image, yet it should also be 'curious' about the specificities of film's cultural, political and economic contexts. The film theorist's curiosity, as Mulvey suggests, 'should also lead back to questions of social understanding, to finding ways to fill in the gaps of ignorance and cultural divergence ... ' (2006, 260). Nancy's reading appears to hesitate over such gaps in cultural divergence, as we have seen. Yet, given that *The Evidence of Film* seeks to present neither a systematic account of Kiarostami nor a coherent theory of film as such, it cannot necessarily be judged in terms of the demands to theory issued by Mulvey here. As we have seen, Nancy's text interweaves a set of loosely structured poetico-philosophical observations which contribute to a post-deconstructive consideration of the ontology of cinema. Mulvey's argument for 'relocating' films in their specific contexts suggests ways in which film theory might seek to combine Nancy's philosophical reflections on evidence with what Mulvey calls here 'a politics of cultural specificity' (2006, 261). An emerging objective may be to supplement Nancy's post-deconstructive configuration of the coming-to-presence of cinematic images with critical analyses of the cultural, political and economic conditions under which these images are produced and circulated. This invites the film theorist to consider the image in terms which are not only ontological but also political, cultural and social – a move from the evidence of film to the curiosity of theory.

LAURA MCMAHON

## Works cited

Derrida, Jacques. 2005. *On Touching: Jean-Luc Nancy*. Translated by Christine Irizarry. Stanford, CA: Stanford University Press.

Farahmand, Azadeh. 2006. 'Perspectives on Recent (International Acclaim for) Iranian Cinema'. In *The New Iranian Cinema: Politics, Representation and Identity*, edited by Richard Tapper, 86–108. London: I.B. Tauris.

James, Ian. 2007. 'The Evidence of the Image'. *L'Esprit Créateur* 47 (3): 68–79.

Mulvey, Laura. 2006. 'Afterword'. In *The New Iranian Cinema: Politics, Representation and Identity*, edited by Richard Tapper, 254–61. London: I.B. Tauris.

Nancy, Jean-Luc. 2001. *The Evidence of Film: Abbas Kiarostami*. Brussels: Yves Gevaert.

——. 2005. *The Ground of the Image*. Translated by Jeff Fort. New York: Fordham University Press.

## Further reading

Colebrook, Claire. 2009. 'Jean-Luc Nancy'. In *Film, Theory and Philosophy: The Key Thinkers*, edited by Felicity Colman, 154–63. London: Acumen.

James, Ian. 2006. *The Fragmentary Demand: An Introduction to the Philosophy of Jean-Luc Nancy*. Stanford, CA: Stanford University Press.

Nancy, Jean-Luc. 2004. 'A-religion'. *Journal of European Studies* 34 (1/2): 14–18.

——. 2008. 'Claire Denis: Icon of Ferocity', translated by Peter Enright. In *Cinematic Thinking: Philosophical Approaches to the New Cinema*, edited by James Phillips, 160–8. Stanford, CA: Stanford University Press.

# EXCESS, CINEMATIC

## Illegibility and the film text

The concept of cinematic excess emerged amid a shift in film theory from critical readings of a film's unifying narrative towards analyses of the conflicting forces in a film conceived as a heterogeneous textual system (Thompson 1986, 130). The textual system cannot contain and unify all the conflicting forces, and what remains outside is called cinematic excess.

In 'The Concept of Cinematic Excess' (1986) Kristin Thompson prioritized the act of interpretation to suggest that excess is invested in the idea of the illegibility of certain aspects of the film. Where configurations of colours and sounds or stanzas and framing remain partial, then the formation of meaning is frustrated (Barthes 1978, 53). For Roland Barthes 'the signifying accidents of which this – consequently incomplete – sign is composed' (Barthes 1978, 53–4) indicate the *too much* that characterizes cinematic excess. An unexpected detail that entices attention, or an elision in the text, can indicate material indeterminate to the system of the film. Barthes proposed a 'theory of supplementary meaning' (Barthes 1978, 55) where a moment of incoherence disturbs the progression of the narrative and the illusory world that unfolds at the cinema.[1] This conceptualization of cinematic excess lies between narrative and narration as an interval in a network of signifiers where 'something in the function of the image "exceeds meaning"' (Barthes 1978, 55) and calls out to the poetic.[2] A textual process akin to a palimpsest revives and emphasizes past traces of the materials and practices that subsist in the structures of film and meaning.

*Don't Look Now* (Nicolas Roeg, 1973), which tracks the journey of John and Laura Baxter to Venice following the drowning of their daughter, operates through a paradoxical alignment of vision and knowledge as images and sounds are repeated. Each new context calls prior meaning into question. The cross-cutting of narrative strands elicits a disorientating effect through the repetition of imagery and sounds: reflective surfaces of mirrors, windows, and water form configurations which shift in relation to the voices, footsteps, and echoes from the walls and depths of the canals. The seemingly innocuous image of light reflecting from the broken glass that the Baxter's son cycles over signals the sequence in which the daughter drowns. This image recurs in the penultimate sequence of the film as the father, John Baxter, is murdered, a repetition which invests this image with new meaning. Similarly the refraction of light on the camera lens during filming registers as an excess of light and effaces the legible composition of the image. This contingent detail is drawn into textual processes that operate between the film's narration and narrative (where the glare forms part of the diegesis).

Thompson initially offers a comparative reading of Roland Barthes and Stephen Heath. Thompson notes that Barthes's theorization of excess does not signal an 'elsewhere of meaning' (Barthes 1978, 62) – a detail anomalous to the system in which it is encountered but which may make sense in another register. Thompson turns to Barthes's analysis of *Ivan the Terrible* (Sergei Eisenstein, 1944–58) to suggest that an emphasis on innately fascinating details that do not progress the narrative signifies the inadequacy of the protagonist. Ornate details such as the emblem of a bird on a sceptre and rug produce seductive images, but call unnecessary attention to the materiality of film where it is without narrative motivation. Thompson's essay, however, moves away from a sense of excess as that which remains obsolete to the film text and towards Heath's analysis. For Heath, excess raises the possibilities of cinematic excess as a paradigm for ideological positions that are considered to deviate from the system of representation. In this model Heath explores the excesses of cinematic representation that reveal the operations of a text. Thompson finds the materiality of the film to be repressed by an emphasis on the homogeneity of the system of representation in classic narrative cinema. Heath goes further, and reads classic narrative cinema as a system that functions by repressing feminine desire. For Heath, 'fractures' in the film text signal deviation from a structure of representation that reproduces dominant views of gender and sexuality (*see* REPRESENTATION).

Heath's analyses of film and system call attention to the problem of sexual difference in terms of enunciation and the formulation of a subject position (*see* ENUNCIATION, FILM AND). A textual process of differentiation is reliant on binary oppositions such as male/female, passive/active to produce the image of woman as the anthropomorphic ideation of passivity. Signification is dependent on feminine desire which cannot be directly represented, but in relation to which meaning is formed.

Thus for Heath the concept of cinematic excess marks the double bind of sexual difference and the preclusion of the specificities of feminine desire as integral but incoherent to a system of representation in which the image of woman is the archetypal image of desire in relation to a masculinized spectator position (*see* GAZE THEORY). For Heath the organization and disruption of the filmic system echo 'the function historically allocated to woman: sexuality, its prohibition' (Heath 1975, 107). However, for feminist cultural analysts such as Teresa de Lauretis (1984) it is the achronology of *Bad Timing* (Nicolas Roeg, 1980) that draws the spectator into a process of recognition and its effacement. Associative editing plays on the frailties of memory in a process of rewriting that addresses the spectator as historical subject.

## Fault lines

For feminist theory such instances reveal the mechanisms of representation that are proscriptive of feminine desire (Johnston 1975). As the politicization of sexuality and the body in critical discourse grew from the social and cultural shifts of the 1960s and 1970s, feminist film theorists argued that although Woman is the archetypal cinematic subject, 'there are no images either of her or for her' in such films (Doane 1981, 22). The language and structure of cinematic representation familiar to classic narrative form are gendered, and in this paradigm the image of woman is constructed as the abstraction of male desire (Mulvey 1989). This image is called into question by de Lauretis's analysis of associative editing in *Bad Timing* (Nicolas Roeg, 1980) as the disillusion of a textual system in which the subject is positioned ideologically. Close proximity to and control of the film's heroine, Milena Flaherty, are implicated as the locus of desire in relation to a masculinized subject position that is temporarily aligned with Stefan Vognic (her dissuaded lover), Alex Linden (a psychoanalyst), and Inspector Netusil (a detective). Each of them temporarily offers a point of orientation for the desire to know that manifests in the sadism of forcing a change in another (Mulvey 1989, 22). However, as de Lauretis notes, the cross-cutting of shots from different locations and the chronological disordering of events disturbs 'visual and narrative identification' (de Lauretis 1984, 88). Fractures in the unifying effect of the film signal the figure of a borderline as a site of exchange and transgression that infers a feminine subject position that resides 'elsewhere' to the filmic system (de Lauretis 1984, 84–102) and so gestures toward the repressed upon which the formation of meaning depends. This approach can be differentiated from Barthes's theorization of material that is excess to the predominant system as it is theorized as a site of resistance to the homogeneity of the film as a gendered system of representation.[3]

For de Lauretis, the destabilizing effect of the discontinuities of montage and the repetitions of associative editing can be manipulated into a narrative form that plays on memory. Rather than reading for unresolved details as excess, de Lauretis analyses *Bad Timing* for a figure of 'non-coherence' in the repetition of an ellipsis that in its replaying remarks a perspective that is not directly represented. The double-take of a gesture shot from two different angles and shown in succession remarks the minute variations. Disorder in the temporality of the film addresses the spectator as historical subject in relation to a narrative form and plot that play on the projective and mnemonic function of images, sounds, and their recurrence within the instabilities of an always and necessarily fragmented text.[4] A sequence in Milena's apartment intercuts shots of Alex Linden's violation of her body with Inspector Netusil's questioning of him in her absence. In a conversation about Milena, the mirroring of a gesture as Linden and then Netusil look off-screen is followed by a shot of her in the stupor of an overdose, an image that disrupts the temporality of the film. Gestures are replayed as images drawn from other sections of the film and situated in their conversation as details explicative of the past are sought. The touch of her hand is juxtaposed with an image of the empty chair she had rested on. The ellipses between shots remark Milena's absence, but insinuate a history which subverts that told by Alex and questioned by Netusil. This practice foregrounds the ineluctably cinematic and elusive immediacy of *now* and the indeterminacy of *nowhere* to position the feminine at the borders enabling the spectator to question the 'imagining' of the film (de Lauretis 1984, 99–102). For de Lauretis it is the achronology of *Bad Timing* that draws the spectator into a process of recognition and its effacement. De Lauretis's theorization of 'elsewhere' resonates with the concept of excess, but relies on the variously disordered or incomplete 'threads' that can be traced through associative editing. Fault lines in the filmic system play on memory and echo the work asked of the spectator to question the historical allocation of a disarticulated image of woman.

Heath and de Lauretis theorize cinematic excess as a rupture in the filmic system. For Heath the historical proscriptions of female sexuality lie in the denaturing effect of the image of woman as the site of the repression of the other on which discourse depends. The inconsistent alignment of a character and the configuration of signifiers through which its position in discourse is articulated infers feminine desire as excess to a narrative in which it remains unexplained, while de Lauretis's analysis of 'non-coherence' demands that the ideation of woman be questioned.

## The disquiet of the everyday

The formation of a specific filmic meaning lies in the spatial and temporal articulation of narrative. Minute details such as the refraction of light on the camera lens that disturbs the legibility of image composition seem to lend themselves to a notion of excess as a signal of the obsolescence of decorous imagery. However, for Rosalind Galt ornate details are not redundant, but the imagining of an affinity that traces a cultural history of sexualities that are considered deviant in the normative discourse of classic cinema. Galt's work addresses the *too much* of visual excess that troubles the critical measure of image and character that narrative relies on; such disruptions demand the evaluation of specifically filmic materials and temporalities (Galt 2011, 11). While the cosmetic and decorous aspects of film are seen as excess to the meanings discerned of the system of representation, they add a dimension to what is sufficient for the text to be grasped (Heath 1975; Bauman 2001) and mobilize a desire that invests in the idea of disruptive details that appear to signal something indeterminate, elusive, or allusive, outside the explanations of the film's plot. The desire to make sense of disparate information drawn into the formulations of a text finds that film continues to register and embody mistiming in prosodic details. The history of cinematic excess is not redundant, but traces a succession of theories which seek to address the ways in which film adjusts to and represents the historicity of the subject in the disquiet of the everyday.

LIZ WATKINS

## Notes

1 For Metz (2007) the cinephile overlooks the infidelities of the image in narrative cinema, while the cineaste invests in tensions between the homogeneity of the film and its anomalies. For Willemen, however, cinephilia designates material that resists or 'escapes existing critical discourse of theoretical frameworks' (Willemen 1994, 228, 231). These modes of analysis trace trajectories of alliance and discord that suggest shifts in the conceptualization of cinematic excess as specific to the historical context in which they are formulated. It is this material that for Barthes is the 'one "too many", the supplement that my intellection cannot succeed in absorbing' (Barthes 1978, 54). The spectator is caught in the interplay of recognition and its effacement, while theory formulates new modes of analysis.

2 There are anomalies that do not point to 'excess'; for example, excess might indicate the heterogeneity of political forces or the limitations and effects of technology in the formulation of a narrative or internet video file beyond the explicit directions of the director. An exception occurs in *Don't Look Now* where lens flare interacts with elements of design such as glare on the window of the boat leaving harbour as Laura Baxter returns to England. In this instance, the anomaly of lens flare becomes part of the mise en scène as the composition dissolves in the over exposure of the photographic image.

3 For Barthes, the materiality of film, such as the colours and grain that the spectator overlooks in favour of the film system, does affect perception. Heath suggests that colour refracts the distancing effect of the look which is otherwise an absence of grain (Heath 1978, 84). Colour operates at the level of film design and as a dimension of the materiality of film; it facilitates and resists legibility and meaning.

4 Barthes and Heath refer to the insights offered by Kristeva into the fascination of the spectator with frayage, which is a trace elicited by the noises or colour frequencies that precede and subsist in moments of recognition (Kristeva 1986, 236–7). Where these aspects of filmic material erupt from the cohesive effect of the film, they cease to reassure the legibility of the image and invite speculation. Kristeva indicates the spectator's interest in cinema as operating on this tension, bringing what eludes identification into the perceptual field: 'condensations, tones, rhythms, colours, patterns – always in excess as compared with the represented, the signified' (Kristeva 1986, 237). Barthes and Kristeva refer to Eisenstein's layering of sound and image as manipulations that figure anguish both in the film and the spectator (Kristeva 1986, 238). The sense of horror enticed by a rhythm, sound, or recurring image is emphasized where the spectator's reaction is echoed in the events depicted. In an unfamiliar configuration of elements the signifier is

diminished and so resists legibility, but the desire for meaning is sustained (Barthes 1978, 62). For Heath this underscores 'intolerable violence' in *Touch of Evil* which is marked by the sudden emptiness of the image (Heath 1975, 110), drawing the film material of light and shadow into the field of the film.

## Works cited

Barthes, Roland. 1978. 'The Third Meaning'. In *Image–Music–Text*, translated by Stephen Heath, 52–68. New York: Hill and Wang.

Bauman, Zygmunt. 2001. 'Excess: an Obituary'. *parallax* 7 (1): 85–91.

de Lauretis, Teresa. 1984. 'Now and Nowhere: Roeg's *Bad Timing*'. In *Alice Doesn't: Feminism, Semiotics, Cinema*, 84–102. Bloomington: Indiana University Press.

Doane, Mary Ann. 1981. 'Woman's Stake: Filming the Female Body'. *October* 17 (Summer): 22–36.

Galt, Rosalind. 2011. *Pretty: Film and the Decorative Image*. New York: Columbia University Press.

Heath, Stephen. 1975. 'Film and System: Terms of Analysis Part II'. *Screen* 16 (2): 91–113.

——. 1978. 'Difference'. *Screen* 19 (3): 51–112.

Johnston, Claire. 1975. 'Women's Cinema as Counter-cinema'. In *Feminist Film Theory: A Reader*, edited by Sue Thornham, 31–40. Edinburgh: Edinburgh University Press, 1999.

Kristeva, Julia. 1986. 'Ellipsis on Dread and the Specular Seduction'. In *Narrative, Apparatus, Ideology: A Film Theory Reader*, edited by Philip Rosen, 236–43. New York: Columbia University Press.

Metz, Christian. 2007 [1985]. 'Photography and Fetish'. In *The Cinematic*, edited by David Campany, 119–23. London: Whitechapel.

Mulvey, Laura. 1989. *Visual and Other Pleasures*. London: Macmillan.

Thompson, Kristin. 1986. 'The Concept of Cinematic Excess'. In *Narrative, Apparatus, Ideology: A Film Theory Reader*, edited by Philip Rosen, 130–42. New York: Columbia University Press.

Willemen, Paul. 1994. *Looks and Frictions: Essays in Cultural Studies and Film Theory*. London: British Film Institute.

# FANTASY AND SPECTATORSHIP

## Feminist reaction to apparatus theory

Jean-Louis Baudry, Jean-Louis Comolli, and Christian Metz, among other theorists of the cinematic apparatus, considered that cinema is a totalizing institution and a powerful ideological instrument that manufactures imaginary subject positions for spectators to occupy when watching films (*see* APPARATUS THEORY [BAUDRY]). Feminist film theorists, including Joan Copjec, Elizabeth Cowie, and Constance Penley, among others, objected to the concept of the cinematic apparatus – which was the dominant strain of psychoanalytic film theory in the 1970s – for its privileging of the male subject and spectatorial position. These feminist scholars argued that, since apparatus theory was deeply rooted in the Freudian Oedipus complex, it demonstrated a disinterest in as well as a denial of female spectatorship. In order to critically address these and other questions concerning female subjectivity, Cowie, along with colleagues Parveen Adams, Beverley Brown, and Rosalind Coward, founded the feminist scholarly journal *m/f* in 1978 (published until 1986), in which Penley's essay 'Feminism, Film Theory and the Bachelor Machines' appeared in 1985. In this text, Penley posits that the cinematic apparatus was a male construction, a 'bachelor machine' structured to provide visual pleasure to the male viewer by resolving the castration complex of his on-screen surrogate – in other words, the film's male protagonist.

In her influential article 'Fantasia', which first appeared in *m/f* in 1984, Cowie puts forth a reading of film as fantasy that allows for multiple and shifting, rather than fixed, spectatorship positions. This idea is at the antipodes of the more rigid structure of spectatorship according to apparatus theory, which contends that 'the cinema works to suppress discourse, to permit only certain "speakers", only a certain "speech"' (Kaplan 1983, 12).

## Fantasy and psychoanalysis

Cowie foregrounds psychoanalytic concepts and terminology in her discussion of film as fantasy and as a *mise-en-scène* of desire. In doing so, she draws primarily upon French psychoanalysts/philosophers Jean Laplanche and Jean-Bertrand Pontalis's writings on fantasy, particularly their article 'Fantasy and the Origins of Sexuality' (1968) and their book *The Language of Psychoanalysis* (1973), as well as Freud's work on daydreams, creative writing, and family romance. Cowie establishes a link between fantasy and film, demonstrating that psychoanalytically theorizing fantasy is productive for film theory since fantasy 'reaches an extraordinary culmination in cinema, the dream factory *par excellence*' (Cowie 1999, 368).

She goes on to explain that film not only 'specularizes' fantasy but also gives the spectator the impression that the fantasy on screen is a real experience at two levels of sensory perception: auditory and visual.

In 'Fantasia', Cowie repeatedly posits the idea that both film and fantasy function as a *mise-en-scène* of desire that allows the subject to assume multiple spectatorial positions, which, like the fantasies themselves, have the potential to evolve depending on various factors. Films are the public disseminations of fantasies that originate in the personal fantasy of the films' creator as well as in universal original wishes (366). According to Freud, these original wishes are *not* usually shared among people, due to their personal and often shameful content, but the cinematic medium allows for such fantasies, when transposed into art forms, to be openly displayed in public. Therefore, cinematized fantasies, transformed into art, work on a larger scale for the general viewing public since spectators can integrate 'ready-made scenarios of fiction' into their own private world (366).

Fantasy, 'the fundamental object of psychoanalysis' (356), is etymologically rooted in the Greek 'to "make visible"', while in German *Phantasie* invokes 'the imaginings ... into which the poet—or the neurotic—so willingly withdraws' (356–7). Fantasies can take on numerous overlapping forms, including nocturnal dreams and daydreams, as they can be both conscious as well as unconscious.

Central to fantasy is how it constructs 'an imagined scene' (356), according to Freud as well as Laplanche and Pontalis, and thereby imposes 'a scenario, a façade of coherence and continuity—in a word, a narrative' (358–9), such as of a novel or a film. The notion of fantasy as scene, a cornerstone of Cowie's discussion, 'enables the consideration of film as fantasy in the most fundamental [psychoanalytic] sense of this term' (358).

## Fantasy and film

Cowie examines how film is an example of the representation of fantasy in the public sphere: 'by far the most common form of public circulation of fantasy is what Freud described as "creative writing"', which includes film (Cowie 1999, 364). Films are based upon original fantasies – themselves derived from universally repressed childhood wishes and desires, some of which spring from the primal scene as described by Freud – and therefore depict common themes which are time and again 'replayed before the cameras, always the same but differently, which has been the key to cinema's success as a mass medium' (365).

Yet Cowie highlights the 'rich diversity of cinema ... [its] range of genres, narrative devices, cinematographic techniques' (365) that rework and reinvent original myths and fantasies through 'complex webs of modern forms of representation' (365). Thus, fantasy scenarios 'can be infinitely various and varied, shifting with the new impressions received everyday, changing to fit the new situations and contexts of the subject' (365), what Laplanche and Pontalis call 'kaleidoscopic material' through which the subject views and filters his or her own experiences. Freud, in 'A Child Is Being Beaten', provides three different subject positions in this fantasy (362). For Freud, fantasy not only involves shifting subject positions, but also conflates three temporal registers: the present ('the material elements of the fantasy'), the past (the wish that originates from 'the earliest experiences'), and the future (the 'fulfillment of the wish') (365). Freud's notions of differing subject positions and chronological shifts within the sphere of fantasy are expanded upon by Laplanche and Pontalis in their concept of 'de-subjectivization'. Here, they claim that within fantasy one undergoes a process of de-subjectivization in which one is no longer defined by gender, geographical location, or time period, but rather can assume numerous identities within the scene: 'in phantasy, the subject ... *cannot be assigned any fixed place* in it ... *as a result, the subject, although always present in the fantasy may be so in a de-subjectivised form*' (Laplanche and Pontalis 1968, 17, emphasis mine).

Cowie extends Laplanche and Pontalis's concept of de-subjectivization in fantasy to the fiction film (Cowie 1999, 362), allowing for multivalent and multi-gendered identificatory possibilities for spectators as they engage with film's staging of desire: the viewer '*takes up more than one position*' (362; emphasis mine) and therefore is not anchored in a single one. As spectators relate with public forms of fantasy material such as narrative film, they are liberated from the patriarchal establishment of the male apparatus and its construction of specific viewing positions.

Numerous prominent film scholars, including Jacqueline Rose, Teresa de Lauretis, and in particular Judith Mayne, acknowledge the significance of the fantasy model of spectatorship as a 'revision of theories of the apparatus whereby the subject of the cinematic fantasy can only always be male' (Mayne 1993, 87). They nonetheless criticize Cowie's notion of fantasy for its limited ability to 'challenge film theory's own compulsory heterosexuality' (90). Fantasy theory allows for multivalent spectatorial/subject positions. In spite of this, Mayne claims that, instead of destabilizing – or doing away altogether with – categories based upon sexual difference, Cowie's fantasy theory is based upon and works within film studies' dominant 'heterosexual master code' (90). Mayne concludes by wondering 'whether fantasy can engage with the complex effects of spectatorship without some understanding of how its own categories – of sexual difference, the couple, and desire – are themselves historically determined and culturally variable' (91).

MARCELLINE BLOCK

## Works cited

Cowie, Elizabeth. 1999. 'Fantasia'. In *Visual Culture: A Reader*, edited by Jessica Evans and Stuart Hall, 356–69. Los Angeles: Sage, in association with the Open University. Originally published in *m/f* 9 (1984): 71–105.

Kaplan, E. Ann. 1983. *Women and Film: Both Sides of the Camera*. New York and London: Methuen.

Laplanche, J., and J.-B. Pontalis. 1968. 'Fantasy and the Origins of Sexuality'. *International Journal of Psycho-analysis* 49 (1): 1–18.

———. 1973. *The Language of Psychoanalysis*. Translated by D. Nicholson-Smith. London: Hogarth Press.

Mayne, Judith. 1993. *Cinema and Spectatorship*. London: Routledge.

Penley, Constance. 2000. 'Feminism, Film Theory, and the Bachelor Machines'. In *Film and Theory: An Anthology*, edited by Robert Stam and Toby Miller, 456–73. Oxford: Blackwell. Originally published in *m/f* 10 (1985): 39–59.

## Further reading

Adams, Parveen, and Elizabeth Cowie, eds. 1990. *The Woman in Question*. Cambridge, MA: MIT Press.

Baudry, Jean-Louis. 1974–5. 'The Ideological Effects of the Basic Cinematic Apparatus'. *Film Quarterly* 27 (2): 39–47.

———. 1976. 'The Apparatus: Metapsychological Approaches to the Impression of Reality in the Cinema'. *Camera Obscura* I: 104–26.

Block, Marcelline, ed. 2010. *Situating the Feminist Gaze and Spectatorship in Postwar Cinema*. Newcastle: Cambridge Scholars Press.

Copjec, Joan. 2000. 'The Orthopsychic Subject: Film Theory and the Recepion of Lacan'. In *Film and Theory: An Anthology*, edited by Robert Stam and Toby Miller, 437–55. Oxford: Blackwell. Originally published in *October* 49 (1989).

Cowie, Elizabeth. 1997. *Representing the Woman: Psychoanalysis and Cinema*. London: Macmillan and Minneapolis: Minnesota University Press.

Doane, Mary Ann. 1990. 'Film and the Masquerade: Theorizing the Female Spectator'. In *Issues in Feminist Film Criticism*, edited by Patricia Erens, 41–57. Bloomington and Indianapolis: Indiana University Press.

Friedberg, Anne. 1990. 'A Denial of Difference: Theories of Cinematic Identification'. In *Psychoanalysis and Cinema*, edited by E. Ann Kaplan, 36–45. London: Routledge.

hooks, bell. 1992. 'The Oppositional Gaze: Black Female Spectators'. In *Black Looks: Race and Representation*, 115–31. Boston, MA: South End Press.

Metz, Christian. 1986. *The Imaginary Signifier: Psychoanalysis and the Cinema*. Bloomington: Indiana University Press.

Rose, Jacqueline. 1980. 'The Cinematic Apparatus: Problems in Current Theory'. In *The Cinematic Apparatus*, edited by Teresa de Lauretis and Stephen Heath, 172–86. New York: St. Martin's Press.

Williams, Linda, ed. 1995. *Viewing Positions: Ways of Seeing*. New Brunswick, NJ: Rutgers University Press.

# FEMINIST FILM THEORY,
## CORE CONCEPTS

Feminist film theory is expanding, as the many narratives describing its history attest. A common narrative runs as follows: though film theory was once grounded in a grass-roots movement, with its supposedly unified category of womanhood, the expanding power of identity politics in the 1980s pushed feminist film theory not only to think about (white) (middle-class) (Euro-American) womanhood, but also to expand its scope to include critical race theory and discussions of class, queer, and postcolonial theories. Similarly, as media technologies, such as television, computer games, and the Internet, entered the discipline of film and media studies, feminist film theory broadened its object to include new media forms. Thus, feminist film theory has been open to an expansion of the category of *womanhood* as well as an expansion of the category of *film*, adding new topics to its scope of inquiry.

It would be easy to divide feminist film theory according to the categories of identity politics: race, gender, sexual orientation, class, and national origin. Some anthologies of feminist film theory explicitly or implicitly divide feminist theory along these lines. Others simply reproduce the dominance of white and/or straight theorists by cordoning off women of colour into their own separate category. The section 'Re-thinking Differences' from Sue Thornham's *Feminist Film Theory* reader comes to mind. However, the division of feminist film theory into topics that retrace existing cultural distinctions risks reifying the distinctions and thereby normalizing the dominant category of white, cisgender, upper-class, straight femininity. Instead, I will discuss how feminist film theory has engaged with three major methodologies within film and media studies: *representation, production,* and *spectatorship*.

The methodology of *representation* asks such questions as: how have women been represented on screen? How have men? What is the relationship between screen representation and the production of gender in our society? Looking at film theory from the perspective of feminist *production* prompts slightly different questions: what would a *feminist counter-cinema* look like? What female and feminist directors are, or should be, part of the Hollywood film canon? How can feminists support women's film production around the world?

Partly because of the early importance and continuing resonance of Laura Mulvey's 'Visual Pleasure and Narrative Cinema', the study of spectatorship has been a central concern for feminist film theory (*see* FEMINIST FILM THEORY, HISTORY OF; GAZE THEORY). Within that area, feminists have developed two different methods for approaching the spectator – the study of *the psyche* and the study of *the body*. *Spectatorship* asks: how are women's images received? What sort of relationships with a screen image can be considered masculine or feminine? How do spectators and fans use representations for their own ends?

*The psyche* has long been a topic of discussion in feminist film theory, largely through the use of psychoanalytic theory to discuss cinema's relationship with constructions of gender and sexuality. The topic of the psyche asks questions such as: what is the relationship between cinema and fantasy? How does cinema shape a relationship with our own gender and sexuality? Recognizing that the mind is not separate from, but part of, *the body*, feminist film theorists also pose questions about phenomenology, scientific imaging, and embodiment that help to refine other topics.

As my discussion of the psyche and the body will demonstrate, the various methodologies interact and overlap. For example, the representation of women is conditioned by the context of production and reception of images and sounds by spectators. Production works within the language of existing cultural representations and the perceived tastes of consumers, and spectators interpret cinema through the lens provided by producers and known representational models. In what follows I will briefly trace the ways in which each methodology has been employed for feminist film theory.

## Representation

One of the first questions that feminist film theorists and students of feminist film theory pose is: how are women represented in the cinema? However, it is difficult to identify a purely *representational* approach, separate from the study of production and spectatorship. Early feminist film scholars, including Molly Haskell, Marjorie Rosen, and the original editors of the foundational journal *Women and Film*, devoted themselves to evaluating what they called *images of women*, relying on their personal viewing experiences and textual analysis to identify a canon of positive and negative female representations in classical Hollywood cinema. These scholars pointed to overarching sexist themes in the representation of (mostly white, mostly straight) women.

There are clear connections between the identification and evaluation of images of women and the process of *consciousness-raising*, whereby women identify and discuss personal issues of gender inequality in their lives. The impetus for studying representation was the belief that if women could begin to understand how patriarchal society was being reproduced through media images, perhaps they would be less hesitant to identify as feminists. However, the representational approach, which often bracketed issues of production and spectatorship, risked reproducing existing cultural inequalities. Because Hollywood continues to be dominated by images glorifying the beauty of white, straight, cisgender women at the expense of other women, it is difficult to discuss these images as representational of women more generally. Scholars who study the representation of under-represented groups tend to focus on canonizing under-rated directors and locating the agency of under-represented women in actresses and below-the-line labourers. Alternatively, these scholars discuss the ways in which under-represented spectators make films work for them by using special interpretive techniques despite their own marginalization.

While the work of British feminists, such as Laura Mulvey and Claire Johnston in the mid-1970s, served to push feminist film theory away from studying images of women outside a production or spectatorship context, this type of work remains dominant in popular discussions of feminism and the media. The documentary *Miss Representation* (Jennifer Siebel Newsom, US, 2011), shown at the Sundance Film Festival and on OWN: The Oprah Winfrey Network, is a prominent example today of the representational methodology in feminist film theory. Feminist blogs such as Jezebel and Feministing also tend to discuss films and media through the perspective of representation.

## Production

Whether feminist theorists encourage a realist style or a more radical style with the aim of destroying visual pleasure, the goal of aiding and documenting women's filmmaking has been an important strand of feminist theory. Examples include feminist film festivals in the US, UK, and Canada in the early 1970s, where 'the sole criterion for exhibiting a film was that it was directed by a woman' (Gaines 1984), the 'In Practice' section of *Camera Obscura*, women's filmmaking workshops, and non-profit organizations for women's film production and distribution, including Women Make Movies.

Jane Gaines identifies a split in feminist theories of production beginning in the 1980s. The search for a *feminist counter-cinema*, kicked off by Claire Johnston and Laura Mulvey in the 1970s, led to what Gaines characterizes as an orthodoxy of film style, dominated by the destruction of visual pleasure. However, many women found this style alienating and many feminist directors disagreed with the argument against visual pleasure, instead favouring a more realist style. Gaines argues that although the destruction of visual pleasure was theoretically dominant in feminist film theory at one point, films that attempted to destroy visual pleasure had little impact on the style of feminist filmmakers worldwide. Instead, Gaines asserts that documentary filmmaking and popular films such as *Flashdance* (Adrian Lyne, US, 1983) resonated strongly with feminist audiences in the 1980s.

The auteur theory, which posits that the director is the main author of a film text, has made its mark on feminist film theory (*see* AUTEUR THEORY). Adding female directors to the canon of identified auteurs has been a goal of production-oriented feminist film theorists since the earliest days, with Dorothy Arzner and Ida Lupino being two of the first Hollywood directors canonized by feminists. Many feminist authors also canonize Julie Dash as the first black woman in the US to direct a feature film for general release (*Daughters of the Dust*, US, 1991), including Anna Everett, who argues Dash represents a unique 'womanist' filmmaking aesthetic. Trinh T. Minh-ha, a feminist film theorist and filmmaker, appeared as one of the earliest representatives of a feminist postcolonial aesthetic in traditionally Western-centric feminist film circles. Christine Vachon has written two autobiographical books about her experiences as a Hollywood film producer that could be employed as guides to help women navigate a male-dominated film industry.

To focus only on female directors and producers raises problems, however, because this approach to production reproduces the overvaluation of above-the-line labour in Hollywood, along with its class-oriented assumptions about who produces value and what types of production are culturally important. Feminist pornography scholars such as Mireille Miller-Young and Celine Parreñas Shimizu focus on labour in the adult film industry, casting porn actresses and performers-turned-producers as the protagonists of their discussion of pornographic film production. This focus on labour situates pornography, a category of film sometimes dismissed by feminists as worthy of extermination, within the larger context of filmmaking and the exploitation of labour in capitalist society. The emergent field of media industries within film and media studies has argued for below-the-line labour as a site for the production of meaning. Miranda Banks discusses the gendered nature of below-the-line labour, focusing on costume designers' experiences as an example of how feminine-coded labour is devalued in Hollywood.

Video game production has become a major area for feminist scholars. Though the masculinist gaming canon tends to devalue the 'girl games' movement of the 1990s, Justine Cassell and Henry Jenkins's anthology *From Barbie to Mortal Kombat* accurately captures the attitudes of producers from that movement through interviews and analyses of games for girls. Anna Anthropy's *Rise of the Videogame Zinesters* is a contemporary call-to-arms for outsider video game designers, and has been cited by feminist game design activists as a good starting point for women, even with little or no computer programming knowledge, to begin to design their own computer games.

## Spectatorship

Laura Mulvey's controversial 'Visual Pleasure and Narrative Cinema' may have defined the *gaze* of cinema as exclusively male, but Mulvey's choice to focus on film through the lens of spectatorship opened the door for the study of male and female spectatorship that helped solidify feminist film theory's place in the academy. The question of female spectatorship, famously under-discussed in Mulvey's original article, produced some of the most nuanced studies in feminist film theory of the relationship between the representation of women and the reception of those images. *Camera Obscura*'s special issue *The Spectatrix* is an excellent snapshot of the early debates surrounding the importance of studying female spectatorship, particularly in relation to the psychoanalytic model used by Mulvey.

The study of female spectators opens up space for a diverse range of voices and interpretive models to enter the realm of feminist film theory. Jacqueline Bobo's *Black Women as Cultural Readers*, Patricia White's *unInvited: Classical Hollywood Cinema and Lesbian Representability*, and Constance Penley's work on female fan fiction authors, 'Brownian Motion: Women, Tactics, and Technology', all demonstrate how under-represented interpretive communities repurpose mainstream cinema and television to justify their own existence. Anna Everett's work on film criticism in the black press and Julie Levin Russo's studies of fan video producers demonstrate how the study of spectatorship in interpretive communities links film spectatorship to social activism. Far from representing spectators as passive recipients of media content, the spectatorship model empowers readers by framing the experience they are most likely to have of cinema as a site of both pleasure and resistance. Focusing completely on the power of spectators at the expense of studying production and the power of representations, however, risks privileging individual or group interpretation over larger power structures. While Mulvey was critiqued for giving female viewers too little power in her interpretive framework, studies that focus too myopically on spectators may give too much power to fan interpretation, ignoring the need for greater opportunities for women in Hollywood. While women make up a vibrant portion of the fan community for male-oriented shows like *Star Trek*, for example, it is usually white male fans that are able to become producers of these franchises, as J.J. Abrams famously did in his 2009 *Star Trek* reboot. It is unlikely that the erotic fantasies of homosexual people and non-binary gender described by Penley would have the same opportunity to be represented on the silver screen.

## The psyche

While the studies described above focus on interpretive communities as well as individual spectators, feminist film theory also concerns itself with theorizing the individual spectator.

The first framework that was adopted for examining the spectator was that of the unconscious psyche. Drawing on Lacanian psychoanalysis and Sigmund Freud's discussion of fantasy, feminist film theorists sought to understand the role cinema plays in constructing a viewer's sense of self, specifically engaging their gender and sexual identity (*see* FANTASY AND SPECTATORSHIP).

Two feminist pornography scholars – Laura Kipnis and Linda Williams – use differing psychoanalytic approaches to discuss the representation of sexuality in cinema. Williams draws heavily on Mulvey's argument that cinematic representations of women are constructed to display the female body for purposes of male spectator pleasure. As such, Williams adopts Mulvey's use of the concept of fetishism to describe representation in cinema, blending the Marxist concept of commodity fetishism with Freud's concept of the fetish. The goal of pornography, Williams argues, is to make the invisible visible – to visualize the female orgasm for the pleasure of an imagined male viewer. Williams assumes that pornography only addresses a male audience – male both in identification and physically. She, like Mulvey, reproduces binary gender distinctions in order to discuss power relations.

By contrast, Laura Kipnis uses the Freudian concept of fantasy to destabilize the link between gender identity and gendered representation for spectators. In *Bound and Gagged: Pornography and the Politics of Fantasy in America*, Kipnis argues that Freud makes a distinction between psychical and physical reality, and that fantasy is allied with psychical reality and is not a simple illusion or lie. Kipnis writes: 'Psychoanalytic theory proposes that in fantasy (and I'm adding, in fantasy genres like pornography), identification is mobile, unpredictable, and not bound by either one's actual gender or practical reality' (Kipnis 1996, 196). Like Carol Clover, who argues that male spectators of slasher horror films identify across gender, fantasizing that they are the killer as well as the victim, Kipnis argues that, in Oedipal fantasy, viewers identify with multiple shifting subject positions at once. Thus what seems straightforward in fantasy narrative is not.

The framework of fantasy in psychoanalysis, particularly Freud's 'A Child Is Being Beaten', has been useful for queer scholars because it offers an escape from the heteronormative assumptions and binary gender system that haunted discussions of the male and the female spectator post-Mulvey. While the fetishistic model used by Mulvey and Williams still has resonance, it is the fantasy model that offers the most possibilities for scholarship on gender, sexuality, and the psyche.

## The body

Feminists have long challenged the ocular-centrism of the humanities. The privileging of vision tends to rely on a strict separation between a viewer-self and a viewed-other. However, senses other than vision are ever-present in the experience of film spectatorship. Sound is the most obvious non-visual sense that spectators experience, particularly after the advent of sound cinema. However, authors such as Laura U. Marks and Vivian Sobchack argue that the sense of touch is also central to spectatorship (*see* AFFECT, FILM AND). Both scholars draw on phenomenology, particularly the work of Maurice Merleau-Ponty, to argue that embodiment is integral to perception, and thus the visual sense is not separate from the other senses. While Marks focuses on theorizing what she calls *haptic visuality*, arguing that the cinema engages viewers' sense of touch through vision, Sobchack discusses a more direct cinematic tactility, by pointing to a tingling in her fingers when viewing a confusing shot in *The Piano* (Jane Campion, Australia/New Zealand/France, 1993).

Though Sobchack's conscious mind and her vision could not identify this shot as representing light streaming through a character's fingers in extreme close-up, her 'fingers knew' what the image meant.

Feminist film theorists have also pointed to science as a site for discussing the body. Lisa Cartwright's work traces a history of visual culture in medicine and biology. N. Katherine Hayles discusses the discursive shifts in computer science that made possible the idea of separating human consciousness from the physical body. While Marks and Sobchack attempt to rectify the disembodiment of spectatorship, Cartwright and Hayles examine scientific models that dehumanize the body. In this way, studies of scientific representations are in conversation with older discussions about the objectification of women's bodies, while phenomenological feminist theory challenges the Cartesian mind/body split that makes such objectification possible.

DIANA POZO

## Further reading

### Representation

de Lauretis, Teresa. 1988. 'Sexual Indifference and Lesbian Representation'. *Theatre Journal* 40 (2) (May): 155–77.

Halberstam, Judith. 1998. *Female Masculinity*. Durham, NC: Duke University Press.

Haskell, Molly. 1973. *From Reverence to Rape: The Treatment of Women in the Movies*. New York: Holt, Rinehart and Winston.

Rosen, Marjorie. 1973. *Popcorn Venus: Women, Movies, and the American Dream*. New York: Coward, McCann & Geoghegan.

Valdivia, Angharad N. 2000. 'A Latina in the Land of Hollywood: Transgressive Possibilities'. In *A Latina in the Land of Hollywood and Other Essays on Media Culture*. Tucson: University of Arizona Press.

'Women and Film: Overview'. 1972. *Women and Film* 1: 3–6.

### Production

Anthropy, Anna. 2012. *Rise of the Videogame Zinesters: How Freaks, Normals, Amateurs, Artists, Dreamers, Dropouts, Queers, Housewives, and People Like You Are Taking Back an Art Form*. New York: Seven Stories Press.

Banks, Miranda J. 2009. 'Gender Below-the-Line: Defining Feminist Production Studies'. In *Production Studies: Cultural Studies of Media Industries*, edited by Vicki Mayer, M.J. Banks, and John T. Caldwell, 87–98. New York: Routledge.

Cassell, Justine, and Henry Jenkins, eds. 1998. *From Barbie to Mortal Kombat: Gender and Computer Games*. Cambridge, MA: MIT Press.

Everett, Anna. 2005. 'Towards a Womanist/Diasporic Film Aesthetic'. In *Film Analysis: A Norton Reader*, edited by Jeffrey Geiger and R.L. Rutsky, 850–71. New York: W.W. Norton & Company.

Gaines, Jane. 1984. 'Women and Representation'. *Jump Cut* 29 (February): 25–7: ejumpcut.org/archive/onlinessays/JC29folder/WomenRepnGaines.html (accessed 5 August 2013).

Johnston, Claire. 2000. 'Women's Cinema as Counter-cinema'. In *Feminism and Film*, edited by E. Ann Kaplan, 22–33. New York: Oxford University Press.

Kaplan, E. Ann. 1983. *Women and Film: Both Sides of the Camera*. New York: Routledge.

Miller-Young, Mireille. 2013. 'Interventions: The Deviant and Defiant Art of Black Women Porn Directors'. In *The Feminist Porn Book: The Politics of Producing Pleasure*, edited by Tristan Taormino,

Celine Parreñas Shimizu, Constance Penley, and Mireille Miller-Young, 105–20. New York: The Feminist Press.

Minh-ha, Trinh T. 1989. *Woman, Native, Other: Writing Postcoloniality and Feminism.* Bloomington: Indiana University Press.

Shimizu, Celine Parreñas. 2007. *The Hypersexuality of Race: Performing Asian/American Women on Screen and Scene.* Durham, NC: Duke University Press.

Vachon, Christine, and Austin Bunn. 2006. *A Killer Life: How an Independent Film Producer Survives Deals and Disasters in Hollywood and Beyond.* New York: Simon & Schuster.

Vachon, Christine, and David Edelstein. 1998. *Shooting to Kill: How an Independent Producer Blasts through the Barriers to Make Movies That Matter.* New York: Avon Books.

## Spectatorship

Bobo, Jacqueline. 1995. *Black Women as Cultural Readers.* New York: Columbia University Press.

*Camera Obscura* 20–21: *The Spectatrix.* May–September 1989.

Doane, Mary Ann. 1982. 'Film and the Masquerade: Theorising the Female Spectator'. *Screen* 23 (3–4): 74–87.

Doty, Alexander. 1993. *Making Things Perfectly Queer: Interpreting Mass Culture.* Minneapolis: University of Minnesota Press.

Everett, Anna. 2001. *Returning the Gaze: A Genealogy of Black Film Criticism, 1909–1949.* Durham, NC: Duke University Press.

hooks, bell. 1996. *Reel to Real: Race, Sex and Class at the Movies.* New York: Routledge.

Mulvey, Laura. 1975. 'Visual Pleasure and Narrative Cinema'. *Screen* 16 (3) (Autumn): 6–18.

——. 1981. 'Afterthoughts on "Visual Pleasure and Narrative Cinema" … Inspired by "Duel in the Sun"'. *Framework* 15–16–17: 12–15.

Penley, Constance. 1991. 'Brownian Motion: Women, Tactics and Technology'. In *Technoculture*, edited by Constance Penley and Andrew Ross, 135–55. Minneapolis: University of Minnesota Press.

Russo, Julie Levin. 2009. 'Sex Detectives: *Law & Order SVU*'s Fans, Critics, and Characters Investigate Lesbian Desire'. *Transformative Works and Cultures* 3.

——. 2009. 'User-Penetrated Content: Fan Videos in the Age of Convergence'. *Cinema Journal* 48 (4): 125–30.

White, Patricia. 1999. *unInvited: Classical Hollywood Cinema and Lesbian Representability.* Bloomington: Indiana University Press.

## The psyche

Clover, Carol. 1992. *Men, Women and Chain Saws: Gender in the Modern Horror Film.* Princeton, NJ: Princeton University Press.

Cowie, Elizabeth. 1997. *Representing the Woman: Cinema and Psychoanalysis.* Minneapolis: University of Minnesota Press.

Creed, Barbara. 1997. *The Monstrous Feminine: Film, Feminism, Psychoanalysis.* New York: Routledge.

Freud, Sigmund. 1920. 'A Child Is Being Beaten: A Contribution to the Study of the Origin of Sexual Perversions'. *International Journal of Psychoanalysis* 1: 371–95.

Kipnis, Laura. 1996. *Bound and Gagged: Pornography and the Politics of Fantasy in America.* New York: Grove Press.

Penley, Constance. 1989. *The Future of an Illusion: Film, Feminism and Psychoanalysis.* Minneapolis: University of Minnesota Press.

Williams, Linda. 1989. *Hard Core: Power, Pleasure and the 'Frenzy of the Visible'.* Berkeley: University of California Press.

## *The body*

Cartwright, Lisa. 1995. *Screening the Body: Tracing Medicine's Visual Culture*. Minneapolis: University of Minnesota Press.

Hayles, N. Katherine. 1999. *How We Became Posthuman: Virtual Bodies in Cybernetics, Literature, and Informatics*. Chicago, IL: University of Chicago Press.

Marks, Laura U. 2000. *The Skin of the Film: Intercultural Cinema, Embodiment, and the Senses*. Durham, NC: Duke University Press.

——. 2002. *Touch: Sensuous Theory and Multisensory Media*. Minneapolis: University of Minnesota Press.

Sobchack, Vivian. 2004. *Carnal Thoughts: Embodiment and Moving Image Culture*. Berkeley: University of California Press.

——. 2005. 'Choreography for One, Two, and Three Legs'. *Topoi* 24 (1) (2005): 55–66.

Treichler, Paula A., Lisa Cartwright, and Constance Penley, eds. 1998. *The Visible Woman: Imaging Technologies, Gender, and Science*. New York: New York University Press.

# FEMINIST FILM THEORY, HISTORY OF

Today we are in many ways far away from the seemingly unified editorial point of view represented in ... early issues of the journal. A diversity of topics, methods, and approaches, particularly as these are fostered in an emphasis on emerging scholars, is characteristic of the current period. But in other ways, the journal remains consistent with its origins: *Camera Obscura* is passionate about ideas, about film, and about its sister media. And its editorial staff are just utopian – or perhaps arrogant? – enough once again to sign the current contribution: The *Camera Obscura* collective.

*Camera Obscura* collective

The foundational American feminist film journal *Camera Obscura* marked its thirtieth anniversary with a historical retrospective discussing the changing shape of feminist film theory. *Camera Obscura*, its editorial collective argues, has been successful because of the tension between its origins as a feminist collective in the tradition of 1960s and 1970s left political activism and its willingness to engage in 'lively and unbridled debate' – to reconsider its methodology in response to theoretical challenges (*Camera Obscura* Collective 2006, 8–10). This narrative, which positions *Camera Obscura*, and feminist film theory itself, as an entity in need of constant re-evaluation, resists the highly critiqued 'wave' model of feminist history. Rather than imagining feminism as a unified concept that is periodically challenged, as one wave gives way to the next, the editorial collective of *Camera Obscura* emphasizes that the definition of feminism has been contested at every point in its history.

In feminist film theory, the questions that define feminism continue to multiply. Feminist film theorists must not only ask 'what is a woman?' and question whether the concept of 'women' is an effective organizing principle for the study of film; they must also question the nature of representation (does gender exist before representation or is it created through representation?), and determine the aspects of film most important for feminist analysis. Should feminists canonize women in the film industry? Or should they focus on producing a feminist theory for all film, regardless of the gender of its producers? What about women as spectators of film? What are the differences between and among women (race, class, sexual orientation, gender identity, gender expression, physical ability, etc.), and how are these central to feminist engagements with film?

Perhaps because of this 'lively and unbridled debate' at the centre of feminist film theory, feminism and feminist scholars have been central to many theoretical developments in film and media studies more generally. Psychoanalytic feminists, including Laura Mulvey and Claire Johnston, contributed to the acceptance of French theory in American and British film studies in the 1970s. Feminist scholars of spectatorship and domestic space, including Tania Modeleski and Lynn Spigel, helped lay the foundation for the field of television studies. Feminist technology scholars, including Constance Penley and Lisa Cartwright, contributed to the centrality of questions of the body in contemporary discussions of 'new media'. Shohini Chaudhuri argues that today feminist film theory is central to mainstream academic film theory and has thus shared its fate, facing critique and cultural backlash since the 1980s (2006, 1).

Contemporary film theory syllabi tend to represent feminist film theory as a moment in the past, signified by Laura Mulvey's 1975 *Screen* manifesto 'Visual Pleasure and Narrative Cinema'. Though the piece is itself almost too well known, students often encounter it out of context (see Merck 2007). I thus begin this entry with a brief discussion of 'Visual Pleasure', before moving on to discuss several feminist film theory approaches to film spectatorship post-Mulvey.

## 'Visual Pleasure' in the feminist film canon

Janet Bergstrom and Mary Ann Doane (1990, 7) write of Mulvey's central place as a signifier of feminism and whipping girl in the feminist film canon:

> 'Visual Pleasure' provided a theoretical framework which feminist film critics henceforth felt compelled to acknowledge – whether to extend and amplify [Mulvey's] insights or to criticize the psychoanalytic or anti-Hollywood assumptions upon which they were based. It was as though her essay produced a stunning recognition effect which thereafter determined the terms of the discussion.

Mulvey was not the first to propose a feminist perspective on film.[1] Instead, as Bergstrom and Doane suggest, Mulvey's 1975 contribution to an existing discussion surrounding the relationship between the feminist movement and the emerging discipline of film theory transformed the field of possibility for feminists interested in film. Whether the effects of Mulvey's article changed the feminist film movement for the better or worse depends on the critic. B. Ruby Rich argues that Mulvey's article helped morph an activist movement she terms *cinefeminism* – which emphasized film production and political organizing – into *feminist film theory*, a 'cottage industry ... captivated by textual analysis, theoreticism, and academic concerns' (Rich 1998, 2). Rich laments the shift from cinefeminism to feminist film theory because she believes that Mulvey introduced a set of complex terms that assimilated feminists into academic film theory and criticism, excluding some of the original cinefeminists from the discussion.

Warren Buckland contextualizes this problematizing of terms within the work of a group of British feminists including Claire Johnston and Elizabeth Cowie. Mulvey, along with Johnston and Cowie, used a variety of theoretical methods – including psychoanalysis, structural anthropology, semiotics, and Marxism – to challenge what Buckland (2012, 117) terms 'the sociological "image-of-women" approach to film analysis'. This approach, represented by Molly Haskell's *From Reverence to Rape* and Marjorie Rosen's *Popcorn Venus*, among others, locates the truth of gender in external reality, of which film is an accurate or inaccurate representation. To write about positive or negative images of women is to assume that gender exists before representation. The British feminists consider instead how ideology is produced by cinema, through its material and signifying practices. It was this approach, Buckland argues, that led British psychoanalytic feminists (notably Mulvey and

Johnston) to propose models of counter-cinema, believing that cinema's constitution of women could only be shifted through revolutionary film practice (Buckland 2012, 120). Though reactions to Mulvey's work sparked a deluge of film theory writing, 'Visual Pleasure' itself calls for feminists to destroy the visual pleasure in classical narrative cinema through their own revolutionary films.

Mulvey's relationship with feminist activism, filmmaking, and film theory is thus more complex than Rich suggests. Though Mulvey was part of 'the Lacan Women's Study Group' and graduated from Oxford University, she was not a professor when she wrote her most famous piece. Thus, Mulvey wrote 'Visual Pleasure' more in the style of an activist manifesto than in that of an academic article. This quasi-academic style was characteristic, however, of the British feminist movement of the time, as women were rare in academia. Mandy Merck (2007, 3) writes: 'In those years before women's studies, feminist theoretical inquiry was largely conducted in reading groups, conferences, occasional extramural classes, and a variety of women's and Left publications.' The shift identified by Rich from *cinefeminism* to *feminist film theory* therefore parallels the general evolution of feminist theory from outside to inside the academy, made possible in part by the gains of the feminist movement.

One of the most enduring critiques of 'Visual Pleasure' is its lack of attention to the question of female visual pleasure, or even of female spectators. This structuring absence, identified by Bergstrom and Doane as the inspiration for the *Camera Obscura* special issue 'The Spectatrix' (1989), has nevertheless been productive for feminist scholars. By structuring their ideas in relation to Mulvey, feminists since the 1970s have been able to articulate the importance of women's film reception, as well as their participation in film production.

## The Spectatrix

However, the construction of a *female spectator* is doubly problematic. The idea that there can be a single female spectator implies a monolithic concept of womanhood that elides differences among women, implicitly privileging white, straight, cisgender[2] women's spectatorship. Secondly, the idea that individual spectatorship should remain central to feminist film theory continues to privilege vision as the primary mode of engagement with films for feminist critics and may privilege film perception and criticism over filmmaking as a mode of feminist practice. This privileging of the film image removed from its social context threatens to elide the many political, institutional, industrial, national, and global power structures that determine film aesthetics and practice.

The founding metaphor in the title of the journal *Camera Obscura* conceptualizes Renaissance models of monocular vision as a productive contradiction for thinking about feminism and film theory (*Camera Obscura* Collective 1976, 7). A camera obscura, or 'dark chamber', refracts rays of light from a brightly lit 'outside' through a small opening or lens and projects the image in colour, inverted, and reversed left-to-right as in a mirror. The single 'eye' of the camera obscura implies that there exists a single, objective viewpoint from which reality can be captured and accurately represented, yet the distortion of the image parallels the ways in which the act of representing must always distort its subject. The spectator of a camera obscura must work to 'right' the image, just as a spectator uses ideology to interpret the rightness of representational images. This optical model of the camera can also serve as a metaphor for human vision. Light rays bouncing off objects in the natural world enter the eye and are projected on the retina as inverted, curved, and reversed. The brain reorients these images in many ways to form a model of the objects being seen.

A simple description of the traditional model of spectatorship follows a similar pattern: a viewer receives images from the film screen, which are absorbed, reoriented, and interpreted in the mind of the viewer. From a feminist perspective, three critiques of this model immediately emerge. First, as suggested by the original editorial collective of *Camera Obscura*, the concept of projection and distortion of the 'real' suggests that something real and singular exists before the distortion of ideology, and offers no model for the operation of this ideology. The collective writes: 'The optical model is thus insufficient as a metaphor for ideology because its presupposition of an anterior reality which is inverted in its representation denies the materiality of ideology' (1976, 9). If ideological distortion is part of the act of perceiving, then ideology structures material reality to such an extent that it becomes more material and more proximate than any reality that may exist.

Second, the optical model privileges the eye, a move which 'unwittingly reinforc[es] the Platonic mind–body split' and 'devalu[es] bodily senses and sensations that are deemed less intellectually compelling' (del Río 2001, 116).[3] Further, mind–body dualism is often mapped onto a binary notion of gender, privileging the rationally coded eye over more 'bodily' senses such as touch, and creating binary gender hierarchies. Third, the traditional model of spectatorship is often rooted in a psychoanalytic and semiotic framework, a theoretical frame that has been criticized by feminists as overly general and essentializing, ignoring individual female spectators and the importance of race and class difference to female subjectivity (Bergstrom and Doane 1990, 8–9).

Linda Williams (1999) offers one answer to the privileging of vision in a model of spectatorship centred around the body through a theory of the 'body genre' originally conceptualized by Carol Clover. Attempting to avoid essentializing the body, bell hooks (1999) proposes a model of the 'oppositional gaze', discussing black women's viewing strategies that respond to and resist dominant readings of cinema.

## Two models of female spectatorship: sameness and difference

Linda Williams's article 'Film Bodies: Gender, Genre and Excess' (1999) begins with three film genres that psychoanalytic feminist theory has deemed the most 'perverse': pornography (sadism), melodrama (masochism), and horror (sadomasochism). Following Sigmund Freud's 'The Psychopathology of Everyday Life', Williams examines in detail the pleasures offered by these three 'body genres'. While the traditional voyeuristic model of spectatorship defines the spectator as separate from the filmic image, Williams locates the difficulty that makes pornography, melodrama, and horror 'gross' in the *lack* of distance between viewer and viewed. Williams writes that 'what may especially mark these body genres as low is the perception that the body of the spectator is caught up in an almost involuntary mimicry of the emotion or sensation of the body on the screen along with the fact that the body displayed is female' (270). While the voyeuristic 'male gaze' derives pleasure from the fetishistic distance between the spectator and the filmed image, Williams argues that the body genre's pleasure can often be found in the very lack of distance from the filmed image that makes the body genre so captivating.

The voyeuristic gaze is 'male' because the viewer must adopt a non-female position in order to voyeuristically view sexualized images of women.[4] Successful body genre films, though their images of excessive sensation are often written on female bodies, produce excessive sensation in both male and female viewers, allowing for what Williams calls 'a strong mixture of passivity and activity, and a bisexual oscillation between the poles of each' in the three body genres (275). Drawing on Freud, Williams also characterizes pornography, melodrama, and horror as 'genres of gender fantasy' (277) for the ways in which viewers are able to oscillate between – and take up different – gendered identifications. While the structure of voyeurism is based on binary gender difference, Williams's discussion of the body genre is based on bisexual gender *fluidity* and viewer–film near-identity.

Another example of how Williams's concept of the body genre is based on establishing similarities rather than differences is that the problems that preoccupy these genres are often the same as their solutions. Williams writes that 'pornographic films now tend to present sex as a problem, to which the performance of more, different, or better sex is posed as the solution ... In horror a violence related to sexual difference is the problem, more violence related to sexual difference is also the solution. In women's films the pathos of loss is the problem, repetitions and variations of loss are the generic solution' (276–7).

By contrast, the 'oppositional gaze', as theorized by bell hooks (1999), is emphatically based on difference, though this difference is not fixed in binary gender or oscillations between the poles of gender. hooks locates the primal scene of oppositional looking in the punishments enslaved blacks suffered from white slave-holders for the wrong sort of look at their masters. These punishments did not stop black people from looking, however. Instead, they produced 'an overwhelming longing to look, a rebellious desire, an oppositional gaze' (308). hooks writes (308): 'By courageously looking, we defiantly declared: "Not only will I stare. I want my look to change reality."' The original form of the oppositional gaze was thus a defiant reaction to the construction of binary race relations, not a reaction to binary gender. The oppositional gaze seeks to reverse the power relationship of voyeurism, allowing the persons 'looked at' to become the bearers of the critical gaze, while those in social power become the objects of examination. The fact that the majority of Hollywood films portray middle-class white characters becomes a source of strength for the oppositional gaze, as these films offer white people as objects to be looked at. In the case of racist representations of black characters, as in *Amos 'n' Andy*, hooks argues that such representations present aspects of white culture and white perception for black scrutiny through the oppositional gaze.

Ultimately, the oppositional gaze is an elective, strategic viewing position, not an essential component of black women's experience. Although all the black women with whom hooks talked while developing her theory were aware of racism, this knowledge did not necessarily lead them to develop the strategies of resistance described by the oppositional gaze. She writes (317): 'Critical black female spectatorship emerges as a site of resistance only when individual black women actively resist the imposition of dominant ways of knowing and looking.' The distance implied in the oppositional gaze therefore must be self-consciously and laboriously created in resistance to dominant modes of spectatorship. This critical gaze is conceived by hooks not as an essential starting point, but as the result of a process of learning, experience, and resistance undertaken by spectators to oppressive regimes of representation.

Williams critiques Mulvey's use of psychoanalysis by shifting focus away from Freud's concepts of fetishism and voyeurism towards the notion of fantasy in Freud's 'A Child Is Being Beaten'. hooks, however, rejects psychoanalysis altogether. By placing her model of spectatorship firmly within the realm of the conscious and the overtly political, hooks resists the tendency of psychoanalysis to describe an unconscious state attributed to ahistorical concepts of gender and sexuality.

## Beyond the spectator: expansion and multiplicity

While general models of spectatorship have been important to feminist film theory, theorists continue to inquire how feminist film theory relates to practice. A comprehensive feminist theory must take into account both specific sorts of feminist viewers and producers. The 'women working' or 'in practice' sections of *Camera Obscura*, in which interviews with women working in the media industries and short descriptions of alternative feminist film movements take their place alongside lengthier theoretical articles, are one example of feminist theory's response to this question. While most early discussions of women and film focused on Hollywood film and European and American avant-garde movements, feminist film theory has more recently examined film spectators and filmmakers outside the US and Europe. Trinh T. Minh-ha, as both film theorist and practitioner, is one of few exceptions to the Eurocentrism of early feminist film theory.

The 'film' in 'feminist film theory' has also come under scrutiny, as has the 'film' in 'film theory' and 'film studies'. Television, with its history of imagining a female audience and its status as a domestic medium, was one of the first media to join film under the rubric of feminist film theory. Video art, zines, online blogs, 'fanvids', and even medical imaging technologies are examples of the many forms that have become part of the arsenal of media analysed by feminist film theorists and employed by feminist media makers. Thus, questions of the 'specificity' of film were displaced in the way that the 'specificity' of gender was dissolved. Clare Hemmings (2011) argues that many narratives of feminist theory rely on the trope of a singular, unitary feminism that has been lost or abandoned, while feminist film theory today more often appeals to a narrative of ongoing diversity and multiplicity. In a retrospective written for *Camera Obscura*'s thirtieth anniversary, the 2006 editorial collective writes (17):

> Offering not a naïve pluralism but, rather, a more informed and more radical one, *Camera Obscura*'s embrace of work on multiple media and subjects, from multiple perspectives and with multiple concerns, has allowed the journal to continue making an impact in film, media and cultural studies without losing sight of either its initial vision or its various options for the future.

As gaze theory and studies of spectatorship fall out of fashion in film and media studies, it is this multiplicity of media and practice that feminist film theory cites as its future strength. Recent writing overwhelmingly attempts to remain rooted in the analysis of specific media objects and producers, rather than adopting a goal of making sweeping theoretical statements about feminism and film. Contemporary scholarship on media and resistance such as Anna Everett's *Digital Diaspora: A Race for Cyberspace* – a history of black 'early adopters' – is feminist in that it focuses on women's contributions to film and media alongside those of other under-represented groups. Just as feminism has expanded to include anti-racist, queer, and postcolonial politics, feminist film theory may need to incorporate a set of theories about power and resistance in the way that it has incorporated fluid spectatorship, multiple media, and multiple forms of media practice.

DIANA POZO

## Notes

1  See Rosen (1973) and Haskell (1973).
2  *Cisgender* people perform, embody, and/or identify with forms of gender presentation and identity that match with societal norms about proper behaviour and presentation for their sex. *Transgender* or *genderqueer* individuals perform and/or identify their gender in ways that diverge from societally sanctioned sex roles.
3  Del Río attributes this critique to Vivian Sobchack (2004) and Linda Williams (1995).
4  Mulvey's model of voyeurism has been critiqued for its exclusion of queer readings of film images. However, I believe that Mulvey's discussion of the 'male gaze' suggests that the viewer is asked to imagine themselves as a straight male being attracted to a female body. In the case of nonheterosexual and/or nonmale viewers, this produces a queer viewing position. Freud allows for this sort of switching of body viewpoints in *fantasy*, which is a mechanism equally available to males and females (see 'A Child Is Being Beaten').

## Works cited

Bergstrom, Janet, and Mary Ann Doane. 1990. 'The Female Spectator: Contexts and Directions'. *Camera Obscura* 20–21: 5–27.

Buckland, Warren. 2012. 'Against Theories of Reflection: Laura Mulvey's "Visual Pleasure and Narrative Cinema"'. In *Film Theory: Rational Reconstructions*. New York: Routledge.

*Camera Obscura* Collective. 1976. 'Feminism and Film: Critical Approaches'. *Camera Obscura* 1: 3–10.

——. 2006. '*Camera Obscura* at Thirty: Archiving the Past, Imagining the Future'. *Camera Obscura* 61: 1–25.

Chaudhuri, Shohini. 2006. *Feminist Film Theories: Laura Mulvey, Kaja Silverman, Teresa de Lauretis, Barbara Creed*. New York: Routledge.

del Río, Elena. 2001. 'The Body of Voyeurism: Mapping a Discourse of the Senses in Michael Powell's *Peeping Tom*'. *Camera Obscura* 45: 115–50.

Everett, Anna. 2009. *Digital Diaspora: A Race for Cyberspace*. Albany: State University of New York Press.

Freud, Sigmund. 1919. "'A Child is Being Beaten' A Contribution to the Study of the Origin of Sexual Perversions," trans. Alix and James Strachey, in *The Standard Edition of the Complete Psychological Works of Sigmund Freud. Volume XVII (1917–1919): An Infantile Neurosis and Other Works*, ed. James Strachey (London: Hogarth Press, 1974), 175–204.

Haskell, Molly. 1973. *From Reverence to Rape: The Treatment of Women in the Movies*. New York: Holt, Rinehart and Winston.

Hemmings, Clare. 2011. *Why Stories Matter: The Political Grammar of Feminist Theory*. Durham, NC: Duke University Press.

hooks, bell. 1999. 'The Oppositional Gaze: Black Female Spectators'. In *Feminist Film Theory: A Reader*, edited by Sue Thornham, 307–20. New York: New York University Press.

Merck, Mandy. 2007. 'Mulvey's Manifesto'. *Camera Obscura* 66: 1–23.

Rich, B. Ruby. 1998. *Chick Flicks: Theories and Memories of the Feminist Film Movement*. Durham, NC: Duke University Press.

Rosen, Marjorie. 1973. *Popcorn Venus: Women, Movies and the American Dream*. New York: Coward, McCann & Geoghegan.

Sobchack, Vivian. 2004. *Carnal Thoughts: Embodiment and Moving Image Culture*. Berkeley: University of California Press.

Williams, Linda. 1995. 'Corporealized Observers: Visual Pornographies and the "Carnal Density of Vision"'. In *Fugitive Images*, ed. Patrice Petro. Bloomington: Indiana University Press.

——. 1999. 'Film Bodies: Gender, Genre and Excess'. In *Feminist Film Theory: A Reader*, edited by Sue Thornham, 267–81. New York: New York University Press.

## Further reading

Bobo, Jacqueline. 1995. *Black Women as Cultural Readers*. New York: Columbia University Press.

Clover, Carol J. 1993. *Men, Women and Chain Saws: Gender in the Modern Horror Film*. Princeton, NJ: Princeton University Press.

Cowie, Elizabeth. 1997. *Representing the Woman: Cinema and Psychoanalysis*. Minneapolis: University of Minnesota Press.

Freud, Sigmund. 2001. *The Complete Psychological Works of Sigmund Freud*. Vol. 24. New York: Vintage Classics.

hooks, bell. 1992. *Black Looks: Race and Representation*. London: Turnaround.

Johnston, Claire. 2000 [1973]. 'Women's Cinema as Counter Cinema'. Reprinted in *Feminism and Film*, edited by E. Ann Kaplan, 22–33. New York: Oxford University Press.

Mulvey, Laura. 1975. 'Visual Pleasure and Narrative Cinema'. *Screen* 16 (3): 6–18.

Penley, Constance. 1989. *The Future of an Illusion: Film, Feminism, and Psychoanalysis*. Minneapolis: University of Minnesota Press.

Trinh, Minh-ha T. 1989. *Surname Viet Given Name Nam*. New York: Women Make Movies.

——. 1989. *Woman, Native, Other: Writing Postcoloniality and Feminism*. Bloomington: Indiana University Press.

White, Patricia. 1999. *Uninvited: Classical Hollywood Cinema and Lesbian Representability*. Bloomington: Indiana University Press.

Williams, Linda. 1989. *Hard Core: Power, Pleasure and the 'Frenzy of the Visible'*. Berkeley: University of California Press.

# FILM FABLE (JACQUES RANCIÈRE)

The *fable cinématographique*, or 'film fable', encapsulates the film theory of French philosopher Jacques Rancière, who, as Tom Conley put it, 'entered a French pantheon of film theory in 2001' (2005, 96) with the publication of his eponymously titled *La fable cinématographique*. Sudeep Dasgupta has summarized Rancière's work on cinema as 'less that of a "film theorist" than a *cinephile*'s poetic engagement with the history of cinema' (2009, 339). However, I would argue that this neglects the systematic aspect of his film writing and, after introducing Rancière's central concept, will engage with Conley's 'Cinema and Its Discontents: Jacques Rancière and Film Theory' in looking at where the 'film fable' fits into a larger theory of film and philosophy of art.

The most recent French philosopher to be granted celebrity status in Anglo-American cinema scholarship, Rancière follows in a prestigious genealogy that extends from Gilles Deleuze back to structural theorists such as Roland Barthes, the postwar humanism of André Bazin, and ultimately to the great modernist harbingers of the Seventh Art. As John Mullarkey has pointed out, Rancière 'takes advantage of coming after so many other theorists by being highly aware of the possible pitfalls awaiting any philosophy of film' (2009, 156). It is therefore apt that, before devoting the final two chapters to Deleuze's epic *Cinéma* project of the 1980s, Rancière should open his seminal and only full-length work devoted entirely to cinema with a passage from 1920s *cinéaste* Jean Epstein. A member of the elite group of filmmakers and film-goers – Delluc, Dullac, *et al.* – charged in the interwar period with delineating film's unique artistry, Epstein has faith not only in an inherent connection between film and the modern condition, but also in film's poetic power to tell much more than just a narrative tale: 'At every moment, the entire room is saturated with drama. The cigar burns on the lip of the ashtray like a threat. The dust of betrayal. Poisonous arabesques stretch across the rug and the arm of the seat trembles … ' (Epstein, quoted in Rancière 2006, 1). This lyrical portrait continues like an elegy to the medium's profound ability to perform what Epstein refers to elsewhere as *photogénie*, an innate ability to draw the soul out of the world of movement, until Epstein concludes: 'Cinema is true. A story is a lie.'

This dualism – as Rancière rephrases it, 'cinema is to the art of telling stories what truth is to lying' (2006, 1) – marks the foundation of Rancière's ongoing analysis of the cinema, which he articulates in its most concentrated form under the concept of the 'film fable'. Following with false naivety the avant-garde's praise for cinema as a medium that is more true to the dynamic complexity of life itself, Rancière writes:

> Life has nothing to do with dramatic progression, but is instead a long and continuous movement made up of an infinity of micro-movements. This truth about life has finally found an art capable of doing it justice, an art in which the intelligence that creates the reversals of fortune and the dramatic conflicts is subject to another intelligence, the intelligence of the machine that wants nothing, that does not construct any stories, but simply records the infinity of movements that gives rise to a drama a hundred times more intense than all dramatic reversals of fortune.
>
> (Rancière 2006, 2)

Rancière's language here is very intriguing, evoking a blend of André Bazin's phenomenology and Henri Bergson's temporal philosophy. The passage opens with the latter, an existential observation concerning the theory of duration ('a long and continuous movement made up of an infinity of micro-movements'), pointing out that cinema provides us at last with a medium that captures not only three spatial dimensions but also that of time, a medium of transformation and constant change that reveals the contradictions of life's narrative flipping and flopping. He then connects the dimensional complexity of the moving image to 'another intelligence', a purely sensory machine of mediation the description of which recalls Bazin's use of *objectif* (the French word for 'camera lens') to argue cinema's objectivity: an 'intelligence of the machine that wants nothing, that does not construct any stories, but simply records the infinity of movements'.

Rancière is careful to point out that he does not refer here to some anachronistic praise for the objective realism revealed through mechanical reproduction, but is instead pointing to something more compromised and, yet, more immaculate: cinema as the meeting point between reality and dream, between representation and art, between mimesis and affect. He continues: '[T]he art of the moving image can overthrow the old Aristotelian hierarchy that privileged *muthos* – the coherence of the plot – and devalued *opsis* – the spectacle's sensible effect' (2006, 2). In very Deleuzean terms (taken from Epstein), Rancière (2006, 2–3) argues that cinema can overthrow this hierarchy because its method of transcribing matter

> is equivalent to mind: a sensible immaterial matter composed of waves and corpuscles that abolishes all opposition between deceitful appearance and substantial reality ... That is the new drama to have found its artist in the cinema. Thoughts and things, exterior and interior, are captured in the same texture, in which the sensible and the intelligible remain undistinguished.

We can read inherent in this an ongoing dialogue between Rancière and the other members of post-structuralist French film-philosophy, most notably Deleuze (1983; 1985) and Jean-Louis Schefer (1980; 1997). Schefer for one offers us a mode of thinking about the moving image that contradicts the representational premise of film art, consequently challenging the cognitive imperative that situates the viewer's experience as being fundamentally based upon narrative engagement. Similarly, Deleuze's most explicit confrontation of previous semiotic models challenges Christian Metz's standard system on the fundamental level of its focus on narration and narrative meaning, redirecting a semiotics of cinema instead towards the unique and definitive features of the image itself. But whereas Schefer and Deleuze reject the hierarchical dominance of representation and attempt to provide a framework for assessing the pre-cognitive or sensory experience of the film image, Rancière views film history as a struggle between representational storytelling ('deceitful appearance') and the medium's affective ability ('substantial reality'). Rancière goes beyond this to seek – in the classic films of Lang, Eisenstein, Rossellini, Mann, and Godard – the balance of different regimes of meaning, or as he puts it 'the sensible and the intelligible'.

As Rancière does not fail to repeat, the film fable is a fable that is contrary to itself, and as Conley summarizes: 'a dialectics inheres in these images that inform so much of canonical film theory' (2005, 97). This dialectics concerns the tension between the visual, narrative, and conceptual power of the moving image; as Mullarkey puts it, films 'can tell stories cinematically that exceed both their scripts and their concepts' (2009, 157). We can find a good example of this in Rancière's analysis of Fritz Lang's *M* (1931), the classic precautionary Weimar film about a mentally deranged serial child-murderer brought to justice by a lynch mob. There is a moment in the film when the killer, between victims, becomes hypnotized before a toy-store window; the camera is placed inside the store, framing his childlike expression of wonderment within the psychedelic reflection of geometric forms cast by the showcase toys. Here, Rancière argues, the film suspends the representational narrative about an evil man and challenges the spectator with a moment of aesthetic expression that combines non-figural visuality (the composition of the image) with non-narrative identification (we can for a moment sympathize with a monster), before the representational regime restores the film to its linear trajectory bearing towards a moral conclusion. For a moment, the aesthetic logic of the image challenges its representational logic, bringing the story to a halt and forcing us to question our alliances as spectators (Rancière 2006, 55).

In Rancière's opinion, this representational compromise is typical of popular cinema and, like Deleuze, Rancière attaches it to a larger historical evolution in the relationship between thought and art. In a larger framework in which regimes are defined by their balance of the intelligible and sensible, the representational regime adheres to a classical organization of relations (between sound and image, voice and meaning, subject and object), the rigidity of which has upheld larger ideological orders from American capitalism to German Nazism, the acquiescence to which proves cinema's tragic weakness throughout history. 'In the age of Joyce and Virginia Woolf, of Malevich and Schönberg, cinema arrives as if expressly designed to thwart a simple teleology of artistic modernity, to counter art's aesthetic autonomy with its old submission to the representative regime' (Rancière 2006, 10). For Rancière this problem goes beyond a simple dichotomy between art and entertainment, though, and arrives at a perpetual conflict tearing at the film fable, which ultimately implodes through 'an indecisiveness at the heart of its artistic nature' (Rancière 2006, 11) – 'a thwarted fable' at all times straddling the paradigms of modernity and classicism and contrasting the pure presence of reality with the reality of philosophical conventions and cultural desires.

Perhaps attesting to his current popularity among English-speaking readers and American academia (he spent spring 2010 in residence at the University of Chicago), Rancière acts as a sort of fulcrum between American cognitive film theory and a more metaphysical French film-philosophy, citing the moving image's constant state of fluctuation as rendering it emblematic of twentieth-century art's movement between the mimetic and the figural. In 'Cinema and Its Discontents: Jacques Rancière and Film Theory', Conley provides a very strong integration of Rancière's film fable into his philosophy of art and cultural ethics, setting out 'to consider how his aesthetic theory inflects cinema' in relation to Rancière's writing of *Malaise dans l'ésthétique* (2004). The later work, like many since *La fable cinématographique* (see *Politics of Aesthetics* [2004], *The Future of the Image* [2007] and *Aesthetics and Its Discontents* [2009]), offers a wider cultural context for the dialectical evolution of artistic regimes demonstrated by the film fable, and Conley traces how the basic premise of the film fable is stretched to analyse the displacement of cinema into the installation space of contemporary museums and how film and video 'become confused when digital processing replaces the material remainders of celluloid and acetate' (2005, 99).

Between these two books Conley teases out Rancière's larger vision of image culture and the wider ramifications of the film fable's conceptual foundations, encouraging us towards necessary horizons that resist a utopia of film-philosophy and, instead, acknowledge the dualistic nature of cinema as both a commercial narrative form and an art, and explore its crystalline connections to other media. In short, Conley concludes that the canonical analysis of Rancière's film fable fights against the titular malaise experienced by contemporary art, urging us 'to awaken a politics from the popcorn-scented consensus we smell in malls and cineplexes all over the world' (2005, 105). Yet, due to its place in a larger puzzle that Rancière assembles involving politics and art, Mullarkey may be apt to criticize the specificity of film to Rancière's breakthroughs. But is this necessarily a negative quality? Might it not benefit us to assess cinema both according to its individual acts of filmic textuality and also according to a wider dialectic that connects it vertically to a genealogy and horizontally to a network of other cultural and political forces? Though Rancière's historical contextualization of cinema may well anchor it to a philosophy of art that precedes the medium by nearly a century, it seems overly dismissive to claim that 'film contributes little that is *new* to Rancière's philosophy of art-politics' (Mullarkey 2009, 162). While his later works may well set Rancière apart as 'among the few that … bring us to the quick of the political aesthetics of cinema' (Conley 2005, 106), it is the kernel of the 'film fable' that best elucidates the dialectical relationship between representation and figuration, the intelligible and the sensible, and this is no doubt what attracted the philosopher to the cinema and us, as readers, to what he writes about it.

HUNTER VAUGHAN

## Works cited

Conley, Tom. 2005. 'Cinema and Its Discontents: Jacques Rancière and Film Theory'. *SubStance* 34 (3): 96–106.

Dasgupta, Sudeep. 2009. 'Jacques Rancière'. In *Film, Theory and Philosophy*, edited by Felicity Colman, 339–48. Durham: Acumen.

Deleuze, Gilles. 1983. *Cinéma I: L'Image-mouvement*. Paris: Les Éditions de Minuit.

——. 1985. *Cinéma II: L'Image-temps*. Paris: Les Éditions de Minuit.

Mullarkey, John. 2009. *Refracting Reality: Philosophy and the Moving Image*. New York: Palgrave Macmillan.

Rancière, Jacques. 2004. *Politics of Aesthetics*. Translated by Gabriel Rockhill. London: Continuum.

——. 2006. *Film Fables*. Translated by Emiliano Battista. Oxford: Berg.

——. 2007. *The Future of the Image*. Translated by Gregory Elliot. London: Verso.

——. 2009. *Aesthetics and Its Discontents*. Translated by Steven Corcoran. Cambridge: Polity.

Schefer, Jean-Louis. 1980. *L'Homme ordinaire du cinéma*. Paris: Cahiers du cinéma.

——. 1997. *Du Monde et du movement des images*. Paris: Cahiers du cinéma.

# FILM-PHILOSOPHY

The idea of film-philosophy – also described as 'film philosophy', 'film and philosophy', and 'film as philosophy' – has gained recognition in recent years as a dynamic strand of contemporary film theory (see Mulhall 2002; 2008; Read and Goodenough 2005; Wartenberg 2007; 2011a; 2011b; Elsaesser and Hagener 2010, 12; Carel and Tuck 2011). As the hyphen suggests, it expresses a way of thinking at the intersection between film and philosophy, linking the two in a shared enterprise that seeks to illuminate the one by means of the other. Inspired by the work of Stanley Cavell (1979; 1981; 1996) and Gilles Deleuze (1986; 1989) (*see* MOVEMENT-IMAGE; TIME-IMAGE; MINOR CINEMA), film-philosophers claim that film and philosophy are intimately related, sharing problems to which they respond in distinctive ways, thereby opening up new possibilities of thought. More generally, film-philosophy can be understood as a style or 'genre' of philosophical film theory with close links to film criticism, aesthetics, as well as earlier traditions of film theory. It seeks to explore the relationship between philosophy and film in a non-reductive, mutually productive manner, and thus overlaps with, but is not reducible to, more traditional philosophy of film. More recently, film-philosophers have claimed that films can make innovative contributions to philosophical understanding by using cinematic means (Mulhall 2002; 2008; Wartenberg 2007; Smuts 2009; Sinnerbrink 2011a; 2011b). From this point of view, one might call Stanley Cavell (1979) a film-philosopher and Noël Carroll (2008) a philosopher of film; they are both concerned with similar problems but philosophize on (and with) film in distinctive, yet complementary, ways.

In what follows, I shall elaborate this sketch of film-philosophy by analysing two influential texts, Stephen Mulhall's *On Film* (2008, 3–11) and Thomas E. Wartenberg's *Thinking on Screen* (2007, 15–31). Both Mulhall and Wartenberg argue that film can make creative contributions to our philosophical understanding via cinematic means. Their work defending the 'film as philosophy' thesis has led to a vigorous debate with other theorists who question whether film can make genuine contributions to philosophy (Livingston 2006; 2009; Russell 2006; Smith 2006). This debate opens up important questions concerning our assumptions about the practice of philosophy, about the power of film to transform our horizons, and about the language we should use in philosophizing on film.

## 'Bold' film-philosophy (Mulhall)

Inspired by the work of Stanley Cavell, Stephen Mulhall's *On Film* (2002, 2008) is one of the more significant and controversial versions of contemporary film-philosophy. In his 'Introduction' (2002, 1–11), Mulhall outlines his reasons for selecting the *Alien* quadrilogy – *Alien*

(Ridley Scott, 1979), *Aliens* (James Cameron, 1986), *Alien³* (David Fincher, 1992), and *Alien Resurrection* (Jean-Pierre Jeunet, 1997) – as a case study demonstrating the idea of 'film as philosophy'. These fascinating genre films are distinguished, for Mulhall, by their sustained interest in questions of human identity and embodiment, concerns that have been central to the modern philosophical tradition since Descartes. Far from being trivial, these films treat identity and embodiment with a 'sophistication and self-awareness' that suggest they are 'making real contributions' to our philosophical understanding (Mulhall 2002, 2). In an oft-quoted passage, Mulhall (2) restates this claim as describing his own approach to film-philosophy:

> I do not look to these films as handy or popular illustrations of views and argu-
> ments properly developed by philosophers; I see them rather as themselves
> reflecting on and evaluating such views and arguments, as thinking seriously and
> systematically about them in just the ways that philosophers do. Such films are not
> philosophy's raw material, nor a source for its ornamentation; they are philosophical
> exercises, philosophy in action – film as philosophizing.

This passage has provoked a storm of debate, with both critics and defenders of film-philosophy arguing over its meaning and implications. Many have taken it as defining Mulhall's 'position' as a film-philosopher, treating his remarks as representative of a general thesis or methodology for the study of cinema (see Baggini 2003; Smith 2006). Mulhall has since defended his approach, stressing that the real argument is to be found in his sustained philosophical interpretations of the *Alien* films, a point mostly ignored by his critics (2008, 130–4).

Mulhall presents this passage at the conclusion of a paragraph highlighting the *Alien* films' philosophical interest in the problem of 'the relation of human identity and embodiment' (2002, 2). These films' thematic exploration of 'the bodily basis of human identity', in turn, raises a question concerning the conditions of cinema, for it is a medium dependent upon 'the projection of moving images of embodied human individuals presented to a camera' (3). These two issues, for Mulhall, suggest that a film like *Alien* explores questions about 'the nature of the cinematic medium' which one might otherwise expect to find in the philosophy of film (3–4). Echoing Cavell's reflections on cinema (1979), Mulhall links the question of how film depicts embodied human individuals with the problem of how cinema can project a 'humanized' world. What is it about movies that both captures and transfigures the human figures they depict? Given the bodily basis of human identity, how can moving images reveal human beings in their unique singularity? For Mulhall, the *Aliens* quadrilogy poses such questions through the medium itself, a cinematic and philosophical exploration of how a camera can reveal the bodily presence of human individuals within a meaningful world.

This Cavellian insight leads Mulhall to specify three senses in which film can be said to 'philosophize'. We can describe films as akin to a *philosophy of/about film*, exploring issues that philosopher-theorists might consider (like 'the nature of the medium'). We can also talk of *film as philosophizing*, where films explore in their own terms recognized philosophical ideas, themes, or problems (like human identity and embodiment). And finally, we can talk of *film in the condition of philosophy*, where films reflect upon their own conditions of possibility (a reflexive enterprise) or the presuppositions of their own practice (the dialectic of 'originality and inheritance', for example, inherent to the creation of cinematic sequels). These are overlapping concerns and the distinctions between them are not always sharp, but they do provide an illuminating way of articulating the different ways in which we might speak of 'film as philosophy'.

There are some ambiguities, however, in Mulhall's account. He cites *Alien*'s concern with human embodiment and identity as suggesting that it engages in 'film as philosophizing' (2002, 2) but also as what relates it to the 'philosophy of film' (4). Reflection upon the nature of the cinematic medium, by contrast, is a sign that the *Alien* films emulate the 'philosophy of film' (3–4) but also that they are instances of 'cinematic modernism' (6), which he then identifies with 'film in the condition of philosophy' (6). Is 'art in the condition of modernism' to be identified only with art that exists 'in the condition of philosophy' (6)? If so, this would seem to exclude non-modernist cinematic works from enjoying philosophical status. Conversely, any work that exhibits elements of self-reflection – say, episodes of *The Simpsons* or recent horror movie franchises – would count as modernist and so as philosophical. I would suggest, however, that film-philosophy need not be tethered to modernist self-reflection; nor should self-reflection be assumed as the only hallmark of a philosophical work.

## 'Moderate' film-philosophy (Wartenberg)

Thomas Wartenberg has addressed these criticisms and defended what he calls a 'moderate' version of film-philosophy (or 'cinematic philosophy', to use his term). In *Thinking on Screen* (2007), Wartenberg questions whether there are good reasons to accept the Platonic 'philosophical disenfranchisement of film' that underpins the most common criticisms of film-philosophy, 'a priori criticisms' that 'do not refer to actual films, but make general claims about what films cannot do' (2007, 16). As a consequence, Wartenberg remarks, critics have tended to posit 'a fundamental theoretical problem' at the heart of film-philosophy, rather than questioning their own assumptions about the relationship between philosophy and film (16).

Wartenberg summarizes these criticisms as the *explicitness*, *generality*, and *imposition* objections (2007, 16–31). The first objection turns on the claim that film, as a visual rather than linguistic medium, 'lacks the explicitness to formulate and defend the precise claims that are characteristic of philosophical writing' (16). Films are taken to be ambiguous, rhetorically driven, and hence epistemically inferior to philosophy (it is difficult to see how they might express logical relations such as negation); or they are taken as making implicit philosophical claims that critics must then make explicit (Russell 2006, quoted in Wartenberg 2007, 19). The idea that only interpreters make arguments in relation to film, however, is misguided. Although viewers or critics may make such arguments explicit, this does not mean that they, rather than the films, are the source or bearers of the arguments as such. Even if arguments are implicit in films, they do not necessarily have to be imprecise; many philosophical arguments are ambiguous, so 'ambiguity' is not a sound criterion for distinguishing between the claims of film and those of philosophy (Wartenberg 2007, 19–20). What such criticisms end up showing, rather, is that film-philosophy is *difficult* rather than impossible, that it requires not only a capacity for theoretical argument but also interpretative skills and an ability to engage in detailed film criticism.

The generality objection, however, challenges this idea. Philosophy, so the objection goes, deals with issues characterized by their 'abstractness and generality', whereas narrative film deals with the particularity of characters, situations, and events (2007, 21).

Wartenberg responds, however, by pointing to non-fiction or documentary films, which can make important contributions to our understanding of historical events or social issues (22–4). What of fictional film? Here Wartenberg underlines the significance of narrative film as way of screening complex 'thought experiments' involving hypothetical narrative situations that prompt us to reflect upon the plausibility and coherence of our beliefs, moral assumptions, or philosophical commitments (24–5, chapter 4). It is worth noting that, although characters and scenarios may be particular or specific, narrative structure depends upon general *causal* relationships (motivations, consequences, implications) that viewers are able to understand and evaluate. So in this respect, it is misleading to suggest that philosophy concerns only 'abstractness and generality', whereas fiction film is concerned exclusively with 'the particular'. Movies (like philosophy) concern the general *and* the particular, the abstract *and* the concrete; they posit definite causal relationships between events, characters, and situations, describe and depict characters, settings, and events in their unique singularity, and engage our powers of inference, reflection, and judgement in order for us to understand and appreciate the film. This is presumably why they can also serve, as Wartenberg argues, as cases of philosophical thought experiment.

The third and most common complaint about film-philosophy is the 'imposition objection': that film theorists are often guilty of 'imposing' inappropriate or unintended theoretical meanings upon their chosen films. This can be reformulated, however, as a maxim that ought to guide philosophical interpretation: namely, to avoid imposing inappropriate interpretations on a cinematic work, and to ensure that any interpretation attributed to it could have been intended by its creator (Wartenberg 2007, 26). Here Wartenberg distinguishes between *creator*-oriented and *audience*-oriented interpretations: reconstructing the meaning that an author of a work could have intended versus that which audiences might find relevant to understanding or appreciating a work. Only the former, Wartenberg claims, 'can justify the claim that the film itself is philosophical', a point he takes up in his Aristotelian interpretation of Carol Reed's *The Third Man* (1948) as an exploration of the philosophical concept of friendship (2007, 26; see also Livingston 2009). One should note, however, Wartenberg's claim that philosophical interpretation (as 'creator-oriented') depends upon attributing a plausible intention to the filmmaker is controversial. Although it can be an important hermeneutic principle, the question of what counts as a valid interpretation of a work of art – particularly one with a philosophical meaning – is not settled by establishing authorial intention (cf. the 'intentionalist fallacy'). The fact that a filmmaker might deny any explicit philosophical intention, for example, does not necessarily render their film devoid of philosophical meaning (see Sinnerbrink 2011a, 129–31). Indeed, the difficult hermeneutic debates over the meaning of movies tend to cut across or confound the poles of 'creator-' versus 'audience-oriented' interpretation.

## Screening philosophy

So how can films 'do philosophy'? There are two ways in which philosophers have sought to show this: a global or 'universalist' approach, which posits an intrinsic connection between film and philosophy (Cavell on film and scepticism for example), and a local, particularist, or empirical approach, which 'investigates the question of film's relationship to philosophy by paying attention both to individual films and specific philosophical techniques' (Wartenberg 2007, 28). Along with other film-philosophers, Wartenberg champions the latter approach, examining what philosophical questions or issues a film raises, and how, in specific terms, films screen these philosophical issues (28). One could add a couple of additional remarks to this point. The first is whether films are bound to treat only established philosophical problems and topics, or whether they can explore such issues in an independent manner or even pose new questions in their own way. The second is whether films might have more complex means of presenting 'arguments' at their disposal, developing multiple conceptual possibilities via complex forms of narrative ('puzzle-plot' or 'mind-game' films). These present challenging cases in which films might be interpreted as engaging in more complex forms of intellectual and moral exploration than conventional philosophical 'thought experiments' (see Buckland 2009).

Wartenberg's pluralist approach implicitly raises a meta-philosophical question, namely, which conception of philosophy do participants in the film-philosophy debate hold? Three distinct conceptions are pertinent here: philosophy as a discipline addressing basic human concerns or 'eternal questions'; philosophy as a discipline that asks questions of other disciplines; and philosophy as a distinctive mode of discourse involving 'the argument, the counterexample, and the thought experiment' (Wartenberg 2007, 30). There are, more-over, many ways in which films can 'screen' philosophy: they can illustrate philosophical ideas in innovative ways; they can make arguments concerning philosophical and moral issues; they can reflect upon the medium of cinema; and they can stage cinematic thought experiments that serve as philosophical counter-examples or provoke reflection on our assumptions and beliefs. From this perspective, a 'moderate' film-philosophy can be defended against the standard objections, and can show, in particular cases, how films make creative contributions to our philosophical understanding using cinematic means.

Wartenberg thus rejects 'bold' versions of film-philosophy, which risk assuming a con-ception of philosophy that is either too encompassing (anything counts as philosophy) or too esoteric (assuming a 'controversial' definition of philosophy). Mulhall's claim that films can philosophize in 'just the ways philosophers do', for example, is criticized for failing to explain 'how a cultural form other than philosophy itself [namely film] can make a sub-stantial contribution to the specifically philosophical discussion of an issue such as that of human embodiment' (Wartenberg 2007, 37). In a similar vein, more radical exponents of film-philosophy are criticized for claiming that film's expressive capacities sometimes out-strip what can be readily articulated in standard philosophical discourse, which means we require a new kind of idiom – perhaps a new kind of thinking – in order to describe and conceptualize what film enables us to experience and think (see Frampton 2006; Sinnerbrink 2011a).

Radical film-philosophy may be defended in two ways. One is to insist that arguments over the validity of film-philosophy require further reflection on the nature of philosophical discourse and its relationship with cinema. If one of the ways in which films contribute to philosophy is by *showing* what philosophy finds difficult to state, then the demand that we need to 'paraphrase' the relevant content of a film into a recognized philosophical dis-course (Livingston 2006) might overlook precisely how film can question our conception of philosophy, how it might raise questions that contemporary philosophy does not typically address, and how such 'cinematic thinking' ought to be communicated (see Sinnerbrink 2011a). The other is to explore the possibility that the language of philosophy has limita-tions when brought to bear on the critical interpretation of aesthetically challenging films. If the aesthetic 'form' of a film is intrinsic to its philosophical meaning, then we require a new language that is at once aesthetically receptive and philosophically reflective if we are to do justice to it as a work of art. Indeed, it raises the question, important for film-philosophy, whether film can express thought in ways that might require us to revise, renew, or transcend our received models of theoretical discourse. Practioners of film-philosophy should therefore reflect further on the kind of language we use in giving voice to film, a question that philosophically challenging films invite us to consider: what is the appropriate language (and style) for appreciating film aesthetically *and* philosophically?

ROBERT SINNERBRINK

## Works cited

Baggini, Julian. 2003. 'Alien Ways of Thinking: Mulhall's *On Film*'. *Film-Philosophy* 7(3): http://www.film-philosophy.com/index.php/f-p/article/view/745/657.

Buckland, Warren. 2009. 'Introduction: Puzzle Plots'. In *Puzzle Films: Complex Storytelling in Contemporary Cinema*, edited by Warren Buckland, 1–12. Oxford: Wiley-Blackwell.

Carel, Havi, and Greg Tuck, eds. 2011. *New Takes in Film-Philosophy*. London: Palgrave Macmillan.

Carroll, Noël. 2008. *The Philosophy of Motion Pictures*. Oxford: Blackwell Publishing.

Cavell, Stanley. 1979. *The World Viewed: Reflections on the Ontology of Film*. Enlarged edition. Cambridge, MA: Harvard University Press.

——. 1981. *Pursuits of Happiness: The Hollywood Comedy of Remarriage*. Cambridge, MA: Harvard University Press.

——. 1996. *Contesting Tears: The Melodrama of the Unknown Woman*. Chicago, IL: Chicago University Press.

Deleuze, Gilles. 1986 [1983]. *Cinema 1: The Movement-Image*. Translated by Hugh Tomlinson and Barbara Habberjam. Minneapolis: University of Minnesota Press.

——. 1989 [1985]. *Cinema 2: The Time-Image*. Translated by Hugh Tomlinson and Robert Galatea. Minneapolis: University of Minnesota Press.

Elsaesser, Thomas, and Malte Hagener. 2010. *Film Theory: An Introduction through the Senses*. New York: Routledge.

Frampton, Daniel. 2006. *Filmosophy*. London: Wallflower Press.

Livingston, Paisley. 2006. 'Theses on Cinema as Philosophy'. In *Thinking through Cinema: Film as Philosophy*, edited by Murray Smith and Thomas E. Wartenberg, 11–18. Oxford: Blackwell Publishing.

——. 2009. *Cinema, Philosophy, Bergman: On Film as Philosophy*. Oxford: Oxford University Press.

Mulhall, Stephen. 2002. *On Film*. London: Routledge.

——. 2008. *On Film*. 2nd edition. London: Routledge.

Read, Rupert, and Jerry Goodenough, eds. 2005. *Film as Philosophy: Essays on Cinema after Wittgenstein and Cavell*. Basingstoke: Palgrave Macmillan.

Russell, Bruce. 2006. 'The Philosophical Limits of Film'. In *Philosophy of Film and Motion Pictures: An Anthology*, edited by Noël Carroll and Jinhee Choi, 387–90. Oxford: Blackwell Publishing.

Sinnerbrink, Robert. 2011a. *New Philosophies of Film: Thinking Images*. London and New York: Continuum.

——. 2011b. 'Re-enfranchising Film: Towards a Romantic Film-Philosophy'. In *New Takes in Film-Philosophy*, edited by Havi Carel and Greg Tuck, 25–47. Basingstoke and New York: Palgrave Macmillan.

Smith, Murray. 2006. 'Film, Art, and Ambiguity'. In *Thinking through Cinema: Film as Philosophy*, edited by Murray Smith and Thomas E. Wartenberg, 33–42. Oxford: Blackwell Publishing.

Smuts, Aaron. 2009. 'Film as Philosophy: In Defence of a Bold Thesis'. *Journal of Aesthetics and Art Criticism* 67 (4): 409–20.

Wartenberg, Thomas E. 2007. *Thinking on Screen: Film as Philosophy*. London and New York: Routledge.

——. 2011a. 'Philosophy of Film'. *Stanford Encyclopedia of Philosophy*: http://plato.stanford.edu/entries/film/.

——. 2011b. 'On the Possibility of Cinematic Philosophy'. In *New Takes in Film-Philosophy*, edited by Havi Carel and Greg Tuck, 1–24. Basingstoke and New York: Palgrave Macmillan.

## Further reading

Bersani, Leo, and Ulysse Dutoit. 2004. *Forms of Being: Cinema, Aesthetics, Subjectivity*. London: BFI Books.

Clayton, Alex, and Andrew Klevan, eds. 2011. *The Language and Style of Film Criticism*. London and New York: Routledge.

Mullarkey, John. 2009. *Refractions of Reality: Philosophy of the Moving Image*. Basingstoke: Palgrave Macmillan.

Rancière, Jacques. 2006. *Film Fables*. Translated by Emiliano Battista. Oxford and New York: Berg Books.

Singer, Irving. 2008. *Cinematic Mythmaking*. Cambridge, MA: MIT Press.

# FORMALIST THEORIES OF FILM

Over the course of the relatively brief history of film studies, a striking number of diverse permutations of formalism have been advanced (Christie 1998; Buckland 2008). These include, for example, approaches developed by Rudolf Arnheim (1957), Christian Metz (1974), Noël Burch (1981), Raymond Bellour (2000), Kristin Thompson (1981; 1988), David Bordwell (1981; 1985; 1988), and Bordwell and Thompson (2012) collaboratively. The present entry explores one of the origins of this tradition, as well as the work of one of its most prominent exponents in contemporary film studies.

The first part of the entry focuses on a seminal essay in Russian formalist literary criticism – Viktor Shklovsky's 'Art as Technique' (1965 [1917]). In this essay, Shklovsky introduces the concept of *ostranenie* or 'defamiliarization', which has proved important to a number of film theorists – perhaps none more so than Kristin Thompson (1981; 1988). The second part of the entry examines the ways in which Thompson's neoformalism makes use of defamiliarization and related Russian formalist ideas.

## Shklovsky's 'Art as Technique'

Although Shklovsky's essay sets out several general claims regarding the nature of perception, the nature of literature, and the nature of art more broadly, it begins with what may initially appear to be a rather insular debate. Shklovsky takes issue with a view, advanced by the largely forgotten Russian philologist Alexander Potebnya, which identifies the essence of art (and poetry, in particular) as the engendering of mental imagery. However, as Shklovsky points out, it seems that something's occasioning 'imagistic thought' (1965 [1917], 7) is neither necessary nor sufficient for it to be art. On his view, it cannot be necessary because various art forms, notably music, seem not to essentially involve imagery, and it cannot be sufficient for two reasons.

One reason imagery is not sufficient for something to be art is that there can be non-artistic uses of imagery – what Shklovsky calls 'prose imagery', (1965 [1917], 9) or 'imagery as a practical means of thinking' (8). This is not an isolated point regarding the nature of imagery. Rather, it owes something to Shklovsky's broader conception of the nature of poetry and language in general. For him, language can be used for practical, non-aesthetic purposes or for non-practical, aesthetic purposes. In the former case, language is prose and in the latter case it is poetry. In both cases, words constitute material that is shaped into either prosaic or poetic language through the use of particular devices like imagery. But neither the materials nor the devices have an essential aesthetic valence or value. Whether or not language is prose or poetry, whether it is non-aesthetic or aesthetic, depends on how it functions in a particular context.

A second and related reason imagery cannot be sufficient for something to be art is that, in the case of poetry, imagery 'is but one of the devices of poetic language' (Shklovsky 1965 [1917], 9). This is a somewhat confusing claim because Shklovsky has just pointed out that imagery can be prosaic as well as poetic. However, what he seems to be suggesting is that imagery is just one of several devices that can be used in poetry. Interpreted this way, Shklovsky is claiming that imagery can be put to prosaic or poetic purposes, but so too can many other devices. Other such devices that can be used poetically include 'parallelism, comparison, repetition, balanced structure, hyperbole, the commonly accepted rhetorical figures, and all those methods which emphasize the emotional effect of an expression' (8–9). As we will soon see, the idea that there is an array of poetic devices, all of which may serve the same purpose equally well, is important to Shklovsky's overall conception of art.

Before explaining what that is, however, Shklovsky first tries to establish a general principle about the nature of perception. 'If we start to examine the general laws of perception, we see that as perception becomes habitual, it becomes automatic' (11). Here, Shklovsky refers not only to visual perception, but all our perceptual modalities – to perception in general. On his view, such 'habitualization' or 'automatization' has deleterious, anaesthetizing consequences. 'Habitualization', he writes, 'devours works, clothes, furniture, one's wife, and the fear of war' (12). That is, habitualized perception is dulled perception – potentially so dulled that experiences may fail to register with us, as if we were sleep walking. But to live life so desensitized to experience is not to really live it at all, as Shklovsky signals by citing an apt passage from Leo Tolstoy's *Diary*: 'If the whole complex of lives of many people go on unconsciously, then such lives are as if they had never been' (quoted in Shklovsky 1965 [1917], 12).

For Shklovsky, the remedy for habitualized perception is art. As he puts it in a well-known remark, 'art exists that one may recover the sensation of life; it exists to make one feel things, to make the stone *stony*' (12). In many texts that cite Shklovsky, the quotation is cut off here, leaving students to ponder the somewhat obscure notion of making a stone stony. But the actual passage from which the quotation is often excised continues with a further explanation: 'The purpose of art is to impart the sensation of things as they are perceived and not as they are known. The technique of art is to make objects "unfamiliar," to make forms difficult, to increase the difficulty and length of perception because the process of perception is an aesthetic end in itself and must be prolonged' (12). In sum, Shklovsky's view is that the purpose of art is the renewal of perception both because perceptual experience is 'an aesthetic end in itself' and because habitualized perception dulls one's experience of life. And this renewal of perception is achieved by making things unfamiliar – by defamiliarizing them. Thus, more simply put, the purpose of art is defamiliarization.

Now we are in a position to understand both Shklovsky's objection to the view that the essence of art is imagery and his emphasis that imagery is just one of many devices that can serve a single function equally well. For Shklovsky, such devices are not ends in themselves, but rather means to realize art's point – means by which to achieve defamiliarization. This brings us to a crucial and often overlooked point about the conception of art held by Shklovsky and the other Russian formalists who adopted his views. Despite being known as a 'formalist', Shklovsky actually propounds a functional theory of art. That is, he identifies

215

the essence of art with a particular function – namely, defamiliarization. This is not to deny that form is important for Shklovsky and the Russian formalists, but rather it is to say that form is significant just because it is what makes defamiliarization possible. And the analysis of form is thus an essential critical activity because it allows us to see how specific devices function in various works to achieve defamiliarization.

It is important to stress, however, that Shklovsky and the Russian formalists have in mind here a somewhat unusual conception of form. Typically, formalism is associated with the views that there is a sharp distinction between form and content and that only form is aesthetically relevant (Thomson-Jones 2009, 132). However, if, as Shklovsky puts it, a given artistic device's 'purpose is not to make us perceive meaning, but to create a special perception of the object' (1965 [1917], 18), then the aesthetic relevance of the form/content distinction seems to dissolve (Thompson 1981, 11; Thomson-Jones 2009, 132–3). Because the purpose of art is the renewal of perception rather than the communication of meaning, form is not a kind of container in which the content or meaning is presented. Rather, form can be thought of as a set of devices used to shape material so that it is perceived a certain way. As Thompson writes, form 'refers in this approach to the sum total of internal relationships in the work' (1981, 12). That is, form is the work's overall system of devices that renders any given material (e.g. words, objects, cinematic or poetic conventions) defamiliarized.

Much of the subsequent discussion in 'Art as Technique' explores defamiliarization in literary contexts, and cinema is not mentioned at all. And although Shklovsky did write both for the cinema and about the cinema throughout the 1920s, he never applied the ideas developed in 'Art as Technique' in the context of cinema in a systematic and sustained fashion. So, too, other Russian formalists turned their attention to film – most notably in the 1927 volume *The Poetics of Cinema* edited by Boris Eikhenbaum – but a comprehensive formalist study of the cinema was never written.

## Neoformalist film analysis

It was not until the 1981 publication of Kristin Thompson's *Eisenstein's* Ivan the Terrible: *A Neoformalist Analysis*, followed by her *Breaking the Glass Armor: Neoformalist Film Analysis* (1988), that the Russian formalists' core assumptions and general approach were systematically brought to bear upon the study of film. Thompson's neoformalism borrows from the foundational principles of the Russian formalists rather than their writings on film for two reasons. First, as we saw above, the formalists never systematized their thinking about cinema. Second, and perhaps for that reason, their writing on cinema tended to apply ideas from their work on literature, assuming that cinema was a kind of language. However, Thompson regards this as an unconvincing line of thought, so in general she adopts the formalists' approach while leaving aside their specific work on cinema.

Nevertheless, there is one sense in which Thompson sees a relevant parallel between film and language. On her view, 'we may take the material elements of cinema to be those components that are equivalent to words in literature; that is, they may be combined to serve practical or non-practical functions' (Thompson 1981, 25). In other words, Thompson suggests, just as language can be used aesthetically or non-aesthetically depending on how it is deployed in a given context, so too are there aesthetic and non-aesthetic instances of film. Thompson identifies the materials of cinema as *mise en scène*, sound, camera/frame, editing, and optical effects (26). Yet, she stresses, 'since these techniques are used in some combination in all films, they are not sufficient to define [aesthetic] cinematicness' (26). (It is not clear whether Thompson conflates materials and devices here, or if she simply does not want to draw the distinction as sharply as I have.)

Here we see some of the most important ways in which neoformalism adopts the core assumptions of Russian formalism. Neoformalism follows Russian formalism in drawing a sharp divide between the realm of the aesthetic and the realm of the everyday. A medium like language or film has no inherent aesthetic valence. It can be used aesthetically or practically, prosaically or poetically. What matters is *how* a particular work's devices organize its materials to perform various functions. What, then, constitutes an aesthetic use of the film medium ('cinematicness') for the neoformalist? When does film function aesthetically?

Again, Thompson follows Shklovsky and the Russian formalists in supposing that an aesthetic use of the medium essentially involves a special kind of perception. 'For neoformalists', she writes, 'art is a realm separate from all other types of cultural artifacts because it presents a unique set of perceptual requirements. Art is set apart from the everyday world, in which we use our perception for practical ends' (Thompson 1988, 8). In contrast to the practical perception required by our engagement with the everyday world, perception in art contexts is, as Shklovsky said, 'an aesthetic end in itself' (1965 [1917], 12). According to Thompson, this is because 'films and other artworks, on the contrary, plunge us into a non-practical, playful type of interaction. They renew our perceptions and other mental processes because they hold no immediate practical implications for us' (1988, 8).

For Thompson, as for Shklovsky, this renewal of perception occurs through defamiliarization, and the neoformalist conception of defamiliarization closely resembles that of the formalists. According to Thompson, 'the nature of practical perception means that our faculties become dulled by the repetitive and habitual activities inherent in much of daily life' (1988, 9). 'Art', she explains, 'defamiliarizes our habitual perceptions of the everyday world, of ideology, of other artworks, and so on by taking material from these sources and transforming them. The transformation takes place through their placement in a new context and their participation in unaccustomed formal patterns' (1988, 11). Thus, like Shklovsky, Thompson adopts a functional conception of art, according to which art's purpose is defamiliarization.

However, it is important to recognize that Thompson adds a number of qualifications here and that, ultimately, neoformalism is less a general theory of art or film than an approach to film analysis. One qualification regards the kind of theory of art that neoformalism adopts. Inasmuch as neoformalism supposes that the purpose of art is defamiliarization because this affords a kind of aesthetic perception, it falls under the broader category of aesthetic theories of art. But neoformalism's aestheticism differs from traditional theories in terms of how it understands the nature of aesthetic experience. In contrast to notions of a detached or disinterested aesthetic attitude, neoformalism invokes a conception of aesthetic experience in which 'the viewer actively seeks cues in the work and responds to them with viewing skills acquired through experience of other artworks and of everyday life. [She] is involved on the levels of perception, emotion, and cognition, all of which are inextricably bound up together' (1988, 10). Thus, the neoformalist conception of aesthetic experience is a deflationary one, according to which there seems to be some penetrability between the aesthetic and the everyday.

A second qualification is that at the same time as Thompson accepts the purpose of art as defamiliarization, she suggests that this is a contingent rather than logically necessary or essential function. In her words, '[t]his is not to say that neoformalism takes art to be a permanent, fixed realm. It is culturally determined and relative, but it is distinctive' (1988, 9). Further moderating neoformalism's commitment to an aesthetic conception of art, Thompson maintains that regarding defamiliarization as the purpose of film art actually constitutes a deep commitment to studying and understanding the historical contexts in which films are made. For, on her view, '[d]efamiliarization depends on historical context; devices that may be new and defamiliarizing will decline in effectiveness with repetition' (1988, 25). Practically speaking, this means that a significant part of the film analyst's job is to locate the film to be in analysed in its historical context and to identify the various norms and deviations – the 'backgrounds' – in operation when it was made.

Here we see that defending a general theory of art as defamiliarization turns out to be significantly less important for the neoformalist than the analytic approach that it makes available. First, for reasons we saw above, it is Thompson's view that conceiving the purpose of art to be defamiliarization dissolves the form/content distinction. On this view, '[m]eaning is not the end result of an artwork, but one of its formal components' (1988, 12). This has the practical consequence of subordinating film interpretation to the analysis of a film's overall formal system: 'for the neoformalist, interpretation is only one part of analysis' (1988, 34 n25). This view closely echoes Shklovsky's assertion, which Thompson quotes, that '[t]he aim of the formalist method, or at least one of its aims, is not to explain the work, but to call attention to it, to restore that "orientation towards form" which is characteristic of a work of art' (quoted in Thompson 1988, 32). Second, given neoformalism's conception of defamiliarization as essentially dependent upon historical context, analysis of the film's overall formal system must be supplemented by historical research.

Finally, it should be clear that the neoformalist conception of films as historically embedded formal systems of devices that perform different functions in different contexts demands a kind of methodological flexibility – a 'constant need for modification' (1988, 6). More specifically, Thompson claims, understanding works of film art this way means that such methodological flexibility is 'built into' the approach. Elaborating, she writes: 'By assuming an overall approach that dictates modification or complete change of the method for each new analysis, neoformalist film criticism avoids the problem inherent in the typical self-confirming method. It does not assume that the text harbors a fixed pattern which the analyst goes in and finds' (1988, 7). Arguably, this was neoformalism's most important intervention in film studies in the 1980s and is still its greatest value as an analytic approach.

TED NANNICELLI

## Works cited

Arnheim, Rudolph. 1957. *Film as Art*. Berkeley: University of California Press.

Bellour, Raymond. 2000. *The Analysis of Film*. Bloomington: University of Indiana Press.

Bordwell, David. 1981. *The Films of Carl-Theodor Dreyer*. Berkeley: University of California Press.

——. 1985. *Narration in the Fiction Film*. Madison: University of Wisconsin Press.

——. 1988. *Ozu and the Poetics of Cinema*. Princeton, NJ: Princeton University Press.

Bordwell, David, and Kristin Thompson. 2012. *Film Art: An Introduction*. 10th edition. New York: McGraw-Hill.

Buckland, Warren. 2008. 'Formalist Tendencies in Film Studies'. In *The SAGE Handbook of Film Studies*, edited by James Donald and Michael Renov, 312–28. London: SAGE.

Burch, Noël. 1981. *Theory of Film Practice*. Princeton, NJ: Princeton University Press.

Christie, Ian. 1998. 'Formalism and Neoformalism'. In *The Oxford Guide to Film Studies*, edited by John Hill and Pamela Church Gibson, 58–64. Oxford: Oxford University Press.

Metz, Christian. 1974. *Film Language: A Semiotics of the Cinema*. Translated by Michael Taylor. Oxford: Oxford University Press.

Shklovsky, Viktor. 1965 [1917]. 'Art as Technique'. In *Russian Formalist Criticism: Four Essays*, edited and translated by Lee T. Lemon and Marion J. Reis, 3–24. Lincoln: University of Nebraska Press.

Thompson, Kristin. 1981. *Eisenstein's Ivan the Terrible: A Neoformalist Analysis*. Princeton, NJ: Princeton University Press.

——. 1988. *Breaking the Glass Armor: Neoformalist Film Analysis*. Princeton, NJ: Princeton University Press.

Thomson-Jones, Katherine. 2009. 'Formalism'. In *The Routledge Companion to Philosophy and Film*, edited by Paisley Livingston and Carl Plantinga, 131–41. New York: Routledge.

# GAMING AND FILM THEORY

In *Theory of the Film*, Béla Balázs (1952, 22) laments a missed opportunity in the early years of cinema to observe

> the emergence of a new form of artistic expression, the only one born in our time ... It would have been worthwhile to seize this opportunity because ... knowledge of the evolutionary process of this new form of artistic expression would per analogiam have provided a key to many secrets of the older arts.

Of course, a partial record of the evolution of cinematic expression remains in the surviving films themselves and in the changes of technique that we can track from one film to another, but Balázs emphasizes the value of observing the development of film art, or of any art, as it is happening. Balázs might have added that it was also an opportunity to observe the evolution of a new form of theory, a chance to seek a 'key' to secrets of older theories of art. By the time Vachel Lindsay (1922) published *The Art of the Moving Picture* in 1915, over two decades had passed since the public unveiling of W.K.L. Dickson's kinetoscope. Early theorists like Lindsay, Hugo Münsterberg, and Rudolf Arnheim were certainly concerned with the evolution of the medium – Münsterberg, for instance, with the close-up as the innovation through which cinema differentiated itself from theatre, and Arnheim with the possible dilution of cinema's visual essence by sound (*see* ATTENTION; CLASSICAL FILM THEORY; SOUND THEORY).

Techno-aesthetic evolution does not necessarily exhibit the transitional forms that characterize biological evolution. Discussing the evolution of cinema, many early theorists tend towards a technological analogue of punctuated equilibrium (cf. Eldredge and Gould 1972), in which periods of stasis are disrupted by rapid change. This can be seen in the gravity with which theorists imbue moments of formal innovation such as the close-up or cross-cutting as well as technological innovations like the introduction of sound or colour. Likewise, in accounts of the originary 'moment' of film, theorists can seem preoccupied by cinema's relationship to other arts, often claiming that cinema incorporates the essential qualities of other arts while also advocating the consideration of film as a wholly distinct medium. Ricciotto Canudo proclaimed film the sixth (later the seventh) art, a synthesis of the classic arts. Meanwhile, Gilbert Seldes (2001) included Hollywood film among the 'lively arts', alongside such roughly contemporaneous developments as jazz and vaudeville, that he felt represented a family of lively new forms of expression. The validation of a medium, it seems, requires both comparison to existing 'legitimate' media and demarcation from those media that preceded it.

Henry Jenkins (2007) has identified video games as a 'new lively art' to join the ones Seldes enumerated a century prior. Much as early film theory sought insight into cinema through comparison to, and differentiation from, other media, video-game theory in its early years has been preoccupied with relationships between video games and narrative cinema. Disciplinary boundaries are at stake as well. In asking how video games are unlike other media, one also asks how video-game theory can (and how it should) differentiate itself from film theory.

Early video-game theory was characterized largely by debates, and even the threat of a 'blood feud' (Jenkins 2004, 118), between 'ludology', or the study of video games as games, and 'narratology', meaning the claim that video games are a narrative medium. This opposition was overstated at the time and is often oversimplified in retrospective accounts. However, the debate was substantial and protracted enough to require a coordinated effort to move on from it. The remainder of this entry looks at two key texts that attempt to do just that. Each reflects on the terms of that early debate while formulating new methodological and conceptual approaches to the study of video games.

In 'Game Design as Narrative Architecture' (2004), Jenkins illustrates how some games map narrative, and thus a temporal component, onto interactive space. In his chapter 'Videogames and the Classic Game Model' (2005), Jesper Juul clarifies his ludological position about video games by showing how the term 'game' can – and how it cannot – be applied to a surprisingly wide range of media and activities. Juul traces commonalities and differences among theories of gameplay extending back to well before the invention of the video game. Each author responds to interactive qualities specific to the medium via discussion of how these qualities contribute to the construction of forms of meaning that transcend media boundaries as conventionally conceived. In doing so, each draws out epistemological continuities between video games and other activities, providing 'a key to many secrets', as Balázs put it, not only to the older arts but to the older theories as well.

## An architectural model

Jenkins (2004) proposes an alternative approach to the relationship between play and narrative. He begins by calling attention to the spatial quality of games, showing that their construction of virtual worlds is substantially different from what is found in other visual media. Navigating game space means both exploring a virtual world and 'navigating narrational space' (126). Jenkins invokes a concept from neoformalist film theory: the fabula/syuzhet dichotomy, which emphasizes the relationship between the temporally linear, causally continuous story (fabula) and the realization of that story moment by moment in a plot (syuzhet). Thinking of games in terms of narrational space allows us to see a game's story – or any story – as 'less a temporal structure than a body of information' (Thompson 1988, 39–40; cited in Jenkins 2004, 126). The relative linearity of the cinematic medium, its unidirectionality of textual progression, and the control over pacing that it affords its creators, allows for precision in 'when and if we receive specific bits of information' (Jenkins 2004, 126). Games tend to favour the measured parcelling of information in spatial arrangements rather than the temporal arrangements typical of film. Jenkins's spatial model accounts for how, in games, the sequence of narrated events can be relatively undetermined. Instead, objects and spaces, all of which coexist in the game world, are charged with informational, narrational, and expressive power. The passing of narrative time is thereby largely displaced onto the player's navigating (in real time) the spatial arrays of the game in search of 'information' under the guise of spatial goals.

Jenkins proposes that we think of 'game designers less as storytellers and more as narrative architects' (121). Jenkins has in mind something broader than what we might immediately think of as 'architecture'. Games depict dynamic and causally complex worlds populated by interacting agents as well as models of causal relationships that fall outside of the purview of the 'architectural' in the conventional sense. The title 'Game Design as Narrative Architecture' emphasizes the connection of the word 'architecture' to an *act* of designing as well as to the resulting structured environment, thus returning to the term's Greek roots: *arkhi* (chief, master) *tektōn* (carpenter, builder). The 'master builder' of game design is a godlike figure, an initiator of worlds. Jenkins provides four examples of how game spaces and interactive schemes can be organized to support narrative development: as evocative spaces, as enactive stories, as embedded narratives, and as emergent narratives. In each case, Jenkins draws comparisons to other spatial storytelling structures, from film to amusement parks. This provides not only an account of the interface between gameplay and narrative in video games, one that helps us to see ludology and narratology as capable of being reconciled as necessary aspects of video-game theory, but also an illustration of how games exist on a continuum with other media, and how video-game theory, as well, is continuous with, but by no means reducible to, other forms of media theory.

Jenkins (2004, 122) grounds his argument in a discussion of the evolution of games' depictions of their spaces and how these depictions connect to previous traditions and innovations:

> The early Nintendo games have simple narrative hooks – rescue Princess Toadstool – but what gamers found astonishing when they first played them were their complex and imaginative graphic realms … When we refer to such influential early works as Shigeru Miyamoto's *Super Mario Bros.* as 'scroll games', we situate them alongside a much older tradition of spatial storytelling: many Japanese scroll paintings map, for example, the passing of the seasons onto an unfolding space.

By observing the evolution of game spaces, we can better understand resonances between games and other spatial media. In suggesting this architectural resolution of the schism in video-game theory, Jenkins offers not only a disciplinary way forward but also a new and compelling way to think across disciplines and across media, to metatheorize.

## A classic model for games

Juul opens his chapter by establishing a 'classic game model' that he says reflects

> the way games have traditionally been constructed. It is also a model that applies to the 5,000-year history of games. Although it is unusual to claim that any aspect of human culture has remained unchanged for millennia, there are strong arguments for this.
>
> (Juul 2005, 23)

Juul outlines a constellation of associations people may have with the word 'game', acknowledging that this outline is itself a kind of game, a language game that Wittgenstein (2009) previously played in his *Philosophical Investigations*. As Balázs suggests, the entry of a new medium into an established field – in this case, the entry of video games into the established range of things that can be called games – facilitates not only a discussion of 'what relates videogames to other games' but also of 'what happens on the borders of games' (Juul 2005, 23). Juul might as well have written 'what happens on the borders of "games"', as his task here is chiefly taxonomic. He outlines conceptual borders, not physical or virtual-spatial ones. But a conceptual border is a kind of virtual border, and we interact with it and feel its contours much as we might the boundaries within a video-game world.

Juul proposes a definition for a classical game:

> a rule-based system with a variable and quantifiable outcome, where different outcomes are assigned different values, the player exerts effort in order to influence the outcome, the player feels emotionally attached to the outcome, and the consequences of the activity are negotiable.
>
> (Juul 2005, 36)

This single sentence addresses the game's internal structures, its higher-level form, the behaviour of its users, something of the cognitive state of its users, and the social frameworks surrounding the practice of gameplay. Juul arrives at this definition through a review of several earlier attempts to define the notion of 'game', during which he finds family resemblances among how scholars have defined the term but no clear agreement on any one quality that all games are supposed to have.

Juul's wide-ranging, but still clearly delimited, definition of what constitutes a game facilitates a separation of video games from other non-game visual media: video games are electronic visual media that fit the criteria of the classical game model. Both Jenkins and Juul see transmediality as a crucial framing concept for video games. For Jenkins, this necessitates understanding games in terms of their relationships to related media properties. Critiquing an earlier argument of Juul's that the video game *Star Wars* (Atari, 1983) illustrates that games are not a storytelling medium because 'you can't clearly deduce the story of *Star Wars* [the movie (Lucas, 1977)] from *Star Wars* the game' (Juul 1998, quoted in Jenkins 2004, 124), Jenkins argues that *Star Wars* the game exists

> in dialogue with the films, conveying new narrative experiences through its creative manipulation of environmental details. One can imagine games taking their place within a larger narrative system with story information communicated through books, film ... In such a system, what games do best will almost certainly center around their ability to give concrete shape to our memories and imaginings of the storyworld, creating an immersive environment we can wander through and interact with.
>
> (Jenkins 2004, 124)

By contrast, Juul is interested in the transmediality of gameness itself. He focuses on how the potential to be a game is not tied to any particular medium. A single game can be implemented in any number of ways, as Juul illustrates with a 'translation' of the traditional Tic-tac-toe into a purely mathematical game, requiring no game board. Either of these games can, of course, be implemented on a computer as well. Since there are also things we do on paper, verbally, or with computers that are not games, and there exist media (such as film) that do not lend themselves naturally to Juul's model of what a game is, 'we can talk about the borders between games and what is not a game' (Juul 2005, 54).

## Establishing boundaries

Borders, wandering, interaction, language games: for both Jenkins and Juul, thinking about video games and gameplay lends itself to thinking about what it means to feel one's way through and around conceptual, disciplinary, and perceptual boundaries and thus to facilitate thinking about their structures, origins, and implications. As Balázs argued, 'knowledge of the evolutionary process of' a new form of expression can provide 'a key to many secrets of the older' ones. While video games invite us to think about films, they also invite us to think about film theory, to consider where its internal boundaries may lie and what we might ask about the relationships between our lives, our gameplay, our story-worlds, and what we might call our theoryworlds. These all would seem to be conceptual spaces that we can wander through and interact with, whose borders we create by finding them and whose contours we find by making them.

DANIEL REYNOLDS

## Works cited

Balázs, Bela. 1952. *Theory of the Film*. London: Dennis Dobson.

Canudo, Ricciotto. 1988. 'The Birth of the Sixth Art', translated by Ben Gibson, Sergio Sokota, and Deborah Young. In *French Film Theory and Criticism, 1907–1939*, edited by Richard Abel, 58–66. Princeton, NJ: Princeton University Press.

Eldredge, Niles, and S.J. Gould. 1972. 'Punctuated Equilibria: An Alternative to Phyletic Gradual-ism'. In *Models in Paleobiology*, edited by T.J.M. Schopf, 82–115. San Francisco, CA: Freeman Cooper; New York: Doubleday.

Jenkins, Henry. 2004. 'Game Design as Narrative Architecture'. In *First Person*, edited by Noah Wardrip-Fruin and Pat Harrigan, 118–30. Cambridge, MA: MIT Press.

——. 2007. 'Games: The New Lively Art'. In *The Wow Climax: Tracing the Emotional Impact of Popular Culture*. New York: New York University Press.

Juul, Jesper. 1998. 'A Clash between Games and Narrative'. Paper presented at the Digital Arts and Culture Conference, Bergen, November 1998: https://www.jesperjuul.net/text/clash_between_game_and_narrative.html.

——. 2005. *Half-Real*. Cambridge, MA: MIT Press.

Lindsay, Vachel. 1922 [1915]. *The Art of the Moving Picture*. New York: Macmillan.

Münsterberg, Hugo. 1916. *The Photoplay: A Psychological Study*. New York: D. Appleton and Co.

Seldes, Gilbert. 2001. *The Seven Lively Arts*. New York: Dover.

Thompson, Kristin. 1988. *Breaking the Glass Armor: Neoformalist Film Analysis*. Princeton, NJ: Princeton University Press.

Wittgenstein, Ludwig. 2009. *Philosophical Investigations*. Hoboken, NJ: Wiley-Blackwell.

## Further reading

Bogost, Ian. 2006. *Unit Operations*. Cambridge, MA: MIT Press.

Frasca, Gonzalo. 2003. 'Simulation vs. Narrative: An Introduction to Ludology'. In *The Video Game Theory Reader*, edited by Mark J.P. Wolf and Bernard Perron, 221–36. New York: Routledge.

Murray, Janet. 1998. *Hamlet on the Holodeck: The Future of Narrative in Cyberspace*. Cambridge, MA: MIT Press.

Wolf, Mark J.P. 2002. *The Medium of the Video Game*. Austin: University of Texas Press.

# GAZE THEORY

## The male gaze and feminist film theory

In the 1970s and 1980s, film scholars including E. Ann Kaplan and Laura Mulvey investigated the intersections of psychoanalysis, looking relations, scopophilia – 'the pleasure in looking at another as an erotic object' (Mulvey 1999, 843) – and cinema. In doing so, they launched feminist film theory.

'Visual Pleasure and Narrative Cinema', Mulvey's provocative and politically charged 1975 article, published in the British journal *Screen*, is the urtext of feminist film theory. According to Mulvey, a British filmmaker and scholar, 'film has depended on voyeuristic active/passive mechanisms' (Mulvey 1999, 844). In 'Visual Pleasure', Mulvey first articulated psychoanalytic feminist film theory's major concepts, such as the male gaze, which is 'built upon culturally defined notions of sexual difference' (Kaplan 1983, 14). The male gaze is the dominant force at work in narrative film – patriarchal culture's 'favorite cinematic form' (Mulvey 1999, 843) – in which women are coded and represented as passive objects for male viewing and sexual pleasure:

> In a world ordered by sexual imbalance, pleasure in looking has been split between active/male and passive/female. The determining male gaze projects its phantasy on to the female figure which is styled accordingly. In their traditional exhibitionist role women are simultaneously coded for strong visual and erotic impact so that they can be said to connote *to-be-looked-at-ness*.
>
> (Mulvey 1999, 837)

The cinematic male gaze is but an on-screen extension, projection, and reproduction of patriarchy: 'the signs in the Hollywood film convey the patriarchal ideology that underlies our social structures and constructs women in very specific ways – ways that reflect patriarchal needs, the patriarchal unconscious' (Kaplan 1983, 24). On-screen representations of gendered subjects serve to replicate and endorse the rigid gender-based socialization and roles created and maintained by patriarchal culture, society, and discourse: 'the image of woman as (passive) raw material for the (active) gaze of man takes the argument a step further into the structure of representation, adding a further layer demanded by the ideology of the patriarchal order' (Mulvey 1999, 843). Patriarchy's values, such as the dominance and power of the male subject over the silent, passive female, find on-screen surrogates in narrative cinema, in which the sexual pleasure of the male auteur/spectator/protagonist is based upon objectification of the female, denying female characters and spectators alike the possibility of an authentic voice or subject position.

225

In her discussion of gaze theory in *Women and Film: Both Sides of the Camera* (1983), Kaplan follows Mulvey, noting how, in 'defining and dominating woman as an erotic object' and 'repressing women through its controlling power over female discourse and female desire', the male gaze, 'carrying with it social, political, and economic as well as sexual power, relegates women to absence, silence, and marginality' (Kaplan 1983, 1–5). Since 'men do not simply look; their gaze carries with it the power of action and of possession that is lacking in the female gaze' (31), the male gaze consigns women to occupying inferior positions that are reminiscent of the Victorian exhortation that 'children should be seen and not heard'. Pioneering feminist attorney Judith Vladek remarked that 'the only way women are tolerated is if they are silent, supine, and submissive' (quoted in Hevesi 2007). These words became a rallying cry for the second-wave feminist movement of the 1970s in the United States. Vladek's statement was written in 1975, a watershed year for feminist activism, filmmaking, and critical theory, as it also witnessed the release of Chantal Akerman's *Jeanne Dielman, 23 Quai de Commerce, 1080 Bruxelles*, a now iconic feminist film, as well as the publication of Mulvey's 'Visual Pleasure'.

## Gaze theory and psychoanalysis

Kaplan's 1983 essay 'Is the Gaze Male?', the introductory chapter of her book *Women and Film*, is, along with 'Visual Pleasure', a foundational text in the (then-emerging) field of feminist film theory. In 'Is the Gaze Male?' Kaplan 'charts the development of this concept of the [male] gaze as it has emerged from recent psychoanalytic, structuralist, and semiotic theories' (Kaplan 1983, 2) in order to consider '*how meaning is produced* in films' (23).

Through unmasking the 'psychic and mythic forces inherent in patriarchy' (3) and the patriarchal underpinnings of narrative cinema's privileging of the male gaze, a dominant force of 'economic and social superiority which results in a demanding authority over women' (5), Kaplan strove to 'create a discourse, a voice, a place' (2) for the female subject and spectator. Kaplan discusses how to create the potential for a female gaze and subject position. Women in mainstream Hollywood narrative films – with underlying theoretical premises structured by the male gaze – are 'ultimately refused a voice, a discourse, and their desire is subjected to male desire' (7–8): 'made to function as an erotic object, woman must sacrifice her desire to that of the male Other, helping to preserve patriarchy by submitting herself to its Law' (5).

Yet Kaplan also notes the following paradox, namely, that fascination with Hollywood films arises because such films 'bring us pleasure', a pleasure that comes from 'identification with objectification': 'our positioning as to-be-looked-at, as object of the (male) gaze, has come to be sexually pleasurable' to women (34). Rather than 'simply enjoy our oppression unproblematically' or 'reappropriate Hollywood images to ourselves, taking them out of the context of the total structure in which they appear', Kaplan strongly advocates the use of psychoanalysis and psychoanalytic theory as means to 'fully understand *how it is* that women take pleasure in objectification' (34) since 'the tools of psychoanalysis and semiology enable women to unlock patriarchal culture as expressed in dominant representations' (3), in particular female masochism. Despite feminist resistance to Freud and Lacan, Kaplan calls 'psychoanalysis a useful tool … since it will unlock the secrets of our socialization within (capitalist) patriarchy' (24) whose cultural and social capital, values, and symbols are reproduced and conveyed by Hollywood. Kaplan relies on a 'psychoanalytic framework' in order to 'deconstruct Hollywood films [thus enabling] us to see clearly the patriarchal myths through which [women] have been positioned as Other', since 'women are excluded from the central role in the main, highly respected Hollywood genres' (25).

In her text, Kaplan raises questions about some of the fundamental premises of gaze theory:

> First, is the gaze *necessarily* male (i.e. for reasons inherent in the structure of language, the unconscious, symbolic systems, and thus all social structures)? Could we structure things so that women own the gaze? If this were possible, would women want to own the gaze? Finally, in either case, what does it mean to be a female spectator? ... When women are in the dominant position, are they in the *masculine* position? Can we envisage a female dominant position that would differ qualitatively from the male form of dominance? Or is there merely the possibility of both sex genders occupying the positions we now know as 'masculine' and 'feminine'?
>
> (Kaplan 1983, 24–5, 28)

Kaplan concludes that 'the gaze is not necessarily male (literally), but to own and activate the gaze, given our language and the structure of the unconscious, is to be in the "masculine" position. It is this persistent presentation of the masculine position that feminist film critics have demonstrated in their analysis of Hollywood films. Dominant, Hollywood cinema is constructed according to the unconscious of patriarchy' (30).

In 'Is the Gaze Male?' Kaplan raises and considers these and other questions about film and female spectatorship as a type of call to action to redress the oppression and marginalization of women in patriarchal society and as a means through which to 'change ourselves as a first step toward changing society' (25): 'the psychoanalytic methodology is thus justified as an essential first step in the feminist project of understanding our socialization in patriarchy ... we have to think about strategies for changing discourse since these changes would, in turn, affect the structuring of our lives in society' (34).

Although posed in 1983, Kaplan's queries about gaze theory as well as her subsequent conclusions about approaching it from a psychoanalytic perspective in order to ultimately challenge the enduring patriarchal structure of mainstream cinema – as a reflection of society at large – do not cease to elicit reaction and produce critical discourse.

## Critiques of the male gaze

Along with Kaplan in 'Is the Gaze Male?', many feminist film theorists have questioned, extended, and amended the male gaze as coined by Mulvey for its presumption of the primacy of the male spectator subject position. These critics also question Mulvey's insistence, in her initial formulation of gaze theory, upon the strict paradigm of male as bearer of the look and female as object of the male gaze. According to Elizabeth Gruber, 'there are certain dangers in adhering too rigidly to the masculine-looker/feminine-object schema' (2010, 229) set out by Mulvey.

Since the publication of 'Visual Pleasure', film critics, theorists, and scholars have reconsidered and complicated Mulvey's stance on the male gaze to 'account for different gazes and subject positions in order to supplement and/or problematize the heteronormative binary of Mulvey's theory of subject–object looking relations' (DeTora 2010,

4–5). Such critics have offered other possibilities, such as plural, shifting gazes and multivalent spectatorial and subject positions that cut across gender identification/boundaries as well as incorporate the performativity of gender, as in Rhona J. Berenstein's theory of 'spectatorship-as-drag' and Mary Ann Doane's concept of the masquerade of femininity. They encompass a wide range of experts, including, among others, Janet Bergstrom, Carol Clover, Elizabeth Cowie, Barbara Creed, Alexander Doty, Cynthia Freeland, Jane Gaines, Christine Gledhill, Miriam Hansen, bell hooks, E. Ann Kaplan, Teresa de Lauretis, Tania Modleski, Constance Penley, Trinh T. Minh-ha, B. Ruby Rich, Julia LeSage, Ilara Serra, Vivian Sobchak, Jackie Stacey, Gaylyn Studlar, Sue Thornham, and Linda Williams. Clover, in her path-breaking work on gender and the slasher film, puts forth 'the possibility that male viewers are quite prepared to identify not just with screen females, but with screen females in the horror-film world, screen females in fear and pain' (Clover 1993, 5).

In her discussion of the 'oppositional gaze' and black female spectators, African-American feminist scholar bell hooks criticized early feminist gaze theory for not acknowledging black female spectatorship. According to hooks, gaze theory 'does not even consider the possibility that women can construct an oppositional gaze via an understanding and awareness of the politics of race and racism ... it speaks about "women" when in actuality it speaks only about white women' (hooks 1992, 123). Moreover:

> Looking at films with an oppositional gaze, black women were able to critically assess the cinema's construction of white womanhood as object of the phallocentric gaze and choose not to identify with either the victim or the perpetrator. Black female spectators, who refused to identify with white womanhood, who would not take on the phallocentric gaze of desire and possession, created a critical space where the binary opposition Mulvey posits of 'woman as image, man as bearer of the look' was continually deconstructed.
>
> (hooks 1992, 122)

Today, much exciting work is being carried out in gaze theory to address, account for, and incorporate a plurality of gazes. Revisions to gaze theory are presented by the current generation of film scholars who problematize it 'by making available the possibility of spectators, regardless of their gender or sexual orientation, to cast themselves into shifting spectatorial roles' (Todd 2010, 59), questioning or even refusing fixed gendered subject positions.

Several essays in Marcelline Block's edited volume *Situating the Feminist Gaze and Spectatorship in Postwar Cinema* (2010) depart from and extend the concept of the male gaze. Sharon Lubkemann Allan, in her chapter about Chantal Akerman, proposes Akerman's 'transgendering' of the gaze: 'Akerman's work represents a translingual and transhistorical as well as transgendered authority and authorship' (Allan 2010, 256). Rachel Ritterbusch, in her reading of the 2003 film *Nathalie ...* by French female director Anne Fontaine, notes that women directors and characters can re-appropriate and possess the gaze – and, with it, objectify other women. DeTora makes use of quantum physics and the quantum gaze to further her contention about the connection between looking relations and monstrous maternity in *Jurassic Park* and *The Thirteenth Warrior*. In her analysis of *Jurassic Park*, DeTora observes how the film 'demonstrates power relations in terms of the [dinosaur's] gaze', since 'power is more significant than gender in these particular looking relations', which 'dovetails with feminist film theories ... that posit shifting subject positions' (DeTora 2010, 17–18, 19). Todd, in his chapter of *Situating the Feminist Gaze* entitled 'Hitchcock's "Good-Looking Blondes"': First Glimpses and Second Glances', proposes queering the gaze (*see* QUEER THEORY/QUEER CINEMA). For Todd, queering the gaze gives a less 'reductionistic model of spectatorship' (Todd 2010, 56) as well as a new way of looking at Hitchcock's female characters that refuses a monolithic categorization: 'the process of queering the male gaze inaugurates significant possibilities for the ways in which images of women and men' (57) emerge, are produced, and are assimilated. In Hunter Vaughan's discussion of Stanley Kubrick's final film *Eyes Wide Shut* (posthumously released), Vaughan rejects the active male/passive female binary by positing the 'poly-gaze': 'the representation of sexual difference through the institution of multi-sexual gazes ... both on the level of the cinematic apparatus as well as among the characters in the film' (Vaughan 2010, 49).

At this juncture, however, it would behove us to recall the significance of early gaze theory, particularly when situated within its socio-historical context of the second-wave feminist movements of the 1970s, when it became a manifesto calling for 'filmmakers to develop a "new language of desire" capable of speaking woman's reality' (Ritterbusch 2010, 34). Ritterbusch notes that 'critics who focus on the weaknesses of Mulvey's arguments overlook the intent of her article, which is to call for radical change ... to create the conditions for an alternative cinema ... that provides an authentic position for the female subject' (35–6).

Amy Woodworth in *Situating the Feminist Gaze* concurs: 'abandoning those theories [of the gaze] is a mistake given the state of current American Cinema ... any encounter with the entertainment media is a reminder of the prevalence of the male gaze' (Woodworth 2010, 141). Undoubtedly, gaze theory 'provides critical tools that enrich readings of film today' (Woodworth 2010, 159), since, in 2004, Kaplan asserted that we are still not

'beyond the gaze' (either male or imperial) as a fact of life, even if feminist film scholars are taking up issues they deem more urgent given today's new global concerns, the proliferation of subjects with agency and stories to tell, and the proliferation of digital technologies ... The impact of new interdisciplinary academic programs and areas of research on feminism and film is still being examined, but clearly the reach of much work is now extremely broad in contrast to the narrow field that many of us worked in the 1980s.

(Kaplan 2004, 1244–5)

Current scholarship continues to push the boundaries of gaze theory to newer realms of film and gender studies, demonstrating its continued significance to twenty-first century film scholars who wish to subvert patriarchy's enduring biases – whether of gender, race, class, and/or nation – which remain much entrenched in the cinematic enterprise. Gaze theory remains a vital component of film studies, even if it has been substantially expanded upon in light of recent developments in the fields of film and gender studies and scholarship. As gaze theory takes on innovative and exciting dimensions, it is important to remember its origins in the second-wave feminist movement of the 1970s, and that it strove to create a genuine space for the female spectator and the formation of female subjecthood – tasks that still remain unfulfilled in the second decade of the twenty-first century, since 'mainstream American film continues to portray a patriarchal fantasy' (Woodworth 2010, 140).

MARCELLINE BLOCK

# Works cited

Allan, Sharon Lubkemann. 2010. 'Chantal Akerman's Cinematic Transgressions: Transhistorical and Transcultural Transpositions, Translingualism, and the Transgendering of the Cinematic Gaze'. In *Situating the Feminist Gaze and Spectatorship in Postwar Cinema*, edited by Marcelline Block, 255–88. Newcastle: Cambridge Scholars Publishing.

Block, Marcelline, ed. 2010 [2008]. *Situating the Feminist Gaze and Spectatorship in Postwar Cinema*. Newcastle: Cambridge Scholars Publishing.

Clover, Carol J. 1993. *Men, Women and Chainsaws: Gender in the Modern Horror Film*. Princeton, NJ: Princeton University Press.

DeTora, Lisa. 2010. '"Life Finds a Way": Monstrous Maternities and the Quantum Gaze in *Jurassic Park* and *The Thirteenth Warrior*'. In *Situating the Feminist Gaze and Spectatorship in Postwar Cinema*, edited by Marcelline Block, 2–26. Newcastle: Cambridge Scholars Publishing.

Gruber, Elizabeth. 2010. '"No Woman Would Die Like That": *Stage Beauty* as Corrective-Counterpoint to *Othello*'. In *Situating the Feminist Gaze and Spectatorship in Postwar Cinema*, edited by Marcelline Block, 226–39. Newcastle: Cambridge Scholars Publishing.

Hevesi, Peter. 2007. 'Judith Vladeck, 83, Who Fought for Women's Rights, Dies'. *New York Times*, 11 January: http://www.nytimes.com/2007/01/11/nyregion/11vladeck.html?_r=1 (accessed 22 April 2012).

hooks, bell. 1992. 'The Oppositional Gaze: Black Female Spectators'. In *Black Looks: Race and Representation*, 115–31. Boston, MA: South End Press.

Kaplan, E. Ann. 1983. 'Is the Gaze Male?' In *Women and Film: Both Sides of the Camera*, 23–35. London and New York: Routledge.

——. 2004. 'Global Feminisms and the State of Feminist Film Theory'. In Beyond the Gaze: Recent Approaches to Film Feminisms, edited by Kathleen McHugh and Vivian Sobchack. Special issue of *Signs: Journal of Women in Culture and Society* 30 (1): 1236–48.

Mulvey, Laura. 1999. 'Visual Pleasure and Narrative Cinema'. In *Film Theory and Criticism: Introductory Readings*, edited by Leo Braudy and Marshall Cohen, 833–44. New York: Oxford University Press. Originally published in *Screen* 16 (3) (Autumn 1975): 6–18.

Ritterbusch, Rachel. 2010. 'Shifting Gender(ed) Desire in Anne Fontaine's *Nathalie ...* '. In *Situating the Feminist Gaze and Spectatorship in Postwar Cinema*, edited by Marcelline Block, 27–43. Newcastle: Cambridge Scholars Publishing.

Todd, Ian Scott. 2010. 'Hitchcock's "Good-Looking Blondes": First Glimpses and Second Glances'. In *Situating the Feminist Gaze and Spectatorship in Postwar Cinema*, edited by Marcelline Block, 52–66. Newcastle: Cambridge Scholars Publishing.

Vaughan, Hunter. 2010. '*Eyes Wide Shut*: Kino-Eye Wide Open'. In *Situating the Feminist Gaze and Spectatorship in Postwar Cinema*, edited by Marcelline Block, 44–51. Newcastle: Cambridge Scholars Publishing.

Woodworth, Amy. 2010. 'A Feminist Theorization of Sofia Coppola's Postfeminist Trilogy'. In *Situating the Feminist Gaze and Spectatorship in Postwar Cinema*, edited by Marcelline Block, 138–67. Newcastle: Cambridge Scholars Publishing.

# Further reading

Berenstein, Rhona J. 1996. *Attack of the Leading Ladies: Gender, Sexuality and Spectatorship in Classic Horror Cinema*. New York: Columbia University Press.

de Lauretis, Teresa. 1984. *Alice Doesn't: Feminism, Semiotics, Cinema*. Bloomington and Indianapolis: Indiana University Press.

Doane, Mary Ann. 1990. 'Film and the Masquerade: Theorizing the Female Spectator'. In *Issues in Feminist Film Criticism*, edited by Patricia Erens, 41–57. Bloomington and Indianapolis: Indiana University Press.

Erens, Patricia, ed. 1990. *Issues in Feminist Film Criticism*. Bloomington and Indianapolis: Indiana University Press.

Gaines, Jane M. 1988. 'White Privilege and Looking Relations'. *Screen* 20 (4): 12–17.

Johnston, Claire. 1973. 'Women's Cinema as Counter-cinema'. In *Notes on Women's Cinema*, edited by Claire Johnston, 24–31. London: Society for Education in Film and Television (SEFT).

Mayne, Judith. 1990. *The Woman at the Keyhole: Feminism and Women's Cinema*. Bloomington and Indianapolis: Indiana University Press.

Mulvey, Laura. 1999. 'Afterthoughts on "Visual Pleasure and Narrative Cinema" Inspired by King Vidor's *Duel in the Sun* (1946)'. In *Feminist Film Theory: A Reader*, edited by Sue Thornham, 122–30. New York: New York University Press.

Penley, Constance, ed. 1988. *Feminism and Film Theory*. New York: Routledge.

Silverman, Kaja. 1988. *The Acoustic Mirror: The Female Voice in Psychoanalysis and Cinema*. Bloomington and Indianapolis: Indiana University Press.

Stacey, Jackie. 'Desperately Seeking Difference'. In *Issues in Feminist Film Criticism*, edited by Patricia Erens, 365–79. Bloomington and Indianapolis: Indiana University Press, 1990.

Thornham, Sue, ed. 1999. *Feminist Film Theory: A Reader*. New York: New York University Press.

# GENRE THEORY

The term 'genre theory' suggests the coming together of two distinct methods of organization. Genres and theories are both ways of unifying disparate material, identifying categories based on shared qualities or principles. Different movies featuring singing and dancing can be called 'musicals'; a variety of contemporary phenomena can be described as 'postmodern'. Many of the issues that genre theory confronts relate to the problems that such categories create. Theorists of genre have had to consider the difficulties entailed in attributing a common character or significance to large groups of films, the critical and historical processes involved in defining genres, as well as the competing claims to authority over what these definitions should be. Major works of genre theory have proposed ways of examining these issues in a rigorous and consistent manner.

Two particular approaches to these problems can be seen in book-length discussions of genre released around the turn of the twenty-first century: Rick Altman's *Film/Genre* (1999) and Steve Neale's *Genre and Hollywood* (2000). Both attempt to establish a logical way to approach key questions of genre theory and accommodate a variety of generic groupings, perspectives, and texts. In his introduction, Neale refers to the publication of *Film/Genre* while his own book was 'in press' (2000, 1), so there is no direct dialogue between the two books. Thus, the two writers address the same traditions of thought in parallel, but contrasting, ways. Despite shared interests and material, Altman's and Neale's conceptions of the meaning and purpose of genre theory are quite different.

## Structure

The differences are evident in the way each writer structures his account. When it was published, Altman's book was described as 'the most explicitly theoretical work on film genre since the 1980s' (Mittell 2000, 88). In *Film/Genre*, Altman aims to reformulate the basic concepts on which genre theory is founded, arguing that genre should be conceived in terms of varied and competing *discourses* rather than fixed and established categories. Altman reinforces this conceptual focus through his chapter headings, which take the form of questions such as 'Are genres stable?' (1999, 49) and 'Where are genres located?' (83). These questions also reflect some of his other aims and aspirations. Their construction is simple, but open-ended, which corresponds to Altman's stated desire to 'lighten the theoretical burden' by writing as clearly and accessibly as possible while still addressing 'important, enduring problems' (ix). The open and general quality of Altman's questions hints at another key aspect of his account: its perceived scope. As the book progresses, Altman argues for the relevance of his revised genre theory to an expanding array of issues. The later chapters introduce general theories of communication (166), historical concerns (179), and finally ask 'What can genres teach us about nations?' (195). In his conclusion, it is apparent that Altman intends his methodology to be applicable beyond the study of film genre: 'The positions presented and defended in this book offer an avenue to a renewed general theory of meaning' (215).

Given the distance travelled by Altman's argument, we might consider the rhetorical advantages that his choice of structure offers him. By posing and then answering a series of questions, Altman is able to define the relevant debates of genre theory as he chooses. This is important because of the extent to which he wishes to depart from previous approaches. His structure allows him to direct his first few questions at the conventions and assumptions of traditional genre theory before moving onto broader issues. The dialogue implied by Altman's question-and-answer structure is also well suited to his emphasis on the discursive qualities of genre and the ways genre interrogates culture.

Neale's chosen structure suggests a different set of aims. Where Altman strives to construct a flexible and versatile conceptual framework for his theory of genre, Neale aspires to producing an extensive picture of the evidence from which his theory emerges. The structure of Neale's book, then, is that of a survey. He divides conceptual matters between the book's introductory and concluding sections. In the first of these, he defines key terms and contexts for the debates about genre. In the second, he looks at the ways in which the significance of genre and its relationship to the American film industry have been theorized. These discussions bracket the book's longer central section, which examines what Neale offers as the major Hollywood genres. Neale outlines and assesses the scholarship on each genre, discussing the ways in which they have been defined and interpreted. Neale's approach to genre theory is based on collating and synthesizing existing theory and criticism.

## Argument and evidence

Another way to characterize the difference between Altman's and Neale's conceptions of genre theory is to consider the relative proportions of description and intervention in each book. Neale is much more descriptive – his aim is to generate a comprehensive account of scholarly and industrial notions of genre. By contrast, Altman moves as quickly as he can from description to intervention. Even his initial outline of traditional genre theory is framed as an examination of its hidden, problematic assumptions: 'in the hope of discovering the origins of our own blindness, the purpose here is to highlight the very claims that genre theorists have failed to recognise they were making' (Altman 1999, 1). Although his engagement is more sympathetic, Neale is by no means an apologist for conventional genre theory. Rather, he wants to build on its insights while addressing its gaps and inconsistencies:

> As I hope I have made apparent, much of this [traditional] work is extremely valuable. However, as I hope I have also made apparent, some of its tenets, some of its practices and some of its presuppositions are open to question.
>
> (Neale 2000, 252)

Where Neale intervenes in the generic debates he describes, it is to identify areas where understanding is incomplete or flawed, for example the limited work on the pre-1940 detective film (72) or the over-reliance on notions of 'frontier mythology' in conceptions of the Western (134–42). The further research that Altman suggests at the end of his book revolves around his revised formulation of genre 'as a multivalent term multiply and variously valorised by diverse user groups' (1999, 214) and his confidence in the wider applications of his methodology (215). While Altman calls for a fundamentally remodelled theory of genre, Neale argues that more conventional genre theory and criticism 'still has a role to play in understanding Hollywood, its history and its films' (2000, 253). Neale promotes the development and strengthening of existing work through more comprehensive coverage, including of 'unrecognised genres' (254), fuller understanding of historical and industrial contexts, and a greater recognition of connections and overlaps through attention to 'hybrids and combinations of all kinds' (254).

When Altman describes a particular area of genre theory or criticism, it is always for a clear rhetorical purpose. He offers an account of how feminist film critics appropriated and redefined the generic terms 'melodrama' and 'the woman's film' (1999, 70–7) as an example of how generic boundaries can shift and change to suit the purposes of different audiences. Neale addresses the same topic in his book, but, rather than noting this departure from historical and industrial definitions of melodrama with approval as 'an interesting test case for [a] process-oriented approach to genre' (Altman 1999, 70), Neale sees it as an inconsistency within generic terminology that does not necessarily need to be resolved, but should be accounted for. Thus, Neale concludes this section of his book by trying to identify historical bases or precedents for different understandings of melodrama (2000, 199–202). Although Neale suggests that he shares Altman's view of genre as a process (217), he seems less interested in exploring the theoretical implications of this than he does in assembling evidence of where shifts in the conception and understanding of genres come from.

If Altman is emphatically rhetorical, even polemical, Neale downplays this stylistic dimension. At the level of language, this can be seen in Neale's repetition of words and phrases. Constructions like this occur throughout the book:

> murder mysteries rub shoulders with long distance bus films, prestige costume films rub shoulders with singing westerns, comedies and woman's films rub shoulders with horror films and musicals, kidnap yarns rub shoulders with race-track pics, comedy dramas rub shoulders with boxing films, spy films rub shoulders with aviation thrillers, and action melodramas about government employees rub shoulders with football, college and military films of all kinds.
>
> (Neale 2000, 241–2)

As this example illustrates, while Neale's style is never inelegant, he is more concerned with comprehensive coverage than with persuasive or evocative language. As it also suggests, one of the standard ways in which he presents his material is through lists. *Genre and Hollywood* is full of lists of films, genres and cycles, critics, quotations, and references. Neale's apparent lack of interest in overt rhetoric can itself be interpreted as a subtle rhetorical strategy, a way of implying that the assembled evidence speaks for itself.

A technique that Altman repeatedly employs is to use an example from everyday life to illustrate a theoretical point. He uses the different ways in which nuts are displayed and stored at the supermarket, in the home, and in a warehouse to demonstrate the extent to which generic definitions depend on the purposes for which they are being used (Altman

1999, 96–9). He extends this same argument by contrasting the ways that Hollywood and its genres are represented by different attractions at Disney World (101–2). He illustrates the interpretative communities that support the understanding and appreciation of genres by referring to a hypothetical graduate student with a growing interest in birdwatching (167–9).

These examples are very effective at giving substance to Altman's concepts and supporting his aim to make theory accessible. Altman's concern with accessibility is a corollary of the level where much of his theorizing takes place – although related to the everyday workings of genre, many of the concepts he proposes are quite general and abstract. His desire to relate his theories to common and familiar experiences can also be connected to his project of reformulating the fundamentals of genre theory. By grounding his conclusions in such experiences, he is able to suggest that they have a logical basis in the wider world. This is also crucial to the expanding scope of Altman's argument across the book. Even before he applies his approach to the formation and structure of nations, and finally declares that it can contribute to a 'general theory of meaning' (215), he has insistently suggested, through his range of 'real-life' examples, the broad application of his methods.

## Theory and criticism

The ambitious breadth of Altman's conception of genre theory can also be related to his choice of intellectual traditions. Unlike Neale, these are not the traditions of genre theory and criticism within the discipline of film studies. Instead, Altman situates his own work in relation to disciplines with a wider and more general theoretical scope. He engages (albeit critically) with philosophers like Aristotle (Altman 1999, 1–4) and Wittgenstein (96–9) and later with social theorists such as Habermas and Benedict Anderson (196–9). His constant point of reference, however, is linguistics. Altman repeatedly returns to its vocabulary of terms and symbols. For example, the diagrams used to illustrate the processes through which genres are defined and redefined are borrowed from the 'conventions of linguistics', using asterisks to indicate 'hypothetical categories never actually observed in the field' (65). When he comes to summarize and define his methodology at the end of the book, Altman proposes an augmented version of the approach outlined in his earlier article 'A Semantic/ Syntactic Approach to Film Genre' (1984). To this formulation, which, as Jason Mittell (2000, 90) points out, is grounded in structuralism, Altman adds a third linguistic term, proposing a 'semantic/syntactic/pragmatic approach' (Altman 1999, 208).

Altman describes pragmatics as an analytical concern with how 'Use grounds linguistic meaning' (209). His choice of the word 'pragmatic' is a way to rhetorically unite his reliance on linguistic and communication theory with an emphasis on everyday usage and changing experience. However, as his employment of philosophy, social theory, and linguistics suggests, his eventual conception of genre theory is somewhat loftier. This conception can be seen in his attitude to genre criticism.

Altman is initially keen to challenge the assumption that '[g]enre critics are distanced from the practice of genre', (28) even offering examples (e.g. melodrama) of the ways that critics can play an active role in the shifting and changing of generic conceptions. As Altman's argument progresses, however, the significance of such criticism seems to diminish. Leger Grindon notes that 'film journalism and scholarship' (2000, 54) do not appear to be included among Altman's 'constellated communities' (1999, 161) whose 'lateral communication' (162) shapes and redefines understandings of genre. Thus, there remains an unresolved tension between the content of Altman's theory – his insistence on the endlessly discursive nature of genre – and the type of theory he is trying to construct. Altman's affiliation with grander, more all-encompassing theoretical traditions ultimately results in a more detached and aloof conception of genre theory, concerned with modelling discourses about genre and historical movements rather than participating in them. With his determination to work with (and, where necessary, around) existing genre scholarship, even while acknowledging its problems, it is Neale who finally seems the more pragmatic.

PETE FALCONER

## Works cited

Altman, Rick. 1984. 'A Semantic/Syntactic Approach to Film Genre'. *Cinema Journal* 23 (3): 6–18.
——. 1999. *Film/Genre*. London: BFI.
Grindon, Leger. 2000. Review of *Film/Genre*, by Rick Altman. *Film Quarterly* 53 (4): 53–5.
Mittell, Jason. 2000. Review of *Refiguring American Film Genres: Theory and History*, edited by Nick Browne, and *Film/Genre*, by Rick Altman. *Velvet Light Trap* 46: 88–91.
Neale, Steve. 2000. *Genre and Hollywood*. Abingdon: Routledge.

## Further reading

Grant, Barry Keith, ed. 2003. *Film Genre Reader III*. Austin: University of Texas Press.
Langford, Barry. 2005. *Film Genre: Hollywood and Beyond*. Edinburgh: Edinburgh University Press.
Thomas, Deborah. 2000. *Beyond Genre: Melodrama, Comedy and Romance in Hollywood Films*. Moffat: Cameron and Hollis.

# IDENTIFICATION, THEORY OF

'Identification' is a term that is widely used in discussions of theatre and cinema to refer to the affective relationship that is established between an audience member and the protagonist of the play or film. A critic may claim that Hitchcock's point-of-view editing encourages audiences to identify with his protagonists. Or an audience member may identify with the emotional suffering and sacrifice of Bette Davis's character in *Now, Voyager* (Rapper, 1942). Usually, two kinds of identification are distinguished. In the first, sympathy, the spectator cares for or is concerned about a character but does not share their emotional state. When the heroine cries in despair, the audience member feels pity but not despair. In the second, empathy, the spectator shares the feeling that is had by a character because the character feels it. A character is afraid of the monster in a horror film and the spectator fears the monster, too, on account of the fact that the character fears it.

While a distinction between sympathetic and empathic emotional responses to fiction is widely accepted in the literature, some have noted the vagueness of usage and that sympathy can be used to mean empathy (Plantinga 2009). However, there is a conceptual distinction to be drawn. Since empathy is a symmetrical relationship in which I share your emotion, I must correctly identify the emotional state you are in in order to feel empathy. Sympathy is an asymmetrical relationship in which I respond emotionally to what I understand to be your mental state. But I might be mistaken in my assessment, in which case my sympathy would be misplaced (Neill 1996; Gaut 1999; 2010a, ch. 6). If the conceptual distinction is granted, then debate turns on which concept is most salient to understanding our emotional responses to fiction or whether both are.

However, theories of identification in the cinema are complicated by the idea that a distinctive sense can be given to the concept of identification that is independent of sympathy and empathy thus defined, one that leads to at least three claims. The first claim is that a new, distinctive concept of identification can help explain central aspects of our general response to fiction, including our emotional responses. Identification has been characterized in many different and incompatible ways but very broadly it can be construed as the capacity to take the point of view, or attitude, of another as one's own. The second claim about identification in the cinema links a proposal about the nature of identification to arguments about cinematic specificity, that is, to arguments about what special qualities distinguish the medium itself. The third claim involves using the concept of identification to support the explanatory role of empathy in our response to fiction, since the concepts of empathy and identification turn out to be closely related.

## Christian Metz's theory of cinematic identification

Christian Metz (1982) developed a theory of cinematic identification based on Freudian and Lacanian psychoanalysis (*see* IMAGINARY SIGNIFIER). Freud claimed that the individual is born into a state of what he called 'primary narcissism' or primary identification lacking a distinction between self and other (Freud 1957). In such a state the infant assumes that objects that are separate from him, like the mother's breast, are in fact part of him. The infant unconsciously assimilates characteristics of something other than itself as its own characteristics. Subsequently, as the infant begins to interact with his parents in the social world, he develops an ideal of selfhood (the ego ideal) that he aspires to become.

Lacan glossed Freud's theory of the ego ideal by returning to the Greek myth that inspired it (Lacan 2002). Narcissus was a youth of exceptional beauty and pride who was led to a pool by Nemesis to stare at his reflection and he promptly fell in love with it, not realizing it was just an image. Subsequently, unable to part from it, he died contemplating the beautiful image. Lacan suggested that the formation of the ego ideal, or what he termed the ideal ego, could be understood as the sight of the infant at his body image in a mirror. Unlike Narcissus, before he encounters the mirror, the child has no self-concept and no clear sense of a self–other boundary. When he sees the reflection, however, he takes what he sees as a something (the ego) and assumes that this ideal form is himself, even though he is merely a nothing without a self–other boundary. Metz refers to this process, too, as a form of primary identification, although it also marks the beginning of secondary identification because it is the moment when the subject begins to move beyond a state of undifferentiation, and is seeking to defend against that loss by imagining itself as something that it is not (i.e. imagining itself as the ideal form in the mirror).

Be that as it may, Metz takes this theory as the basis of primary identification in the cinema. The cinema, Metz argues, is like Lacan's mirror in which a child can recognize a world of differentiated objects save for the fact that its own image is absent. Indeed, it is no longer needed since self–other boundaries have already been established and the ego formed. So where is the spectator's ego in the cinema? Metz initially proposes that the spectator '*identifies with himself*, with himself as a pure act of perception' (Metz 1982, 49). Presumably, this identification is to be understood as a special case of the ego ideal, where the ego ideal is defined purely in terms of perceptual capacities, i.e. seeing and recognizing an image. However, the spectator's identification is also with the point of view of the camera. The spectator assimilates the visual field of the camera to his own perceptual field. Even while the spectator knows the visual array pre-exists him and that he is only watching a film, that knowledge is 'disavowed' in favour of the belief that the visual field of the film comes into being for and in his sight. In this sense, the identification is a regressive, narcissistic one since the spectator imagines there is no distinction between what exists and what he perceives to exist. This serves to define the uniqueness of identification in the cinema, in contradistinction, say, to the theatre or to a mirror.

Metz conceptualizes character identification primarily in terms of the relationship the spectator takes up to the visual field of a character's glance in a shot/reverse shot eye-line match. One character looks at another who is offscreen and the spectator is invited to look at this scene of a character looking through the eyes of the offscreen character, even when the on-screen shot is not a literal point-of-view shot. Sharing a character's attention is sufficient. Subsequently, the character who was off-screen will become the on-screen character within the visual field of the gaze of the character whom we had recognized in the initial shot. This initial character, now off-screen, becomes the new locus of spectator identification. But how exactly does secondary, character identification, thus conceived, act as a 'relay' of primary identification? Where I previously merged with the point of view of the camera, I now merge with the character who is the owner of the glance whose object is represented in the point-of-view shot, and that merger is ensured by a similar process of disavowal. 'I must both "take myself" for the character (= an imaginary procedure) so that he benefits, by analogical projection, from all the schemata of intelligibility that I have within me, and not take myself for him (= the return to the real)' (Metz 1982, 57).

## Cognitive and analytic theories of identification

Cognitive and analytic theorists are in broad agreement in challenging the assumption that identification consists in the imagined assimilation of self and other that requires a theory of disavowal or 'splitting of belief' in order to explain how a form of assimilation can coexist with the knowledge that the other is different from the self. Cognitive and analytic film theories argue that, on the contrary, we are under no illusion when we perceive a fiction film, and that our responses actually depend on our knowledge that we know it is only a fiction, for we do not run away when the monster attacks in a horror film (Carroll 1988; 1990). To this Metz might respond that, of course, we do not run away because we know, in spite of our belief in its reality, that it is only a movie. However, the point is that our behaviour is *prima facie* evidence for us knowing that it is a film we are watching, but what is the countervailing evidence that we take the film to be real? The burden of proof is on the psychoanalytic theorist to show why, in the face our behaviour, we still also believe that we are actually seeing the events depicted. Nor can it plausibly be maintained that when we identify with a character, we take ourselves to be that character, for while the characters are fleeing the monster, we are staying put.

Cognitive and analytic theorists are in broad agreement that psychoanalysis misconstrues the role of beliefs in our response to fiction. Fiction films mandate that we imagine what it is that they represent, not that we believe what it is they represent (Carroll 1990; Currie 1995; Smith 1995). The type of imagination involved is not fantasy, that very particular kind of visual imagining, privileged in psychoanalysis, in which we conflate what is real and what is imagined; rather, it is akin to entertaining a proposition in thought (Carroll 1990). Some philosophers and film theorists characterize imagination in terms of simulation where, in Currie's words, we run our beliefs 'off-line' (Currie 1995; Coplan 2004; 2009). However, there is still room for disagreement as to what fictions enjoin us to imagine and when. A weaker, and perhaps more defensible, version of the primary identification thesis is what Gregory Currie has dubbed the 'imagined observer hypothesis'. This is the thesis that fiction films enjoin us to imagine that we see what they represent from the point of view of the camera; he attributes this view to Wilson (1986). This requires an utterly implausible phenomenology of spectatorship in which we would be required to move, sometimes in extreme rapidity, across space and time, from one location to the next (*see* IMAGINED OBSERVER HYPOTHESIS). In its place, Gregory Currie argues that my imagining in film is impersonal or external: 'my imagining is not that I see the characters and the events of the movie; it is simply that there are these characters and that these events occur' (Currie 1995, 179). However, it is also perceptual. What distinguishes imagining a film from imagining the events of a novel is that films, unlike novels, give rise directly to 'perceptual imaginings' that depend in their content and structure on what it is that we see in a film.

Nevertheless, we might reject the imagined observer hypothesis as a general theory of identification and still claim that personal or internal imagining can contribute to an understanding of character identification by explaining how, in, say, the point-of-view shot, we identify with the perceptual point of view of a character by imagining seeing from their point of view (Smith 1997). For Berys Gaut (1999; 2010a, chap 6), the capacity to imagine seeing from a character's point of view is just one of many ways in which we can imagine what it is like to be in the situation of a character and forms part of a broader 'aspectual' theory of identification. When we identify with a character, we don't imagine being that character, for we do not share all their responses, but we imagine being in the character's situation, a situation that we identify with only partially. Thus, in the point-of-view shot of a monster in a horror film, we may identify perceptually with the monster but not motivationally and affectively. Gaut distinguishes four aspects of identification: perceptual, affective, motivational, and epistemic, although there may be others. In this way we can imagine, separately or in combination, seeing what a character sees, feeling what a character feels, wanting what a character wants, believing what a character believes.

Gaut (2010b) provides a richly pluralistic explanation of how cinema solicits an emotional response in the spectator since he discriminates a distinctive role for the concepts of affective identification, empathy, and sympathy which can be prompted or cued by the strategies of narrative alignment and focalization discussed by Smith (1995) and others. Gaut defines empathy as feeling what a character feels because they are feeling it and argues that it usually presupposes that we imagine what it is they are feeling from their point of view. However, the concepts are logically independent. One might share someone else's feeling without imagining what it is that they felt. This could be the case in examples of mirroring, when, for example, we weep automatically when we see someone else weeping. One may affectively identify with someone without either empathizing or sympathizing, as in the case of the imaginative torturer who imagines how it feels for his victims in order to torture them better. Sympathy requires us neither to affectively identify with someone nor for us to share their emotion, and although sympathy is usually packaged with empathy, we may share another's feelings and yet be callously indifferent to their fate.

The most serious challenge to Gaut's arguments is that such pluralism is misguided and that emotional responses to character can be satisfactorily explained without recourse to either identification or empathy. For example, some have questioned whether indeed the point-of-view shot needs to be explained as something that is internally imagined rather than simply delivering information that this is what a character sees (Currie 1995; Choi 2005). A rapid shot/reverse shot point-of-view sequence seems to invoke an implausible viewer phenomenology akin to that of the imagined observer hypothesis, though here the jump is from one imagined point of view to another. Noël Carroll (1990) goes further and proposes that our normative response is fundamentally external to character. According to Carroll's assimilationist view: 'We respond to fictional situations as outside observers, assimilating our conception of the character's mental state into our overall response as a sort of onlooker with respect to the situation in which the character finds himself' (Carroll 1998, 350). We assess a character's situation from the outside and emotionally respond to that situation rather than sharing the emotions of a character, and thus there is a radical asymmetry between what a spectator feels and what a character feels (Carroll 1990; 2007).

For Carroll, on the grounds of explanatory parsimony, it is not necessary to invoke concepts of identification and empathy when we can develop a satisfactory account of emotional response without them. Gaut's response to Carroll is that there is nothing in these arguments that explicitly precludes either affective identification or empathy. Given the fact that spectators customarily report these experiences, the theorist who denies the salience of identification and empathy needs to explain why spectators are in error about the nature of their emotional responses to film.

RICHARD ALLEN

## Works cited

Carroll, Noël. 1988. *Mystifying Movies: Fads and Fallacies in Contemporary Film Theory*. New York: Columbia.

——. 1990. *The Philosophy of Horror or Paradoxes of the Heart*. New York: Routledge.

——. 1998. *A Philosophy of Mass Art*. Oxford: Clarendon Press.

——. 2007. 'On the Ties that Bind: Characters, the Emotions and Popular Fictions'. In *Philosophy and the Interpretation of Popular Culture*, edited by William Irwin and Jorge J.E. Gracia, 89–116. Lanham, MD: Rowman and Littlefield.

Choi, Jinhee. 2005. 'Leaving It up to the Imagination: POV Shots and Imagining from the Inside'. *Journal of Aesthetics and Art Criticism* 63: 17–26.

Coplan, Amy. 2004. 'Empathic Engagement with Narrative Fictions'. *Journal of Aesthetics and Art Criticism* 62: 141–52.

——. 2009. 'Empathy and Character Engagement'. In *The Routledge Companion to Philosophy and Film*, edited by Paisley Livingston and Carl Plantinga, 97–110. New York: Routledge.

Currie, Gregory. 1995. *Image and Mind: Film, Philosophy and Cognitive Science*. New York: Cambridge University Press.

Freud, Sigmund. 1957. 'On Narcissism: An Introduction'. In *Standard Edition of the Complete Psychological Works of Sigmund Freud*, vol. XIV, edited and translated by James Strachey, 73–102. London: Hogarth Press.

Gaut, Berys. 1999. 'Identification and Emotion in Narrative Film'. In *Passionate Views: Film, Cognition, and Emotion*, edited by Carl Plantinga and Greg M. Smith, 200–16. Baltimore, MD: Johns Hopkins University Press.

——. 2010a. *A Philosophy of Cinematic Art*. New York: Cambridge University Press.

——. 2010b. 'Empathy and Identification in Cinema'. *Midwest Studies in Philosophy* XXXIV: 136–57.

Lacan, Jacques. 2002. 'The Mirror Stage as Formative of the Function of the I as Revealed in Psychoanalytic Experience'. In *Ecrits*, translated by Bruce Fink, 3–9. New York: Norton.

Metz, Christian. 1982. *The Imaginary Signifier*. Bloomington: Indiana University Press.

Neill, Alex. 1996. 'Empathy and (Film) Fiction'. In *Post-theory: Reconstructing Film Studies*, edited by David Bordwell and Noël Carroll, 175–94. Madison: University of Wisconsin Press.

Plantinga, Carl. 2009. *Moving Viewers: American Film and the Spectator's Experience*. Berkeley: University of California Press.

Smith, Murray. 1995. *Engaging Characters: Fiction, Emotion, and the Cinema*. Oxford: Clarendon Press.

——. 1997. 'Imagining from the Inside'. In *Film Theory and Philosophy*, edited by Richard Allen and Murray Smith, 412–30. Oxford: Clarendon Press.

Wilson, George M. 1986. *Narration in Light: Studies in Cinematic Point of View*. Baltimore, MD: Johns Hopkins University Press.

# IDEOLOGY, CINEMA AND

## 'Cinema/Ideology/Criticism'

'Cinema/Ideology/Criticism' (Comolli and Narboni 1971) was the title of an editorial in the important French cinema journal *Cahiers du Cinéma* in 1969, shortly after the student and worker uprisings of May 1968 in France which had nearly brought down the government. May '68 drew on and magnified intense political radicalism. Because it involved students and many of their lecturers, it also sparked a culture of intense intellectual activity, which was felt especially in film circles (Harvey 1978). This editorial, translated in *Screen* in 1971 – one of the leading journals in the UK to propagate French political culture in English – marked *Cahiers*'s commitment to radicalism. This was all the more significant because *Cahiers* had been the home of André Bazin (1918–58), a founding figure of French film culture, whose commitment to realism was at the point of being disowned by the younger radicals who now took over the journal.

The *Cahiers* essay displays its rationale only at its conclusion, where it rejects impressionistic and interpretive film criticism. Giving Bazin a nod, they thank him for drawing attention to the specifics of film practice, before pointing towards the linguistic inspiration of the unnamed Christian Metz, whose work of the late 1960s reformulated film as a semiotics based on the model of language. They refuse 'phenomenological positivism' and 'mechanical materialism' – the former associated with Maurice Merleau-Ponty, then at the height of his influence, and the latter with the old guard Marxism of the Second International which sanctified the relation between economy and ideology as that of base and superstructure. In their stead they propose drawing on the Russian revolutionary filmmakers of the 1920s, especially Eisenstein (who of course continued making films and theorizing until the 1940s) (*see* MONTAGE THEORY II [SOVIET AVANT-GARDE]).

The fundamental appeal, however, was to Louis Althusser, communist and structuralist philosopher – not to his influential theory of ideology which was first published in 1970, after this editorial, but to his distinction between ideology and science (Althusser 1979 [1965]; Althusser *et al.* 1979 [1965]). The new *Cahiers* would be dedicated to scientific analysis, not impressionistic interpretation. The appeal to linguistics reflects a then current faith in linguistics as 'queen of the human sciences', the one discipline in the humanities to have embraced the procedures and goals of the hard sciences. The school of linguistics the authors refer to is the semiotic tradition that began with Ferdinand de Saussure (1857–1913), who introduced some key distinctions: between the whole system of a language and the activity of speaking or writing in it; between a sign and what it refers to; and between the material form of the sign and its semantic component, the 'signifier' and 'signified' respectively.

The difference between signifying (representing, depicting) and the world it refers to (loosely speaking, reality) is where ideology operates. Ideology is an obfuscation of the relation between signifying systems – such as cinema – and the reality of the world and human life. Science is an accurate account of those relations. Rather paradoxically, the essay sets out to give a scientific account of the ignorance and lies. Hence the opening phrase 'Scientific criticism' and the would-be disciplinary methodology: to establish its object and methods (Althusser's *problématique*), and to analyse the truth-conditions of its own way of proceeding.

In this case the conditions are first a group of people involved in film culture and producing a magazine, and second the capitalist economy of France, which is the objective and unavoidable framework of printing and distributing it. They reject the 'parallel', alternative culture, common enough at the time, of self-regulating communes holding themselves apart from mainstream society, both because they are easy targets and because repressive tolerance (Marcuse 1965) brackets them off as evidence of a freedom of speech, effectively turning them into another object of consumerist lifestyle choice.

Given this political frame, Comolli and Narboni assert the critical distinction they will abide by: to distinguish between films which reproduce dominant ideology and those that in one way or another challenge it. They distinguish first the film from cinema as a whole, a topic too large for the magazine to take on, instead specifically orienting themselves to 'the film today'. The second section opens with an even more tightly focused part of this larger inquiry: what is a film? They specify two aspects, which relate almost as signifier and signified, and very clearly as the Marxist categories of exchange-value and use-value: the film is an industrial product sold for profit, and it is an ideological vehicle. They present the core of the new project for *Cahiers*: 'Because every film is part of the economic system it is also part of the ideological system' (Comolli and Narboni 1971, 29–30). But this does not mean that all films are equally ideological, or in the same way. Instead, since filmmakers differ, so do their films. As a result, they stress that '*every film is political*' (30). The function of criticism will be to identify the manner and tendency of that politics.

Two qualities of films make them especially favourable to conveying ideology. First, because they require teamwork, they typically mobilize economic forces and are tied to monopoly suppliers like Kodak. Second, cinema has the reputation of being a realist medium, tied by technology to what later critics would refer to as indexicality: a privileged relation to the world based on the involuntary physics of light and light-sensitive film-stock. However, they argue that 'concrete reality' is an eminently ideological idea. The cinema typically reproduces not things as they are but as they appear, and therefore according to the relationships established between people and their world under actually existing social and historical conditions. Disrupting this replication of the world as self-evident is the political task of film.

Underpinning this argument is a dialectical relation between the world and its depictions. Cinema, they say, is one of the 'languages through which the world communicates itself to itself' (30). This is the nature of *re*-presentation: doubling up, as if to confirm that the world actually is as it is. But according to the authors, what is reproduced is not the world but an ideological refraction of it. Ideology in this sense is an imaginary relation to the real conditions of existence. So the cinema is not the *world* communicating itself to itself, as Bazin might have had it, echoing the poet Mallarmé, but rather ideology 'talking to itself'. Thus, far from reinforcing the realty of the world, cinema reproduces its ideological constitution. Yet as we have heard, Comolli and Narboni do not believe that all films

243

are the same. How differently can filmmakers respond to this problem, this political challenge?

## Seven categories of films

They suggest that there are seven categories of films: (a) ideological mainstream films; (b) films that resist in content as well as form; (c) artistic films that resist formally without being overtly political; (d) films with political content but realist form; (e) films that should belong in the first category but are sufficiently self-contradictory to disrupt pure ideological functioning; and finally (f) and (g), two modes of *cinéma direct* documentary, the former accepting the dominant realism, the latter resisting and disrupting it. Some films address ideological issues – mainly political ones – without also innovating formally; others are formally inventive without clear political commitment.

The majority form of film is the ideological vehicle pure and simple. Such films repackage social needs as discourse, such that 'audience demand and economic response have also been reduced to the same thing' (31). The very idea of a public, and thence of public taste, was created ideologically: giving the public what it wants is thus a closed loop of ideology once again talking to itself. Even more than profit, the reassuring repetition of common sense from ordinary life into the film seems to motivate the film industry's production of these ideological movies.

In the second, and much the most praiseworthy, group are films which break open the dominant in style and content. Among the films they mention here are *Unreconciled (Nicht versöhnt oder Es hilft nur Gewalt wo Gewalt herrscht)* (1965), directed by Jean-Marie Straub from a novel by Heinrich Böll, and Robert Kramer's political thriller *The Edge* (1968), indicating that there is no intrinsic bias away from Hollywood and towards Europe; just as ideological films can be mainstream or art-house, so political films can appear in the guise of genre movie-making. It is clear by now that the critical political task of cinema is to break down the ideology of depiction, the realism once championed by the journal in the immediate postwar years.

If critics have a role in revealing the ideological in majority filmmaking, and celebrating its breakdown in category (b) films, they have a special role in the interpretation of artful and innovative productions which, however, have no obvious political bone to pick. The selection of films here indicates again the breadth of their sympathies: Ingmar Bergman's quintessential angst-ridden vanguard fiction *Persona* (1966); *Méditerranée*, an almost abstract forty-minute 1963 documentary by Jean-Daniel Pollet and Volker Schlondorff, with a script by *Tel Quel* founder Phillippe Sollers; and Jerry Lewis directing himself in the 1960 comedy *The Bellboy*. This last is difficult for anglophone audiences to quite get to grips with: French cinephiles adored Lewis, seeing his work as the legitimate heir to Keaton and Chaplin. This indicates the importance of critical interpretation to rescuing films from their apparently merely aesthetic qualities.

Categories (c) and (d) mirror one another: the former attempt to be artistic without politics, and the latter political without formal innovation. The authors are clear where they stand: it is far more important to make formal attacks on the ideological work of depiction than to make populist political films. This stance would inform the debate in the UK over Ken Loach's early television series *Days of Hope*. Comolli and Narboni's examples are Costa-Gavras's 1969 political thriller *Z* and a rather quirky political melodrama from 1969, *Le temps de vivre* by Bernard Paul. It is unclear quite why the latter figures in this classification. A similar division exists in the examples from *cinéma direct*: *Chiefs*, an eighteen-minute 1968 documentary by Richard Leacock about a Hawai'ian convention of thousands of police chiefs, is singled out for not challenging the normal functions of depiction, oddly compared with *Les Grandes familles*, a 1958 fictional portrait of a wealthy family starring Jean Gabin, while *Le règne du jour*, Pierre Perrault's 1967 documentary about a French-Canadian family's search for ancestral roots in France, and Jacques Willemont's 1968 documentary *La reprise du travail aux usines Wonder* (whose title is slightly misquoted), a brief documentary on the defeat of a strike in May 1968, are singled out for breaking up the traditional methods.

But of all their taxonomy, it is category (e) films which have received the most attention. Here are films which set out with little aesthetic or political ambition but which nevertheless express in their internal contradictions the problematic nature of ideological representation. Here they echo literary critic Georg Lukács's defence of Balzac, the supporter of a defeated royal party whose bitter insights into the corruption of mid-nineteenth century Paris were of greater value precisely because more misplaced than the explicitly socialist novels of his contemporary Zola. 'Frankly reactionary' purposes (32) can be suppressed when, as they express it, the ideology becomes subordinate to the text, that is when the work of making the film takes over from the labour of reproducing the ideology – when, for example, a narrative or a way of shooting in a location take on a logic of their own. Such films begin to dismantle the system from within. Among their examples is Ford's *Young Mr. Lincoln* (1939), which would provide *Cahiers* with the material for a model analysis of a category (e) film (*Cahiers du cinéma* 1972) (*see* SYMPTOMATIC READING).

This category would be a benchmark for film studies throughout the 1970s and 1980s, driving passionate research into the radical potentialities of various genres, as Barbara Klinger (1984) points out. Finding the troublesome edge between the practice of filmmaking and the ideological project of cinema as a whole would employ film scholars who felt the necessity to provide a political analysis, since that proved that film studies were important, while at the same time preserving their enjoyment of even apparently exploitative horror, B-movie and blaxploitation films. As Klinger argued, however, genres are integral to the industry's overall evolution, and, as Rick Altman (1992) demonstrated six years later, the ostensibly liberating genre of melodrama was integral to classical Hollywood.

Intriguingly, though they were at pains to place cinema as an economic activity, there is little here to propose a political economy of the cinema industry. Nor is there any proposal for studying audiences, commercial or 'parallel'. More surprising, given their distrust of the old realism once espoused by the journal, is their cheerful acceptance of the auteurism of the *nouvelle vague* who had preceded them at the journal. This auteurism would endear them further to the rather literary and textual tradition that began to emerge in the 1970s and 1980s in English-speaking film studies, where the lionizing of directors like Hitchcock would become a small industry within film studies.

On more positive notes, the proposal was made in this editorial for an empirical engagement with the material of the films themselves and with film technique. While criticizing the apolitical formalism of a barren antiquarian style of analysis, this principle demanded that theory be melded with critical analysis. Each category of film required a different mode of analysis, reflecting Althusser's three stages of research: defining the object, the method, and the kind of knowledge you wish to produce. If, in the afterglow of near revolution in 1969, that kind of knowledge was politically radical and intellectually utopian, it is important to the history of film studies that at one time it was strongly directed towards a radical platform of social and cultural change.

SEAN CUBITT

## Works cited

Althusser, Louis. 1979 [1965]. *For Marx*, translated by Ben Brewster. London: Verso.

Althusser, Louis, Etienne Balibar, Roger Establet, and Jacques Rancière. 1979 [1965]. *Reading Capital*. Translated by Ben Brewster. London: Verso.

Altman, Rick. 1992. 'Dickens, Griffith and Film Theory Today'. In *Classical Hollywood Narrative: The Paradigm Wars*, edited by Jane Gaines, 9–47. Durham, NC: Duke University Press.

*Cahiers du Cinéma*. 1972. 'John Ford's *Young Mr. Lincoln*: A Collective Text by the Editors of *Cahiers du Cinéma*', translated by Helene Lackner and Diana Matias. *Screen* 13 (3): 5–44.

Comolli, Jean-Louis, and Jean Narboni. 1971. 'Cinema/Ideology/Criticism'. Translated by Susan Bennett. *Screen* 12 (l): 27–36.

Harvey, Sylvia. 1978. *May '68 and Film Culture*. London: BFI.

Klinger, Barbara. 1984. '"Cinema/Ideology/Criticism" Revisited: The Progressive Text'. *Screen* 25 (1) (Jan.–Feb.): 30–44.

Marcuse, Herbert. (1965). 'Repressive Tolerance'. In *A Critique of Pure Tolerance*, edited by Robert Paul Wolff, Barrington Moore, Jr., and Herbert Marcuse, 95–137. Boston, MA: Beacon Press.

## Further reading

Comolli, Jean-Pierre, Gérard Leblanc, and Jean Narboni. 2001. *Les Années pop: cinéma et politique, 1956–1970*. Paris: BPI-Centre Georges Pompidou.

# ILLUSION

Throughout the history of film theory, the notion of illusion has been used mainly to discuss two characteristics of the cinematic apparatus:

(1)  its ability to become invisible, to the extent that spectators believe they are faced with the world, not its representation (*perceptive illusion*);
(2)  its ability to serve as a reliable source of information about the world, even if the film is fictional (*descriptive illusion*).

I shall discuss each in turn.

## Perceptive illusion

The notion of illusion is quite difficult to analyse as it is based on the presupposition that there is an *actual* state of things. For me to fall victim to an illusion, things *actually* have to not be what I think they are. Such a definition is not problematic in some visions of the world, such as the ones Ancient Greece built on the idea of a presumed final essence. Plato thought that with a proper education one might move from step to step acquiring more accurate knowledge; Aristotle suggested gifted artists could reach for the essence of something by accurately representing it. By contrast, in the Darwinian system – to which cognitive-evolutionary film theories often resort when describing the cinematic apparatus – our senses are not required to distinguish in our environment what is true from what is not. They are required to build a representation of the world that is good enough for us to move around with a view to ensuring our survival. Perception is here linked with cognition to allow the body to move within space: whether *reality* (i.e. the representation I have of the world) actually corresponds to *the real* (i.e. the world as represented by other forms of analyses of its aspects – the world such as it appears, for instance, to a bat, a whale, a Geiger counter, or a microscope ...) does not really matter. It is, however, crucial that my representations should be useful to me, that they should show me the obstacles, preys, and predators along my way, as well as make clear what affordances may arise around me.

This concept of perceptual fitness allows one to invert the usual apprehension of illusion: one sometimes believes one is faced with a false representation when this representation is truer than one thinks. Russian Formalists asserted this lying–true effect could achieve *ostrannenie*, i.e. the useful defamiliarization provided by some works of art (for an application to movies, see Jullier 2010) (*see* FORMALIST THEORIES OF FILM). Ernst Gombrich assumed it too in his *Art and Illusion*: Botticelli's *Venus* is obviously 'false' (on an anatomical point of view) but she tells a lot more about womanliness than Bouguereau's one, though the latter is anatomically correct (1963, 37).

In the Darwinian system, the fact that my perceptive/cognitive system tells me that there are 'moving pictures' in the movie theatre while scientific reason has it they are fixed and their apparent movement is a mental construction ('moved pictures') is not of utmost importance. In terms of physiological resources, it is simply easier for me to perceive these pictures as moving – my survival is not at stake here. Still, in the same logic of 'magic' properties attributed to images, American law rules that the following warning should be engraved on rear-view mirrors: 'objects in the mirror are closer than they appear'. Literally, this statement is not true, as the image reflected in the mirror is not the object itself – it simply stands for it. The inscription should rather read: 'objects whose image is reflected in the mirror are closer than they appear'. In terms of survival, however, the short cut is better.

If illusion is, as defined and popularized by Freud (1928), a belief leading to the supremacy of the mental over the concrete, then movement in cinema is not an illusion. Religion – the example chosen by Freud – is an illusion because I obviously do not perceive any direct clue of God's existence, either using my senses or through scientific investigations. But if I freeze a frame or watch film frames unfolding in slow motion, I can understand that what I thought was movement on the screen was just a personal interpretation. The same holds for audiovisual mirages, such as when an actor filmed in CinemaScope is pacing back and forth on the screen of a theatre with monophonic sound. I am convinced I can hear the sound of the man's footsteps moving left and right as he is walking, due to cross-modal checking, i.e. my brain's engagement with a situation read holistically. But if I simply close my eyes, the mirage vanishes. Once again, it is simply more economical and reliable for me to perceive the world this way (in the form of audiovisual sources in which sound and image cannot be dissociated from one another). This is not a hoax.

Yet a system inspired by Platonism, such as the system of the 'metaphysics of the image/trace' developed by André Bazin in the 1940s to 1950s (*see* ONTOLOGY OF THE PHOTOGRAPHIC IMAGE), may be held as an illusion as Freud defined it. In this approach, cinema acts as a pointer, giving us access to the real (often capitalized 'Real' in this theory) by disregarding the limitations of our senses. It makes us 'see the world before it is seen', to quote Maurice Merleau-Ponty, whose phenomenological approach is close to Bazin's.[1] This explains why a Rossellini film written about by Bazin is like a Cézanne painting written about by Merleau-Ponty: it produces an *epiphany* – a religious expression – which breaks the illusion induced by our senses. But this advantage is the spectator's responsibility: you have to *believe* in the possibility of reaching the Real, beyond material evidence. The camera, after all, is a human construction that has been designed to create images that look like the world as perceived by human beings. It is not obvious that the camera can overcome this limitation, even when Rossellini is handling it.

Yet instead of setting *contra*-illusion Darwinian systems against *pro*-illusion Platonic systems, one may see them both as forms of the *factish* figure. The word *factish* was coined by Bruno Latour (2011) to describe the mythic anecdote of the first encounter between the European missionaries arriving in America and the 'savages' they found there. The missionaries were exasperated by the bad faith (both literal and figurative) of the savages, who presented their visitors with two contradictory propositions: yes, they sculpted their amulets with their own hands, and, yes, these amulets *were* deities with magic powers. How was this possible? The missionaries preferred to think of the savages as cynical (they used the amulets to manipulate others) or naive (they eventually believed in their own lies). Yet, as Latour explains, the savages simply 'made something beyond them'. The manipulator of fetishes gives voice to the object he or she makes, and the object conversely gives voice to him or her. The term describing this compromise between external reality (the *fact*) and the subject's beliefs (the *fetish*) is the *factish*. Its makers are literally 'overtaken by events'. In the same way as the fetish is not a piece of sculpted wood but an event for an audience, the film is less an illusory text than an *in-situ* spectacle.[2] Both of them allow different practices – of interpreting, informing, exchanging, and prescribing – to quite literally *take place*. These practices lead one to consider the 'film text' as a provider of ideas, projects, and desires which are not in themselves dramatized in the film ('this movie changed my life').

Caution is thus advisable before applying to cinema S.T. Coleridge's famous quote asserting that it is simply a 'willing suspension of disbelief for the moment, which constitutes poetic faith' (*Biographia Literaria*, 1817). Instead of religion and illusion, one may speak concretely of interactions and play (see Winnicott 1971).

## Descriptive illusion

The films produced by cultural industries, as opposed to art films or modernist works, are often accused of participating in what Pierre Bourdieu (1998) calls *illusio*, which is the (illusory) feeling of the natural obviousness of social structures. Films are said to produce illusory descriptions of the human world. One of the most famous texts of the sociology of the Frankfurt School is entitled 'The Culture Industry: Enlightenment as Mass Deception'. In this chapter of their *Dialectic of Enlightenment* (1997 [1944]), Theodor W. Adorno and Max Horkheimer describe Hollywood as a static world where the arbitrariness of hierarchical relationships between human beings has been reified and frozen in place. The film spectator, for example, 'learns' there will always be rich and poor people, and that there is no conflict between merit, aspirations, and achievement. The poor will be poor and the rich will be rich because they deserved it, which is no big deal as 'money does not bring happiness' (*You Can't Take It with You*; *Has Anybody Seen My Gal*). Besides, love is stronger than social barriers (*The Designing Woman*; *Titanic*) and, at worst, if this love cannot flourish on earth, then it will in heaven (*Peter Ibbetson*; *A Place in the Sun*).

The theories of passive spectators taking at face value what the cultural industries give them, as well as theories of spectators being 'on drugs' (cultural dopes and dupes), have two forerunners. The first of them is Nietzsche: 'Oh who will narrate to us the whole history of narcotics! – It is almost the history of "culture," the so-called higher culture!' (Nietzsche 1924, 122). Adorno will later express the same type of idea, using the same behaviourist tone that systematically dooms the spectator to be deceived:

> The sound film, far surpassing the theatre of illusion, leaves no room for imagination or reflection on the part of the audience, who is unable to respond within the structure of the film, [nor] yet deviate from its precise detail without losing the thread of the story; hence the film forces its victims to equate it directly with reality.
>
> (Adorno and Horkheimer 1997, 126).

The second, major forerunner is Marx. Cinema participates in 'false consciousness' as the spectator has a wrong idea of his own place in society and of the relation he has to his own material and human environment. Remarkably enough, Marx uses a metaphorical description of vision to express this idea:

> In the act of seeing, there is at all events an actual passage of light from one thing to another, from the external object to the eye. There is a physical relation between physical things. But it is different with commodities. There, the existence of the things *quâ* commodities, and the value relation between the products of labour which stamps them as commodities, have absolutely no connection with their physical properties and with the material relations arising therefrom.
>
> (Marx 1867)

Ideally, we should only exchange commodities obtained through an equivalent quantity of work. But this is not the case with the 'fetishism inherent in commodities', as Marx calls it, which enshrines these commodities in an illusory aura (apart from the labour value of their production). Exactly as the object does not bring light to the eye, the commodity does not offer any special magic power to its buyer. Nowadays, capitalism organizes this commerce of magic by, for example, producing 'limited series' of objects (e.g. DVDs for collectors) whose rarity is artificially created to enhance their value:

> The culture industry perpetually cheats its consumers of what it perpetually promises ... The promise, which is actually all the spectacle consists of, is illusory: all it actually confirms is that the real point will never be reached, that the diner must be satisfied with the menu.
>
> (Adorno and Horkheimer 1997, 139)

But is it legitimate to transpose a Marxist reasoning about commodities onto the question of works of art in general and film in particular? First, as Noël Carroll (1998) has shown, many successful films fight against opposition to change and describe social inequalities, sometimes inciting their spectators to go on struggling. The favourite film of IMDb users (the largest web source on cinema) has long been Frank Darabont's *The Shawshank Redemption* (1994). This 'traditional' film, built as an homage to Hollywood's golden age, does not owe its success (i.e. the recognition of its *use value*, to adopt Marx and Adorno's terminology) to its advertising campaign or to the enthusiasm of critics and academics, but only to word of mouth. And yet it attempts to tell the story of someone who continues to fight, even though he cannot change the unfairness of a world of inequalities of which he is a victim.

By declaring that a film shows, in an illusory way, a certain state of the world (such as 'love triumphs over social inequalities'), a researcher has, in effect, *taken* the spectator's *own place*. He or she produces an interpretation without witnessing what actual spectators *do with* the film, i.e. without witnessing which *usage value(s)* they give it. For, contrary to what Adorno thinks when he only uses the notion of use value for modern high art, the works of cultural industries do have, as *factishes*, a use value as well, and not only one linked with the notion of escapism (I'm exchanging the price of my ticket for a two-hour escape from my concerns). Since Richard Hoggart's *The Uses of Literacy* (1957) and the development of the discipline of cultural studies, the academic world has understood that 'to a rationalized, clamorous, and spectacular production corresponds another production called "consumption," [which] does not manifest itself through its own products, but rather through ways of using the products imposed by a dominant order' (De Certeau 1984, xii–xiii). Many pragmatic and sociological analyses are thus opposed to Marxist–Nietzschean *Kulturpessimismus*. They argue that the spectator is all the less subjected to deceptive illusion when he or she behaves like a poacher (De Certeau 1984, xii), and in our case a textual poacher (Jenkins 1992) who re-encodes narrative information in a private way for his or her own purposes (see Hall 1980) by using image and sound polysemy (see Fiske 1986). Whether or not film has a narcotic power, it is never able to impose its meaning and instead leaves ample room for the agency of its public.

As with the so-called perceptive illusion discussed above, the notion of agency avoids the question of whether a film 'depicts' true or untrue things about the world, and instead focuses on which actions the film can prompt a spectator to undertake when endowing the film with meaning. If, thanks to the film, the spectator discovers sufficient energy to carry out personal projects or solve intimate conflicts, then whether the film offers a true or untrue description is of no importance.[3] In fact, the notion of descriptive illusion holds sway only if one forgets that the meaning of a film is not automatically given, but rather inferred and constructed *in situ* by a spectator who is using screen data merely as a starting point.

LAURENT JULLIER

## Notes

1 'Cézanne wanted to paint this primordial world, and his pictures therefore seem to show nature pure, while photographs of the same landscapes suggest man's works, conveniences, and imminent presence' (Merleau-Ponty 1964, 13–14).
2 That is, a *situation*, in the meaning of an 'organization of experiences' coined by interactionist sociology (see Goffman 1959).
3 See, for example, Will Brooker on *Star Wars*: 'Some kids are inspired to get into computers, filmmaking, or the police force by early exposure to the saga' (2002, 19).

## Works cited

Adorno, Theodor W., and Max Horkheimer. 1997 [1944]. Dialectic of Enlightenment. London and New York: Verso.
Bourdieu, Pierre. 1998. *Practical Reason: On the Theory of Action*. Stanford, CA: Stanford University Press.
Brooker, Will. 2002. *Using the Force: Creativity, Community, and Star Wars Fans*. London and New York: Continuum.
Carroll, Noël. 1998. A Philosophy of Mass Art. Oxford: Clarendon Press.
De Certeau, Michel. 1984. *The Practice of Everyday Life*. Berkeley: University of California Press.
Fiske, John. 1986. 'Television: Polysemy and Popularity'. *Critical Studies in Mass Communication* 3 (4): 391–408.
Freud, Sigmund. 1928. *The Future of an Illusion*. New York: Horace Liveright.
Goffman, Erving. 1959. *The Presentation of Self in Everyday Life*. Garden City, NY: Doubleday Anchor Books.
Gombrich, Ernst H. 1963. Art and Illusion. Princeton, NJ: Princeton University Press.
Hall, Stuart. 1980. 'Encoding/Decoding'. In *Culture, Media, Language*, edited by S. Hall, D. Hobson, A. Lowe, and P. Willis, 128–38. London: Hutchinson.

Hoggart, Richard. 1957. *The Uses of Literacy*. London: Chatto & Windus.

Jenkins, Henry. 1992. Textual Poachers: Television Fans and Participatory Culture. New York: Routledge, Chapman and Hall.

Jullier, Laurent. 2010. 'Should I See What I Believe? Audiovisual Ostrannenie and Evolutionary-Cognitive Film Theory'. In *Ostrannenie*, edited by Annie van den Oever, 119–40. Amsterdam: Amsterdam University Press.

Latour, Bruno. 2011. *On the Cult of the Factish Gods*. Durham, NC: Duke University Press.

Marx, Karl. 1867. *Capital*. Volume One, Part I: 'Commodities and Money': http://www.marxists. org/archive/marx/works/1867-c1/ch01.htm.

Merleau-Ponty, Maurice. 1964. 'Cézanne's Doubt'. In *Sense and Non-Sense*, translated by H. and P.A. Dreyfus. Evanston, IL: Northwestern University Press.

Nietzsche, Friedrich. 1924. *The Joyful Wisdom*. Translated by O. Levy: http://www.archive.org/ details/completenietasch10nietuoft.

Winnicott, Donald W. 1971. *Playing and Reality*. London: Tavistock.

## Further reading

Allen, Richard. 1995. *Projecting Illusion: Film Spectatorship and the Impression of Reality*. New York: Cambridge University Press.

Anderson, Joseph. 1996. *The Reality of Illusion: An Ecological Approach to Cognitive Film Theory*. Carbondale: Southern Illinois University Press.

Anderson, Joseph, and Barbara Anderson, eds. 2005. Moving Image Theory: Ecological Considerations. Carbondale: Southern Illinois University Press.

Carroll, Noël. 1997. 'Fiction, Non-Fiction, and the Film of Presumptive Assertion: A Conceptual Analysis'. In *Film Theory and Philosophy*, edited by Richard Allen and Murray Smith, 173–202. Oxford: Clarendon.

Walton, Kendall. 1990. *Mimesis as Make Believe: On the Foundations of the Representational Arts*. Cambridge, MA: Harvard University Press.

# IMAGINARY SIGNIFIER

French film theorist Christian Metz published a long essay on 'The Imaginary Signifier' in 1975 (Metz 1982). It was the culmination of over a decade of publications on film semiotics. The essay represents Metz's 'second semiotics', the combination of semiotics and psychoanalysis in the study of film and spectatorship.

There is no central argument in 'The Imaginary Signifier'. Rather, Metz investigates some of the ways in which theories of psychoanalysis – from Freud, Lacan, and Melanie Klein – might be useful for understanding the nature of the 'cinema signifier'. He is therefore not especially interested in unpicking psychoanalytic themes in the plots of films, whether explicit or implicit. He focuses instead on the cinema 'signifier'; that is, on questions of how the cinema happens to be meaningful in the first place and also of how audiences in general understand what cinema is and does. In short, one of the main questions he tries to answer is: what do people think they are doing when they 'go to the cinema'?

Metz's question is not a naive one, for he points out that people (generally speaking) are not forced to go to the cinema and indeed they usually must pay money in order to do so. If people stop going to the cinema and stop paying money for the privilege of doing so, then the cinema will quite simply cease to exist. What films must therefore do, argues Metz, is deliver pleasure to their audiences.

> In a social system in which the spectator is not forced physically to go to the cinema ... there is no other solution than to set up arrangements whose aim and effort is to give the spectator the 'spontaneous' desire to visit the cinema and pay for his ticket.
>
> (Metz 1982, 7–8)

In the light of psychoanalytic theory Metz's question thus becomes one which asks: what spontaneous mechanisms are in place which give the spectator the desire to go to the cinema (and to pay money for the experience)? What *psychical* mechanisms, in other words, operate along with the social and economic imperatives that drive any member of the public to go to the cinema? Why might someone feel the need or desire to do such a thing?

In order to answer such broad-ranging questions, Metz has to speculate on what an average viewer might expect from an average 'movie'. And what such a spectator expects, Metz claims, is a fiction film: '[I]t is the film felt ideologically to be ordinary (the fiction film) that serves as a reference point and opens the paradigm [of "what a film is"], and on the contrary the category of "all the rest" groups fewer films and ones that society regards

253

as slightly strange' (39). There are thus 'mainstream' films and this, for Metz, should serve as a marker for what is generally understood as a film in general. 'Every film is a fiction film' is one of Metz's more contentious claims (44).

Slightly less contentious is Metz's more ideologically influenced categorization of the 'ordinary fiction film' as one that covers the traces of its own making (such statements are no doubt influenced by Comolli and Narboni [1990], Baudry [1985], and others). The ordinary fiction film typically functions in the guise of transparency, so that it is far less 'the cinema' that one sees when one goes to the cinema and far more 'the story being portrayed' that is essential to the film experience.

> The fiction film is the film in which the cinematic signifier does not work on its own account but is employed entirely to remove the traces of its own steps, to open immediately on to the transparency of the signified, of a story.
>
> (Metz 1982, 40)

Here are the beginnings of Metz's claim that the cinema signifier is 'imaginary', for it is a signifier that removes the traces of its own steps. It is not 'there' in a material sense, but is instead merely imaginary.

In what way does the cinema spectator make sense of this imaginary signifier, a signifier that is not 'there' but which also must still be there, signifying its absence, signifying by way of its removal? Metz tries to answer this question by asking with what the cinema spectator identifies during a film. He claims that the spectator identifies in a certain way with the characters in a film, but this, Metz cautions, is an identification with the *signifieds* of a film, rather than being any sort of identification with cinema's *signifier*. It is an identification with things that are 'in' the film and not a grounding identification, for there must, claims Metz, be a prior identification to this which in its turn makes identifications with characters possible. Thus he will call this type of identification a *secondary* form of cinematic identification. To identify with that activity or pastime which is that of 'going to the cinema' requires something else, an identification with the situation or expectations which all add up to make a film a *film*.

In order for this identification of the cinema signifier to occur, that identification which then makes the notion of a 'film' possible for the spectator, Metz puts forward a very contentious claim: *I identify with myself*. 'I am myself this place where this really perceived imaginary accedes to the symbolic by its inauguration as the signifier of a certain type of institutionalized social activity called the "cinema"' (48–9). The spectator needs to identify with her/himself as the person who is there and who is watching (and hearing) this socially organized and institutionalized activity known as and understood as the cinema. It is as though on one level – perhaps at a level that psychoanalysis would like to call 'unconscious' – the spectator must declare, while watching a film, 'I am here at the cinema and what I am doing is watching a film'. And if I am here, then the film is there: '[T]he spectator identifies with himself, with himself as a pure act of perception (as wakefulness, alertness): as the condition of possibility of the perceived and hence as a kind of transcendental subject, which comes before every *there is*' (49) (*see* IDENTIFICATION, THEORY OF).

Metz works up to these statements after having compared the cinema screen with a mirror. The reason he does so – and he again follows Jean-Louis Baudry (1985) in this respect – is to bring French psychoanalyst Jacques Lacan's notion of the mirror stage to bear on the cinematic situation (Lacan 2006) (*see* APPARATUS THEORY [BAUDRY]). According to

Lacan's theory, one way to conceive of how the child develops a sense of itself as a distinct and individual person is to consider what occurs when a child first understands that its mirror image is something separate from itself. 'If that is my image there, then I must be here', we might imagine the child thinking to itself. It is in this way that the child, Lacan argues, first gains a sense of 'self', a sense of being able to think to itself 'I am'.

Metz thus examines the cinematic experience alongside the mirror experiences posited by Lacan, for the cinema spectator declares a similar 'I am' in front of the cinema screen to the child in front of the mirror. Metz qualifies the comparison by stating that the experiences are in *some* ways similar, but they are by no means the same. For one, the spectator at the cinema has already gone through the mirror stage so there is certainly no question of the spectator going through the mirror stage again while at the cinema. Secondly, unlike the body-image of the child looking in the mirror, the spectator's own body does not appear there on the cinema screen. Nevertheless, what the spectator does see there are images, and so too does the child see an image in the mirror of the mirror stage.

Metz will examine closely the notion of the cinema's 'images' in order to take his observations to a conclusion. What he emphasizes for much of the essay is that the cinema's qualities are for the most part immaterial: they are in one way or another fictional, fantastical, absent, and removed – they are imaginary. 'What is characteristic of the cinema is not the imaginary it may happen to represent but the imaginary that it *is* from the start, the imaginary that constitutes it as a signifier' (Metz 1982, 44). He argues that this imaginariness of the signifier makes the cinema truly different from other arts and entertainments. While cinema is, he claims, 'more perceptual' than arts like painting, literature, and photography (for cinema's images move and contain sounds too), it is perceptually similar to opera, theatre, and vaudeville or music hall. And yet these other forms differ from the cinema in an important respect (43):

> Their difference from the cinema lies elsewhere: they do not consist of *images*, the perceptions they offer to the eye and the ear are inscribed in a true space (not a photographed one), the same one as that occupied by the public during the performance; everything the audience hear and see is actively produced in their presence, by human beings or props which are themselves present.

The cinema, for its part, is composed of images and nothing of those images that a spectator hears and sees at the cinema can be touched, for we are not in their presence in the way we are with an opera or theatre performance.

Metz extends these observations by claiming that the visual and auditory senses employed by a spectator during a film screening are ones which keep their objects at a distance: to touch, taste, or smell requires coming into contact with objects, while seeing or hearing typically involves maintaining objects at a distance. This distance, combined with the imagistic nature of what the cinema presents to our senses, ultimately means that, Metz argues, 'the screen presents to our apprehension, but absents from our grasp, more "things"' than the other arts (61). The cinema presents and absents things from us at one and the same time.

Metz's major points of comparison are between cinema and theatre. Unlike cinema, the theatre does not engage in this act of simultaneously giving and taking away things. Rather, argues Metz, 'the theatre really does "give" this given, or at least slightly more really: it is physically present, in the same space as the spectator' (61). If what the theatre (or music hall or opera) gives are things which are physically present, the cinema does not: 'The cinema only gives it in effigy, inaccessible from the outset, in a primordial *elsewhere*, infinitely desirable ( = never possessible) on another scene which is that of absence and which nonetheless represents the absent in detail' (61).

The cinema thus becomes, for Metz, a machine for presenting images in a mode of absence. Strangely though, this is why the cinema to some extent seems more real than does the theatre. We know while at the theatre that what we are seeing are props and actors who are performing something in this space here and now, but which gestures to an elsewhere. These are real actions and props directed towards unreal scenes (the action of the play). By contrast, in the cinema the spectator has much more of a sense of looking in on reality because what is seen there are images which are already in some sense unreal. These are unreal scenes and props and settings directed towards unreal scenes (the action of the film). The cinema's primordial elsewhere, its grounding imaginariness, nonetheless infuses that experience with a keenly felt sense of reality. Such is Metz's argument. 'Thus the theatrical fiction is experienced more ... as a set of real pieces of behaviour actively directed at the evocation of something unreal, whereas cinematic fiction is experienced rather as the quasi-real presence of that unreal itself' (67).

Finally, at the end of his long essay, Metz engages in some detail with Freud's psychoanalytic theories of fetishism in order to explain the psychical mechanisms triggered by the cinema's imaginary signifier (Freud 1977). Fetishism, according to Freud, involves the presence of an object invoked by its absence. In the classic scenario, for the child the absence of the mother's penis is invoked as present; an 'imagined', fetishized penis – the signifier of an absent object – is put in place of the absence of a penis. Metz thus claims that the cinema signifier functions in a similar way, 'the quasi-real presence of that unreal itself' (Metz 1982, 67). The logic of the cinema's imaginary signifier is thus equated with the psychoanalytic theory of fetishism. Ultimately it is this kind of logic which provides an answer to Metz's question of why a spectator goes to the cinema. It is, to a large extent, so that the spectator might undergo an experience of pleasure akin to that which is provided by fetishism.

Many scholars have mistakenly criticized Metz as making an argument very similar to that made by Baudry (1985), especially on the relation between the screen and mirror. Joan Copjec (1994), for example, argues that scholars like Metz and Baudry place the cinema spectator in a position of mastery over the cinematic image (21). As a result, this spectator becomes a 'transcendental subject', as Metz puts it, a subject who completes and fills up the image by being in control of it: 'It is I who make the film' is another of Metz's claims (Metz 1982, 48). Against such claims, and drawing on a range of concepts from Lacan, Copjec argues that the cinematic subject is in fact the product of what is *hidden from* that subject's view, that the cinema subject is produced by what it *searches for* in the image but which it cannot find. It is this perennial 'what is missing?' from the image that stimulates a spectator's desire, keeps it open, unstable, and stimulated. Copjec concludes by stating that 'the conflictual nature of Lacan's culpable subject sets it worlds apart from the stable subject of film theory' (Copjec 1994, 38).

Such claims might be well and good for a critique of Baudry, but they simply do not pertain to Metz (Copjec treats these two scholars interchangeably in her essay). Rather, Metz conceives of the cinematic situation as a 'series of mirror-effects' rather than as a mirror *per se* (Metz 1982, 51). Furthermore, Metz already has a conception of the 'gap' which stimulates desire inasmuch as that gap is produced by the spectator's perceptual distance from the screen. For Metz, it is this imaginary object – an object present only as absent – that stimulates a spectator's desire to go to, and to keep going back to, the cinema.

RICHARD RUSHTON

## Works cited

Baudry, J.-L. 1985. 'Ideological Effects of the Basic Cinematographic Apparatus'. In *Movies and Methods*, vol. II, edited by B. Nichols, 531–42. Berkeley: University of California Press.

Comolli, J.-L., and J. Narboni. 1990. 'Cinema/Ideology/Criticism'. In *Cahiers du cinéma, Volume III: The Politics of Representation*, edited by N. Browne, 58–67. London: BFI.

Copjec, J. 1994. 'The Orthopsychic Subject: Film Theory and the Reception of Lacan'. In *Read My Desire: Lacan against the Historicists*, 15–38. New York: MIT Press.

Freud, S. 1977. 'Fetishism'. In *The Pelican Freud Library, Volume 7: On Sexuality*, translated by James Strachey, 351–8. London: Penguin.

Lacan, J. 2006. 'The Mirror Stage as Formative of the *I* Function as Revealed in Psychoanalytic Experience'. In *Ecrits*, translated by B. Fink, 75–81. New York: Norton.

Metz, C. 1982. *Psychoanalysis and Cinema: The Imaginary Signifier*. Translated by C. Britton *et al*. London: Macmillan.

# IMAGINED OBSERVER HYPOTHESIS

The imagined observer hypothesis (IOH) is a label used by philosopher Gregory Currie for the idea that the spectator thinks that he watches the events in the film from the position of the camera (Currie 1995, 164ff.). The strongest version of this can be found in illusionist film theory, which holds that the spectator is made to believe he is present in the diegetic space, watching it from the position of the camera. A weaker version of the theory is that the spectator *imagines* that he watches the events in the film from the camera's position in the diegetic universe without actually believing this. Currie argues that many classical film theorists, such as V.I. Pudovkin (1970; see also Bordwell 1985, 9–12), and contemporary theorists, such as George Wilson (1986, 55–6), support a version of IOH. Currie rejects IOH.

Currie's critique of IOH latches onto a debate in philosophical aesthetics about pictorial representations in general, and whether we imagine seeing what pictures represent. What is at stake in his discussion is what characterizes the relation between the imagination and vision when watching a fiction film. Currie wants to pin down what is essential about film as a visual medium. His philosophy of film (Currie 1995) is regarded as one of the central works in cognitive film theory, typical for this movement in its scepticism towards the psychoanalytic paradigm. Currie rejects psychoanalysis, and his discussion of IOH is one example of critical scrutiny of an idea he sees as influenced by this line of thinking (xiv–xv). IOH is nonetheless important in Currie's account as motivation for his own, rival account of what is distinctive about the spectator's imagining in relation to fiction film. He acknowledges that the question 'What characterizes cinematically induced imaginings?', to which IOH is one reply, is an interesting one.

Currie argues that a consequence of IOH is absurd imaginings. It seems unlikely that I as spectator imagine myself

> on the battlefield, mysteriously immune to the violence around me, lying next to the lovers, somehow invisible to them, viewing Earth from deep space one minute, watching the dinner guests from the ceiling the next[.]
>
> (Currie 1995, 171)

This is what imagining myself seeing from the point of view of the camera would seem to entail. As the world of the film is typically much like the real world, imagining such a magical mode of observation as part of the fictional world would be prohibited. Furthermore, imagining seeing the fictional events from the point of view of the camera would be 'disorienting and distracting, and quite unlike the normal experience of watching the scene' (177).

Another problem IOH gives rise to is how a spectator can imagine himself seeing a murder that is supposed to be unseen in the fiction (173). IOH entails that the spectator imagines himself seeing the events in the fiction (what Currie labels *personal imagining*), but Currie argues against this. The alternative theory Currie proposes is that the spectator imagines *that* the events of the film occur. The type of imagining appropriate to fiction film viewing is *impersonal imagining*. The spectator does not imagine any perceptual relation to the events of the film. He does not imagine seeing or hearing these events, but imagines propositionally – he imagines believing what he sees. One way to formulate this would be to say that the spectator simulates acquiring beliefs, 'the beliefs I would acquire if I took the work I am engaged with for fact rather than fiction. Here I imagine myself acquiring factual knowledge' (148). What the spectator first and foremost imagines when watching fiction film is what is fictional in the story – what would be true if the events of the film were actually taking place. The spectator imagines that Spider-Man can climb walls, for example. It is fictional that he can do so.

So far, this description of the spectator's imaginative activity does not account for the specificity of cinematically induced imaginings, as readers of literature also imagine what is fictional in the story they read. Currie argues that what is particular about film viewing, as compared to reading literature, for example, is that the spectator imagines the events of the film as they are depicted. Just as we have perceptual beliefs about the real world, so we have perceptual imaginings about fiction film. If I see a black cat outside my window, this will make me *believe* that the cat is black. This is a *perceptual belief*, as my perception determines what I believe about the cat. The fiction film makes the spectator *imagine* that the things he sees have such and such qualities – if the film depicts a cat being black, the spectator will imagine that the cat has this property. When watching a fiction film, the spectator has *perceptual imaginings*. This is what is typical of imaginative engagement in fiction film: the spectator's perceptual imaginings are counterfactually dependent on the filmic picture – were the cat depicted otherwise, as black with white spots for example, the spectator would have imagined it otherwise. Fictional film thus encourages perceptual but impersonal imaginings. What the spectator primarily does when watching a fiction film is to imagine propositionally that the events he sees on the screen are such and such as perceived in the film. He does not imagine having a perceptual relation to these events. IOH is right in claiming that imaginings are tied to vision in a special manner when watching film, as compared to reading literature, but wrong in arguing that the spectator imagines seeing the events on the screen from the point of view of the camera. The spectator actually sees the events on the screen, and imagines about them propositionally.

Currie's account avoids putting the spectator in the unlikely position of having to imagine himself in a kind of magical mode of observation in the fictional world, and it avoids absurd imaginings. Nonetheless, his take on these issues remains controversial. For example, one reply to Currie is that the spectator need not imagine the implications of imagining seeing things from the middle of the battlefield, or unseen murders, for example (Walton 1997; 2008), and that it is indeterminate how he has access to the point of view given by the camera (Wilson 1997; 2011). Nonetheless, I will pursue a different line of critical inquiry of Currie's account here (but see also Gaut 2004; Carroll 2006; 2009).

Even if one agrees with him that it is unlikely that the spectator always imagines seeing from the point of view of the camera, and thus discards IOH, one might still argue that the spectator often, or even typically, imagines seeing in another sense: the spectator might typically imagine seeing from the characters' point of view.

Murray Smith argues that the point of view (POV) shot might be seen as a counterexample to Currie's account of impersonal imagining. Smith writes:

> If we were to identify with a character on the basis of a POV shot from that character's vantage-point, that would surely mean that we would imagine seeing the diegesis from just that vantage-point.

(Smith 1997, 421)

To maintain his critique of imagining seeing, Currie must therefore account for the contents of POV shots without stating that the spectator is encouraged to imagine seeing. In relation to the example of a POV shot rendering a character's experience of vertigo in *Vertigo* (Alfred Hitchcock, 1958), he admits that this is an example of imagining seeing, but states that it is an extraordinary case (Currie 1995, 170–1). Smith points out that the POV is not exceptional in the way Currie suggests – it is a common device in fiction film. Smith concludes that Currie's admittance raises more problems for Currie's account than he grants.

Currie's theory is equipped to explain character engagement. Currie does not restrict use of the imagination in relation to fiction film to impersonal imagining. He gives simulation or empathy with the characters a role in watching fiction film. While he refutes personal imagining, and argues that the spectator typically does not imagine anything about himself when watching fiction film, he remains open to empathy, where the spectator imagines experiencing what the character experiences. Through empathy the spectator may have imaginary versions of thoughts and feelings as a result of 'putting [him]self, in imagination, in the character's position' (153; see also Currie 2004, 179). Currie argues that empathy with the characters is not required for imaginative engagement in a fiction film. Frequently, one need not empathize with one or other of the characters in order to imagine propositionally what is fictional in the story. Thus, empathy with characters is given a role in Currie's philosophy of film, but not a prominent one.

A problem at this point is that Currie does not address what relation personal imagining has to empathy. Empathy is not the same as personal imagining. Nevertheless, his critique of personal imagining and imagining seeing may have consequences for his account of empathy, as empathy may also from time to time entail imagining seeing. Currie dismisses personal imagining because, on his account, it entails that the spectator imagines not only the events of the film, but also himself and his own seeing of these events. He argues that the spectator does not imagine himself being in the narrative where the protagonist is (e.g. Currie 1997 and 1999). He seems to assume that if the spectator imagines seeing or hearing the events in the film, this must mean that the spectator imagines himself seeing or hearing this. However, in his critique of Currie's account Kendall L. Walton points out that '[i]magining seeing does not reduce to imagining that I see' (Walton 1997, 64). In Currie's account, imagining seeing seems to be conflated with imagining that 'I imagine seeing', where 'I' and 'seeing' are part of what the spectator imagines. An underlying problem with Currie's discussion of imagining seeing is that it gives no clear account of imaginings that are not of the propositional, impersonal kind.

Giving empathy a more prominent role in his theory could solve some problems in Currie's philosophy of film, such as the question of why fiction films are only sometimes engaging. A fiction film may bore me one day, but watching it again later I may be caught up in its story. The spectator engages in impersonal, perceptual imagining in both cases: he watches the film and imagines the events to be such and such as depicted in the film. What is different when the spectator engages more fully in the film? One reply could be that it is engaging to evaluate the art and argument made by the director. This will, at least momentarily, pull the spectator out of internal, fictional engagement in an external evaluation of the film as an object made by someone (cf. Lamarque and Olsen 1994, 143ff.). Arguably, this mode of film appreciation is more typical of aesthetically trained spectators (cf. Tan 1996, 34, 64ff.). While we as spectators are always aware of the external perspective at some level, more is needed in order to explain ordinary spectators' fiction film engagement.

Another reply is that fiction film experience is particularly engaging when the spectator empathizes with the characters. Although Currie makes a similar observation – pointing out that it is 'when we are able, in imagination, to feel as the character feels that fictions of character take hold of us' (Currie 1995, 153) – he does not accommodate it fully in his theory. Through imagining what one or several characters' experience is like, the spectator may latch onto the experience of seeing and hearing the fictional events from within the fictional universe. As a grenade is heading towards the frightened characters in the middle of a battlefield, for example, the spectator may imagine what the experience is like for them – and simulate the thoughts and feelings evoked by seeing what they see. This kind of internal engagement in the fiction may be at the core of ordinary spectators' idea of an engaging fiction film experience. Furthermore, it may entail imagining seeing, in the sense of imagining the fuller, phenomenal experience of seeing something (Smith 1997; Vaage 2009; 2010).

An intuition behind IOH is that 'putting us in the picture is something that film naturally succeeds in doing unless "distancing" or "alienating" measures are taken by the film maker to prevent it', but Currie argues that 'film does not have this capacity to any marked degree' (Currie 1995, 167; see also Currie 2010, 194). IOH explains this experience of presence in the fictional world by postulating that the spectator imagines seeing from the perspective given by the camera. Nevertheless, the notion of empathy can be used to explain the intuition that we as spectators naturally feel a certain presence in the fictional world, without resorting to any magical modes of observation. Moreover, giving empathy a more prominent role in fiction film engagement is consistent with Currie's view of impersonal, perceptual imagining as a description of the imagination's connection to perception when watching fiction film, and with his critique of IOH.

MARGRETHE BRUUN VAAGE

## Works cited

Bordwell, David. 1985. *Narration in the Fiction Film*. London: Routledge.

Carroll, Noël. 2006. 'Introduction to Film Narrative/Narration'. In *Philosophy of Film and Motion Pictures*, edited by Noël Carroll and Jinhee Choi, 175–84. Malden, MA: Blackwell.

——. 2009. 'Narration'. In *The Routledge Companion to Philosophy and Film*, edited by Paisley Livingston and Carl Plantinga, 196–206. London: Routledge.

Currie, Gregory. 1995. *Image and Mind: Film, Philosophy and Cognitive Science*. Cambridge: Cambridge University Press.

——. 1997. 'The Film Theory That Never Was: A Nervous Manifesto'. In *Film Theory and Philosophy*, edited by Richard Allen and Murray Smith, 42–59. Oxford: Oxford University Press.

——. 1999. 'Narrative Desire'. In *Passionate Views: Film, Cognition, and Emotion*, edited by Carl Plantinga and Greg M. Smith, 183–99. Baltimore, MD: Johns Hopkins University Press.

———. 2004. *Arts and Minds*. Oxford: Clarendon Press.

———. 2010. *Narratives and Narrators: A Philosophy of Stories*. Oxford: Oxford University Press.

Gaut, Berys. 2004. 'The Philosophy of the Movies: Cinematic Narration'. In *The Blackwell Guide to Aesthetics*, edited by Peter Kivy, 230–53. Oxford: Blackwell.

Lamarque, Peter, and Stein Haugom Olsen. 1994. *Truth, Fiction, and Literature: A Philosophical Perspective*. Oxford: Clarendon Press.

Pudovkin, V.I. 1970 [1926]. *Film Technique and Film Acting*. New York: Grove.

Smith, Murray. 1997. 'Imagining from the Inside'. In *Film Theory and Philosophy*, edited by Richard Allen and Murray Smith, 412–30. Oxford: Oxford University Press.

Tan, Ed S. 1996. *Emotion and the Structure of Narrative Film: Film as an Emotion Machine*. Mahwah, NJ: Lawrence Erlbaum.

Vaage, Margrethe Bruun. 2009. 'The Role of Empathy in Gregory Currie's Philosophy of Film'. *British Journal of Aesthetics* 49: 109–28.

———. 2010. 'Fiction Film and the Varieties of Empathic Engagement'. *Midwest Studies in Philosophy* 34: 158–79.

Walton, Kendall L. 1997. 'On Pictures and Photographs: Objections Answered'. In *Film Theory and Philosophy*, edited by Richard Allen and Murray Smith, 60–75. Oxford: Oxford University Press.

———. 2008. 'Depiction, Perception and Imagination'. In *Marvelous Images: On Values and the Arts*. New York: Oxford University Press.

Wilson, George M. 1986. *Narration in Light: Studies in Cinematic Point of View*. Baltimore, MD: Johns Hopkins University Press.

———. 1997. '*Le Grand Imagier* Steps Out: The Primitive Basis of Film Narration'. *Philosophical Topics* 25: 295–318.

———. 2011. *Seeing Fictions in Film: The Epistemology of Movies*. Oxford: Oxford University Press.

# INAESTHETICS

## A Platonist film

Film has clearly contributed a good deal to Alain Badiou's philosophy – as the title of an interview with him implies: 'Le Cinéma m'a beacoup donné' ('Cinema Has Given Me So Much'; see Badiou 2010, 13–40). Though his engagement with it has not been as systematic as it has been with music, theatre, and literature, since the 1970s Badiou has written in excess of thirty pieces on cinema in general as well as on particular films, some of them quite brief, others prolonged reflections on the power of cinema as a form of philosophical thought and experimentation. Whereas the other visual arts have been mostly ignored by Badiou – he acknowledges this as a blind-spot in his work – film has been a constant companion in his articulation of art as a form of truth-making event. As Alex Ling has written, 'cinema plays an important ... role in Badiou's proclaimed recommencement of philosophy under the aegis of a return to Plato' (Ling 2010, 2). And Badiou himself has recently stated in a talk, entitled 'Cinema as Democratic Emblem', that 'there is a clear requistion of philosophy by cinema – or of cinema by philosophy', and this relation, he maintains, must be tackled in terms of Platonism: film as the creation of unworldly truths (see Badiou 2010, 375). By 'unworldly truths', Badiou means those eternal verities – often mathematical in form – that cannot be directly experienced through our worldly senses but only intelligently grasped through a non-sensory act of mind.

Of course, these persistent references to Platonism raise what is the perpetual hobgoblin for many working in the interdisciplinary field of film and philosophy: is cinema only being used here to illustrate philosophy rather than genuinely create it? At the heart of this question is the concern that cinema is reduced to the role of Grand Illustrator: the problem of free will in *Minority Report* (Spielberg, 2002); of justice and virtue in *Crimes and Misdemeanours* (Allen, 1989); of mortality in *The Seventh Seal* (Bergman, 1957); and so on. Here, there is only a one-way inquisition of film *by* philosophy. The claim that film can *also* philosophize in original ways (one that Badiou also makes), on the other hand, implies that it is doing more than simply illustrating prevailing ideas or debates, but thinking through its *own* visual and auditory modes of logic. This shared capacity for thought would be a proper, reciprocal relationship between the two. With Badiou, the question of reciprocity is all the more pertinent inasmuch as he argues that because film does in fact rehearse Plato's arguments – especially those concerning the immaterial, non-sensory nature of truth – *it is being philosophical in the only way that it, or indeed anything else, can be.*

This last idea is captured in the following formula: film can create truths *for* philosophy no less than any other art form. Indeed, for Badiou, philosophy is wholly dependent on other fields, or 'conditions', for its truths: science, politics, art, and love.

Philosophy itself does not produce truth, but only collects together the truths that are created within these fields in any particular era. Philosophy is conditioned by the local truths of these other, non-philosophical domains, one of which, art, includes film as well. His neologism of 'inaesthetics' attempts to inaugurate a new relationship between philosophy and art, one of philosophy's submission to *its* truths and modes of thinking. There is no philosophy *of* art, as the older name of 'aesthetics' implied (nor indeed is there one *of* science, *of* love, or *of* politics). If aesthetics traditionally denoted the philosophical practice that stood in judgement over art, adjudicating what counts as true and false, as the beautiful and the sublime, then inaesthetics reverses the relationship. Film, here, instructs philosophy on these topics.

## Subtractive cinema

Badiou's writings on film, recently gathered together in a volume starkly entitled *Cinéma*, mostly comprise short, left-wing (that is, Maoist) readings of various films, old and new, alongside brief aphoristic or manifesto-like interventions into the French film theory scene. Among the more explicitly film-philosophical pieces, probably the most important is 'The False Movements of Cinema' (Badiou 2004, 78–88).[1] Here, Badiou finally offers us his ontology of film, though it is one which, characteristically, says very little about film – a minimalist ontology. For Badiou, almost all ontologies (including cinematic ones) are 'generative' – they always add their own philosophical history to the object. By that, Badiou understands them to frame their ontology within a set of presuppositions about film and philosophy (what is true, real, art, and so on). His own ontology is 'subtractive' – it says as little as possible about the object: less rather than more. Behind this stance is Badiou's fundamental view that ontology is a non-philosophical discourse. In fact, ontology, the science of being as such, belongs to mathematics, one of philosophy's 'conditions' in his view (Mullarkey 2006, chapter 3). The truth of an object as such, then, is not found in what can be said of its *qualities* (which, he believes, are only our subjective impressions of it), but in as little as can be said of it at all, that is, *only* in what can be said of it quantitatively or mathematically. A subtractive ontology strips away our subjective, additive, qualitative impressions of the object to find the thing itself, and though this need not literally entail using mathematical symbolism, the language of an object, even an artwork, must aspire to express as little as possible in case it only produces individual illusions. In other words, the language must be as objective as possible, mathematical models – set theory for instance – offering the best examples of such a depersonalized approach.

With this background in mind, then, the little that Badiou does say about cinema is significant, for he gives it an even more subtractive characterization than the other arts. Indeed, cinema is the point of intersection of the other six arts according to Badiou, having no essence of its own save for the barest outline of what minimal essence there is in literature, theatre, music, painting, dance, and sculpture. Film cuts out and splices together these minimal essences. As 'The False Movements of Cinema' puts it:

> Cinema is the seventh art in a very particular sense. It does not add itself to the other six while remaining on the same level as them. Rather, it implies them – cinema is the 'plus-one' of the arts. It operates on the other arts, using them as its starting point, in a movement that subtracts them from themselves.
>
> (Badiou 2004, 79)

Badiou does admit that there is, in fact, no way of moving from one art to another; 'the arts are closed' to each other, and no painting could ever become a piece of music. Yet, all the same, cinema is still the 'organization' of just such an impossible movement among the arts. Only it works by subtraction, not addition. This makes cinema *the* impure art. It is, he says, 'internally and integrally contaminated by its situation as the "plus-one" of arts'. In Visconti's *Death in Venice* (1971), for example, alongside a script based on the novel by Thomas Mann, we also have the intersection of various other arts: Mahler's music, artistic echoes of Venetian style, pictorial themes from Guardi and Canaletto, literary themes from Rousseau and Proust, and the acting of Dirk Bogarde – especially through his face (see Badiou 2004, 82, 86, 84).

However, leaving film with no essence of its own (save as the intersection or 'plus-one' of the other arts) also leaves philosophers with very little to say *about* film. Certainly, recounting the qualities of a film is insufficient:

> It is clear that film criticism is forever suspended between the chatter of empathy, on the one hand, and historical technicalities, on the other. Unless it is just a question of recounting the plot (the fatal novelistic impurity) or of singing the actors' praises (the theatrical impurity). Is it really so easy to speak about a film?
>
> (Badiou 2004, 83)

Film itself, Badiou continues, 'operates through what it withdraws from the visible', through editing, framing, through holding up or suspending movement: all in all, 'the controlled purge of the visible' (Badiou 2004, 78). But, then, he asks, 'what here is, strictly speaking, the film?':

> After all, cinema is nothing but takes and editing. There is nothing else. What I mean is this: There is nothing else that would constitute 'the film'. It is therefore necessary to argue that, viewed from the vantage point of an axiomatic judgment, a film is what exposes the passage of the idea in accordance with the take and the editing.
>
> (Badiou 2004, 86)

Given that there is nothing to film other than a subtraction from the other arts, such that it is subtraction and impurity in person, film can only *do* rather than *be*; it can only be the *passage of ideas* rather than have an idea of itself (an essence). Film *is* simply thought on its way to philosophy (rather than the other way about). Against normative judgements of film ('this is good', 'this is beautiful'), Badiou proposes an *axiomatic* attitude that inquires into 'the effects for thought' of each particular film. We don't ask what the film is, but rather what it makes us think, how it transports ideas: 'to speak about a film axiomatically comes down to examining the consequences of the proper mode in which an Idea is treated thus by *this* particular film' (Badiou 2004, 84).

## Anti-image cinema

Despite this 'inaesthetical' approach, however, it is arguable whether Badiou continues to fix cinema within a strict and traditional aesthetic domain (it is the 'seventh art' after all for him too), and whether his method is manipulative in various ways, choosing very specific films (mostly from the European canon – Murnau, Welles, Visconti, Tati, Straub, etc.) that fit his Platonist approach. One apparant exception is the essay 'Dialectics of the Fable' that tackles three science-fiction films, *Cube*, *The Matrix*, and *eXistenZ*, which were all released in France in 1999. Here, Badiou tells us that cinema

> can only put philosophy to the test with some degree of rigour if it demands *a variation in the regime of the sensible*. Basically, we must verify that the cinema enjoys a certain aptitude for the concept, once it has the power to render the certainty of the visible visibly uncertain.
>
> (Badiou 2008, 21)

The art of cinema now lies precisely in 'showing that it is only cinema, that its images only testify to the real to the extent that they are *manifestly* images'. This is the reason why Badiou concludes his essay by commending *The Matrix*'s philosophy over that of the other two films, because its challenge to 'the image on the basis of the image itself, in the direction of its foundational beyond, is the very question of cinema'. Or, to be precise, *The Matrix* advances 'the most robust' cinematic inquiry *because* it is 'the Platonist one'. No image of any one actual horse existing in the world will match the perfect concept of a horse ('horseness'), which can only be grapsed through intellect – a concept that consequently allows us to recognize each of the myriad different kinds of horse we percieve with our senses as, nonetheless, examples of horse (see Badiou 2009, 18).

Accordingly, *The Matrix* is philosophical because it repeats Plato's *anti-imagistic*, written thought, and not because it possesses its own cinematic one. Here, it seems that Badiou requisitions film for his own philosophy (or his own interpretation of Plato's philosophy). That said, however, Badiou still offers us a significant attempt to think through what it means for cinema to develop its own aesthetics (and even philosophy, more broadly construed), 'bottom up', so to speak, rather than have a theory *of* film imposed upon it 'top down', from some form of philosophical master-discourse. The irony, of course, is that this attempt should be implemented under the 'aegis' of a heavenly (i.e. top-down) Platonist approach, though Badiou would argue that this stance remains the only coherent method available, given the uniquely bare, subtractive ontology that Platonism provides. Whether this unadorned, quasi-mathematical/quantitative perspective is sufficient to film's more qualitative aspects remains debatable. For Badiou, the visual and sound qualities of cinema are inessential (and illusory) – in film there are only 'takes and editing'; for many other film theorists, of course, colour and sound, for example, cannot be subtracted from a film without losing something essential in the work. In Badiou's eyes though, what is less, or minimal, is also what is most true.[2]

JOHN MULLARKEY

## Notes

1  This text was originally published in *L'Art du cinéma* 4: 1–5, reprinted in Badiou (2010, 147–54).
2  For more on Badiou's notion of truth in relation to his film philosophy, see Mullarkey (2010, chapter 5).

## Works cited

Badiou, Alain. 2004. *Handbook of Inaesthetics*. Translated by Alberto Toscano. Stanford, CA: Stanford University Press.

——. 2008. 'Dialectics of the Fable: Philosophical Myths and Cinema', translated by Alberto Toscano. *Science Fiction Film and Television* 1 (1): 15–23; 'Dialectique de la Fable'. In Badiou, *Cinéma*, 307–21.

——. 2009. *Logic of Worlds*. Translated by Alberto Toscano. London: Continuum.

——. 2010. *Cinéma: Textes rassemblés et présentés par Antoine de Baecque*. Paris: Nova Editions.

Ling, Alex. 2010. *Badiou and Cinema*. Edinburgh: Edinburgh University Press.

Mullarkey, John. 2006. *Post-Continental Philosophy: An Outline*. London: Continuum.

——. 2010. *Philosophy and the Moving Image: Refractions of Reality*. Basingstoke: Palgrave Macmillan.

# INTERFACE

The cultural theory of Slavoj Žižek is founded on a number of philosophical schools of thought: German idealism (especially Hegel's dialectical philosophy), Marxism, and Lacanian psychoanalysis. His writings on film are numerous (Žižek 1992; 1993; 2001). Here I will focus on his concept of the 'interface', which he developed in section 1 of his book *The Fright of Real Tears*, devoted to the Polish film director Krzysztof Kieślowski (Žižek 2001). Section 1 is called 'The Universal: Suture Revisited' (2001, 13–68), and its theory of the interface is based on a series of interrelated concepts: 'negativity', 'the universal', 'the particular', 'hegemony', 'suture', and 'symptom'. We shall look at each in turn.

## Negativity

Žižek inherits from Hegel and Lacan a philosophy of negativity – a philosophy founded on alienation, contradiction, division, and instability. Negativity is manifest in the logic of the Hegelian dialectic, which is premised on the contradiction between opposing ideas. Hegel's dialectic is a dynamic model of transformation that proceeds from an idea to its negation. Crucially, the negation does not simply extinguish the initial idea; instead, the negation absorbs or 'sublates' it. What this means is that, in negating the initial idea, the dialectic preserves some aspects of it. For Žižek, concepts are founded on the dialectic. They are not stable, fixed entities, but are in constant transformation, for they contain their own negation within themselves. This negativity triggers the necessity for fantasy and ideology, which attempt to repress the negativity and create the *impression* of totality, fullness, and stability. Fantasy and ideology are therefore necessary because concepts only gain value, meaning, and significance when this negativity is concealed. But these attempts to conceal necessarily fail; it is impossible to achieve fullness and stability within a system that contains within itself its own negation. Negativity therefore exists at the core of concepts, which are never fixed.

## The universal and the particular

Žižek's main aim in 'The Universal: Suture Revisited' is to conceptually link up the concept of suture with the universal, the particular, hegemony, and the symptom. Before outlining the role of suture, we first need to address the concepts of the universal and the particular, and specify their relationship. For Žižek, the concept of the universal can only be understood in relation to the particular. Their conjunction results in a 'concrete universal', which combines universal abstract truths with particular (empirical, historical) facts; that is, the universal is an empty category, but is filled in with particular facts. Žižek's main point is that the particular can never adequately manifest the universal; the particular struggles with and displaces the universal (2001, 26). The universal is not, therefore, a transcendental, static category which is filled in by particular substances; instead, we *begin* with various concrete instances, which at various times temporarily become universal. However, there is always a remainder or excess between the universal and the particular (the symptom, discussed below).

## Hegemony

Hegemony is a temporary moment of stability created between diverse contingent groups within an otherwise unstable society. By means of consent, the diverse groups temporarily adopt the ideology of the ruling group as the universal norm. Therefore, it is via hegemony that the universal is temporarily filled in with a particular substance. Consensus is created by welding together the diverse groups into the ideology of the dominant group.

## Suture

In Žižek's formulation, negativity, the universal, the particular, and hegemony all follow the logic of suture:

> *suture* ... concerns precisely the gap between the Universal and the Particular: it is this gap that is ultimately 'sutured'.
>
> (Žižek 2001, 31)

Because the concrete can never adequately signify the universal, a permanent gap or split opens up, which can only be sutured temporarily. Suture is therefore a general conceptual process of hegemony that temporarily brings together the universal and the particular. In the cinema, suture joins together an individual spectator and universal but empty 'subject position' inscribed in each film (*see* CONTEMPORARY FILM THEORY); their conjunction, in which the individual spectator temporarily fills the universal subject position, creates an impression of coherence and unity in both the film and the spectator.

The spectator is therefore sutured into a film by temporarily taking up the universal subject position. This is achieved via the process of transformation: the transformation of a spectator's vision from the film's *objective level* to its *subjective level*. The objective level describes the look of the camera outside the fiction, as in a shot of a character; the subjective level describes the camera representing the look of a character inside the fiction, as in a reverse or counter-shot of the objective shot of a character (*see* SUTURE). This transformation takes place by means of the spectator identifying with the character's look on the subjective level, rather than the camera's look on the objective level, thereby suturing the spectator into the film. Through the transformative process of identification, the camera's look is negated by the character's look. However, this process of transformation is not fixed and static, but is continually restaged throughout a film.

In 'The Universal: Suture Revisited', Žižek collects examples from a variety of films in which the suturing process clearly breaks down:

(1) *Impossible subjectivity*, which subverts the standard, straightforward transformation of an objective shot into a subjective shot, as in the murder of Arbogast, as he falls down the stairs in the Bates house in *Psycho* (1960) (2001, 35–6); or the birds' apparent point of view of the burning of the petrol station in *The Birds* (1963) (2001, 36). In these examples, the subjective shot is not controlled by a character inside the fiction, and therefore the suture does not take place.

(2) The *sudden intrusion of a violent event* in the transformation of the objective shot into a subjective shot, as in the moment in *The Birds* when Melanie in the rowing boat on Bodega bay is suddenly struck on the head by a sea gull (2001, 38).

(3) The *unexpected objectivization of a subjective shot*, as when a character enters their own point of view shot (Žižek mentions examples from Kieslowski's *Blind Chance* [1981] and Antonioni's *Cronaca di un amore* [1950]; 2001, 38–9).

(4) *Interface*, a concept Žižek invents to name the new problematic data he examines, which consists of the *combination of the subjective and objective in the same shot*, which thereby takes on a spectral/fantasmatic dimension (an imaginary scenario which stages an impossible scene).

## Interface

Although interface is the fourth type of failed suture, it also stands in for all four, as the name of the process of failed suture in general. 'Interface' names the moment that suture does not quite work. More positively, it names a fantasmatic or impossible dimension.

How does interface differ from standard suture? The term 'interface' is defined by the *Oxford English Dictionary* as 'a surface lying between two portions of matter or space, and forming their common boundary'. In chemistry, for example, interface names a common boundary between two substances (air/liquid, liquid/solid, etc.). In cinematic terms, Žižek implies that two different substances come into contact, although the contact is not seamless, is not completely sealed at the boundary. The interface 'operates at a more radical level than the standard suture procedure: it takes place when suturing no longer works' (2001, 52). In the interface, the exchange between the two 'substances' – the universal and particular, or the subjective and objective shots – fails to suture; the gap between them is not filled in. The interface is a form of artificial suturing, in which the normally invisible boundary becomes visible.

For Žižek interface is manifest as a shot that contains its own counter-shot – the two levels of suture are represented in the same frame:

> [I]nterface could appear as a simple condensation of shot and reverse-shot within the same shot; but it is not only that, since it adds to the included reverse-shot a *spectral* dimension, evoking the idea that there is no cosmos, that our universe is not in itself fully ontologically constituted, and that, in order to maintain an appearance of consistency, an interface-artificial moment must suture-stitch it (a kind of stage-prop that fills in the gap, like the printed background that closes off reality).
>
> (Žižek 2001, 52–3)

Žižek develops what he means by the added spectral dimension: 'when the gap can no longer be filled in by an additional signifier, it is filled in by a spectral *object*, in a shot which, in the guise of the spectral screen, includes its own counter-shot. In other words, when, in the exchange of shots and counter-shots, a shot occurs to which there is no counter-shot, the only way to fill this gap is by producing a shot which contains its own counter-shot' (2001, 54).

Žižek's main example is what he calls a 'double interface' in *Opfergang* (Veit Harlan, 1944). In the final moments of the film, Albrecht and his mistress Aels are lying in separate beds – Albrecht in hospital recovering from typhus, and Aels at home dying. Yet, they 'meet' in a fantasmatic space in which they say goodbye to each other. Žižek calls this the 'supremely condensed "suturing" shot/counter shot' (2001, 43):

> [O]n the right side of the screen, we get the close-up of the dying Aels, and, on the left side, the American shot of Albrecht, these two appearances communicating … Albrecht tells Aels the big secret that he really loves [his wife] Octavia and that he is here to bid her [Aels] farewell; after a mysterious exchange about what is real and what a mere phantasmagoric appearance (a kind of reflexive comment on what we see), Aels wishes him the best of luck in his marriage; then, Albrecht's image disappears, so that we see just a slightly blurred image of her as an island of light on the right side of the screen, surrounded by blue darkness. This image gets gradually more and more blurred – she dies.
>
> (Žižek 2001, 43)

Žižek tries to determine whose fantasy this image belongs to. As Aels's fantasy, the image represents the real Aels and her fantasy image of Albrecht. But Žižek argues that this shot of Aels and Albrecht can be codified at a higher level as Albrecht's fantasy. His fantasy therefore absorbs and mediates Aels plus Aels's fantasy of him. He fantasizes about Aels forgiving him, in order to rescue his marriage: 'The two fantasies are thus interwoven in a kind of spatial warp, and this impossible fantasy of the double sacrifice provides the only consequent solution to the male problem of being divided between a loving wife and a loving mistress – it provides a formula for getting out of the deadlock without betraying anyone' (2001, 48). Žižek concludes that: 'Shot and counter-shot are here not only combined within the same shot – it is *one and the same* image which is *at the same time* the shot (of the hallucinating Aels) and the counter-shot (what appears as a counter-shot to Albrecht in his hospital bed)' (2001, 49). In other moments of interface, the spectral fantasy is introduced into everyday reality. In *Opfergang* the spectral fantasy takes over completely, embedding one fantasy into another.

As a spectral screen, the interface is a visible flat surface area between the two levels of suture: the universal on one side, and the particular on the other side. As a visible surface, the interface cannot efface traces of the outside; it remains visible. Its opacity produces a supplement, an excess, what Žižek calls the symptom, or the exception.

## Symptom (the exception, individual)

In suture, there is always an excess, something left over that 'sticks out'. In philosophical terms, the symptom is the failure of the particular to completely stand in for the universal. (In Lacanian terms, the symptom is a surplus value: the *objet petit a*.) The symptom exists between the universal and particular, holding them together while blocking their complete assimilation.

## Critique

'The Universal: Suture Revisited' successfully presents an expanded theory of suture, one explicitly premised on the logic of the Hegelian dialectic, hegemony, and the concrete universal. Many reviewers of *The Fright of Real Tears* celebrated Žižek's bravura performance in bringing high theory, European culture, and American popular culture together, while denouncing his lack of a specific film studies perspective. David Bordwell (2005) called it a book of 'impressionistic criticism', 'a fairly conventional book of free-associative film interpretation'. These criticisms are levelled at the bulk of the book devoted to Kieslowski, although Todd McGowan (2007), Robert Bird (2004), and Matthew Flisfeder (2011) do suggest that there is more to the book than mere impressionistic criticism.

The section of the book devoted to suture encounters a danger in the formulation of the standard theory, of being reduced to a particular instance: shot/reverse shot for the standard theory, a single shot combining the subjective and objective for Žižek's concept of suture as interface. Nonetheless, the broadly conceptualized notion of suture as interface is sufficiently different from the standard theory; it thereby transforms our pre-existing ideas, and is sufficiently distinct from the standard conception.

WARREN BUCKLAND

## Works cited

Bird, Robert. 2004. 'The Suspended Aesthetic: Slavoj Žižek on Eastern European Film'. *Studies in East European Thought* 56 (4): 357–82.

Bordwell, David. 2005. 'Slavoj Žižek: Say Anything': http://www.davidbordwell.net/essays/zizek.php.

Flisfeder, Matthew. 2011. 'Between Theory and Post-theory; or, Slavoj Žižek in Film Studies and out'. *Canadian Journal of Film Studies = Revue canadienne d'études cinématographiques* 20 (2): 75–94.

McGowan, Todd. 2007. 'Introduction: Enjoying the Cinema'. *International Journal of Žižek Studies* 1 (3): 1–13: http://zizekstudies.org/index.php/ijzs/article/view/57/119.

Žižek, Slavoj, ed. 1992. *Everything You Always Wanted to Know about Lacan (but Were Afraid to Ask Hitchcock)*. London: Verso.

——. 1993. *Enjoy Your Symptom! Jacques Lacan in Hollywood and out*. New York: Routledge.

——. 2001. *The Fright of Real Tears: Krzysztof Kieślowski between Theory and Post-theory*. London: British Film Institute.

## Further reading

Buckland, Warren. 2012. *Film Theory: Rational Reconstructions*, chapter 8. Abingdon: Routledge.

Taylor, Paul A. 2010. *Žižek and the Media*. Cambridge: Polity.

# LONG TAKE

Equating the essence of cinema with human life itself, Italian filmmaker Pier Paolo Pasolini once declared: 'The substance of cinema is therefore an endless long take, as is reality to our senses for as long as we are able to see and feel (a long take that ends with the end of our lives); and this long take is nothing but the reproduction of the language of reality' (1980, 5). As a term the *long take* refers to the relatively extended temporal duration of an unedited cinematic shot. Along with scale-oriented concepts like depth of field or the close-up, there is no precise numerical value that qualifies a filmic sequence as being 'long' (or 'deep' or 'close'). Its definition depends on the textual (within a given film) and extra-textual (compared to other films across cultural and historical traditions) contexts in which it occurs. One could argue that this variability contributes to its rich status across various writings on cinema, allowing film theorists to speculate about what ontologically and epistemologically constitutes a long take. Even more pertinent than its inexact nature, however, as Pasolini's words tellingly suggest, is discourse claiming that the long take is bound up with cinema's ability to engage powerfully with real life.

## The long evolution

As a cinematic unit, the long take intersects with issues of editing and cinematography, and, in turn, the articulation of time and space. In reviewing its position in film theory, it is helpful to offer an analogy: depth of field is to space as the long take is to time (*see* DEPTH OF FIELD). Both technical devices allow a viewer to see into and linger on the image and what it contains, coinciding with what we might think of, and perhaps even problematize, as a patient kind of spectatorship. Both the long take and depth of field often go hand in hand in theories of film. The long take also is often contrasted with a montage style, a quick-cutting style of images based on a Gestalt principle of juxtaposition, elaborately theorized and practised by Soviet filmmakers Sergei Eisenstein and Lev Kuleshov (*see* MONTAGE THEORY II [SOVIET AVANT-GARDE]). One can observe these connections and disconnections by closely considering *Cahiers du cinéma* critic and theorist André Bazin's figuring of the long take in his writing about cinema.

Bazin discusses the long take in a number of essays, and especially important components of his approach appear in a famous text, 'The Evolution of the Language of Cinema'. This essay is widely cited in different critical discussions in relation to a wide range of topics in film studies – from semiotics, historiography, and realism to sound, cinematography, and editing. But, for present purposes, we can focus on the ways in which Bazin develops an account of cinema that reserves a privileged rhetorical place for the long

273

take. Later I will consider Daniel Morgan's reframing of Bazin's film theory and its reception, changing the status of the long take in film theory.

Note that the use of the word 'evolution' in the title of Bazin's essay suggests steady, incremental, and continuous movement, like a long-take progression through time. 'The Evolution' essay opens with Bazin declaring his plan: 'holding it to be less an objective statement than a working hypothesis, I will distinguish, in the cinema between 1920 and 1940, between two broad and opposing trends: those directors who put their faith in the image and those who put their faith in reality. By "image" I here mean, very broadly speaking, everything that the representation on screen adds to the object there represented' (1967, 24). With these words, Bazin is often understood to characterize Soviet montage directors and German expressionists as those filmmakers who have 'put their faith in the image'. For these filmmakers, the artistic process involves *doing things with and to* the cinematic image – whether creating fantastic visual effects and distortions or by editing images in provocative ways to generate new forms of expression. Bazin contrasts this mode of filmmaking with directors who, rather than constructing meaning by approaching the cinematic image as a sort of plastic material to be sculpted, have a different relationship to the image. This other relationship involves a 'faith in reality', allowing the camera to act as a tool that observes and records, rather than interferes with or reconstructs, the objects, contexts, and scenes it encounters. Bazin favours an image that 'is evaluated not according to what it adds to reality but what it reveals of it', an image that provides the viewer with enough time to discover 'reality' for him or herself (28). A similar division of film history into two camps was elaborated upon earlier in the same decade by Siegfried Kracauer, who proposed 'two main tendencies' of filmmaking – a 'realist' tradition that could be traced back to the early actualities of the Lumière brothers, and a 'formalist' mode originating in the early trick films of George Méliès – a binary which resurfaces in film theories to this day, and which has been particularly intriguingly revisited and problematized in an amassing body of scholarship examining documentary animation.

Focusing on later decades in film history, Bazin writes of films by Erich von Stroheim, F.W. Murnau, and Robert Flaherty, claiming:

> In their films, montage plays no part, unless it be the negative one of inevitable elimination where reality superabounds. The camera cannot see everything at once but it makes sure not to lose any part of what it chooses to see. What matters to Flaherty, confronted with Nanook hunting the seal, is the relation between Nanook and the animal; the actual length of the waiting period. Montage could suggest the time involved. Flaherty however confines himself to showing the actual waiting period; the length of the hunt is the very substance of the image, its true object. Thus in the film this episode requires one set-up. Will anyone deny that it is thereby much more moving than a montage by attraction?
>
> (Bazin 1967, 26–7)

## Styleless style, a standard reading

A reader might first of all note that Bazin's writing style contains references not to philosophers and scholars, as film theory often does, but instead is textured with passionate descriptions of specific film scenes, and its tone is marked by a spirit of cinephilia found in film criticism (Flaherty's style is 'much more moving'). From this short passage, a reader can also discern some components of Bazin's film theory. The meaning of this scene from *Nanook of the North* (1922) depends on, even equals, its extended temporal duration ('the length … is the very substance'). Portraying a sequence in a long take is a way for the filmmaker to seemingly transport the spectator to the very scene unfolding before the camera. Bazin feels that Flaherty's long take brings us there alongside both him and Nanook, compelling us to observe and wait, and to feel the weight of time and the presence of the present.

Note, too, how Bazin imagines an alternative, hypothetical way of filming this scene to more fully appreciate how Flaherty has in fact decided to film it: 'Montage *could* suggest the time involved' (emphasis mine). In other words, if we were to see a succession of shots in sequential stages of the progress in the hunt, the spectator would still discern that Nanook is involved in a time-consuming hunt, and the film would not thereby betray its documentary pact with the viewer that s/he is ethnographically witnessing a 'real' Inuit Eskimo perform a routine survival ritual. But, as Bazin would have us bear in mind, such a hypothetical montage sequence would not capture the impact of the long take and its power, which allows us to almost share Nanook's experience of the waiting that structures the *labour* of the hunt, being *in* a hunt.

We might more generally understand the strategy Bazin draws upon here as setting the relationship between theory and practice into sharper focus: it can often be instructive to conceptualize film theory as a reverse engineering of sorts of film practice. If a filmmaker faces a series of decisions when making a film, a film theorist or analyst views the final film and then can imagine another set of hypothetical images or shooting styles that could have been employed in order to better understand what it has become. Indeed, the most useful way to approach the theoretical possibilities of the long take might be found in considering the theoretical possibilities and limits of montage. For this reason, one can find more on Bazin's theory of the long take in his essay 'The Virtues and Limitations of Montage', where he again mentions *Nanook* alongside other notable long takes in film history in films such as Orson Welles's *The Magnificent Ambersons* (1942) and Alfred Hitchcock's *Rope* (1948).

A well-known formulation by Bazin in this essay comes in the context of his discussion of Italian neorealism. He writes that 'neorealism tends to give back to the cinema a sense of the ambiguity of reality' (1967, 37). Bazin's interpreters generally stress that Bazin's idea about the 'ambiguity of reality' involves neorealism being characterized as a 'styleless style' – with long takes that don't interrupt the flow of time, deep space, and action by non-professional actors in real locations utilizing no staging or special lighting. With the crucial help of a long-take style, neorealist cinema is designed to preserve the experiences of everyday life, bound up as they are with no clear definitions and narratives (hence the 'ambiguity').

## Reassessing Bazin's realism

The account of Bazin's film theory I have so far provided roughly corresponds to what Daniel Morgan, in his essay 'Rethinking Bazin: Ontology and Realist Aesthetics' (2006), describes as the 'standard reading'. Morgan argues that this interpretation of Bazin, while it follows from important passages and beliefs found in his writing, does not fundamentally hold up when weighing the entire oeuvre of his criticism. In turn, Morgan claims, this also explains why Bazin is largely dismissed in many subsequent discussions of film theory. As he puts it, Bazin's 'intelligence and insight in grappling with difficult problems of style and ontology has been misunderstood and therefore mostly rejected' (Morgan 2006, 444). In other words, Bazin's ideas appear fragmented across many writings and subservient to (and evolving according to) his encounters with specific films in his role as a film critic.

Morgan explains (457) that in this standard reading:

> The use of deep space and the long take in Renoir's films, for example, are seen as techniques that are inherently realistic; neorealism, another favorite of Bazin's, involves the use of real locations, non-actors, natural light, and an emphasis on contingent and ordinary events. According to this account, these films not only provide an experience of the world of a film that replicates our habitual way of being in the world; they employ styles that emphasize it … It's almost a normative claim, reading Bazin's insistence that realism ought to follow from ontology as a quasi-moral position.

Morgan identifies the belief that a technique such as the long take comes close to re-creating the experience of our everyday modes of witnessing our physical environments as *perceptual realism*. It is precisely on these grounds, for example, that Noël Carroll finds fault with Bazin's theory when he writes that 'there is no necessary connection between realism and the techniques … that constitute the Bazinian style of spatial realism' (Carroll 1988, 139).

By contrast, Morgan argues:

> Ultimately the problem with perceptual realism is not that it fails to describe what Bazin takes the world of a film to be: how it is constituted by the film and held in place by the viewer. Nor is it that Bazin never talks about realism in such terms. The problem lies in its equation of the creation of a coherent world on film with realism. What becomes apparent when we look at more examples of Bazin's criticism is that the correspondence of the world of a film to our world – the cornerstone of both versions of the standard reading – is simply *not* the criterion for realism.
>
> (Morgan 2006, 458)

Morgan is here pointing out that the tendency to dismiss Bazin in film theory for inadequately theorizing realism – by prominent figures such as Noël Carroll, who also asserts that 'fiction wreaks havoc with Bazin's theory' – have not adequately considered Bazin's nuanced conceptualization of realism (Carroll 1988, 158). Rather than realism being necessarily marked by a styleless style, a more holistic way to understand Bazin lies in his claim that realism names a set of practices that has a positive and productive relationship with reality. From this perspective, Morgan argues that we need to view the remarks in the 'Evolution' essay about not evaluating an image for what it 'adds to reality but what it reveals of it' in a larger context, and therefore as an 'overstated' exception in an otherwise coherent and consistent theory that bolsters and spans hundreds of articles (Morgan 2006, 476).

As Morgan notes, Renoir's style 'does not simply provide a blank background (the ambiguity of reality) on which action takes place but makes us aware of the connection between the individual and the group, and the scale of the consequences an individual action may have' (460). Drawing on the aesthetic theories of Stanley Cavell and Michael Fried, Morgan proposes that we consider Bazin's realism through the concept of *acknowledgement*, an open-ended 'process by which a relation between style and reality is generated', which is defined by an artist's *doing something with or responding to* knowledge – in this case, a filmmaker's positivist decision to respond in a specific, but not prescribed, way to the facts of reality (471). Understanding Bazin's notion of realism in terms of acknowledgement asks us to consider a relation generated by a film's overall method of developing a style that maintains a certain commitment or contract with the spectator about his or her 'reality' – but is not defined by the use of any particular cinematic technique. With these terms, Morgan aims to loosen the tight association that has been built over the course of the history of film theory – as seen, for example, in Pasolini's remarks on the long take – that links style with ontology, and which Morgan observes to have been too quickly attributed to Bazin's own theory. In other words, a long-take style does not, in and of itself, equate with or belong to a realist style. Rather, Morgan points out that realism for Bazin is even more complicated: realism is both a style and something more – a mode with the potential of teaching us something new about reality. The long take thus does not, indeed cannot, exist apart from film as an exalted technique, but it makes meaning within a dynamic relationship among film, filmmaker, and spectator. And, in effect, the question of the long take cannot be disentangled from the broader question of 'what is realism?'

JEFF SCHEIBLE

## Works cited

Bazin, André. 1967. 'The Evolution of the Language of Cinema'. In *What Is Cinema?*, vol. 1, translated by Hugh Gray, 23–40. Berkeley: University of California Press.

Carroll, Noël. 1988. *Philosophical Problems of Classical Film Theory*. Princeton, NJ: Princeton University Press.

Morgan, Daniel. 2006. 'Rethinking Bazin: Ontology and Realist Aesthetics'. *Critical Inquiry* 32 (Spring): 443–81.

Pasolini, Pier Paolo. 1980 [1967]. 'Observations on the Long Take'. *October* 13 (Summer): 3–6.

## Further reading

Andrew, Dudley, and Herve Joubert-Laurencin, eds. 2011. *Opening Bazin: Postwar Film Theory and Its Afterlife*. New York: Oxford University Press.

Bazin, André. 1967. 'The Ontology of the Photographic Image'. In *What Is Cinema?*, vol. 1, translated by Hugh Gray, 9–16. Berkeley: University of California Press.

——. 1967. 'Theater and Cinema'. In *What Is Cinema?*, vol. 1, 76–124.

——. 1967. 'The Virtues and Limitations of Montage'. In *What Is Cinema?*, vol. 1, 41–52.

——. 1971. 'An Aesthetic of Reality: Cinematic Realism and the Italian School of the Liberation'. In *What Is Cinema?*, vol. 2, translated by Hugh Gray, 16–40. Berkeley: University of California Press.

——. 1973. *Jean Renoir*. Translated by W.W. Halsey II and William H. Simon, edited by François Truffaut. New York: Da Capo Press.

Bordwell, David. 1997. *On the History of Film Style*. Cambridge, MA: Harvard University Press.

——. 2006. *The Way Hollywood Tells It: Story and Style in Modern Movies*. Berkeley: University of California Press.

Deleuze, Gilles. 1989. *Cinema 2: The Time-Image*. Translated by Hugh Tomlinson and Robert Galeta. London: The Athlone Press.

Henderson, Brian. 1980. 'The Long Take'. In *A Critique of Film Theory*. New York: E.P. Dutton.

Kracauer, Siegfried. 1985. 'Basic Concepts'. In *Film Theory and Criticism*, 3rd edition, edited by Gerald Mast and Marshall Cohen, 10–17. New York: Oxford University Press.

Margulies, Ivone, ed. 2002. *Rites of Realism: Essays on Corporal Cinema*. Durham, NC: Duke University Press.

Rhodes, John David. 2006. 'Haneke, the Long Take, Realism'. *Framework: The Journal of Cinema and Media* 47 (2) (Autumn): 17–21.

Rosen, Phil. 2001. *Change Mummified: Cinema, Historicity, Theory*. Minneapolis: University of Minnesota Press.

Salt, Barry. 1974. 'The Statistical Style Analysis of Motion Pictures'. *Film Quarterly* 28 (1): 13–22.

Williams, Christopher, ed. 1980. *Realism and the Cinema: A Reader*. London: BFI.

# MEMORY AND FILM

## Hugo Münsterberg's 'Memory and Imagination'

The first scholarly study of the relation of film and memory occurs in what is considered one of the very first works of film theory: Hugo Münsterberg's 1916 *The Photoplay: A Psychological Study and Other Writings* (2002). In the chapter 'Memory and Imagination', Münsterberg's groundbreaking psychological study of early silent film anticipates subsequent analyses of phenomena such as the flashback, as well as other formal strategies for the cinematic representation of either subjective memory or an objective past, or some combination of both. Münsterberg focuses on the mental experience of the viewer, anticipating contemporary theories of film spectatorship in a discourse free of Freudian concepts. Here Münsterberg introduces the reader to the new terminology of the 'photoplay', including the 'cut-back', which would eventually give way to the more popular term 'flashback' as an 'objectification' of the 'mental act of remembering' (Münsterberg 2002, 90; see Turim 1989, 1–20).

With his axiomatic observations about what constitutes a successful narrative film in the early silent era, Münsterberg's book reads today like a combination of a prescriptive Aristotelian poetics, emphasizing an ideal unity of form, and the kind of instrumental reason that informs modern notions of industrial efficiency – a field to which Münsterberg also applied his psychological expertise (Münsterberg 2002, 23). The latter set of ideas – that the scientist can break down any occupation, trade, or technology into its component parts in order to better understand how to maximize its inherent efficiencies – is reflected analogically in the initial reception of cinema as the 'seventh art' with its own distinctive and medium-specific formal features (see Arnheim 1957; Canudo 1988). In this regard, it makes sense that Münsterberg would ground his discussion of memory and imagination in cinema spectatorship in relation to the nature of attention in theatre spectatorship, where memory augments and amplifies the viewer's attention (*see* ATTENTION). The theatre, however, 'cannot do more than suggest to our memory' the kind of 'looking backward' memory demands when engaged with live-action narrative (90). The photoplay, argues Münsterberg, is characterized by precisely this capacity to go further than the theatre in its ability to represent, through the judicious deployment of editing, not only present but also past actions, whether seen before in the story or provided as backstory, as context for the main narrative. What Münsterberg calls the 'cut-back' refers to the former, when the action returns to an earlier scene. In this he sees a true 'objectivation of our memory function'. The formal device of the 'cut-back', representing 'the mental act of remembering', is thus seen to be parallel to the close-up, which represents 'the mental act of attending' (90). The schema invoked, where memory relates the diegetic past, attention the present, and imagination the future, is as old as St Augustine's *Confessions* (39, n. 73). Münsterberg emphasizes cinema's unique ability to show all three temporalities within the same narrative, however, without engaging with the question of the very tense of the image *per se*, a debate that would not be articulated until the late 1960s. Münsterberg accords special significance to the other type of flashback (mentioned above), wherein the film includes images from the past of specific characters, rather than the story's objective past, which, according to Münsterberg, accords with the viewer's own frame of reference. Münsterberg closely observes the formal device of the dissolve, in the early silent era already established as the dominant convention for representing the passage from one time to another, where the second temporality is embedded within the first, in the form of a character's reverie-cum-flashback. In Hollywood cinema this evolves into the classical subjective flashback, as in *Casablanca* (1941), when Rick, thanks to Sam's song, remembers with bitterness his blissful time in Paris with Ilsa. As in this example, Münsterberg's account shows that the character-specific subjective flashback amounts to a literal re-staging of past events, which the spectator has not seen before, but which are clearly marked off as such by means of what he calls the 'cumbersome method' of the dissolve. As he nevertheless recognizes, this device had already (in 1916) come to 'symbolize' the 'appearance and disappearance of a reminiscence' (92).

What Münsterberg could not be expected to foresee, however, is the possibility that such cinematic conventions as the flashback-dissolve – a transitional device Christian Metz would refer to as 'minimum segments', non-mimetic 'punctuation' between larger, more complex syntagma (1974, 137–8) – could become naturalized for the cine-literate spectator as not merely a representation of the action of memory but as memory itself in action. Münsterberg's general approach, however, is characterized by his implicit position that seeing and knowing are for all intents and purposes indistinguishable; that consciousness is equivalent to vision, a theme that has since become a major point of contention in theories of film in a broader visual cultural context (96) (cf. Jay 1994). Münsterberg also anticipates here what David Bordwell would label the 'intensified continuity style' characteristic of both post-classical Hollywood and the international art film (Bordwell 2002). Münsterberg criticizes Raoul Walsh's *Carmen* (1915) for its superfluity of 'scene changes', or cuts, which, in one ten-minute section, in his estimate, reach a high of 167 – an average shot length of only three seconds. Münsterberg sees this as an exaggerated instance of what was recognized early on as one of cinema's most productive potentials, the representation of life in all its simultaneous and manifold complexity: 'Life does not move forward on one single pathway. The whole manifoldness of parallel currents with their endless interconnections is the true substance of our understanding … The photoplay alone gives us our chance for such omnipresence' (Münsterberg 2002, 95). Münsterberg anticipates here a constellation of ideas around cinema's engagement with memory elaborated by Gilles Deleuze in a wholly different terminology.

## Gilles Deleuze's 'From Recollection to Dreams: Third Commentary on Bergson'

On the surface, Gilles Deleuze's mid-1980s two-volume work *Cinema 1 and 2* appears far removed both stylistically and philosophically from Münsterberg – not to speak of the major trends in classical and contemporary film theory that intervened. What is not obvious at first, however, is Deleuze's influence on subsequent theories of subjectivity and identity that foreground or privilege affectivity and the body; Deleuze, after all, is one of the most important philosophers in the line stretching from Nietzsche in the late nineteenth century, presenting the major alternative to the privileged position within the humanities accorded Freudian theory and psychoanalysis generally for much of the twentieth century, and for film theory in particular. (Unlike Marx, Nietzsche could not be retrofitted to articulate with Freud.) Needless to say, the consequences of this difference for theories of memory are far-reaching. In *Cinema 1 and 2*, moving beyond what he terms the 'movement image' of pre-war classical film, Deleuze elaborates the 'time image' characteristic of the postwar art cinema, ushering in a highly influential, if sytlistically forbidding, philosophical approach to the cinematic representation of time, simultaneously a diagnosis of European subjectivity in the aftermath of the Second World War (*see* MOVEMENT-IMAGE; TIME-IMAGE). Deleuze's time-image, and the subject it entails, also chimes with film theory's privileging of vision and the image since Münsterberg: for Deleuze, the primary 'action' in the postwar time-image film is no longer acting but *looking* (see Deleuze 1989, 126).

The chapter 'From Recollection to Dreams: Third Commentary on Bergson' in *Cinema 2* (Deleuze 1989, 44–67), while not focused exclusively on the flashback, nor on film narrative in any conventional sense, illustrates Deleuze's major contribution to rethinking the cinematic representation of time and memory, from a generally Bergsonian perspective. In his reading of Bergson, Deleuze teases out the point that what links the images in the kind of film governed by the time-image is not movement but memory, via the 'recollection image' (44–6). Coupled with this is the Bergsonian observation that such recognition signifies even more when it fails than when it succeeds (54); hence the postwar art film's preoccupation with amnesia, hallucination, dream, and madness. For Deleuze, then, the conventional flashback, *à la Casablanca*, as hallmark of classical Hollywood style, is not an instance of the time-image but of the movement-image: 'we know very well that the flashback is a conventional, extrinsic device: it is generally indicated by a dissolve-link, and the images that it introduces are often superimposed or meshed. It is like a sign with the words: "watch out! recollection". It can, therefore, indicate, by convention, a causality which is psychological, but still analogous to a sensory-motor determinism, and, despite its circuits, only confirms the progression of a linear narration' (48). At such moments Deleuze could be in direct dialogue with Münsterberg, but it is not only the discourse which differs; this passage illustrates Deleuze's marked antipathy towards what he deems the bankrupt psychologism of the movement-image.

Significantly, Deleuze attributed his notion of the time-image to Proust (e.g. 82), grounding his theory in one of the key texts for modern memory theory, and complicating his relation to Bergson. Deleuze's debt to literature, as opposed to philosophy, in this regard extends to Borges, whose metaphysical fictions underpin Deleuze's discussion of Joseph Mankiewicz's use of the flashback in such a classical Hollywood film as *All about Eve* (1950), which, in its form, manages to transcend the conventional recollection image: 'There is no longer any question of an explanation, a causality or a linearity which ought to go beyond themselves in destiny. On the contrary it is a matter of an inexplicable secret, a fragmentation of all linearity, perpetual forks like so many breaks in causality. Time in these films "is exactly as Borges describes it in 'The Garden of Forking Paths': it is not space but time which forks, … embracing every possibility"' (49). It is here that the flashback finds its justification, at each point where time forks. The multiplicity of circuits thus finds a new meaning, and cinema's capacity for capturing time approaches Deleuze's ideal of a 'deeper memory, a memory of the world directly exploring time, reaching in the past that which conceals itself from memory' (39). This is the potential of the time-image, which would only appear with the full flowering of the art cinema as both product and symptom of the postwar period in which the old certainties – especially received notions of history and memory, of ways of relating to and making use of the past to justify the present – could no longer serve.

## Alison Landsberg's 'Prosthetic Memory: The Ethics and Politics of Memory in an Age of Mass Culture'

In his prescient acknowledgement of the 'astonishing numbers of people who attend the moving pictures' (Münsterberg 2002, 24), Münsterberg foreshadows subsequent theories of 'high' vs. mass cultural forms, of which popular cinema is the key instance. Modern mass culture was famously theorized by members of the Frankfurt School in the 1930s and 1940s, negatively in the 'culture industry' thesis of Theodor Adorno and Max Horkheimer, more positively in the work of Siegfried Kracauer and Walter Benjamin, both of whom showed themselves open to cinema's emancipatory potential (see MIMETIC INNERVATION; REDEMPTION [KRACAUER]). In his crucial emphasis on the de-linking of the 'authentic' experience of the artwork as auratic cult object and its contemporary manifestation as alienated commodity, Benjamin in particular can be seen as prescient of subsequent post-modern theories of mass culture and media studies, especially film, where the visual image has triumphed as the ultimate commodity form (see Benjamin 2002).

Despite a shared foundation in embodied identity, affect, and a non- or post-Freudian subjectivity, Alison Landsberg's theory of prosthetic memory, advanced in a handful of articles and in the 2004 book *Prosthetic Memory: The Transformation of American Remembrance in the Age of Mass Culture*, represents a very different tendency in theories of memory and cinema. Rather than the art film, Landsberg emphasizes popular cinema, in accordance with a post-Marxian left-wing analysis of capitalist-consumer culture, but more in the recuperative spirit of Benjamin than Adorno and Horkheimer's scathing critique. Landsberg advances prosthetic memory as a lens through which to re-evaluate contemporary popular culture's, and especially film's, relation to global capitalism and the universal commodification it prescribes. Rather than proscribing such processes, however, Landsberg reads the commodification of memory optimistically, as the opportunity for empathic relations among peoples otherwise widely separated in both space and time: 'It has become possible to have an intimate relationship to memories of events through which one did not live: these are the memories I call prosthetic. "Prosthetic memories" are indeed "personal" memories, as they derive from engaged and experientially-oriented encounters with the mass media's various technologies of memory' (Landsberg 2003, 148–9). According to Landsberg, 'prosthetic memories' are: neither 'authentic' nor natural, like a literal *prosthesis*, 'worn on the body; these are sensuous memories produced by an experience of mass-mediated representations' (149). Prosthetic memory implies that, long before television or web-based venues, preceded of course by photography, a mass medium like cinema already constituted a form of memory as both storage place and retrieval mechanism, existing independently of the body and in a complex relation to the mind. Cinema as 'prosthetic memory' is both a form of collective memory and a medium from which the viewer may glean information about the past – however banal or trite or inaccurate it may be. Landsberg, unlike Marianne Hirsch, is concerned less with questions of historical 'accuracy' and more with the *empowering* potential for the individual of an artificially expanded memory. In this respect it is perhaps her insistence upon the bodily or *sensuous* nature of such memories that justifies Landsberg's otherwise utopian claims. In other words, insofar as prosthetic memories function primarily at a pre-intellectual level of affect, feeling, and physical sensation, then Landsberg's theory can be said to illuminate the operation of contemporary mass-produced popular cultural objects more generally, putting such commodified experiences into the best possible light. On the other hand, it remains difficult to reconcile this aspect of Landsberg's theory with her other major claim that prosthetic memories exemplify the kind of commodifed object or experience which lends itself to creative and counter-hegemonic re-purposing by the media-savvy viewer-consumer – a process necessarily dependent upon critical scepticism towards contemporary popular culture's emancipatory potential.

With Deleuze as the major exception, discussions of memory in/and film since the 1980s have generally taken place between the ideological poles represented by the theories of Landsberg (as above) and a previous generation of thinkers, such as Fredric Jameson (1992). In Jameson's post-Marxist critique, the 'postmodern sensibility' can be defined in terms of a *lack* of historical awareness or knowledge coupled with a *nostalgic desire* for a non-existent past. The cinematic historical roots of this sensibility in contemporary culture in fact precede Jameson and postmodern theory, while the ideological underpinnings of prosthetic memory are the new critical orthodoxy. According to Astrid Erll, 'cultural memory' theory contests the nostalgic position articulated in 1967 by Godard that 'memory has been *replaced* by technology', positing a different relation between memory and the various media forms characteristic of modern, postmodern, or other contemporary social reality. 'Media of memory ... which can be understood [after McLuhan] as "extensions" of our organic memories, bring about consequences in that they shape cultural remembrance in accordance to their specific means and measures. In this sense, "the medium is the memory"' (Erll 2011, 115).

Even more than Jameson's critical category of postmodern 'nostalgia', theories such as Hirsch's postmemory, and especially Landsberg's prosthetic memory, raise significant ethical, epistemological, and aesthetic questions around the 'ownership' of specific memories, or of cultural memory more broadly. Such conceptions of memory encourage us to question the difference between first-hand organic memory and second-hand artificial memory, not to speak of the formerly clear line between memory and history. Postmodern theories of memory such as Landsberg's direct attention to transformations in constructions of subjectivity or individual human identity, and the degree to which these quantities are mediated through technologies of representation. The social-constructivist discourse that underpins these ideas is, on the surface at least, far removed from either Deleuze's still vital or Münsterberg's now historical significance for contemporary film theory. Together, however, these diverse approaches provide a picture of film studies' perspective on the complexity and contradictions of modern memory.

RUSSELL J.A. KILBOURN

## Works cited

Arnheim, Rudolf. 1957. *Film as Art*. Berkeley: University of California Press.
Benjamin, Walter. 2002. 'The Work of Art in the Age of Its Technical Reproducibility'. In *Selected Writings, Volume 3: 1935–38*. Translated by Edmund Jephcott, edited by Howard Eiland and Michael W. Jennings, 101–33. London: Harvard University Press.

Bordwell, David. 2002. 'Intensified Continuity: Visual Style in Contemporary American Film'. *Film Quarterly* 55 (3): 16–28.

Canudo, Riccioto. 1988. 'Birth of a Sixth Art [1911]'. In *French Film Theory and Criticism: A History/Anthology, 1907–1939*. Edited by Richard Abel, 58–65. Princeton, NJ: Princeton University Press.

Deleuze, Gilles. 1989. *Cinema 2: The Time-Image*. Translated by Hugh Tomlinson and Robert Galeta. Minneapolis: University of Minnesota Press.

Erll, Astrid. 2011. *Memory in Culture*. Translated by Sara B. Young, edited by Astrid Erll. New York: Palgrave Macmillan.

Jameson, Fredric. 1992. *Postmodernism, or, The Cultural Logic of Late Capitalism*. Durham, NC: Duke University Press.

Jay, Martin. 1994. *Downcast Eyes: The Denigration of Vision in Twentieth-Century French Thought*. Berkeley: University of California Press.

Landsberg, Alison. 2003. 'Prosthetic Memory: The Ethics and Politics of Memory in an Age of Mass Culture'. In *Memory and Popular Film*, edited by Paul Grainge, 144–61. Manchester: Manchester University Press.

——. 2004. *Prosthetic Memory: The Transformation of American Remembrance in the Age of Mass Culture*. New York: Columbia University Press.

Metz, Christian. 1974. *Film Language: A Semiotics of the Cinema*. Translated by Michael Taylor. Oxford and New York: Oxford University Press.

Münsterberg, Hugo. 2002 [1916]. 'Memory and Imagination'. In *The Photoplay: A Psychological Study and Other Writings*. New York: Routledge.

Turim, Maureen. 1989. *Flashbacks in Film: Memory and History*. New York and London: Routledge.

# MIMETIC INNERVATION

In film studies, 'mimetic innervation' refers to the potential of film to awaken a quality of sensory experience and memory that is capable of undoing the numbing effects of mass–mediated modernity on the human sensorium. The concept was proposed by Walter Benjamin to theorize the possibility of an 'antidote' to the alienation of the senses caused by the encounter with technology. Miriam Hansen's essay 'Benjamin and Cinema: Not a One-Way Street' (1999) argues that mimetic innervation is a pivotal concept in Benjamin's theorization of cinema, but one that has been sidelined in many contemporary under-standings of Benjamin's thinking. Benjamin's 'The Work of Art in the Age of Mechanical Reproduction' (1969), which has become a canonical text in contemporary film and media studies, is commonly read as an attempt to seek a positive, redemptive reading of the new forms of perception and reception brought about by mechanical reproduction, character-ized by shock and distraction. Hansen argues that other texts of Benjamin's are far more important and productive for film studies, citing 'One-Way Street', his essays on surrealism, Proust and Kafka, and his reflections on the mimetic faculty, among others. In these texts, he attempts 'to imagine an alternative reception of technology' (Hansen 1999, 328) – one that is empowering and enabling, and has the capacity to 'pierce the scar tissue formed to protect the human senses in the adaptation to the regime of capitalist technology' (308) and to recover sensory affect.

Hansen emphasizes Benjamin's ambivalence about the decline of aura and the con-templative mode: as much as he attempts to redeem the new, distracted forms of engage-ment, she argues, he also laments the decline of experience and memory. However, by placing the artwork essay in the context of the other texts, and by excavating the many earlier, unpublished drafts of the essay, Hansen draws out the significance of a third posi-tion: an 'antidote' to the anaesthetic effects of shock experience, encapsulated in the 'counter-concept' of mimetic innervation. Her aim in the essay is to 'reactivate the trajectory ... between the alienation of the senses that preoccupied the later Benjamin and the possibility of undoing this alienation that he began to theorize as early as "One-Way Street" (1928), particularly through the concept of innervation' (309).

In this essay, Hansen works through a series of Benjamin's key texts to highlight how these two opposing forces are constantly caught in a dialectic in Benjamin's thinking. In Hansen's account, the significance of this dialectic is missing from many readings of Benjamin's work. She argues that these antinomies in Benjamin's thinking emerge directly from his engagement with historical actuality: they are irreconcilable contradictions in mass–mediated modernity, brought about by the confrontation between the human senses and technology. Hansen contextualizes these concerns in Benjamin's own historical

285

moment: in Europe in the 1930s this crisis takes on an urgency, as the numbing effects of technology have the potential to 'spiral' into 'a vortex of decline' (313). The aesthetic 'phantasmagoria' of fascism come to offer a compensation for this loss of sensation and experience. For Benjamin, she argues, this is the political horizon against which it is imperative to find a new mode of engagement between the senses and technology to counter this decline and enable new collective forms of reception and transformation. Benjamin sees the human sensorium as the site on which these contradictions are played out. The concept of mimetic innervation comes to function as a way of imagining an alternative to this logic of accelerated desensitization: a reception of technology that could counter these effects of sensory alienation and restore the capacity for sensory affect, experience, and memory.

Hansen traces the origin of the term innervation. She writes that 'innervation refers, broadly, to a neurophysiological process that mediates between internal and external, psychic and motoric, human and mechanical registers' (313). In its original use in physiology, the term refers to a bodily stimulation or excitation that travels inwards in one direction: a pathway from a nerve to an organ or muscle. Freud, she argues, revised the concept as a psychic excitation, which also travels in one direction: from an internal psychic or emotional excitation, such as trauma, outward to the body in the form of a somatic symptom. In Benjamin, she writes, innervation is a process that travels in two directions: in the first, affective or psychic energy provokes a somatic response; in the second, a somatic or motoric stimulation has the capacity to travel in the other direction to restore or recover psychic energy. Innervation here is an awakening of bodily energies that has the capacity to 'recover split-off psychic energy' (317). In Benjamin's model, this two-way movement of psychic energy challenges Freud's concept of a defensive psychic shield induced by shock and excessive stimulation (316), like an 'armour' around the senses that blocks innervation (317). As Hansen reads Benjamin, the 'boundary ... of the bodily ego [is less like an armour and more of a] porous interface between the organism and the world' (317).

In Benjamin, cinema is the one site that has the potential to activate this two-way sensory engagement with the world, and his argument centres on the concept of the mimetic faculty. The term 'mimetic' has become a commonplace in much of aesthetic theory, where it refers to a semblance to the real: a copy or verisimilitude. Hansen traces a second strand in the understanding of the mimetic, one which has predominated in anthropology and zoology, which focuses on performative dimensions of play. Benjamin's 'comprehensive' understanding of the mimetic retains this dual nature. The explanation Hansen cites (324), from Benjamin, clarifies this:

> Since the oldest forms of imitation, "language and dance", knew only one material of creation, the imitator's body, semblance and play were two sides of the same process, still folded into one another: "The person imitating makes a thing apparent. One could also say, he plays [or performs] the thing. Thus one touches on the polarity that rests at the basis of mimesis."

This second understanding of the mimetic, which emphasizes process, activity, performance and play, becomes central to Benjamin's theorization of cinema.

Here the mimetic entails 'a mode of cognition involving sensuous, somatic and tactile forms of perception' (329). It is an 'engagement with the other that opens the self to experience' (329): it involves 'a form of practice that transcends the traditional subject–object dichotomy' (329).

Children's play provides a prototype for Benjamin of this 'inventive reception of this new world of things' (330) that involves both mimicking the thing and performatively becoming it, but Benjamin is specifically concerned with the possibility of reviving the mimetic faculty in modernity. In his account, there is 'no outside of technology' (325), and technology must be a part of the solution. He argues that cinema has the capacity to reawaken and '[reconnect] with the discarded powers of mimetic practices that involve the body' (321) and to expand the potential space for mimetic experience in modernity.

Hansen draws out the importance in Benjamin's thinking of a 'reconfiguration of "body-image space"' (335). This idea is partly dependent on a sense of proximity: a collapse of the traditional distance between the viewer and the object. Benjamin links the reception of cinema to the transformations in reception across other terrains of modern life, such as the experience of advertising, which produce 'a momentary fusion of vision and object' (336). This blurring of boundaries between subject and object informs Benjamin's attempt to theorize 'new forms of subjectivity' (321). For Benjamin, the body is 'the "preeminent instrument" of sensory perception and moral and political differentiation' (321), and these new forms of subjectivity depend on the capacity to 'reactivate the [mimetic] abilities of the body' (321). Hansen argues that this concept is very far from the way some contemporary media theory suggests an 'abdication to the regime of the apparatus' (325), and radically different from Brechtian ideas of distanciation (*see* BRECHT AND FILM). The empowering potential of cinema to revive mimetic experience is at the core of the cultural and political aspirations Benjamin has for cinema.

Hansen emphasizes that for Benjamin this is a two-way process: 'a decentering and extension of the human sensorium … into the world … and an introjection, ingestion or incorporation' of the technological apparatus into the body (332). In a statement that signals the enormously productive potential of this understanding for contemporary film studies, Hansen writes: 'I'd like to think that Benjamin recognized something of this affectively charged excentric perception at work as well in the dispersed subjectivity of the cinema experience' (332).

In Hansen's reading, Benjamin pays close attention to the 'specificity of the cinema experience' (341), through what she describes as the 'double mediation' of film: the 'mediation between the film and the depicted world' (337), which we could gloss as the level of representation or 'inscription', and the mediation 'between the film and the audience' (337): reception, which he explores on the phenomenological level of sensory-aesthetic effects, and which he envisages as a collective, social mode of reception. She traces Benjamin's theorization of the 'optical unconscious', which intersects with the concept of mimetic innervation, within this dual frame. In the 'canonical' published version of the Artwork essay, mimetic innervation has gone from the argument, and Benjamin simplifies his thinking to talk of the optical unconscious only on the level of inscription or indexicality – the potential of the camera to reveal the hidden, invisible dimensions of things. In this version of the Artwork essay, the theorization of the 'sensory-somatic immediacy' (341) of cinema experience, which holds so much potential for our contemporary understanding, has vanished.

Benjamin's aspirations for cinema depend on the interlinking of innervation with new forms of collective reception: it is only through producing new forms of collective 'reflexivity' that the 'technologically altered sensorium' (341) could transform the catastrophic effects of modernity. This is perhaps the most problematic aspect of Benjamin's theorization of innervation, and Hansen speculates that Benjamin's ambivalence about the emerging mass audience led to his erasure of the concept of innervation from the Artwork essay. It is here that the genuine antinomies and ambivalences of Benjamin's thinking, as he reworked and revised his key essays, are most starkly revealed. Hansen identifies a messianic/utopian dimension to Benjamin's aspirations for the potential of cinema, an 'overvaluation' of its potential (323, quoting Koch 1994, 208). In Benjamin's own life, she argues, this project failed, unravelling in the actual progression of historical events in Europe. And in a contemporary context, collective reception is no longer the predominant mode of cinema reception. However, Hansen claims that Benjamin recognized that the concept was to some extent 'based on miscognition' (324), on a metaphor, a concept that was not actualized but 'could unleash creative transformative energies' (324). In this sense, the essay suggests an imaginative horizon for thinking the possibilities of cinema's engagement with the world of things and the senses.

Hansen's essay is not purely a historical excavation: in restoring the political dimension to Benjamin's thinking, it seeks to impress upon the reader the need to engage similarly with our own actuality. Benjamin serves as an exemplar of a mode of cultural and aesthetic theoretical work that attempts to take on the urgent challenges faced by human society in all of its ramifications – on the level of the political collective and the individual sensorium, and the imbrication between the two. Hansen gives this historical inquiry a framing story that places its implications firmly in the present. She opens the essay with two examples from recent Hong Kong cinema that take up, thematically, the challenges of mass mediated modernity that Benjamin explores. At the end of the essay, she emphasizes that there are similar antinomies that drive our own contemporary mediated culture, 'now more so than ever' (310). These contradictions, she argues, are 'the framing condition of any cultural practice today' (343), and the essay emphasizes the importance of engaging with the ways they play out in contemporary electronic and digital media.

This is a dense, layered, and at times difficult essay but one that richly rewards a careful reading, and that reveals more with each subsequent reading. There are many more layers and connections to the argument that cannot be covered here: in particular, arguments about the temporality of the image, the mimetic capacities of writing, and the reconfigured relationships between the human senses and things. However, by retrieving the concept of mimetic innervation, Hansen makes a significant contribution to moves to restore the body and the senses to our understanding of film spectatorship. The essay can be very productively read together with Hansen's excavations of Siegfried Kracauer's work on materiality, the senses and spectatorship. As film studies grapples with a range of ways of thinking about cinematic affect, the concept of mimetic innervation offers a material base for us to understand the ways in which cinema can engage embodied spectators to enhance affective experience.

A hazard of focusing on this material base, however, in our explorations of its resonance with contemporary experiences of cinema, is the potential to valorize the awakening of the mimetic faculty *per se*, without exploring how this articulates with social, cultural, and political dimensions. If, for Benjamin, the enabling progressive potential is specifically dependent on collective reception, where does this leave us in a contemporary context? Divorced from this context, the concept can lead to a kind of euphoric celebration of the atomized, innervated body/subject as an end in itself. And, clearly, history teaches us that the transformative energy unleashed by affective mimetic engagement can equally be deployed in the service of the most destructive goals. It is this historical counter-tendency that Martin Jay (1993, 81) describes as 'the fascist combination of mimesis and instrumental rationality'. Jay furthers this critique with a claim that Benjamin's hopes for film are 'naïve' (82), but when he claims that 'film is an unlikely candidate for the restoration of touch over sight' (82), he grounds his comments specifically in the 'distraction' polarity in Benjamin's thinking.

Michael Taussig's work suggests directions in which our understanding of mimetic innervation needs to be elaborated. Taussig (1993) highlights the dual nature of Benjamin's concept of the mimetic – as copy and contact – and he emphasizes that these are two sides of the same coin, inseparable. For the concept of mimetic innervation to open up our understanding of cinematic experience more fully, in a way that resonates with the constantly reconfiguring horizons of our sensorial engagement with and reception of contemporary technologies, perhaps it is this relationship between the semantic and the somatic that the concept of mimetic innervation must grapple with.

ANNE RUTHERFORD

## Works cited

Benjamin, Walter. 1969. 'The Work of Art in the Age of Mechanical Reproduction'. In *Illuminations*, translated by Harry Zohn, edited by Hannah Arendt, 217–52. New York: Harcourt Brace & World.

Hansen, Miriam Bratu. 1999. 'Benjamin and Cinema: Not a One-Way Street'. *Critical Inquiry* 25 (2): 306–43.

Jay, Martin. 1993. 'Sympathetic Magic'. *Visual Anthropology Review* 9 (2): 79–82.

Koch, Gertrud. 1994. 'Cosmos in Film: On the Concept of Space in Walter Benjamin's "Work of Art" Essay', translated by Nancy Nenno. In *Walter Benjamin's Philosophy: Destruction and Experience*, edited by Andrew Benjamin and Peter Osborne, 205–15. London: Routledge.

Taussig, Michael. 1993. *Mimesis and Alterity: A Particular History of the Senses*. New York and London: Routledge.

## Further reading

Benjamin, Walter. 1928. 'One-Way Street'. In *Selected Writings, 1913–26*, translated by Edmund Jephcott, edited by Marcus Bullock and Michel Jennings. Cambridge, MA: Belknap Press, 1996.

——. 1969. 'Franz Kafka'. In *Illuminations*, translated by Harry Zohn, edited by Hannah Arendt, 111–40. New York: Harcourt Brace & World.

——. 1969. 'The Image of Proust'. In *Illuminations*, 201–16.

——. 1969. 'On Some Motifs in Baudelaire'. In *Illuminations*, 155–200.

——. 1978. 'On the Mimetic Faculty'. In *Reflections*, edited by Peter Demetz, 333ff. New York: Harcourt Brace Jovanovich.

——. 1978. 'Surrealism: The Last Snapshot of the European Intelligentsia'. In *Reflections*, 177ff.

Hansen, Miriam Bratu. 1987. 'Benjamin, Cinema, and Experience: "The Blue Flower in the Land of Technology"'. *New German Critique* 40: 179–224.

——. 1993. 'Of Mice and Ducks: Benjamin and Adorno on Disney'. *South Atlantic Quarterly* 92: 27–61.

——. 1993. '"With Skin and Hair": Kracauer's Theory of Film, Marseille 1940'. *Critical Inquiry* 19 (3): 437–69.

Rutherford, Anne. 2011. *'What Makes a Film Tick?': Cinematic Affect, Materiality and Mimetic Innervation*. Bern: Peter Lang. [For an application of the concept of mimetic innervation in contemporary film analyses, see 75–83 and 190–2.]

# MINOR CINEMA

The term 'minor cinema' is most commonly a term adapted from the work of French philosopher Gilles Deleuze, in collaboration with psychotherapist Félix Guattari (1986; first published 1975). They devised the concept of the 'minor' in literature, before Deleuze reworked the concept into his *Cinema* books, in particular articulating the notion of a 'minor cinema' in *The Time-Image* (1985) (*see* TIME-IMAGE).

I shall discuss the key characteristics of the minor, before looking at how film scholars have typically adopted this term. I then propose shortcomings with the concept, by way of future directions in which we might take the idea.

## Taking the minor from literature to cinema

Deleuze and Guattari explore the revolutionary potential of minor literature in their book *Kafka: Toward a Minor Literature*. Minor literature is revolutionary because it involves the creation of works that take a 'major' language and 'deterritorialize' it. That is, minor works make us rethink the way in which a major language is perhaps unthinkingly deployed, thereby refreshing its potential for novelty and change. In the case of Kafka, then, we see a Czech Jew writing works in German that upset the major language and which make that major language 'stutter'.

While the rethinking of a major language is arguably revolutionary in and of itself, Deleuze and Guattari further the political credentials of minor literature by saying that it can 'express another possible community' by 'forg[ing] the means for another conscious-ness and another sensibility' (1986, 17). That is, a minor literature can bring together people that share a particular identity that is otherwise hidden within or at the margins of the 'major' community. This in turn troubles any monolithic interpretations of what con-stitutes a particular community, and instead posits the possibility for a community in fact to be made up of many, heterogeneous communities. Producing minor literature helps bring one of those communities into being, meaning that the minor is implicitly linked to the future: the minor in literature is of a 'people to come'.

Arguing against the linguistic and semiotic turn in film studies, Gregory Currie (1995) has contended that cinema is not a language, meaning that the 'minor' in cinema might need from the very beginning to be rethought. In other words, unlike a minor literature, a minor cinema cannot make the *language* of cinema 'stutter', because cinema is not a language at all. However, while this contention could conceivably stand, the word 'lan-guage', when we transpose the concept of minor literature on to cinema, is best understood as cinema's various modes of representation. In this sense, the 'major' becomes the dominant filmmaking practices of Hollywood, while the minor can, as we shall see, be co-opted to define other/alternative modes of representation, and/or to challenge representation itself.

## The collective politics of minor cinema

To stick to Deleuze's elaboration of 'minor cinema' in *The Time-Image* (1985, 281–91), it is worth remembering that the idea of 'dominance' with regard to film practices takes on a political role: cinema can be, when deployed for propaganda purposes, used to dominate (the thoughts of) a people. As such, a 'minor' cinema is a revolutionary cinema that seeks to articulate different, perhaps as yet non-existent or at the very least unrecognized, identities; hence, once again, the notion of 'a people to come'.

For Deleuze, minor cinema also blurs the boundary between the political and the private. When an individual from a 'minor' community acts, her actions have political ramifications that are understood not simply as her own, but as those of the whole community. Similarly, the wider actions of the community are transposed on to the individual, such that individual (private) and community (political) are inextricably intertwined. Deleuze uses as an example of this the way in which Alexandria becomes conflated with Egyptian filmmaker Youssef Chahine in *Alexandria … Why?* (1978): the film asks 'why Alexandria?' as well as 'why me?' in such a way that the two become interlinked.

What seems to be true of characters within a minor cinema, in that the individual's actions stand for those of the community and vice versa, is also true of the minor work itself. That is, even though a minor film, such as Ousmane Sembène's *Ceddo* (1977), is nominally the work of a single author (Sembène), it is in fact a *collective enunciation*. In order to explain what this means, we need to consider how a minor filmmaker might question the myths that surround a particular people, be they created by others (the 'majority') or by the 'minor' people themselves. Challenging these myths, however, does not involve a simple act of accurate ethnography; rather, both sets of myths must be brought into question (or, to use a Deleuzian term, deterritorialized) without being reterritorialized. It is not a question, in other words, of reifying the people, such that they become incarcerated in a certain, set mythology, but a question rather of *fabulating*. Fabulating involves a mix of the real and the imagined, the documentary and the fictional, in such a way that the boundary between the two is blurred. This process similarly involves an element of futurity: as opposed to 'capturing' the essence of a people (by delimiting the boundaries of what it is and what it is not), minor cinema suggests that a people is always changing (we do not know where the 'truth' of that people begins or ends), and in this sense the people is 'to come'. We can use this consideration of fabulation to explain what is meant in part by 'collective enunciation', then, because, by involving documentary and fictional elements that blur the boundary between fiction and reality, the film uses real people (or 'intercessors') as well as fictional characters – and the intercessors speak for themselves and the community that they represent (and are not necessarily under the control of the filmmaker). These intercessors, as the name suggests, 'intercede' in the film, arguably destabilizing its credentials as the work of a single author, but reinforcing the sense that the work is collective, or a collective enunciation.

Finally, the minor film's 'liminal state' – on the boundary between fiction and reality – means that it is not just an oppositional work, a work created in a 'minor' language that can only be 'spoken' or understood by a few people. Rather, it is a work that 'speaks' – at least in part – the 'major' language, but in such a way that it troubles it, makes it 'stutter'. Furthermore, the major language is not rejected for the sake of some 'return' to a prior existence (which would be to root the minor in the past), but it is reappropriated by the minor such that the minor exists *within* the major. This reappropriation helps, after Deleuze, to express the impossibility of living under domination.

## Interpretations of the minor

D.N. Rodowick makes clear in his treatment of Ousmane Sembène's *Borom Sarret* (1966) that 'minor cinema' does not apply simply to the cinema of demographic minorities (Rodowick 1997, 152). Rather, it applies to the cinema of dominated and disempowered groups. This accounts for Deleuze's own decision to mention Sembène, Yilmaz Güney, Lino Brocka, Glauber Rocha, Pierre Perrault, Youssef Chahine, Haile Gerima, and Charles Burnett as exemplars of minor cinema, even though they come from different political, ethnic, and national backgrounds. It would seem, from this perspective, that *cinema* is the 'major' language that these filmmakers make stutter, and that the 'majority' version of this language is the dominant cinema of Hollywood and its various regional/national imitators. As much seems confirmed by Dudley Andrew (2000, 226), when he invokes the minor as a means of defining any non-Hollywood cinema that must (romantically, it seems) be bicycled to various outposts in order to be seen, before more or less labelling this cinema as *festival cinema*.

In fact, because of this general anything-but-Hollywood definition of minor cinema, it is a concept that has been applied to all manner of cinemas. Tom Gunning (1989) has applied the term to experimental filmmakers such as Phil Solomon and Peggy Ahwesh, while in *An Accented Cinema* (2001) Hamid Naficy briefly uses the term to discuss exilic and diasporic filmmakers now based in the West who make films that 'speak' with an 'accent'. The term has also been applied to various 'national' cinemas, or rather cinemas of nations that do not have a clear-cut state, such as Québec (Marshall 2001; 2008), Hong Kong (Yau 2001), and Scotland (Martin-Jones 2004). Mette Hjort (2005), meanwhile, has used the term in relation to the fully fledged national cinema of Denmark, considering it as minor in relation to Hollywood. Both Alison Butler (2002) and Patricia White (2008) have used the term in relation to women's cinema, particularly that which does not belong to the mainstream, with White applying the term in particular to lesbian cinema. David Martin-Jones has also applied the term to queer cinema (2008). Finally, Isaac Julien and Kobena Mercer (1988), citing June Givanni (1988), have used the term in relation to black British cinema.

In other words, and perhaps fittingly, minor cinema seems to span a plethora of contexts, the shared features of which become hard to trace the more the term is co-opted in relation to other cinemas. Furthermore, if conceptual 'cleanliness' were a desired goal of considering minor cinemas, then it becomes even harder to find, given that it shares overlapping traits with other movements or forms of cinema such as 'counter-cinema' and 'third cinema', see separate entry on Third World Cinema.

Patricia White argues that '[i]f major is to minor as film is to video, feature to short, cinema to television, fiction to documentary, women – and thus lesbians and often transpeople – tend to labour in the latter category of each of these pairs' (2008, 410). If this is in part her basis for contending that lesbian cinema is 'minor' cinema, then this surely does not apply to a good number of the filmmakers mentioned by Deleuze, or indeed Naficy,

Marshall, Yau, Martin-Jones, and Butler. In other words, while minor cinema spans multiple contexts, it also seems to take on multiple forms.

## Suggestions for the minor

Rather than cleaning up this conceptual mess, however, I should like briefly to propose two possible alternative, and in some respects complementary, approaches to the minor, both of which might only further trouble our understanding of this phenomenon, but which, paradoxically, might allow us to push on through to some clarity concerning the mess.

David E. James (2005) applies the concept of the minor to non-mainstream cinemas in Los Angeles. This involves nods to, if not major considerations of, B-movies. The B-movie can also be reinterpreted historically as the 'minor' form that made the 'major' language of cinema 'stutter', while at the same time reinforcing its hegemony. However, in an era when, since the advent of the New Hollywood blockbuster with *Jaws* in 1975, B-movie aesthetics have come to dominate Hollywood, as is argued by Geoff King (2003) and Warren Buckland (2006), we might say that Hollywood has long since co-opted and thereby nullified the revolutionary potential of minor cinema. Arguably the commercialization of film festivals, which Dudley Andrew sees as the symbolic home of minor cinemas, is evidence of this. The 'truly' minor cinema now is perhaps unheard of, and, indeed, as soon as it becomes heard of, it ceases to be minor. Alternatively, perhaps the truly minor, by which I mean revolutionary, cinema is not the cinema that is celebrated by Deleuzian scholars for its opposition to Hollywood (dispersed and globalized entity that it now is), but which, after James, lies somewhere already within Hollywood, a cinema that makes itself powerfully understood, but which at the same time disrupts the 'major' language of Hollywood. Perhaps its revolutionary power lies precisely in its unrecognizable revolutionariness. This conception does indeed lend to minor cinema a sense of futurity, whereby what the 'people to come' is is not overtly based on the national/regional model proposed by various Deleuzian scholars (Hong Kong, Québec, Scotland, Africa), but on something much more vague and without a basis in history: a people the nature of which we do not yet know.

Indeed, to lead to my second proposal regarding minor cinema, perhaps the concept of the people is no longer sufficient for the purposes of a revolutionary cinema. Whereas many scholars who invoke the minor appeal to a certain type of cinema (experimental) or to a certain kind of pre-established identity (lesbian, queer, female, Québecois, Scottish, Hong Kong, African, black British), perhaps minor cinema can be reconsidered in a different way. Perhaps both major and minor cinema need to be challenged by a new conception of cinema which tentatively we might call *common cinema* based not upon the people but upon the multitude. Paolo Virno (2004), along with Michael Hardt and Antonio Negri (2000; 2004), point to shortcomings in the term 'people' in a political sense, since it is 'centripetal' (i.e. unifying, in the sense that it abolishes difference), while multitude acknowledges difference and variety. Only when *all of cinema* is considered as a commons of the multitude, in which there is not just an opposition between major and minor (a direction in which Deleuzians, if not Deleuze himself, seem to take the minor) but a democratic recognition of all of its manifestations as legitimate and equal, will cinema have begun to realize some of its vast potential.

WILLIAM BROWN

# Works cited

Andrew, Dudley. 2000. 'The Roots of the Nomadic: Gilles Deleuze and the Cinema of West Africa'. In *The Brain Is the Screen: Deleuze and the Philosophy of Cinema*, edited by Gregory Flaxman, 215–49. Minneapolis: University of Minnesota Press.

Buckland, Warren. 2006. *Directed by Steven Spielberg: Poetics of the Contemporary Hollywood Blockbuster*. London and New York: Continuum.

Butler, Alison. 2002. *Women's Cinema: The Contested Screen*. London: Wallflower.

Currie, Gregory. 1995. *Image and Mind: Film, Philosophy and Cognitive Science*. Cambridge: Cambridge University Press.

Deleuze, Gilles. 1985. *Cinéma II: L'image-temps*. Paris: Éditions de Minuit.

Deleuze, Gilles, and Félix Guattari. 1986. *Kafka: Toward a Minor Literature*. Translated by Dana Polan. Minneapolis: University of Minnesota Press.

Givanni, June. 1988. *Black and Asian Film List*. Edited by Nicky North. London: British Film Institute Education.

Gunning, Tom. 1989. 'Towards a Minor Cinema: Fonoroff, Herwitz, Ahwesh, Lapore, Klahr and Solomon'. *Motion Picture* 3 (1/2): 2–5.

Hardt, Michael, and Antonio Negri. 2000. *Empire*. Cambridge, MA: Harvard University Press.

——. 2004. *Multitude: War and Democracy in the Age of Empire*. London and New York: Penguin.

Hjort, Mette. 2005. *Small Nation, Global Cinema: The New Danish Cinema*. Minneapolis: University of Minnesota Press.

James, David E. 2005. *The Most Typical Avant-Garde: History and Geography of Minor Cinemas in Los Angeles*. Berkeley: University of California Press.

Julien, Isaac, and Kobena Mercer. 1988. 'Introduction: De Margin and De Centre'. *Screen* 29 (4): 2–10.

King, Geoff. 2003. 'Spectacle, Narrative, and the Spectacular Hollywood Blockbuster'. In *Movie Blockbusters*, edited by Julian Stringer, 114–27. London and New York: Routledge.

Marshall, Bill. 2001. *Québec National Cinema*. Montreal: McGill-Queen's University Press.

——. 2008. 'Cinemas of Minor Frenchness'. In *Deleuze and the Schizoanalysis of Cinema*, edited by Ian Buchanan and Patricia MacCormack, 89–101. London: Continuum.

Martin-Jones, David. 2004. '*Orphans*: A Work of Minor Cinema from Post-devolutionary Scotland'. *Journal of British Cinema and Television* 1: 226–41.

——. 2008. 'Minor Cinemas'. In *Deleuze Reframed*, by Damian Sutton and David Martin-Jones, 51–64. London: I.B. Tauris.

Naficy, Hamid. 2001. *An Accented Cinema: Exilic and Diasporic Filmmaking*. Princeton, NJ: Princeton University Press.

Rodowick, D.N. 1997. *Gilles Deleuze's Time Machine*. Durham, NC: Duke University Press.

Virno, Paolo. 2004. *A Grammar of the Multitude: For an Analysis of Contemporary Forms of Life*. Translated by Isabella Bertoletti, James Cascuito, and Andrea Casson. New York: Semiotext(e).

White, Patricia. 2008. 'Lesbian Minor Cinema'. *Screen* 49 (4): 410–25.

Yau, Ka-Fai. 2001. 'Cinema 3: Towards a "Minor Hong Kong Cinema"'. *Cultural Studies* 15 (3/4): 543–63.

# MISE EN SCÈNE

'Mise en scène Is Dead, or: The Expressive, the Excessive, the Technical and the Stylish' (Martin 1992) is a 16,000-word text, published in 1992 in *Continuum*, an Australian journal of media studies. It is a distillation of university courses I taught on film style and aesthetics over the ten preceding years. The aim of the article is to survey and evaluate the different, major approaches to analysing and understanding the formal work of *style* in cinema – all of the significant choices that a director and his or her collaborators make in relation to the use of colour, movement (of both the camera and the actors), rhythm, lighting, editing, music, and so on. This approach to cinema goes under various names: close analysis, formal analysis, detailed analysis, and the extravagant misnomer frame-by-frame analysis.

In every medium or art form, aesthetic issues focus on a key question: what is the relationship of *form* (or style) to *content* (the narrative world and its implied meaning for the spectator)? Both in teaching and writing this material, I was struck by the historic tension (sometimes an all-out, polemical war) between two broad schools or types of analysis – schools that take diametrically opposed stances on the style/content relationship.

On the one hand, there is a *classical* approach associated with critics such as V.F. Perkins and Robin Wood (from *Movie* magazine in UK), Jean-Loup Bourget and Alain Masson (*Positif* magazine in France), and André Bazin and Éric Rohmer (*Cahiers du cinéma* in the 1950s). The classical aesthetics of these critics is what I term the *expressive* approach. It rests on a *thematic* premise: films, like literary or theatrical works in a narrative-based tradition of drama or comedy, are seen to possess *themes* – distillations of ideas, questions, or propositions. What expresses and embodies these themes are, in the first place, the scripted properties of plot and character, and then, more decisively, the integrated, systematic ensemble of stylistic choices made by the director.

Some filmmakers favoured by critics of an expressive tendency include Max Ophuls, Nicholas Ray, Jean Renoir, Kenji Mizoguchi, and Clint Eastwood. Classical film aesthetics – just like accounts of classical architecture, music, or the nineteenth-century novel – stresses qualities such as balance, order, elegance, logic, symmetry, patterning, and the meaningful repetition of motifs. Even more crucially than these surface qualities, expressive criticism seeks what popular vernacular calls *deep* meaning: epiphanies or insights that emerge through the film's unfolding, often fully unveiled in the final scene, offering a profound knowledge of how people live within a social, personal, or philosophical context. It is important to add, as Perkins (1990) insists, that so-called deep or rich meanings are not literally *hidden* in a film; rather, they are *implied*, and thus form a pattern that demands to be noticed and explicated.

The second loose school or group emerged in the 1960s and 1970s. Associated with the rise of intellectual movements including structuralism, semiotics, Lacanian psychoanalysis, and the neo-Marxist political theory elaborated by Louis Althusser, this is the *excessive approach*, as I call it in relation to aesthetic analysis. It can be aligned most closely with the form of theory and critique that labelled itself *post-structuralism*. The first crucial 'move' of the post-structuralist school was to downplay the role of the auteur or director as the central, controlling consciousness behind a work; rather, following the lead of Roland Barthes in literary theory, a film was seen as a *text*, 'a tissue of quotations drawn from the innumerable centres of culture' (Barthes 1977, 146) – formed more by storytelling habit, stylistic convention, and the reigning cultural ideology than by any specific, artistic intent.

By the same token, all film texts are (according to this hypothesis) inherently *heterogeneous*, multi-layered, made up of many types of often clashing materials – not *homogeneous*, as in the classical ideal of a smoothly combined, polished fusion of elements. Thus, filmic texts can easily 'lose control' of themselves, producing surprising, hybrid combinations of elements – and this is the positive phenomenon of *excess* (or *rupture* as it was often called at the time). Key exponents of the excessive approach included, internationally, Peter Wollen, Stephen Heath, Tom Conley, and Marie-Claire Ropars (*see* CONTEMPORARY FILM THEORY).

In aesthetic terms, this means that style in cinema is no longer interpreted as the servant of content, or the vehicle that orders and articulates meaning, as in the expressive approach. Style, on the contrary, performs on the *surface* of a film, no longer providing clues for the spectator's grasp of a deep meaning. Style, therefore, *exceeds* the process of its thematic interpretation – and its does so because of its evident *materiality* as a screen phenomenon, something akin to what Alfred Hitchcock, Brian De Palma, and other directors have described as *pure film*. The idea of materiality (which is an indispensable one for film studies) indicates two things: first, that a film is an evidently constructed, composed work; and second, that it generates *effects* (as well as emotional *affects*) within spectators, such as shock, surprise, delight, anxiety, arousal, contemplation, introspection, and so on.

Certain filmmakers seem to offer a close fit with this theoretical approach, Jean-Luc Godard, Federico Fellini, Raúl Ruiz, Pedro Almodóvar, and Vincente Minnelli among them. Particular forms of underground and queer cinema (such as the short films of the Kuchar brothers) were 'redeemed' by the excessive outlook, while being excluded from discussion or recognition within the classical canon. The excessive viewpoint also favours certain genres that are stylistically *histrionic* by their very nature: melodrama, the musical, horror, thriller, and action films.

Writing in 1992, I attempted to break the seductive binary opposition of classical vs. post-structural approaches, by noting some intermediary stylistic options already very prevalent in film production of the period. These options were what I termed the *loose fit* relationship between style and content, where a broad set of stylistic strategies (such as a particular colour scheme, use of music, or intermittent montage sequences) was 'laid upon' the story, as in films by Michael Mann or Oliver Stone, and the *mannerist* method (named after the movement in painting), where style draws attention to its own display (as in the work of Tim Burton or Lynne Ramsay), while stopping short of wholesale excess or chaotic heterogeneity.

By multiplying the stylistic options, I sought to free the relationship of style to content from the prevalence of stark metaphors of *power*: style in the service of content, or style overpowering content. I attempted to introduce a less heated and more finely graded concept: *economy*. The idea is that each film, or each type of film, proposes a particular *balance* or *interrelationship* of style and content; no proportion is inherently superior to any other. It is this balance, different from case to case, which I describe as an economy.

In the context of 1992, my essay also placed itself within a debate about the *neoformalist* method of film studies, as practised by David Bordwell, Kristin Thompson, and others. Neoformalism tends to reject the analytical strategies of both classicism and post-structuralism (*see* FORMALIST THEORIES OF FILM). While finding its narrow self-definition of a commitment to the *historical poetics* of cinema too limiting, I wished to credit neoformalism for continuing an attentiveness to form that can be traced back through many significant critics who belong to no particular school, including Manny Farber, Frieda Grafe, Jonathan Rosenbaum, and Noël Burch.

General discussions of style or aesthetics in cinema tend to congregate – sometimes misleadingly – around the term *mise en scène*. In its strict, conventional sense, *mise en scène* is a practice derived from theatre, referring to the staging or choreography of bodies within a set. This strict definition carries over to the cinema, in the arrangement of what many critics refer to as 'bodies in space' – no longer the space defined for the theatre audience by the traditional proscenium arch, but the mobile, ever-changing space primarily defined by the camera, its positions and movements. Some critics (such as Alain Bergala 2004) continue to insist on this operation – the moment of the director filming bodies in space, whether in fiction or documentary mode – as the central, crucial aspect of *mise en scène*, indeed even the essence of cinema itself.

However, when most critics (such as Gibbs 2002) speak of *mise en scène* in film, they tend to use it as a designation for *all* aspects of style, including pre-production conceptualization (shot lists, storyboarding, set and costume design), and the post-production processes of picture editing, sound design, and (increasingly in our time) digital treatments of the image. Although we risk imprecision by using the term in this way, there is no doubt that, to the general film-literate public, *mise en scène* has come to mean something like 'the director's creative resources' – and, as such, it is still a useful shorthand.

The argument of my 1992 essay sets out from the bold declaration in 1975 by V.F. Perkins that changes in cinematic style and language since the 1960s can be considered in terms of 'the death of *mise en scène*' (Perkins *et al.* 1975, 6). In order to interrogate this claim, I distinguish between *mise en scène* as an artistic or professional practice (i.e. something that filmmakers themselves do, even if not necessarily under this label) and *mise en scène* as an idea, theory, or approach (i.e. something conceptualized and debated by critics and theorists). While there is overlap and sometimes synchronicity between these two practices, there can also be a disconnection or a time-lag: films may be exploring new areas or configurations of style that commentators have not yet noticed, absorbed, or analysed in depth.

My intuition was that while one kind of *mise en scène* may well have seemed to be dead or dying by 1975, newer forms of style in cinema were indeed also emerging, and continue to do so today in the twenty-first century. What Perkins perceived as a lost art was, in effect, the classical style of cinema that he, like the other critics of his ilk, favoured. Classical filmmaking has never completely died (we see refined versions of it today in the work of Bertrand Tavernier or Lone Scherfig), but there can be no doubt that filmmaking, on all its diverse levels (commercial, independent, experimental, documentary, animation, etc.), has developed in many fruitful directions since the highpoint of classicism in the 1950s. This diversification of stylistic options went hand-in-glove with the popular movement of *postmodernism,* particularly strong in the 1980s and 1990s, that revelled in the simultaneous existence of multiple aesthetic strategies drawing from both high and low culture (*see* POSTMODERN CINEMA).

Since the writing of my essay, a crucial advance in the theorization of film aesthetics has been provided by Jacques Aumont's edited collection *La mise en scène* (2000). Two key ideas emerge here. First, there is the rigorous concept of a *social mise en scène,* which seeks to draw filmic creation a little further away from the abstraction of an auteur's sheer creativity, and to ground it within what Umberto Eco once described as the *kinesic* and *proxemic* dimensions of any civilization's social codes: i.e. how people are allowed to move, how they are meant to behave in any given situation, how close they are able to stand next to each other, whether they can touch one another and in what specific ways, and so on. With the hindsight provided by this idea, we can discern which directors are particularly adept at drawing out and playing upon such codes: Hitchcock, Luis Buñuel, Luchino Visconti, John Ford, and Roy Andersson offer strong examples.

The second concept that has emerged in the general rethinking and expansion of *mise en scène* – and has been born from recent developments in international art – is the idea of the *dispositif.* This term, translatable as apparatus, sometimes refers to the general 'set-up' of the cinematic viewing experience (seated spectator, screen, projector, darkened room) (*see* APPARATUS THEORY [BAUDRY] and APPARATUS THEORY [PLATO]). In aesthetic terms, however, it refers to the *rules* or *strategies* by which a film (or any audiovisual work) can be generated: a game-like approach that often involves (as in the experimental writings of the Oulipo authors) the canny invention and imposition of *constraints.* Lars von Trier and Jørgen Leth's film *The Five Obstructions* (2003) is the best-known illustration of a *dispositif* procedure, and much contemporary installation art (such as that of Agnès Varda) explores the possibilities of procedure-based work; looking back, however, we also can see that some of cinema's most celebrated auteurs, including Robert Bresson, Yasujiro Ozu, and Chantal Akerman, derived their 'signature style' from a specific set of self-imposed restrictions (such as deliberately inexpressive acting, the eschewal of shot/reverse shot structure, or minimal camera movement).

In a more general sense, the *dispositif* idea opens *mise en scène* to a more inclusive, holistic conception of aesthetic method than it has previously enjoyed: according to Raymond Bellour (2012), *mise en scène* in its classical formulation is only one possible way of organizing the relation of images and sounds in cinema. His powerful example is Godard's groundbreaking 'film essay' series *Histoire(s) du cinéma* (1988–98): it has little *mise en scène* in the conventional sense of staging bodies in a fictive space, but a great deal of arranging and relating of shot-fragments and soundtrack snippets, thus giving rise to a slew of new terms: *mise en phrase* (the 'dropping in' of a verbal or written quotation), *mise en page* (the graphic design or layout of the screen's rectangle), and so on. All these diverse forms of stylistic organization today deserve to be classified and integrated by film theory and criticism.

Since writing the essay in 1992, I have found the recent method of *figural analysis* (Brenez 1998) to be an approach that combines the lesson of cinematic heterogeneity with a regard for formal logic and hermeneutic meaning (see my contribution to Balcerzak and Sperb 2009). And my 2014 book *Mise en scène and Film Style* attempts to trace the full range of productive applications of the term *mise en scène,* from its initial classical conception in the work of Louis Delluc (1919) through to the many and varied *dispositifs* of contemporary digital, audiovisual art.

ADRIAN MARTIN

# Works cited

Aumont, Jacques, ed. 2000. *La mise en scène*. Brussels: De Boeck.

Balcerzak, Scott, and Jason Sperb. 2009. *Cinephilia in the Age of Digital Reproduction: Film, Pleasure and Digital Culture*. Vol. 1. London: Wallflower Press.

Barthes, Roland. 1977. *Image–Music–Text*. London: Fontana.

Bellour, Raymond. 2012. *La Querelle des dispositifs*. Paris: P.O.L.

Bergala, Alain. 2004. 'De l'impureté ontologique des créatures de cinéma'. *Trafic* 50: 23–36.

Brenez, Nicole. 1998. *De la figure en général et du corps en particulier: L'invention figurative au cinéma*. Brussels: De Boeck.

Delluc, Louis. 1919. *Cinéma et cie*. Paris: Grasset.

Gibbs, John. 2002. *Mise en scène: Film Style and Interpretation*. London: Wallflower Press.

Martin, Adrian. 1992. 'Mise en scène Is Dead, or: The Expressive, the Excessive, the Technical and the Stylish'. *Continuum* 5 (2): 87–140.

——. 2014. *Mise en scène and Film Style*. London: Palgrave Macmillan.

Perkins, V.F. 1990. 'Must We Say What They Mean? Film Criticism and Interpretation'. *Movie* 34 (5): 1–7.

Perkins, V.F. *et al*. 1975. 'The Return of *Movie*'. *Movie* 20: 1–25.

# MODERNISM VERSUS REALISM

There is much disagreement about the precise meanings of the terms modernism and realism, and they have been applied to a bewildering array of artists, artworks, and theories. Nevertheless, scholars usually concur that modernism refers at the very least to the increasing tendency of artists in Europe and North America from the late nineteenth century onwards to reject traditional artistic styles and invent new ones. In his history of the term, Matei Calinescu argues that this has been modernism's principal meaning since the early twentieth century, as illustrated by Laura Riding and Robert Graves's 1927 *Survey of Modernist Poetry*: 'Characteristically, Riding and Graves define "modernist" poetry (as distinct from "modern" poetry in the neutral chronological sense) by its willful deviation from accepted poetic tradition, by the attempt to "free the poem of many of the traditional habits which prevented it from achieving its full significance"' (Calinescu 1987, 83).

This impulse to 'make it new', in the famous words of the poet Ezra Pound (himself a major modernist), is called modernism because it can be viewed as a manifestation in the arts of the desire to modernize – the wish to make progress and ameliorate human life by rejecting older, outmoded ways of doing things and finding new and better ones – that is a hallmark of modern societies. Modernist artists typically conceived of themselves as improving human life by heroically pushing art forward in previously unexplored directions, and they often inflected their artistic experimentation with explicitly political, even utopian, agendas. This does not mean modernists saw no relation between their work and artistic tradition. Indeed many, such as Pound, believed that innovation guaranteed 'a link to tradition' by enabling them to discover what was most 'durable' about the artistic mediums in which they worked, which is one reason the critic Harold Rosenberg referred to modernism as 'the tradition of the new'. Modernists often quoted, alluded to, and borrowed from artworks of the past, and they frequently appealed to the doctrine of medium-specificity, the claim that an artistic medium has features specific to it that an artist working within that medium should exploit.

Meanwhile, one of the older, traditional artistic styles against which modernists reacted was realism, which is why the two are often opposed (as in the title of this entry). Modernism's 'adversary', claims Malcolm Bradbury, 'is, to put it crudely, realism or naïve mimesis' (Bradbury 1983, 323). Realism, as a stylistic movement in the arts, preceded modernism and was dominant in parts of Europe in the mid-nineteenth century. 'Its aim', argues Linda Nochlin, 'was to give a truthful, objective and impartial representation of the real world, based on meticulous observation of contemporary life', and realism is usually defined as the accurate imitation or description of perceptible quotidian reality using a transparent, even invisible, style that focuses the viewer's or reader's attention on that

reality as clearly and directly as possible (Nochlin 1971, 13). Due to the premium modernists placed on novelty, their styles were enormously varied. But in general, in a modernist
artwork, form is just as visible and important as representational content, sometimes to the
point that the representation of visible reality is eschewed in favour of organizing purely
formal elements into patterns (such as shape and colour in abstract painting) (*see* COUNTER-
CINEMA; STRUCTURAL/MATERIALIST FILM). Hence, modernism often shades into formalism,
the doctrine that artistic value lies primarily or even exclusively in an artwork's formal,
sensuous qualities rather than its representational content. This did not mean modernists
were uninterested in reality, however. In fact, they often maintained that their artistic
innovations enabled them to access reality more truthfully and accurately than the
transparent, invisible style of traditional realism.

Modernism and realism have exerted a profound influence on film theory, and in particular have informed theoretical debates about what makes cinema an art (*see* ART, FILM AS).
Although differing fundamentally in their conceptions of art, both modernist and realist
film theorists typically isolate a feature of cinema that, in their view, makes film *essentially*,
in its very nature, a modernist or realist art form. After surveying the modernist film theory
of Soviet filmmaker Vsevolod Pudovkin, who argued that editing is a medium-specific
property of cinema that allows the filmmaker to transform reality and thereby create art,
I will examine André Bazin's theory of the 'ontology' of the photographic image, which
claimed that cinema is an intrinsically realist art due to the mechanical manner in which its
photographic images come into being.

## Pudovkin's modernist film theory

Pudovkin was a prominent member of the Soviet montage movement in the late 1920s,
which was one of the first modernist group styles in film; like fellow members such as
Sergei Eisenstein, he proposed a theoretical rationale for the movement's innovations (*see*
MONTAGE THEORY II [SOVIET AVANT-GARDE]). When the cinema first emerged in the 1890s, he
argued in his book *Film Technique* it was nothing more than 'an interesting invention that
made it possible to record movements' (Pudovkin 1976, 79). It became an art only when
American filmmakers discovered ways of manipulating the appearance of reality on film
using editing. For instance, editing allows the filmmaker to expand or contract time, and
Pudovkin gives the example of filming a person falling from a window. The filmmaker can
eliminate much of the fall through editing, he points out, thereby creating a divergence
between the way the event occurs in reality and its appearance on film. Editing makes
cinema an art, Pudovkin claims, in part because of this divergence: 'Between the natural
event and its appearance upon the screen there is a marked difference. It is exactly this
difference that makes the film an art' (86).

Editing also makes cinema an art because it is one of the 'peculiar possibilities' of film,
and Pudovkin compares cinema to theatre in order to show why editing is a medium-
specific technique (81). When filmmakers first became interested in creating art, he suggests, they merely recorded the pre-existing art of theatre: 'The film remained, as before,
but living photography. Art did not enter into the work of him who made it. He only
photographed the "art of the actor"' (80). Cinema only departed from theatre and became
an autonomous art when editing was discovered because editing distinguishes cinema from
theatre in two ways. First, when editing is used, the film camera is no longer like the
'motionless spectator' of theatre (82). Rather, due to variations in the scales and viewpoints

of different shots, it resembles an 'active observer' who can move around and view something from a number of angles and distances (82). Second, the theatre is subject to the laws
of space and time. There can be no instantaneous movement between different points in
space and time in the theatre. By contrast, due to editing, the cinema is free of such laws.
For instance, it can omit space and time, as in the example of the person falling from a
window when most of the fall is not shown. Thus, when editing is exploited, 'the film
assembles the elements of reality to build from them a new reality proper only to itself; and
the laws of space and time, that, in work with living men, with sets and the footage of the
stage, are fixed and fast, are, in the film, entirely altered' (90).

Editing was therefore the most important cinematic technique for Pudovkin and other
Soviet montage filmmakers in the late 1920s due to their modernism, their belief that an
art form must eschew the imitation of reality through exploiting techniques specific to it.
Moreover, while they were indebted to the tradition of editing that had been established
by American filmmakers by the late 1910s, which privileged the maintenance of spatial,
temporal, and causal continuity between shots, like modernists in general, they sought to
move beyond tradition by innovating their own style. Hence, in their films, they pioneered
a more elliptical, discontinuous form of editing than continuity editing, one which,
Pudovkin felt, more fully exploited cinema's capacity to diverge from the imitation of reality and theatre by multiplying viewpoints and departing from the laws of space and time
to a greater degree than continuity editing. Yet, while he maintained that editing gives rise
to a uniquely 'filmic space and time', this does not mean he believed film art was divorced
from reality (87). In fact, he argued that it allowed for the possibility of 'giving a clear,
especially vivid representation of detail' due to the elimination of unnecessary spatial,
temporal, and causal information through editing, along with close-ups that draw the
viewer's attention to only the most crucial information (91):

> The power of filmic representation lies in the fact that, by means of the camera, it
> continually strives to penetrate as deeply as possible, to the mid-point of every
> image. The camera, as it were, forces itself, ever-striving, into the profoundest
> deeps of life: it strives thither to penetrate, whither the average spectator never
> reaches as he glances casually around him.

Such claims are legion in modernist film theory, showing that, although opposed to
realism, modernists often saw their formal and stylistic innovations as enabling a more
authentic representation of reality than is possible through the transparent, invisible style of
realism (Turvey 2008).

## Bazin's realist film theory

Pudovkin and the other Soviet montage filmmakers were forced to modify if not abandon
their artistic innovations by the mid-1930s due to the imposition of socialist realism on all
artists in the Soviet Union, and, in general, the 1930s and 1940s were not hospitable to
modernism due to political and economic turmoil, the hostility of communist and fascist
regimes, and the resurgence of realism. It was during this period that Bazin came of age.
In his essays on the history of film style, Bazin argued that the introduction of synchronized
sound in the late 1920s heightened film's potential as a realistic recording medium and
thereby changed the way filmmakers conceived of the cinema. Whereas many silent

filmmakers, such as the Soviet montage group, were modernists who believed that 'the art of cinema consists in everything that plastics and montage can add to a given reality' (Bazin 1967, 26), sound filmmakers increasingly 'evaluated' the image 'not according to what it adds to reality but what it reveals of it' (28). Bazin was primarily a critic and historian, but he also briefly sketched a realist theory of film art in his famous essay 'Ontology of the Photographic Image' (1945) in order to explain why cinema, at heart, is a realistic medium (see ONTOLOGY OF THE PHOTOGRAPHIC IMAGE). It should be noted that he employs a number of different conceptions of realism in this essay, some of which I attempt to untangle below.

Bazin's major argument is that 'Photography and the cinema … are discoveries that satisfy, once and for all and in its very essence, our obsession with realism' (1967, 12). The explanation for this is not to be found in the way photographs look, Bazin claims, but rather in the way they come to be (which is why his essay is about the 'ontology' of the photographic image, ontology being the study of the nature of being). This is in contrast to painting, where it is the perceptible features of the painted image, such as perspective, that create the realistic 'illusion' of reality. (Although he occasionally uses the word 'illusion' in connection with cinema, Bazin's theory of film's realism is not an illusion theory.)

Rather, for Bazin, the realism of photographs is due primarily to the fact that they come into being mechanically (13):

> Originality in photography as distinct from originality in painting lies in the essentially objective character of photography … For the first time, between the originating object and its reproduction there intervenes only the instrumentality of a nonliving agent. For the first time the image of the world is formed automatically, without the creative intervention of man.

Photographs, in other words, have a causal relation to the subjects they depict. Light bounces off the subject in front of a camera, is focused by the camera's lens onto the photochemical surface of the photograph inside the camera, and reacts with the chemicals to create a photographic depiction of the subject. Although the camera operator must frame the subject and press the button to take the photograph, the process through which light is registered on the photochemical surface of the photograph is causal. Handmade images such as paintings, however, have an intentional relation to their subjects. They are dependent on the beliefs and other intentional states of their makers. If I paint what is in front of me, the resulting painting depicts what I believed was in front of me when I painted it. If I photograph what is in front of me, the resulting photograph depicts what was in front of me when I took it regardless of what I believed was in front of me. Thus, if I paint what is in front of me and I am experiencing an hallucination, I will paint the hallucination, while no such hallucination will appear in a photograph of what is in front of me. One consequence of this is that photographs are, in the words of philosopher Berys Gaut, ontologically realistic (Gaut 2010, 67–8). 'We are forced to accept as real the existence of the object reproduced' in a photograph (Bazin 1967, 13). Another is that photographs are epistemically realistic. They have more 'credibility' than handmade images (13).

Bazin also draws a further ramification (14):

> The photographic image is the object itself, the object freed from the conditions of time and space that govern it. No matter how fuzzy, distorted, or discolored,

no matter how lacking in documentary value the image may be, it shares, by virtue of the very process of its becoming, the being of the model of which it is the reproduction. It *is* the model.

This is the most mysterious of Bazin's arguments about photographic realism, and there has been much debate about how to understand it. Bazin seems to be suggesting not just that a causal process produces a photographic depiction of the subject, but that part of the subject's being is transferred to the photograph during this process. As he goes on to say: 'The photograph as such and the object in itself share a common being, after the fashion of a fingerprint' (15); the photograph is able to 'reach out beyond baroque resemblance to the very identity of the model' (16).

What is the 'common being' that photographs and the subjects they depict putatively share? One possibility is that, just as a finger leaves part of itself behind in a fingerprint, so an object leaves part of itself in the photograph, namely, the light that bounced off it. But however one understands this claim, it gives rise to another notion of realism: transparency. A photograph, Bazin seems to be arguing, doesn't just represent its subject, it *re*-presents it, setting it before us. We actually see it, not just a representation of it (13–14):

> We are forced to accept as real the existence of the object reproduced, actually *re*-presented, set before us, that is to say, in time and space. Photography enjoys a certain advantage in virtue of this transference of reality from the thing to its reproduction.

Some of Bazin's metaphors indicate that he thinks that we look through a photograph and literally see the subject it depicts. The photograph, he writes, 'preserves the object, enshrouded as it were in an instant, as the bodies of insects are preserved intact, out of the distant past, in amber' (14). Just as we look through the amber at the body of a preserved insect, so we look through a photograph at the subject it preserves.

For this reason, Bazin maintains (14) that photography satisfies a deep, universal, transhistorical psychological need in humans to preserve the past in the present.

> Hence the charm of family albums. Those grey or sepia shadows, phantomlike and almost undecipherable, are no longer traditional family portraits [i.e. paint-ings] but rather the disturbing presence of lives halted at a set moment in their duration, freed from their destiny ... Photography ... embalms time, rescuing it simply from its proper corruption.

As for film, because it consists of a series of photographic images that record events unfolding in time, Bazin describes it as 'objectivity in time' (14), proclaiming that: 'Now, for the first time, the image of things is likewise the image of their duration, change mummified as it were' (15). This is why, Bazin concludes, cinema is an essentially realistic medium and filmmakers should pursue realism in their films: The 'aesthetic qualities' of cinema, he suggests (15),

> are to be sought in its power to lay bare the realities. It is not for me to separate off, in the complex fabric of the objective world, here a reflection on a damp

sidewalk, there the gesture of a child. Only the impassive lens, stripping its object of all those ways of seeing it, those piled-up preconceptions, that spritual dust and grime with which my eyes have covered it, is able to present it in all its virginal purity to my attention and consequently to my love.

MALCOLM TURVEY

## Works cited

Bazin, André. 1967. *What Is Cinema?* Vol. 1. Berkeley: University of California Press.

Bradbury, Malcolm. 1983. 'Modernisms/Postmodernisms'. In *Innovation/Renovation: New Perspectives on the Humanities*, edited by Ihab Habib Hassan and Sally Hassan. Madison: University of Wisconsin Press.

Calinescu, Matei. 1987. *Five Faces of Modernity: Modernism, Avant-Garde, Decadence, Kitsch, Postmodernism.* Durham, NC: Duke University Press.

Gaut, Berys. 2010. *A Philosophy of Cinematic Art.* Cambridge: Cambridge University Press.

Nochlin, Linda. 1971. *Realism.* New York: Penguin Books.

Pudovkin, V.I. 1976. *Film Technique and Film Acting.* New York: Grove Press.

Turvey, Malcolm. 2008. *Doubting Vision: Film and the Revelationist Tradition.* New York: Oxford University Press.

# MONTAGE THEORY I
# (HOLLYWOOD CONTINUITY)

It takes skills to tell a story. What skills it takes depends on the medium we choose. Film is the medium of showing. What to show? What to show closer? What to show longer? What to show next and what to show again? Such questions may sound simple, yet thinking about them made people come up with medium-specific explanations known as montage theories in film studies.

Montage, editing, cutting. In present-day English, the three terms mean more or less the same: the act of putting sounds and images together at the final stage of film production. Historically, however, each of the terms has its own date of birth and its own reason for being named as it is. *Cutting* must have been the oldest of the three; according to an early filmmaking tutorial, to cut a picture is to remove the unneeded: 'There may be too much of a particular episode of the picture or an uninteresting patch, or a section showing no action, or it may be desired for some reason or another to shorten the film either at the beginning or at the end. The superfluous piece of the film must be cut off or cut out, and the ends then neatly joint up, so that the pictures follow in their proper sequence' (Bedding 1909, 587). *Editing* is cutting according to continuity rules; borrowed from print media, the term (as the term *continuity*) came into use early in the 1910s when the way action would be segmented and assembled came to be seen as the responsibility of those who wrote for films rather than those who staged and cut their scenes. Studio employees known as *picture story editors* specialized in revising freelance scenario acquisitions to ensure that the number of scenes, inserts, characters, and sets were in line with the film's genre and format, and lived up to production practices and regulations. In the mid-1910s, the term *editor*, or *cutting editor* (Sargent 1916, 6), slipped from pre- to post-production, and is in use to this day. *Montage* may mean one of two things: a fast-paced sequence designed to bridge a lapse of days or decades, or the practice of editing in the mirror of theory. While German examples may have served as a source of inspiration for montage sequences in Hollywood films (Bordwell 1985, 73–7), the term itself came from the French word *montage* via Russian *montazh* and settled in English in or soon after the 1920s.

## The emergence of editing

Was there a theory of cutting? While some thought has been given to pre-1910 forms of cutting by a number of modern film historians (Salt 1983; Bottomore 1990; Bowser 1990; Musser 1991; Keil 2001; Gunning 2010), not much of it comes from contemporary writings. From the little we learn from trade sources about cutters, clever selection from ready material was seen as their basic skill: 'Very often the success of the picture will depend on the inclusion of a greater or less amount of the narrative action. Therefore the man who examined the film after it is made, should, besides his technical knowledge, have some sense of proportion; a nice appreciation of the author's and producer's intention in the making of the film' (Bedding 1909).

Arguably, the first medium-specific view on cutting known to early film historians comes from the pen of a Czech writer from 1908: 'The cinematograph is, of course, able to make use of scenes arranged in a theatrical fashion, yet in such cases it is too easy to see through the illusion. Alternately, the cinematograph can break up the action and follow it in rapid intervals from various perspectives; however, this technique has yet to overcome the diffi-culty of maintaining the interconnected coherence between individual moments of a highly active scene' (Tille 2008, 80). There is hardly more in the way of cutting theory to be found in film literature before the 1910s.

Things started changing when people in the film industry recognized that writing for pictures required some understanding of the logic of pictures, not only of writing. 'It is in transition from the primitive and elemental to the professionally artistic that the picture play now finds itself', wrote one of these people early in 1911. 'The one who would be a skillful and artistic picture dramatist must study his play and revise it constantly, with the patient thoroughness of a German savant. He must arrange and rearrange every situation in order to get the best effect in the most natural and logical way ... His is a new techni-que, based on the elements of the old [drama], and demanding not only the training of the old, but a genius for the new' (Craw 1911, 126–7).

The new technique entailed new expertise and a new occupation: 'Owing to the fact that so many good [story] ideas are submitted incorrectly developed, the larger film com-panies find it necessary to employ reconstruction experts. In fact, practically all the scripts that are purchased have to be entirely reconstructed before they are suitable for the director to produce' (Carr 1914, 118).

## Continuity theory

Word on how pictures (should) tell a story spread beyond studio walls through various screenwriting manuals that mushroomed across the United States after 1913. Authored mainly by *picture story editors* (a less pompous name for *reconstruction experts*), these books offered advice to short-story writers, stage playwrights, and sundry amateurs eager to try their hand at writing for films. It was on the pages of such manuals (and in attendant trade journal essays) that medium-specific film theory found its first home.

While early screenplay manuals have been successfully used to trace the emergence of continuity style in filmmaking practice of the 1910s (Thompson 1985), the theoretical thoughts on editing that their pages harboured are not as well known as they deserve. Here are two good reasons for listening to them. First, taken together, early textbooks of screenwriting offered the first coherent theory of filmmaking, a platform of knowledge worth inspecting. The other reason is that here we find a self-portrait of editing perceived as 'typically American' across the rest of the world, specifically in Soviet Russia, where a quite different, coherent theory of editing was about to emerge, much of it in response to what they called *American montage*. Photoplay writing manuals, the cradle space of film theory, warrant attention.

Making a virtue of necessity was the first lesson these books and booklets taught. On the one hand, the absence of spoken lines makes it trickier for the screen actor to bring home what the stage actor can simply state in words; on the other, film actors have devised an ingenious method of instantly *registering* thoughts and emotions which would take a soliloquy to express on the live stage: to get some of these across, a *close-view* can be used in films, which, of course, is unthinkable on-stage. Prose writers are free to use as many words as they need to make clear a complex story twist or situation; filmmakers, in turn, use *leaders*, *flash-backs*, *busts*, *visions*, *cut-ins*, and suchlike contrivances to make picture narratives as supple as those found in stories or novels. The italicized terms come from period glossaries and were used in *photoplays* and studio talk in the 1910s.

Time and space imposed their own conditions on filmmaking, early film theorists explained, hence the cult of precision and the worship of measure which was part of the film making and editing culture from the start. 'Photoplays are put on', said one prominent producer, 'with a stop-watch in one hand and a yardstick in the other' (Esenwein and Leeds 1913, 147). Mastery over time and space was what this two-tool figure allegorized.

Before you cut, you measure, and so you do before you shoot. The yardstick was to be used to resolve problems of staging and framing, manuals asserted. 'For practical purposes the photographic stage is but six feet wide and four to six feet deep, no matter how much more can be included in the scene' (Sargent 1916, 11). This claim was based on pure optics. Unlike the theatre stage which can be taken in at a glance, the beam of camera vision is narrow and tapers at the lens. When the player is close, only part of his or her body remains in frame, blocking the rest of the photographic stage.

This yardstick was also a yardstick of style. Using it, the director would draw a *working line* separating the camera and the playing stage which the players were not supposed to cross. The distance to the line was a variable, not a constant value. If the working line is set far enough in the distance, the result will be what we nowadays call 'tableau staging' (Bordwell 2012); alternatively, if actors are allowed to come closer to the camera, spaces and actions will have to be shown piece by piece, not all at once. The second option entailed what scholars nowadays call 'scene dissection' (Salt 1983) and 'analytical editing' (Thompson 1985).

Here is where the label 'American' comes in. Where the *working line* would lie was also seen as a borderline between geographical currents of filmmaking. Thus, an early French director and theorist spoke of 'the European and American schools' of framing (Jasset 1911, 57); by the same token, American authors made a distinction between the full-length *French stage* and the *American stage* which licensed that 'the lower part of the legs of a player standing on the front line is not shown' (Sargent 1916, 11).

In those times, facial close-ups had a distinct American feel about them, too. 'The development of the "close-up" action, whereby the figures are sometimes so large as to show only heads and torsos is an American innovation, although we owe the earlier methods of photoplay pantomime to the French and Italian producers', Eustace Hale Ball observed in his 1913 book *The Art of the Photoplay*, the Harvard library copy of which bears the stamp 'From the Library of Hugo Münsterberg, Professor of Psychology, 1892–1916' (Ball 1913, 19). It may have been in the wake of reading Eustace Ball that Münsterberg proclaimed: 'Here [with the close-up] begins the art of the photoplay' (Münsterberg 1916, 37) (*see* ATTENTION).

As space, so time. The time span for actors to act before one shot gives way to another is counted in seconds, sometimes less. Actors may hate this, but it is the brevity of scenes that gives the photoplay author a tremendous advantage over the playwright. As distinct from theatre, '[i]t is *abrupt* shifting from one locality to another that constitutes a "change of scene" in the photoplay' (Esenwein and Leeds 1913, 127; original italics). Filmmakers are always at liberty to shift, and it is due to this that the 'practice of switching from one scene to another, and then back to the first' (131) emerged, called *cut-back*, *switch-back* or *flash-back* (Griffith 1928, 185) in the 1910s, and *crosscutting*, *intercutting*, or *parallel montage* at later times.

Another medium-specific feature that photoplay guidebooks would proudly point to was that in films one could *discover* characters after a change of scenes instead of *entering* them on the stage as live playwrights were compelled to. 'To have the characters enter into a room or an exterior is a waste of film. Unless for some valid reason it is desirable to show this action, this extra time should be omitted. As often as possible, the characters should be "discovered" in the scene when it begins for in many cases the entrance "eats up" many valuable feet of film' (Ball 1913, 51). Narrative economy equals the economy of time and footage – during the 1910s this, too, was perceived as a specifically American ethos of filmmaking.

What we call a 'shot' today was called a *scene* in the 1910s, and what they called a *scene change* we call a 'cut'. How many scenes should there be in a one-reel subject, an aspiring free-lance might ask, and how long should a scene last before we cut? American trade press and screenwriting manuals alike burst with know-how and know-for-how-long, their authors vying and quarrelling with one another. The figure most experts writing between 1913 and 1916 recommended varied: around 40 scenes for a drama and 50 to 100 for a comedy.

Others proposed that different types of shots require different lengths. 'Don't be foolish and say, "I have read somewhere that about thirty-five or forty scenes constitute a reel",' explained Louella O. Parsons, a one-time Essanay story editor. 'No one in the world can possibly tell how many scenes there are to a reel. You cannot tell how many apples in a bushel. Of course not. The number of apples would depend upon their size' (Parsons 1916, 46–7).

No set rules applied to the length of consecutive scenes, except one best summarized in Griffith's brilliant essay 'Pace in the Movies':

> I have alluded to the semi hypnotic effect on the audience of the enforced concentration of its vision upon the screen. The effect is of incalculable value to the director ... but it is fraught with danger. If the picture were made so that each scene contained the same (or even approximately the same) number of frames, the 'semi hypnotic effect' would become the 'hypnotic effect,' and the audience would drop into the Land of Nod.
>
> (Griffith 1926, 7)

William Gordon's *How to Write Moving Picture Plays* stated: 'One scene may take four minutes and the next scene thirty seconds' (Gordon 1914, section 20). The only rule there could be about this was one of diversity justified by analogy to prose writing. Marguerite Bertsch, a picture story editor with the Vitagraph scenario department, wrote this in *How to Write for Moving Pictures*:

> While there are stories that are best carried out in the rapid action of short, snappy scenes, and while there are themes that require the longer scenes, few stories can be told to advantage by the use of one or the other exclusively. How

tedious would be our conversation, or how wearisome the pages of a story, given entirely in long, sonorous sentences! How maddening, too, would be the incessant pound of short, terse sentences! It is in the use of both of these, delicately playing one upon the other, that we get an artistry in style like that wonderful variation in landscape, of sharp elevations and rolling plains. So in pictures the long, stirring scenes create a mood from which we turn to brisker action, only to revert again to the long, low harmony.

(Bertsch 1917, 92)

How to learn what it is that makes scenes long or short? The best piece of advice picture story editors had to offer about this was not to look in the book but to frequent movies instead, armed with some gauging tool or other. '[M]ake a practice of carrying a few small cards, with a line drawn down the middle of each. As the card is held in the hand, mark with a pencil a short stroke on one side for every change of scene, and on the other side a stroke for each leader, letter or other insert – this will serve as a convenient record device', one manual suggested (Esenwein and Leeds 1913, 211). 'The inexperienced writer labors under a handicap, and one that he could overcome in a measure', another one chimed in. 'If he would take the trouble to count the scenes and note the length of them by consulting his watch as the story is unfolded, he would discover that some would-be wiseacre had given him a wrong steer' (Carr 1914, 106–7). Timing, counting, and cataloguing shots was a research practice much advocated in the 1910s.

Since the first thing said to single out American editing was speed, it makes sense to ask what types of shots were shorter than others and which sequences were the speediest of all. The most obvious variance you will discover, photoplay manuals would point out, will be between the length of scenes proper and that of intertitles, then called *leaders*, whose size depended on the number of words they contained, one second per word, the fewer the better (Nelson 1913, 21; Radinoff 1913, 35). While leaders were short, they were not the shortest of shots. It was the so-called *flashes* and *busts* that were the shortest particles of action.

What were these busts and flashes for and how quickly would they flash by? The word *bust* was a misnomer. What the bust meant in the screenwriters' vernacular was a close-up of any part of the body other than the head and shoulders, e.g. a hand with a gun shown to tip off the killer. A flash, in its turn, was what we might call a *cutaway* today, namely, '[a] brief glimpse of a scene, just enough to account for the presence of some character in a particular place' (Carr 1914, 34). Busts and flashes are inserts that never last; some are but two or three seconds long. About the shortest flash Epes Winthrop Sargent remembered having seen was a 'flash scene of six frames, the duration of the scene on the screen being three-eighth of a second' (Sargent 1916, 182).

As to sequencing, most observers agreed that the technique of cross-cutting (or *cut-back scenes*) was by far the fastest way of cutting films. 'For instance, in one release there were a hundred and seven scenes, twelve leaders, the title and the censorship tag – all on the thousand feet of film', J. Esenwein and Arthur Leeds complained in their 1913 book *Writing the Photoplay*. 'One scene ran four-fifth of one second, by a stop-watch, and it is not a difficult task to compute the average number of feet given to each scene!' (Esenwein and Leeds 1913, 174). We do not know if the authors had actually computed the value they suggested; if they had, the resulting figure would show an average of 8.3 seconds per shot – a fast, though by no means the fastest, instance of American cross-cutting in the mid-1910s.

To give a sense of the timing our two authors are talking about, it suffices to say that *The Mothering Heart* (1913) by D.W. Griffith has an average shot length of 8.2 seconds.

As tends to be the case with montage theories at large, early American continuity was theorized primarily (though not exclusively) by those who worked in the film industry or who aspired to join their ranks. This fact should not imply, however, that how to make your picture work was the only thing on their mind. Some reached to look behind the fence, asking questions that it might take a psychologist to answer. How do moving pictures work on the film viewer and how does the viewer's mind work as they watch scenes change?

Marguerite Bertsch came up with a theory of mental metrics and psychological harmony:

> Watching a picture, our minds get to working at a tempo prompted by the nature of the idea conveyed. If the scenes are, in length and action, in perfect harmony with this tempo, we are carried along, yielding ourselves to the subject until our very pulse beats in time with the movement. Should any one scene be not perfectly timed to the spirit of the play, it would throw out our count, breaking up the metrical response of mind and heart and causing us that discomfiture which comes with a 'drag' in the action ... For even where the story develops through a slow, meandering process, our minds adjust themselves so finely to its scarcely perceptible metre that we feel almost as keenly as in the above a departure from the same.
>
> (Bertsch 1917, 90)

The wind blows where it will. There must be holes in the fence that human fancy erects between academic film studies and teach-yourself literature of the kind cited above, for isn't it plausible to assume that Bertsch's 1917 excursion into the workings of a film viewer's mind had been encouraged by Hugo Münsterberg's *The Photoplay: A Psychological Study* (1916) – the first film theory book authored by an academic – as much as the latter may have been informed by guides like *The Art of the Photoplay* (1913) by Ball?

American continuity theory was part and parcel of continuity as a practice; with both, the goal was to square the editing techniques with what were seen as basic properties of viewers' perception. Given this, it is hardly surprising that the first editing theorist who was not a film industry practitioner was a student of Wilhelm Wundt and a colleague of William James. Münsterberg was an experimental psychologist; hence the measurements and calculations he used on films hardly differed from the methods used to study mental processes at his psychology lab at Harvard:

> If the scene changes too often and no movement is carried on without a break, the [photo]play may irritate us by its nervous jerking from place to place. Near the end of the Theda Bara edition of *Carmen* [1915] the scene changed one hundred and seventy times in ten minutes, an average of a little more than three seconds for each scene. We follow Don José and Carmen and the toreador in ever new phases of the dramatic action and are constantly carried back to Don José's home village where his mother waits for him. There indeed the dramatic tension has an element of nervousness, in contrast to the Geraldine Farrar version of *Carmen* [1915] which allows a more unbroken development of the single action.
>
> (Münsterberg 1916, 45–6)

Scientists like Münsterberg were as curious about the technique of editing as Hollywood story editors like Marguerite Bertsch were about the working of the human mind. The pivotal thought of Münsterberg's film theory was that film editing replicates mental processes. His 1916 study book links the 'cut-back' to memory and 'visions' to imagination; in turn, the close-up technique exteriorizes our attention's propensity to focus.

The film-as-mind analogy central to Münsterberg's book remained productive for the art and the science of motion pictures throughout their history. The attention argument has been used more than once to account for continuity and staging. 'The director counterfeits the operation of the eye with his lens', D.W. Griffith explains in a later essay (Griffith 1926); in Soviet Russia, Dziga Vertov and Vsevolod Pudovkin would resort to the observer-eye metaphor in their theories of film. In more recent times, attention has resurfaced in a number of differently conceived studies one can loosely describe as cognitive film theories. Here, editing is seen as responding to: natural ways for the human eye to navigate the space of the screen (Smith 2012); optimal ways in which our attention fluctuates over time (Cutting *et al.* 2010); filmmakers' choice of tools to guide the viewers' attention (Bordwell 2013). The two former approaches square with the Münsterberg tradition, the latter with the tradition of Soviet poetics of montage.

YURI TSIVIAN

## Works cited

Ball, Eustace Hale. 1913. *The Art of the Photoplay*. New York: Dillingham.

Bedding, Thomas. 1909. 'The Modern Way in Moving Pictures Making'. *Moving Picture World* 4 (19): 587 (8 May).

Bertsch, Marguerite. 1917. *How to Write for Moving Pictures*. New York: George H. Doran Company.

Bordwell, David. 1985. 'The Classical Hollywood Style'. In *The Classical Hollywood Cinema: Film Style and Mode of Production to 1960*, by David Bordwell, Janet Staiger, Kristin Thompson, 1–84. New York: Columbia University Press.

——. 2012. 'Not-Quite-Lost Shadows'. http://www.davidbordwell.net/blog/2012/07/22/not-quite-lost-shadows/.

——. 2013. 'How Motion Pictures Became the Movies'. A video-lecture. http://davidbordwell.net/video/movielecture.php.

Bottomore, Stephen. 1990. 'Shots in the Dark: The Real Origins of Film Editing'. In *Early Cinema: Space, Frame, Narrative*, edited by Thomas Elsaesser, 104–13. London: British Film Institute.

Bowser, Eileen. 1990. *The Transformation of Cinema*. New York: Charles Scribner's Sons.

Carr, Catherine. 1914. *The Art of Photoplay Writing*. New York: The Hannis Jordan Company Publishers.

Craw, Rockhill George. 1911. 'The Technique of the Picture Play'. *Moving Picture World* 3 (8): 126–7.

Cutting, James, J.E. DeLong, and C.E. Nothelfer. 2010. 'Attention and the Evolution of Hollywood Film'. *Psychological Science* 21: 440–7.

Esenwein, J. Berg, and Arthur Leeds. 1913. *Writing the Photoplay*. Springfield, MA: The Home Correspondence School.

Gordon, William Lewis. 1914. *How to Write Moving Picture Plays*. Cincinnati, OH: Atlas Publishing Company.

Griffith, D.W. 1926. 'Pace in the Movies'. *Liberty* (13 November): http://web.grinnell.edu/courses/spn/s02/spn395-01/RAF/RAF02/RAF0202.pdf: 1–9.

——. 1928. 'How Movies Are Made'. In *The Griffith Project*, edited by Paolo Cherchi Usai, vol. 11, 184–5. London: BFI Publishing.

Gunning, Tom. 2010. 'Editing: Spatial Relations'. In *Encyclopedia of Early Cinema*, edited by Richard Abel, 104–5. London and New York: Routledge.

Jasset, Victorin-Hippolyte. 1911. 'An Essay on Mise-en-scène in Cinematography'. In *French Film Criticism: A History/Anthology 1907–1939*, edited by Richard Abel, vol. 1, 55–65. Princeton, NJ: Princeton University Press, 1988.

Keil, Charlie. 2001. *Early American Cinema in Transition: Story, Style, and Filmmaking, 1907–1913*. Madison: Wisconsin University Press.

Münsterberg, Hugo. 1916. *The Film: A Psychological Study*. New York and London: D. Appleton and Company.

Musser, Charles. 1991. *The Emergence of Cinema*. New York: Charles Scribner's Sons.

Nelson, J. Arthur. 1913. *The Photo-play: How to Write, How to Sell*. Los Angeles, CA: Photoplay Publishing Company.

Parsons, Louella O. 1916. *How to Write for the 'Movies'*. Chicago, IL: A.C. McClurg & Co.

Radinoff, Florence. 1913. *The Photoplayers' Handy Text-Book*. New York: Manhattan Motion Picture Institute.

Salt, Barry. 1983. *Film Style and Technology: History and Analysis*. London: Starword.

Sargent, Epes Winthrop. 1916. *Technique of the Photoplay*. New York: The Moving Picture World.

Smith, Tim J. 2012. 'The Attentional Theory of Cinematic Continuity'. *Projections* 6 (1): 1–27.

Thompson, Kristin. 1985. 'The Formulation of the Classical Style, 1909–28'. In *The Classical Hollywood Cinema: Film Style and Mode of Production to 1960*, by David Bordwell, Janet Staiger, and Kristin Thompson, 167–85. New York: Columbia University Press.

Tille, Václav. 2008 [1908]. 'Kinéma'. In *Cinema All the Time: An Anthology of Czech Film Theory and Criticism, 1908–39*, edited by Jaroslav Andel and Petr Szczepanik, 71–91. Ann Arbor: Michigan Slavic Publications.

# MONTAGE THEORY II
## (SOVIET AVANT-GARDE)

Cutting fast was the American speciality throughout the 1910s; soon after the First World War the practice spread to Soviet Russia and to France, where they called it *montage*. The two notions are not identical, however. What happened to cutting on the way to Europe was what Russian Formalist theorists might call a change in its constructive function (Tynianov 1927). Distinct from the American way of joining shots, montage in the French and Soviet sense did not hinge so much on storytelling needs. When *montage* was evoked by a French cinephile or cineaste after Abel Gance, it was more likely to be about the rhythm and musicality of action than about action *per se* (Epstein 1924); and when *montazh* was theorized in Soviet Russia, the conversation would typically pivot around the construction of meaning that emerges not within but *between* shots.

Soviet montage theory is an umbrella term that covers a number of theories developed by seven film directors. The names of those whose writings were translated and became known in the West are Lev Kuleshov, Dziga Vertov, Vsevolod Pudovkin, and Sergei Eisenstein; Semion Timoshenko and Sergei and Georgii Vasiliev are lesser known. We might add to this list a handful of literary scholars whose ideas about film gained currency in filmmaking circles – Viktor Shklovsky, Boris Eikhenbaum, Yuri Tynianov.

Although most of these individuals used to lecture and teach, or publish scholarly books, Soviet montage theory was anything but academic. As it happened, every film director or film theorist interested in montage belonged to or had a leaning towards innovative scholarship or an avant-garde art movement, be it futurist poetry, constructivist art, or formalist poetics. Accordingly, montage theory was less a systematic affair than an amalgam of polemical addresses, artistic manifestos, and post-analyses of one's own experiments on film. Here, practice constantly segued into theory and theory into practice.

## Origins and models

Why in Russia and why in the wake of the First World War? A convergence of factors helps to account for the montage explosion. One was the elaborate slowness of Russian quality pictures of the mid-1910s. 'The speed it moves at is no more than "four kilometers per hour",' a newspaper reviewer complained about Yevgeni Bauer's *Silent Witnesses* (*Nemye svideteli*, 1914), turning into a critical metaphor the speed of motor cars, the production of which was an industry as new as film (Teatral'naya Gazeta 1914, 11); indeed, the average shot length of Bauer's film is as high as 41.3 seconds, which is quite slow, at least by American standards. There is a mindset that stands behind this number. For Bauer the faster the film, the less room it leaves for thought and feeling. At later times this kind of logic resurfaces in the anti-montage arguments of Andrei Tarkovsky and André Bazin (*see* LONG TAKE).

At one point, cut less, move less, feel more took the form of a stylistic doctrine promoted in no humble terms by Russian trade paper philosophers. It was the actor, not film footage, that was alleged to be the cornerstone of filmmaking. A selection of statements will suffice to give an idea of where Russian cinema was heading in the teens and of the role of the actor in the crusade against cutting:

> The [Russian] film story breaks decisively with all the established views on the essence of the cinematographic picture: it repudiates *movement* ... In the world of the screen, where everything is counted in meters, the actor's struggle for the freedom to act has led to a battle for long (in terms of meters) scenes or, more accurately, for 'full' scenes ... A 'full' scene is one in which the actor is given the opportunity to depict in stage terms a specific spiritual experience, no matter how many meters it takes. The 'full' scene involves a complete rejection of the usual hurried tempo of the film drama. Instead of a rapidly changing kaleidoscope of images, it aspires to rivet the attention of the audience on to a single image ... This may sound like a paradox for the art of cinema (which derives its name from the Greek word for 'movement') but the involvement of our best actors in cinema will lead to the slowest possible tempo.
>
> (Petrovskii 1916, 3; italics in the original)

In writings like this, the 'true essence' of cinema was seen to lie in acting not action.

Indeed, if a race existed in which the slowest won, Russian tsarist cinema would be the winner. It is here, however, that another factor intervenes, less intrinsic to Russian cinema as such, but no less historic in terms of its development. In October 1917 the Bolshevik revolution took place and left no stone unturned, the cornerstone of Russian filmmaking included. This is where Lev Kuleshov comes in. Bauer's understudy since 1916, this 20-year-old embarked in 1918 on a project that was nothing short of revolutionary: to restructure the way films were made in pre-revolutionary Russia and upshift the pace of Russian films.

The method Kuleshov chose is best described as stylistic engineering. 'First of all, we divided the cinema into three basic types: the Russian film, the European, and the American.' Kuleshov explained what he and his friends did in order to crack the code of cutting fast: 'When we began to compare the typically American, typically European, and typically Russian films, we noticed that they were distinctly different from one another in their construction. We noticed that in a particular sequence of a Russian film there were, say, ten to fifteen splices, ten to fifteen different set-ups ... while in the American film there would be from eighty, sometimes upward to a hundred, separate shots' (Kuleshov 1974, 187). The study brought results: Kuleshov's *Engineer Prait's Project* (*Proiekt inzhenera Praita*, 1918) was an exercise in Hollywood-style continuity complete with flashes, busts, and a number of other cutting devices from the arsenal of analytical editing (Thompson and Bordwell 2006, 107), which enabled Kuleshov to raise his cutting rate to an average shot length of 6.2 seconds.

*Americanitis* was a trendy disease among the Soviet left. 'We are short of raw stock. Give it to us and you will see what the American montage is all about, how gifted our film players [*kinonaturshchiki*] are and how beautifully American a city can look, even if this city is as un-American as Moscow', Kuleshov promised in 1922 (Kuleshov 1979, 146). And another voice from the same year stated: 'The American montage is no news. Today we can consider it classics' (Vertov 1922, 10). Classics or not, as late as 1922 Vertov was still calling rapid cutting American.

There existed a difference, however, between what American photoplay manuals wrote about editing and what people made of editing in Russia. If in the eye of the former cutting was but a means to an end, a way of solving storytelling problems, in Russia the technique itself was seen as a problem, something to be explored, explained, and experimented with. Will spaces match if someone walking along a street in Moscow waves her hand to someone descending Capitol Hill in Washington? Will she dance if one dancer's hands are spliced together with another dancer's legs? And if one and the same close-up is combined with three different shots, will the viewer attribute to the same facial expression three different moods? For Kuleshov and Vertov questions like these sounded fully legitimate.

Such explorations occurred in a constructivist environment. In avant-garde circles of the early 1920s montage was as hot a notion as American. In Russian the word *montage* had previously been employed to refer to housing construction and mechanical engineering. To make, to build, and to assemble were the right words to be used in Constructivist studio talk instead of 'create', as was the word *things (veshchi)* instead of 'works of art'. To build a new city out of two cities or to assemble a perfect person out of parts was a challenge that experimenters like Kuleshov and Vertov saw ingrained in the very word *montage*.

## Montage vs. editing

'The *plot* is the thing', the American editor Captain Leslie T. Peacocke states in his *Hints on Photoplay Writing* (Peacocke 1916, 13). This commandment was never quite observed in the Soviet Union of the 1920s. While it is true that most Soviet films were action-driven, Soviet montage theorists were ambivalent about plots. Even Kuleshov, who never shunned plotting, made sure the spectator bore in mind that stories in his films were treated as mere material; what really mattered was 'not the demonstration of the content of the shots as such, but their organization, combination and construction, that is, the interrelationship of shots, their sequence, the replacement of one shot by another' (Kuleshov 1974, 46).

In other words, for Kuleshov, as for Soviet theorists at large, the ultimate element of cutting was not the shot, but the cut. Whether it was hunger, desire, or mourning that a face on the screen expressed was decided not by what happened within the shots but by what happened between them. In his editing practice, Kuleshov was a minimalist to the maximal degree: the average shot lengths of the three feature films he made between 1924 and 1926 were as low as 4.3, 3.6, and 4.1 seconds.[1] Only the fastest of Keystone slapstick comedies had been cut as fast in the United States.

In Kuleshov's case this led to what an American photoplay expert would reject. Continuity remains continuity as long as we take no notice of it; by increasing the speed, Kuleshov made cutting more salient than the story it served. For Kuleshov and his like cutting, not acting or action, was the 'true essence' of film.

## Montage as art, poetry and music

It was his shift of emphasis from the story material to the techniques of cutting and piecing it together that makes Kuleshov's films resemble Dadaist and Constructivist photomontages. It may not have been by chance that as many as five of Kuleshov's pictures hinge on American themes and feature grotesque versions of Hollywood types from comedies and melodramas; and it was by no means by chance that Kuleshov's essay 'Montage', published in the Constructivist magazine *Kino-fot* in 1922, appeared illustrated with collages by Aleksandr Rodchenko in which cut-outs from stills found in American film fan magazines were shown frozen in their most dramatic and suggestive poses. In Constructivist montages, explicit constructed-ness is the thing, and so it is in Kuleshov's films.

The cut, not the shot, is where Soviet montage theory began. What happens when two shots touch one another with their naked ends? Vertov, Pudovkin, and Eisenstein had their own ideas about this. Vertov's idea was prompted by what he knew from music theory. What is found between two shots should be called *interval*, Vertov claimed. In music, each note has its own pitch, yet it is not the pitch as such but intervals between pitches that turns discrete sounds of music into music. So in films: every film shot has its own length and scale and is characterized by the speed and direction of the moving objects being shown, and yet it is not these parameters *per se* but intervals and variations between them that give to films their dynamic form.

What Vertov wanted from editing was structure. A die-hard advocate of documentaries, Vertov's writings condemned all fiction films as fakes. Cinema which wants to tell the truth must free its hands from the fetters of the plot. Yet Vertov knew such freedom would come at a price. The price was structure, the armature that holds the work together. Fiction has structure, non-fiction seemingly has none. If not the plot, then what? Vertov's answer was poetry and music, two media whose ways of arranging elements into a whole did not hinge on narratives of any kind.

Early on Vertov saw to it that his films were structured on several levels. The low-level structures were what Eisenstein (speaking of Vertov) labelled *metric montage* (Eisenstein 1949, 72–4). Vertov used to count frames between cuts as a composer might measures or a poet syllables and feet, and was the first to have theorized frame counting (Belenson 1925, 11). Shots of different lengths recur at regular times, the metric doctrine decreed.

It took more than frame-counting to give shape to unscripted films. Thematic parallels and repetitions were what defined Vertov's method of sequencing. The power of parallelism was the lesson Soviet montage directors learned from D.W. Griffith's *Intolerance* (1916) when the film was shown in Russia in 1918. 'After this happened, it became easier to talk', Vertov admitted (Vertov 1966, 116). The fiction of four fictions as *Intolerance* was, its multi-story construction and Whitmanesque refrain were perceived in Russia as a poetic alternative to standard fiction.

Vertov's parallels meet on a higher level. Throughout Vertov's writings and across his films runs the blended-name *kino-eye*, a theoretical metaphor, both a visual object and a para-narrative agency all at once. In the latter capacity, Vertov's kino-eye was his substitute for a narration that simply chronicles what happens; the kino-eye lists the things it sees. Lists upon lists of things to see were what drew together Vertov's montage and the 'catalogue poetry' of Walt Whitman, Vertov's favourite read.

What a theorist believed happens between shots depended on which analogy was in force. Both editing and montage theorists looked to literature to explain film, but, distinct from the Americans, Soviets leaned towards poetry, not prose. In prose, the length of the shot was determined by how much an author intended to say. '[S]imple and complex structure in scenes is very like the corresponding structure in writing. The simple sentence tells one thing only; so also does the simple scene', Marguerite Bertsch explained to aspiring photoplay authors, whereas 'parts of the complex scene, like the clauses in a complex sentence, will introduce into the same a multitude of ideas and suggestions' (Bertsch 1917, 91).

The montage school, by contrast, treated shots as lines in a poem. Prior to the Bolshevik revolution in October 1917, cuts between shots were seen as transitions, and the smoother the better, Tynianov wrote in 1927. Not so now. 'Cinema jumps from shot to shot, just as verse does from line to line. Strange as it may seem, if one is to draw an analogy between cinema and the verbal arts, then the only legitimate analogy would be between cinema and verse, not prose' (Tynianov 1927, 93). Editing hides behind the story; montage, as verse, lays its presence bare.

What happens between two shots became a matter of a debate, a shorthand summary of which dates back to the mid-1920s. 'In front of me lies a crumpled yellowed sheet of paper', Eisenstein wrote in his 1929 study of montage:

> 'Linkage—P' and 'Collision—E.' This is a substantial trace of a heated bout on the subject of montage between P (Pudovkin) and E (myself). This has become a habit. At regular intervals he visits me late at night and behind closed doors we wrangle over matters of principle. A graduate of the Kuleshov school, he loudly defends an understanding of montage as a *linkage* of pieces. Into a chain. Again, 'bricks'. Bricks, arranged in series to *expound* an idea. I confronted him with my viewpoint on montage as a *collision*. A view that from the collision of two given factors *arises* a concept. From my point of view, linkage is merely a possible *special* case.
>
> (Eisenstein 1949, 37–8; italics in the original)

Pudovkin conceded, but never fully. Polarized as they may have been in the radical eye of Eisenstein or Vertov, montage and editing walked hand in hand in Pudovkin's films and writings. Pudovkin's *invisible observer* – the hypothetical demon conjured up to motivate framing and sequencing of shots – may impersonate plain point-of-view editing at one point in a film and turn out to be as volatile and ubiquitous as Vertov's kino-eye demon at another. Pudovkin's *Mother* (*Mat'*, 1926) is a centaur of a movie: it begins as a story and ends as a verse in which formal structures take precedence over narrative ones, as Shklovsky observed in his essay 'Poetry and Prose in Cinema' (Shklovsky 1927, 176–8).

## Eisenstein's montage theory

Of all Soviet montage theories of the 1920s, Eisenstein's has been the most influential and all-embracing. Beneath a stream of topics and references one discerns a few basic principles Eisenstein never tired of reasserting. One was the principle of *conflict* or *collision* which he upheld in his debate with Pudovkin. Another was that of totality, which Eisenstein labelled *monistic ensemble*, which definition itself contained an internal conflict, namely the idea of being single or alone (monism) combined with a collectivity (ensemble). Third, Eisenstein's idea of form was dynamic, never static. It makes sense to look at these three principles one by one, starting with the latter.

Form in art should be conceived as an ongoing process rather than as a fixed mould. Eisenstein used this distinction to account both for the artist's creative work and for the way art works (or should work) on the viewer. For example, according to Eisenstein the art of drawing, like dance, is that of movement not of moulding static space.

In 1923 Eisenstein published an essay entitled 'The Montage of Attractions', which argued that the task of the (theatre) director was to push the spectator through a pre-planned series of *shocks* regardless of whether the play really occasioned them (*see* ATTRACTION). As on stage, so in film. Some sequences in *Strike* (1925) were designed to promote this theory by way of downplaying the film's narrative coherence in order to favour a *montage of film attractions*. The further vicissitudes of this tenet took Eisenstein the thinker to his theory of *intellectual montage*, according to which meaning is generated via colliding rather than linking neighbouring shots. In *October* (1928) Eisenstein tested this principle, hoping to generate 'abstract concepts' by way of juxtaposing artefacts found in the Winter Palace (icons, Fabergé eggs, Rodin's sculpture, Napoleon statuettes, a clockwork peacock) and historical figures of 1917.

His next step was to propose that montage as dynamic form replicates the process of human thinking, which took Eisenstein the filmmaker to a few stream-of-consciousness sequences in (unrealized) films of the 1930s. During the last decade of his life, Eisenstein developed his *pathos and ecstasy* theory, which defined how, exactly, the process (called *dialectics*) of art form works to achieve a specific type of emotional involvement (called *pathos*) necessary to jolt the spectator 'out of the stasis' of everyday experience. The state of *ecstasy* thus achieved obliterates the boundary between the *self* and *others*. This theory Eisenstein would typically illustrate with the 'Odessa steps' sequence from his earlier *Battleship Potemkin* (1925), in which the images of the descending firing squad and those of the massacred crowd interact to create the implacable montage rhythm due to which the 'jumping sculpture' of the stone lion that crowns the sequence is perceived not as a visual joke but as stone itself woken up at the high point of the tragedy. 'For the stone shall cry out of the wall', Eisenstein quoted from the Bible in explaining this visual trope.

*Conflict* was another key word in Eisenstein's theory of montage. For Eisenstein, conflict was not solely what happened between two shots or within a single one, but the principle of art in general. In the 1920s he found collisions everywhere. Unlike most of the modernist acting reformers of the 1920s (Vsevolod, Meyerhold, Kuleshov, Nikolai Foregger), Eisenstein's idea of expressivity foregrounded conflict rather than harmony and adjustment within the moving body (gravity vs. effort, volition vs. inertia, etc.). As the musical analogy gained weight in Eisenstein's later aesthetics, he would use the term *counterpoint* instead, to stress that conflict was a constituent of dynamic unity.

Art separates formal elements from their everyday contexts (Eisenstein called this operation *de-anecdotization*) – this idea was key to his theories of sound and colour in cinema. For the artist, an element becomes instrumental only when separated from its real-life connections. The creaking of boots will work emotionally when we do not see the boots on the screen. Otherwise in black and white, *Ivan the Terrible* (1944/6) suddenly acquires colour towards the end – similarly, with no apparent motivation, a character's face turns blue at the high point of tragedy. Separated from its source, sound becomes a matter of artistic choice; when colour is not predicated by the object, but is chosen by the filmmaker, true colour cinema is born.

Polyphony was Eisenstein's third favourite principle of montage. Unlike most other artists and theorists gathered around LEF (Left Front of Arts), who would insist on exclusive use of 'correct' material or techniques (Vertov, Osip Brik), in his first manifesto, 'The Montage of Attractions' (1923), Eisenstein asserted the primacy of impact over devices:

319

since the basic material of theatre is the audience itself, the correct means are those that best lead to the desired effect. Late in the 1920s, Eisenstein's aesthetic pluralism showed up in his proposed typology of montage: *metric, rhythmic, tonal,* and *overtonal,* the last one being superior to the first three because, rather than operating through a single dominant, it works on the viewer through multiple *stimulants* found within shots.

The principle of poly-stimulant impact was reinforced by the Japanese Kabuki theatre, during whose visit to Moscow in 1928 Eisenstein was struck by what he termed a *monistic ensemble*: a technique of acting and staging based on a precisely measured-out impact by means of several sensory channels (acoustic and visual) in relay fashion rather than simultaneously. This experience proved handy when Eisenstein found himself faced with the problem of sound. He envisioned sound cinema as a promising medium for the stream-of-consciousness technique that he saw as a monistic ensemble of senses (images without sound, sounds without images, words alone, music alone, etc.). A firm believer in synaesthesia, Eisenstein argued that sounds and images could thus interact in *vertical montage,* creating a *polyphony* of multi-sensory impacts, a theory he tested in *Alexander Nevsky* (1938) and developed into an audiovisual polyphony in the two-part *Ivan the Terrible,* one of the most ambitious ventures in all of film history.

It may sound like a paradox, but montage theory in the Soviet sense descends directly from the Hollywood continuity techniques minus the very thing they served: the fluent and unobtrusive rendering of the film story. Theorizing American experience was what Soviet directors started with; taking the water and leaving the baby were what Soviet montage theory ultimately recommended. Various avant-garde ideas took the place which Hollywood story editors reserved for the storyline. Starting with the end of the decade when Hollywood continuity rules caught the eye of young Soviet avant-garde artists, a number of other currents of thought emerged, each linking the technique of editing to this or that set of radical ideas. This was a place and time with no respect or patience for rules. Here, invention and experiment were the rule of the day. Every film had to be a montage experiment and every theory had to invent montage anew.

YURI TSIVIAN

## Note

1 *Extraordinary Adventures of Mr. West in the Land of the Bolsheviks (Neobychainye prikliucheniia Mistera Westa v strane bol'shevikov)* (1924) had an average shot length (ASL) of 4.3 seconds, *The Ray of Death (Luch smerti)* (1925) an ASL of 3.6 seconds, and *By the Law (Po zakonu)* (1926, Soviet Union) an ASL of 4.1 seconds. Samples of American and European silent films for the period 1918–23 studied by Barry Salt have a mean ASL of 6.5 and 8.7 seconds; see figures 2.2 and 2.3 in Baxter (2012).

## Works cited

Baxter, Mike. 2012. 'Chapter 2 – Examples'. In *Cinemetrics Data Analysis*: http://www.mikemetrics.com/#/cinemetrics-data-analysis/4569975605.

Belenson, Aleksandr. 1925. *Kino segodnia [Cinema today]*. Moscow.

Bertsch, Marguerite. 1917. *How to Write for Moving Pictures*. New York: George H. Doran Company.

Eisenstein, Sergei. 1949. *Film Form: Essays in Film Theory*. Edited by Jay Leyda. New York: Harcourt, Brace & World.

Epstein, Jean. 1924. 'Rhythm and Montage'. *Afterimage* 10 (Autumn 1981): 16–17.

Griffith, D.W. 1926. 'Pace in the Movies'. *Liberty* (13 November): 1–9: http://web.grinnell.edu/courses/spn/s02/spn395-01/RAF/RAF02/RAF0202.pdf.

Kuleshov, Lev. 1922. 'Montage'. *Kino-fot* 3: 12.

——. 1974. *Kuleshov on Film*. Edited by Ronald Levaco. Berkeley, Los Angeles, London: University of California Press.

——. 1979. *Stat'i: Materialy*. Moscow: Iskusstvo.

Peacocke, Leslie T. 1916. *Hints on Photoplay Writing*. Chicago, IL: Photoplay Publishing Company.

Petrovskii, I. 1916. 'Kinodrama ili kinopovest?' ['Film Drama or Film Story?']. *Proektor* 20.

Shklovsky, Viktor. 1927. 'Poetry and Prose in Cinema'. In *The Film Factory: Russian and Soviet Cinema in Documents 1896–1939*, edited by Richard Taylor and Ian Christie. London and New York: Routledge, 1988.

Teatral'naya Gazeta. 1914. 'Nemye Svideteli' [Silent Witnesses]. *Teatral'naya Gazeta* 19: 11.

Thompson, Kristin, and David Bordwell. 2006. *Film History: An Introduction*. New York: McGraw-Hill.

Tynianov, Yuri. 1927. 'On the Foundations of Cinema'. In *Russian Formalist Film Theory*, edited by Herbert Eagle. Ann Arbor: Michigan Slavic Publications, 1981.

Vertov, Dziga. 1922. 'On i ia'. *Kino-fot* 2.

——. 1966. *Stat'i, dnevniki, zamysly*. Edited by Sergei Drobashenko. Moscow: Iskusstvo.

# MOVEMENT-IMAGE

*Cinema 1: The Movement-Image*, which was first published in France in 1983, is the first of two volumes on cinema by French philosopher Gilles Deleuze. It was followed in 1985 by *Cinema 2: The Time-Image* (*see* TIME-IMAGE), and, combined, the two books attempt to set out a taxonomy of cinematic images, with Deleuze drawing his examples from a range of films from all periods of film history and from most continents.

Trying to summarize Deleuze's books is no mean task, let alone listing all the film scholars who subsequently have used and abused them. The reason for this is that the books, as Ronald Bogue puts it, 'make significant demands of the reader, who must follow Deleuze through thickets of dense reasoning and sweeping synthetic exegesis across the domains of both cinema and philosophy' (Bogue 2003, 2). However, in spite of this obstacle, in this entry I shall draw a basic outline of Deleuze's movement-image, before explaining briefly how and perhaps why scholars have since both rejected and embraced the concept.

## The influence of Bergson

If above I described Deleuze's cinema books as a taxonomy of images, that is because the books do involve a list of types of image, such as the perception-image, the affection-image, and the action-image, which I shall explain below. However, underwriting Deleuze's books, and in accordance with his day job as a philosopher, there is a conception of time, space, and movement that draws heavily on the works of one of Deleuze's philosophical predecessors, Henri Bergson, and which needs to be explained. It is with a summary of Bergson's and Deleuze's philosophical outlook, then, that this entry shall begin.

In *Creative Evolution* (1907), Bergson criticizes cinema for offering a succession of still images, which do not reflect the fundamentally continuous and indivisible nature of time itself. Although Deleuze draws heavily upon Bergson in the *Cinema* books, at the beginning of *The Movement-Image*, he criticizes his master, arguing that cinema does not offer us a succession of still images to which movement is added, but rather cinema offers us a direct *movement-image*. That is to say, cinema does not break movement down into discrete units, in each of which there is a figure described at a unique moment; instead, with cinema, it is continuous (and indivisible – though I shall refine this term later on) movement that describes the figure (Deleuze 1983, 14). This relates to Bergson's concept of duration (*durée*), which is the term he uses to describe the constantly changing 'whole' that is the 'open' universe, which mistakenly, though perhaps for good reason, humans all too often take to be fixed, or 'closed'. For Bergson and Deleuze, the universe is constantly changing, since it is always in movement. Moreover, for Deleuze if not for Bergson, cinema shows moving images of this always-moving universe/whole. From this we can conclude that cinema is a philosophical tool, in that it visualizes the open, while the human mind all too often is, I might argue, 'closed' (but we know that humans are truly open-minded because the 'closed-minded' often do change their minds!).

If duration is an indivisible whole, and if cinema for Deleuze shows the constant movement of this indivisible whole, then an inevitable problem arises: how do we understand the frame? For, if the whole is indivisible, then the frame by its very nature divides the external and supposedly indivisible world into fixed (and closed) spaces. Here we can refine the use of the term indivisible: patently the universe is divisible, as the fragmentation of space that is the frame exemplifies. However, for each 'division' that is made, the 'whole' changes (1983, 26). That is, the very act of framing can be seen to contribute to the changing nature/to the movement of the whole. Furthermore, while framing itself contributes to the movement of the whole, Deleuze argues that camera movement, as well as the use of off-screen space generally, indicates that the 'whole' is there, even if we cannot see it directly. In other words, in the same way that we ourselves cannot see all of reality, but we can derive its presence/be conscious of it from the fragment that we do see, the camera, too, can suggest or indirectly show to us 'the whole', particularly when it moves.

What is more, the comparison between the camera and human consciousness does not end there: Deleuze also proposes that the camera has its own 'consciousness', particularly when it does not follow the actors but performs movements that seem 'unmotivated'. In addition, even when the camera remains motionless, editing or montage can create movement. In other words, Deleuze suggests that the cinematic image is 'open' and that movement is its defining characteristic, much as openness and movement are defining characteristics of duration (and consciousness, which is a fragment of duration that changes the whole).

## A history of montage

Hereafter, Deleuze begins to discuss montage in more detail, outlining differences between American, Soviet, German Expressionist, and pre-war French montage. American montage, especially the work of D.W. Griffith, is defined as expressing the whole, or giving us an indirect image of duration/time, by contracting the present moment such that the present becomes the whole itself (Deleuze 1983, 50). In *Intolerance* (1916), we can see this happening by the acceleration of the cutting rhythm as the film reaches its climax: the interval between actions becomes so small as the film mingles stories from different time periods and places (Babylon in 539 BC, Jesus' crucifixion, France in 1572, and America in 1914) that each seems to co-exist as pure presence.

Soviet montage is defined as dialectic. By showing contrasting images (as in Dziga Vertov's films, as well as those of Sergei M. Eisenstein), the 'whole' is continually split in two by the Soviet filmmakers, but these pieces recombine to form a new whole. In other words, the films in some senses can be seen to reflect the revolutionary Soviet project: to reshape the world anew.

Meanwhile, French pre-war cinema puts an emphasis on the movement of both people and objects. For Deleuze, this happens in such a way that not just machines (animate objects) come to the fore, but such that the interaction between people and the objects and places that surround them forms a single 'dancing machine' (1983, 62). This in turn leads to a conception of French pre-war cinema as not a cinema involving solid objects moving, but a fluid cinema that is reflected in the emphasis on the sea and rivers in the works of Marcel L'Herbier, Jean Renoir, Jean Epstein, Jean Vigo, and Jean Grémillon. Here, and in the films of Abel Gance, Deleuze perceives a depiction of the immensity of the moving whole, or the universe, an excess of movement such that these films surpass the powers of the imagination, or 'reduce it to impotence' (1983, 72). This takes us to the limits of thought, where we contemplate the totality of things that is ungraspable because it is always in motion.

Finally, where French pre-war cinema involves an emphasis on movement, German Expressionist cinema involves an emphasis on light. For Deleuze, light is movement (we can conceive of this by thinking about light speed: light is the very limit of movement), and the light-images of German expressionism fulfil a similar function to the movement-images of French pre-war cinema: in my own words rather than Deleuze's, they attempt to shed light on the invisible 'darkness' (because invisible) that is the whole. Here, too, there is an emphasis on the 'non-organic life of things' (1983, 75), which is reflected in the films by the presence of zombies, sleepwalkers, and golems: everything is alive, and German Expressionist cinema as a whole suggests for Deleuze that *life* drives the universe, even when the moving person or thing is supposedly 'dead'. This *life* (inorganic and non-psychological) is what Deleuze calls *spirit*, and which he labels the 'divine' part in all of us (1983, 80).

## Back to Bergson: Deleuze's image types

Deleuze then reconsiders Bergson, in particular his *Matter and Memory* (1896), in order to construct three principle image-types: the perception-image, the affection-image, and the action-image. Bergson's thesis is that everything is an image, including ourselves, and that every image acts upon and reacts to other images. In short, this seems to be a way of saying that we are not voyeurs of the world who are abstracted from it and who clearly can see it; on the contrary, we are in the world, and we are changing along with it at each and every instant. It is not that my brain contains images, then; my brain is simply another image, and it acts upon and reacts to the images that compose the moving universe, since images = movement (Deleuze 1983, 84).

Because humans and their language differentiate subjects from objects, the Deleuze–Bergson thesis is perhaps counter-intuitive to many people, and although Deleuze defines all of these as *movement*-images, he distinguishes perception-, affection-, and action-images in order to demonstrate the way in which cinema reflects human experience (i.e. is anthropocentric).

In general terms, the perception-image is a master or long shot, in which we see what characters (and/or objects) see in the film world; the affection-image is the close-up or the reaction shot; and the action-image is the middle shot in which the reaction is put into action. However, Deleuze also is clear to differentiate between sub-types, or what we might call degrees, of these images – and it is through this that we can bring cinema back from anthropocentrism to the cosmic/universal arguments that precede Deleuze's taxonomy.

For while the perception-image may offer us a point-of-view, or subjective, shot, very often in cinema it does not. If we see shots in films that are not from a particular character's point of view, then we might, as Deleuze does, attribute these shots to the camera.

As a result, the camera becomes its own character/becomes 'conscious', as Deleuze sees happening especially in the cinema of Pier Paolo Pasolini and Jean-Luc Godard, among others (1983, 108–9).

If French pre-war cinema was a 'liquid' cinema, not just because it featured fluid matter, but also because it became a flowing, 'dancing machine', then Deleuze also distinguishes this from 'solid' cinema (which is a cinema rooted in character-bound point-of-view shots – i.e. a cinema that conforms to the norms of human perception) and from 'gaseous' cinema, which involves perception-images that show us not just people and objects but the 'molecular gaps' between them (1983, 123). What Deleuze means here is a cinema that offers us a non-human perspective, not just in terms of shots and angles but also perhaps in terms of montage: hyper-rapid cutting, as in the films of Stan Brakhage, such that perception is unhinged from action.

The affection-image, meanwhile, shows objects in close-up – and close-ups are typically of faces. However, Deleuze says that affection-images are not necessarily close-ups of human faces, but close-ups that bring out the 'faceness' of any object (1983, 126). By this, Deleuze means that a close-up can show us the unity of force (*puissance*) and 'quality' (in the sense of attribute or property, as well as 'suchness'/*quale*) of an object: intensities of emotion that are not just the particular emotion of a character in a film at that moment in time ('such as it is'), but also the emotions of the whole 'consciousness' of the film (expressed as the feelings of the collective in the close-ups of Eisenstein, for example).

Since a close-up involves the decontextualization of the object/face it depicts, in that we can no longer see the space that surrounds it as it fills the entire screen, it reflects the fear of literally 'losing face'. For a close-up does not so much help to individuate a character (as we might typically believe) as to dissolve individuation; in Ingmar Bergman's *Persona* (1966), the close-up serves to make Alma (Bibi Andersson) and Elisabeth (Liv Ullmann) indistinguishable. As such, the affection-image not only shows desire and wonder in the faces of those we see, but it also reflects the fear of erasure and nothingness (1983, 144). Furthermore, this decontextualization leads Deleuze to the conception of the any-space-whatever, which can be linked back to the 'gaseous' perception described earlier, in that it, too, helps us to see spaces and faces anew.

After a consideration of the 'pulsion-image', in which the potential for action (the affection-image) begins its materialization as action, Deleuze finally considers the action-image, which he divides into two sub-types as well: the large form and the small form. The large-form action-image is characterized by action that changes an initial situation such that there is a visible progression from situation to changed situation via action, or what Deleuze abbreviated as SAS'. The weak-form action-image, meanwhile, is abbreviated as ASA', here, as this abbreviation suggests, we see a situation shaping an action such that a changed action is the result. Naturally this latter form is less anthropocentric than the former, since it involves feedback from the 'situation' or world/universe on the character doing the acting, and Deleuze sees this in the films of Keaton and Chaplin, while he sees the large-form action-image in classical westerns and films by Billy Wilder and Robert Flaherty.

Finally, Deleuze provides a consideration of the 'crisis of the action image', which will lead into his consideration of the time-image. Briefly, Deleuze sees cinema as a machine for thought (1983, 278), but, after Hitchcock, cinema has become infested with clichés (281). Clichés do not involve original thought; rather, they involve the stasis of thought (repetition and sameness) and, as such, they do not reflect/help us to think about the ever-changing universe or 'whole'.

## Responses to Deleuze

If the above summary of *The Movement-Image* fails in its bid not to reproduce the opacity of Deleuze's writing, then it is understandable that many film scholars have responded negatively to the work itself, which is equally, if not more, opaque. Both Edward Dimendberg (1988) and Ronald Bogue (2003) pick up on the fact that Deleuze pre-requires a substantial amount of knowledge to read his work, since Deleuze himself will often simply evoke the name of a director in order to illustrate points that he makes – without giving any further concrete textual examples of what he means. Furthermore, Dimendberg accuses Deleuze among other things of failing to engage with 20 years of (English-language) film theory, in particular the notion of ideological critique. Dimendberg says that Deleuze does not address the actual plots of films, preferring instead simply to refer to the 'movement' therein, thereby flattening 'the logic and structure of the story into a shapeless mass of events' (Dimendberg 1988, 203). As a result, what individual films might 'mean' – particularly to real spectators who could interpret films in a wide variety of manners – is lost. Finally, Dimendberg criticizes Deleuze's use of Bergson in order to reconcile subject and object within cinema as a refusal to acknowledge the real history of the Holocaust, which strongly challenges such idealism.

However, while Deleuze may not have engaged with English-language film theory, he is well versed in French film theory and criticism, as his many footnotes in *The Movement-Image* testify. Furthermore, while Deleuze may not address history in any depth in *The Movement-Image*, this is something that he does (at least to a greater extent) in *The Time-Image*.

Surprisingly, given that both parties write substantially on cinematic affect, Deleuze has not so much been critiqued by cognitive film theorists as roundly ignored. Aside from some brief swipes from Noël Carroll in *Post-theory* (1996, 37) and from David Bordwell in *On the History of Film Style* (1997, 116–17, 148), Deleuze does not feature prominently in their work.

Deleuze has inspired several other scholars of affect in film, however, with Steven Shaviro's *The Cinematic Body* (1993) being perhaps the first, and still one of the best, treatments of Deleuze in relation to films that the Frenchman himself does not consider, including George A. Romero, Jerry Lewis, David Cronenberg, Rainer Werner Fassbinder, and Andy Warhol. The book offers a consideration of bodies on film, as well as the body of film, that is cinema's potential to inspire a visceral response in audiences.

To offer up a different explanation of the seeming lack of critical engagement with or use of *The Movement-Image*, the book is perhaps more a work of philosophy than a work of film studies, not least given Deleuze's pedigree. Deleuze wrote extensively on art and literature during his career, but he used these as a means of investigating the creative mind and the human engagement with novelty more generally. Indeed, this perhaps in part explains, if not excuses, Deleuze's 'opaque' style: in order to draw creative and philosophical thought from his reader, his work is not necessarily easy to follow, but it does force the reader to think. Deleuze perhaps wishes to raise questions more than he wants to answer them, to produce an 'open' as opposed to a 'closed' text, an approach that, contrary to Dimendberg, does have a political and historical foundation: Deleuze wants to make propositions and to create concepts rather than to offer up any final solutions regarding cinema.

Finally, it is perhaps as a result of the perceived hierarchy between the movement-image and the time-image that more scholars use Deleuze's second *Cinema* book as the basis for their work, not least because it deals with the scholar-friendly New Wave cinemas of Europe and political cinemas from elsewhere in the world.

WILLIAM BROWN

## Works cited

Bergson, Henri. 1896. *Matière et mémoire*. Paris: Presses universitaires de France.

——. 1907. *L'évolution créatrice*. Paris: Presses universitaires de France.

Bogue, Ronald. 2003. *Deleuze and Cinema*. London and New York: Routledge.

Bordwell, David. 1997. *On the History of Film Style*. Cambridge, MA: Harvard University Press.

Carroll, Noël. 1996. 'Prospects for Film Theory: A Personal Assessment'. In *Post-theory: Reconstructing Film Studies*, edited by David Bordwell and Noël Carroll, 37–68. Madison: University of Wisconsin Press.

Deleuze, Gilles. 1983. *Cinéma I: L'image-mouvement*. Paris: Les Éditions de Minuit.

——. 1985. *Cinéma II: L'image-temps*. Paris: Les Éditions de Minuit.

Dimendberg, Edward. 1988. 'The Grand Deleuzian Fog: A Review of *Cinema 1: The Movement-Image* by Gilles Deleuze'. *Canadian-American Slavic Studies* 22 (1–4): 199–209.

Shaviro, Steven. 1993. *The Cinematic Body*. Minneapolis: University of Minnesota Press.

## Further reading

Beugnet, Martine. 2007. *Cinema and Sensation: French Film and the Art of Transgression*. Edinburgh: Edinburgh University Press.

Kennedy, Barbara M. 2000. *Deleuze and Cinema: The Aesthetics of Sensation*. Edinburgh: Edinburgh University Press.

Marrati, Paola. 2008. *Gilles Deleuze: Cinema and Philosophy*. Translated by Alisa Hartz. Baltimore, MD: Johns Hopkins University Press.

Pisters, Patricia. 2003. *The Matrix of Visual Culture: Working with Deleuze in Film Theory*. Stanford, CA: Stanford University Press.

Rodowick, D.N. 1997. *Gilles Deleuze's Time Machine*. Durham, NC: Duke University Press.

# NARRATION

The nature, form, and functioning of the term 'narration' are the object of study of narratology, an area of film theory dominated by the writings of David Bordwell. In his monumental book *Narration in the Fiction Film* (1985), Bordwell presented the first comprehensive theory of narration in the cinema. In what follows, we will look into the key elements of his approach to film narration and discuss the main issues that arise from this influential work.

In the first two chapters of *Narration*, Bordwell lays out the historical and theoretical foundations of the term 'narration' by dividing all previous theories of narration into two categories, namely mimetic theories and diegetic theories of narration. In the mimetic tradition, Bordwell explains how Aristotle's concept of 'mimesis' has been employed to signify narration as the presentation of a spectacle, as an act of showing (3). In this scheme, whether it applies to theatre, literature, or film, the function of narration centres on the act of vision, whereby the narrator is somebody *who shows* and the spectator is somebody *who perceives*. In such a visual transaction, the notion of 'perspective' plays a key role insofar as it determines the coordinates of the spectacle for an ideal observer. In cinema, Bordwell notes that most theorists up to the 1960s (Arnheim, Münsterberg, Bazin) worked under the assumption that a film is a string of images that, above all, amount to a spectacle. This implicit supposition is openly spelled out in V.I. Pudovkin's monograph *Film Technique* (1970 [1926]), where narration is considered to represent a story through the eyes of an 'invisible observer', ideally mobile in space and time. Bordwell is critical of the anthropomorphism entailed in this line of reasoning and rejects the 'invisible observer' model for lacking coherence, breadth, and discrimination (Bordwell 1985, 12).

In the second category of narrative theory, the diegetic theories of narration, it is Plato who offers the founding conception of narration as a linguistic activity. Here the act of storytelling presupposes a 'voice' which performs an act of 'telling' rather than 'showing', thus guiding us to explore the analogies between film and language (17). The Russian formalist critics of the 1920s and 1930s (Bakhtin, Tynianov, Eichenbaum) were the first to promote the study of the cinema in comparison to literature, but a more rigorous and systematic analysis of film through linguistics would only materialize in the 1960s with the rise of French structuralism. At this stage, Bordwell does not engage with the work of the formalists but chooses, instead, to debunk a number of structuralist concepts, including Colin MacCabe's 'meta-language' and Emile Benveniste's 'enunciation' (18–26). A recurring criticism involves the discrepancies that result from the application of linguistic categories to filmic elements, while the general concern that Bordwell expresses about both diegetic and mimetic theories is how they fail to account for the entirety of the formal universe of a fiction film.

To rectify the situation, Bordwell puts 'form' at the very heart of his theory of narration and seeks to construct a narrative model that not only does justice to all the premises of the filmic medium but also provides a framework for narration across media. According to Bordwell, narration is a formal activity that comprises three building blocks: the *fabula* (story), the *syuzhet* (plot), and the *style*. The fabula/syuzhet distinction descends from the Russian formalists, whose writings surface over and over again in Bordwell's account, giving away a certain affinity with the diegetic tradition. It is a distinction that tries to specify the dual nature of what an average viewer vaguely calls 'the story of a film'. This story is, in fact, two fairly separated entities; the fabula is the *mental* reconstruction of a series of events portrayed in the film, while the syuzhet is the *actual* arrangement and presentation of those events on the screen (49–50). The third element, the style, also refers to the on-screen manifestation of these events, but it is limited to the technical choices that are employed to represent them. The complete definition of narration in the fiction film is 'the process whereby the film's syuzhet and style interact in the course of cueing and channeling the spectator's construction of the fabula' (53). In other words, narration is a dynamic process between something tangible, which includes what we see on the screen (the events, the way they are rendered), and something fluid, which is created in our minds based on what we see and according to how we are trained to process it (cognitive schemata). What is distinctive about Bordwell's definition of narration is the blending of the formal elements with the viewer's activity, which places his work at the intersection of narratology and cognitive theory. Indeed, his third chapter, entitled 'The Viewer's Activity', paved the way for a group of younger scholars who would explore further the cognitive side of film narration (Branigan, Buckland, Smith). Yet, the weight of Bordwell's theory in *Narration* clearly falls on the formal issues and it is those that require further elaboration.

The relation between the fabula, the syuzhet, and the style of a film is organized along three analytical axes: the narrative logic, time, and space. The events of the syuzhet as well as the style of the film are motivated according to a certain logic (compositional, realistic, generic, or artistic) that helps us formulate the fabula in a coherent manner. Similarly, the syuzhet and the style signify both temporal and spatial qualities that allow us to determine the time and the space of the fabula. What is not always uniform, however, is the way the three building blocks of the narration treat each other. Bordwell outlines the workings of narration in the majority of films, but he is careful enough to account for possible exceptions to these rules. Specifically, there are some limit cases, where the syuzhet and the style obstruct the construction of a coherent fabula, as in Alain Resnais's *L'année dernière à Marienbad* (1961). Moreover, the syuzhet and the style are not always close collaborators, as in most classical Hollywood films. Instead, style has the potential of working autonomously from the demands of the syuzhet by setting up a pattern of its own. Rare as this case may be, Bordwell's theory acknowledges the heuristic value of such a pattern and even reserves an entire paradigm of narration, the parametric mode, for those films whose style defies interpretation (275). As to whether there is something in a film that is not narrational, he chooses to address Kristin Thompson's concept of 'excess' only to declare, in a rather blatant manner, that it lies outside his concern in this book.

Apart from the central definition of narration that I summarized above, Bordwell enriches his narrative theory with three concepts that he borrows from Meir Sternberg: *knowledge*, *self-consciousness*, and *communicativeness* (57). These terms are useful for describing the ways in which the process of narration transmits information to the viewer. First, the knowledge of the narration is characterized by a specific *range* and *depth*, depending on the way it handles the characters as sources of information. For instance, an omniscient narration exceeds the awareness of the characters and possesses a wide range, whereas its depth depends on the degree of subjectivity or objectivity that it acquires. Second, self-consciousness involves the extent to which the narration acknowledges that it is addressing an audience (58). The more aware the spectator becomes of the narrating act, the more self-conscious the narration is. Finally, the communicativeness of a narration is measured by the amount of information that the film communicates to the viewer. Regardless of how much the narration knows, its communicative aspect depends solely on how much of its knowledge it is willing to share with us; it may know little and tell us all (communicative) or it may know it all and tell us little (suppressive). With these three narrative qualities, Bordwell tries to solve some of the quandaries that resulted from the use of the terms 'point-of-view' and 'unreliability' (60).

Finally, the last key issue in Bordwell's theory regards the role of the narrator/author. His position is summarized in the following statement: 'To give every film a narrator or implied author is to indulge in an anthropomorphic fiction' (62). In other words, the narration in the fiction film does not entail the presence of a narrator, and we should not be tempted to attribute the entire narrative edifice to a specific author. Instead, we are invited to understand narration as a process that presupposes a 'message' and a 'receiver' but not a 'sender'. At this point, Bordwell's rationale cuts off its ties with the diegetic tradition, which assumes there is the voice of the author that speaks to us, while he also explicitly rejects the standard communication model, which is based on the sender/message/receiver triptych.

In summary, the narrative theory that Bordwell puts forward in this book is undoubtedly one of the most thorough and groundbreaking theories of film narration. The breadth and width of his approach are unparalleled to this date, and the impact of his arguments, not only within narratology but in other theoretical realms as well, is entirely justified.

## Criticisms of Bordwell's theory of narration

Before engaging with a number of contemporary scholars who have criticized Bordwell's theory of narration, I would like to dwell for a while on the relation between the concept of 'narration' and that of 'narrative', which are often regarded as equivalent. Bordwell clearly states on the first page of his introduction to *Narration* that he will study narrative as a process and that he will call this process narration. From then on, the word narrative does not appear in the book again and for him all relevant conceptual distinctions appear to be settled. However, the meaning of 'narrative' in the works of other narratologists, particularly those who come from literary studies, is not as easy to handle. I would like to refer to Gérard Genette's *Narrative Discourse Revisited* (1988), where he discusses various approaches to narrative, most of which rely on binaries such as story/discourse, narrative/discourse, story/narrative, and story/plot. For him, the 'narrative fact' is better understood as a triad of story/narrative/narrating, while the order of these three terms can vary depending on whether the circumstances of this fact are real or fictive (Genette 1988, 14–15). For instance, in a non-fictional narrative, first comes the *story* (the completed events), then the *narrating* (the act of recounting in a pragmatic sense), and finally the *narrative* (the product of that act in oral or written form). On the other hand, in a fictional context the narrating precedes and produces both the story and the narrative at the same time.

With these distinctions in mind, I would like to turn to the criticisms levelled at Bordwell's theory of narration, which, instead of debating his preference for narration over narrative, concentrated almost exclusively on the issue of the 'narrator'. In *Coming to Terms* Seymour Chatman opts for the term 'narrative' instead of 'narration' (without differentiating between the two), and puts Bordwell's argumentation under the microscope in order to single out a key point of contention, namely the presence or not of a creator/narrator. As he explicitly states: 'my only real criticism is that [he] goes too far in arguing that film has no agency corresponding to the narrator and that film narrative is best considered as a kind of work wholly performed by the spectator' (Chatman 1990, 124). According to Chatman, if we conceive narration as a 'process', as Bordwell suggests, then we either consider it a natural happening or we acknowledge that someone or something has set it in motion (128). Since we can hardly claim that a film narration is a natural phenomenon, we are forced to identify a certain source of agency behind this process. Chatman's solution to the problem of agency lies in the concept of the 'implied author' who 'is an agent intrinsic to the story whose responsibility is the overall design – including the decision to communicate it through one or more narrators' (132). In other words, a film may employ various narrators, such as character narrators or heterodiegetic narrators, but the entire narration is the invention of an implied author, who is not a biographical person but a principle within the text (133).

A similar rationale was put forward by Robert Burgoyne in an article entitled 'The Cinematic Narrator: The Logic and Pragmatics of Impersonal Narration', which came out the same year. Burgoyne criticizes Bordwell for adhering to the 'non-narrator' tradition of narratology, together with Ann Banfield and Shlomith Remon-Kenan, and he insists that the category of the narrator is a 'fundamental component of fictional expression in the cinema' (Burgoyne 1990, 15). Instead of aligning with Chatman's 'implied author', however, Burgoyne prefers to establish a slightly different distinction between the 'impersonal' and the 'personal narrator'. The impersonal narrator is the one who creates the fictional world and sanctions the truth and authenticity at the fictional level, while the personal narrator is either a witness or a participant in the fiction (7).

The most comprehensive response to all these worries about the existence of the narrator and its various guises came from Edward Branigan in *Narrative Comprehension and Film* (1992). Using the terms 'narration' and 'narrative' sometimes distinctively and at other times interchangeably throughout the book, Branigan addresses the issue of narrative comprehension as a 'constructive activity' that helps us bypass the need to discuss film as language or even as communication (Branigan 1992, 17). He discusses in detail the aforementioned positions of Bordwell and Chatman, among others, in order to take up an intermediate stance. He notes: 'It may well be that "narrator" is a metaphor, but if so, one that permeates our thinking about the world, and is in need of explanation on that basis ... Personifying narration would seem to have a real function in our lives even if narration is not a personality made real nor a communication made public' (110).

His attempt to acknowledge the usefulness of the term 'narrator' without reducing it to a 'sender' of a 'message' led him to the formulation of a tremendously elaborate narrative schema, which contains eight hierarchical levels of narration, each delineating an epistemological context for describing data (chapter 4). In the top four levels we have the presence of *narrators* (historical author, extra-fictional narrator, non-diegetic narrator, and diegetic narrator), who are in charge of the transmission of data. In the bottom four we find the characters either as *actors* (non-focalized narration and external focalization) or as *focalizers* (surface and depth internal focalization). This means that the characters transmit information through their actions as well as through their awareness of the fictional world. The definition of 'narration' that results from this schema is the following: 'Narration in general is the overall regulation and distribution of knowledge which determines when and how a reader acquires knowledge from a text. It is composed of three related activities associated with three nominal agents: the narrator, actor, and focalizer. These agents are convenient fictions, which serve to mark how the field of knowledge is being divided at a particular time' (106).

Overall, Bordwell's and Branigan's theories of narration, despite their discrepancy with respect to the role of the narrator, converge in two significant ways. First, they are both keen on organizing *all* the visual and aural aspects of the film into a pattern, thus recuperating the shortcomings of the previous mimetic or diegetic theories of narration. Second, they both place the spectator at the centre of the narrative activity. Bordwell was the first to discuss the viewer's activity in the handling of the cinematic narration, and Branigan promptly followed with a more systematic model for explaining the multiple ways in which the elements of a film could be processed by the viewer.

ELEFTHERIA THANOULI

## Works cited

Bordwell, David. 1985. *Narration in the Fiction Film.* Madison: University of Wisconsin Press.
Branigan, Edward. 1992. *Narrative Comprehension and Film.* London and New York: Routledge.
Burgoyne, Robert. 1990. 'The Cinematic Narrator: The Logic and Pragmatics of Impersonal Narration'. *Journal of Film and Television* 17 (1): 3–16.
Chatman, Seymour. 1990. *Coming to Terms: The Rhetoric of Narrative in Fiction and Film.* Ithaca, NY: Cornell University Press.
Genette, Gérard. 1988. *Narrative Discourse Revisited.* Ithaca, NY: Cornell University Press.
Pudovkin, V.I. 1970 [1926]. *Film Technique and Film Acting,* New York: Grove.

## Further reading

Bordwell, David. 1989. 'Historical Poetics of Cinema'. In *The Cinematic Text: Methods and Approaches,* edited by Robert Barton Palmer, 369–98. New York: AMS Press.
Buckland, Warren. 2000. *The Cognitive Semiotics of Film.* New York and Cambridge: Cambridge University Press.
Casetti, Francesco. 1999. *Theories of Cinema, 1945–1995.* Austin: University of Texas Press.
Chatman, Seymour. 1978. *Story and Discourse: Narrative Structure in Fiction and Film.* Ithaca, NY: Cornell University Press.
Gaudreault, André. 1987. 'Narration and Monstration in the Cinema'. *Journal of Film and Video* 39: 29–36.
Genette, Gérard. 1980. *Narrative Discourse: An Essay in Method.* Ithaca, NY: Cornell University Press.
Henderson, Brian. 1983. 'Tense, Mood, and Voice in Film'. *Film Quarterly* 36 (4): 4–17.
Smith, Murray. 1995. *Engaging Characters: Fiction, Emotion, and the Cinema.* Oxford: Clarendon Press.

# ONTOLOGY OF THE
# PHOTOGRAPHIC IMAGE

## A shocking idea

He may be known for his modesty, yet André Bazin did not hesitate to set the stakes of his life's work as high as he could. He titled his first serious publication 'The Ontology of the Photographic Image'. At 26 years old and having published fewer than a score of pieces for a university broadside, he constructed an essay that was destined for an impressive 450-page volume, *Problèmes de la peinture,* whose table of contents includes the names Picasso, Matisse, Bonnard, Braque, Rouault, Desnos, Dufy, Cocteau, and Gertrude Stein. You can imagine the care with which he crafted this coming-out piece, for here was a chance to put both himself and the cinema on the intellectual map right at the Liberation of France when ideas about art, philosophy, and politics were moving into a new, turbulent modernist stage. More important than its prestige, this essay was clearly the point of departure for a young man who had recently decided on a career of full-time – and lifetime – writing about film.

Although that career would last but fifteen years, he published more than 2,500 pieces. When, just before his death from leukaemia at the age of 40, he organized his most significant fifty-two essays into four small volumes under the overall rubric *Qu'est-ce que le cinéma?* (*What Is Cinema?*), he placed 'The Ontology of the Photographic Image' in lead position. So, from first to last, and while addressing every conceivable genre and topic (including acting, special effects, television, film festivals, censorship – you name it), Bazin pursued the nature of cinema's being. For that is what 'ontology' is: the study of being, the study of the basic categories of existence, and the manner of existence of such-and-such an entity.

Eric Rohmer, who took over the editorship of *Cahiers du cinéma* from Bazin, published in that journal the very first review that *Qu'est-ce que le cinéma?* received, stressing that: 'Each article, but also the whole work, has the rigor of a real mathematical proof ... All of Bazin's work is centered on one idea, the affirmation of cinematic "objectivity", in the same way that geometry centers on the properties of the straight line' (Rohmer 1988, 95). This objectivity axiom is laid down in 'The Ontology of the Photographic Image', which Rohmer later claimed Bazin had come up with in response to Jean-Paul Sartre's existentialist aesthetic, and which he never relinquished.

Rohmer's review appeared in January 1959, the fabled year that saw him, François Truffaut, and Alain Resnais bring out their first feature films. To some degree Bazin's fate would be linked to that of the French New Wave; his ideas spread in the 1960s as all four volumes of *Qu'est-ce que le cinéma?* became available in France and as filmmakers and critics in Japan, Latin America, Germany, the USSR, and Eastern Europe rode new waves of their own. Rohmer, as well as the recently baptized '*cinéma vérité*' movement (Chris Marker, Jean Rouch, Edgar Morin, who had all known Bazin), believed that cinema was fast evolving into what, at its heart, it really always was; and whatever it was had to do with the objectivity Bazin had shown was essential to it, i.e. its ontology.

## The mystery of photography: being and belief

As the study of 'Being', ontology puts particular pressure on the copular verb 'to be' or 'is'. The title of his book already indicates that Bazin realized he was in the domain of ontology, for the word 'est' (is) can be heard twice in the standard French form of the question 'Qu'est-ce que c'est le cinema?' Bazin immediately tests the limits of his ideas by using this verb, as well as this philosophical term, in the most daring and controversial sentences of the ontology essay: photography gives us 'the object itself, but liberated from its temporal contingencies. The image ... has been created out of the ontology of the model. It is the model' (Bazin 2009a, 8; see also 2009b, 14). The original French knowingly alludes to the theological mystery of the Trinity for '[*l'image*] *procède par sa genèse de l'ontologie du modèle; elle est le modèle*' echoes the Roman Catholic Creed: 'The Holy Spirit proceeds from the Father and the Son' and they are 'one in spirit'. Or, to use another theological (but also Platonic) notion, the image 'participates in the being' of the model. In the 1958 French publication of the essay that Bazin oversaw, the section just quoted faces a full-page reproduction of a photo of the Holy Shroud of Turin, which Bazin comments on in a footnote. His example is superb since the shroud is venerated for having touched the body of Christ, whose image was left on it as in a contact print. Furthermore, the shroud became particularly famous when Secundo Pia was given permission to remove protective glass in front of it and expose it to his camera. Around midnight on 20 May 1898, he stood by for twenty minutes during which low light reflected from the shroud made contact through a lens with a sensitive emulsion that, in a state of excited anticipation, he promptly developed: the negative seemed to show the visage of Christ (Mondzain 2005)! Every photograph that was later made (and millions were sold at churches and shrines) could now claim to be a relic because, in an 'ontological' sense, each shared an actual connection to the original body of Christ, so long as all intermediaries had been produced 'automatically', that is by photochemical contact without human interference. For it is all about contact: a wallet-sized print – or the full page in each copy of Bazin's book – had been stamped out through contact with the negative (or intermediate photos going back to the negative), whose properties had been fixed when light from the shroud etched itself on the emulsion, giving it the same form in outline that the shroud had itself received while wrapped around the bloodied body of Christ. A photo could be venerated since it had been in touch with what it purports to show, light having passed directly from shroud ('model') to emulsion ('image'). Even after the shroud was determined to be false – scientific tests suggest that it dates from the thirteenth century – these photographs are not in themselves fakes. The sceptical scientist still believes something: that the photo in Bazin's book is 'of' a thirteenth-century piece of cloth, and not of something else.

So you can see how useful ontology is in distinguishing cinema (which is 'the completion in time of photography's objectivity') from drawing, painting, etching, and other forms of mimetic representation. But you can also see that more than ontology is involved, since the photograph does not share the DNA of the model. It shares instead the attitude of belief we bring to both, the one having been produced by the light coming from the other. Bazin's ontology is bound up in something similar to the photographic *arché*. *Arché* is the Greek term French aesthetician Jean-Marie Schaeffer (1987) came up with to indicate that which is distinctive about a photograph beyond its physical form; a photo's *arché* concerns not its look but instead the way it came into being, or, more accurately, the way the spectator believes it to have come into being. So long as we credit the direct and automatic participation of reality at some point in what we see, even a rotoscoped movie like Richard Linklater's 2001 *Waking Life* (which features a scene all about Bazin) partakes of this peculiar ontology of cinema.

Actually Bazin complicates his ontology in the very first sentence of the essay when he proposes to put the arts under 'psychoanalysis'. In civilization's infancy, mummification was invented to preserve the 'being' (ontology) of the departed human in 'the appearance of being' (psychology). Through a chemical process the body becomes art. He concludes: 'A history of the visual arts is ... above all a history of their psychology. It is also a history of resemblance or, if you prefer, of realism.' And in this history, the invention of photography (and correlatively of cinema) stands as the most dramatic event, effecting the greatest change. What changed in the nineteenth century was precisely the psychological attitude (the belief) of viewers. Spectators have treated photographically produced images as if they were different in kind from artists' renderings, with a different ontology, one inevitably and automatically related, by the arché, to the model pictured.

You might ask how there can be a 'different ontology', for isn't something either existent or not? This is the thrust of the title, and much of the argument, of *Being and Nothingness*, Jean-Paul Sartre's masterpiece, published in 1943 when he was known to have attended Bazin's ciné-club. But Bazin would later claim that the film image partakes of an intermediate ontology between being and nothingness (Andrew 2010, 15). Towards the end of the ontology essay he salutes the surrealists for whom the 'logical distinction between the imaginary and the real was eliminated. Every image should be experienced as an object and every object as an image. Photography was thus a privileged technology for Surrealist practice because it produces an image which shares in the existence of nature: a photograph is a really existing hallucination' (Bazin 2009a, 9–10). Bazin's French gets back to that philosophical and theological mystery already mentioned; he evokes it by the term 'participation' translated above as 'shares': '*elle réalize une image participant de la nature: une hallucination vraie*'. Looking backwards, Jean-Francois Chevrier has traced Bazin's ideas and vocabulary beyond the surrealist André Breton to Hippolyte Taine and Gustav Flaubert, nineteenth-century writers who fretted about the status of hypnogogic and other hallucinatory images that seem to be both natural and psychological at the same time (Andrew 2011, 42–5). Looking forward, Louis-Georges Schwartz has pointed out the remarkable way that Bazin's ideas about the trace of objects (as in the mummification of the corpses of human beings) anticipate well-known positions of Jacques Derrida (Andrew 2011, 95–103).

## The ontology axiom in our experience of movies

In his fine 340-page doctoral dissertation consecrated to Bazin's eight-page essay, Steven Rifkin (2010) examines its three separable but interlocking components (following Bazin's three sections in the 1945 text): representation (ontology), desire (psychology), and presence (art). Most of the debate around the essay has focused on whether the photographic nature of film truly changes the stakes, or even the notion, of representation in comparison with earlier media. Tom Gunning (2004) measures all sides of this debate in 'What's the Point of an Index?', an essay that brings up Bazin only in its final considerations, but does so crucially. Gunning reminds us that in film theory the term 'index' came from Peter Wollen's attribution of C.S. Peirce's semiotics to Bazin's ideas (see Wollen 1969). True, Bazin often compared the film image to a 'fingerprint', a 'death mask', the 'veil of Veronica', and, as we have seen, the 'Shroud of Turin'. These are all indexes in Peirce's scheme, where the index differs in the way we use it from signs that Peirce names the icon and the symbol. Rudolf Arnheim and Vsevolod Pudovkin had been concerned with the 'iconic' look of the image in relation to the look of visible reality, but Bazin was indifferent to resemblance. Occasionally a theorist has discussed cinema as a 'symbolic' sign system, as when Sergei Eisenstein related film language to Japanese graphic script or contemplated adapting Karl Marx's *Das Kapital* to the screen, but Bazin was opposed to considering cinema a conventional symbolic language, being antipathetic to coded editing strategies that viewers learn to 'read'. He definitely cared most about film as an indexical image; still, Gunning thinks Wollen's view doesn't really get at what Bazin saw in mechanically recorded images: for him they are conduits to a world that the model belonged to. The richness of this world stimulates our 'phenomenological fascination with photography' (Gunning 2004, 45).

Of Rifkin's three categories, Gunning downplays *representation* and *desire* in favour of *presence*, thanks to cinema's prodigious manner of bringing us through the image into the sensory richness of the world it pictures. Such plenitude escapes Wollen's dry semiotic notion that a photograph stands as an index of its referent, like a falling barometer needle standing for the dangerous weather conditions that produce it. In the case of a photograph or of a film scene, we don't read its meaning, but rather experience something of the referent itself. (Here Gunning edges close to Bazin's 'it is the model'.) And this remains the case even after the so-called digital revolution, which initially brought on euphoria or panic among scholars because every image became suspect once the human hand could manipulate pixels to synthesize rather than present recorded images. Gunning reminds us that the 'push–pull' between the accuracy of raw recording and its transformation for artistic, rhetorical, or entertainment purposes has been a part of photography and cinema from the outset. Bazin often noted the same thing.

Relying in part on Gunning, Daniel Morgan's 'Rethinking Bazin: Ontology and Realist Aesthetics' forthrightly proposes a subtle reading of Bazin in the face of the challenge of those who prematurely concluded that digital processes had obviated his importance. Also mainly interested in 'presence', Morgan, however, shifts attention from the past world that the photograph or film invites the viewer to enter, instead treating the 'image as an object' just the way Bazin said the Surrealists have done (Morgan 2006, 449). The mechanically produced image requires a process (and a pre-existent model) to come into existence, but does not depend on that model for its later significance. Adopting a key concept from Stanley Cavell, Morgan believes that, thanks to the photographic process, filmmakers, and audiences after them, 'acknowledge' the 'object itself, but liberated from its temporal contingencies' (Bazin 2009a, 8). A film establishes its own set of temporal relations, giving value to objects and acknowledging them, by putting images together according to one style or another; and Bazin had many ideas about the kinds of processes or filmic styles that would enhance the sense of an original model, e.g. lateral depth of field. This lets us experience the object anew, 'offer[ing] it up unsullied to my attention and thus to my love'. The ontology essay concludes by insisting that we admire the object photographed in ways we previously failed to 'acknowledge' (Cavell's term: Cavell 1971). So the image *is* the model, but seen in a very different time-space context, and projected under a certain slant we call style.

By focusing on what happens to the image after its creation (i.e. focusing on its claim on the viewer, its relation to other images in a film, the style under which it, rather than the model, appeals to us), Morgan extricates Bazin (and photographic images) from being shackled both to a dying photo-chemical technology and to the pro-filmic events during which those images were captured. His opponents have often strenuously argued that Bazin's theory is limited to 'realist' directors and genres (Carroll 1988, chapter 2) and thus shackled to realist ideology. When the New Wave receded, and especially after the violent social upheavals of 1968 in Paris, even *Cahiers du cinéma* turned on its founder for this reason. In a contentious 1970 interview the magazine's new, politically radical editors attacked Eric Rohmer, who had been ousted: 'The Bazinian conception [was of] cinema as a window on the world. All of us are totally against this conception.' Rohmer replies: 'I still think Bazin was right ... It is above all in respect for the world that the genius of the cinema bursts out. Whether you like it or not, this is the nature of taking photographs. Bazin, therefore, put his finger on what was unique about the art of cinema in relation to all the other forms of art' (in Bonitzer *et al.* 2010).

However, the variety of Rohmer's own films, including *Percival* (with its visibly fake décor) and *The Lady and the Duke* (with its CGI backdrops), suggest that it would be a mistake to assume that the objectivity axiom places the documentary at the centre of Bazinian cinema. He did consecrate many of his most impressive essays to forms of documentary, but for him every type of film is affected by the cinema's ontology. This includes films about paintings, films taken from novels, and films that restage theatrical events such as operas and plays. The second volume of *Qu'est-ce que le cinéma?* shows the peculiar advantages of the hybrids that result when cinema's 'materialism' (capturing whatever the lens takes in, planned or not) confronts cultural monuments (physical ones such as paintings or mental ones such as novels). Styles and genres can be distinguished according to the ratio between the 'push–pull' of accuracy and transformation that they establish. This is why Bazin wanted to investigate all sorts of films and could assume new sorts would develop after he was gone.

And the digital age doesn't change the stakes, for photo-chemistry was always only a sufficient, partial, and never necessary part of what Bazin is getting at in the ontology essay. Not tied to subject matter or genre, and having little to do with the literary or pictorial movements and manifestos bearing the name *realist*, Bazin's notion of cinematic objectivity designates a condition of experience whereby the viewer regards what is on the screen as the actual trace of something pre-existent, and perceives this trace using many of the same presuppositions that govern the routine of everyday perceptual acts (searching, recognizing, verifying impressions, etc.). In short, we manage to maintain some belief in (or feel for) the photograph's relation to the real even in films that are fantastical. The ghost genre and science fiction depend on this.

## Ontology under attack

All in all, arguments aiming to refute the 'objectivity axiom' can be grouped into two types: the categorical and the historical. The first type proposes that the process by which a photograph becomes a representation of a scene or of an object is a variant of picture-making processes that go on in all the visual arts, and so photography and cinema are not unique in this regard. The hand of the artist may not be evident in the taking of the photograph, but it is surely there in the selection and arrangement of the subject, and it is indisputably there in the optical and chemical processes that result in the particular focus, illumination, and colour that re-present the subject on a screen. This type of objection, however, must still explain the authority that the photographic media claim (over drawings or other man-made images) as evidence in scientific experiments, law cases, and insurance reports.

The historical argument against the objectivity axiom is more recent, triggered by technological developments that have, for instance, reduced the authority of photographs in court cases. Photography and other technologies producing analogue images may have dominated the twentieth century, but their reign has been cut short by digital technology. The challenge comes from the fact that digital images are capable of unusually detailed illusion that can be produced entirely without relation to a referent in the world. Bazin might have treated this development as a step in the evolution of images in culture, a step potentially demoting the authority of cinema. In 'The Myth of Total Cinema', he enthu-siastically forecast technological developments that may permit the increasingly perfect 'reproduction' of the visual world. He might have argued, however, that digitally synthe-sized images imitate rather than reproduce the world. They may amaze the spectator with *trompe l'oeil* effects but, being fabrications rather than imprints, they are guides less to the world they depict than to the fascinations and needs of those who do the depicting, i.e. they are guides to ourselves.

I believe this to have been his attitude towards animation. Despite writing about it often as an art and as a social phenomenon, Bazin's ontology should exclude it from what we identify as cinema. For even though in his day animated pictures may have come on reels of celluloid to be projected at twenty-four frames a second onto a reflecting screen, their ontology is related to that of the traditional arts of drawing and design, since the spectator senses these human skills to be at their genesis. The animated image is produced by an artist, not by light in contact with some model, although of course the animator may make 'eye contact' with a model when imitating it while drawing.

The troublesome case of animation has mushroomed in the age of synthetic computer imagery. This should lead us to repeat, more loudly than he did, Bazin's ques-tion 'What is Cinema?' Never expecting a final answer, he wrote that '[c]inema's existence precedes its essence', paraphrasing Sartre. Rather than lay out principles defining cinema once and for all, the critic ought to deal with whatever comes under the name of cinema, even as this changes over time. How then do we reconcile the ontology axiom, which ought to be ahistorical, with this existential relativism attuned to cinema's shifting historical existence? Animated films and synthesized blockbusters play alongside feature-length documentaries at multiplexes today. The point is that we still crave cinema's special rapport with reality and that we acknowledge reality most fully when the image has been transformed by style into something striking. Illuminating how reality becomes art, Bazin's ontology essay keeps us forever alert to the world beyond art which photography and cinema have touched. This amazingly rich essay funded a life-time's worth of criticism about films that Bazin often admired and always wrote about brilliantly.

DUDLEY ANDREW

## Works cited

Andrew, Dudley. 2010. *What Cinema Is!* Malden, MA: Wiley-Blackwell.

——. 2011. 'André Bazin'. In Oxford Bibliographies on-line: Cinema and Media Studies. http://www.oxfordbibliographies.com/view/document/obo-9780199791286/obo-9780199791286-0006.xml?rskey=zS4xlo&result=13&q=.

——with Hervé Joubert-Laurencin, eds. 2011. *Opening Bazin*. New York: Oxford University Press.

Bazin, André. 1958. 'Ontologie de l'image photographique'. In *Qu'est-ce que le cinéma?*, vol. 1 (*Ontologie et Langage*), 9–17. Paris: Cerf. [This is an updated and somewhat altered version of 'Ontologie de l'image photographique', in *Problèmes de la peinture*, edited by Gaston Diehl. Lyon: Confluences, 1945.]

——. 2009a. *What Is Cinema?*. Translated and edited by Timothy Barnard. Montreal: Caboose Books.

——. 2009b. *What Is Cinema?*. 2 vols, translated by Hugh Gray, new foreword by Dudley Andrew. Berkeley: University of California Press, 2004.

Bonitzer, Pascal, Jean-Louis Comolli, Serge Daney, and Jean Narboni. 2010 [1971]. 'New Interview with Eric Rohmer'. By Pascal Bonitzer in *Cahiers du cinéma* 219 (April). Translated by Daniel Fairfax at www.sensesofcinema.com issue 54 (4 April).

Carroll, Noël. 1988. *Philosophical Problems of Classical Film Theory*. Princeton, NJ: Princeton University Press.

Cavell, Stanley. 1971. *The World Viewed: Reflections on the Ontology of Film*. New York: Viking Press.

Gunning, Tom. 2004. 'What's the Point of an Index, or Faking Photographs?'. *Nordicom Review* 25 (1–2): 39–49.

Mondzain, Marie-José. 2005 [1996]. 'A Ghost Story'. In *Icon, Image, Economy*. Stanford, CA: Stanford University Press.

Morgan, Daniel. 2006. 'Rethinking Bazin: Ontology and Realist Aesthetics'. *Critical Inquiry* 32 (Spring): 443–81.

Rifkin, Steven. 2010. 'André Bazin's "Ontology of the Photographic Image": Representation, Desire, and Presence'. Doctoral dissertation, Carleton University, Ottawa, Canada.

Rohmer, Eric. 1988 [1959]. 'André Bazin's "Summa"', in *A Taste for Beauty*. Cambridge, UK: Cambridge University Press.

Schaeffer, Jean-Marie. 1987. *L'Image précaire: du dispositive photographique*. Paris: Seuil.

Wollen, Peter. 1969. *Signs and Meaning in the Cinema*. London: Secker and Warburg.

## Further reading

Rosen, Philip. 2001. 'Subject, Ontology, and Historicity in Bazin', in *Change Mummified: Cinema, Historicity, Theory*. Minneapolis: University of Minnesota Press.

# 'ORDINARY MAN OF CINEMA'
# (SCHEFER)

Discussing the introspective turn of Jean-Louis Schefer's philosophical writings on film, Dudley Andrew summarizes with an apt balance of clarity and paradox: 'Schefer evocatively reminds us that film theory will only progress by interrogating concrete instances for their systematic ramifications, and that in turn these ramifications are of interest only insofar as they return us to those aspects of our experience which are particular and unsystematic' (Andrew 1984, 190). Despite attempts by Andrew, Paul Smith, and Tom Conley (2010), Schefer's work – unlike that of Gilles Deleuze and Jacques Rancière, seemingly ubiquitous in Anglo-American circles today – has yet to successfully make the transatlantic voyage. It is true, as Katya Mandoki critiques, that Schefer is 'very hard to read' (1998, 1), but D.N. Rodowick (2010) has noted that there was a similar reaction to Deleuze's work, now probably the most commonly engaged film-philosophy. As such, Schefer's eccentricity should not deter us from his offerings but, instead, encourage our engagement for the very reason that it offers us something lacking in Anglo-American paradigms: a link between the ideological critique of apparatus theory and the personal experience championed by cultural studies. This intersection takes place in what Schefer refers to as the 'ordinary man of cinema', a methodological foil constructed by Schefer in order to return thinking and writing of the film experience to a personal level, the level of the common individual.

Schefer sets out to understand the cinematic experience as something that is inseparable from the individual's own history, instilling into film theory a notion of Pierre Bourdieu's *habitus*, which functioned in Bourdieu's sociology as a way of restoring the subject to structural analysis. This is the crux of Schefer's best-known work, *L'Homme ordinaire du cinéma* ('The ordinary man of cinema', 1980), which has not been fully translated into English, though excerpts were published in English in Smith's 1995 collaboration with the French philosopher entitled *The Enigmatic Body*. This may be because, unlike the empirical tone of Anglo-American film studies, Schefer utilizes a non-academic prose mode to describe the cinematic experience in terms of the abstract interactivity at the heart of the subjective viewing experience. The ordinary cinematic experience produces a paradoxical being in the spectator, a schizophrenic subject split between two worlds: his or her own (which also contains personal memory) and that of the camera or apparatus (which offers an image without memory, but with an ideological genealogy). Schefer's 'ordinary man' is indefinite and transforming, and Schefer's writing is an essayism that accommodates the mutability with which we engage a medium bent on constant change. For Schefer, this ordinary experience is an enigma, and 'the enigma consists in that part of ourselves and our histories that has been disinherited in the attempt to represent, rationalize, and regulate' (Smith 1995, x). His methodological turn away from the empirical and towards the complexity of mundane personal experience situates his work in an intellectual history best demonstrated through Maurice Merleau-Ponty's phenomenology of perception and Wittgenstein's later philosophy of language, which focus on walking step-by-step through the ordinary experiences, respectively, of perception and speech.

Rejecting the catechism of academic empiricism for more personal reflections on ordinary viewership, Schefer frees himself to produce what is often lyrical, profound, and subjectively personal to the point of occasionally being difficult (if not sometimes impossible) to follow. In his preface to Smith's 1995 collection of translated essays, Schefer begins: 'first of all I have to avow that I have neither the inclination nor the patience to be a scholar' (Smith 1995, xvii). This echoes the opening declaration of *L'Homme ordinaire du cinéma*: 'the ordinary man of cinema would say nothing here except this one inessential thing: cinema is not my job' (Schefer 1980, 5). The casual self-deprecation of these continuous negations ('nothing but', 'inessential', 'not my job') calls subtle attention to Schefer's affection for the critical tradition of the outsider, which in the world of academic scholarship is the philosophical essayist. Schefer makes telling references to Robert Musil's *A Man without Qualities*, a model for the dissolution of individualism in the modern era of overwhelming external influence and sensory overload; this reference draws a connection between Schefer's avowedly non-scholarly style and a great figure of the essayistic practice, tying Schefer to an eclectic but particular prose tradition. When introducing his own work, Schefer self-consciously extols the ambiguous virtues of the 'essayist', whom he describes as 'an indolent historian, a novelist beset by doubts about the material of fiction, a philosopher without a system' (Smith 1995, xix).

Yet, there is a stylistic dichotomy at play in Schefer's ordinariness: while cinema may not be Schefer's line of work, it is this imperfect function that enables his revelations. While he held academic posts earlier in his career, Schefer is clearly suspicious not of the objective rigour but of the subjective limitations of academic research, resisting the confines of any monolithic position and rejecting conventional modes of textual analysis. The few critics who have granted Schefer due interest categorically note that this methodological stance is part of Schefer's larger resistance to conventional understandings of cinema as essentially representational, an argument that makes him a prototype for the central arguments and theories developed by both Gilles Deleuze and Jacques Rancière (*see* FILM FABLE [JACQUES RANCIÈRE]; MOVEMENT-IMAGE; TIME-IMAGE). His work, as Smith points out, provides an implicit rejection of much film theory, in particular the apparatus and ideology theories provided by the *Tel Quel* group, the militant *Cahiers du cinéma* of the 1970s, and the subject-positioning analysis erected by Christian Metz and the *Screen* tradition (Smith 1995, 109) (*see* CONTEMPORARY FILM THEORY; IMAGINARY SIGNIFIER). Although Schefer does not align himself with any conventional theory of construction, he perhaps falls closest to spectator theory, as he is concerned with revealing the private and personal experience of the viewer (though without psychoanalytic or Marxist undertones). Highly influenced by the later works of his friend and mentor Roland Barthes, Schefer's writing on art and cinema can be seen as part of a larger post-structuralist or postmodern movement – initiated by Barthes and inherited by Irigaray, Schefer and others – away from the impersonal and anonymous approaches provided by structuralist rhetoric. As Conley points out, there lies in this postmodern movement a rethinking of the notion of the 'ordinary', which for Barthes registers a similar cachet as the 'natural', that which is claimed to be eternal and without history, without ideology, without formation (Conley 1985, 4).

Writers such as Barthes, Irigaray, and Schefer focus their attention on the 'ordinary' experience as one that is laden with personal history instead of merely providing a blank vessel for the structural meaning of the text. Unique to our understanding of the function of the arts, there reigns in the cinematic experience a distinct osmosis between viewer and image that, for Schefer, challenges theories of spectatorship from Plato to Jean-Louis Baudry (1974) (see APPARATUS THEORY [BAUDRY]), to Noël Carroll's virulent rebuttal of Baudry's take on Plato (1988). When watching a film, Schefer writes, 'I do not believe that we are crouched in Plato's cave; we are, for an inestimable eternity, suspended between a giant body and the object of its gaze. I am not seated, but floating in a prism of light' (Schefer 1980, 87–8). Whereas Baudry adjusts the Platonic cavern myth for the cinema spectator, inanimate in an enclosed and dark space and convinced of the reality of the shadows seen dancing on the wall, Carroll rejects this very notion through the liberation of action and critical interpretation granted to the spectator. Schefer attempts to reconcile these two extremes, envisioning an interaction not composed of disconnected concepts or projections but, instead, a shifting, fluid realm of meaning in which we are immersed while watching. Schefer also insists that part of our engagement with the image does not take place within the spatio-temporal limits of our physical entity, but within a larger mental and historical universe that transcends both the darkened space of the movie theatre and also the temporal duration of the text and its viewing. This strikes a strong rapport with Anglo-American cultural studies, and in particular Robert Stam's utilization of Bakhtinian concepts to argue that the spectator sits in dialogical engagement with the image (see DIALOGISM).

The spectator acts therefore as an arena for the experimentation of meaning whereby the image empties itself of its content, a vessel – albeit unstable and impermanent – for the fiction's unfolding. This appropriation marks a high degree of escapism (we take our problems into the cinema and let the movie whisk them away), a social function of cinema causing Schefer tremendous guilt that he accepts as inescapable because we of the twentieth century have had our memories – our modes of registering and preserving experience – structured by the fact that we are and have from birth been movie spectators, paradoxical beings existing as two beings, offering ourselves up to an open window of alternative universes with the implicit ritualistic sacrifice of our own world. The role of personal context and memory has particularly resonant importance in Schefer's auto-biographical inclusions of his own childhood growing up in Paris during the Second World War and the German Occupation. Then, as in any other time, there was no full escape from the world, no complete disappearance into the text; we always remain part of the world on our side of the screen, presences inside the theatre. For this reason, no cinema is a silent cinema, and we carry with us for life not only the texts we have seen but also the people we were when watching them:

> Even silent cinema could never be silent: it is a cinema caught up in whispers (the subtitles, for example, read softly to children during the show). And in the whispered silence of those first films, the first images, the dust, the light of the cinema's gray bodies returns within us: as if there were a child seated within us, clinging to our hand.
>
> (Smith 1995, 126)

The cinema he viewed as a child would forever bind Schefer's cinematic experience to two things: the historical context of that childhood and the terrorized child that would eventually be buried away within the grown man. The viewings to follow would be a process of 'digging out a sort of childhood unconsciousness' in search of that interior, enigmatic being. One's experience of films during youth forms a unique bond, a link between the text and spectator. Serge Daney would not be overstating it when he writes, in his assessment of the influence of film-going on his own childhood:

> I know of few expressions more beautiful than the one coined by Jean-Louis Schefer when, in *L'Homme ordinaire du cinéma*, he speaks about the 'films that have watched our childhood'. Because it is one thing to learn to watch movies as a 'professional' – only to verify that movies concern us less and less – but it is another to live with those movies that watched us grow and that have seen us, early hostages of our future biographies, already entangled in the snare of our history.
>
> (Daney 1992, 1)

Daney's specific phrasing, 'already entangled in the snare of our history', is useful in understanding Schefer's 'ordinary man of cinema' as an animal caught in a bind, jerking recklessly to escape the metal teeth of a real world that we have contaminated, that will never fully let us go, whose tetanus will torture us even once we manage to break free.

Schefer's vocabulary of the 'ordinary' world of cinema experience is rife with such metaphors and symbols – traps, animals, dwarves, monsters, mutants – used to indicate humanity's perpetual state of transformation and hybridization with that which is alien to us or existent primarily in our imagination. Returning to Mandoki's criticism, it may be the very mysticism of personal experience that many find inaccessible in Schefer's work, which runs contrary to the objective language of most scholarly writing in the arena of visual studies. Indeed, Mandoki and others may view Schefer's essayistic writing and non-conformist methodological openendedness as antithetical to conventional scholarship and institutional criticism, concluding as she does: 'I personally think that his questions are more interesting than his answers' (Mandoki 1998). On the other hand, the eccentricity and unconventionality of his language belie the presence, in an autobiographical film-philosophy, of the sublime impact of a historical moment and interior process that, be they ordinary, defy the parameters of typical film writing. Moreover, the premise of critical theory inherent in cultural studies and the gradual shift in visual studies towards philosophy may soon demand that we start to value questions as much – if not more – than answers. I personally look forward to such a day, and when it comes I will be grateful to have glimpsed the inspired writing of the little-known Jean-Louis Schefer.

HUNTER VAUGHAN

## Works cited

Andrew, Dudley. 1984. *Concepts in Film Theory*. Oxford: Oxford University Press.

Baudry, Jean-Louis. 1974. 'Ideological Effects of the Basic Cinematographic Apparatus'. Translated by Alan Williams. *Film Quarterly* 28 (2): 39–47.

Carroll, Noël. 1988. *Mystifying Movies: Fad and Fallacies in Contemporary Film Theory*. New York: Columbia University Press.

Conley, Tom. 1985. 'Reading Ordinary Viewing'. *Diacritics* 15 (1): 4–14.

——. 2010. 'Jean-Louis Schefer: Screen Memories from *L'Homme ordinaire du cinéma*'. *New Review of Film and Television Studies* 8 (1): 12–21.

Daney, Serge. 1992. 'The Tracking Shot in Kapo'. *Trafic* 4 (Fall): 1.

Mandoki, Katya. 1998. 'An Enigmatic Text: Schefer's Quest upon a Thing Unknown'. *Film Philosophy* 2 (April): 1.

Rodowick, D.N. 2010. 'Introduction: What Does Time Express?'. In *Afterimages of Gilles Deleuze's Film Philosophy*, edited by D.N. Rodowick. Minneapolis: University of Minnesota Press.

Schefer, Jean-Louis. 1980. *L'Homme ordinaire du cinéma*. Paris: Gallimard.

Smith, Paul. 1995. *The Enigmatic Body: Essays on the Arts by Jean Louis Schefer*. Edited and translated by Paul Smith. Cambridge: Cambridge University Press.

# PERSPECTIVISM VERSUS REALISM

## Language, images and the question of realism

Film theory and analysis create associations between words and images (and sounds). A theory that explains why we laugh at humorous incongruities on screen – secret agents aren't usually seen riding motorized gondolas through the Piazza San Marco (*Moonraker*, Gilbert, 1979) – uses language demonstratively. It is believed that the theory finds support in what can be pointed to in *this* image. Analytical descriptions also endeavour to *show things* to the reader: *Skyfall*'s (Mendes, 2012) long take showing the villain Silva (Javier Bardem) as he spins an elaborate tale of rats and his grandmother's island for James Bond (Daniel Craig), the camera gently tilting upward as he strolls into the foreground, reveals the character's penchant for histrionics, for performance. The difference between theoretical and analytical uses of words is one of mood. As an abstraction, a theoretical proposition about comic incongruity is ratified by many images like this one. The analytic words about *Skyfall*, by contrast, fine-tune our sense of *this particular shot*.

Whatever their differences, an underlying assumption in the language of film theory and analysis is that words have the capacity to shape our understanding, sharpen our perception, of images. Indeed, we often measure the value of a theory or a description by its ability to explain the perception we have of an image or expand our appreciation by revealing aspects in it we had overlooked. Words confirm or expand what is in a picture. The relationship is one of verification, however hurried, intuitive, retroactive, or informal. Something like a triadic scheme applies: the reader of a theory or an analysis (A) checks the words invoked (B) against the image (or against memories of it) (C) (Figure 7).

But does this assumption survive strict scrutiny? Is there an image to match our words against, or is (C) a superfluous term in this dynamic? These questions point to the perennial philosophical problem of realism versus perspectivism (and the related matter of relativism). The debate is about whether we know only what we make (with words). Either word choices are constrained by the world or the theories and analyses elaborated in film studies are limited to the horizon of language, where words simply refer to other words, concepts to other concepts.

The philosophical realist posits that an entity like a film can be grasped *non-* or *pre-linguistically*. A work of art has an innate potential that is 'spotted' and then confirmed and perhaps even reshaped or warped when brought under a description. To rephrase as an epistemological process, we *intuit* a subsisting artefact (a 'movie' or an 'image') and then marshal words to articulate its visual and acoustic qualities and effects. As this reasoning goes, all verbalizations are *of* some prior thing that is stable enough to perception to

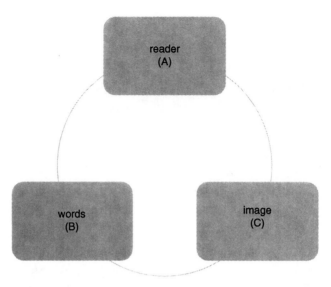

*Figure 7* Word-to-image verification.

prompt us to 'dance' with it cognitively or to 'play' with it more in language. Yet, however we verbalize such an entity, knowing it is not just a productive process; it is also *acquisitive*. There are things to *discover* in the artefact. In other words, there is some real, 'meaningful' entity apart from anyone's linguistic (re-)constructions.

Sceptical of the realist's faith in a world 'out there', the advocate of perspectivism might ask: how could we know this prior entity unless by moving about in words? *Skyfall* cannot be known except through the meaning-making process of language use. And what we each make of it is different – potentially radically different – because of the variations in the lexical and conceptual frames we bring to bear. Put differently, there is no reason to believe that a movie exists independently of the positions – of the perspectives – we occupy on it. What we know of movies is limited to some combination of (1) what our linguistic horizon sanctions (the language-games thesis that we do not invent the words and the meanings we use) and (2) what we each individually make of movies in our personal encounter with them (the relativist thesis that we each 'make' in unique ways, such that there is neither a 'real' entity nor a legitimate 'ordinal measure' upon which to evaluate the verbalizations we each devise). The relatively recent philosophical turn in film theory gives us the opportunity to examine this difficult question further.

## The language-games of film studies: a perspectivist impulse

If traditional film theory seeks to explore cinema as an art form, a language, or an ideology, or the subject's pleasure in or cognitive or emotional engagement with cinema, film studies' philosophical turn pursues questions about the deep epistemological and moral roots of film theory. Film-philosophy (*see* FILM-PHILOSOPHY) includes the following research programmes (examples of each are provided in parentheses):

1. A Wittgensteinian language-therapy of film theory (Allen and Turvey eds. 2001; Branigan 2006; Turvey 2007).

2. Intellectual and critical histories and genealogies that find the roots of film theory in a variety of philosophical traditions (Szaloky 2005; Tognolotti 2005).[1]
3. Investigations of the concepts developed by or found in films and/or the study of filmmakers as philosophers (Cavell 1996; Rodowick 2001; Frampton 2006).
4. Exegetical studies of philosophers, both ancient and modern, whose thought provides a basis for scrutinizing anew perennial questions of film theory and/or presuppositions of theorists and historians (Rodowick 1997; Lefebvre 2007a; 2007b).
5. Inspired largely by continental philosophy, a return to Grand Theoretical speculation about cinema's place in society and the limits of 'historicism' in film studies (Žižek 2001; Price 2008a; 2008b).

This list, while certainly not exhaustive, gives one a sense of the range of philosophizing film studies people now rely upon. With the possible exception of the rather amorphous third category, these parallel projects take a conspicuous metatheoretical posture. In 'An Elegy for Theory', D.N. Rodowick identifies this recent theoretical trend as an effort to carve out 'a metacritical space of epistemological and ethical self-examination' (Rodowick 2007, 102).

Explicitly concerned with the philosophical problem of the relationship between words and reality, Edward Branigan's *Projecting a Camera: Language-Games in Film Theory* (2006) seeks to answer several intermeshed questions. Based on what conceptual materials are film theories built? Does language dictate the world or vice versa? Do things like physical cameras prompt verbalizations or is it only in words that these same things materialize? For Branigan, answers can be gleaned from the various conceptions of 'camera' at play in film writing (*see* CAMERA). He theorizes that 'cameras' as words in descriptions of cinematic texts do not reference concrete things but rather *a phase in the viewer's stream of thought* (about a film). The cameras invoked in film theory, criticism, and the viewer's attempt to make sense of a narrative are mental, *not* physical.

We are all actors in language-games. This stems from the basic textual nature of sense-making. Making meaning of a movie or indeed of 'film' involves moving about in grammar. What we see in a movie, in other words, is 'the result of a person speaking about his or her knowledge and feelings on an *occasion* of reading and seeing' (Branigan 2006, 5). One finds support in the philosophy of Wittgenstein:

> For Wittgenstein, each grammar [whether narrowly linguistic or broadly considered as a 'manner of acting in the world'] is a kind of map created to solve a set of closely related problems. In fact, for Wittgenstein we make a world by accumulating a large number of these sets of problems and their associated grammars. That is, we fashion a significant world out of problems and grammars into which our various desires and acts may be fitted and made significant. Wittgenstein proposes that these many grammars should be understood as a series of 'language-games' where each game requires one to learn in order to be able to make a significant 'move' (i.e. to play, act in, the 'game'). Playing a game is a practice, though we may also practice playing a game.
>
> (Branigan 2006, 5–6)

A language-game will sanction only certain moves *vis-à-vis* the objects that the game puts in play. In terms of film theory, this means it will address those 'games' that a community of theorists and readers expect it to play, like those (in the case of the 'cameras' we talk about) of 'fictiveness' (how various cameras are said to be motivated narratively), 'mobility' (whether a camera is made to move by a character, a Narrator or an Author, or the frames of thought set in motion by the viewer), 'causation' (how the camera reveals lines of the plot), 'subjectivity' (the camera's role in the expression of character point of view), and what 'concrete reality' will consist of ('photographicity,' pro-filmic, post-filmic, etc.). The expectation of a film theory is that it will have something to say about some or all of these things.

Which use of 'camera' is most effective in sharpening our perception of the film image? Focusing instead on the connections between words, Branigan denies that a single, comprehensive theory of film – any accurate verbalization that links words with a real camera or a real image – is possible because every theory is a product of circumstance and a linguistic artefact. How, then, is the value of a film theory to be assessed, if not against an artefact 'out there'?

Branigan recommends two kinds of analysis. He proceeds by way of a connective analysis of theories (borrowed from philosopher P.F. Strawson) and a complementary analysis of the radial meanings of polysemous words of which 'camera' is one (a tool borrowed from cognitivist George Lakoff). An analysis looking for connections along a horizontal axis can be contrasted to an analysis that is 'reductionist', which proceeds vertically, dissecting things into parts looking for the essential constituent elements. Branigan's handling of the various theories both 'classical' and 'contemporary', from Münsterberg to Žižek, Arnheim to Deleuze, crossing historical periods, divergent institutional contexts, and deep-felt theoretical commitments, puts on display the virtues of *lateral* analytical thinking, finding 'links and knots' between and among systems of theoretical explanation (Branigan 2006, 16).

The radial method, no less flexible, is critical to his conception of theorizing and, specifically, to the relations between the 'cameras' projected by viewers. A polysemous term will have no basic frame to which all cognate meanings can be distilled and no all-encompassing one in which all cognate meanings can be contained. In the case of 'camera', there is no physical camera to which a theorist or critic can point as the core or source or as the unifying sense of the various meanings of 'camera' that theorists, critics, and viewers rely upon to think over a text seen. The reason for this follows directly from Branigan's conception of film theory itself as:

> *the grammar of an ensemble of words*, such as frame, shot, camera, point of view, editing, style, realism, auteur, performance, spectatorship, and medium specificity, accompanied by selected radial extensions of these words. I believe that a film theory is not simply a set of objective propositions about film, because 'film' – that is, the grammar (the vocabulary) of the words that describe film – is not fixed but is tied to culture, value, and a consensus about, for example, the present boundaries of the medium (i.e. the properties we select that presently interest us relating to the materials of the medium) as well as the present ideas that are used 'to clarify our experience of film.' What we think of as cinema comes from the uses we make of our thinking.
>
> (Branigan 2006, 115–16)

In Branigan's heterarchical rather than hierarchical understanding of the numerous images of 'camera', the world of words is self-sufficient:

*no critic uses the term 'camera' to refer to a piece of equipment.* Rather, a critic speaks of the camera in the ways most helpful to his or her interpretive and evaluative projects. The camera, absorbed into these projects of responding to films, acquires a flexible, metaphorical identity, better adapted to the causality of ever-new and emerging contexts that are being summoned from a spectator's memory.

(Branigan 2006, 201)

And later (also using italics):

I would like to suggest that the question about how to employ the term 'camera' when looking at a film needs to be rephrased as follows: We must inquire through *what set of judgments*, based on which beliefs and desires, is a 'camera' *seen to have* certain properties, that is, *when* does a camera come to exist *under descriptions that we offer* of the functioning of the text, under labels that we apply to the text in order to *picture* (to model) a series of photographs (or film) as having been seen picturing (modeling) motion and change.

(Branigan 2006, 217)

'Cameras,' in short, are projections of our interests and serve our goals.

This text challenges the student of film to take up the perennial philosophical problem of the relations of words to worlds, of words to pictures. No philosopher of art can deny that this is central concern; the odd task of matching terms to texts implicates every film theory, all film criticism, and every viewer's activity. Branigan expresses amazement that we continue to believe that there is a '*right description*' to shoot for that encapsulates the camera or the experience we have of its having guided us through a film (Branigan 2006, 216; italics in source). For this reason he espouses Richard Rorty's view that 'a thing materializes only "under a description"'(218). In a passage on the nature of truth, he contends that only by moving away from theoretical and critical inquiries into a given descriptor's correspondence to the world (220), a description's objective validity, can we uncover the complex contours of the process of description itself. In film's case, '[it] is greater than what meets the eye because it must be taken up by consciousness, which imposes (often verbal) descriptions onto an object of interest and onto other objects in relation to objects of interest' (223).

## Reality bites back? The targets of ostensive description

According to a Wittgensteinian analysis of film studies language, words do not refer to images; words connect with other words. In response, the realist evokes the basic *ostensivity* of language. That is, the realist would argue that the film theorist or critic trusts that the reader will on some level supply precision to his words by reflecting on the terms chosen and the object described. This implies that there is an entity, whether physical or abstract,[2] that can be perceived independently of word choice. The beholder can look and decide whether the words stick. It is hardly incompatible with a moderate conception of language-games that some film writing operates under the expectation that readers are capable of and interested in thinking about the relations – some close, some remote – between words and art objects. Art historian Michael Baxandall calls this 'the ostensivity of critical description' (Baxandall 1985, 8) – a word-to-object relation that the Wittgensteinian paradigm seems ill-equipped to explain, except perhaps to say that it is based upon a metaphysical delusion.

Far from delusory, the notion of ostensivity speaks to our ordinary experience of images: viewers' perceptions and objects under consideration reciprocally sharpen or fine-tune one another through the tool of descriptive words. Whatever 'camera' I adhere to, it seems unlikely that any description of a film still will do, or that any description at all would be able to make the shot materialize as sharply in the mind's eye. It also seems unlikely that two rival critics would be able to decide on a full, 'objective' description. But does this leave us with the view that our object materializes only under whatever description we see fit to invent given our commitment to this or that language-game? This relativistic conclusion hardly follows from the premises. Clearly some descriptions would be too soft to be of interest and others still would be flat out false. There must be a target to hit if one's description is to be accepted by a critical community as one belonging to a shot from the scene in Robert Bresson's *Journal d'un curé de campagne/Diary of a Country Priest* (1951) in which Séraphita (Martine Lemaire) confesses to the *curé* (Claude Laydu). Were I to claim that *this shot shows that the cinematographer decided to throw the focus onto the foreground male figure, leaving the centrally positioned and slightly elevated mid-ground female figure with hazy features*, aspects of this description (the term 'focus' as applied to the foreground figure, for instance) would be demonstrably false.[3] However much I wish to have the shot work this way, however much my community ratifies the description, the picture simply does not do what I want it to do. It pushes back against my interests, scuttling my efforts to make it materialize in the verbal incarnation I have tried to impose. Our projections are valuable only insofar as they take aim at the appropriate target.

The grammar of film studies often depends upon the reader's ability to play a matching game with the original (by proxy or directly). And this suggests that the practices of film studies are at odds with what might be called Wittgensteinian perspectivism, where a description is a sheer projection given context and sense by virtue of the interests of the theorist or critic as a member of a discursive community. According to this logic, an analysis of the words used plays itself out with reference only to discursive fields and the 'ways of life' that support them. But for Baxandall, a description does not use words 'absolutely', as he puts it, but uses them 'in tandem with the object, the instance' (Baxandall 1985, 8). While the Wittgensteinian wants to claim a unidirectional relation between words and moving pictures – pictures become what we say of them, limited only by what a community will accept – Baxandall acknowledges that words take some of their meaning from the reciprocal interaction between them and a visibly present object (or one that has or can be accessed).

The word-to-picture relations that interest us point to a horizon beyond language-games. If there is no real picture to perceive, then there is no sense bothering with focusing our eyes more sharply to see it as a whole or in its parts.[4] Ostensive words target a perception or an object of perception, whose logical priority is a prerequisite for our sense that certain words tweak our perceptions.

COLIN BURNETT

## Notes

1 In this list I restrict myself to relatively recent (read: published in the last 15 years) sources. But it would be remiss of me not to mention that, in the case of the second project, the founding text is perhaps Dudley Andrew's *The Major Film Theories*, first published in 1976.

2 I say 'physical or abstract' because film philosophers, it seems to me, will have to decide whether the entity referred to needs to be an actual physical or material thing or if it is rather better construed as an abstract object. One philosopher favours the latter; he says about realism: 'Realism is the position that there are abstract objects. Realism *per se* does not say what kinds of abstract objects there are, only that the world contains them. A realist view of an object-theory says that it is about abstract objects and that its truth consists in the abstract objects' having the properties and relations that the theory ascribes to them' (Katz 1990, 250–1).

3 In fact, Wittgenstein himself gave some thought to the possibility of the certainty for claims of this sort. He writes:

> But why *am* I so certain that this is my hand? Doesn't the whole language-game rest on this kind of certainty?
> Or: isn't this 'certainty' already presupposed in the language-game? Namely by virtue of the fact that one is not playing the game, or is playing it wrong, if one does not recognize objects with certainty.
>
> (Wittgenstein 1972, 58e, §446)

Even as recognition of a hand and the analysis of a shot's selective focus might not be identical forms of knowledge (although, at the moment, I cannot see how such an argument would go), it should be said that Branigan does not consider such passages in Wittgenstein.

4 Some film theorists have claimed for themselves properly realist epistemological positions. Cf. Casebier (1991) and Currie (1995; 1999).

## Works cited

Allen, Richard, and Malcolm Turvey, eds. 2001. *Wittgenstein, Theory and the Arts*. London: Routledge.

Andrew, Dudley. 1976. *The Major Film Theories: An Introduction*. New York: Oxford University Press.

Baxandall, Michael. 1985. *Patterns of Intention: On the Historical Explanation of Pictures*. London: Yale University Press.

Branigan, Edward. 2006. *Projecting a Camera: Language-Games in Film Theory*. New York: Routledge.

Casebier, Allan. 1991. *Film and Phenomenology: Toward a Realist Theory of Cinematic Representation*. New York: Cambridge University Press.

Cavell, Stanley. 1996. *Contesting Tears: The Hollywood Melodrama of the Unknown Woman*. Chicago, IL: University of Chicago Press.

Currie, Gregory. 1995. *Image and Mind: Film, Philosophy, and Cognitive Science*. Cambridge: Cambridge University Press.

——. 1999. 'Cognitivism'. In *A Companion to Film Theory*, edited by Tony Miller and Robert Stam, 105–22. Malden, MA: Blackwell.

Frampton, Daniel. 2006. *Filmosophy*. New York: Wallflower Press.

Katz, Jerrold J. 1990. *The Metaphysics of Meaning*. Cambridge, MA: MIT Press.

Lefebvre, Martin. 2007a. 'Peirce's Esthetics: A Taste for Signs in Art'. *Transactions of the Charles S. Peirce Society* 43 (2): 319–44.

——. 2007b. 'Théorie, mon bon souci'. *Cinémas* 17 (2–3): 143–92.

Price, Brian. 2008a. 'Labor Thought Theory: On Frampton and Beller'. *New Review of Television and Film Studies* 6 (1): 97–109.

——. 2008b. 'The Latest Laocoon: Medium Specificity and the History of Film Theory'. In *The Handbook of Film and Media Studies*, edited by Robert Kolker, 38–82. New York: Oxford University Press.

Rodowick, D.N. 1997. *Deleuze's Time-Machine*. Durham, NC: Duke University Press.

——. 2001. *Reading the Figural: Or, Philosophy after the New Media*. Durham, NC: Duke University Press.

——. 2007. 'An Elegy for Theory'. *October* 122: 91–109.

Szaloky, Melinda. 2005. 'Making New Sense of Film Theory through Kant: A Novel Teaching Approach.' *New Review of Film and Television Studies* 3 (1): 33–58.

Tognolotti, Chiara. 2005. 'L'Alcool, le cinéma et le philosophe: l'influence de Friedrich Nietzsche sur la théorie cinématographique de Jean Epstein.' *1895* 46: 36–53.

Turvey, Malcolm. 2007. 'Theory, Philosophy and Film Studies: A Response to D.N. Rodowick's "An Elegy for Theory"'. *October* 122: 110–20.

Wittgenstein, Ludwig. 1972. *On Certainty*. Edited by G.E.M. Anscombe and G.H. von Wright. New York: Harper & Row.

Žižek, Slavoj. 2001. *The Fright of Real Tears: Krzystof Kieslowski between Theory and Post-theory*. London: British Film Institute.

# PHENOMENOLOGY AND FILM

Phenomenology is the philosophy of experience. Film both records experience and presents itself as an object to experience. It is this double movement that phenomenological approaches to film attempt to address. Rather than speculating about the nature of reality, or indeed of the self, phenomenology tries to investigate the very boundary between the self and reality. In this sense, it is a philosophy of reduction; attempting to strip away everything inessential and leaving only those facts of which we can be certain, that is, the fact of our experience. Film is a paradigm example of a medium that functions at the very border between ourselves and the world, and this is perhaps why it is so attractive to phenomenology.

Although phenomenological thinking can be traced back to the very earliest philosophers, we can place its origins in René Descartes's *Meditations on First Philosophy* (1641), where the French philosopher tries to surmise the nature of reality from his armchair. Descartes questions the existence of everything around him – famously postulating an 'evil demon' whose sole purpose is to create an illusion of reality around the thinker – until Descartes is left with only one certainty: that there is an 'I' who thinks and who doubts. In cinema, this problem is perhaps most clearly presented in *The Matrix* (Wachowski Brothers, 1999) but also in any number of other films, notably *The Thirteenth Floor* (Josef Rusnak, 1999) in which a group of researchers create a digital virtual reality only to realize that they are computer simulations themselves. It is consciousness, conscious of itself as such, that is the ground zero of experience. When we say that we 'experience' something, we in fact mean that we experience ourselves experiencing. It is this self-reflexive thinking that is developed into phenomenology proper by Edmund Husserl (1859–1938), Martin Heidegger (1889–1976), Ludwig Wittgenstein (1889–1951), Jean-Paul Sartre (1905–80), and Maurice Merleau-Ponty (1908–61).

When we speak of a phenomenological approach to film we can mean two things. First, we can mean the experience we have when we watch a film, and, second, although this is less often discussed, we could also mean the relationship that film has to the reality which forms its basis. One of the interests of phenomenology in film is in understanding what we experience when we watch a film. In this sense, phenomenology is epistemological – that is, it is interested in how and what we know, rather than in ontological questions of being. Sometimes this is expressed as an interest in description rather than interpretation. Wittgenstein's aphorism from *The Philosophical Investigations* sums up this position:

There must not be anything hypothetical in our considerations. We must do away with all *explanation*, and description alone must take its place.

(Wittgenstein 1953, I, 109)

Thus it is the task of the phenomenologist not to explain why something is, but rather to describe it as accurately as possible. Of course, it quickly becomes crucial to understand what we might mean by 'description' as opposed to explanation or interpretation. Is it possible to describe something without also positing an interpretation of that thing? In order to describe a valley, we must already have an interpretation of what a mountain might be and its relationship to that valley. It is not possible to describe that valley without already having an explanation of what a valley might be. Nevertheless, let us put this problem aside for the moment, and explore the way in which phenomenology has been used in thinking about film.

The work I will discuss here is Vivian Sobchack's *The Address of the Eye: A Phenomenology of Film Experience* (1992), a book that, alongside Allan Casebier's less well-known *Film and Phenomenology: Towards a Realist Theory of Cinematic Representation* (1991), forms the basis of phenomenological approaches to film in the English-speaking world. It may be useful to consider Sobchack's and Casebier's books as reflecting two different approaches to film phenomenology. Sobchack considers the experience of film viewing, while Casebier investigates the relationship of film to reality. Sobchack takes as her basis Don Ihde's short and accessible *Experimental Phenomenology: An Introduction* (1986).

## Vivian Sobchack and the experience of film

Sobchack's *The Address of the Eye* is often cited as the most rigorous of the film-phenomenology books and indeed she does meticulously explore Merleau-Ponty's work in particular, but the book is rather dense and the development of her argument is often difficult to follow. Unlike Ihde she never systematically approaches her subject – perhaps purposely so – and the book reads more as an impressionistic essay than a concerted explication of the matter at hand as she ranges from the historical development of phenomenology to existentialism, semiotics, and Lacanian psychoanalysis.

Sobchack distinguishes between Husserl's 'transcendental phenomenology' and Merleau-Ponty's 'existential phenomenology' and grounds her own approach in the latter. Sobchack explains that both phenomenologies 'seek their subjective grounding in the ontology of conscious experience from which all epistemes and science are generated' (Sobchak 1992, 32). Thus it is consciousness itself which is the object of phenomenology, but this is of course complicated by the fact that consciousness is the supreme subject of the world and so there is a radical confusion between subject and object which, in phenomenological terms, is not so much a contradiction as the essence of being in the world.

Husserl, according to Sobchack, claims that 'all knowledge of the world arises in experience and emerges as a *mediated* relation between consciousness and phenomena' (33). Key for Husserl is the concept of 'intentionality' since consciousness can never exist on its own but only as a '*consciousness of something*' (34). Here Sobchack introduces the important phenomenological terms '*noema*' and '*noesis*'. She writes that 'the phenomena of our experience (the *noema*, or intentional objects of consciousness) are always correlated with the mode of our experience (the *noesis*, or intentional acts of consciousness)' (34). It is important not to confuse this specialized understanding of 'intentionality' (as the *consciousness of* something) with the more usual definition of the word (as expression of will). It is intentionality, then, 'that structures and directs our experience and, from the first, infuses it with meaning' (34). It is the correlation of subject and object – the subject-as-consciousness comes into existence through its experience of the object – which defines phenomenology but also begs the question of origin. How does the subject come into existence if its being is predicated on its experience of an object (which is itself brought into that particular being through its being experienced)? This, however, is a metaphysical question with which phenomenology is not particularly concerned. We are in the world and our job is to deal with the world as we experience it.

The Husserlian project is one that aims to bring to the fore this experience of the world: to make strange, to use a Russian formalist term, our perception of reality so that we become aware of the ways in which we perceive. Perception is therefore not a pure anteriority but is itself a historical and contingent part of the world, and phenomenological *reduction* or *epoché* is a 'controlled and rigorous bracketing of presuppositions' (35) which aims to find the 'invariant' in the world. In other words, the phenomenological method, like Descartes in his armchair, aims to ignore everything that is not essential to perception.

Sobchack presents Ihde's formulation of Husserl and Merleau-Ponty's method of reduction (48–9):

> The rules that inform the act of *phenomenological description* are (1) Attend to the phenomena of experience as they appear and are immediately present and given to experience; (2) Describe, don't explain; and (3) Horizontalize or equalize all immediate phenomena and do not assume an initial hierarchy of 'realities.' (4) Seek out structural or invariant features of the phenomena; [and finally] (5) Every experiencing has its reference or direction towards what is experienced, and contrarily, every experienced phenomenon refers to or reflects a mode of experience to which it is present.

Thus we try to see not only the world but also our seeing of it and seek to understand the ways in which the world is brought into being through our perception of it.

Crucial to the terminology of phenomenology are the 'I', the subject of experience; the *noesis*, the way which we experience the world; and the *noema*, the phenomena that we experience. Crudely put, the I perceives noema through noesis. In practice, the I sees a *core* surrounded by a *field* which is bounded by a *horizon*. Phenomenology attempts to identify this structure in our experience as precisely as possible: What do we see? How do we see it? Who is it that sees? These three questions cannot be separated.

Sobchack stresses the self-conscious experience of viewing which is highlighted while seeing a film. We are aware not only that there is somebody being killed, but that we are seeing that act in a pre-recorded, and probably fictional, representation. We are aware of our own act of seeing and therefore aware of ourselves as perceiving beings. Sobchack defines the human as that which is 'uniquely capable not only of the experience of vision but also of the consciousness of vision' (53). For Sobchack, '[s]eeing is an act performed by both the film (which sees a world as visible images) and the viewer (who sees the film's visible images both as a world and the seeing of a world)' (56). Sobchack argues that perception is *synaesthetic* (one perception is 'commutable' to any other – seeing, for instance, can be understood as touch) as well as *synoptic* (it gives an overview of our encounter with the world). Thus, in using a phenomenological approach to film we are able to explain both the meaning of a film and the meaning of ourselves, since these two elements exist only in their encounter with each other.

## Don Ihde, Allan Casebier, and phenomenological film criticism

Ihde makes a distinction between hermeneutic and transcendental phenomenology. In essence he means that we can approach a phenomenological analysis either from the side of noesis (the way in which we perceive) or from that of the noema (the appearance that we perceive). In the hermeneutic mode we can change our perception of an object – Ihde uses the example of the Necker cube, the line drawing of a cube that can appear to be facing in two different directions – by telling ourselves an imaginary story about what the object might be. For example, the Necker cube is usually only discussed in terms of two possible apparent cubes in the single figure. Ihde shows that by telling ourselves different stories about the cube (that the central parallelogram is the body of an insect, which allows us to see a two-dimensional entity, or that the centre of the cube is in fact one plane of a gem, giving us a non-cuboid three-dimensional shape) we are able to perceive any number of different objects. Similar perceptual transformations are possible by using a transcendental approach which scans the figure itself for different ways in which we might perceive it. Ihde says that this is a much more cumbersome and time-consuming way of achieving the same insights given by the hermeneutic approach.

It would seem, however, that transcendental analysis must underlie the hermeneutic method since how would we know what story to tell about an object if we had not already seen this perceptual possibility. In other words, we make up the story to allow others easier access to that perceptual possibility. However, we ourselves must have perceived that possibility *without* the story in the first place. We can then consider the story as a sort of mnemonic allowing us to remember our intuitive analysis. Allan Casebier makes this move explicit in his discussion of film criticism which he sees as making available critics' intuitions about film:

> Critical communication, the act of critics writing to their readers, involves the use of the communicative skills at the critics' disposal to guide the readers to perceive what the critics have perceived in the film. By use of vivid images, metaphors, similes, whatever, the critics enable their readers to intuit in the film for themselves what the critics have at a prior time intuited.
>
> (Casebier 1991, 56–7)

We can therefore consider each individual film to be a form of puzzle with an almost infinite number of possible views or interpretations. While all these interpretations must already exist within the structure of the film itself, it is the task of the critic to allow others to see a particular way of looking at that film. In this sense, phenomenological film criticism does not have to be 'true' in the sense of pointing out 'what the film really means'; rather, the criticism is successful – and therefore true – if others are able to see what the critic is pointing out. Phenomenological film criticism is therefore really a criticism of persuasion rather than of fact.

## Phenomenological filmmaking

What impact has phenomenology had on filmmaking itself? While any number of film-makers have shown an explicit interest in philosophy, it is always difficult to make direct connections from expressed interests to actual films. Nevertheless, Terrence Malick is a good example of a filmmaker who has professional expertise as a philosopher and whose interest in phenomenology is evidenced by his work on Heidegger. Malick himself translated Heidegger's *The Essence of Reasons* (1969) into English. If we can assume that Malick is aware of the essence of phenomenological thinking, we should then be able to make some guesses as to how this knowledge may be reflected in the materiality of his own films.

On a stylistic level, Malick's films, such as *The Tree of Life* (2011), *The Thin Red Line* (1998), or *Badlands* (1973), tend to use long shots and to concentrate on moments of stillness, which do not have much apparent narrative consequence. Isolating one peculiar technique may be useful here. All of Malick's films are interested in the quality of light, particularly sunlight, but also the dimness of interiors in contrast to the lucidity of the outdoors. There is a certain romanticism associated with this celebration of the natural which I will not discuss further here (but see Ben McCann's [2003] discussion of landscape in Malick's films). Malick's interest in light is given a material form through his use of intense backlighting which sometimes results in prominent lens flare effects in the image. Since these effects are a condition of the recording of the image, this technique encourages an audience to consider not so much the light itself, as the recording of that light and their own perception of that recording. Thus the audience is asked not to experience light but rather to consider their own perceiving of the recording of that light. In phenomenological terms, noesis is stressed and noema given a less privileged position. We are asked to reflect on our perception and not on the supposed reality of that which is represented on the screen (although, of course, we are paradoxically asked to consider the reality of the image on the screen and not the image's faithfulness to some anterior reality).

One of the effects of phenomenological thinking about film has been to encourage a style that stresses the surface texture of objects and, particularly, human skin. This is a metaphorical transposition of phenomenology's interest in experience into the visual realm. Extreme close-ups of finger-tips touching surfaces – such as we see at the beginning of Lynne Ramsay's *Morvern Callar* (2002) when Morvern runs her hand over her dead boy-friend's skin – encourage an imaginative mirroring in the viewer: what would it be like to touch the same thing as those fingers, so very much like ours, right here right now? Andrea Arnold's *Wuthering Heights* (2011) stresses the touch of fingers on skin or fur to highlight the sensuous nature of Emily Brontë's novel. It seems that it is fairly easy for humans to conjure up a phantasmic or fictional experience such as this. See, for instance, the many experiments on rubber hands being mistaken for and felt as a person's own real hand through optical illusion (Westerhoff 2012, 62–3). The films of the surrealist Czech film-maker Jan Švankmajer similarly stress the texture of objects and also explicitly depict human touch. See, for instance, the importance of skin contact in *Conspirators of Pleasure* or Švankmajer's frequent and visceral portrayal of eating and drinking where we are asked to imagine what it would be like to touch or taste that which is on screen. During a period when he was disallowed from making films by the then communist government, Švank-majer published the samizdat *Touch and the Imagination* (1983) in which he quotes liberally from phenomenological philosophers. This does not mean to say these films are 'more' phenomenological than any other film, but merely that they highlight an interest in experience through the metaphorical slippage of physical touch to mental touch (as in 'being touched' on an emotional level). Another way of saying this would be that phenomenological thinking stresses subjective experience in the cinema rather than objective presentation.

## Film phenomenology and the crack in the mirror

In *The Address of the Eye* Sobchack asks us not only to consider film as an object of experience, but also to concentrate on our own experience of viewing a film. Sobchack exhorts us to experience our experience. While this approach can lead to many interesting insights, a problem does arise. Surely this will lead us into merely reinforcing our prejudices by valuing only what we already know. If we elevate personal experience above all else, we can find ourselves trapped in a hall of mirrors where all we see in what we look at is a reflection of ourselves. Phenomenology's emphasis on experience must be tempered by a critical understanding that there is indeed a mirror in the world and that our reflection in it is more than just a corroboration of what we understand ourselves to be. Phenomenology, done properly, can perhaps point to the flaws and joins in the mirror that allow us to see something that we are not. The project of phenomenology is not to find the human in the world but rather to discover the impossible inhuman world.

DAVID SORFA

## Works cited

Casebier, A. 1991. *Film and Phenomenology: Towards a Realist Theory of Cinematic Representation.* Cambridge: Cambridge University Press.

Heidegger, M. 1969. *The Essence of Reasons.* Translated by Terrence Malick. Evanston, IL: Northwestern University Press.

Ihde, D. 1986. *Experimental Phenomenology: An Introduction.* Albany: State University of New York Press.

McCann, B. 2003. "'Enjoying the Scenery": Landscape and the Fetishisation of Nature in *Badlands* and *Days of Heaven*'. In *The Cinema of Terrence Malick*, edited by Hannah Patterson, 75–85. London: Wallflower.

Sobchack, V. 1992. *The Address of the Eye: A Phenomenology of Film Experience.* Princeton, NJ: Princeton University Press.

Westerhoff, J. 2012. *Reality: A Very Short Introduction.* Oxford: Oxford University Press.

Wittgenstein, L. 1953. *Philosophical Investigations: The German Text, with a Revised English Translation.* 3rd edition. Translated by G.E.M. Anscombe. Oxford: Blackwell, 2009.

# PIXEL/CUT/VECTOR

Sean Cubitt introduces the three cinematic categories of pixel, cut, and vector in *The Cinema Effect* (2004). Cubitt's categories synthesize several philosophical triads, notably the Firstness, Secondness, and Thirdness of the triadic logic of American philosopher Charles Sanders Peirce, and Jacques Lacan's psychic realms Real, Imaginary, and Symbolic (see Table 1).

Cubitt applies the terms pixel, cut, and vector, associated with computer-based media, retroactively to film. His purpose in using these terms is to 'supplant the metaphors of film as language supplied by Metz ... and film as psychology as pursued by Bordwell ... with a more digital analysis of the mathematical bases of motion' (Cubitt 2004, 7–8). In Cubitt's thought, digital media are not mathematical abstractions but material entities (as he argued in *Digital Aesthetics*, Cubitt 1998). Pixel, cut, and vector are thus more materialist analytic categories than the metaphoric systems imposed on cinema by Metz and Bordwell.

The philosophy of Gilles Deleuze, including his writing on cinema, clearly influences Cubitt's thought, though Cubitt only occasionally acknowledges it directly. Cubitt's materialist politics of the Open resonates with the materialist ethics of Deleuze and Félix Guattari. Like Deleuze, he takes the Bergsonian position that cinema consists of images in movement, as the world itself does (*see* MOVEMENT-IMAGE). Also similarly, and with the same non-dualistic intention, he argues that cinematic images do not represent the world but are part of the world. Deleuze based three of his categories of movement-image – affection-image, action-image, and relation-image – on Peirce's triadic logic, according to which all phenomena possess one of three modes of being: Firstness, Secondness, and Thirdness. (Deleuze proposed that the perception-image is a degree zero of the image. He introduces the relation-image, also called the mental image, towards the end of *Cinema 1*, with Hitchcock as his main example: an image that puts two things into relation and invites a mental comparison.) Cubitt's three categories have much in common with Deleuze's categories.

Like Deleuze, Cubitt derives a cinematic ethics from Henri Bergson's vitalist proposition that the universe is open and consists of constant change, undetermined by past or imagined future events. For Deleuze, this means that the best films are those that take part in the universe's becoming by revealing the total freedom of each instant: direct images of time. Cubitt, in contrast, shifts attention to human communities' potential to become. Not only individuals but society as a whole needs to be able to evolve creatively (to use Bergson's term) through collective action, by creating relations in the free present moment of duration. For this reason, Cubitt does not adopt Deleuze's distinction between movement-image and time-image. Instead, he seeks the potential for creative human action in

*Table 1*

| Pixel | Cut | Vector |
|---|---|---|
| iteration of time | objection of space | production of meaning |
| Firstness | Secondness | Thirdness |
| sensation | perception/representation | communication |
| event | object | sign |
| pre-individual | individual | social |
| indifference (zero) | unity/multiplicity | infinity |
| real | imaginary | symbolic |
| timelessness | destiny | hope |
| referent | signified | signifier |

Cubitt's Elementary Aspects of Cinema.
Source: Cubitt (2004, 97–8).

all categories of cinema. '*Pace* Deleuze, film began in the time-image' (Cubitt 2004, 51), he writes, attributing to the early cinema the freedom from causality that Deleuze identified primarily in postwar cinema.

A social emphasis also characterizes Cubitt's adaptation of terms from Lacanian psychoanalysis, in which he emphasizes human community rather than individual psychic construction; I discuss this below. In Peirce, Cubitt finds an ally who already bases his categories in the social, for meaning and consequence in Peirce's thought usually take place in human interaction.

In Peirce's triadic logic, Firstness, Secondness, and Thirdness indicate respectively 'the being of positive qualitative possibility, the being of actual fact, and the being of law that will govern facts in the future' (Peirce 1955, 75). Firstness is 'the mode of being which consists in its subject's being positively such as it is regardless of aught else' (76). It is one in itself. Insofar as we cannot conceive of a thing except as distinct from other things, Firstness is a possibility, 'a mere may-be' (81) as redness is a possibility before it is embodied in something red. 'The idea of First is predominant in the ideas of freshness, life, freedom' (78). We may compare Firstness to Deleuze's concept of virtuality, which is also a realm of free potentiality that has not yet been constrained to manifest in actuality. As Deleuze pointed out, Firstness characterizes the pre-temporal: it 'concerns what is new in experience, what is fresh, fleeting, and nevertheless eternal' (Deleuze 1986, 98).

## Pixel

A pixel is a fundamental, indivisible 'pixel element'. In computer-based media, each pixel is assigned a numerical address. Like the atoms of Greek and Islamic atomism, pixels do not affect each other (see Galloway 2009 and Marks 2010), but differences among them give rise to a picture and, in successive frames, create a sense of movement. Cubitt, retrofitting the digital term to film, designates the pixel as Firstness, proposing that a single film frame, at the moment it is projected, constitutes a pixel. The projected film frame is the zero point of a film, where zero signifies not nothing or absence but the sum of activities up to the present, like the zero of double-entry bookkeeping. Because cinema is movement, a film frame is necessarily incomplete, existing in a state of potentiality; it does not stand on its own like a photograph. Cubitt asserts that films cannot be scrutinized for indexical evidence, because every frame is incomplete.

In terms of subjective states, Peirce's Firstness corresponds to feeling or sensation that occurs prior to perception. Peirce wrote that the state of consciousness characteristic of Firstness is 'Feeling, the consciousness which can be included with an instant of time, passive consciousness of quality, without recognition or analysis' (1955, 95). Firstness characterizes a pre-cognitive state in which one is not aware of differences, including the difference between oneself and others. In the pixel state, both cinema and spectators are like an infant that cannot distinguish self from environment. Cubitt argues that this occurs in the early films of the Lumières, which consisted of movement that was not yet cut up into significant parcels. He agrees with James Lastra and Dai Vaughn that early audiences welcomed the random movement of clouds, water, smoke, steam, and dust in films like *Arrivée d'un train à La Ciotat* and *Barque sortant du port.* They did not attempt to isolate and master the objects of vision but enjoyed immersion in a dreamlike, pre-cognitive state. The flicker effect that resulted from early films' unstable registration, the imperfect fit between sprockets and sprocket holes, certainly contributed to audiences' inability to visually comprehend the image. Cinema's utopian moment, Cubitt suggests, occurred when the random movement of early films existed in itself, and could not be summarized or subsumed to a general meaning or a narrative.

The pixel state characterizes not only the earliest flickering films but also films that immerse themselves in the world with little sense of causality. In the magical cinema of Georges Méliès and the Indian pioneer Dadasaheb Phalke, causality (and thus the cut) occurs outside the world of the film, in religion or myth. The fetishistic realism of Jean Renoir's *La Règle du jeu* multiplies the effects of Firstness, of a world perceived but not measured. The cinema of the pixel implies a spectatorial openness to the future – 'Cinematic zero inscribes the dynamic equilibrium of spectatorship as unfinished process' (Cubitt 2004, 40) – without, as yet, a capacity to act.

We can compare the films to which Deleuze attributes Firstness, namely films in which quality or affect predominate. Quality, Peirce stated, is a state of potentiality that precedes action. Like Cubitt, Deleuze associates images of water with Firstness, in the 'liquid perception' of Renoir, Jean Epstein, and Jean Vigo's *L'Atalante.*

## Cut

Peirce's Secondness is the realm of actuality, in which one thing is constrained by another or two things struggle with one another. In Cubitt's system, the *cut* establishes a distinction, for example between figure and ground or cause and effect. Since pixels give rise to images only because of differences among them, the cut is responsible for establishing differences. The cut comprises not only the edit, but also techniques that isolate objects: framing and compositing. Framing divides space into on-screen and off-screen, implying alternative views: it establishes the difference between what is visible and what is not. Compositing techniques include staging in depth, the parallax effect, the use of mattes, and optical printing: all techniques that separate figure from ground. This retrofitting of the digital-editing term *compositing* allows the term to comprehend a variety of techniques from the history of moving-image media. As Lev Manovich has pointed out, analogue precedents of digital compositing include layering images, which can be achieved with optical printing of film, and inserting images, which can be achieved with video keying (Manovich 2000, 145–55). Thus what Cubitt intends by 'cut' occurs in single-shot films that use framing and compositing. The Lumières' single-shot *L'Arroseur arrosé* differentiates figures by composing action in depth, and, by reframing at the conclusion, it establishes a horizon that retrospectively organizes the film.

In terms of spectatorial states, Secondness corresponds to objective perception. According to Peirce, while Firstness appears to exist in an eternal present, Secondness constitutes a sharp distinction that necessarily occurs in time: 'something more than can be contained in an instant' (Peirce 1955, 96). Thus while Firstness is a state of indifferentiation, Secondness differentiates both past from present and world from perceiver. 'In the pixel', Cubitt writes, 'film, retina, and mind are not distinguished. The cut distinguishes them, then reorganizes them into an apparatus for organizing space and time' (Cubitt 2004, 66). If the pixel corresponds to non-differentiation, the cut, because it renders space an object, corresponds to identity, fixity, and difference.

From this follows Cubitt's ideological critique of narrative. While cinema's ontology, according to Cubitt, is to move, narrative works against movement, attempting to instigate identity. In contrast to Jacques Aumont, André Gaudreault, and the many others who contend that cinema is narrative simply by virtue of taking place in time, Cubitt argues that cinema is not inherently narrative. Rather, narrative is instigated by the cut. While pixel films appear undifferentiated, existing in Firstness, films of the cut establish differences, Secondness. Through their suggestion of off-screen space, framing and compositing create diegesis; only at this point does a film become narrative. Thus *L'Arroseur arrosé* is a narrative film, while *Workers Leaving a Factory* is not. Another early example is Porter's *Pan-American Exposition by Night* of 1901, composed of two panning shots. The reframing of the panning shot is diegetic, reminding the spectator that there is more to see beyond the borders of the frame. Reframing also demands that the spectator wait for the scene to make sense, in the sense of Maurice Merleau-Ponty's term *Rückgestaltung*, making a whole in retrospect. Cutting, for example in a shot–reverse shot sequence, does this too, of course. The cinema of the cut is teleological: 'the effect shapes the cause' (2004, 67). A reactive kind of spectatorship ensues: the spectator is not immersed in an undifferentiated scene but seeks to establish causal relations.

Here Cubitt's cinema of Secondness is closely similar to Deleuze's category of the action-image. Following Peirce, Deleuze wrote that in the realm of Secondness, of 'brute facts', qualities become 'actualised directly in determinate, geographical, historical and social space-times' (Deleuze 1986, 141). In action movies, characters respond to situations, simply enough. The action-image, Deleuze wrote, tends to be dominated by clichés, replacing fresh perceptions with pre-given meanings. Similarly, but drawing out a political implication, Cubitt writes that 'narrative conjures up identity as a method for controlling the unfixed dynamic of the event, and by implication the democratic upwelling' (Cubitt 2004, 40).

At this point it makes sense to introduce the triadic categories Cubitt adapts from Lacanian psychoanalysis. If the pixel is like an infant that cannot distinguish between itself and the environment, the cut, separating the viewer from the world viewed, repeats the moment where the infant first distinguishes itself from the world. The cut makes the moving image 'an instrument by which the world can be possessed'. In this way the cut produces subjectivity, giving the viewer an illusion of mastery, as Lacanian film theory conventionally holds. The cinema of the pixel corresponds to the Lacanian Real, the world as it exists in itself, antedating and indifferent to human subjectivity. The cinema of the cut corresponds to the Lacanian Imaginary, the world organized from the point of view of a subject. It appeals to a narcissistic subjectivity based on identity. While the flux of the pixel is social in a kind of pre-cognitive way, the cinema of the cut appears asocial, mired in the illusion of individual unity.

But unlike the loss Lacan emphasizes with the splitting of self from world in the construction of subjectivity, Cubitt's theory of the cut sees it as a gain. The dispersed, atomic sensation characteristic of the pixel becomes unified in the cinema of the cut. As Elizabeth Grosz points out, the etymology of *de-scision* means to cut out. She writes: 'The teeming flux of the real ... must be symbolized, reduced, to states, things, and numeration in order to facilitate practical action. This is not an error that we commit, a fault to be unlearned, but a condition of our continuing survival in the world' (Grosz 2001, 131). Secondness is the realm of practical, cumulative activity. Greater complexity is possible, as the cinema of the cut produces unities that in turn take part in hierarchies of unities.

Also differing from conventional psychoanalytic film theory, Cubitt implicitly rejects the notion that the cut 'sutures' a spectator into the subject position demanded by the film. 'The cut is always lacking, always inadequate to the plenum it depicts', he writes. 'Its unity not only implies multiplicity; it exists in a dialectical relation to the flux of pixels without which it has nothing to organize' (Cubitt 2004, 70). Since to cut is to choose, the very fact of a cut emphasizes that something has not been chosen. Cubitt suggests, then, that the relation between the 0 of the ground and the 1 of the figure cut from it is reversible.

## Vector

Cubitt's emphasis on the plenum from which an object is cut out indicates that a third relation is possible – a comparison between what was chosen and what was not. In Thirdness, a third element enters to carry out a relation between two things, as in comparison, judgement, prediction, and interpretation. Deleuze's films of Thirdness instigate mental relations of comparison, judgement, prediction: Hitchcock is his main example. Cubitt's films of Thirdness differ from Deleuze's, again in his emphasis on the social and ethical attitudes they invite.

Here the third term enters: *vector*. The mathematical definition of vector is any quantity that has magnitude and direction. In analogue electronic media like the oscilloscope and radar, the vector is a line fixed at one end: it draws the image from the centre of the screen. (Computer-based vector graphics adapt this means of drawing, which is more efficient than bit-map graphics.) The example Cubitt elicits from early cinema is the animation *Fantasmagorie* (1908) of Émile Cohl, in which a line seems to redraw itself in real time. Depicted objects transform: the puppet Pierrot becomes 'a bubble, a hat, a valise' (Cubitt 2004, 76). Cohl used no key frames, so the animation does not return to a stable identity but is constantly transforming. Cubitt's description of *Fantasmagorie* echoes Deleuze's characterization of the 'cartoon film': 'If it belongs fully to the cinema, this is because the drawing no longer constitutes a pose or a completed figure, but the description of a figure which is always in the process of being formed or dissolving through the movement of lines and points taken at any-instant-whatevers of their course' (Deleuze 1987, 5).

An ethics of openness to others and to the unknown governs the vector. In terms of Peirce's semiotics, Cubitt points out that the cinema of the vector is a Peircean symbol in that it requires the action of the interpreter. A symbol is 'a sign that would lose the character which renders it a sign if there were no interpretant' (Peirce 1955, 104). Like the vector, the symbol becomes meaningful only when it is received. The pixel precedes being. The cut makes being possible, by creating entities. The vector destabilizes identities into relations. Since the vector continually constructs new relations in time, it cannot revert to what is known already but remains open. The vector makes becoming possible. Where the cut is teleological, the vector is eschatological: 'its future is open, governed only by hope' (Cubitt 2004, 80).

Once again, Cubitt gives an optimistic spin to the corresponding category of Lacanian psychoanalysis, the Symbolic. Lacan proposed that we enter language and the Symbolic by accepting to communicate according to rules, with a corresponding loss of freedom. Cubitt stresses that the Symbolic is a social universe, unlike the narcissistic Imaginary.

In films more complex than Cohl's 1908 animation, we can recognize a vectorial structure when the film invites interpretation and creative action.

LAURA U. MARKS

## Works cited

Cubitt, Sean. 1998. *Digital Aesthetics*. London: Sage.

———. 2004. *The Cinema Effect*. Cambridge, MA.: Harvard University Press.

Deleuze, Gilles. 1986. *Cinema 1: The Movement-Image*. Translated by Hugh Tomlinson and Barbara Habberjam. Minneapolis: University of Minnesota Press.

Galloway, Alexander. 2009. 'The Pixel'. In *The Object Reader*, edited by Fiona Candlin and Raiford Guins, 499–502. New York and London: Routledge.

Grosz, Elizabeth. 2001. 'The Thing'. In *Architecture from the Outside: Essays on Virtual and Real Space*. Cambridge, MA: MIT Press.

Manovich, Lev. 2000. *The Language of New Media*. Cambridge, MA: MIT Press.

Marks, Laura U. 2010. 'Baghdad, 1000: Origin of the Pixel'. In *Enfoldment and Infinity: An Islamic Genealogy of New Media Art*, 189–218. Cambridge, MA: MIT Press.

Peirce, Charles Sanders. 1955. *Philosophical Writings of Charles Sanders Peirce*. Edited by Justus Buchler. New York: Dover.

# POETIC CINEMA

## Shklovsky and Pasolini

Two canonical essays on poetic cinema, Viktor Shklovsky's 'Poetry and Prose in Cinematography' (1927) and Pier Paolo Pasolini's 'The Cinema of Poetry' (1965), both identify lyrical, or verse-like, films as those where the patterning of technical and formal features attracts as much, or more, attention than plot. Shklovsky's essay, written on the cusp of the sound era, takes as its touchstone the Soviet avant-garde, specifically Dziga Vertov's *A Sixth Part of the World* and Vsevolod Pudovkin's *Mother*, both from 1926. He claims that these films, like poetry, resolve themselves through compositional means rather than through the solution to a problematic story-world situation or the provision of key narrative information. The repetition of images at the end of *A Sixth Part of the World*, for instance, 'recall[s] the triolet form', a circular stanza that ends with the same two lines with which it begins (Shklovsky 1973, 129).

Pasolini's essay describes tendencies in modernist European art cinema of the late 1950s and early 1960s. His key references are Michelangelo Antonioni's *Red Desert* (1964), Bernardo Bertolucci's *Before the Revolution* (1964), and unspecified work by Jean-Luc Godard, and he places as much emphasis on the actualization of a poetic subjectivity as on composition. Surprisingly, he takes a critical term associated with prose as the foundation of his definition of cinematic poetry. He borrows the concept of free indirect discourse from theories of the novel and considers its transposition to film. The stylistic distinction between the hero's inner speech and the author's discourse becomes, in film, a difference between the visual modes of heroine and auteur. Since it is not so much discourse at stake as sensual and affective perception, Pasolini calls this device of marking an enunciative difference between the world as perceived by author and hero '"the free indirect subjective" which establishes the possible tradition of a "technical language of poetry" in cinema'. He chooses as central examples moments where the vision of a character 'contaminates' that of the author. Two shots in succession, for instance, 'frame the same portion of reality – first from close in, then from *a little* farther away; or else first head-on, then *a little* obliquely; or else, finally, quite simply, on the same alignment but with two different lenses' (Pasolini 1976, 552–3). The vision that pollutes the narration in these films belongs to a neurotic heroine, and she provides a pretext for 'obsessive framings and montage-rhythms' that transcend plot 'function' and appear as '"language in itself," style' (Pasolini 1976, 555). By calling the heroine's modern malaise a 'pretext', Pasolini signals his awareness that we can always recuperate narrative motivation behind the stylistic excess her point of view generates (he accepts as historical fact that cinema is primarily a narrative art). But such recuperation, for Pasolini, would be beside the point. He is interested in the way the excess suggests a film 'behind' the film, 'the one the author would have made without the pretext of *visual mimesis* with the protagonist' (Pasolini 1976, 555).

Pasolini does not valorize this 'cinema of poetry'. While Shklovsky is writing about a young art in a revolutionary context – 'In cinematography we are still children' (Shklovsky 1973, 130) – Pasolini, 38 years later, sounds jaded:

> All this belongs to the general movement of recuperation, by bourgeois culture, of the territory it had lost in the battle with Marxism and its possible revolution. And this is a part of the somehow grandiose movement of the evolution ... of the bourgeoisie, along the lines of an 'internal revolution' of capitalism, i.e. of a neo-capitalism, which questions and modifies its own structures and which, in the case which concerns us, re-attributes to the poets a pseudohumanistic function: myth and the technical awareness of form.
>
> (Pasolini 1976, 557–8)

Pasolini thus sees 'the cinema of poetry' of his time as the antithesis of revolutionary film: it does not promise radical progress, it negates it, functioning instead as an eddy in a current that carries once revolutionary forms into the neo-capitalist mainstream.

What does it matter to Shklovsky and Pasolini that they can point to a cinematic category they call poetical? Shklovsky's three-page essay proposes as its main examples two films that explicitly celebrate the Russian Revolution, but focuses narrowly on their technique. Pasolini takes interest in the striking formal features of his central examples, and dismisses their political significance as one of stasis. Is poetic cinema, then, 'empty formalism'?

A complex set of aims clusters around the traditions and descriptions of film poetry. An elastic conceptual category – Shklovsky begins his essay by stating that 'poetry and prose are not sharply differentiated one from the other' (Shklovsky 1973, 128) – 'poetry' threatens to expand to a broad inclusivity that would render it irrelevant. Significantly, both Shklovsky and Pasolini use as examples hybrid films that both tell a story and break from the function of providing narrative information in order to emphasize relatively independent elements of form. But how does the sequence of superimpositions at the end of *The Mother*, singled out by Shklovsky, differ from what Eisenstein might call 'tonal montage' (Eisenstein 1998, 117–20), where an expressive pictorial quality pervades the sequence? How do the techniques described by Pasolini differ from what David Bordwell, borrowing from Noël Burch, calls 'parametric narration', where 'the film's stylistic system creates patterns distinct from the demands of the syuzhet [plot] system' and 'may be organized and emphasized to a degree that makes it at least equal in importance to syuzhet patterns' (Bordwell 1985, 275)? For Bordwell, 'in this context, "style" simply names the film's systematic use of cinematic devices' (Bordwell 1985, 50). Is poetry, then, just another word for (an unusual) 'style'?[1]

## Negotiating the boundaries of the genre

The formalist definition of film poetry depends on quantitative as well as qualitative distinctions. Formal patterns occur in all narrative films, but may not distract attention from plot. Compositional or technical patterning needs to reach a threshold of autonomy, or dominance, before a film tips into the category of poetry. A sense of this threshold helps define the category and prompts critics to identify certain films as belonging to it. These films, in turn, reshape conceptions of what poetry might mean for cinema and presumably point towards new directions and future sorts of poetry: Shklovsky and his contemporary Adrian Piotrovsky cite the early films of Vertov, Pudovkin, and Eisenstein; Pasolini addresses the films of the 1965 Locarno film festival and those of Antonioni, Bertolucci, and Godard; a 'Poetic School' of filmmakers, including Sergei Paradjanov, Yuri Illienko, and Bolotbek Shamshiev, emerged in the Soviet Union in the 1960s and 1970s, drawing inspiration from Alexander Dovzhenko. In his book on Derek Jarman, Steve Dillon (2004) identifies a canon of poetic cinema that includes films of D.W. Griffith, Jean Cocteau, Sergei Paradjanov, and Andrei Tarkovsky.

## Beyond formalism

All of these films realize what Roman Jakobson called the poetic function of language, which is to draw attention to itself (Jakobson 1990, 62–94); but some critics see poetic film as doing something other than reflexively drawing attention to its form. Like Shklovsky, Piotrovsky cites Vertov's documentary *A Sixth Part of the World* and identifies a category of 'plotless genres' that 'could be called "poetry" in order to distinguish it from prosaic genres' (Piotrovsky 1981, 145–6). But he also points to a 'lyrical principle' that can exist within narrative fictions. The expressive close-up realizes this principle, as do '"atmosphere" segments' in the works of Louis Delluc, Marcel L'Herbier, and Jean Epstein, 'which function to build lyrical images of life in progress by moving completely away from the narrative' (Piotrovsky 1981, 144–5).

Piotrovsky goes beyond making an analogy between editing techniques and poetic metres, line breaks, or caesuras; he does not limit 'lyricism' to style or device: instead he suggests that certain film sequences capture a specifically poetic subjectivity. (He does not specify whether this belongs to the narrator, character, or spectator.) His discussion of lyricism in reference to what some scholars call 'Impressionist' cinema echoes the writing of French filmmaker and theorist Jean Epstein. In 'On Certain Characteristics of Photogenie' (1924), Epstein writes: 'this landscape or this fragment of drama staged by someone like Gance will look nothing like what would be seen through the eyes and heart of a Griffith or a L'Herbier. And so the personality, the soul, the poetry of certain men invaded the cinema.' He concludes that, in cinema, 'poetry, which one might have thought but verbal artifice, a figure of style, a play of antithesis and metaphor – in short, something next to nothing – achieves a dazzling incarnation. "So poetry is thus true, and exists as truly as the eye." The cinema is poetry's most powerful medium' (Epstein 1988, 318).

Sceptical of Epstein's Impressionist arguments, David Bordwell cites the 1921 essay 'La Poésie d'aujourd'hui', where Epstein emphasizes cinema's power to express fleeting feelings, and writes:

> The Impressionist's stress on art's evocation of feeling sidesteps the question of the nature of feeling ... What is a feeling? ... How does the Impressionist theorist avoid an idealism which posits the feeling as an entity existing solely in the minds of the artist and perceiver? Not only is the status of the work reduced to that of the consequence or cue for purely private feelings, but a more fundamental

question enters: How can the artist's 'expression' be known as such by a perceiver?

(Bordwell 1980, 96–8)

Bordwell's insistence on terminological precision ('What is a feeling?') and empirical evidence (how can the form of a film reliably communicate that feeling?) makes sense if the goal is to understand how film style cues shared psychological responses. If we shift our frame of reference, however, to include beyond what appears on screen, the discourses surrounding cinema, then persistent comparisons of film to poetry do not merit dismissal for the sometimes muddled thought that underlies them, but instead deserve further historical and conceptual investigation.[2]

Why, for instance, does Maya Deren, 30 years after Epstein, at Amos Vogel's 1953 symposium 'Poetry and Film' at Cinema 16, again claim that poetic film expresses particular feelings? She compares the difference between poetry and prose in film to that between soliloquy and dramatic action in a play: just as soliloquy constitutes a pause where a character reflects on, or establishes an attitude towards, action, film poetry explores the depth of an experience rather than moving on to its causal effects, or to another situation. For Deren, poetry is 'concerned in a sense not with what is occurring, but with what it feels like or what it means'. In this sense, it has a 'vertical' development while film prose develops 'horizontally'. Here 'horizontal' development resembles Shklovsky's 'narrative resolution', but Deren explicitly de-emphasizes such formal patterns as 'assonance, or rhythm, or rhyme' in favour of 'feeling' and 'meaning' (Deren et al. 1963, 56). Amos Vogel himself places poetic form in dialogue with modern hard sciences, psychoanalysis, and Marxism: 'The discoveries by Marx, Einstein, Freud, Heisenberg, and Planck … have revealed poetry and non-linear art as more suitable to the complex fluidities of the modern world view' (Amos Vogel 1974, 19). For him, poetic forms of film speak to a subjectivity shaken by relativity and uncertainty.

This promise of realizing a 'soul', or 'world view', generates the allure of poetic cinema for filmmakers ranging from Griffith to Stan Brakhage, Isaac Julien, and Terrence Malick. This 'lyrical' realization of subjectivity does not always rely on montage for its connection to verse. Stan Brakhage's *Mothlight* (1963), for instance, has no shots or edits, consisting, in its initial incarnation, of the wings of dead moths stuck to celluloid. But P. Adams Sitney categorizes it as 'lyrical film' and credits Brakhage with 'invent[ing] a form in which the film-maker could compress his thoughts and feelings while recording his direct confrontation with intense experiences of birth, death, sexuality, and the terror of nature' (Sitney 2002, 168). Just as lyric is a subgenre of poetry, Piotrovsky's 'lyrical segment', and Sitney's 'lyrical film', belong to a 'poetic cinema' capacious enough for Impressionist 'atmosphere', Brakhage's 'feelings', and Vertov's 'film facts'.

## The desire behind the theory

'A poem conveys heightened forms of perception, experience, meaning, or consciousness in heightened language', claims the *Princeton Encyclopedia of Poetry and Poetics* (Brogan 1993, 938). If we return to Shklovsky and Pasolini, we see that while their formal analysis emphasizes 'heightened [film] language', the desire for, or belief in, 'heightened … perception, experience, meaning, or consciousness' underlies their arguments. Shklovsky does not explicitly address this approach in 'Poetry and Prose in Cinematography', but the concept of 'heightened experience' grounds his broader theory of art and its effect of *ostranenie*, or 'making strange', which he begins developing in 'Art as Technique' (1913). For Shklovsky, art disrupts our habitual modes of experience. Confronting the beholder with its mediation, art makes perception difficult and thus creates an intensified sense of its objects. Pasolini's concept of film poetry emphasizes a different kind of heightened perception. He associates the 'significant images' or 'im-signs' of the poetic with those 'of memory and dream, that is, the images of communication with oneself' (Pasolini 1976, 544, 548).

Within Shklovsky's formalism and Pasolini's semiotics, we can trace the desire for a poetic mode that provides us with something lacking in conventional narrative film. (It is the felt contours of this lack that are really at stake in any discussion of what poetry might mean to film.) Still, their definitions of 'poetry in cinematography' or a 'cinema of poetry' soberly rely on negation: poetry exists primarily in its difference from the classical conventions of storytelling. They make no explicit claim that attaches positive political or social value to this mode. In their influential essays, 'poetry makes nothing happen'.

But just as W.H. Auden's blunt statement of 1939 left room for interpretation, their relative silence concerning any generative significance of poetry in film has allowed for speculation. There are a number of post-Pasolini arguments that claim poetic films do more than call attention to a marked mode of discourse. The lyricism of Derek Jarman's work, or of the American underground, often emerges in and through its straining against social and sexual norms. And while Pasolini explicitly dismisses any connection between 'a cinema of poetry' and social progress, Homay King, revisiting his essay in 2004 (and reading its underlying political desire), again makes a case for the didactic value of 'free indirect subjectivity'. Writing about John Cassavetes's *Opening Night* (1977) and *Faces* (1968), she takes the 'free indirect subjectivity' which, for Pasolini, is a defining feature of poetry as a cinematic mode, and tweaks it, emphasizing it as 'free indirect affect': 'It is as if Cassavetes' films attempt to exteriorize affect; that is, to dispossess the actors of their emotions and to locate their source in a diffuse visual situation ... If affects cannot be localized, then the characters to whom they ostensibly belong cannot be pathologized in a clear-cut manner ... Instead emotional states are linked to a group situation or dynamic, and the responsibility for them is likewise collectivized' (King 2004, 107, 109). Like Pasolini, King chooses films where the perspective of middle-class, female characters seems to shatter not only the reductive, frozen assumptions of their storied social milieu, but also the enunciatory control of a male auteur. While Pasolini sees this jostling of white, bourgeois viewpoints as ultimately going nowhere, King's 2004 essay implicitly tries to recuperate its political, and specifically feminist, value.

As that which negates, or breaks free from, the conventions of classical narration (whether of the Hollywood type or, in the case of the Soviet poetic school, the conventions of socialist realism), the term 'poetic', applied to film, absorbs, and sustains, many critical projects. Queer, unreified, underground, and surreal, it stands for the unconscious, or repressed, of narrative logic. It abides as a critical term, and it persists as a creative aspiration: among the many films of the past 50 years that aim to realize poetry on screen are Forough Farrokhzad's *The House Is Black* (1962), Andrzej Wajda's *Pan Tadeusz: The Last Foray in Lithuania* (1999), and Isaac Julien's *Looking for Langston* (1989) and *Paradise Omeros* (2002).

Just as Shklovsky makes only a tentative distinction between poetry and prose in cinematography, definitions of poetry as a cinematic mode or category remain provisional. Its difference may entail aspects of composition and intensified experience. Its aims or effects can range from stirring nationalism to making us sense the limitedness of our particular world-view. Its 'heightening' of language and expression can disclose a Marxist critique of modernity, or a theological impulse. Bordwell asserts that we can just as well call the poetic 'parametric', 'style-centered', 'dialectical', or 'permutational'. But such terms fail to call forth the specific history that is bound to the word 'poetry'. Its multiplicity makes it impossible to conclusively define what it means for film culture. We can, however, aim to describe and historicize the desires that underlie its invocation as a kind of cinema.

KARLA OELER

## Note

1 As noted above, Pasolini equates 'a cinema of poetry' with '"language in itself," style' (Pasolini 1976, 555). And Bordwell writes of his use of the term 'parametric' that he could also 'call it "style centered," or "dialectical," or "permutational," *or even "poetic"* narration' (Bordwell 1985, 274; my emphasis).
2 Malcolm Turvey, for instance, does such work in his 2008 book *Doubting Vision: Film and the Revelationist Tradition*.

## Works cited

Bordwell, David. 1980. *French Impressionist Cinema: Film Culture, Film Theory, and Film Style*. New York: Arno Press.

——. 1985. *Narration in the Fiction Film*. Madison: University of Wisconsin Press.

Brogan, T.V.F. 1993. 'Poetry'. In *The New Princeton Encyclopedia of Poetry and Poetics*, edited by Alex Preminger and T.V.F. Brogan. Princeton, NJ: Princeton University Press.

Deren, Maya *et al*. 1963. 'Poetry and the Film: A Symposium'. *Film Culture* 29: 55–63.

Dillon, Steve. 2004. *Derek Jarman and the Lyric Film: The Mirror and the Sea*. Austin: University of Texas Press.

Eisenstein, Sergei. 1998 [1929]. 'The Fourth Dimension in Cinema'. In *The Eisenstein Reader*, edited by Richard Taylor, 111–23. London: British Film Institute.

Epstein, Jean. 1988. 'On Certain Characteristics of Photogenie'. In *French Film Theory and Criticism*, vol. I, edited by Richard Abel, 314–18. Princeton, NJ: Princeton University Press.

Jakobson, Roman. 1990. 'Linguistics and Poetics'. In *Language in Literature*, edited by Krystyna Pomorska and Stephen Rudy, 62–94. Cambridge, MA: Harvard University Press.

King, Homay. 2004. 'Free Indirect Affect in Cassavetes' *Opening Night* and *Faces*'. *Camera Obscura* 56 (vol. 19, no. 2): 104–39.

Pasolini, Pier Paolo. 1976. 'The Cinema of Poetry'. In *Movies and Methods*, vol. I, edited by Bill Nichols, 542–58. Berkeley: University of California Press.

Piotrovsky, Adrian. 1981. 'Toward a Theory of Cine-Genres', translated by Anna M. Lawton. In *Russian Formalist Film Theory*, edited by Herbert Eagle, 131–46. Ann Arbor: Michigan Slavic Materials.

Shklovsky, Viktor. 1973. 'Poetry and Prose in Cinematography'. In *Russian Formalism: A Collection of Articles and Texts in Translation*, edited by John E. Bowlt, 128–30. New York: Harper and Row, Inc.

Sitney, P. Adams. 2002. *Visionary Film: The American Avant-Garde, 1943–2000*. Oxford: Oxford University Press.

Turvey, Malcolm, *Doubting Vision: Film and the Revelationist Tradition*. Oxford: Oxford University Press.

Vogel, Amos. 1974. *Film as a Subversive Art*. London: Weidenfeld and Nicolson.

# POINT OF VIEW

The term 'point of view' can denote many things, among them the narrator's or filmmaker's stance towards the fictional events in the film. The only focus here is on the idea that some narrative techniques in film can communicate to the spectator the subjective experience, or point of view, of characters in the fictional world. In *Point of View in the Cinema* (1984), Edward Branigan points to several critics' astonished reviews of Henning Carlsen's *Hunger* (1966). For example, one critic argues that the film is

> a true invention of subjective cinema. It stays inside [the main character's] skull, and everything in it expresses that man. We see the world through a singular mind housed in the body of an indigent. His moods sweep the film: bile, pride, phantom hope, fury, fantasies of due grandeur that are outwardly unapt in a bum ... The experience of the film is the experience of being this character.
>
> (Penelope Gilliatt, quoted in Branigan 1984, 5)

Branigan's pivotal study describes narration that is subjective in the sense that 'the telling is *attributed* to a character in the narrative and received by us [as spectators] *as if* we were in the situation of a character' (73; original emphasis).

Branigan defines character narration, or subjectivity, as narration given by a character in the narrative (later Branigan also refers to this as focalization; see Branigan 1992, 100–7, on how his use differs from use in literary theory) (*see* NARRATION). The narrative is in this case linked to a character as origin. This stands in contrast to *reference narration* or *objective narration*, 'not unified by a coherence ascribed to a diegetic character or character's mind' (Branigan 1984, 76). The basic element in subjective narration is the *point of view (POV) structure*. On the most fundamental level, this structure consists of two shots. In shot A, labelled by Branigan 'point/glance shot', the camera shows the character looking at something, usually off screen. In shot B, the POV shot or what Branigan refers to as the 'point/object' shot, the camera assumes the position of the character in order to show the spectator what the character sees. The spectator sees what the character sees from the character's position in the diegetic universe. The spectator perceives the two shots as temporally simultaneous or continuous, and understands the POV shot as the character's visual experience.

Branigan gives a comprehensive account of the many variations of the POV structure, such as *prospective* (where shot A precedes shot B) versus *retrospective* POV structures (shot B, then shot A), *closed* POV structures (A, B, A), and *delayed* POV structures, where shot B is delayed for a number of shots or scenes. Deviation of the temporal continuity between shot

A and B may give us the *flashback*, where shot A shows us a character smiling at something, for example, and in the next shot we see his beloved greeting him, but at an earlier time than the narrative present, as we know from the narrative context that the lover is now dead. Additional marks may be used to signify that it is the character's memory we now see, such as dissolves, and repeating shot A after the flashback to emphasize the character's memory as origin of what we just saw. Likewise, *dream sequences* are typically enclosed by close-up shots of the character who is dreaming to clearly mark the sequence as subjective, lest the dream sequence be ambiguous. Furthermore, the POV structure signals the character's normal awareness of something. In the *perception structure*, a *perception shot* signals the character's mental condition as well. In this case, an optical POV shot mimics, so to say, the character's mental condition stylistically. For example, an out-of-focus shot may signify drunkenness (Branigan 1984, 80).

In addition to the direct link between narration and the character's visual experience in the POV and perception structures, there are other, indirect forms of subjective narration. Here, the narrative is linked to the character's experience metaphorically. What is shown is not restricted to the optical vantage point of the character, but is still perceived by the spectator, through a series of inferences, as the character's experience. In *projection*, for example, the character's state of mind is made explicit. Branigan (1984, 133–4) exemplifies this with a sequence from *White Heat* (Walsh, 1949). The psychotic gangster Cody Jarrett is obsessively devoted to his mother. While in prison, he is worried about his mother coming to harm. He is wheeling a cart through the prison's machine shop when there is a series of subjective shots. Among these is a sequence of close-up shots of machinery. It is unlikely that Cody actually looks at the machinery in this way, but nevertheless the whole sequence is subjective, Branigan argues: the steam, lights, sparks, heat, violent action, and rasping noise relate to his pounding rage and are interpreted by the spectator as metaphors for Cody's disorder.

In a later study, Branigan labels the subjective techniques discussed so far *internal focalization*, and points out that no other character or hypothetical observer in the story world can witness this – a witness cannot see from the character's point in space, and neither can he see the character's drunken perception nor what the character dreams about or remembers (Branigan 1992, 103). Subjective narration of this kind gives access to the character's 'fully private and subjective' experience (103). Focalization can, however, also be *external*, such as through *eyeline matches*, where we see what the character sees, when he sees it, but not from his point in space. Another character or observer present in the story world would be able to see what the character is looking at in this way. An eyeline match is semi-subjective – it renders 'a measure of character awareness but from outside the character' (103).

The POV shot holds a special place in Branigan's theory of subjective narration as it is a direct way of linking what is shown to the character's experience: we as spectators actually see what the character sees, from his position in the diegetic space (Branigan 1984, 73). Nevertheless, he contends that there is 'nothing "natural" about the POV shot' (73). The spectator must learn its elements and significance. However, Branigan does not explore in depth the idea that subjective narration is not just telling 'attributed to a character in the narrative' but also 'received by us *as if* we were in the situation of the character' (73). His account of subjective narration is first and foremost a description of POV editing with roots in narratology, and not an explanation of its effect on the spectator.

Branigan's influence on the then emergent field of cognitive film theory was considerable. In a later elaboration of his theory, the influence of cognitive psychology is prominent, and his theory of subjective narration is reframed within a cognitive theory of narration (Branigan 1992). I will not go into detail about this here, however, but look at the influence his account of POV editing has had on cognitive film theory. First, Noël Carroll takes Branigan's description as a starting point and gives an explanation of why POV editing is such an important technique in film, and why it works so effectively (Carroll 1993; see also Persson 2003, 66ff.). Second, while Branigan merely assumes that POV editing is linked to spectatorial identification with the characters in some way or another, Murray Smith discusses in detail the effect of various narrative techniques on the spectator's engagement with the characters (Smith 1995; 1997).

Although Carroll does not openly disagree with Branigan, he is at odds with Branigan's claim that there is nothing natural about the POV shot. Carroll argues that POV editing mimics our natural tendency to track another human's gaze to see what he is looking at (in what was labelled the POV shot above), and to use his facial expression to learn what he is thinking and feeling about what he sees (in what I will refer to as the reaction shot). Carroll writes that point of view editing is

> a representation whose recognition is hard to avoid since it is keyed in intimate ways to our perceptual makeup. Structurally, it delivers the glance and the target, the nodal points of our perceptual prototype, while functionally it serves the congruent purpose of supplying information about the agent whose gaze concerns use.
>
> (Carroll 1993, 129)

As POV editing is 'keyed to biologically rooted and transculturally distributed features of perception, it guarantees fast pick-up and a high degree of accessibility to mass, untutored audiences' (138). In Carroll's account, both the POV shot and the reaction shot are important in this natural tendency, as these two shots inform each other reciprocally.

One could be tempted to read Carroll's account as an explanation for why POV editing is particularly effective in prompting the spectator to identify with a character. However, Carroll criticizes the notion of identification (see, for example, Carroll 2008, 147ff.) and rejects the claim that POV editing is linked to identification (Carroll 1993, 129). Carroll's resistance towards linking POV editing to identification is grounded in his critique of illusion theories of cinematic representation, which claim that we as spectators lose consciousness of the fact that we are seeing a film when watching conventional film (see Carroll 1988, 182–99). According to this line of thought, when shown a POV shot, we perceive ourselves as the character. In a similar critique of illusion theories of cinematic representation, Murray Smith argues that the psychoanalytic *suture theory* (*see* SUTURE) is underpinned by the simplistic view that the POV shot "wires' us directly into the mind of a character' – an assumption Smith calls *the fallacy of POV* (Smith 1995, 156).

While Smith points out that the POV shot has always held a privileged position in discussions of identification in film, he emphasizes how terms such as 'identification' or 'point of view' conflate different ways of engaging with a character (1995, 144, 156) (*see* IDENTIFICATION, THEORY OF). In Smith's theory of character engagement, sympathy and empathy replace the notion of identification. In cognitive film theory, the question of identification with the characters in film is thus typically recast as the question of what makes the spectator sympathize with them, in the sense of liking and becoming attached to them, and empathize with them, in the sense of sharing their experiences to some degree.

Smith replaces Branigan's notion of subjective narration or focalization with *alignment*. Alignment is 'the process by which spectators are placed in relation to characters in terms of access to their actions, and to what they know and feel' (1995, 83). Alignment has two subcategories: a narrative can be more or less restricted to what the character experiences (*spatio-temporal attachment*), and give more or less access to the character's thoughts and feelings (*subjective access*) (1995, 142ff.; see also Bordwell 1985, 57ff., on narrational range and depth). Alignment is not the same as fully fledged sympathy with a character, which also entails a moral evaluation. The spectator evaluates to what degree the character represents morally desirable or preferable traits, a process Smith labels *allegiance* (Smith 1995, 187ff.). While alignment with a character, and more specifically access to a character's motivations and reasons for doing something, may encourage sympathy for him, and perhaps 'exonerate actions' that would otherwise be 'easier to condemn', it does not necessarily have this effect (1995, 223).

While Branigan gives the POV shot a special role in his theory of subjective narration, he also stresses the narrative context. This latter emphasis is taken one step further by Smith, who argues that '[c]haracter subjectivity is an emergent quality of the narration as a whole, not the product of any single technique' (1995, 158). The POV shot does not necessarily give access to a character's subjectivity, and it is not 'privileged in providing us with uniformly greater access to characters' states than other devices' (1995, 83). POV shots are linked to alignment, but are neither necessary nor sufficient for it.

Furthermore, both Carroll and Smith stress the importance of the reaction shot more than Branigan does. Smith neatly formulates the importance of the reaction shot for spectator engagement as a paradox in the use of the POV shot:

> [T]he more a film attempts to render in a literal fashion the subjectivity of a character through the adoption of optical POV, the more it surrenders the power to evoke the full range of a character's mental states, through the powerful mechanism of facial expression.
>
> (Smith 1995, 160)

Thus one can say that it is not the POV shot that communicates character subjectivity most effectively, but the reaction shot. Carl Plantinga makes a similar point and shows how close-up shots of characters in emotionally laden situations are commonly used at dramatic peaks in film in what he labels as *scenes of empathy* (Plantinga 1999).

Smith sums up his discussion of the POV shot by suggesting that it has two functions. First, it functions as a marker in shifts of alignment, or as an emphasis of continual alignment with a character (Smith 1995, 161); second, it can be used to limit the spectator's knowledge of a narrative situation to what the character knows, for example in order to create similar reactions of shock and fear in the spectator (1995, 163–4). He returns to the question of the POV shot in a later paper (Smith 1997). He considers again whether there is something to the intuition that POV is connected to 'identification', and suggests what we might add as a third function of the POV shot in his theory. According to this third function, POV does have a special relation to *optical* experience. It 'render[s] certain aspects of visual experience' in a way that no other shot can (1997, 417). This may prompt the spectator to imagine having that visual experience. As part of a POV structure and a larger structure of alignment, POV shots may indeed encourage the spectator to imagine the character's experience of seeing something. This, Smith sums up, 'gives POV its due, recognizing its unique role with respect specifically to imagining seeing, without falling into the fallacy of POV' (1997, 417–18).

MARGRETHE BRUUN VAAGE

## Works cited

Bordwell, David. 1985. *Narration in the Fiction Film*. London: Routledge.

Branigan, Edward. 1984. *Point of View in the Cinema: A Theory of Narration and Subjectivity in Classical Film*. Berlin: Mouton Publishers.

———. 1992. *Narrative Comprehension and Film*. London: Routledge.

Carroll, Noël. 1988. *Mystifying Movies: Fads and Fallacies in Contemporary Film Theory*. New York: Columbia University Press.

———. 1993. 'Toward a Theory of Point-of-View Editing: Communication, Emotion, and the Movies'. *Poetics Today* 14 (1): 123–41.

———. 2008. *The Philosophy of Motion Pictures*. Malden, MA: Blackwell Publishing.

Persson, Per. 2003. *Understanding Cinema: A Psychological Theory of Moving Imagery*. Cambridge: Cambridge University Press.

Plantinga, Carl. 1999. 'The Scene of Empathy and the Human Face on Film.' In *Passionate Views: Film, Cognition, and Emotion*, edited by Carl Plantinga and Greg M. Smith, 239–55. Baltimore, MD: Johns Hopkins University Press.

Smith, Murray. 1995. *Engaging Characters: Fiction, Emotion, and the Cinema*. Oxford: Clarendon Press.

———. 1997. 'Imagining from the Inside'. In *Film Theory and Philosophy*, edited by Richard Allen and Murray Smith, 412–30. Oxford: Oxford University Press.

# POSTMODERN CINEMA

The term 'postmodern' is simultaneously historical and aesthetic, indicating both a particular time period and a distinctive style. Matters are made more complicated by acute disagreement over both aspects: where to draw the lines delineating a specific postmodern epoch, and how to evaluate the defining elements of postmodern style. Many would agree that key features of postmodern texts include: acute stylization, a self-conscious concern with 'the very act of showing/telling stories', and multiple references to other texts (Degli-Esposti 1998, 4). The crucial aesthetic debate is whether such stylized, reflexive, and intertextual films can be regarded as either critical or original.

This entry will explore two articles, written within a year of each other, which have helped define postmodern cinema: Noël Carroll's 'The Future of Allusion: Hollywood in the Seventies (and Beyond)' (1982) and Fredric Jameson's 'Postmodernism and Consumer Society' (1983). While Carroll only addresses the postmodern in a single footnote (Carroll 1982, 70, fn. 14), his article has recently come to play a formative role in the definition of postmodern cinema (Dika 2003; Garrett 2007). Jameson's hugely influential article presents the nostalgia film as the epitome of postmodern aesthetics and philosophy. I will trace the notable similarities and differences between these two articles before demonstrating the ways in which they intertwine, thereby founding an integrated paradigm of postmodern cinema. Unfortunately this paradigm creates a number of additional problems that I will outline before setting out some positive alternatives.

## Carroll

Carroll seeks to delineate a distinctive feature of films made in the 1970s and 1980s, arguing that they contain unprecedented levels of allusion (Carroll 1982, 51). The period demarcated by the piece shifts to incorporate the 1960s (64–5, 73, 80–1) and corresponds to the era of post-classical or New Hollywood, which emerges with the rise of independent production after the break-up of the vertical integration of the studio system (74). Carroll defines allusion as an 'umbrella term' including: 'quotations, the memorialization of past genres, the reworking of past genres, homages, and the recreation of "classic scenes," shots, plot motifs, lines of dialogue, themes, gestures and so forth from film history' (52). His first example, *Body Heat* (Lawrence Kasdan, 1981), exhibits allusion at every level: the plot, character archetypes, costume, lighting style, and tone – a 'mood of pessimism-cum-destiny' – are all drawn from 1940s film noir (51).

Importantly, Carroll argues that allusion does not constitute 'plagiarism or uninspired derivativeness', but should be seen as 'part of the expressive design of the new films' (52).

In this first definition, allusion both draws on and sustains auteurism (*see* AUTEUR THEORY). For example, 1970s directors are said to refer to Howard Hawks's films in order to 'assert their possession of a Hawksian world view, a cluster of themes and expressive qualities that has been … expounded in the critical literature' (53). Thus an allusion to Hawks is not just a reference to his films' diegetic world; it also draws on a critical conception of the distinctive perspective of Hawks-the-auteur (55). In turn, the use of allusion constructs the new directors themselves as auteurs in that their engagement with the films and critical literature allows them to 'unequivocally identify *their point of view* on the material at hand' (53, my italics).

Carroll argues that this explosion of allusion is the result of a general discovery of film history that seized America in the 1960s and early 1970s (54). The rise of independent cinemas gave audiences unprecedented access to European films as well as the archives of classical Hollywood (Balio 1985, 405–6). This deepened sensibility, coupled with education at film schools, resulted in a new generation of cinematically literate directors who began to make films for the 'expanding cinema-learned coterie' (Carroll 1982, 55). Thus the practice of allusion creates a two-tier model of the audience: those with the cultural capital to play 'the game of allusion' (55) and those who naively watch 'the genre film pure and simple' (56). In this way allusionism constructs a new cultural elite within mass culture, enabling the film critic 'to adopt the role of guardian of specialized knowledge' (57, fn. 5).

Carroll next attempts to set up a distinction between Hollywood allusionism and postmodernism: 'Hollywood allusionism is undertaken for *expressive* purposes whereas postmodernism … refers to artifacts of cultural history for *reflexive* purposes, urging us to view the products of media as media' (70, n. 14, my italics). The problematic binary of expressive versus reflexive is sustained by pitting Hollywood films against the work of postmodern visual artists, such as Cindy Sherman. This binary, however, is undermined by Carroll's own analysis of how the widespread practice of allusion changed 'the nature of Hollywood symbol systems' (55). He charts a movement away from a natural integration of form and content to a system of shorthand: 'organic expression for a Hawks was translated into an iconographic code by a Walter Hill or a John Carpenter' (55). Later, Carroll delineates a specific type of allusion that works via 'iconic reference rather than … expressive implication', dubbing it 'style-as-symbol' (69). The shift away from the natural and expressive to the code/symbol is compounded by comments on the 'strident stylization' of Hollywood films from the mid-1960s onwards (78), strongly suggesting that such films have a reflexive quality, a foregrounding of film as film, thereby merging with Carroll's definition of the postmodern.

The shift from natural expression to an iconographic code parallels another transition charted across the article: the decline of Hollywood allusion, exemplified by the career of Brian de Palma (Carroll 1982, 73–4). In his analysis of *Blow-Out* (1981), Carroll notes that merely '"mentioning" great themes' from Antonioni's *Blow-Up* (1966) does not amount to 'saying anything substantive' (74). For Carroll, truly expressive allusionism is bound up with a distinctive utopian social project: a desire 'to establish a new community, with film history supplying its legends, myths and vocabulary' (79). However, this utopianism is located firmly in the 1960s, and later forms of allusion are in danger of deteriorating into 'mere affectation [and] nostalgia' (80). In this second definition, allusion becomes the practice of the despised *metteur en scène* rather than the auteur, 'presenting the artist in terms of ultra-competence rather than genius, as technically brilliant rather than profound, as a manipulator rather than an innovator' (80, n. 16).

## Jameson

The postmodern lurks at the periphery of Carroll's article yet the piece has some intriguing parallels with Jameson's later work. Both authors present cinema of the 1960s to the 1980s as a distinctive epoch marked by a particular aesthetic style, namely the repeated referencing of previous texts, defined as allusion and pastiche respectively. However, for Jameson, the new aesthetic style reflects fundamental socio-economic shifts, and he uses 'the postmodern' to indicate the correlation between 'the emergence of new formal features in culture with ... a new type of social life and a new economic order' (Jameson 1983, 113). The 1960s is set up as a crucial transitional time, ushering in 'the newly emergent social order of late capitalism' (113). Late capitalism is the most excessive form of capitalism. It is formed through the rise of advertising, which results in the purchasing of goods for the lifestyle they symbolize, and the creation of global markets for the production and consumption of goods and services.

For Jameson, postmodern art takes the form of pastiche, an artistic practice that comprises 'the mimicry of other styles' (113). Pastiche is defined in opposition to parody. The latter involves the imitation of unique styles created by modernist authors, such as D.H. Lawrence or Wallace Stevens. Parody 'capitalizes on the uniqueness of these styles and seizes on their idiosyncrasies and eccentricities to produce an imitation which mocks the original' (113). Using humour to send up the stylistic tics of modernist authors demonstrates their 'excessiveness and eccentricity with respect to the way people normally ... write' (113). Thus parody relies on a general sense of linguistic norms from which the great modernists diverge. Jameson asserts that such norms no longer exist within the era of late capitalism: 'there is nothing but stylistic diversity and heterogeneity' (114). As a result, laughter at divergence from the norm has become impossible, and thus the imitation of previous styles can constitute only pastiche, which is famously defined as 'blank parody, parody that has lost its sense of humour' (114). Importantly, the stylistic heterogeneity of pastiche is a play of differences that rests on the obliteration of key distinctions, specifically the division between high and low art, thereby undermining the foundations of aesthetic value.

Jameson argues that the rise of pastiche marks the end of the modernist author, the individual genius who generates his or her 'own unique vision of the world and ... own unique, unmistakable style' (114). Unlike Carroll, whose initial definition of allusion draws on and sustains auteurism, Jameson consistently conceptualizes pastiche as a practice that marks the end of Romantic conceptions of authorship. Pastiche occurs 'in a world in which stylistic innovation is no longer possible, [where] all that is left is to imitate dead styles' (115). The focus on the loss of innovation echoes Carroll's definition of debased allusion where the director is merely a manipulator, rearranging rather than revitalizing his/her material (Carroll 1982, 80, n. 16). While Carroll's narrative of the decline of allusion ends by presenting true auteurism as a very remote possibility, Jameson is more extreme in that, strictly speaking, the phrase 'postmodern auteur' is a contradiction in terms.

Such differences are partly the result of differing conceptions of the nature of quotation. While Carroll sets out a wide variety of textual practices that count as allusion (Carroll 1982, 51), Jameson sets up pastiche as a failure to quote properly, contrasting it with the correct method presented by modernist texts. Thus, for Jameson, modernist works quote texts such as adverts, popular generic literature, and B-movies, maintaining a clear distance from these low cultural sources and thereby providing a properly critical commentary on them (Jameson 1983, 112). In contrast, postmodern texts incorporate such elements, obliterating the boundaries between high and low culture (112). Like Warhol's Campbell's soup can paintings of the 1960s, postmodern texts utilize the themes and techniques of advertising, thereby becoming adverts themselves. Such works are said to lack any capacity for political or social critique of the economic system of late capitalism; they are simply expressions of the capitalist system (124).

The breakdown of key boundaries also applies to specialized fields of knowledge, such as philosophy, history, and social sciences, which postmodernism reconstructs as a single "'theoretical discourse'" (Jameson 1983, 112). Unlike Carroll, for whom allusion created a new type of specialized knowledge of mass cultural forms for a cultural elite, Jameson conceptualizes pastiche as merely destructive, undermining the boundaries required to protect traditional disciplinary areas. At stake here are fundamentally different conceptions of the value of mass culture, enabling Carroll to celebrate some aspects of New Hollywood, while Jameson vilifies such films for being complicit with the capitalist system.

The differences between the theorists become clear in their analyses of films that evoke nostalgia for the past, such as *Star Wars* and *Raiders of the Lost Ark* (Carroll 1982, 62–4; Jameson 1983, 116). Carroll reads these films as examples of 'memorialization, the loving evocation through imitation and exaggeration of the way genres were' (Carroll 1982, 62). The quotation acknowledges the distance between the original low budget B-movie cliffhangers and the later lavish homages. For Jameson, *Star Wars* is not only generic homage; it also appeals to our sense of history: 'by reinventing the feel and shape of characteristic art objects of an older period … it seeks to reawaken a sense of the past associated with these objects' (Jameson 1983, 116). Crucially, for Jameson, this sense of our own history is actually erased by the nostalgia film.

Carroll's and Jameson's differing conceptions of time and history can be seen in their analyses of the allusions to 1940s film noir in *Body Heat* (Carroll 1982, 51, 69; Jameson 1983, 117). For Carroll the retro-style costuming works to position 'the film as shifting between past and present' (Carroll 1982, 51). In contrast, Jameson argues that the small-town setting sidesteps key contemporary references, such as technology and architecture, presenting the film as 'a narrative set in some indefinable nostalgic past, an eternal '30s, say, beyond history' (Jameson 1983, 117). Thus the evocation of a non-specific past is a move beyond history that collapses the timeline of past to present, ultimately leaving us unable to understand the past or conceptualize our own present. This 'collapse' parallels the 'reduction' of high to low culture. Importantly, the consumption of nostalgia films actually fuels the loss of the past: 'we seem condemned to seek the historical past through our own pop images and stereotypes about that past'; the images come between us and the past, ensuring it 'remains forever out of reach. (118). Thus, paradoxically, the nostalgia film is the product of 'a society that has become incapable of dealing with time and history' (117).

While Carroll and Jameson discuss many of the same films, Jameson clearly goes beyond Carroll's analysis of a specific tendency in post-classical Hollywood cinema to make a series of claims about the nature of the postmodern condition. Unfortunately, Jameson simply characterizes the postmodern as a nihilistic negation of modernity, marking the end of art, authorship, originality, critique, knowledge, and history. It is interesting that both theorists offer narratives that are centred on loss. Carroll's lament for the passing of the utopian social project driving American films of the 1960s can be paralleled with Jameson's lament for the passing of proper modernist critique. Jameson later reconceptualizes this move in explicitly utopian terms whereby the utopian dimension of art that was crucial to the imaginative creation of alternatives to the capitalist system is finally lost (Jameson 1991, 6–10). Both theorists offer narrative trajectories that chart a downward spiral: the demise of authentic expressive allusion and the degeneration of art into pastiche.

## A new paradigm

The narrative trajectories of Carroll and Jameson have been conjoined to create an overarching, linear model of the development of postmodern cinema. Roberta Garrett sets out a three-stage model of allusion that begins with Carroll and ends by conflating his position with that of Jameson. In 'the first wave of auteurist allusionism ... new Hollywood directors sought to pay homage to the best of classical and European art cinema' (Garrett 2007, 42). This is followed by 'the blockbuster celebration of older action and adventure forms', a second wave that fuses Carroll's and Jameson's writing on *Star Wars* and *Raiders of the Lost Ark* (12). The third stage of 'postmodernist self-reflexivity is marked by its range of "lowbrow" subcultural, popular references' (42). Here the sheer quantity and diversity of popular allusions displayed by the postmodern text mark its status as a ragbag of intertextual references. The link between the third, most debased form of allusion and the practices of global capitalism is then made clear: 'it reflects the music, fashion, TV and film industries' tendency to plunder, cannibalize and repackage older forms' (42–3). As a process of repackaging and recycling, postmodern allusionism epitomizes the logic of late capitalism.

While Garrett is concerned to challenge this model, and, more specifically, the masculinism of a paradigm developed through focusing on directors such as Quentin Tarantino and David Lynch (Garrett 2007, 44–50), she argues that it constitutes a key map of the development of postmodern cinema within the discipline of film studies (20–33, 42–4). Nonetheless, its limitations are obvious. The historical transitions between the three stages loosely correspond to a history of Hollywood comprising: the rise of New Hollywood in the 1960s and 1970s, the development of the blockbuster from the mid-1970s to the 1980s, and the advent of postmodernism from the 1980s onwards. The blurry delineation of the temporality of the three waves worsens when considering their relation to global capitalism. Jameson argues that late capitalism begins in the 1960s; however, Hollywood films of this decade are not deemed postmodern. The economic strategies of the blockbuster – simultaneous release patterns supported by saturation marketing and global advertising – are clearly forms of late capitalism. Yet the allusionism displayed by films from this second stage is characterized as celebratory, while the allusionism of films from the third stage is unacceptably debased because of its relation to the practices of global capitalism. If the distinction between the stages is based on the sheer quantity of allusions alone, one is forced to pose the absurd question: how many intertextual references make a text postmodern? Indeed, the attempt to define postmodern film on the basis of a single criterion, allusion, is clearly problematic. Overall, the blurry temporal lines delineating the three stages indicate that postmodern cinematic aesthetics cannot be neatly confined to a discrete epoch in the history of Hollywood cinema (Constable 2014).

The most important feature of this map of the development of Hollywood cinema is that it unites the downward trajectories of the narratives offered by Carroll and Jameson, to present postmodern cinema as synonymous with the death of creativity, originality, and critique. The account intersects with a number of widely held cultural assumptions about the postmodern that become evident when looking at the critical reception of *Pulp Fiction* (Quentin Tarantino, 1994). The film's content is lambasted as pastiche – a magpie collection of film references – thereby sustaining repeated criticisms of its lack of depth, triviality, and superficiality (Brooker and Brooker 1997, 89–90). These criticisms re-emerge in one of the few book-length studies of postmodern Hollywood: M. Keith Booker's adaptation of Jameson's theoretical position, whereby *Pulp Fiction* is characterized as '[o]ne of the most self-consciously cool films ever made' (Booker 2007, 13) and 'the perfect, postmodern, cinematic stew' (48). Booker's glib analysis constructs the film as hip and superficial, foregrounding an important problem. Defining postmodern style as *inherently* debased and superficial is a self-fulfilling prophecy because it effectively sets up the limits of what the viewer is prepared to see in any given postmodern film.

## Some ways out

Brooker and Brooker argue rightly that it is absolutely crucial to explode the stranglehold of thinking via negation that underpins analyses of postmodern style as the superficial antithesis of the true depths presented by humanist or modernist aesthetics. 'We have ... to think with more discrimination ... about the aesthetic forms and accents of postmodernism – so famously "all about style" but not by that token always and only about "merely" style' (Brooker and Brooker 1997, 91). In order to accomplish this goal it is important to recognize the dangers of straightforwardly linking stylistic strategies to aesthetic value. As postmodern aesthetics is characterized by the use of reflexive techniques and quantities of intertextual references, it is helpful to think of each of these qualities as possessing a range of possible deployments. This could involve returning to Carroll's broad umbrella term of allusion, removing it from the unworkable binary opposition between expressive and reflexive, as well as disengaging it from the reductive overarching narrative of decline. Richard Dyer's work on the multiform nature of pastiche challenges Jameson's narrow and eccentric definition by examining the wide variety of textual practices encompassed by the term (Dyer 2007, 7–63). He also provides a nuanced reading of the ways in which *Body Heat* both evokes and diverges from 1940s film noir, locating its temporal shifts more precisely (119–24).

One important postmodern theorist who has yet to become central to thinking about postmodern film is Linda Hutcheon. Her work underpins some of the most interesting essays in the collection edited by Degli-Esposti (1998). Hutcheon effectively and convincingly challenges Jameson's nihilistic conception of the postmodern (Hutcheon 1989, 24–9, 113–14). Carefully placing postmodern film in relation to previous aesthetic forms, she suggests: 'it is more wilfully compromised, more ideologically ambivalent or contradictory. It at once exploits and subverts that which went before, that is, both the modernist and the traditionally realist' (107). This shifting balance of exploitation and subversion also informs Hutcheon's account of the dominant aesthetic practice of postmodern film: namely parody. 'What postmodern parody does is to evoke ... the horizon of expectation of the spectator, a horizon formed by recognizable conventions of genre, style, or form of representation. This is then destabilized and dismantled step by step' (114). This definition opens up a range of possibilities: from the humorous questioning of the politics of representation presented by De Palma's reworking of *Faust* in *Phantom of the Paradise* (1974) to a radical undermining of the key tenets of objectivity and truth within the documentary genre, as in Maximilian Schell's *Marlene* (1984) (114–16).

While Hutcheon does celebrate the critical possibilities of postmodern film and literature, she retains certain categories of cultural production that are simply complicit with capitalism: television, shopping malls, and music videos (Hutcheon 1989, 10, 12, 106–7). Importantly, the distinction between mere products and art forms that have the potential to offer new types of compromised critique does not involve positioning the latter outside capitalism. 'Postmodern film does not deny that it is implicated in capitalist modes of production, because it knows it cannot. Instead it exploits its "insider" position in order to begin a subversion from within' (114). Hutcheon thus avoids the reductive reasoning that characterizes Jameson and his protégés whereby all commercially successful films – no matter how thought-provoking – are ultimately dismissed for being complicit with the capitalist system.

What is important about Hutcheon's concepts of postmodern parody and subversion from within is that they set up the postmodern as a move away from modernism and humanism that is not based on simple negation. While postmodern film cannot offer a modernist critique of the sort Jameson craves, this does not mean the end of all forms of critique. Indeed the very possibility of pure critique that opens up various spaces outside the capitalist system is regarded with suspicion because it draws upon a traditional conception of thinking as a form of objective reasoning that rises above its own socio-cultural location. For Hutcheon, and indeed all postmodern feminist theorists, it is vital to acknowledge that we are within the systems that we analyse, utilizing the concepts and discourses that they provide. As a result, our status as critical thinkers within postmodern culture takes the same compromised form as the subversive insider dealings offered by postmodern films.

Hutcheon aligns her conception of compromised critique with new forms of creativity: 'Postmodern parody is both deconstructively critical and constructively creative, paradoxically making us aware of both the limits and powers of representation' (Hutcheon 1989, 98). While she tends to eschew the vocabulary of originality, Hutcheon's film readings trace the ways in which the textual strategies offered by parody invite us to gain new perspectives through referencing and revitalizing past texts. At stake here is a challenge to the traditional conception of originality promulgated by the Romantic ideal of the self-generated and self-sufficient Author who creates his or her own, unique, world-view. Thus Hutcheon's work delineates ways in which postmodern films might be both original and critical by interrogating and rethinking key aspects of traditional aesthetics. Hutcheon sketches out a model of postmodern film that enables us to trace the ways in which a variety of intertexual references and reflexive devices are used to make us laugh, think, and question the unexamined concepts we take and have taken for granted. 'Were we to heed the implications of such a model, we might have to reconsider the operations by which we both create and give meaning to our culture through representation. And that is not bad for a so-called nostalgic, escapist tendency' (Hutcheon 1989, 117).

CATHERINE CONSTABLE

## Works cited

Balio, Tino. 1985. 'Part IV: Retrenchment, Reappraisal and Reorganisation'. In *The American Film Industry*, edited by Tino Balio, 401–47. Madison: University of Wisconsin Press.

Booker, M. Keith. 2007. *Postmodern Hollywood: What's New in Film and Why It Makes Us Feel So Strange.* London: Praeger.

Brooker, Peter, and Will Brooker. 1997. 'Pulpmodernism: Tarantino's Affirmative Action'. In *Postmodern After-Images: A Reader in Film, Television and Video,* edited by Peter and Will Brooker, 89–100. London: Arnold.

Carroll, Noel. 1982. 'The Future of Allusion: Hollywood in the Seventies (and Beyond)'. *October* 20: 51–81.

Constable, Catherine. 2014. *Postmodern Hollywood.* New York: Wallflower and Columbia University Press.

Degli-Esposti, Cristina, ed. 1998. *Postmodernism in the Cinema.* New York: Berghahn Books.

Dika, Vera. 2003. *Recycled Culture in Contemporary Art and Film: The Uses of Nostalgia.* Cambridge: Cambridge University Press.

Dyer, Richard. 2007. *Pastiche.* London and New York: Routledge.

Garrett, Roberta. 2007. *Postmodern Chick Flicks: The Return of the Woman's Film.* Basingstoke: Palgrave Macmillan.

Hutcheon, Linda. 1989. *The Politics of the Postmodern.* London and New York: Routledge.

Jameson, Fredric. 1983. 'Postmodernism and Consumer Society'. In *The Anti-aesthetic: Essays on Postmodern Culture,* edited by Hal Foster, 111–25. Seattle, WA: Bay Press.

——. 1991. *Postmodernism, or, The Cultural Logic of Late Capitalism.* London: Verso.

## Further reading

Constable, Catherine. 2004. 'Postmodernism and Film'. In *The Cambridge Companion to Postmodernism,* edited by Steven Connor, 43–61. Cambridge: Cambridge University Press.

Denzin, Norman. 1991. *Images of Postmodern Society: Social Theory and Contemporary Cinema.* London: Sage Publications.

# QUEER THEORY/QUEER CINEMA

Descriptions of queer theory/cinema need to address several complications. First, they must consider how *queer* functions as a noun, verb, and adjective. Second, when analysing the *queer* aspects of films, they must consider queer filmmakers, queer content and production, queer distribution and exhibition, queer reception, and the myriad combinations of these aspects. Third, they must consider how *queer* changes over time and from place to place. Taken together, these three complications make *queer theory/cinema* notoriously difficult to articulate.

Historically, gay and lesbian criticism arose from and as a critique of feminist film theory in the 1970s. Like feminist criticism, gay and lesbian criticism criticized (mis)representations of gender and sexuality on screen and examined how the cinematic apparatus positions us as gendered and sexed spectators. Working from these basic tenets of feminist theory, though, gay and lesbian film theory began to critique the heterosexist assumptions of its precursor. Thus, if feminist theory showed us how we are sexed by the cinema, gay and lesbian theory showed us how we are heterosexed by it. By the late 1980s/early 1990s, gay and lesbian theory became 'queer' as it began to associate gender and sexuality critique with other identity markers, such as race, class, and ethnicity. This concentration on the intersections of gender and sexuality with other aspects of personhood remains a key trait of queer theory.

But what do we mean by *queer*? In *Tendencies* (1994), Eve Sedgwick reminds us that questions of queerness revolve around the complex questions of sexual identity, gender, and either/or thinking. As Sedgwick explains, queer alludes always to gender and sexuality issues, especially same-sex object choice and the complexities of gay and lesbian identity, orientation, and presentation. Given the history behind the term *queer* and the contemporary debate over its definitional boundaries, it remains ethically and politically suspect – as well as publicly impractical – to remove or disavow this reference at the core of the term. Yet, same-sex object choice, as important as it is, denotes only one aspect of *queer*. Sedgwick asserts, as central as issues of gender and sexuality remain to the concept, that

> a lot of the most exciting recent work around 'queer' spins the term outward along dimensions that can't be subsumed under gender and sexuality at all: the ways that race, ethnicity, postcolonial nationality criss-cross with these *and other* identity-constituting, identity fracturing discourses, for example.
>
> The gravity (I mean the *gravitas*, the meaning, but also the *center* of gravity) of the term 'queer' itself deepens and shifts.
>
> (Sedgwick 1994, 8)

Thus, queer embodiment derives from and intersects with desire, language, incarnation, the state, recognition, race, class economics, domesticity, labour, kinship, migration, ability, inheritance, law, location in time and place, and a long line of other factors that affect our being-in-the-world. Its roots stem from gender and sexuality issues, but its branches extend into many other areas of what make human beings recognizable or unrecognizable to other human beings.

## Three looks

Books and documentaries such as *The Celluloid Closet* (book by Vito Russo, 1981; film by Rob Epstein and Jeffrey Friedman, 1995) and *Lavender Lens: 100 Years of Celluloid Queers* (David Johnson, Sister Boy Productions, 1995) have shown us that questions of queer cinema are as old as cinema itself. Questions of queer cinema surround the reception of the 1894/5(?) 'Dickson Experimental Sound Film' (also known as 'The Gay Brothers'). *A Florida Enchantment* (Sidney Drew, Vitagraph, 1914) is seen as one of the earliest feature films to delve into and openly extend *queer* beyond issues of gender and sexuality. As well, even the debate over the role of Alice Guy Blaché in the invention of the cinema and her place as the first director of a story film serves to queer the accepted history of how the movies began. Connect these early film debates with wider censorship and obscenity laws, and we can see *queer* issues at the roots of all film history.

Contemporary debates over queer theory/queer cinema might be traced to a series of reactions to Laura Mulvey's article 'Visual Pleasure and Narrative Cinema', written in 1973 and published in *Screen* in 1975 (*see* GAZE THEORY; FEMINIST FILM THEORY, HISTORY OF). In this article, Mulvey points to three looks – the look of the camera, the looks between characters on screen, and the look of the audience at the screen. What these three looks share in mainstream narrative cinema, she argues, is their ability to position all spectators into a sexed viewing position. According to Mulvey, mainstream narrative film situates us to see from a male point of view and view women on screen as objects to be seen (*see* GAZE THEORY). Some feminist, gay, and lesbian critics agreed with but extended Mulvey's concern with the cinema's three looks and her description of the cinematic apparatus's ability to position spectators to see in a certain way. The beginnings of queer theory came when certain theorists questioned the heterosexual assumptions of Mulvey and other feminist film theorists. They asked how gay men and lesbians might *look* differently – on screen and at the screen. If the cinema positions us as sexed and gendered, early queer theorists argued, then it (and some attendant theories) also position us as heterosexed. To challenge mainstream narrative cinema's structures (and descriptions of the structures), they declared, we must challenge their sexism, heterosexism, and overall normativity.

## *How Do I Look? Queer Film and Video*, edited by Bad Object-Choices

Where might we begin to locate these early interventions into Mulvey's 'Visual Pleasure' and other (heterosexual) feminist film theory? We might specifically locate the beginning of this extension and critique addressing queer theory/queer cinema in the work of Teresa de Lauretis, who is said to have introduced the term 'queer theory' as the title of a 1990 conference at the University of California, Santa Cruz, and as the focus of a special issue of *differences: A Journal of Feminist Cultural Studies*, which emerged from that conference. As well, we might locate its origin in the writings of B. Ruby Rich, especially her 1992 article in *Sight & Sound*, where Rich uses the phrase 'New Queer Cinema' to describe the themes, aesthetics, production, and distribution practices of a number of independent films from the late 1980s and early 1990s. Both de Lauretis and Rich mark crucial turns in feminist/gay and lesbian/queer criticism, theory, and filmmaking.

Perhaps, though, it is possible to begin a step earlier than these accepted examples. It may be best to begin with an event and text that mark a transitional stage from gay and lesbian film production and criticism to queer theory/queer cinema. The conference entitled 'How Do I Look? Queer Film and Video', held at Anthology Film Archives in New York City, 21–22 October 1989, and the collected conference proceedings – papers and discussions – edited by Bad Object-Choices, published in 1991, demonstrates that transition. More than the other potential starting points for this discussion, the Bad Object-Choices collection concentrates on the intersections of gender and sexuality with other aspects of personhood – especially race, ethnicity, and class – rather than relegating them to derivative positions. Also, as a scan of the participants indicates, the collection is deeply invested in examining film and video from many sides, including production, distribution, exhibition, and reception. Furthermore, in its very collective authorship 'Bad Object-Choices' marks a queering of normative authorial representation from the start. Grounded in questions of the three looks, it queers that very grounding.

According to the collective authors,

> The idea for a conference on queer film and video emerged from the casual, nonlinear development of our group's [Bad Object-Choices] interest in theoretical and political questions raised by lesbian and gay media. Or, rather, it arose from our frustration at the scarcity of work on this topic, a scarcity we knew resulted from a lack of institutional support from the academy and the publishing industry. We also knew that our interests were shared by many who make, distribute, and program lesbian and gay films and videos and by their audiences.
>
> (Bad Object-Choices 1991, 11)

Compiled in the shadow of the deaths of historian Vito Russo (*The Celluloid Closet*, 1981) and artist and activist Ray Navarro, the further devastation wreaked by HIV/AIDS under the Reagan/Bush regimes, the pervasive institutional apathy and disdain for gay and lesbian work, and the self-contradictory censorship and obscenity laws of such obstructions as the Hays Code and the Meese Report, the goal of this collection appears twofold: to articulate a critical reception of *queer* works and to *queer* the limits of the established institutions and codes.

Beginning with its title, *How Do I Look?* announces its relationship with and challenge to accepted film theory by questioning the relationships between desire, the gaze, spectatorship, and representation on and off screen. Bad Object-Choices leaves the question of *looking* open and ambiguous – redeploying the psychoanalytical assumption that the homosexual object-choice is wrong and putting all three looks into conversation 'with just the right camp inflection to suggest a queer event' (Bad Object-Choices 1991, 12). In short, the collection asks 'how we look – at/in film and video' (12). Thus, it turns the question back on those who have demanded we explain ourselves and our desires not just to challenge representations of homosexual identities, subjectivities, and differences, but also to problematize institutional assumptions of the very meanings of abnormality, deviancy, aberrance, perversion, and pathology. This examination of traditional presumptions marks a turn from established 'representation critique' to queering of film function. *How Do I Look?* asks not just about what is depicted on screen but also how that depiction and its attendant apparatus position us in response – inside and outside the cinema. For, as Bad Object-Choices makes clear: 'All of the essays in this collection describe intersections of theoretical study with collective political struggle – each with a different emphasis and implication' (13). In other words, the participants here ask not just after how they look or are looked at but also how they can make others look and look at them differently. The point is to circulate among queer cinema, criticism, theory, practice, and activism. To this end (and others) *How Do I Look?* includes the primary participants in Bad Object-Choices – writers Teresa de Lauretis, Judith Mayne, Kobena Mercer, and Cindy Patton (who is also a community activist) along with film and videomakers Stuart Marshall and Richard Fung – as well as responses from a broad community of artists, critics, historians, and activists, including B. Ruby Rich, Jean Carlomusto, Gregg Bordowitz, John Greyson, Dennis Altman, Ray Navarro, Martha Gever, Alexandra Juhasz, Jim Fouratt, Isaac Julien, Marusia Bociurkiw, Tom Kalin, Douglas Crimp, José Arroyo, Victoria Starr, Diana Fuss, Tom Waugh, Mandy Merck, Peter Bowen, Lei Chou, Robert Garcia, Ada Griffin, Cora Kaplan, Michelle Parkerson, Robert Mignott, Nancy Graham, Jeff Nunokawa, Terri Cafaro, and Liz Kotz.

Following especially Russo's lead, this collection challenges the assumption that gays and lesbians do not look and do not exist to be looked at. Judith Mayne discusses filmmaker Dorothy Arzner at the intersection of feminist and lesbian film theories – theories especially suspicious of simplistic links between gender, sex, and sexuality – to examine the 'tension between Arzner as a lesbian image and Arzner as a female signature to a text' (108). Kobena Mercer argues that Isaac Julien's film *Looking for Langston* not only queers expectations of documentary realism, but also questions links between authorial identity and authentic identity. The film's aesthetic collage and viewer ambivalence, according to Mercer, reconnect authorial integrity and identity to 'fantasy, memory, and desire', and this queering of authenticity 'serves as an imaginative point of departure for speculation and reflection on the social and historical relations in which black gay male identity is lived and experienced in diaspora societies such as Britain and the United States' (198). Both representation and construction of viewership are brought into dialogue here in considerations of sexuality/gender, race, class, culture, nation, and other differences.

Reconsidering these different looks in the light of the gender gap between lesbian and gay film and video theory is at the centre of several other arguments in *How Do I Look?* Cindy Patton's essay considering safe-sex and pornography for lesbians and gay men, and the ensuing discussion of her admitted self-censorship of images of lesbian sex highlight the gender gap within sexuality studies. While women may be uncomfortable exhibiting images of lesbian sex on screen, men may not feel the same discomfort with public depictions of gay sex. The tension between the looks of women on screen and the looks of women in the audience highlights what is gained and lost by queer theory's roots in feminist film theory. As well, it raises questions about what gay men gain and lose because they look at/in pornography differently. In a similar way, Teresa de Lauretis's essay on Sheila McLaughlin's *She Must Be Seeing Things* focuses on representations of lesbian visibility/invisibility on screen. The film addresses issues of a lesbian, mixed-race couple involved in butch-femme role-playing, where the looking is ever more multiplied by different aspects of personhood. Yet, that multiplication remains locked in the either/or relationships of institutional heterosexism. According to de Lauretis, even as it tries to escape heterosexism, the film reinforces it because in two-sexed society 'sexuality is not only *defined* but actually *enforced* as heterosexuality, even in its homosexual form' (253). The binaries may be multiple here, but they remain binaries: visible/invisible, lesbian/straight, black/white, butch/femme.

Still further complexities emerge as the different looks expose differences within differences. Stuart Marshall and Richard Fung highlight these further complexities of race, ethnicity, embodiment, and ambivalence when they ask:

> What are the patterns of reinforcement and resistance that define relations between scopic homoeroticism and racism? How can minority queer subjectivities imagine or produce a place for their own desires and their own desireabilities in a representational regime that appears to define itself through their exclusion or subordination? Can we characterize the relation between homophobia and racism as homologous, and what are the consequences of such a characterization?
>
> (Bad Object-Choices 1991, 24)

Marshall investigates the role of imaginary identification in the reclamation of the pink triangle for contemporary gay rights. What does it say, about 'us', Marshall asks of gay and lesbian and AIDS activists, when we mobilize around an image of former genocidal oppression? What do we mean when we say, 'we'? Fung questions the compensatory use of racial stereotypes in contemporary gay pornography. He asks after the visibility/invisibility of a 'politically palatable' pornographic representation of gay Asian men (160). What, for example, might it mean to make pornography where Asia is a location, rather than a sign for a certain kind of sexuality? What, for example, might it mean for Asian men to have sex with each other, rather than serve as a commodity of exchange between white men? What, for example, might it mean to construct Asians as subjects who look at, as well as objects that are looked at, in these films? With both writers, fantasy and the intersection of gender, race, and ethnicity with other differences queer any simple understanding of the tensions among the look of the camera, the looks between characters, and the looks of spectators.

## How does queer theory/cinema look?

*How Do I Look?* closes with an energetic discussion focusing on confluences and rifts, the power of ambivalence and the slippage between meanings, the dangers of representations, the role of autobiography in queer writing and images, the relations among theory, history, and practice, and the places of institutions, codes, and censure in future work. The key questions of that discussion remain relevant for any rethinking of queer theory/cinema. What issues remain contemporary? To whom? In which locations? For what reasons?

Queer theory remains perversely difficult to define and delimit. For some, this inarticulation is its strength. The fact that everything is queer or can be queered has great ethical, aesthetic, and political potential. For others, this muddle makes it too broad to be of use. They argue that if everything is queer or can be queered, then the concept drifts into meaninglessness. Beyond these definitional boundaries, disputes, and evaluations, though, several key critiques remain of queer theory. Some critics question queer theory's anti-essentialism, arguing that medical and evolutionary findings may indicate a more essential understanding of sexual orientation. Other thinkers also question queer theory's prioritizing of desire, performance, and recognition. These critics argue for a more incarnated theory of gender and sexuality, one that gives priority to the body and the material existence of bodies. Such questions and others add to the complications involved in descriptions of *queer theory/cinema*, which continues to ask: 'How do I look?'

BRIAN BERGEN-AURAND

## Works cited

Bad Object-Choices. 1991. *How Do I Look? Queer Film and Video*. San Francisco, CA: Bay Press.

Mulvey, Laura. 1989. 'Visual Pleasure and Narrative Cinema'. In *Visual and Other Pleasures*, 14–26. Bloomington: Indiana University Press.

Sedgwick, E. Kosofsky. 1994. *Tendencies*. Durham, NC: Duke University Press.

## Further reading

Aaron, Michele, ed. 2004. *New Queer Cinema: A Critical Reader*. New Brunswick, NJ: Rutgers University Press.

Benshoff, Harry, and Sean Griffin, eds. 2004. *Queer Cinema: The Film Reader*. New York: Routledge.

Creekmur, C.K., and A. Doty, eds. 1995. *Out in Culture: Gay, Lesbian, and Queer Essays on Popular Culture*. Durham, NC: Duke University Press.

Dyer, Richard. 2003 [1990]. *Now You See It: Studies in Lesbian and Gay Film*. 2nd edition. New York: Routledge.

Gever, M., J. Greyson, and P. Parmar, eds. 1993. *Queer Looks: Perspectives on Lesbian and Gay Film and Video*. New York: Routledge.

Hanson, E. ed. 1999. *Outtakes: Essays on Queer Theory and Film*. Durham, NC: Duke University Press.

Stacey, Jackie, and Sarah Street, eds. 2007. *Queer Screen: A Screen Reader*. New York: Routledge.

# RECEPTION THEORY

'Reception theory' refers both to a model for literary history developed by Hans Robert Jauss in 1967 and to a more general approach in literary and film and media studies. In its recent incarnation, reception theory does not denote a theory *per se* but rather a collection of models, practices, and heuristics that are concerned with historicized and active responses by readers and viewers as opposed to intended meanings by authors and filmmakers. The British cultural studies paradigm is arguably the first instance of a modern and sustained concern with audiences, though film theorists have always carved out a place, albeit limited, for the dynamics of spectatorship. Such is the contention of Janet Staiger, who arguably more than any other contemporary film and media scholar has worked to extend the tradition initiated by Jauss. What follows will concentrate on Jauss's earlier 'aesthetic of reception' and Staiger's later 'historical-materialist approach to reception studies' – as each scholar frames their respective contributions as a challenge to the status quo.

## Jauss's challenge

Jauss elucidated his model most forcefully in a speech entitled 'Literary History as a Challenge to Literary Theory' in 1967 at the University of Konstanz. In it, Jauss opens the possibility of a true literary history – a history based not on author biographies and publication dates of first editions, but on a history of readers' reactions to aesthetic experiences. He provocatively lays out seven aphoristic theses – challenges to the status quo in West Germany of historicist and positivist approaches to literary history (Holub 1995, 320). Jauss explains his theses in some depth while stopping short of proposing a step-by-step methodology. While there is not space here to elucidate all of the theses, several are noteworthy for this discussion.

His first thesis is that the history of literature must shift from facts (such as dates of publication) to experiences (such as impact on readers). A work of literature is not static but, in his words, 'more like an orchestration that strikes ever new resonances among its readers' (Jauss 1982, 21). This is a historical process that unfolds slowly, with subsequent audiences, authors, and critics engaging and re-engaging with a particular work over time (22). He asserts that the text cannot be freed from its material domain – the text cannot be activated or have any aesthetic effect – unless it enters into the experience of readers. His task is to 'objectify' this process in order to chart a new history of literature (22). In his second thesis, he offers suggestions for identifying the tropes, conventions, contexts, materials, and phenomena that form the historical reader's 'horizon of expectation', including, somewhat simplistically and tautologically, relying upon 'familiar norms' and 'familiar works' (24).

The fourth thesis is inspired most directly by Hans-Georg Gadamer, a professor of Jauss's and a philosopher of twentieth-century hermeneutics. Gadamer believes that any timeless or objective interpretation of history is impossible; rather, the task is to determine the relevant present-day questions that the past might help to answer. For Gadamer this is not a case of postmodernist self-consciousness, since he believes that the present is already a part of past tradition and thus also part of a single trajectory. The challenge is to understand the interconnectedness of both past and present 'horizons of understanding' (30). Jauss seeks to bring this historical insight of Gadamer to the historical study of the reception of literature.

Formalist concerns become most apparent in the fifth thesis, which charts a work's changing significance over time – in linguistic terms, its 'diachronic' changes. Jauss adopts the formalist preoccupation with formal and stylistic innovation, but, in a nod to Gadamer, stresses that this must take into account a perceiver's unique horizon. 'To recognize the problem left behind to which the new work in the historical series is the answer', Jauss argues, one 'must bring his own experience into play, since the past horizon of old and new forms, problems and solutions, is only recognizable in its further mediation, within the present horizon of the received work' (34). Once a work's form is thus histor-icized, it becomes apparent that there is often a gap between initial and subsequent receptions of a form. As Jauss describes it, a work's 'virtual significance' – the significance a work's formal innovations had on audiences and other artists at the time of its emergence – does not always line up with its 'actual' or later significance (34–5). The actual significance of a work may only arise later, upon further reappropriations by subsequent artists – such as the development of classical themes and tropes during the Italian Renaissance. This 'interaction between production and reception in the historical change of aesthetic attitudes' is the evolution that Jauss is ultimately interested in charting along a diachronic axis (35).

The sixth thesis concerns the synchronic axis, that is, a work's import at a single moment in history. Interestingly, Jauss does not oppose the synchronic with the diachronic as much as he locates the diachronic *within* the synchronic. That is, for Jauss, each synchronic and diachronic point – insofar as it is even possible to separate them – is constitutitive of and constituted by each other. His project is not to create a static universal grid of literary history, but, in the way that mass bends space-time around planets and stars, he is inter-ested, following Kracauer, in exploring 'the "coexistence of the contemporaneous and non-contemporaneous"' and 'moments of entirely different time-curves, conditioned by the laws of their "special history"' (36). The synchronic, when viewed from an aesthetic of reception, is best understood not as a timeless slice of diachronic time but as a hetero-geneous, dynamic mixture of past and future currents, in which different literary works are viewed from multiple angles and become, alternately, 'modish, outdated, or perennial, as premature or belated' (37). In addition to studying vanguard exemplars, then, it is also important to take into account mainstream and even passé works available to readers in order to obtain a more accurate, if necessarily less distinct and fuzzy, picture of each synchronic moment (37).

For his final thesis, Jauss pushes the Formalist belief in the power of new and novel perceptions to a different register. According to Jauss, the Formalists accurately understood the power of new artworks and art forms to affect perceptions of subsequent forms, but they stopped short and failed to understand the 'socially *formative* function of literature' as well (40, his emphasis). This formative link serves as a junction between the Formalists and Gadamer's question-and-answer approach to history. Jauss declares that a literary work's 'social function in the ethical realm is to be grasped according to an aesthetics of reception in the same modalities of question and answer, problem and solution, under which it enters into the horizon of its historical influence' (42). Jauss thus maps the Formalist project of novelty onto morality and ethics. He cites the reception of *Madame Bovary* as an example, illustrating how the new narrational form of Flaubert's narrative forced a confrontation with ethical questions that had not previously been posed as precisely. Jauss explains: a 'literary work with an unfamiliar aesthetic form can break through the expectations of its readers and at the same time confront them with a question, the solution to which remains lacking for them in the religiously or officially sanctioned morals' (42–3). For Jauss, then, literary history is not a 'reflection' of general history, but a dynamic process that is constitutive of general history (45).

## Staiger's historical materialism

Staiger's reception project begins with *Interpreting Films: Studies in the Historical Reception of American Cinema* (1992). Here she demarcates the landscape of literary theory into three categories: 'text-activated', 'reader-activated', and 'context-activated theories' (Staiger 1992, 34–48). 'Text-activated theories' are those positing a strong text that determines the meaning for a reader – envisioned as a more or less passive participant in the process. Structuralism and formalism are examples of text-activated theories for Staiger. On the flip side of the coin, 'reader-activated theories' are those that posit a weak text and a strong reader. Here, a reader's personal experiences and psychology explain the meaning of a text better than any intended meaning by an author; Staiger cites various works of Norman Holland, David Bleich, and Jonathan Culler as examples (43).

Staiger places both herself and Jauss in the third category. 'Context-activated theories' are a middle-ground of sorts concerned with the historical and social contexts surrounding the process of reading. These theories posit that meaning arises from the interplay between a reader, the text, and surrounding historical and social forces. She cites Jauss's 'horizon of expectation' and Macherey and Bennett's discussion of successive historical 'encrustations' of meaning – though she notes that the text does not fade into oblivion, as it does for the reader-activated approach (46).

Similarly to Jauss, Staiger presents *Interpreting Films* as a challenge to a particular model of history. Just as Jauss is interested in thinking through a new type of literary history, Staiger is interested in thinking through a new type of film history. She argues that, contrary to received wisdom, even the earliest film theories carved out at least a meagre place for the spectator. Moreover, she opines that post-1960s film theory did not do much better (50–1). Harking back to Gadamer and Jauss, she wonders if the questions of film history need to be expanded. Instead of asking 'what is cinema's function?' that leads towards Dudley Andrew's formalist vs. realist split model of film history, she proposes a new question for contemporary film theory: 'What is the spectator's relation to the cinematic text?' (50–1). Using this question, Staiger interrogates classical film theories, psychoanalytic theories, linguistics, cognitive psychology, and British cultural studies – discovering a sustained, if latent, interest in the spectator, an interest with many blindspots and untenable assumptions (52–78). Though British cultural studies, for example, is often lauded for its attention to spectators, Staiger is critical of its tendency to reduce audiences to simplistic socio-economic demographics (73).

Staiger proposes a new method, which she labels a 'historical materialist approach to reception studies' (78). As Staiger defines it, this approach 'assumes an interaction among context, text, and individual' and posits relatively active viewers who may or may not realize which parts of their overdetermined selves are being activated by overdetermined texts and historical contexts (79). As opposed to focusing on either texts or idealized readers/ viewers, such a method examines a variety of interpretive modes and tracks 'historically constructed "imaginary selves", the subject positions taken up by individual readers and spectators' (81). By so doing, Staiger argues that her approach does not seek to create a new hermeneutic method, but instead seeks 'a historical *explanation* of the event of interpreting a text' (81, Staiger's emphasis).

Staiger presents an analysis of the reception accorded to Hitchcock's *Rear Window* (1954). Retreading the same ground as Jauss, she suggests that one may 'attempt to constitute the era's reactions by historical research' but, with more finesse than Jauss, adds that this entails 'ferreting out information from nonstandard historical sources (such as diaries, let- ters, small mimeographed newsletters, oral histories, etc.)' in order to include non- dominant readings (87). She chooses to focus her analysis of the reception of *Rear Window* on reviewers of the 1950s, while foregrounding the limits of this sample. Via an analysis of movie reviews, she examines 'the contextual reading strategies available to a spectator in the mid-1950s' (89) and identifies several particular discourses, such as psychoanalysis, to gauge varying responses within her chosen interpretive community. What counts for Staiger is not the veracity of the discourses themselves, but their availability *as* discourses (95). Similarly to Jauss, she advocates a 'diachronic analysis' that would take successive interpretations into account (93).

Staiger's analysis of *Uncle Tom's Cabin* (Porter, 1903) demonstrates how such an approach may be used to rethink commonly held assumptions in film history. Questioning the tra- ditional view that cinema shifted from an emphasis on 'attractions' and tableau scenes towards, around 1909, more sophisticated and complex narratives when audiences alleg- edly become more sophisticated, Staiger argues that a historical materialist study shows this is not the case. She points out that audiences were obviously able to follow the com- plex narrative of the theatrical play of *Uncle Tom's Cabin* (117–18). What may seem to be awkward tableau shots with little narrative logic in the film version may be explained via the large number of ancillary materials – such as the novel, theatrical versions, and 'pos- ters, programs, lithograph cards, and handbills' – that would have provided audiences with much of the information they would need (109). Supplying this information in the film would be redundant (117). Thus we might view this 'highly extrareferential, nonredundant, intertextual film practice' as a mode of transmedia before its time – 'more sophisticated than some later cinema, at least in its assumptions about what its audience could do' (119). Staiger's analysis of reception via a plurality of media offers a compelling reason to rethink the conventional wisdom about spectators being unable to comprehend complex narratives prior to 1909.

In *Perverse Spectators* (2000), a collection of essays written after *Interpreting Films*, Staiger takes stock of more recent work on fandom and active audiences in order to propose a model for reception studies that charts responses between the 'very general' and the 'very specific' (Staiger 2000, 1). The deployment of the term 'perverse spectators' is a way for Staiger to avoid Stuart Hall's three-part categorization of 'dominant', 'negotiated', and 'oppositional' meanings (2). Staiger argues that most readings are, at the end of the day, negotiated, and the term 'perverse' allows a scholar to avoid assuming that a spectator is somehow complicit or knowledgeable about any intended meaning of the text – an argument she also launches, to a lesser extent, in *Interpreting Films*. Provocatively, Staiger insists in *Perverse Spectators* that such a mode of spectatorship is not the exception but the rule (7). Perverse spectators seemingly speak for themselves under the pressures they feel in their lives, and may or may not speak for the text or an author.

*Perverse Spectators* pushes further the insights of *Interpreting Films*. Staiger notes that even an individual spectator is not the same spectator, in a sense, from one moment to the next. She grounds this claim through a discussion (179–87) of her own changing attitudes – from horror to humour – during successive viewings of *The Texas Chainsaw Massacre* (Hooper, 1974). Interestingly, similarly to Jauss, Staiger brings aesthetics – and, specifically, formalist and neoformalist aesthetics – into the mix in order to anchor her model of perverse spectatorship. Staiger now is interested in such matters as charting how spectators may diverge from the aesthetic ideals operating in the classical Hollywood cinema: 'to write the history of the reception of the classical Hollywood cinema is to examine the interplay between the produced films and their consuming publics' (41). Aesthetic conventions operate here, then, as background conditions in a text to which spectators react differently from one moment to the next.

In a 2007 article, '*Kiss Me Deadly*: Cold War Threats from Spillane to Aldrich, New York to Los Angeles, and the Mafia to the H-Bomb', Staiger places a greater emphasis on textual and filmic production by considering the act of adaptation as a form of reception. In this essay, she examines the 'articulated reception' of Robert Aldrich and A.I. Bezzirdes as they adapt Mickey Spillane's novel into a screenplay and film (Staiger 2007, 280). Spillane's novel is regressive, she argues, gaining energy thematically from the paranoia of the House Un-American Activities Committee hearings and McCarthyism. Aldrich's film adaptation, on the other hand, takes these themes and historical influences, and reverses their polarity so that McCarthyism may be seen as a societal problem and not a solution (282). Staiger illustrates several formal and narrational tactics by which Aldrich and Bezzirdes effect their articulated reception, and then charts the various iterations of popular reception to Aldrich's film (284). Via an analysis of movie reviews, Staiger concludes that the film's broader political meanings were clear to audiences at the time, and that French critics understood the critique of McCarthyism even if American critics did not (285). Realizing that such claims invite problems with authorial intended meanings, which are notoriously difficult to pin down, Staiger opines that she is 'unsure that I am willing to give up critically analyzing intentional discourse by audiences or authors as audiences' (285). By thus considering authors as audiences, Staiger reframes the intentionality question in a new light and perhaps makes it a legitimate one to consider anew, especially via the lens of adaptation

## Conclusion

By proposing a study of historicized reception – with varying degrees of attention to the text and aesthetics – both Jauss and Staiger seek to frustrate conventional models of history. Janet Staiger, writing a quarter-century after Jauss, takes up much of his challenge and reframes it for film and media studies. Both Jauss's and Staiger's approaches may be faulted for seeking to stabilize historical moments in a bit too facile a manner. Arguably,

Jauss celebrates Formalist ideals too uncritically, whereas Staiger overstates the malleability of the spectator. For the most part, however, both theorists succeed in their respective challenges. The study of the reception of specific texts by historically situated readers and spectators existing in specific contexts is now a mainstay of literary and film and media studies.

CHRIS DZIALO

## Works cited

Holub, Robert C. 1995. 'Reception Theory: School of Constance'. In *The Cambridge History of Literary Criticism, Volume 8: From Formalism to Poststructuralism*, edited by Raman Selden, 319–46. Cambridge: Cambridge University Press.

Jauss, Hans Robert. 1982. *Toward an Aesthetic of Reception*. Translated by Timothy Bahti. Minneapolis: University of Minnesota Press.

Staiger, Janet. 1992. *Interpreting Films: Studies in the Historical Reception of American Cinema*. Princeton, NJ: Princeton University Press.

——. 2000. *Perverse Spectators: The Practices of Film Reception*. New York and London: New York University Press.

——. 2007. '*Kiss Me Deadly*: Cold War Threats from Spillane to Aldrich, New York to Los Angeles, and the Mafia to the H-Bomb'. In *New Directions in American Reception Study*, edited by Philip Goldstein and James L. Machor, 279–88. Oxford and New York: Oxford University Press.

## Further reading

Gadamer, Hans-Georg. 2004. *Truth and Method*. 2nd, revised edition. Revised translation by Joel Weinsheimer and Donald G. Marshall. London and New York: Continuum.

Holub, Robert C. 1984. *Reception Theory: A Critical Introduction*. London and New York: Methuen.

Stam, Robert. 2000. 'The Birth of the Spectator'. In *Film Theory: An Introduction*, 229–34. Malden, MA: Blackwell.

# REDEMPTION (KRACAUER)

## The redemptive power of cinema

In *Theory of Film: The Redemption of Physical Reality* Siegfried Kracauer argues that film has 'affinities with such aspects of the natural world as "unstaged reality," "chance," "the fortuitous," "the indeterminate," "the flow of life" and "endlessness"' (Kracauer 1997, 173). Thanks to the homology between the indeterminate, transient, and undramatic nature of the *Lebenswelt*[1] and the equally indeterminate nature of the film image (298), film can *redeem* the *Lebenswelt* from its repression by the objectifying discourses of modern science. Nevertheless, Kracauer attributes a redemptive power to cinema *selectively*: first, only certain subjects, which he identifies as 'properly cinematic', hold the potential to redeem physical reality, and, second, cinema's redemptive potential concerns only 'the inherent affinities of the medium', cinema's 'essence', not its 'technical properties'.

First, Kracauer maintains that 'there are certain subjects within the world which may be termed "cinematic" (e.g. the chase, dancing, nascent motion, and inanimate objects) because they seem to exert a peculiar attraction on the medium. It is as if the medium were predestined (and eager) to exhibit them' (41). Paradoxically, Kracauer begins every new section of his book with an account of the uncinematic and then proceeds to derive the cinematic from it, endlessly qualifying his distinction between the two so as to 'redeem' the uncinematic as, after all, potentially cinematic. For instance, he argues that when the 'uncinematic' subject is placed in the context of a 'cinematic' one, the former 'boosts' the cinematic nature of the latter and, in fact, becomes palatable itself merely by virtue of its difference from the cinematic subject.[2]

Second, in Kracauer's view film differs from the other arts in that it does not offer an idealistic conception of the world. Unlike the established arts, film does not completely process the raw experience it draws upon. Because it 'incorporates aspects of physical reality with a view to making us experience them' (40), film cannot be an art but only a medium which channels, redirects, and intensifies our experience rather than representing or interpreting it to us (309). Thus, Kracauer dismisses film's technical properties as not being part of what he calls 'the properly cinematic'. In terms of its 'inherent affinities' film is a *medium*, but in terms of its 'technical properties' it is an *art*. The 'medium of film' is ontologically anterior to the development of its technical (i.e. artistic) properties. For instance, inasmuch as special effects, such as slow and accelerated motion, belong to the *history* of the medium, not to its *essence*, they are deprived of a redeeming potential.

According to Kracauer, the fundamental quality that camera-reality shares with physical reality, the essential quality that embodies and guarantees cinema's redeeming potential, is *indeterminacy*. While indeterminacy pertains to the ontology of the photographic image (referring to the perceptual inexhaustibility or illegibility of the image irreducible to signification or verbal summary), it also describes the nature of cinematic spectatorship and the type of narrative Kracauer considers most cinematic, the episodic narrative. Kracauer's account of spectatorship demonstrates that, far from advocating a factual or documentary type of realism, he locates the essence of film in its ability to give us 'stuff for dreaming', to both shock us (awaken our senses) and relax us into a state of reverie. The dreaming state that film images may induce can take two forms: 'dreaming toward' the object and 'dreaming away' from the object, the former producing a passive state of mind and the latter drawing the spectator into his subjective (Proustian) reveries. The film spectator alternates between these two states, first responding passively and purely viscerally to sense data and then, while remaining in this involuntary, indeterminate state, activating the secret reserves of his or her unconscious (166).

## The redemptive potential of certain types of film narrative

In Kracauer's view, narratives range from 'embryonic patterns', through Flaherty's 'slight narrative', which privileges the typical and the collective over intrigue and individual protagonists and actions, to the truly cinematic, indeterminate, episodic narratives, whose 'stories emerge from and again disappear in the flow of life' (Kracauer 1997, 251). Not every content can be treated in an episodic form: often an uncinematic content (usually an abstract idea) clashes with the episodic cinematic form. For instance, *The Defiant Ones* (1958) is uncinematic because the idea behind the story (racial tolerance) becomes the prime mover, violating the 'natural' permeability of the episodes. 'Permeability' may refer to the setting of an episode – e.g. transitory public spaces such as railway stations, bars, and any public space through which people continuously circulate – or to a character, e.g. adrift and directionless characters who seem to 'follow a course strangely devoid of purpose and direction … as if they drifted along, moved by unaccountable currents' (256). Episodic narratives (e.g. films by Rossellini, De Sica, and Fellini), especially those featuring drifting characters, approximate most closely the 'flow of life', thereby 'curing' our melancholy and reanimating our connection to the material world in all its complexity and endlessness.

Films with an episodic structure built around multiple intersecting stories and involving some kind of spatial displacement are cinematic because they draw attention to 'the solidarity of the universe' (64) revealed, for example, in the representation of things and events coexisting in different spaces. Kracauer's definition of 'the cinematic' betrays his tendency to conceive both reality and camera-reality in predominantly spatial terms; thus, he writes of the 'nostalgia for the vast *spaces* of life' (233) and describes the *flâneur*'s shock perceptions almost exclusively in terms of spatial rather than temporal sense data.[3] Not only is 'camera-reality' described as a space – rather than space-time – continuum, but Kracauer demands that films adhere to the theatrical *unity of time* despite his insistence that film is *not* an extension of theatre but of photography. Whereas *spatial displacements* are cinematic, temporal displacements – e.g. historical films or science fiction films – are not. Referencing Lukács's *Theory of the Novel*, Kracauer observes that the modern novel and film share an 'affinity for endlessness'. The time of the modern novel and film differs from the time of the epic: epic time is eternity, from the point of view of which chronological time makes no sense. In the novel and film, both products of modernity's 'groundlessness', eternity has been replaced by a 'chronological ["fallen"] time without beginning and end' (233). The modern novel and film embody the dominance of a chronological notion of time, which arranges events in a never-ending series of 'one after another' with no hope for transcendence, i.e. absolute meaning or value.

## Redeeming Kracauer's 'realist' theory from common misinterpretations

Kracauer's notion of 'redemption through cinema' exposes the inadequacy of viewing his film theory as 'naively realist'. In his introduction to *The Mass Ornament: Weimar Essays* (2005) Thomas Levin challenges the misconception of Kracauer's theory as naively realist:

> Although Kracauer's turn to [the] mass media in the mid-1920s was ... certainly overdetermined by the evidentiary quality of the photograph and photogram (their iconic and indexical semiotic specificity), the 'realist vocation' common to both resided in their unstaged depiction of the 'real' negativity of the metaphysics of modernity.
>
> (Levin 2005, 20–1)

In other words, for Kracauer the realism of the new media resided not in their ability to represent the world but in their status as indices of a specific socio-historical reality, i.e. in their ability to reflect the problems of modernity in an unmediated way. In Levin's reading of Kracauer, the redemptive potential of photography and film lies in their ability – derived from their affinity with (or resemblance to) the 'surface' of reality – to present us with an unmediated image of life under the conditions of capitalism. *The realism of film is a function of film's demythologizing, rather than of its indexical and iconic potential (i.e. its causal and resemblant relationship to reality).*

For instance, for Levin (via Benjamin) photography annihilates the person, thereby foregrounding the increasing abstraction of the human under capitalism. Montage foregrounds another typical feature of modernity – the fragmentation or loss of coherent meaning – but, at the same time, the fragmentation constitutive of montage has an emancipating potential for 'only once the current state of things is revealed as provisional (that is, not a result of nature) can the question of their proper order arise' (Levin 2005, 22). By revealing the arbitrariness and contingency of existing relations (including social ones), montage hints at the possibility of change and contributes to the disenchantment and demythologization of Reason as a mechanism supporting the dominant ideology. For Levin, not only is cinema capable of revealing the metaphysical void at the core of modern life, but it can also expose the provisionality of the established sociopolitical order and prepare the way for its overcoming. In this sense, Kracauer's 'realism' points to film's *deconstructive and/or corrective potential,* to its revelation of the anachronistic politics of bourgeois culture.

In her Introduction to Kracauer's *Theory of Film* (1997) Miriam Hansen also seeks to rehabilitate Kracauer's theory from critiques by Dudley Andrew, Pauline Kael, and the journal *Screen*. Using Kracauer's Marseille notebooks (his original notes for the book, on which he began working in Marseille in 1940–1), Hansen traces Kracauer's theory back to his Weimar writings, a genealogy that is largely obscured in the final version of *Theory of Film* (1960). The Marseille notebooks reveal that, contrary to those who read *Theory of Film* as expounding a realist film ontology rooted in cinematic indexicality, Kracauer never really abandoned his earlier preoccupation with cinema as an alternative public sphere with a revolutionizing and democratizing potential. The trajectory from Weimar through Marseille to New York demonstrates that Kracauer's concept of realism, 'his insistence on film's affinity with the "material," "physical," "external reality," "existence," and "environment" – is bound up with the problematic of the subject (historical viewer), rather than simply with film's referential relation to the material world' (Hansen 1997, xvi). Kracauer grounds his film aesthetics in the medium of photography not because of its surface authenticity and verisimilitude but because of its ability to both depict the world and render it *strange*, i.e. because of its crucial work of *alienation*, which it shares with history.

## Kracauer's redemption of the negative aspects of modernity

The theory of redemption – the claim that cinema can redeem or reclaim physical reality for us – depends on Kracauer's similar *redemption of the negative aspects of modernity into positive aesthetic qualities, which he posits as 'the basic affinities of film'*: film's affinities for the indeterminate, the unstaged, the infinite, the fortuitous, and the transient disguise the negative effects of mass culture, including fragmentation, distraction, groundlessness, relativism, and solitude. Kracauer proceeds in the following manner: (1) he isolates the fundamental problems of modern mass culture; (2) he attributes these problems to cinema, i.e. he argues that the invention of cinema has, in one way or another, caused or exacerbated these problems (fragmentation, alienation, loneliness, groundlessness, moral relativism, nostalgia or longing for an immediate, unreflexive experience of life, and scepticism); (3) he asserts that these negative *effects* of the invention of cinema are, in fact, *inherent* in cinema, that they constitute the 'basic affinities' of the film medium; but (4) he insists that film's 'basic affinities' are also precisely what will 'solve' the problems of modernity and 'redeem' physical reality.

The analogy Kracauer draws between the film spectator and the nineteenth-century *flâneur* serves to redeem the fragmentary, abstract, and transient nature of life in modern mass culture. Like the *flâneur*, the film spectator is highly susceptible to the transient real-life phenomena crowding the screen. Transient public spaces (e.g. bars and hotels) that foster social alienation and superficial human contacts are *redeemed* by Kracauer as authentic and cinematic: bars are no longer places where lonely strangers come and go but instead mysterious dark venues holding out the promise for 'strange adventures'; people do not engage in inconsequential small talk with strangers but form *improvised* (rather than *random* or *superficial*) gatherings that hold out the promise for 'fresh human contact'; the increasing pace of life and the fragmentation of time and space are not disorienting or alienating but instead offer 'unforeseeable possibilities' (Kracauer 1997, 170). Abstracted from its usual social connotations and considered from a purely disinterested (aesthetic) point of view, alienation is no longer a symptom of the disintegration of social ties; instead, it reveals its hidden *liberating* potential.

To put a positive spin on the depressingly abstract, fragmented existence of modern man, in which things are reduced to their bare schemata, Kracauer reinterprets *fragmentation* as *multiplicity* and contrasts it with the already suspect 'totalitarian' notion of *totality*. He proposes that we can reconnect with reality not by trying to revive an impossible sense of wholeness but by fragmenting reality even more, specifically by breaking it down into unfamiliar configurations (e.g. through composition and editing). *Fragmentation* is redeemed as a positive quality in terms of *autonomy* and *indeterminacy*: things are 'cinematic' (whether appearing in a film or not) when they are *fragmented*, detached from other things, represented for their own sake, and de-narrativized; conversely, as long as a thing remains embedded in a network of relations to other things, it is in danger of simply being reduced to a symbol or a metaphor, a mere mental representation. Likewise, Kracauer emphasizes the principles of *multiplicity* and *fragmentation*, which increase the impression of *endlessness*. Just as things become more cinematic when they are presented from *multiple perspectives* (the multiplication of perspectives is not to be confused with montage: montage arranges the multiple perspectives of an object to express a certain idea – hence Eisenstein's notion of 'intellectual montage' – while Kracauer's idea of the perspectivization of an object points to the inexhaustible difference of the object from itself), so events become more cinematic when they are multiplied, when large 'blocks' of time are made up of *multiple episodes*. Kracauer redeems the fragmentation of time into episodes as a liberating and democratizing instance of *multiplicity* (as opposed to the illusion of *unity*).

Kracauer reinterprets positively the degradation of absolute value and the weakening of morals, beliefs, and norms characteristic of modernity by suggesting that it is precisely the insignificance of events and their relative value that makes them cinematic. In a truly cinematic film, major plot events are replaced by multiple, indeterminate 'incidents' with no clear causal relation between them. The fragmentation of narrative into episodes or incidents renders them self-sufficient, neutral, valueless, and thus equally insignificant, but, rather than taking 'randomness' and 'arbitrariness' as pointing to the absurdity of existence (as Beckett would), Kracauer emphasizes their *democratizing* potential. In short, Kracauer redeems *distraction* as *episodicity*, which he praises for challenging the 'totalitarianism' of plot. *Moral and existential relativism* or *groundlessness* are redeemed as *ambiguity* and *indeterminacy*, while *solitude* and *alienation* – fragmentation on a social level – are refigured as states of (Kantian) *aesthetic disinterestedness*. Finally, *melancholy*, experienced as a certain loss of selfhood, is redeemed as a more *ethical* way of relating to reality, whereby we open ourselves up to other experiences, other types of durations, to the physical world as such. In each of these cases, a particular negative aspect of modernity is recast as a redeeming aesthetic quality essential to film and hence to film's *realism*.

TEMENUGA TRIFONOVA

## Notes

1 Edmund Husserl introduced the concept of the *Lebenswelt* (life-world) – the world as lived prior to reflective analysis – in his *Crisis of the European Sciences* (1970 [1936]).
2 See Kracauer's discussion of stillness and movement (pp. 43–44), the staged and the unstaged (pp. 60–62), language and pure sound (pp. 104–111).
3 The *flâneur* (from the French verb *flâner*, 'to stroll') is an emblematic figure of *fin de siècle* modern urban experience. Drawing on Charles Baudelaire's poetry, Walter Benjamin transformed the *flâneur* into an object of scholarly interest in the twentieth century.

## Works cited

Hansen, Miriam. 1997. 'Introduction'. In *Theory of Film: The Redemption of Physical Reality*, Siegfried Kracauer, vii–xlv. Princeton, NJ: Princeton University Press.

Husserl, Edmund. 1970 [1936]. *Crisis of the European Sciences*. Evanston, IL: Northwestern University Press.

Kracauer, Siegfried. 1997 [1960]. *Theory of Film: The Redemption of Physical Reality*. Princeton, NJ: Princeton University Press.

Levin, Thomas. 2005. 'Introduction'. In *The Mass Ornament: Weimar Essays*, 1–33. Cambridge, MA: Harvard University Press.

# REPRESENTATION

Representation is the depiction of things, classes, relationships, experiences, and other phenomena by means such as signs, images, models, formulas, and narratives. In an important sense the notion of representation – something standing for something else – implies that the real world is not simply out there for us to perfectly copy or experience without mediation. We may assume material reality exists irrespective of our consciousness, but only representations enable us to create a meaningful and workable relationship to that reality.

A point Paul Ricoeur has made about *mimesis* applies to representation. He thinks of mimesis not merely as an 'imitation' of reality (as the word has usually been translated) but, rather, as a creative act through which attention is focused on certain features of a thing by making them salient in terms of a particular way of modelling our perceptions and experience (Ricoeur 1978, 39–40). In drama and other forms of narration, such modelling is achieved by constructing a plot that brings forth aspects of the motivations and conditions, effects and moral consequences of human action.

The notion of the social constructedness of representation – that the real world is not simply directly reflected objectively in our minds, but is rather the result of the historical development of certain ways of depicting things within a community – has led to a 'crisis of representation'. How can representation tell us something true about the world? Behind this concern there is the ancient philosophical quest for certain knowledge. However, even the observation and representation of the material world in the natural sciences are always tied to a certain point of view and a faith in methods that set forth guidelines for formulating questions within prevailing research paradigms. This is all the more true in the field of the humanities, where subjective experience is often a crucial aspect of the object of study. A film, for example, is not only a material object, but also exists through the ways it is perceived and experienced as part of a shared culture and tradition.

## Film as representation

Filmic representation takes place first of all on the level of sound and moving image. These serve as a basis for capturing and shaping the phenomenal world as it supposedly exists (as in observational documentary), or as staged for expressive purposes – ranging from various forms of documentary to fictional films shot in studios. From the way such material is arranged emerges narration, which represents characters and the world they inhabit. Our attention tends to oscillate between these two levels. As Siegfried Kracauer suggested, any element in a film might be 'intended to advance the story to which it belongs ... [I]t also affects us strongly, or even primarily, as just a fragmentary moment of visible reality, surrounded, as it were, by a fringe of indeterminate visible meanings. And in this capacity the moment disengages itself from the conflict, the belief, the adventure, toward which the whole of the story converges' (Kracauer 1960, 303). Here, representation is observed as taking place on two distinct levels: (1) images as re-presentations of fragments of the actuality that has existed in front of the camera while it has been operated (the pre-filmic event); and (2) as modelling by means of narrative organization which assigns those fragments a more precise meaning and function as part of a discourse. In terms of (1), the image projected on screen may be recognized as something actual and specific, say, an existing person or a certain location. Capturing something by a camera produces a representation which is, by virtue of the photomechanical or photoelectronic nature of the image, *indexical*, to use the term from C.S. Peirce's semiotics. What this means is that the image functions as a sign by virtue of the causal relationship it has to the object depicted. (Animated films are an important exception, but for the sake of brevity the focus here will be only on live-action film.) Because of its indexicality, the photographic image has a different kind of ontological relationship to the thing represented than does a painting (*see* ONTOLOGY OF THE PHOTOGRAPHIC IMAGE). However, this process also gives the image a highly *iconic* quality, to use another term from C.S. Peirce's semiotics. What this means is that the image refers to something by resembling it. Because the photographic reproduction emerges from the indexical, there are no clear boundaries between the indexical and iconic as regards the function of the representation. In order to clarify this we have to carry out a brief examination of a major branch of classical film theory.

Because of film's ability to create a highly verisimilar image of the phenomenal world, the question of representation in film has been closely tied to the notion of realism. One of the key figures of this line of thought was André Bazin. He drew attention to what he called 'our appetite for illusion by a mechanical reproduction in the making of which man plays no part' (Bazin 1967, 12). One hastens to add that the supposed objectivity in the production of such images is only possible once certain photographic parameters such as framing, focal length, aperture, and length of exposure have been chosen – not to speak of the position of the camera and the decision about when to start and stop filming. One may well think of the adjustments made in choosing to shoot something in a particular way as a 'creative intervention of man' (13). But the main point in Bazin's thinking is that the filmic image actually 're-presents' something that existed in front of the camera at the time of shooting. He even went so far as to state that 'the photographic image is the object itself' (14). Bazin emphasized that the photograph 'carries with it more than mere resemblance, namely a kind of identity' (96). In other words, to him the realism of the photographic image lies in its indexical rather than in its iconic quality.

Bazin's ideas have often been criticized, but seldom as incisively as in Noël Carroll's *Philosophical Problems of Classical Film Theory* (1988, chapter 2). Here the main target is Bazin's claim that a relationship of identity exists between the photographically generated image and the thing it stands for. It is true that a live-action film image represents something that has existed previously. For Bazin, however, the main point is the idea of film as a re-presentational medium, the true vocation of which is spatial and temporal realism: the camera can capture things as they once existed – the pre-filmic event. This connects closely with phenomenological realism, how we *perceive* space. In Bazin's view, deep focus cinematography enables the same kind of relation to the visual field that takes place in our natural perception, including a degree of ambiguity in that the spectator's attention is not guided as forcefully as in rapid Eisensteinian montage, which often relies on close-ups (*see* DEPTH OF FIELD; MODERNISM VERSUS REALISM). It even 'brings the spectator into a relation with the image closer to that which he enjoys with reality' (Bazin 1967, 35). Carroll, however, thinks that Eisenstein and other Russian montage theorists of the 1920s were much more successful than Bazin in their analysis of how representation takes place in fiction film, as they insisted that 'editing can give a shot a meaning and reference different from what the shot physically portrays' (Carroll 1988, 151).

Carroll further emphasizes recognizability as the crucial point of our ordinary understanding of representation. Photographic representation enables us to recognize the thing depicted because our attention is drawn to certain salient and invariant features with which we are familiar through our interaction with our natural and social environment. Because of the remarkable flexibility of our perceptual apparatus in recognizing objects, remarkably few features suffice to do the job. The image of historical figures can be so highly conventional (Napoleon with his famous pose and hat) that the idea of him or her can be conveyed by mere suggestion. This may be taken as an instance of the third category of signs in Peirce's semiotics, namely *symbolic* (signs referring to something by virtue of convention). Representation need not be all that life-like: drawn caricatures can serve as a form of representation. As such they can even draw our attention to a person's features that we have previously not been aware of.

## Levels of filmic representation

As regards film, we have to make distinctions according to the ontology of the filmic image, the way it functions as the basis for fiction, and the ways in which we might appropriate that fiction into our imaginary representations. First of all, we have to discern what different levels of filmic representation actually stand for. Carroll states that 'we should agree that there are a number of different types of representation available in film, types determined by and best analyzed in terms of the uses they serve' (Carroll 1988, 170). He then proceeds to clear away certain fallacies that he thinks mar Bazin's theory of realism by identifying three levels of representation (which he borrows from Monroe Beardsley): physical portrayal, depiction, and nominal portrayal.

Arguably, Bazin's insistence on the near identity between the filmic image and the object which its represents as the foundation of its realism does seem to end up with problems as he deals with fictional films. Carroll suggests that, following Bazin's line of thought, *Casablanca* (Curtiz, 1942) could be said to re-present Humphrey Bogart. However, 'that seems beside the point if we are interested in appreciating the film as fictional representation – in which case it is about Rick and not about Bogart' (Carroll 1988, 148). We might add that while Bogart may be said to be represented in a film on the level of an indexical sign function (the character has been played by a historical person of this name, familiar to us from other films and other related representations), what matters for the spectator is the iconic sign function, which in conjunction with certain conventions enables us to recognize his image as a representation of a fictional character (we observe a verisimilar diegetic world with characters familiar to us as types on the basis of similar films we have seen previously).

Carroll's threefold distinction sorts out these complications. The first of these is *physical portrayal*. In live-action film, every shot portrays 'a definitive object, person, place, or event that can be designated by a singular term' (149). In this sense *Casablanca* may indeed be said to re-present Humphrey Bogart. Following Paul Messaris, we may observe that this is possibly because of the flexibility of our perceptual recognition system: we recognize objects and persons in real life for what they are because their structural features match our internal encyclopaedia of familiar objects similarly organized, and adjusting to photographic representation of such things takes place quite effortlessly (Messaris 1994, 73).

What is much more to the point as regards a fiction film is that a film also, in Carroll's words, '*depicts* a class or collection of objects designated by a general term' (Carroll 1988, 150). An individual represented might potentially be categorized in many ways, but the narrative context cues only a limited number as salient, thus leading the spectator to a categorization serving the appropriate narrative purposes – although the spectator may indulge in alternative categorizations according to his or her preferences or ideological position. Thus we may recognize the character played by Bogart in *Casablanca* as representing a cynical and dexterous person facing certain moral decisions emerging from the combination of a frustrated love affair and circumstances created by war.

However, usually it is more pertinent that a fictional context gives rise to what Carroll calls *nominal portrayal*. That is, a character within the story world is given a certain fictional name and identity establishing that the things shown in the image 'stand for particular things other than the ones that caused the image' (Carroll 1988, 151). Here, factual and fictional narration part ways. In a documentary film, the narration is founded on people captured on film as representing themselves. However the narration is constructed, it tells their individual story. When watching what we know to be a fiction film, however, we are aware that actors – apart from the occasional cameo appearance – represent fictional characters. We form a mental image of them on the basis of their traits and qualities which we recognize through the way they fit categories in terms of which we make sense of the real world, on the one hand, and fiction, on the other.

Carroll's categories can be mapped onto C.S. Peirce's categories:

- Physical portrayal – indexical (*Casablanca* portrays Humphrey Bogart).
- Depiction – iconic (*Casablanca* depicts a man facing certain moral choices; classification).
- Nominal portrayal – symbolic (*Casablanca* portrays the fictional character Rick).

But not everything in human life can be simply reduced to these basic levels. To complete the picture we must broaden our notion of representation by discerning two further levels. First, there is *film as historically contextualized discourse representing psychological concerns and ideology*. This became the main concern of much of film studies in the 1970s and 1980s, mainly under the aegis of neo-Marxist sociology and Lacanian psychoanalysis (*see* CONTEMPORARY FILM THEORY), as well as cultural studies inspired above all by Raymond Williams and Stuart Hall. It should be appreciated that even if one would not find the background philosophies of these approaches congenial, the issues they have focused on are fundamental for a critical understanding of the representation of social relationships and the psychological appeal of films.

Finally, we can identify a level called *representation of aesthetic and ethical values*. Art has traditionally been seen as one of the principal means of articulating human concerns, sorting out conflicts of values, and maintaining faith in some transcendent meaning of human pursuits. More recently, such ways of conceiving the role of art have been reduced to social and psychological symptoms, on the one hand, or to the more basic cognitive operations that have had evolutionary significance, on the other. But as everyday experience tells us, we cannot live our lives in terms of reductionist philosophies and naturalistic accounts of human behaviour. We have to operate in terms of genuinely felt motivations guided by a sense of values and notions about things worth pursuing. The paradox here lies in that while we cannot ignore the findings of evolutionary anthropology and cognitive science any more than those of sociology and psychology as regards the foundations of our being, we still have to act in terms of values that furnish us with both reasons and a genuinely felt wish to act in certain ways and not others. Thus, on top of this level of ideological critique of representation we still find the level of appreciating narratives as standing for a meaningful assessment of the moral foundations of life and action – what might be called a *symbolic sphere* (only indirectly related to Peirce's notion of the third category of signs). (For further discussion on all these levels see Bacon 2005.)

## Representation, ideology, and ethics

In terms of ideological representation, films represent psychological features and social relationships. In the most straightforward cases this amounts to telling stories about people who posses ideas and adhere to certain values. Characters may state these explicitly or they may manifest them in their actions. There may be a discrepancy between what they say and what they do – or what they appear to be doing, and characters may be pitted against one another in these terms so as to question their integrity and offer a more subtle representation of the complexities of ethical choices. The ending is likely to be interpreted as a statement about what the filmmakers take as being the correct moral stance. Much of the pleasure afforded by mainstream cinema is based on the restoration of a just state of affairs after a successful struggle – if this does not take place, the film will probably appear like a very cynical statement about the way of the world. It has often been argued that the very pleasure offered by a standard happy ending is inimical to serious social or political criticism.

In 'The Politics of Representation' Michael Ryan and Douglas Kellner explore whether 'dominant representational codes' can be used in producing radical alternatives to established notions of form and content. This is a crucial question because, certain 'prevailing patterns of thought, perception, and behavior ... are determined ... by representations, the dominant forms or modes through which people experience the world'. Accordingly, even to imagine, say, 'a more egalitarian social arrangement would require different representations' (Ryan and Kellner 2005, 213). Ryan and Kellner point out that while commonly accepted forms of cinematic realism are thought to be hopelessly entangled with dominant ideology, it may be possible for filmmakers to represent political events so as to provide an accessible critical view of them. Films do not simply depict or reveal reality: 'Rather, films construct a phenomenal world and position the audience to experience and live the world in certain ways' (218).

Ryan and Kellner argue that although Hollywood films foreground the efforts of individual characters in a way that might not do justice to the complexities of the political and social issues involved, such characters can serve as points of identification that enable an audience to find the representation interesting and involving. In the case of the Costa-Gavras film *Missing* (1982), this might lead to becoming aware of the historical issues depicted, such as the US involvement in the atrocities connected with the overthrow of the democratically elected Allende regime in Chile. Ryan and Kellner quote an audience survey indicating that many people did become more aware of the political issues related to the coup through this film. Thus the writers come to the conclusion that not all classical forms of film narration are inherently conservative (Ryan and Kellner 1988, 220). It is possible to represent complex political and social issues by means of standard cinematic narration.

A more refined form of representation, the ethical, is that of ideas and values treated as something that cannot be simply reduced to social or psychological symptoms and which we absolutely need in order to live our lives. Kieślowski's *Blue* (1993) tells the story of Julie, who loses her husband and daughter in a car accident. Julie continues her life, but it is as if she has lost her ability to experience life as rich and meaningful. Nothing seems to matter. Through certain plot twists we reach a point where Julie succeeds in restoring a symbolic sphere for herself. Thus the film represents a spiritual trajectory which the spectator is invited to share. Just as Julie is once again able to find meaning in life and return to other people through reassuming creative activity – a spiritual act made possible through resuming contact with other people – the film itself can serve to strengthen the spectator's own sense of meaningfulness. Making this claim is in a sense a return to traditional notions of the function of art as not only something that serves certain emancipatory social functions and has therapeutic and curative properties, but that is fundamentally constitutive of our lives as conscious beings, constantly facing the need to make choices and maintain faith in the possibility to live a purposeful life.

HENRY BACON

## Works cited

Bacon, Henry. 2005. 'Synthesizing Approaches in Film Theory'. *Journal of Moving Image Studies* 4: 4–12.
Bazin, André. 1967. 'The Ontology of the Photographic Image' and 'The Evolution of the Language of Cinema'. In *What Is Cinema?*, vol. I, essays selected and translated by Hugh Gray, 9–16, 23–40. Berkeley: University of California Press.
Carroll, Noël. 1988. *Philosophical Problems of Classical Film Theory*. Princeton, NJ: Princeton University Press.
Kracauer, Siegfried. 1960. *Theory of Film: The Redemption of Physical Reality*. New York: Oxford University Press.
Messaris, Paul. 1994. *Visual Literacy: Image, Mind, and Reality*. Boulder, CO: Westview Press.
Ricoeur, Paul. 1978. *The Rule of Metaphor: Multi-disciplinary Studies of the Creation of Meaning in Language*. Translated by Robert Czerny with Kathleen McLaughlin and John Costello SJ. London: Routledge and Kegan Paul.
Ryan, Michael, and Douglas Kellner. 2005 [1988]. 'The Politics of Representation'. In *The Philosophy of Film: Introductory Text and Readings*, edited by Thomas E. Wartenberg and Angela Curran, 213–24. Oxford: Blackwell Publishing.

## Further reading

Bacon, Henry. 2009. 'Blendings of Real, Fictional, and Other Imaginary People'. *Projections* 3 (1): 77–99.
Donald, Merlin. 2001. *A Mind So Rare: The Evolution of Human Consciousness*. New York and London: W.W. Norton & Company.

# RHETORIC, FILM AND

Rhetoric is the technique and theory of discourse composition, with particular reference to persuasive speech. It originated in classical Greek and Latin culture, and was revived in the context of the linguistic and semiotic wave in the 1970s (*see* SEMIOTICS OF FILM). Rhetoric has been applied to film studies with three different meanings: (1) The study of film as a persuasive discourse, that is, as a kind of discourse implying, conveying, and naturalizing ideologies (for instance within the colonial film studies field). David Bordwell (1989) argues that many theories and analyses of film are determined by networks of underlying assumptions. (2) The study of film as narrative discourse, both in its fictional (Chatman 1990) and non-fictional (Plantinga 1997) manifestations. (3) The study of rhetorical figures present in the film; within the modern film studies field, this trend implies an analogy between the discourse of the film and conscious or unconscious mental processes. In this entry we focus on this third sense, as it constitutes the most original contribution of film studies to the renewal of rhetoric.

Christian Metz introduced the debate with his essay 'Metaphor / Metonymy, or the Imaginary Referent' (1982), based on linguistic and psychoanalytic studies of rhetorical figures. Many scholars commented on Metz's arguments during the 1980s, and pointed out both the limits and the potentiality of his essay. However, the most radical criticisms of Metz's work (as well as a more profitable recovery) were made in the 1990s, after the so-called 'visual turn'.

## Metaphor, metonymy, condensation, displacement

Linguist Roman Jakobson (1956) argues that each utterance requires two operations: the 'selection' of units within a repository of possibilities, and their 'combination' in the context of a discourse. Therefore, every word is related to the other units of language on the basis of two sets of relationships: 'substitution' and 'contexture'.

Within each set, two kinds of relations are possible: similarity or contiguity. On the axis of selection, the words are linked by similarity (I can say 'fire' instead of 'gaslight') or by contiguity, spatial, temporal, and causal (I can say 'glass' for 'window'). Otherwise, on the axis of combination, the connections of concepts in the discourse can be made by similarity (as in poetry) or by contiguity (as in narrative prose or film). There are, therefore, two methods of connecting words and concepts; Jakobson uses rhetorical terms and calls them respectively 'metaphor' (connection by similarity) and 'metonymy' (connection by contiguity).

Lacan (2006, originally published in 1966) recovers some of Jakobson's ideas in the context of his own rethinking of Freud's theories. Lacan argues that Freud's concept of the unconscious is to be reformulated as 'the Other's discourse' (436); that is, a discourse uttered by a subject other than ourselves who nevertheless is 'the core of our being' (437). The laws of the unconscious are manifested especially in the analysis of dreams. Here the discourse of the unconscious appears as a flow of signifiers (equivalent to letters and words of verbal discourse) which refer to their meanings through two major operations of distortion (Freud's concept of *Entstellung*): 'displacement' (*Verschiebung*) and 'condensation' (*Verdichtung*). As the unconscious is identified with a discourse, and since this discourse is essentially modelled on verbal speech, Lacan identifies displacement with metonymy and condensation with metaphor. More generally, Lacan assimilates metonymy into the wish or desire, as a force of constant and infinite progress which moves the discourse of the unconscious, and metaphor into the symptom, as a form of expression which can use either the body or the words of the subject (for example, in slips of the tongue or jokes).

Lyotard (2011, originally published in 1971) radically criticized Lacan's thesis from a philosophical point of view. According to Lyotard, two opposite types of spaces are present in written text: the 'discourse', represented by the conceptual and formal entity of the letter, and the 'figure', linked to the energetic and innovative line. Western culture has been dominated by the model of knowledge and thought of the discourse (logocentrism); indeed, the figure has intervened just to distort the forms of discourse with its vital strength (for example, in medieval miniatures, graphic experiments of Mallarmé, drawings by Paul Klee, etc.). Lyotard identifies the figure with Freud's psychic primary processes (*Primär-vorgang*) and the discourse with the secondary processes (*Sekundärvorgang*): the figure is the blind and free energy of the unconscious desire, which the discourse must 'bind' and organize at a conscious level.

From this point of view, the unconscious and the dream cannot be assimilated to a discourse whose model is verbal speech – as in Lacan's theory. The unconscious is purely figurative and a-discursive, while the 'dream-work' (Freud's *Traumarbeit*) is the distortion of the traces of secondary materials (discourse) handled by the primary process (figure). Lacan, by recovering Jakobson's linguistic categories, confuses the 'signified' with the 'signification', that is the meaning as formally encoded with the meaning as constantly reinvented.

## Christian Metz's 'Metaphor / Metonymy, or the Imaginary Referent'

In his essay, Metz applies the ideas of Jakobson, Lacan, and Lyotard to film studies. This shift of concepts is legitimized by a homology between verbal utterances, the unconscious, and films; indeed, these three 'machines' all adopt the same operating principle: the discourse. Metz exposes this framework both in the introduction and in the conclusion of his essay.

In the first part of the essay, Metz discusses Jakobson's ideas. He introduces a distinction that is not always so clear in Jakobson. On the one hand, there are the modes of appearance of linguistic terms within the discursive string (i.e. the 'positional' or 'discursive' axis, also called 'syntagm' by structural linguistics). On the other hand, there are the kinds of relationship between their meanings (i.e. the 'semantic' or 'referential' axis, or 'paradigm'). Metaphor and metonymy are defined within the referential axis: in the case of metaphor, we find a relation of 'comparability' (a term which Metz prefers to that of Jakobson's 'similarity') between meanings; otherwise, in the case of metonymy we find relations of 'contiguity'. Yet, the two rhetorical figures may have different positions within the discursive axis. Here, Metz retains the same locutions of 'contiguity' and 'similarity', not without a slight confusion and imprecision; accordingly, he defines 'discourse contiguity' as the presence of two contiguous terms of the rhetorical figure within the discursive chain, and 'discourse comparability' as the substitution of one term by another.

A typology with four terms derives from here: (1) 'Referential comparability and discursive contiguity, that is, a metaphor presented syntagmatically' (189): for example, the flock of sheep juxtaposed to a crowd of workers in the opening of Charlie Chaplin's *Modern Times* (1936). (2) 'Referential comparability and discursive comparability. This is the metaphor presented paradigmatically' (189). For instance, the stereotyped representation of flames in the place of a love scene. (3) 'Referential contiguity and discursive comparability, or metonymy presented paradigmatically' (190), as in the case of the lost balloon which stands for the murdered child in Fritz Lang's *M* (1931). (4) 'Referential contiguity and discursive contiguity, or metonymy presented syntagmatically' (190), as in the preceding images of the same film, when we see the child still alive and holding the balloon.

In the second part of the essay, Metz discusses the psychoanalytical approach to rhetoric. First, he borrows the Freudian distinction between primary and secondary processes; furthermore, he borrows from Lyotard the equivalence between the primary processes and linguistic innovations, on the one hand, and the secondary processes and coding, on the other. However, in contrast to Lyotard (and in the wake of Lacan) Metz believes that the two processes are not reciprocally opposite and isolated. On the contrary, innovation and coding define a common space of mutual action: 'the word then appears as a secondarised deposit – this is the moment of the code – forever "positioned" between two primary forces of attraction, one of which has preceded it in the history of the language, the other (the same one, resurrected) having the capacity to "take it back" at any moment, in poetry, in dreams, in spontaneous conversation, and set in motion again' (240).

Second, Metz discusses the concepts of condensation and displacement. In this case his thinking deviates from Lacan, as Metz argues that the two concepts cannot be identified with metaphor and metonymy. Indeed, condensation and displacement are kinds of movement of meaning – that is, ways of building relationships between referential elements – while the rhetorical figures are the results of such movements and processes. As a consequence, we can find both a movement of condensation which produces a metonymy (e.g. when the image of a face overlaps with that of the subject's recollections) and a movement of displacement which produces a metaphor (e.g. when a tracking shot or an editing cut puts a human face and a resembling animal side by side).

In conclusion, psychoanalytic tools provide two new axes for the analysis of filmic figures. Scholars have to situate figures 'in relation to four independent axes: any one figure is secondarised to a greater or lesser extent; closer to the metaphor, or closer to metonymy; manifests condensation especially or displacement especially, or an intimate combination of the two operations; is syntagmatic or paradigmatic' (275). As an example, Metz analyses the lap-dissolve.

In the final part of his long essay, Metz observes a further possibility: that condensation and displacement operate directly on the visual signifier. In this case 'a semantic trajectory brings about an alteration, however slight or localised, in a previously constituted and stable unit of signifier' (284). In other words, we find a manipulation of the visual signifier which de-secondarizes already coded figures. Regarding this point, Metz reapproaches Lyotard's key idea: primary processes directly work on and distort the products of secondary processes in a creative and unusual way.

## The development of the debate

Marc Vernet claims that Metz's essay has been little utilized within film theory (1990, 223). Nevertheless, many scholars discussed the essay during the 1980s.

Williams (1981) retrieves Metz's categories within her analysis of surrealist films; at the same time she revisits many of Metz's positions. First, not all films are homologous to the discourse of the unconscious: surrealist films reproduce the dynamics of dream better than ordinary fiction movies. Second, this peculiarity is due to the disturbed hierarchy between 'figures' and 'diegesis' (that is the usually coherent fictional narrative world): 'the peculiar emphasis of figure over diegesis ... reverses the usual function of the figure in narrative film' (214). Thanks to such proceedings, the 'figures of desire' rework and distort the film diegesis. Williams then borrows Lyotard's opposition between discourse and figure; however, she replaces the verbal with the narrative on the side of discourse, and the iconic with the rhetorical on the side of the figural.

Andrew (1984) also points out, in opposition to Metz, the value of 'innovation' of filmic rhetorical figures, with particular reference to metaphor. Andrew borrows from the French philosopher Paul Ricoeur the idea that metaphor constitutes an event of reconfiguration and reinvention of the discursive semantic spaces. In this sense, 'we may say that metaphor can occur as the calculated introduction of dissonance into any stage of the film process [i.e.] into perception, signification, structure, adaptation and genre' (Andrew 1984, 167). As a consequence, metaphor shifts the theory from the structural approach of the 1970s, such as that of Metz, to a hermeneutic one: 'structuralism will not recognize the event of cinematic discourse. It will always and only provide a description of the system, which is put into use in the event. If, as I claim with Ricoeur, the system is altered by the event, if (to make a stronger claim) the system was born and exists only as a residue of such events of figuration, then we need a broader vision of the creation of meaning in films' (170).

## Rhetorical figures and film after the 'visual turn'

During the 1990s, the humanities were involved in a 'visual' or 'pictorial' turn. Within this new framework, images are studied as spaces of development and manifestation of invisible forces and events, such as sensory, mental, psychic, or intellectual processes. Hence, the logocentrism is radically deconstructed: image produces signification by its own means; it neither reproduces verbal signification, nor needs to distort verbal discourse (as Lyotard thought). This new intellectual environment has had a contradictory effect on Metz's positions. On the one hand, it implies a critique of the transfer of linguistic–rhetorical categories to the film; on the other hand, however, the visual turn allows film scholars to recast several issues introduced by Metz.

In this respect Aumont's (1996, especially chap. 8) is an exemplary intervention. He insists that images, and therefore films, 'think': images are sensory and material objects that are able to visualize the process of creating, combining, manipulating concepts. Aumont calls this force of thought of the image 'figure'. The film work is figural and figurative: therefore, film produces concepts.

However, Aumont distinguishes between the term 'figure' as designating iconic, material objects and the same term as referring to rhetorical tropes: in particular, Aumont traces (in the wake of the philologist Eric Auerbach) two different developments of the same term. Moreover, figural processes of signification are completely independent from verbal rhetoric.

In conclusion, most recent interventions radicalize both Metz's intuitions and the critiques of the 1980s scholars. As a consequence, they recast the rhetoric of film in two respects. First, they locate processes of meaning on the filmic signifiers, which are seen in all their sensory richness and conceptual inventiveness. Second, they transform the kind of relationship between film and psychic processes. This relationship is no longer based on homology, but on causation: film figures neither reproduce nor reveal psychic process; they produce and drive the movements of thinking. Using the key terms of this entry, we can say that the relationship between cinema and thought has shifted from a metaphorical to a metonymical position. On this basis, the project of a new rhetoric of film is still largely to be built.

RUGGERO EUGENI

## Works cited

Andrew, Dudley. 1984. *Concepts in Film Theory*. New York: Oxford University Press.

Aumont, Jacques. 1996. *A quoi pensent les films?* Paris: Séguier.

Bordwell, David. 1989. *Making Meaning: Inference and Rhetoric in the Interpretation of Cinema*. Cambridge, MA: Harvard University Press.

Chatman, Seymour. 1990. *Coming to Terms: The Narrative Rhetoric in Fiction and Film*. Ithaca, NY: Cornell University Press.

Jakobson, Roman. 1956. 'Two Aspects of Language and Two Types of Aphasic Disturbance'. In *Fundamentals of Language*, edited by Roman Jakobson and Morris Halle, 55–82. The Hague: Mouton & Co.

Lacan, Jacques. 2006. 'The Instance of the Letter in the Unconscious or Reason since Freud'. In *Écrits: The First Complete Edition in English*, translated by Bruce Fink, Héloïse Fink, and Russel Grigg, 412–41. New York: Norton & Co.

Lyotard, Jean-François. 2011. *Discourse, Figure*. Translated by Antony Hudek and Mary Lydon. Minneapolis: University of Minnesota Press.

Metz, Christian. 1982. 'Metaphor / Metonymy, or the Imaginary Referent'. In *The Imaginary Signifier: Psychoanalysis and the Cinema*, translated by Celia Britton and Annwyll Williams, 149–314. Bloomington: Indiana University Press.

Plantinga, Carl R. 1997. *Rhetoric and Representation in Nonfiction Film*. Cambridge: Cambridge University Press.

Vernet, Marc. 1990. 'Le figural et le figuratif, ou le référent symbolique'. In *Christian Metz et la théorie du cinéma*, edited by Michel Marie and Marc Vernet, 223–34. Paris: Klincksieck.

Williams, Linda. 1981. *Figures of Desire: A Theory and Analysis of Surrealist Film*. Berkeley: University of California Press.

## Further reading

Blakesley, David, ed. 2003. *The Terministic Screen: Rhetorical Perspectives on Film*. Carbondale: Southern Illinois Press.

# SCEPTICISM

The exploration of diffuse borders between reality and illusion, fact and fiction, the waking state and dreaming, certainty and doubt are integral narrative and aesthetic traditions throughout the history of cinema. From the stage-magician-turned-filmmaker George Méliès through the art-house cinema of Federico Fellini, Michelangelo Antonioni, and David Lynch to the alternative mainstream films of Christopher Nolan, filmmakers have experimented with cinema's potential to manipulate cinematically rendered impressions of reality, and they have exploited the affinity of human beings to mistake daydreaming, fantasy, or hallucination for reality.

While silent films like *The Cabinet of Dr. Caligari* or *Sherlock Jr.* focus on characters who confuse their dreams or hallucinations with reality, contemporary films like *The Matrix*, *The Truman Show*, or *The Island* shift the focus to ontological questions about the 'reality' of reality by locating their unwitting film characters in artificial or even simulated environments. *Inception* revolves around the idea that it is possible to enter the dream worlds of others – shared environments which can resemble real life to such an extent that eventually it becomes nearly impossible to distinguish dreaming from a waking state.

Such films directly or indirectly address the perennial problem of philosophical *scepticism*. This doctrine raises the possibility that (1) the world we believe we are living in and that we believe to know things about might not be the way we think it is, and that (2) our limited human perspective on the world might prevent us from discovering how the world truly is. The first option can be called ontological scepticism because it raises doubts about the properties or even the existence of the world; the second option can be called epistemological scepticism because it raises doubts about the reliability or sufficiency of our claims to know the world.

Cinema relates to scepticist concerns in at least two ways. First, films such as the ones mentioned explore the theme of a gap between reality and human notions of reality. Second, the process of filmmaking and the medium's basic properties raise fundamental questions about the relationship between the 'reality' of created filmic worlds and the (physical) reality of its machinery, creators, and spectators, as well as raising questions about the meaning of the term 'reality' itself when applied to cinema.

Film theorists like Bazin, Kracauer, and Epstein implicitly or explicitly address the analogy between film and scepticism. They are fascinated by the notion that the (photographic) camera might be able to 'bridge' the gap between the world 'in all its virginal purity' (Bazin 1967, 15) and the imperfect, incomplete, or inaccurate world-view of its human inhabitants. In the 1970s, the French film theorist Jean-Louis Baudry illustrated his account of cinema as a *dispositif* by claiming a close analogy between the situation of the

413

film spectator in a dark theatre and the situation of prisoners trapped in a cave watching moving shadows in the famous Allegory of the Cave elaborated by the Greek philosopher Plato (*see* APPARATUS THEORY [PLATO]; APPARATUS THEORY [BAUDRY]).

## Cavell

Baudry's analogy suggests that cinema and scepticism are partly correlated because cinema *screens* reality, and that this screened reality differs from whatever it is that we call the real world. According to this notion, in cinema reality is transformed into something else, and it becomes a task of film theory to ask what it is that reality is transformed into in cinema. Alternatively, one can try to find reasons why the notion that cinema 'screens' reality is misinformed. The film philosopher Stanley Cavell subscribes to the former task in his book-long film-philosophical essay *The World Viewed*, often characterized as 'the last great work of classical film theory' (Rodowick 2007, 79), by asking: 'What happens to reality when it is projected and screened?' (Cavell 1979, 16).

Cavell plays with the ambiguity of the English word 'screen', which can both be used as a verb ('to screen [out]') and as a substantive ('a screen'): He describes the screen of the movie theatre as a double 'barrier' (24) between the fictional film world and the world of the audience: it 'screens me from the world it holds that is, makes me invisible. And it screens that world from me – that is, screens its existence from me' (24). One might call this the ontological Janus-face of cinema: it screens a reality which is both present and absent (to its audience). On the one hand, this reality is *present* to an audience while the latter is 'invisible' to the characters/actors of the fictional world projected on the screen. On the other hand, the screened reality of the film is simultaneously absent from the audience, precisely *because* it is a projected (and not simply reproduced or re-presented) world which has been thought up, recorded, and assembled in another space and time. Audiences are therefore *ontologically absent* to film reality by occupying a different ontologi-cal or spatial realm and *temporally absent* due to the temporal difference between assemblage and screening of a film. Paradoxically, however, simultaneously the film world is present to its audience when (literally) screened.

These remarks on the simultaneous presence and absence of screened reality prepare Cavell's explicit correlation of film and scepticism later in the book, where he states that 'film is a moving image of scepticism: not only is there a reasonable possibility, it is a fact that here our normal senses are satisfied of reality while reality does not exist – even, alarmingly, *because* it does not exist, because viewing it is all it takes' (Cavell 1979, 188f.).

According to this, it is the (basic) properties of the *medium* of film, its peculiar mechanism of screening reality, which render it a moving image of scepticism, not the phenomenon that individual films deal with scepticism.

Cavell grounds his claim on an analogy between film perception and reality perception as envisioned by a scepticist. In both cases 'our normal senses are satisfied of reality while reality does not exist'. Accordingly, film as well as the world we live in cause sensory per-ceptions which are – a further step Cavell does not explicitly mention here – interpreted as being 'of' reality. But 'outside' of our sensory perceptions this reality, in fact, does not exist in that form. In other words, for our senses, being satisfied of reality is all that is required in order for us to make-believe that whatever they are perceptions 'of' is real. But for Cavell, in cinema it is even 'a fact', not only a possibility, that reality does not exist. Strictly speaking, film reality does not 'exist' apart from its being perceived. That's why, as Cavell claims, 'viewing [reality] is all it takes' in order to render film a 'moving image of scepticism'.

A few sentences later, Cavell reflects further on cinema's ambiguous relation to reality: 'In screening reality, film screens its givenness from us; it holds reality from us, it holds reality before us, i.e. withholds reality before us. We are tantalized at once by our subjection to it and by its subjection to our views of it' (Cavell 1979, 189). Here, Cavell deliberately exploits the ambiguity of the word 'to screen', but his extensive use of various prepositions does not exactly aim at clarification. Important, however, is the notion of a mutual dependency between film spectators and the reality screened for/before/from/to them: spectators are subjected to a screened reality they cannot actually interact with, but this reality is subjected to its spectators since it becomes 'actualized' or 'to life' only qua the spectators' 'views of it'.

The subjection of the film world is not the only limitation imposed on film. There is also the epistemic limitation of the camera, as Cavell notes:

> I am content to proceed on the assumption that the camera is no better off epistemologically or scientifically than the naked eye – that the camera provides views of reality only on the assumption that we normally do, apart from the camera, see reality, i.e. see live persons and real things in actual spaces.
>
> (Cavell 1979, 192f.)

Cavell is basically asserting that from an epistemological perspective the film camera is on a par with the naked (human) eye: both simply provide views of reality. And the camera can only do so if we, too, normally 'see live persons and real things in actual space'. The camera, though generating film as a moving image of scepticism, thus does not answer, overcome, or solve the scepticist dilemma.

So, for Cavell, film is a moving image of scepticism because its recording mechanisms and viewing conditions are analogous to the everyday situation claimed by sceptical positions. However, one could also claim that the very fact that the world of the film is *constituted* by the possibility of spectating it subverts Cavell's analogy, since traditional scepticist worries are directed at the correspondence between our notions of the world and the factual constitution of that world. If the subsistence of the film world depends on its presence to at least one spectator, the analogy between film and scepticism fails at this point because the philosophical scepticist's worry is precisely that we are not able to grasp the world that exists *independently of us* (only extreme scepticist positions, idealism, challenge the *existence* of such a world). This would be a possible starting point for a critical discussion of Cavell's analogy.

## Animation

Cavell's philosophy of film, while essentially a philosophy of the ontological implications of the experience and memory of films, is intricately tailored to the conditions of analogue filmmaking, to the indexical relation between the world and its audiovisual traces on a celluloid film strip. But how do Cavell's reflections stand the test of time with the rise of digital cinema in the twenty-first century, which profoundly changed the ontological correlation between the image and its (digitally) captured objects as well as the way in which films are produced, marketed, and screened to audiences? (*See* DIGITAL CINEMA; ONTOLOGY OF THE PHOTOGRAPHIC IMAGE; REPRESENTATION.)

Cavell does not address this issue in *The World Viewed*, the second, enlarged edition of which was published in 1979, nor in his later writings on film. However, in the section 'More of *The World Viewed*' (Cavell 1979, 162–230), he discusses a criticism launched by film scholar Alexander Sesonske against Cavell's claim that the 'material basis of the media of movies' consists in 'a succession of automatic world projections' (167). Cavell sees films as 'projections of the real world' (167), but this, as Sesonske points out, excludes the popular genre of the animated cartoon. The Cavell–Sesonske discussion provides a shop window view of a 'digital version' of Cavell's film ontology under the assumption that animated cartoons share basic features with forms of digital cinema, such as extensive use of animated elements, which in turn have a weaker indexical relation (or none whatsoever) to whatever it is we call reality.

Sesonske argues that the world and characters of animated cartoons 'never existed until they were projected on the screen' (quoted in Cavell 1979, 167). They exist only '*now*, at the moment of projection' (quoted in Cavell 1979, 168), and this differs profoundly from the experience of the projected world of a real-footage film. In animated film, '[t]here is *a* world we experience here, but not *the* world – a world I know and see but to which I am nevertheless not present, yet not a world past' (quoted in Cavell 1979, 168).

For Cavell, animated cartoons are indeed not 'successions of automatic world projections' but rather 'successions of animated world projections' (Cavell 1979, 13), whose animated characters – contrary to real-footage film – 'abrogat[e] … corporeality' (170). For Cavell, the audience's temporal absence from the world projected on screen is what makes films philosophically special (155). He is fascinated by the movies' ability to make *present* (in both senses of the word) a world which has, in whatever form, existed in the past. The world of a real-footage film is not entirely invented; it draws on, re-combines, fictionalizes, and elevates into a different ontological dimension actual elements of the world. The status of animated cartoons in Cavell's film ontology thus depends on the definition of the term 'world projections' as either 'projections of *the* world' or 'projections of *a* world'.

Cavell does not assume a definite position on animated cartoons, since, first, he is not interested in a comprehensive, i.e. essentialist, definition of the medium of movies ('the answer [to the question "what is the essence of movies?"] seems to me more or less empty' [Cavell 1979, 165]), and, second, he is rather interested in the '*role* reality plays in this art' (165). And the role it plays for Cavell is intricately connected to the *experience* of movies as the unique experience of a world *past*, a world which is already gone.

Cavell's conception of cinema can hardly explain the ontological and epistemological implications of present-day digital cinema, which is often an indiscernible mix of real footage and animated footage. The integral role of animation in digital cinema challenges Cavell's philosophy of film, which works with a narrow set of realist or neorealist films or character-centred screwball comedies, all of which deliberately avoid extensive use of visual effects and props.

## Rodowick and digital cinema

How does digital cinema change the ontology of film and the 'material basis of the movies'? Despite being a book on the fate of (analogue) film theory in the age of digital computation of the (cinematic) image, David Rodowick's *The Virtual Life of Film* is to a large extent also a meditation on Cavell's *The World Viewed*. For Rodowick, a committed cinéphile, the vanishing of the celluloid film strip entails a radical shift in the character of film: in digital cinema, the indexical, recorded photographic image is replaced by 'a computational simulation that enables new forms and modalities of creative activity' (Rodowick 2007, 184), since whatever a digital photographic lens captures is immediately 'transcod[ed]' (117) into computational language. Real-world input captured by a lens becomes ontologically on a par with animated or graphic material – and thus, in comparison to analogue photography, easier to manipulate (even though not necessarily manipulable).

Since digital technology now dominates all forms of image and sound capture, cinema has become part of a wider-ranging digital screen culture, which has almost completely intruded on and restructured our everyday lives, and populated it with interactive computer and tablet screens. This radically affects our relation to the world we live in (our *Lebenswelt*), and consequently our ontologies, since 'the material content of physical reality is not simply nature but rather what phenomenology calls the *Lebenswelt*: the global accumulation of the events, actions, activities, and contingencies of everyday life, an asubjective world overwhelming individual perception and consciousness' (Rodowick 2007, 77).

The new 'transcoded ontologies' (174) which influence the *Lebenswelt* create an array of often virtual (or at least simulated) events, actions, activities, and contingencies of everyday life which do not have a direct correlation to the material content of physical reality, and they raise fundamental questions about the 'epistemological and ethical relations to the world and to collective life [which these] simulation automatisms presuppose' (174). Rodowick invokes the philosopher Roger Scruton in suggesting that 'what fades in film is the historical dimension of photographic causality' (86), while digital images become 'the art of synthesizing imaginary worlds' (87) – worlds which are 'less anchored to the prior existence of things and people' (86). Méliès trumps Lumière.

Rodowick is perhaps most indebted to Cavell in this appreciation of film's intricate connection to the real world: film 'relied on a perception of the shared duration of people and things as expressed in the condition of analogy' (179). But where for Cavell film is a moving image of scepticism, for Rodowick analogue film *overcame* scepticism because – unlike painting or other arts – it automatically records the duration of events in the world and does not merely render a *re*-presentation of it. The film recording in its analogue condition reassures us of the existential fact that there *is*, or at least was, a spatio-temporal world, and it allows us to explore and reflect on this world without being directly immersed in it. Digital screen technology still provides this opportunity – but the ontological intimacy of the digital with its projected world is weaker than in analogue cinema. Digitality does not assure us of the prior existence of the projected world, and hence 'is not an overcoming of scepticism, but a different expression of it' (175).

So, in the digital era, with its interactive screen technologies, the problem of scepticism is reformulated. The problem of knowledge of the world gives way to the problem of other minds: in a society governed by constant indirect interaction via computing devices there can be no final reassurance about the identity of the users of the interfaces we interact with. Consequently, the digital paves the way to a sort of 'acceptance of scepticism' which updates Cavell's claim:

> In the world of computers and the Internet, we have little doubt about the presence of other minds and, perhaps, other worlds. And we believe, justifiably or not … in our ability to control, manage or communicate with other minds and

worlds, but at a price: matter and minds have become 'information'. In this sense, the cultural dominance of the digital may indicate a philosophical retreat from the problem of scepticism to an acceptance of scepticism. For in the highly mutable communities forged by computer-mediated communications, the desire to know the world has lost its provocation and its uncertainty. Rather, one seeks new ways of acknowledging other minds, without knowing whether other selves are behind them.

(Rodowick 2007, 175)

Where before knowledge was, metaphorically speaking, in the possession of the world that we insufficiently tried to grasp, it is now computer technology which is the keeper of the kind of knowledge the sceptic yearns for:

Our disappointment in failing ever to know the world or others now becomes the perpetual disappointment of failing to attain the more nearly perfect (future) knowledge of computers and computer communications, whose technological evolution always seems to run ahead of the perceptual and cognitive capacity to manipulate them for our own ends.

(Rodowick 2007, 176)

As the composition of our *Lebenswelt* changes, so does the concept of knowledge and its attainability from which arise the various forms of scepticism. Rodowick downgrades the epistemological dimension of scepticism in favour of more existential questions which surround the emergence of digital screen culture. The digital world radically postpones the question of the human relation to the world 'as it is' – simply because the digital world is never 'as it is' because it is in a permanent state of (unforeseeable) transformation. It is created by the 'intervention' of the human hand, and its computational character entails that it is always changing, always being reconfigured. Thus the nature of scepticism is always changing, or else no longer matters.

PHILIPP SCHMERHEIM

## Works cited

Bazin, André. 1967 [1945]. 'The Ontology of the Photographic Image'. In *What Is Cinema?*, vol. I, translated by Hugh Gray, 9–15. Berkeley: University of California Press.
Cavell, Stanley. 1979. *The World Viewed: Reflections on the Ontology of Film*. Enlarged edition. Cambridge, MA: Harvard University Press.
Rodowick, David N. 2007. *The Virtual Life of Film*. Cambridge, MA: Harvard University Press.

## Further reading

Baudry, Jean-Louis. 1986. 'Ideological Effects of the Basic Cinematographic Apparatus' [orig. 1970] and 'The Apparatus: Metapsychological Approaches to the Impression of Reality in Cinema' [orig. 1975]. In *Narrative, Apparatus, Ideology*, edited by Philip Rosen, 286–318. New York: Columbia University Press. [Develops the analogy between the cinematic apparatus and Plato's Allegory of the Cave.]
Cavell, Stanley. 1979. *The Claim of Reason: Wittgenstein, Skepticism, Morality, and Tragedy*. New York: Oxford University Press. [Cavell's influential but notoriously inaccessible magnum opus on philosophical scepticism.]

——. 2005. *Cavell on Film*. Edited and with an introduction by William Rothman. Albany, NY: State University of New York Press. [This almost complete selection of Cavell's film-theoretical and film-philosophical articles is a good introduction to his thought on film.]

Deleuze, Gilles. 1986. *Cinema 1: The Movement-Image*. Translated by Hugh Tomlinson and Barbara Habberjam. London: The Athlone Press; 1989. *Cinema 2: The Time-Image*. Translated by Hugh Tomlinson and Robert Galeta. London: The Athlone Press. [Together with Cavell, the most influential philosopher of film. Deleuze does not directly address scepticism but claims that the 'power of modern cinema' lies in its ability to '[r]estor[e] our belief in the world' (*Cinema 2*, p. 166) which was lost in the modern world.]

Manovich, Lev. 2001. *The Language of New Media*. Cambridge, MA: MIT Press. [Influential work on digital cinema and a main point of reference in Rodowick's book.]

Rothman, William, and Marian Keane. 2000. *Reading Cavell's* The World Viewed*: A Philosophical Perspective on Film*. Detroit, MI: Wayne State University. [Page-by-page exegesis of Cavell's book.]

Turvey, Malcolm. 2008. *Doubting Vision: Film and the Revelationist Tradition*. New York: Oxford University Press. [Accurately unveils the scepticist underpinnings of classical film theory.]

Wartenberg, Thomas E. 2007. *Thinking on Screen: Film as Philosophy*. New York: Routledge. [Chapter 4 contains a wonderful analysis of 'A Skeptical Thought Experiment: *The Matrix*'.]

# SEEING/PERCEIVING

In the mid-1980s, a small group of film theorists proposed that cognitive science might offer a productive path towards illuminating how we engage with cinema, and why movies tell stories in the way they do. For example, in *Narration in the Fiction Film* (1985) David Bordwell used cognitive science to demonstrate how a film spectator is cued by a film rather than positioned by it. Noël Carroll proposed in his 1985 essay 'The Power of Movies' that commercial, mass-consumed movies are easy to engage with because they seamlessly interface with our perceptual systems (Carroll 1996) (*see* COGNITIVE FILM THEORY).

Joseph Anderson's book *The Reality of Illusion: An Ecological Approach to Cognitive Film Theory* (1996) expanded on Carroll's claim that filmic perception depends very little on specialized code-reading, offering a comprehensive account of cinematic perception and comprehension within the framework of James J. Gibson's ecological approach to cognitive psychology – an influential theory that places human perceptual capacities in an evolutionary context. The following will outline Anderson's model of filmic perception along with some critiques of his theory.

## Ecological theory of perception

Anderson's *The Reality of Illusion* explores the evolutionary development of human eyes and minds, and how this development has shaped film style and storytelling. He approaches this topic by following Gibson's proposal that all the capacities humans developed for perceiving the world were tailored towards survival during our long history as hunter-gatherers. Charles Darwin's theory of evolution explains how nature selects those individuals who are most suited to their surroundings; those who can survive the climate, catch and digest food, evade predators, and find a mate will survive and produce offspring with the same abilities, which are enhanced and refined over time.

Our perceptual systems, according to Gibson's ecological theory, were developed in the same way. For example, a creature with simple visual sensitivities which can discern shadows and light from darkness is more likely to escape from potential predators than an organism with no visual faculties. Likewise, evolution favours those with developed cognitive skills who can make sense out of their surroundings by gauging the intentions of others and understanding causal relationships between events. By such a process of perceptual and cognitive evolution, humans have acquired a complex and well-integrated system with which to engage with the natural world. Ultimately, this leads to visual and auditory abilities, and it also factors in to more complex facilities such as narrative comprehension and character engagement.

Anderson summarizes Gibson's position by commenting that 'our brains and sensory systems, indeed our very consciousness, our sense of self, our mind in all its implications, is the present result of past evolution, when our capacities were being cruelly sorted by the processes of natural selection, [and] the contingencies of existence were quite different from what they are today' (Anderson 1996, 13–14). Our relationship with motion pictures, then, can be understood as 'ancient biology interfacing with recent technology' (28).

The subject of depiction, including depiction within cinema, raises questions for the ecological model of perception, since films operate as a man-made, surrogate environment and exploit our evolved perceptual facilities in a distinctive way. The perception and comprehension of motion pictures may be understood as a subset of perception and comprehension in general, since it is non-veridical and artificially constructed. Anderson suggests that once we begin to understand how our perceptual systems work in the natural environment, we can also start to understand how we engage with the constructed, surrogate environments found in films. An ecological theory of film perception, then, must be grounded in a broader theory of how we perceive the world in general – not just for vision, but also for narrative comprehension and involvement with characters. While we interact with motion pictures in many of the same ways we interact with the natural world, studying the ways in which filmmakers evoke surrogate environments may provide insight into the nature of the evolved mind.

In summary, Anderson adopts Gibson's ecological model of perception and comprehension to understand some of the ways we respond to the manufactured world of film. Anderson discusses the perception of cinema by examining the evolved habits of mind that were developed to survive and engage with the natural world.

## Joseph Anderson's *The Reality of Illusion*

Chapter 1 of Anderson's book outlines the differences between cognitive theory and other approaches within film studies. The second and third chapters build an understanding of the ecology of cinema – that is, the manner in which film was developed to suit the auditory and visual systems of humans. Chapters four and five address perception (i.e. the reception of information in the form of stimuli) by exploring visual perception (flicker, motion, form, depth, and colour) and sound and image relations (synchrony, sound effects, and music); chapters six to nine discuss cognition (the higher processing of information) by exploring continuity, diegesis, character engagement, and narrative comprehension. As an illustration of his approach, I will focus on Anderson's discussion of visual perception in chapter four. Here, Anderson considers questions that have caught the attention of film scholars, such as how it is possible for a succession of still frames to create a compelling illusion of smooth, continuous motion. Also, what is the nature of depth in the motion picture, and is perspective a convention of culture?

To put vision into an ecological context, Anderson explains that the origins of the human visual system vastly pre-date the emergence of humans. To hunt successfully and move with agility, animals needed accurate information about their surroundings. By the time that humans emerged, the visual system in mammals was fundamentally in place, and the central organizing principle was *veridicality*, meaning that an individual's perception of their surroundings had to be a close approximation to what was there. If an organism's perceptions were not sufficiently accurate, the consequences were severe – a creature's chances of survival and reproduction would be diminished if it could not detect and evade potential predators. Likewise, if it were not accurate in locating its prey, it would starve and so would its offspring.

Although perceptual development has tended towards veridicality, we still have non-veridical perceptions, or *illusions*. Not only do we hallucinate when drugged or deranged, and experience visions when we dream or meditate, but we also experience illusions when we are awake and sceptical. For instance, we may perceive depth on a flat surface when the visual system, following its own internal instructions, arrives at a percept that is in error when compared to physical reality. For perceptual psychologists and those who seek to understand motion picture viewing, illusions are of special interest because they reveal the ordinarily invisible rules according to which the perceptual system functions.

One widely recognized illusion is the impression of movement that is evoked by the presentation of still images in rapid succession. In outlining motion perception, Anderson explains that film originally ran at 40 frames per second (fps) to minimize flicker. In seeking an economical alternative, the technicians at Edison films discovered in the late nineteenth century that 16fps was the lowest frame rate they could use without perceiving a distracting flicker. Since projectors were hand-cranked, however, this produced annoying fluctuations in the image between motion and flickering. The frame rate was finally raised to 24fps, and this became the industry standard. This convention came about through trial and error together with convenience and economy. While the technicians at Edison films knew little about the mechanisms of visual perception, it was the human perceptual system that set the lower limits for the operation of cinematic projection.

Within Anderson's ecological model, the viewer and filmmaker are characterized in a unique way. The viewer can be thought of as a standard biological audio/video processor, and '[the] central processing unit, the brain along with its sensory modules, is standard. The same model with only minor variations is issued to everyone. The basic operating system is also standard and universal, for both the brain and its functions were created over 150 million years of mammalian evolution' (Anderson 1996, 12). Filmmakers may be understood as 'programmers' who develop programs to run on a computer that they do not understand, and whose operating systems were designed for another purpose. Anderson states that '[since] the filmmakers/programmers do not understand the operating system, they are never sure exactly what will happen with any frame or sequence of their programs. They therefore proceed by trial and error. They follow certain filmic conventions and then go beyond them by guessing' (13).

To summarize, Anderson claims that the perception of motion pictures is non-veridical (i.e. it does not coincide with reality); narrative films function as surrogates for the physical world, in which we apply many commonplace perceptual and cognitive facilities developed during evolution; and filmmakers can be understood as practical psychologists who intuitively attempt to interface with evolved habits of mind, even if they do not understand the underlying mechanisms.

## Criticisms of and alternatives to Anderson's ecological model

At the time *The Reality of Illusion* was written, Anderson's ecological discussion of film perception was unique in the sense that it did not offer, nor did it attempt to provide, a discussion of cultural, historical, or political influences on film and its viewers. Anderson's book consciously framed itself as an alternative to psychoanalytic, Marxist, feminist, and semiotic film theories. It also offered a unique perspective among other cognitive works of film scholarship. However, influential cognitive film scholars, such as Bordwell, have written about narrative comprehension, Murray Smith (1995) has explored emotional responses to fictional characters, and Ed Tan (1996) has provided a more general study of viewers' emotional responses to cinema. Recently, Greg Smith (2003), Torben Grodal (2009), and Carl Plantinga (2009) have discussed affective responses to narrative cinema. The central goal of Anderson's cognitive discussion of film perception was to demonstrate how it meshed with our perceptual and cognitive endowment in a systematic manner, through Gibson's ecological model.

Some of the criticisms levelled at *The Reality of Illusion* are carried over from Gibson's ecological theory, rather than being unique to Anderson's argument. David Large (1997), for example, comments that while Anderson regards the ecological approach as a metatheory of cognitive theories, it is a controversial position that needs significant elaboration, since the ecological approach has not found universal favour among contemporary cognitive psychologists and philosophers. In addition to this, the ecological model claims that perception is direct, which Large suggests downgrades the role of cognition when building an overall mental impression. The notion of 'direct perception' within the ecological model, therefore, requires a more detailed explanation than is found in Anderson's book.

Thomas Stoffregen (1997) comments that there are unresolved issues in Gibson's theory of depictions both in still and moving pictures which might be clarified through a closer consideration of perception as an exploratory act, and of film as an instrument that guides exploration. Additionally, Stoffregen suggests that Anderson does not appear to share the view, common to many ecological theorists, that ecological theory is fundamentally incompatible with many other theories of behaviour. The result is that, in its details, Anderson's presentation is eclectic. This raises problems because many of the arguments made by Anderson in an ecological context are shared by others who explicitly reject the ecological approach, for example Hochberg (1986).

Other criticisms relate more specifically to Anderson's own work. James Cutting (1999) comments that Anderson's discussion of sound effects and music is slim, but this may be due to the relative paucity of cognitive research into that area at the time *The Reality of Illusion* was written. Harold Hatt (1996) suggests that more films could have been discussed, as well as film style, storytelling, and perception in general. Only *Citizen Kane* (1941) and *Casablanca* (1942) receive any detailed discussion, and only four other films are mentioned in the book.

Another way of discussing the cognitive dimension of visual perception when viewing films that doesn't follow Gibson's ecological model is offered by Tim Smith. Smith has conducted eye-tracking experiments that empirically demonstrate how filmmakers are able to use lighting, staging, dialogue, and editing to steer our visual attention quite minutely within the frame. Experimental subjects in Smith's experiments have demonstrated how we shift our gaze within the frame, continually seeking out maximal information about the on-screen action (Smith *et al.* 2012).

In summary, Anderson proposed a plausible and unique theory of filmic perception that was supported with a logical line of reasoning. He shifted the focus of the questions that could be asked within film theory from the political and social to the perceptual, and staked out a unique space within film theory generally, but also within the field of cognitive film theory, by offering large-scale theorizing with the first systematic ecological approach to film perception.

PAUL TABERHAM

## Works cited

Anderson, Joseph. 1996. *The Reality of Illusion: An Ecological Approach to Cognitive Film Theory*. Cardondale: Southern Illinois University Press.

Bordwell, David. 1985. *Narration in the Fiction Film*. London: Methuen.

Carroll, Noël. 1996. 'The Power of Movies'. In *Theorizing the Moving Image*, 78–93. Cambridge: Cambridge University Press.

Cutting, James. 1999. '[Review of] The Reality of Illusion: An Ecological Approach to Cognitive Film Theory'. *Journal of Film and Video* 51 (3–4) (Fall/Winter): 97–9.

Grodal, Torben. 2009. *Embodied Visions: Evolution, Emotion, Culture, and Film*. New York: Oxford University Press.

Hatt, Harold. 1996. 'Review of Anderson, Joseph D., The Reality of Illusion: An Ecological Approach to Cognitive Film Theory'. H-PCAACA, *H-Net* (April): http://www.h-net.org/reviews/showrev.php?id=405 (accessed 3 February 2013).

Hochberg, Julian. 1986. 'Representation of Motion and Space in Video and Cinematic Displays'. In *Handbook of Perception and Human Performance*, vol. 1, edited by K.R. Boff, L. Kaufman, and J.P. Thomas, 22–64. New York: Wiley.

Large, David. 1997. 'Ecology and Reality: Notes towards an Ecological Film Theory'. *Film-Philosophy* 1 (2) (April): http://www.film-philosophy.com/vol1-1997/n2large.htm (accessed 3 February 2013).

Plantinga, Carl. 2009. *Moving Viewers: American Film and the Spectator's Experience*. Berkeley: University of California Press.

Smith, Greg. 2003. *Film Structure and the Emotion System*. Cambridge: Cambridge University Press.

Smith, Murray. 1995. *Engaging Characters: Fiction, Emotion, and the Cinema*. Oxford: Clarendon Press.

Smith, Tim, Daniel T. Levin, and James Cutting. 2012. 'A Window on Reality: Perceiving Edited Moving Images'. *Current Directions in Psychological Science* 21: 101–6.

Stoffregen, Thomas. 1997. 'Filming the World: An Essay Review of Anderson's *The Reality of Illusion*'. *Ecological Psychology* 9 (2): 161–77.

Tan, Ed. 1996. *Emotion and the Structure of Narrative Film: Film as an Emotion Machine*. Mahwah, NJ: Erlbaum.

## Further reading

Anderson, B. and J. Anderson, eds. 2007. *Moving Image Theory: Ecological Considerations*. Carbondale: Southern Illinois University Press.

Bordwell, D. 'The Viewer's Share: Models of Mind in Explaining Film'. http://www.davidbordwell.net/essays/viewersshare.php (accessed 3 January 2013).

Gibson, J. 1986. *The Ecological Approach to Visual Perception*. Hillsdale, NJ: Lawrence Erlbaum Associates.

Münsterberg, Hugo. 2002 [1916]. *The Photoplay: A Psychological Study and Other Writings on Film*. Edited by Allan Langdale. New York: Routledge.

# SEMIOTICS OF FILM

What is the specific nature of film, according to film semiotics? Christian Metz tried to answer this question in his breakthrough essay 'Cinema: Language or Language System?' (1974a, 31–91; first published in 1964). Although the actual results of this essay were negative and are now dated, we need to recognize that it was a pioneering, exploratory piece that completely transformed the way film theory is carried out.

Before outlining Metz's essay and the theory behind it, we must first note that the very idea of 'film language' for film semiotics is not a simple analogy, but suggests that film is a coded medium like natural language and possesses a specific underlying system – again, as does natural language. In principle (if not always in practice), the semioticians' claim that film is a language was therefore made not through any direct resemblance between film and natural language, but on methodological grounds: film's specific, underlying reality could be reconstructed by the methods of structural linguistics. At least from this methodological viewpoint, film semioticians were justified in using structural linguistics to study film because this discipline is the most sophisticated for analysing a medium's underlying reality.

## Structural linguistics

The work of Ferdinand de Saussure (his *Course in General Linguistics*, first published in 1916, the foundational text of structural linguistics: Saussure 1983) offered film and cultural theorists in the 1950s and 1960s one of the most sophisticated methods for analysing underlying systems of codes. Structural linguistics, and semiotics based on it, are modernist theories in that they aim to identify the specificity of each medium (or language), and they locate that specificity in the underlying system.

Structural linguistics is founded upon the hierarchy between *langue* and *parole*. *La parole* simply means speech, which is the manifestation of *la langue*, the underlying system of natural language. Some of the concepts semiotics developed to analyse *la langue*/language system include: articulation, arbitrariness, recursivity, language as speech circuit, commutation, plus syntagmatic and paradigmatic relations. These concepts are fundamental to understanding Metz's semiotic theory of film.

The concept of articulation refers to the joining together of basic elements, or signs, following rules of combination to create new messages. To understand the significance of articulation, we simply need to contrast it with a non-articulated sign, which has a direct (iconic) relation to what it represents. In a non-articulated language, each particular aspect of reality or experience has a corresponding sign. This is an uneconomical, cumbersome

425

way to communicate, for it leads to the proliferation of a long list of signs. Language does not consist of a long list of non-articulated signs, but of a small number of articulated signs organized as a hierarchal system:

> We might imagine a system of communication in which a special cry would correspond to each given situation or fact of experience. But if we think of the infinite variety of such situations and these facts of experience, it will be clear that if such a system were to serve the same purpose as our languages, it would have to comprise so large a number of distinct signs that the memory of man would be incapable of storing it. A few thousand of such units as *tête, mal, ai, la,* freely combinable, enable us to communicate more things than could be done by millions of unarticulated cries.
>
> (Martinet 1964, 23)

Making a message more nuanced or original does not involve the invention of new signs, but the combination of pre-existing signs into a specific order, or the unusual manipulation of these signs (as in poetry). From a semiotic perspective, language (*la langue*) is essentially an articulated system of finite signs. Speech (*la parole*) is simply the partial manifestation of this underlying system.

André Martinet argues that language is organized as a double-levelled or doubly articulated system (1964, 22–4). The first articulation involves the minimally meaningful units, where there is a correlation between signifier and signified, creating a sign (Martinet calls these minimally meaningful signs 'monemes'). These monemes in turn are composed of non-signifying significant units (phonemes), which constitute the second level of articulation: 'Thanks to the second articulation language can make do with a few dozen distinct phonic products which are combined to achieve the vocal form of the units of the first articulation' (24). Meaning is generated from the recursive combination of the small number of phonemes to generate a large number of monemes, and the recursive combination of monemes to generate a potentially infinite number of sentences. Double articulation therefore accounts for the extraordinary economy of language and is, according to Martinet, language's unique, defining characteristic (22). And because the phonemes on the second level have no direct relation to meaning, then meaning is generated from the interrelations between phonemes rather than from what they signify. The phonemes are autonomous from reality (they do not 'reflect' reality, but are arbitrary); meaning emerges out of non-meaning – from the selection and combination of phonemes into monemes, rather than simply reflecting a pre-existing meaning.

Saussure delimited the specific object of linguistic study – *la langue* – by the metaphor of speech as a circuit; as Roy Harris explains, the *Course in General Linguistics* 'is the first treatise on language to insist that speech communication is to be viewed as a "circuit", and to attach any theoretical significance to the fact that individuals linked by this circuit act in turn as initiators of spoken messages and as recipients of such messages' (1987, 24–5). The metaphor 'speech circuit' enabled Saussure to conceive of a language as a system of communication.

To study a language as a system of communication, Saussure developed the commutation test, which is a method for segmenting *la parole* into the small number of underlying codes that it manifests. Saussure described *la parole* as infinite and *la langue* as finite. Generating an infinity of speech utterances with finite means is possible by recognizing that all utterances are composed from the same small number of signs used recursively in different combinations. All the infinite manifestations could thereby be described in terms of the finite system underlying them. Furthermore – and here Saussure located the 'ultimate law of language' – signs are defined only in terms of their relation to, or *difference* from, other signs, both the paradigmatic relations they enter into in *la langue* and the syntagmatic relations they enter into in *la parole*.

## 'Cinema: Language or Language System?'

The problem analysed in Metz's first essay in film semiotics is conveniently stated in the essay's very title – is there a filmic equivalent to *la langue*/language system? An answer to this question would offer a definition of filmic specificity, the primary objective of film semiotics. In other words, filmic specificity should be defined in terms of an underlying reality (modelled on natural language's underlying reality – *la langue*), not in terms of the immediately perceptible level of film, as classical (pre-semiotic) film theorists had attempted to do. Metz's background assumption in this essay is that film must possess an equivalent to *la langue* to be defined as a language (*langage*).

Metz studied the film image according to the principles of structural linguistics. Not surprisingly, the results came out negative: he concluded that cinema is a language without a language system. Much of his description involves documenting how the underlying reality of film does *not* resemble *la langue*.

The negative results are not unexpected, for the semiotic language of film does not possess the same system specific to natural language. Metz states: 'the image discourse is an open system, and it is not easily codified, with its non-discrete basic units (the images), its intelligibility (which is too natural), its lack of distance [i.e. lack of arbitrariness] between the [signified] and the signifier' (1974a, 59). Metz emphasized that the image does not derive its meaning in opposition to other images, but from a direct correspondence to pro-filmic events. In other words, film has no paradigm on the level of the image; consequently, it has no *langue*, and no double articulation.

The reasons are twofold. (1) At this stage of his research, Metz believed that the image is analogical, not coded – it directly resembles the thing it represents; and (2) 'The image is always actualized' (1974a, 67). What he means is that filmic images do not belong to a semiotic system existing prior to usage; rather, each image is at the outset a complete, manifest, and individual unit of discourse. In Metz's famous example: 'A close-up of a revolver does not mean "revolver" (a purely virtual [non-manifest] lexical unit [moneme]), but at the very least, and without speaking of the connotations, it signifies "Here is a revolver!"' (67). This led Metz to state that 'the cinematographic image is primarily speech [*parole*]' (69), which is the same as saying that 'The filmic shot is of the *magnitude of the sentence*' (86; emphasis in the original).

But the terminology in this quotation – 'magnitude of the sentence' – has often confused the way the linguistic status of the image is understood. Metz merely characterized the relation between image and sentence in *exterior* terms, in which there is no structural similarity between them, because the sentence is also analysable into units that signify paradigmatically: 'The difference [between sentence and image] is that the sentences of natural language eventually break down into words, whereas in the cinema, they do not: A film may be segmented into large units ("shots"), but these shots are not *reducible* (in Jakobson's sense) into small, basic, and specific units' (1974a, 88). The 'irreducibility' of filmic images suggested that they do not involve articulation, because they are potentially infinite in number and each one is unique. This explains why they cannot be theorized in terms of articulation and formed into a closed paradigm.

Metz also concluded that the cinema does not form a speech circuit: 'The cinema is not a language system, because it contradicts three important characteristics of the linguistic fact: a language is a *system* of *signs* used for *intercommunication*. Three elements to the definition. Now, like all the arts, and because it is itself an art, the cinema is one-way communication' (1974a, 75; original emphasis). Language as a 'speech circuit', so crucial for Saussure, does not, therefore, apply to film.

Metz's failure to establish a film semiotics on the level of the image is due to the genuine inability to develop a new perspective on film by means of Saussure's concepts of the arbitrary relation between signifier and signified, and the metaphor of language as a speech circuit – for these two criteria do not hold on the level of the filmic image. To achieve his objective – to define filmic specificity in semiotic terms – Metz sought the above two criteria on the level of image sequences. (In fact, it was evident that film does not form a speech circuit on any level, so Metz attempted to establish a principle of arbitrariness in sequences of images.) Because the filmic image does not conform to the same system of articulation as that revealed by the structural linguistic analysis of natural language, Metz concluded that the structural linguistic research into the specificity of film language on the level of the image is an inappropriate starting point from which to establish a semiotics of film.

## Metz's critique of 'Cinema: Language or Language System?'

In 'Problems of Denotation in the Fiction Film' (1974a, 108–46), Metz moved on to explore the syntagmatic dimension of film, under the background assumption that filmic specificity is to be identified with narrativity (a single, super-structural code): '*it is precisely to the extent that the cinema confronted the problems of narration that* ... it came to produce a body of specific signifying procedures' (95; emphasis in the original). The main purpose of the essay is to employ the structural linguistic method of segmentation and commutation to identify a prior set of sequence (or syntagmatic) types in classical cinema, a paradigm of syntagmas from which a filmmaker can choose to represent pro-filmic events in a particular sequence. Each syntagma is identifiable by the particular way it structures the spatio-temporal relations between the pro-filmic events it depicts. Syntagmas are commutable because the same events depicted by means of a different syntagma will have a different meaning.

These spatio-temporal relationships between the images constitute filmic specificity for Metz because they articulate the pro-filmic events in terms of a *specific* cinematic space and time. In other words, this cinematic space and time confers upon these events a meaning that *goes beyond* their analogical relation to the image. These image orderings therefore conform to the principle of arbitrariness, since there is no strict motivation governing the choice of one syntagma over another in representing a particular pro-filmic event.

Metz detected eight different spatio-temporal relationships in total, which constitute eight different forms of image ordering (*syntagmas*). Metz called the resulting 'paradigm of syntagmas' the *grande syntagmatique* of the image track. These image syntagmas form a paradigm to the extent that they offer eight different commutable ways of constructing an image sequence. As Metz himself has said: 'These montage figures [film syntagmas] derive their meaning to a large extent in relation to one another. One, then, has to deal, so to speak, with a paradigm of syntagmas. It is only by a sort of *commutation* that one can identify and enumerate them' (Metz 1976, 587).

The *grande syntagmatique* identifies syntagmatic units only when a change in shot produces a change in meaning – that is, when a spatio-temporal transition (the cut, etc.) on the level of the filmic signifier correlates with a change in meaning on the level of the signified (= the spatio-temporal relationship between the pro-filmic events). Each filmic syntagma is constituted by the same spatio-temporal relationship between its images. As long as the same relation holds across cuts, there is no commutation. A commutation, or change in meaning, therefore occurs when a spatio-temporal transition on the level of the filmic signifier is correlated with a *new* spatio-temporal relation between pro-filmic events, for a new relation signals the end of one syntagma and the beginning of another. (See Metz [1974a, 124–33] for an outline of the eight syntagmatic types.)

'Problems of Denotation in the Fiction Film' successfully identified an autonomous level of articulation in the cinema (syntagmas) and constructs a paradigm of eight syntagmas (thus overcoming cinema's paradigmatic poverty). As Stephen Heath points out: 'The focus on syntagmatic relations "saves" semiology (in so far as it is held in the *langue* or *langage* debate) in the face of the paradigmatic poverty of cinema' (1981, 144). Yet two problems remained: Metz's identification of filmic specificity with narrativity, and the uncoded, transparent nature conferred on the image (a problem carried over from 'Cinema: Language or Language System?' and merely displaced in the *grande syntagmatique*). Metz approached and overcame both problems in *Language and Cinema* (1974b).

Despite the limited success of his results in 'Cinema: Language or Language System?', Metz established a new object of study, new problems to address, and a new methodology with which to approach film. The new object of study was that of a new level of filmic reality – the unobservable, latent level that makes filmic meaning possible and which defines its specificity.

WARREN BUCKLAND

## Works cited

Harris, Roy. 1987. *Reading Saussure*. London: Duckworth.
Heath, Stephen. 1981. 'The Work of Christian Metz'. In *Cinema and Semiotics: Screen Reader 2*, edited by Mick Eaton and Steve Neale, 138–61. London: Society for Education in Film and Television.
Martinet, André. 1964. *Elements of General Linguistics*. Translated by Elisabeth Palmer. London: Faber and Faber.
Metz, Christian. 1974a. *Film Language: A Semiotics of the Cinema*. Translated by Michael Taylor. New York: Oxford University Press.
——. 1974b. *Language and Cinema*. Translated by Donna Jean Umiker-Sebeok. The Hague: Mouton.
——. 1976. 'On the Notion of Cinematographic Language'. In *Movies and Methods*, edited by Bill Nichols, 582–9. Berkeley: University of California Press.
Saussure, Ferdinand de. 1983. *Course in General Linguistics*. Translated by Roy Harris. London: Duckworth.

## Further reading

Buckland, Warren. 2000. *The Cognitive Semiotics of Film*. Cambridge: Cambridge University Press.
——. 2012. *Film Theory: Rational Reconstructions*, chapter 4. Abingdon: Routledge.

# SOUND THEORY

## Narrative theory and film sound aesthetics

Film sound theory has nearly slipped into the general register of sound studies, which is an amalgamation of related disciplines that prioritize the acoustic field of perception in the expanding realm of media studies (as attested by two recent edited volumes: Sterne 2011; Bull 2013). In film theory, however, sound theory became established through a descriptive vocabulary that relates its narrative function to the moving image on screen. An illuminating series of film studies has foregrounded the narrative semiotics of music and speech (Chion 1994), the philosophical nature of the soundtrack (Branigan 2010), as well as a wide array of scholarship focused on case studies of films within an adapted literary taxonomy. Individual films have been analysed as analogous to great works of literature; auteur directors with an ear for sound are likened to poets; and film genres, like the musical (Altman 1987), are described within a narratological framework. All of these approaches have opened possibilities for hearing sound in cinema.

The location and qualities of a sound may be elaborately specified in relation to aspects of a narrative situation (Bordwell 1985). Christian Metz developed a semiotic formulation of the aural source as an object that identifies sound as a perceptual event (Metz 1985). Scholars such as Claudia Gorbman have grappled with the complexities of types of film music that create a 'point of experience in the film narration' (Gorbman 1987, 2), while Sarah Kozloff (1988), among others, has examined the narrative effects of voice-over narration. The analysis of narrative film sound as a well-recognized category of film theory has also influenced filmmaking practice, however fleetingly or simply in line with the ballooning budgets for marketing films, as with the Dogme 1995 manifesto (Geuens 2001). Just as narrative film sound theory continues to serve as an important analytic reference point for understanding new media objects, early sound film theory serves as an essential foundation for modern sound film theory in spite of what might seem at first to be arcane and quixotic formulations. For this reason it will be useful to examine more closely two early attempts to theorize sound in film.

## Rudolf Arnheim and the Gestalt of silent film art

Rudolf Arnheim's uneasiness with the advent of sound film remains a significant perspective on the nature of synchronized sound in the history of film theory (Arnheim 1957). Although the attribution of 'silence' to silent cinema has always been a misnomer (Altman 2004), popular film production and exhibition changed significantly with the economic and

430

technological consolidation of the synchronized talking film by the late 1920s. This transformation served to clarify Arnheim's understanding of silent film and its aesthetics, which he claimed the newly developed sound film worked to undercut (Arnheim 1997, 30). By contrast with Béla Balázs's approach to sound film (to be discussed later), Arnheim's sceptical view not only highlights the complex relationship between film and art, but also contributes to an appreciation of the aesthetic and perceptual uniqueness of sound theory (*see* ART, FILM AS; CLASSICAL FILM THEORY).

In 'Film Sound (1928)' (Arnheim 1997, 29–32), first published as part of an 80-page chapter on sound in *Film als Kunst* (1932) and translated in the first, now out-of-print, English version under the title *Film* (Arnheim 1933), Arnheim outlined the infelicitous effects of sound film (see Alter 2011). The argument begins with the assertion that sound turns the film screen into a spatial stage, such that it imitates a theatrical mode from which it had already become emancipated. In other words, sound film marked a return to an earlier phase of the peep show, prior to the embrace of film as a form of artistic expression. As Anton Kaes (Kaes and Levin 1987) has explained, it was thanks to the influence of American film of the 1920s, along with films featuring Asta Nielsen, that the non-literary origins of film gained recognition in Germany among the bourgeoisie, who became increasingly convinced of its artistic value.

Arnheim advocated that film become a visual art in relation to theatre, photography, sculpture, painting, and poetry in order to preserve the distinctiveness of film art, under the inspiration of G.W.F. Lessing in 'A New Laocoön: Artistic Composites and the Talking Film (1938)' (Arnheim 1957, 199–230). Arnheim criticizes synchronized sound film for doing away with the significant *interplay* between the 'division of the picture and movement within an area … [along with the] … three-dimensional body and movement in space' (Arnheim 1997, 30). In other words, synchronized sound distracts from the significant play of visual interpretation among all the elements of the image and instead locks the viewer into the space of a locale. Further, the musical-like interplay of imagery in establishing contrasts, point of view, and sizes of objects is inhibited by the use of sound, which, he claims, 'lends each scene with so much importance and burdens it with naturalism … such that it cannot compete with the dance of form which is running roughshod over all its contents' (31).

These assertions require some explanation, particularly given that the first German edition of *Film als Kunst*, published in 1932, was banned by the Nazis in 1933, which in turn delayed its critical reception (Hake 1993, 283). Arnheim's unhappiness with synchronized sound underscores the perceptual wonder associated with silent film as a distinct aesthetic and psychological category of experience. As Getrud Koch makes clear, Arnheim draws on the experience of film as an anthropological concept derived from Gestalt psychology that incorporated neo-Kantian structures of perception and form. While these objective, mental structures were not conceived as autonomous, they were pre-existing human capacities for perception (Koch 1990, 171). In Arnheim's turn against synchronized sound, he emphasizes the differences between film and reality as a key artistic quality of film form. That is, with the reduction of three-dimensional objects onto a two-dimensional screen, film's relationship to reality is not imitative, but is a constitutive process from which derive its most stunning effects (172).

For Arnheim, the performative nature of perception engaged with silent film as art because the process of perceptual interaction was always more than a sum of component parts, and was subject to inner structural (Gestalt) laws. The success of a work of art relied upon its coherence as a whole, and Arnheim persuasively argued that the addition of syn-chronized sound does not significantly contribute to film as art but partially defeats it through an emphasis on imitating reality. This was not to claim, however, that sound recording is a less significant source of artistic expression, but rather that it was better served through other forms of electronic media, particularly radio (see Arnheim 1971 [1936]). To better illustrate this point, Arnheim recalls a scene from *The Immigrant* (1917) where Chaplin is depicted bent over the side of a rocking boat during a transatlantic crossing, making it seem as though he is suffering from sea sickness. However, the latter section of this scene is 'switched out', in the language of Gestalt psychology, as he reels in the catch of the day with a sense of triumph. This effect of surprise is also reliant upon a technique of restrictive framing so well deployed in the silent cinema (Arnheim 1957, 36).

## Béla Balázs and the synchronized sound film

In contrast to Arnheim (1904–2007), Béla Balázs (Herbert Bauer [family name], 1884–1949) developed an approach to understanding cinema allied with his literary career and avowed interest in scriptwriting and film producing. He conceived the advent of sound film as an extension of cinema's narrative capacities, especially in relation to the fairy tale (see Loewy 2006). While Balázs *et al.*'s *Spirit of Film* (2001 [1930]) is often contrasted with *Film als Kunst* as a defence of sound film (Carter 2010, xxxix), their writing about sound tends to overlap and shares a certain degree of scepticism about its function in shaping audience aspirations (*see* CLOSE-UP).

Balázs introduces his approach to sound film by explaining that 'silent film was on its way to acquiring a psychological subtlety, a creative power almost unprecedented in the arts. Then the technical invention of the sound film burst upon the scene, with catastrophic force' (Carter 2010, 183). This initial claim regarding the 'primitivism' of the newly developed sound film is then tempered by its demotion to simply another representational 'crisis' in the arts, and a prediction that the new machine of cinema will most certainly come to be 'assimilated as a human organ. It [will] become our fingertips' (183). This language is also suggestive of the intelligence of fingertips, allied with Henri Bergson's intuitive notion of *élan vital*, or vital force of evolutionary consciousness, integral to Balázs's own intellectual itinerary. Later mobilized in the contemporary lexicon of the digital, derivations of the digits, the fingerprint, and the sense of touch as implied by the 'haptic', 'becoming our fingertips' refers to the intuitive and emotional capacity for extended cine-matic expression. From this frame of reference, Balázs argues that cinema at its most compelling 'reveals the relations between forms and the psychic rhythm of mental associations' (184).

In *The Spirit of Film*, Balazs also makes a compelling case for sound film as the first audiovisual medium to effectively represent silence, returning us once again to the mis-nomer of 'silence' in silent film. That is, silence does not function as a condition of the subject, but as a significant dramatic event which evokes the quality of a cry turned inwards, for example, a screaming hush, the holding of one's breath, and finally the flair of a 'negative detonation', as he terms it. Here he writes: 'Like the circus music, [or drum roll,] that falls silent at the moment of the death-defying feat. A silence, then, follows necessarily from sound' (191).

Balázs proposes that sound film offers opportunities for the visual qualities of film to guide us to a new aural sensitivity, teaching us to listen more attentively. By contrast to

Arnheim's insistence on neo-Kantian a priori mental forms, Balázs specifies the role of 'sound close-ups' that allow us to hear isolated intimate sounds previously inaccessible. Against Arnheim's claim that radio is aesthetically better suited to the task of shaping the acoustics of magnification and amplification, Balázs retorts that the radio play is a narrative or dramatic representation with acoustic illustrations burdened by the need to explain what is heard to fulfil expectations of legibility. Sound film, by contrast, allows us to receive acoustic expression in its unmediated form. Unlike Arnheim, who is less interested in probing the nature, qualities, and potential of synchronized sound because it devalued the heightened aesthetic qualities of silent film, Balázs describes how the experience of sound may become more spatially defined. By contrast with a two-dimensional image, the temporal nature of sound becomes related to the hearing subject's own location in any given space. The potentially spatial characteristics of sound, which Altman (1992) has further described as the 'material heterogeneity' of sound, may then be better guided, Balázs insists, through a visual representation. The image assists in disentangling the location of voices speaking, for example, as attached to different speakers appearing on screen with their own distinct qualities and physiognomies of expression.

While Balázs remains uncertain regarding the future of synchronized sound film, he points to the close-up and montage as prominent features that contributed to transforming silent film into a form of artistic expression, and considers a developing toolbox of techniques including asynchronous sound. On the relative significance of asynchronous sound as part of an extended commentary by Pudovkin (1985) and Eisenstein, among others, and in the films of René Clair, Arnheim and Balázs disagree about its utility as a technique. However, it was their contrasting orientation towards the masses and approach to visual instruction that remain more significant. As described by Sabine Hake, Arnheim had little emotional investment in questions of mass culture and was less enthralled by its subversive potential: 'Film is not an art of the masses, except in the sense that quantity alone counts at the box office' (Hake 1993, 279).

## Concluding remarks

Whereas Balázs's approach to film criticism was indebted to a utopian aesthetics of literary and political engagement, initially allied with his Hungarian compatriot György Lukács (see Levin 1987), Arnheim continued to develop a psychologically informed, modernist aesthetics of artistic expression. The contrasting positions for their writing about film took shape in the Berlin-based German weekly journals as commentaries that were later compiled and edited into longer published works on film. Arnheim's notion that the verisimilitude of nature and realism is the antithesis of film art remains a productive means by which to understand the organic nature of artistic expression. Balázs, enthralled by the flexibility and transformational qualities of film techniques, claimed that the boundaries between silent and sound film remain permeable in the service of narrative form and function. We could also say that whereas Balázs's approach to film sound remains contemporary in outlook, Arnheim's scepticism may better stimulate new categories and qualities of expression.

These debates about the relative value of particular devices of film continue within the context of computer-generated special effects and, most notably, the aesthetics of 3D for which Arnheim was an early advocate. Differing criteria for modes of artistic expression are relevant to understanding the specificity of sound theory in film, and it is here that

Arnheim's work continues to be relevant. The contrasting imperatives of narrative studies and aesthetic categories lead us back to silent sound film as a perceptual frontier that enables assessments of emerging forms of cinema.

PETER J. BLOOM

## Works cited

Alter, Nora M. 2011. 'Screening out Sound: Arnheim and Cinema's Silence'. In *Arnheim for Film and Media Studies*, edited by Scott Higgins, 69–88. New York: Routledge.

Altman, Rick. 1987. *The American Film Musical*. New York: Columbia University Press.

———. 1992. 'The Material Heterogeneity of Recorded Sound'. In *Sound Theory, Sound Practice*, edited by Rick Altman. New York: Routledge.

———. 2004. *Silent Film Sound*. New York: Columbia University Press.

Arnheim, Rudolf. 1932. *Film als Kunst*. Berlin: Rowohlt.

———. 1933. *Film*. Translated by L.M. Sieveking and Ian F.D. Morrow. London: Faber & Faber.

———. 1957. *Film as Art*. Berkeley: University of California Press. [This edition still remains the most widely read and available English edition. In this edition, a detailed analysis of film and ideology and a chapter on sound film have been substituted by four essays written after *Film als Kunst* was first published in 1932.]

———. 1971 [1936]. *Radio*. Translated by Margaret Ludwig and Herbert Read. London: Faber & Faber. Reprinted in New York by Arno Press and the *New York Times*.

———. 1997. *Film Essays and Criticism*. Translated by Brenda Benthien. Madison: University of Wisconsin Press. [This translation of Arnheim's early essays includes film essays that appeared in the *Weltbühne* weekly journal published between 1928 and 1933, and additional material from the 1932 edition of *Film als Kunst*.]

Balázs, Béla, Hanno Loewy, and Rudolf Arnheim. 2001 [1930]. *Der Geist des Films* (*The Spirit of Film*). Frankfurt am Main: Suhrkamp. [For the English translation, see Carter (2010, 91–230).]

Bordwell, David. 1985. *Narration in the Fiction Film*. Madison: University of Wisconsin Press.

Branigan, Edward. 2010. 'Soundtrack in Mind'. *Projections* 4 (1) (Summer): 41–67.

Bull, Michael, ed. 2013. *Sound Studies*. New York: Routledge.

Carter, Erica, ed. 2010. *Béla Balázs: Early Film Theory*. Visible Man *and* The Spirit of Film. Translated by Rodney Livingstone. New York: Berghahn Books.

Chion, Michel. 1994. *Audio-vision: Sound on Screen*. Edited and translated by Claudia Gorbman. New York: Columbia University Press.

Geuens, Jean-Pierre. 2001. 'Dogma 95: A Manifesto for Our Times'. *Quarterly Review of Film and Video* 18 (2): 191–202.

Gorbman, Claudia. 1987. *Unheard Melodies: Narrative Film Music*. Bloomington: Indiana University Press; London: BFI Publishing.

Hake, Sabine. 1993. *The Cinema's Third Machine: Writing on Film in Germany, 1907–1933*. Lincoln: University of Nebraska Press.

Kaes, Anton, and David J. Levin. 1987. 'The Debate about Cinema: Charting a Controversy (1909–29)'. *New German Critique* 40 (Winter): 7–33.

Koch, Gertrud. 1990. 'Rudolf Arnheim, the Materialist of Aesthetic Illusion: Gestalt Theory and Reviewer's Practice'. *New German Critique* 51 (Autumn): 164–78.

Kozloff, Sarah. 1988. *Invisible Storytellers: Voice-over Narration in American Fiction Film*. Berkeley: University of California Press.

Levin, Tom. 1987. 'From Dialectical to Normative Specificity: Reading Lukács on Film'. *New German Critique* 40 (Winter): 35–61.

Loewy, Hanno. 2006. 'Space, Time, and "Rites de Passage": Béla Balázs's Paths to Film'. *October* 115 (Winter): 61–76.

Metz, Christian. 1985. 'Aural Objects'. In *Film Sound: Theory and Practice*, edited by Elisabeth Weis and John Belton, 154–61. New York: Columbia University Press.

Pudovkin, Vsevolod I. 1985. 'Asynchronism as a Principle of Sound Film'. In *Film Sound: Theory and Practice*, edited by Elisabeth Weis and John Belton, 86–91. New York: Columbia University Press.

Sterne, Jonathan, ed. 2011. *The Sound Studies Reader*. Abingdon: Routledge.

# SPECIFICITY, MEDIUM I

Since the beginning of cinema, writers have speculated about the origin and defining characteristics of the medium. Having witnessed the moving image for the first time in 1896 at a screening by the Lumière brothers, for instance, Maxim Gorky wrote in negative terms about the minimal but significant differences between film and life that addressed cinema's defining features: 'Before you a life surges, a life devoid of words and shorn of the living spectrum of colours, a grey, silent, bleak and dismal life' (1988, 25). In 1915, the American poet Vachel Lindsay spoke more enthusiastically about film's privileged relation to physical existence. Singling out the close-up as a unique aspect of the motion picture – as many European and Soviet film theorists would do a decade later – Lindsay declared that: 'It [cinema] gives [us] also our idiosyncrasies. It is gossip *in extremis*. It is apt to chronicle our petty little skirmishes, rather than our feuds' (1970, 50–1).

What both writers share is an attentiveness to film's relation to the textures of physical existence, from which a general theory of what cinema uniquely does would later be derived. In this way, film theory has long been animated by a preoccupation with medium specificity and realism, by a concern to distinguish film from the other arts, and by an effort to understand how those distinctions are to be located in the material limitations of the medium. Limitation, here, is understood not in the usual sense of the foreclosure of possibility; rather, limits make style happen. More simply, to ask a medium-specific question is to inquire about what a film can do that a novel or a painting cannot. If paintings may imply movement, film is motion itself. If epic poetry generalizes human existence with its pronouncements about heroes and crowds in a condensed economy of line and metre, cinema – owing to its ability to both record and reveal unforeseen aspects of physical existence in close-up – is better suited to smaller subjects. Hence, Lindsay's suggestion that film is 'gossip *in extremis*'. Cinema is on the side of gossip because it can record intimate gestures in motion, details unsuited to grand pronouncements and generalization. Medium-specific theorizing, then, inquires about the essence of the medium and then proposes that an appropriate style follow from those limits. Moreover, style, having been conceived in relation to what defines cinema against other art forms, in turn begets a particular sort of content: gossip, human vicissitude, ephemera.

Historically, film theorists have utilized the trope of specificity for different reasons. Primarily, these theories were devised in an effort to establish cinema as an art form (*see* ART, FILM AS). To describe film as an instance of real rather than implied movement is to suggest that filmmakers are concerned with the same problems as painters. If cinema is movement itself, then painters must find a new subject, come to better terms with what is unique about their own medium. This is one way of understanding the turn to figureless abstraction in twentieth-century painting by artists like Mark Rothko and Barnett Newman who stressed the two-dimensional character of the canvas, the 'essence' of which is flatness rather than depth, which is now understood as the exclusive domain of photography and film. Thus, if cinema can be said to both share and master a concern with painting, which has already been legitimized institutionally, then cinema can become art, too, and seek to acquire its own institutional distinction within the art world.

In addition to exploring cinema's relation to established art forms, the medium-specificity theorist is also concerned to make a distinction between cinema as an art form and film as an escapist medium of industrial manufacture – claims typically predicated on common-sensical notions about mass culture. Early film theorists worried that, as a product of industrial manufacture and mass dissemination, film style would mimic and popularize the stylistic conventions of more 'respected' art forms, as we see in the many debates about film as a form of filmed theatre during the transition to sound in the early 1920s. Or else, cinema would carry on the diversionary aesthetics of the fairground attraction.

It should be said that filmmakers themselves helped to generate the discourse of medium specificity. As such, medium-specific theories of film almost always take the form of a manifesto and tend largely towards exaggerated and adversarial claims about what various art mediums make possible. And they do so in order to create an institutional space for the recognition of film as art, and thus a place for themselves as artists. And while medium-specific film theories are largely concerned with style that follows from the 'essence' of a medium, this very same concern can be read in terms of discourses of stylistic fidelity to mediums that transcend the specificity of place, institution, or philosophical orientation.

## Germaine Dulac and early Soviet film theory

Germaine Dulac's 1925 essay 'The Essence of the Cinema: The Visual Idea' provides a good example of the search for essence that defines medium-specificity theory. Dulac was a major French avant-garde filmmaker of the 1910s and 1920s. Her discourse resonates with other filmmakers and theorists of her time, despite the seemingly substantial differences in the world-views held by so many of these filmmakers. The 1920s is a particularly fecund period for claims about medium specificity, especially in the Soviet Union and France, where the writing of theory was regularly understood as preparatory to practice. However, if the means were meant to be the same – between filmmakers across national contexts – the ends were not.

In the Soviet Union, for instance, filmmakers such as Sergei Eisenstein, V.I. Pudovkin, Dziga Vertov, and Lev Kuleshov were eager to understand editing or montage as the essence of film, and they did so in ways that mimicked and promoted the constructivist ethos of the Soviet Union (see CLASSICAL FILM THEORY). These filmmakers were united by a belief that nothing stable or necessary inheres in a single shot, that the meaning or effect of any sequence is not derived from something essential or unalterable in a body or object presented in a single framing, but from the context in which this body or object now appears in combination with some other. If the Soviet Union was itself predicated on the belief that the world is made and not found, that identity – personal and political – is constructed rather than innate, then cinema could be said to mirror, in material terms, the logic of the state. The defining characteristic of cinema – the creation of new worlds from pre-existing material by way of editing – could also be said of the Soviet subject.

In France, the discourse of medium specificity was less political, animated, as it often was, by metaphysical suppositions that would have been anathema to the Soviets. Yet, the rhetorical conceit of these claims had the effect of unifying practices across nations with rather different social, political, and metaphysical beliefs. In addition to Dulac, filmmakers/theorists like Jean Epstein, Louis Delluc, and Réné Clair pursued the idea of cinema as a purified visual form uniquely capable of revealing the unforeseen richness of the smallest detail like a microscope. Such was the mantra of Jean Epstein, who understood cinema's essence in terms of *photogénie*: '*an aspect is photogenic if it changes positions and varies simultaneously in space and time*' (1978, 25; emphasis in original). Where Soviet film theorists routinely understood the essence of cinema to be montage – and the essential purpose or content of this style to be the production of a new Soviet subject that would experience a social unification born of fragmentation and contingency – French filmmakers generally understood the essence of cinema to involve the provocation of ways of seeing that more faithfully observe the purity of perception. If the essence of cinema produced solidarity in the Soviet Union, in France the very same appeal to an 'essence' was intended to yield an entirely different result: an aesthetic autonomy that implied social autonomy and the revelation of a 'soul', individual or collective. This autonomy, however, was figured more explicitly in aesthetic rather than political terms.

In 'The Essence of the Cinema', Dulac appeals to the autonomy of the 'genuine' filmmaker in paradoxical terms. She opens with a gesture common to the manifesto: 'I will be concerned, in these few pages, not with discussing technique, but rather with discussing the moral essence of the cinematic art, an art born of our own time, and for which we must make an effort, in order to avoid the misunderstanding which so often meets unexpected revelations' (Dulac 1978, 36). Cinematic art has a *moral* essence, according to Dulac, which is also an 'unexpected revelation'. But if something is unexpected, can it also be moral?

To behave morally is to restrict one's actions to a set of values that define what is necessarily good, and thus what is possible. Though it is possible to act otherwise, acting otherwise is to become immoral, to stand outside of a given moral consensus in a community, especially as that consensus follows from a set of values that must be known in advance and admit of no variation. One cannot be pure *and* immoral at the same time. People can change, styles can vary, and we can try to imagine ways to make recalcitrant acts fit, but the categories that define our actions must remain stable in a moral economy since they are construed strictly in terms of identity and essence. Thus, if cinema has a moral essence, style has to be understood as something predictable precisely because the limits have been determined in advance.

For Dulac, the unexpected *is* the moral essence of cinema. She regards cinema as an 'idea with no precedent [that] springs from a prophetic brain, with no preparation' (36). Dulac, in other words, describes pure cinema as an idea that emerges prior to the materials necessary for its realization. Dulac's belief in a pure idea of the cinema contradicts the claim that she will likewise make for remaining true to what the medium can uniquely do, which can only be made comparatively. The only way to negate the contradiction in this instance would be to understand cinema in metaphysical terms, whereby an idea of cinema as a form that precedes its existence is eventually given a harmonious material expression of that otherwise unforeseen ideal.

This is why Dulac retains the idea of the unforeseen, cinema as an expression of purity. She does so by eliminating everything that does not effect such an alignment between the idea of cinema and its material expression. Note the rhetoric of divine election:

A caste of artists has been born which is unwilling to express its sensibility and its intelligence in any of the pre-existing forms. They are neither writers nor dramatists nor painters nor sculptors nor architects, they are Filmmakers, for whom the art of movement, as contained in cinema, is a unique form of expression.

(Dulac 1978, 37)

Cinema is distinguished by way of a series of 'neither–nors' that does not go on indefinitely. If the series went on indefinitely, cinema risks being defined as a mongrel medium. 'Nor', in this case, would imply 'sometimes this' and 'occasionally that' but never really all at once and never solely. Dulac's 'nor' is instead a purifying chain of adverbs that dramatically presents cinema as a pure category, despite her simultaneous effort to retain a sense of ambiguity within the category of the cinematic now 'purely' defined.

Having described what film is not, Dulac offers a statement of film's essence, which has been derived not from something that exists but instead from what the idea of pure cinema negates. These are the material practices or stylistic prescriptions that are to be derived from the series of distinctions produced by the chain of 'neither–nors', which should be considered as an expression of what any other medium can do. For Dulac, the answer lies in cinema's capacity to preserve and depict real motion as only the camera – which has the revelatory potential of the microscope – can uniquely do. Dulac notes that early filmmakers merely understood the real motion of film as a method for producing literature in a new form, insofar as the film – like the novel or play before it – moves from place to place; both film and novel are capable of condensing space and time. Instead, Dulac asks us to understand cinema not as a mode of scenic or character transport in more literal terms, but as the movement of light *as* light: 'For cinema, which is moving, changing, interrelated light, nothing but light, genuine and restless light can be its true setting' (39).

Considering film as a microscopic instrument, Dulac suggests (39) that:

One of its first characteristics is its educational and instructive power; in documentaries we see film as a sort of microscope with which we are able to perceive, within the realm of reality, things which we would not perceive without it … life appears before us in its infinite detail, its evolution, all that that the eye is normally unable to follow.

Cinema is understood not only as something that magnifies nature, but also as something that corrects vision, as enhanced seeing. Hence, Dulac's investment in the as-yet-unforeseeable, which results strictly from the camera's capacity to show things as they *truly are*. And if we are seeing something as it truly is, then our vision – which is now fully capable of beholding the mysterious, or the formerly mysterious – can be described in moral or essential terms.

Curiously, Dulac's rhetoric in this passage resembles that of Dizga Vertov, her contemporary from the Soviet Union, who likewise understood the camera as an improvement of human vision. In 'The Council of Three', written in 1923, Vertov declares that:

The mechanical eye, the camera, rejecting the human eye as crib sheet, gropes its way through the chaos of visual events, letting itself be drawn or repelled by movement, probing as it goes, the path of its own movement.

(Vertov 1984, 19)

Vertov's analogy of 'the human eye as crib sheet' suggests that natural perception is always reductive, that it routinely makes phenomena appear simpler and more unified than they truly are. If phenomena can be described as a unity, it is only on the basis of what cinema can reveal about the world. Ideally, for Dulac, film is a 'perceptual inspiration evolving in its continuity' (Dulac 1978, 41). Just like Vertov, Dulac imagines cinema, conceived along the lines of medium specificity, as having the capability of revealing a larger truth of the world. If the camera is a corrective, in other words, the world can be known in only one way.

Dulac speaks of essence, spirit, and soul. Vertov, by contrast, is keen to understand the Soviet subject – much like the movie camera itself – as a machinic apparatus receptive to and productive of the Soviet state – which was predicated on atheistic terms that can only understand 'being' and the world as something made, never divined. This is a markedly different relation to metaphysics than we find in Dulac, and it raises serious questions about how seemingly incompatible world-views could be derived from the same aesthetic strategy. How can we believe in two different ideas about existence even though the questions are posed in precisely the same terms?

The discourse of medium specificity is perhaps the only rhetorical context in which a paradoxical proposition such as this one can make sense. Insofar as this discourse constitutes an appeal to the essence of a medium and to that medium's potential for discovering the truth of the world, then truth itself must be defined as that which appears when the limitations of the medium are strictly observed. While Vertov worked in a climate hostile to metaphysical explanation, his rhetoric nevertheless lends itself to moral claims about a medium which demand that style conform to essence, the result of which is the display of a world infinitely greater and more unified than the human eye can perceive. The price of institutional legitimacy, in both cases, is a moral severity that imagines a world 'properly' seen in strikingly similar terms, despite conflicting ideas about the nature of existence itself. Such differences disappear on the basis of medium-specific claims about film.

While medium-specificity theories thrived in the 1920s, they are in no sense limited to that period. On the contrary, many of the major achievements of classical film theory – contrapuntal sound/image relations, the realist theories of Kracauer and Bazin, to name just two types – were predicated on medium-specific claims. Likewise, this tendency is at the heart of theories of the digital that seek to define the ontological 'purity' of computer code. Such efforts typically fall foul of D.N. Rodowick's useful suggestion that medium is better understood as 'a terrain where works of art establish their mode of existence, and pose questions of existence to us' (2007, 42). Mediums, then, are better understood as material vehicles of expression that can do much more than display their essential features. Art mediums afford more than the restrictions placed on them by medium-specificity theories, which impose limitations that are based less on what a medium *actually* do than on what a medium *alone* can do. The productive limitations of medium-specificity theory, then, are merely rhetorical and always follow a moral logic of exclusion and purity that may very well fall foul of the putative world-views of its authors.

BRIAN PRICE

## Works cited

Dulac, Germaine. 1978 [1925]. 'The Essence of the Cinema: The Visual Idea'. In *The Avant-Garde Film: A Reader of Theory and Criticism*, edited by P. Adams Sitney, 36–42. New York: Anthology Film Archives.

Epstein, Jean. 1978. 'The Essence of Cinema'. In *The Avant-Garde Film: A Reader of Theory and Criticism*, edited by P. Adams Sitney, 24–5. New York: Anthology Film Archives.

Gorky, Maxim. 1988. 'The Lumière Cinematograph'. In *The Film Factory: Russian and Soviet Cinema Documents, 1896–1939*, edited by Richard Taylor and Ian Christie, 25–6. Cambridge, MA: Harvard University Press.

Lindsay, Vachel. 1970. *The Art of the Motion Picture*. New York: Liveright Publishing.

Rodowick, D.N. 2007. *The Virtual Life of Film*. Cambridge, MA: Harvard University Press.

Vertov, Dziga. 1984 [1923]. 'The Council of Three'. In *Kino-Eye: The Writings of Dziga Vertov*, edited by Annette Michelson, translated by Kevin O'Brien, 14–21. Berkeley: University of California Press.

# SPECIFICITY, MEDIUM II

If we had a good definition of the essence of cinema, it would be easy to say what the specificity of the apparatus of the cinema is. But such a definition does not exist as cinema is more often seen as a 'total social fact', to quote Marcel Mauss (1990), and it is better to give a working definition of it that is sensitive to context rather than a definition of its essence. For most people, cinema is a form of the performing arts that consists in collectively watching a narrative feature film in a theatre specifically devised for this effect. But this working definition is far from perfect. For some people, going to the movies does not necessarily imply going to a theatre. They may organize a 'movie screening party' at home with friends, in front of a suitably named *home cinema*. Or they may watch experimental movies, which will be neither feature films nor narratives, and still say they 'are going to the movies'. There are Wittgensteinian family similarities among these cases, but it would be useless to try to list all the characteristics that a form of the performing arts should include in order to be called 'cinema'. Besides, in these times of transmediality (Jenkins 2003) and relocation (Casetti 2009), the 'audiovisual narrative' object has a greater importance and clarity in daily life than the 'cinema' object, and whether the story is being told in a TV series or a feature film does not much matter as long as it is a good one.

There are additional angles, however, that may reveal the specificity of the cinematic apparatus: (1) the artistic and intermedial dimension; (2) the audiovisual content; (3) the socio-cognitive usage.

## The artistic and intermedial dimension

Not long after the first commercial screenings of moving pictures, people attempted to turn cinema into a machine, a medium, or a *particular* art. Cinema initially appeared as a realization of the double romantic vow of fighting against the inexorable passing of time, being both:

- a mechanized extension of the 'mummy complex', as André Bazin would say in 1945, i.e. a way of preserving living beings beyond their own deaths (*see* ONTOLOGY OF THE PHOTOGRAPHIC IMAGE); and
- a flat 2D form of the 'Frankenstein syndrome', as Noël Burch would say in 1990, i.e. a way of bringing the dead back to life (through images, which is better than nothing).

But this slightly morbid conception of moving pictures immediately had to compete with other, more cheerful, ones. For cinema is also a performing art, and a deeply intermedial one at that. It shares with photography the capacity to keep alive luminous traces of the world; with chronophotography the possibility to break down movement; with scientific toys the transformation of fixed into animated images; with the magic lantern the notion of screening images in the dark; with theatre the use of actors, décors, and artificial lighting; with literature the use of words; with opera the use of music from the orchestra pit; with conjuring arts the way of unexpectedly summoning people and things and making them disappear; and with fairy tales the staging of marvellous worlds. Later, when dialogues were introduced, it also borrowed techniques and codes from the radio and the phonographic industry.

And not only did cinema appear as the heir (or the poacher, or even the murderer in the case of fairy tales) of all these arts, but throughout the decades some of its character-istics were inherited or poached by others. Comics, television, video art, video games, etc. also have points in common with it, while cinema itself has borrowed from its 'cousins'. There is definitely something Frankensteinian about the cinematic apparatus, but it has to be looked for within the monster rather than in Baron Victor. For the specificity of the cinematic apparatus is probably that it is made of borrowed *pieces* that fit together – neither the scars nor the bolts can be seen – which makes it somewhat different from the monster created by the Baron. Cinema, rather, merges together characteristics of other arts and media. This is what is called *fusional* intermediality.

One of the first commentators to advance a claim for the artistic specificity of cinema, Riccioto Canudo, thought this way; to him, as early as 1911, cinema was 'a beautiful *reconciliation* of the Rhythms of Space (the Plastic Arts) and the Rhythms of Time (Music and Poetry)' (Canudo 1988, 59). As leader of the lobbying campaign that would anoint cinema as the Seventh Art, Canudo did not bet on the 'mummy complex', or else he would have counted photography as the seventh art, thus making cinema the eighth. In his eyes, photography – which is also able to support the 'mummy complex' – was nothing but 'the copy of a subject: the condition that prevents [it] from becoming an art' (61). Cinema did know how to make time stand still, but what mattered to Canudo was that it did so in a very *new* way: 'The arrival of cinema heralds the renovation of all modes of artistic creation, of all means of "arresting the fleeting", conquering the ephemeral' (296). Here Canudo was in line with the spirit of the avant-garde movements of his time, of the neo-philiac spirit – the demand for novelty – associated with modernity. The specificity of cinema also and especially consisted in the fact that the special synthesis it made of other arts was new – in other words, it was 'absolutely modern' (59).

## The audiovisual content

As Noël Carroll has shown, there is a *medium-specificity thesis* which 'recommends that artists exploit the distinctive possibilities of the medium in which they ply their trade and that they abjure the effects that are discharged better or equally well by the media of other artforms'. When they succeed in this task, 'they are *cinematic* – that is, they engage in and exploit the distinctive properties of the medium' (Carroll 2008, 36 and 38; *see* ART, FILM AS; CLASSICAL FILM THEORY).

But this thesis raises at least two issues. The first one is the difficulty in locating these 'distinctive properties' as we deal with a Frankenstein medium synthesizing other (chan-ging) arts and media. Strictly speaking, of course, these properties do exist. No other art, for instance, can produce tracking, a dolly shot, a cutaway, not to mention a simple cut.

But more generally, a moving backdrop produced by unrolling a painted canvas on stage may produce the same impression as a tracking shot; a magic lantern with a mobile lens may produce the impression of moving forward or backward as in a dolly shot; literature and comics can produce cutaways; and the Bian Lian technique (changing-face performance) of Chinese opera gives the same feeling as a cut. One also should not forget that these so-called 'distinctive properties' are all based on the perceptual/cognitive system common to all human beings. I 'can read' the tracking because I know what happens from a visual point of view when I move sideways, forwards, or backwards and am used to looking through the window when travelling by train; I understand the cutaway because I often briefly glance at a detail; and a cut does not disturb me because I regularly blink (see Cutting 2005). The second issue is that the *medium-specificity thesis* is highly debatable as a judgement or standard of taste, though not as descriptive assertion. Hitchcock is more cinematic than Bergman, and Renoir more than Pagnol – fine – but saying that *for this very reason* Hitchcock and Renoir are *better directors* is untenable: 'Even if a film that engages the medium more directly is better as film art, it is not evident that it follows that it is a better artwork qua art. For the quality of the artist as such and the artwork as such depends on the overall excellence of the output' (Carroll 2008, 46).

Under the *medium-specificity thesis* hides the romantic definition of art as the personal expression of a creative genius. This was already the argument used by Canudo to try to transcend the photographic dimension of cinema that threatened to reduce cinema from an art to a thing producing merely 'copies of a subject': for this purpose, the director had to become conscious that 'his mission [was] to transform objective reality into his own personal vision' (Canudo 1988, 298). Yet if this definition of art is highly successful among *cinema enthusiasts* and in the Art World, most spectators expect something else (or something more) of motion pictures than the expression of a singular sensitivity.

## The socio-cognitive usage

Instead of looking for specificity in the filmic text or in the apparatus, maybe one should look for it in the way films have been used and developed throughout the world. Two other arts have had the same universal success as cinema, namely literature and music. But access to literature requires the ability to read, and music does not tell stories. As for motion pictures, they tell stories that are comprehended immediately by an untutored audience. From contact with motion pictures – and especially from their collective contact, even when the collectivity is reduced to a mere couple – a feeling of togetherness arises. Even though he was preoccupied with artistic and textual issues, Canudo noted as early as 1911: 'What is striking, characteristic and significant, even more than the spectacle itself, is the uniform will of the spectators ... the desire for a new Festival, for a new joyous unanimity, realized at a show, in a place where together, all men can forget in greater or lesser measure, their isolated individuality' (Canudo 1988, 65).

Evolutionary psychology would make a similar assertion a century later, speaking of narrative arts: narratives may be seen as an 'information storage and transmission system', a 'mimetic simulation of human experience' (Scalise 2005, 191), i.e. a cognitive modelling process or thought experiment. And 'art is an adaptation whose functions are shaping and sharing attention, and, arising from that, fostering social cohesion and creativity' (Boyd 2005, 151).

Thinking of all the fans and textual poachers who reproduce and transform audiovisual figures, the notion of dissemination generally, often referred to as 'flow' and 'spreadability' (see Jenkins 2007), should probably be added to these two elements. It would be a mistake, however, to believe that this dispersal had to wait until the Internet age to flourish. As soon as cinema reached international success, it left traces in everyday life. One of the fathers of anthropology, Marcel Mauss, understood this very early, and in 'The Techniques of the Body' he already underlined a specificity of cinema which makes it different from other narrative arts, namely the fact that it is a kinesthetic form of imagery:

> A kind of revelation came to me in hospital. I was ill in New York. I wondered where previously I had seen girls walking as my nurses walked. I had the time to think about it. At last I realized that it was at cinema. Returning to France, I noticed how common this gait was, especially in Paris: the girls were French and they too were walking the same way. In fact, American walking fashions had begun to arrive over here, thanks to the cinema.
>
> (Mauss 2006, 80)

Mauss reveals here the contribution of cinema to what Michel Foucault would later call the 'techniques of the self' – not only ways of moving around, but also of being, feeling, perceiving, remembering, and understanding. In this perspective, including, once again, the idea of being 'alone together', cinema is simply the narrative art which best combines contributions to the 'techniques of the self' with the faculty to produce social cohesion. Or rather it *was*, as television and other individual, often handheld, screens have now outdone it in terms of numbers of spectators, due to transmediality and relocation.

LAURENT JULLIER

## Works cited

Boyd, Brian. 2005. 'Evolutionary Theories of Art'. In *The Literary Animal: Evolution and the Nature of Narrative*, edited by Jonathan Gottschall and David Sloan Wilson, 147–76. Evanston, IL: Northwestern University Press.

Burch, Noël. 1990. 'Charles Baudelaire versus Doctor Frankenstein'. In *Life to Those Shadows*. Berkeley: University of California Press.

Canudo, Ricciotto. 1988. 'The Birth of a Sixth Art' (1911) and 'Reflections on the Seventh Art' (1923). In *French Film Theory and Criticism: A History/Anthology, 1907–1939*, vol. 1, edited by Richard Abel, 58–65 and 291–302. Princeton, NJ: Princeton University Press.

Carroll, Noël. 2008. *The Philosophy of Motion Pictures*. Malden, MA: Blackwell.

Casetti, Francesco. 2009. 'Elsewhere: The Relocation of Art'. In *Valencia09/Confines, Valencia, IVAM*, edited by C. Ciscar Casabàn and V. Trione, 226–33. Valencia: Institut Valencia d'Art Modern.

Cutting, James E. 2005. 'Perceiving Scenes in Film and in the World'. In *Moving Image Theory: Ecological Considerations*, edited by J.D. Anderson and B.F. Anderson, 9–27. Carbondale: University of Southern Illinois Press.

Jenkins, Henry. 2003. 'Transmedia Storytelling'. *Technology Review*, 15 January: www.technologyreview.com/biotech/13052.

——. 2007. 'Slash Me, Mash Me, Spread Me … '. Weblog text, 24 April: http://www.henryjenkins.org/2007/04/slash_me_mash_me_but_please_sp.html.

Mauss, Marcel. 1990 [1925]. *The Gift*. Chicago, IL: University of Chicago Press.

——. 2006. *Techniques, Technologies and Civilisation*. New York: Durkheim Press.

Scalise, Michelle. 2005. 'Reverse-Engineering Narrative: Evidence of Special Design'. In *The Literary Animal: Evolution and the Nature of Narrative*, edited by Jonathan Gottschall and David Sloan Wilson, 177–96. Evanston, IL: Northwestern University Press.

## Further reading

Carroll, Noël. 1996. 'Concerning Uniqueness Claims for Photographic and Cinematographic Representation'. In *Theorizing the Moving Image*, 37–48. Cambridge: Cambridge University Press.

Leveratto, Jean-Marc. 2010. 'The Techniques of the Body by Marcel Mauss: American Culture, Everyday Life and French Theory'. In *Transatlantic Voyages and Sociology: The Migration and Development of Ideas*, edited by Cherry Schrecker, 82–96. London: Ashgate.

# STRUCTURAL/MATERIALIST FILM

This entry presents structural/materialist film through a discussion of Peter Gidal's important essay 'Definition and Theory of the Current Avant-Garde: Materialist/Structural Film' (1974). Gidal's essay is based on an uncompromising anti-illusionism, formulated against dominant ideological filmic practices. Gidal's anti-illusionism entails a polemical rejection of narrative, image, and meaning.

## Peter Gidal

Peter Gidal is a practitioner as well as theorist of structural/materialist films, a form of counter or avant-garde film movement developed in Europe, the USA, and especially Britain in the 1960s (*see* COUNTER-CINEMA). Gidal's uncompromising formal experiments in film (*Key, Clouds, Room Film 1973, Condition of Illusion, Denials, Volcano*, etc.) are matched by the radical political aims of his theoretical writings (Gidal 1974; 1975; 1976; 1979; 1989).

Gidal's 1974 essay does not study individual films but reads more like a manifesto, stating in polemical terms the ideas behind structural/materialist filmmaking. He mentions in passing its predecessors, such as Andy Warhol, and also lists European avant-gardes of the 1920s (such as surrealism), and American visionary films – such as those of Stan Brakhage, which rely on the Romantic notion of the expression of the artist's personal 'vision'. But Gidal mentions these only to demarcate the differences between them and structural/materialist film. He also sharply differentiates structural/materialist filmmaking from commercial narrative cinema and art-house cinema. In his 1975 essay, Gidal lists a small canon of structural/materialist films, including Malcolm Le Grice's *Little Dog for Roger* and *Yes No Maybe Maybenot*; Michael Snow's *Wavelength, Back and Forth*, and *The Central Region*; Kurt Kren's *Trees in Autumn, TV, Szondi Test*, and *Auf der Plaueninsel*; Peter Kubelka's *Adebar* and *Schwechater*; Hollis Frampton's *Process Red* and *Zorns Lemma*; Paul Sharits's *Word Movie*; and his own films *Clouds, Hall*, and *Room Film 1973*.

Gidal shares with art critic Clement Greenberg (1982) the sense that visual art can escape illusion and content through abstraction. Both authors focus on medium specificity (on what is unique and irreducible to a medium; *see* SPECIFICITY, MEDIUM I AND II), for it is the specificity of painting or film that limits its illusionistic, representational function. Whereas illusionistic art tries to conceal the limitations of its medium, modernist art draws attention to its own limitations, its specific qualities (in painting: the flat surface of the canvas, the frame, the paint pigments, brush strokes; in film: the flat surface of the screen, the frame, film grain, the beam of projected light, movement, repetition, duration). By foregrounding medium specificity, modernist art achieves self-definition.

If this were the main agenda of Gidal's essay, it would be an unremarkable aesthetic theory. But Gidal went much further; he used theories of French structuralism (structural linguistics, structural anthropology, and semiotics), and, most importantly, added 'materialism' to his definition of structural film – meaning not simply the physical material (the specific qualities/limitations of a medium) but more significantly materialism in the sense developed in dialectical materialism. Gidal constructs a dialectical theory of film, a theory that conceives film in terms of the interaction of two opposing terms, consciousness and material, in which the material, although primary, is inseparable from the process of knowing it. From this dialectical materialist definition Gidal identifies structural film's political agenda – not a positive agenda to express a political message through film, but a negative agenda to undermine dominant ideology's grip on filmic practices (*see* CONTEMPORARY FILM THEORY; IDEOLOGY, CINEMA AND). Structural/materialist film is non-narrative, non-illusionistic, non-representational, and impersonal, for it aims to present the film material and process.

From his threefold theoretical perspective (modernism, structuralism, dialectical materialism), in his 1974 essay Gidal formulated an initial definition of structural/materialist filmmaking. Gidal's theory is a solution to the problem of defining a modernist, structural, political avant-garde filmic practice.

## The six issues Gidal's essay addresses

1. *The avant-garde is a didactic avant-garde*: 'A re-educative process is at work from the moment a creative act that differs formally from its predecessors is attempted' (Gidal 1974, 53). There are two components in Gidal's opening proposition: avant-garde art breaks radically from the past; that radical break is epistemological. He gives the example of avant-garde film needing to unleash itself from 'inherently authoritarian and manipulative, and therefore reactionary', narrative structures (53). Narrative creates an illusionistic representation; it negates the materiality of filmic space and time in favour of an imaginary, fictional space and time of the story world. The issue here is to develop a filmmaking practice that returns film to its own materiality, rather than exploit film to represent something outside itself.

2. *The dialectical function of the current avant-garde*: Gidal singles out British structural films as dialectical, in opposition to the non-dialectical American visionary avant-garde, still influenced by Romanticism (film as expressive of an artist's inner life), as well as commercial and art-house narrative films, which rely on passive identification with characters. The issue here is to condemn commercial narrative film because it negates its own material space and time by creating an illusory fictional space and time. By contrast, structural/materialist films are dialectical because they increase the viewer's perception of filmic materiality, its mode of production. Structural/materialist films are therefore reflexive.

3. *Many filmmakers of the current avant-garde started out as painters, rather than writers or journalists.* Gidal traces the influence of abstract expressionism and minimalism on structural/materialist filmmakers. These filmmakers follow abstract expressionism's 'ethic of process': 'the act of creation remains visible in the product' (54), and they borrow minimalism's austere aesthetics, its 'paring down the artwork to a minimum of "essential" qualities' (54). The issue here is to identify film's essential qualities and to praise films that foreground those qualities. Gidal singles out 'duration' as a basic structural unit of

film, in combination with flatness, grain, light, movement, and repetition, for duration, of course, is not specific in itself to film but is a characteristic of all temporal media.

4. *Reflexivity.* Gidal employs the modernist concept of reflexivity to displace the dichotomy thinking/feeling. Reflexiveness involves a dialectical interaction between viewer and film, not simply a rational contemplation of film or an emotional-cathartic engagement with fictional characters. A reflexive act, Gidal informs us, is one whereby the film spectator remains critical and self-aware: 'the act of self-perception, of consciousness *per se*, becomes the basic context of one's confrontation with the work' (54). The issue here shifts from the filmic material to the viewer's act of perception and cognition of that material (hinted at in proposition 2). By involving perception and cognition, Gidal avoids mechanistic materialism (which reduces film to its physical properties).

5. *Defining structural film.* In this long section Gidal addresses the main issue in his essay – to define structural film. A definition consists of two parts: the genus, or general qualities of a concept, and differentia, the qualities that distinguish a concept from other concepts. Together, the genus and differentia specify the necessary and sufficient conditions for identifying a concept. Gidal's definition is analysed below.

6. *Categorization.* Gidal identifies the activity of categorization as problematic but necessary. He sets up strict boundaries around structural/materialist film. Not only does Gidal add 'materialism' to the theorization of structural film; he also defines structuralism according to the tenets of French structuralism.

Gidal's theory condemns an experience dominant in commercial film and art cinema: absorption in an illusionistic representation. He characterizes this experience as 'a passive mental posture in the face of a life unlived, a fantasy identified with for the sake of 90 minutes' illusion' (54). He challenges this ideologically conditioned experience, not only theoretically but also in his own filmic practice, where he attempts to replace illusionistic experience of film with a dialectical materialist experience. In a structural/materialist film, ideologically conditioned everyday lived experiences are transformed into a more rarefied, pared down, reflexive experience, in which the image is (almost) emptied of represented content, replaced with the actual filmmaking processes that have constructed the image on screen.

## The six concepts in Gidal's essay

We can identify six interrelated concepts in Gidal's essay that enable him to define structural/materialist film: (1) presentation of process; (2) reflexivity; (3) dialectical materialism; (4) structure; (5) the subject-in-process; and (6) relativistic time (duration). Note that there is no simple one-to-one mapping between the six issues identified above and the six concepts listed here. Instead, the relation between issues and concepts is more fluid, open-ended, and diffuse.

1. To define the genus of the structural/materialist film, Gidal employs a standard trope of modernist art: the medium's form becomes the (non-fictional) content. In other words, the presentation of the process of making, or the traces of the film's coming into being, constitutes the primary content of a structural film, rather than an illusionistic reproduction of a fictional content.

449

2. This focus on the presentation of process in turn activates in the spectator a self-aware reflexive stance, a conscious experience of film's form and materiality. It is therefore the spectator's experience of the process of making which is central to defining the structural/materialist film: 'viewing such a film is at once viewing a film and viewing the making of the film, i.e. the *system of consciousness* that produced the work' (55; emphasis in original).

3. The differentia of the structural/materialist films Gidal examines is that the viewing experience is not simply aesthetic, but dialectical: 'The mental dialectical activation of the viewer is necessary for the procedure of the film's existence' (55). And: 'The attempt to retain the self during experience, the attempt to not feel the need for separation of feelings from thoughts, is basic to this form of consciousness' (54).

4. How is Gidal's definition structural? The structural/materialist film's structure is not perceived instantaneously, but gradually and indirectly, through its effects. A structural/materialist film does not aim to create a coherent Gestalt; it does not aim to present a unified, coherent experience of a film, but an heterogeneous experience. Stephen Heath emphasized that the heterogeneous structural/materialist film produces spectatorial activity 'at the limit of any fixed subjectivity, materially inconstant, dispersed in process, beyond the accommodation of reality and pleasure principles. [It is based on] the loss of the imaginary unity of the subject-ego and the very grain of drive against that coherent fiction' (Heath 1981, 167).

5. Julia Kristeva's concept of the 'subject-in-process' presents a precise conception of the dispersed subjectivity generated by structural/materialist films. The subject-in-process 'accentuates *process* rather than identification, *projection* rather than desire, the *heterogeneous* rather than the signifier, *struggle* rather than structure' (Kristeva, quoted in Coward and Ellis 1977, 145–6; original emphasis). However, this dispersed subjectivity remains implicit in Gidal's 1974 essay, for he writes primarily about reflexive self-perception without pursuing the split nature of this perception.

6. Finally, the concept of duration. This raises the problematic of experiencing time, which Gidal divides into three categories: real time (as in Warhol's films, or in long takes in commercial and art-house cinema); illusionistic time (manipulation of time in commercial cinema via editing and montage); and relativistic time (the dialectical experience of a structural film). Whereas the first category refers to pure, physical duration, as in real time, and the second to a purely artificial, fictional time, the third conception refers to reading duration – the dialectical interaction of consciousness with the structural/materialist film's physical duration. Gidal goes beyond dialectical materialism to characterize this interaction in terms of the theory of relativity: 'The third aspect of time is post-Newtonian, Einsteinian time. There is, in the latter, no absolute value other than the interaction of film-moment and viewer' (Gidal 1974, 55). Presumably Gidal uses Einstein to dispel the notion that real time is a fixed, invariant reference frame for understanding the heightened, reflexive duration in the structural/materialist film. Instead, this reflexive duration is a relative experience constituted entirely between the shifting relations between film and the spectator's consciousness.

In sum, Gidal presents in this early formulation an already complex definition that does not simply involve listing the specific qualities of structural/materialist film, but crucially also involves a dialectical experience of film, an experience Gidal characterizes as relativistic time (rather than real or illusionistic time).

## Critique: Constance Penley

Gidal's theory of structural/materialist film sets out to be rigorously modernist, structuralist, dialectical, and materialist. And the aim of structural/materialist films is not simply to provide an aesthetic experience; instead, they attempt to oppose dominant ideology's grip on filmic practices. Gidal's 1974 essay marks the beginning of his well-formulated theory (although the reader should be warned that these formulations are sometimes hidden in an opaque and deliberately contradictory writing style).

Whether Gidal's theoretical edifice is based on correct assumptions or not can be seen in the way he developed his theory. In his 1975 essay, he downplayed the value of French theories in theorizing structural/materialist film: 'Advanced (mainly French) theory (not necessarily directly concerning film) is either not capable of dealing with film or else posits retrograde, illusionist, post-Bazinian manifestations of such' (Gidal 1975, 193). He goes on to say: 'The lamentably derivative watered-down [film theory] regurgitated by the editors of *Screen* is merely importation from at most three Paris sources, which though at moments useful is not directed correctly, is not made to interact with avant-garde film practice in this country (or any other)' (193). And later, in *Materialist Film*, he downplayed the significance of the (Greenbergian) modernist agenda, placing emphasis on an individual film's materiality, rather than film in general: 'It was never up to the structural/materialist filmmaker to recover films' essential nature, i.e., film as film. If anything, it is *a* film's concrete existence which must interest; its possibilities of militating against transparency; its presentation/formation of processes of production' (Gidal 1989, 20). What remains at the core of Gidal's work is a dialectical materialist theory and practice that aims to demystify filmic representation.

The widespread response his theory received indicates its relevance and significance in expanding knowledge of avant-garde film. Gidal's work quickly became the focal point around which to discuss and theorize avant-garde filmmaking. However, in 'The Avant Garde and Its Imaginary' (Penley 1989, 3–28; first published in 1977), Constance Penley questioned the significance of his work by asking: 'In what ways does it offer solutions to those problems basic to any attempt to formulate a filmmaking practice that would not reenact the illusions and manipulations of dominant cinema?' (4). Referring to key French psychoanalytic film theory texts of the 1970s – including Christian Metz's essay on the imaginary signifier (1975) (*see* IMAGINARY SIGNIFIER) and Jean-Louis Baudry on the cinematic apparatus (1974, 1976) (*see* APPARATUS THEORY [BAUDRY]) – Penley sounded a sceptical note concerning the possibility of structural/materialist films escaping the imaginary of the cinematic signifier and the ideology of the cinematic apparatus. It is not sufficient for Gidal to critique narrative and identification, she argues, for the filmic signifier and the cinematic apparatus themselves are ideological. She criticizes the attempts to present structural/materialist filmmaking as existing outside of ideology, in which the materiality of film can be directly perceived:

> If one can successfully eliminate a certain kind of imagery ('symbolic,' 'associative' images, ones that are 'representations' or 'reproductions') and a particular ordering of images (editing that suppresses material space and time) [as Gidal argues] then the spectator would be confronted with an image, a film, that would call forth a direct and conscious response, a response focused on the subject's own act of perception ... Such 'materialization' strategies refuse or disavow any

knowledge of the imaginary inherent in the cinematic signifier itself. The imaginary can only be endlessly played out; its infinite metonymy can only be stopped into *fictions* of materiality, never materiality itself.

(Penley 1989, 11–12; original emphasis)

The question Penley posed at the beginning of her essay receives a negative reply – Gidal is unable to formulate a filmmaking practice that escapes the illusions and manipulations of dominant cinema; for her Gidal's theory is not well-formed. Yet, her negative assessment downplays the positive value of non-meaning in Gidal's work, which lies in its rejection of the given, the taken-for-granted, of the ideological coding of events, subjectivity, and meanings as 'natural', stable, and fixed. The structural/materialist film is not guaranteed by an external truth or reality. Neither does the structural/materialist film strive to create a fixed, static, immediately perceivable coherent shape, or Gestalt. Instead, 'the question of anything being held, finalized, stopped, is constantly problematic in such a film' (Gidal 1989, 8).

WARREN BUCKLAND

## Works cited

Baudry, Jean-Louis. 1974. 'Ideological Effects of the Basic Cinematographic Apparatus'. *Film Quarterly* 27 (2): 39–47.

——. 1976. 'The Apparatus'. *Camera Obscura* 1: 104–26.

Coward, Rosalind, and John Ellis. 1977. *Language and Materialism: Developments in Semiology and the Theory of the Subject*. London: Routledge and Kegan Paul.

Gidal, Peter. 1974. 'Definition and Theory of the Current Avant-Garde: Materialist/Structural Film'. *Studio International* 187 (963) (February): 53–6.

——. 1975. 'Theory and Definition of Structural/Materialist Film'. *Studio International* 190 (978) (November/December): 189–96.

——. 1976. 'Theory and Definition of Structural/Materialist Film'. In *Structural Film Anthology*, edited by Peter Gidal, 1–21. London: BFI.

——. 1979. 'The Anti-narrative'. *Screen* 20 (2): 73–93.

——. 1989. *Materialist Film*. London: Routledge.

Greenberg, Clement. 1982 [1965]. 'Modernist Painting'. In *Modern Art and Modernism: A Critical Anthology*, edited by Francis Frascina and Charles Harrison, 5–10. London: Harper and Row.

Heath, Stephen. 1981. 'Repetition/Time: Notes around "Structural/Materialist Film"'. In *Questions of Cinema*, 165–75. London: Macmillan.

Metz, Christian. 1975. 'The Imaginary Signifier'. *Screen* 16 (2): 14–76.

Penley, Constance. 1989. *The Future of an Illusion: Film, Feminism, and Psychoanalysis*. Minneapolis: University of Minnesota Press.

## Further reading

Le Grice, Malcolm. 1977. *Abstract Film and Beyond*. London: Studio Vista.

Rodowick, D.N. 1988. *The Crisis of Political Modernism: Criticism and Ideology in Contemporary Film Theory*, chapter 5. Chicago: University of Illinois Press.

Michelson, Annette. 1971. 'Foreword in Three Letters'. *Artforum* 10 (1) (September): 8–9.

# SUTURE

In *A Seventh Man*, John Berger describes a passport photograph of a young boy belonging to a migrant worker (Berger and Mohr 1975). To us the photo suggests a presence, but to his father it represents an absence. This dialectic of presence and absence is one clue to the concept of suture, except that suture is not about the missing boy, but the address the image makes to its reader. Suture describes the relations between a film and its spectator, specifically to two apparently contradictory qualities of film viewing: that the action of the film and its style produce meanings in us, but at the same time we produce meanings in the stream of images we watch.

The word suture was used with subtle differences by a small group of thinkers and critics inspired by Jacques Lacan, especially some specific theories about how meaning is created. For the film theorists, the first important thesis is that any film is a discourse. Here the word 'discourse' means simply something spoken by someone and addressed to someone else. Lacan refused to accept the thesis that individual human beings exist before their socialization through language and other symbolic systems (table manners for example, or any rule of behaviour). As discourse, the film produces the subject – the part of us that experiences subjectivity, our experience of existing – as an effect of its discourse (*see* CONTEMPORARY FILM THEORY).

## J.-P. Oudart's 'Cinema and Suture'

When the spectator is addressed by the film, who is actually speaking? In the first film theory to take on the concept of suture, J.-P. Oudart (1977/8) argues that the viewer imagines a source the film comes from. Oudart suggests four stages. At first the viewer is lost in the flicker of the image, mesmerized. Then something – his example is a visual gag in Keaton's *The General* (1926) – makes them aware of the artifice of the scene they are watching. At first it is a delightful surprise, but it also brings the spectator back to themselves: just someone in a cinema staring at the pictures, the signifiers. Then they ask themselves who is 'speaking' the discourse of the film, and the troubling answer comes back: no one, an absence. But when the very next shot reverses the angle, we see the person, animal, or thing from whose point of view the previous shot was seen. Of course, the subject cries out, that is who is making the film, who is telling the story, who is calling the shots. This last move, imagining a subject who recounts the film, heals the absence created in the previous moment: it is a suture in the sense of a surgical stitch which both confirms the meaning of the film and the construction of the viewing subject as subject of – and to – the film. At this basic level, suture is a theory which accounts for the way we carry attention across edits without losing narrative, intellectual, or emotional connection with the movie.

There are a number of reasons why this simplified version of the concept needs to be unpacked. In the first instance, as Barry Salt had demonstrated in an early response, shot/reverse-shot transitions accounted for only 30 to 40 per cent of classical Hollywood edits. The theory needed a more general sense of the oscillation of the viewing subject into and out of the surface of the film. This is one challenge taken on by Stephen Heath's 1977/8 'Notes on Suture'. A second is that the title is very accurate: the four sections of the essay seem to have rather different tasks in mind. Third, one of those tasks is to work out how to reconcile three main versions of the concept, or to get one version that works. The essay appeared in a 'Dossier on Suture' in *Screen*, including translations of essays by Miller and Oudart, and Heath also refers to three essays published in the journal *Film Quarterly* by Dayan (1974), Rothman (1976), and Salt (1977). Here we will follow the structure of Heath's essay: two sections of critical commentary, a critique of reductive use of the concept, and a suggestion as to the future of suture in film theory.

## Stephen Heath's 'Notes on Suture'

In the first section of 'Notes on Suture', Heath shows how J.-A. Miller (1977/8) develops the term from Lacan. Miller uses an analogy from mathematical logic: a proof that all numbers can be derived from zero. There are two main steps: first, to define zero as the non-identical (everything that exists is self-identical, so nothing, which does not exist, must be non-identical); and second, that the set of non-identical things – the empty set – is nonetheless a set, and must be counted as one set. All subsequent numbers come from adding one to the primary one which 'names' the empty set. (A demonstration: how many numbers on a blank page? None. Write '0'. How many now? One. Write '1'. How many now? Two. And so on.) The analogy is with the non-identical nature of the human psyche. Naming it gives it a sense that it is a unit, whole, complete. Yet the name actually names non-identity. And every other word that follows keeps moving between non-identity (emptiness) and unity (fullness). This oscillation as an effect of naming, of discourse, is what Oudart has applied to the discourse of film. Incidentally, it also explains why suture theory always refers to the 'logic' of the signifier.

Miller was trying to demonstrate that at the origin of logic, the science of truth, there is a repressed lack or absence. Classically, logic refuses to accept subjectivity: truth is a formal property of well-made statements. For Miller, the non-identical zero is not just an analogy: it is the excluded figure that speaks and is spoken to in logical discourse. The subject both exists and does not exist, just as zero is represented by one (or indeed, as he puns, by the symbol Ø, the empty set).

In Lacan, language is representation. What is represented is not present in language, but only re-presented. The subject is no exception: it is only presented, never present. The subject is absent from language: as a kind of zero, by analogy with Miller's argument about logic, its exclusion actually causes language. The purpose of language is to speak the subject which started it off, each new signifier adding another 'plus 1' to the chain in an attempt to control, and perhaps to conclude the attempt to make the subject whole again. This leads Lacan to argue, in a phrase repeated by almost all the authors involved in suture theory, 'a signifier represents a subject for another signifier'. This, as Heath is at pains to describe, is the obverse of the more familiar statement 'a signifier represents something for a subject'. As an effect of language, the 'something' that is represented by a signifier is the subject to whom it is addressed. Therefore the subject is present in language after all. For Miller this contradictory condition is the basis of suture: a flickering in and out of existence which is managed through the succession of signifiers in the unfolding of language.

But film is not language. Heath now turns to film theory, to Oudart's essay, and to his commentators and critics in *Film Quarterly*. Oudart's essay is elliptical and obscure even by the standards of the day. Heath clarifies it to a great degree, without losing its complexity. Language can be analysed into two parts: a system of rules, and the actual use of them to make statements. The second of these can be split again into the things spoken, and the act of speaking. Oudart emphasized the latter: the *enunciation*. The question for the subjectivity called into existence by the address of the film is: who is calling me? Who enunciates? The problem is greater because the moment it is posed, it makes it obvious that everything the subject sees is a signifier. Which means, once more, a representation which actively excludes what it represents – like the little boy absent from his photograph in Berger's story.

Here Oudart's expression gets murky. He names the absent 'speaker' of the film the Absent One, presumably in reference to the role of numbers in Miller's article: not just an absence, but the absence of a unified subject capable of speaking the film as a complete account of the subject. That complete account he calls the signifying Sum. This is the goal of the film, but it is illusory or, more specifically, imaginary, a term with a special significance for Lacanians. The imaginary is the realm of images of ourselves we create in response to the splitting and loss that characterize infancy – separation from the mother, discovering you are separate from the rest of the world, discovering that your body is made of parts that could be lost. To describe the Absent One and the signifying Sum as imaginary suggests that they are self-images characterized by being imagined as whole and indivisible. This will be something Heath takes exception to, because it de-emphasizes other aspects of the process. What Heath does accept is the formulation describing suture as 'cinema's necessary representation of the subject's relation to its discourse' (Oudart 1977/8, 38). Note the words 'representation' and 'relation': there must be a relation for there to be a representation, but representing excludes what it represents, that is, the relation which makes representation possible.

To get over this problem, cinema uses cutting. This is one of the formal elements of cinema that can work as suture: in fact Oudart discusses depth of field at length, and one key example from *The General* involves not a cut but characters entering the frame. Suddenly aware of the frame, the spectator realizes that where she was previously free-floating, immersed in the screen, now she is included in the construction of virtual space in the scene before her. The indefinite becomes definite; but in place of the proximity she felt in the first phase of her involvement, the trick reveals the irreducible distance between camera and what it portrays. The image is then composed of three elements: frame, distance (depth of field), and object depicted. Concentrating on any one of them makes it impossible to see the others: again, the subject flickers between modes of perception. For Oudart the object has a key role: it can be simply the end stop of distance (what the camera is distant from) or a mere signifier, but if it does appear as object, it seems to appear from out of pure absence, as the representative of the Absent One whose imaginary gaze – synonymous with the omni-voyant gaze of the camera – is the imaginary unifying principle of both the film and the subject. The object 'sutures the cinematic discourse'.

Heath now moves on briefly to Dayan's commentary, which seeks to place Oudart's suture in terms of the theory of ideology. He goes back to earlier work of Oudart's on classical painting, where it was argued that the object depicted always signifies a subject who will look at it. But that viewer can never be represented (with the famous exception of Velàzquez's *Las Meninas*) because the place must be left empty so that any one passing by can occupy it. So a classical painting proposes both itself and how it is to be viewed. But in cinema each shot posits a different subject, setting up the conditions for ideological communication in the cinema.

According to Dayan, in the first shot we see from the point of view of the Absent One. In the second we see a figure we presume (imagine) to *be* the Absent One, but at that moment the Absent One moves from the enunciation to the fiction – the enunciated, what is spoken – of the film. This also means that shot two is the 'meaning' of shot one: meaning is deferred, but also operates retroactively, 'remodeling memory'. Dayan's conclusion is neat: the spectator finally realizes that in the cinema no one speaks. It is as if things speak themselves. And that is the very definition of ideology.

Heath begins to assemble these three disparate variants into his own thesis. Oudart, he says, emphasizes the imaginary too much. By ignoring the symbolic, Oudart has allowed it the power to create meaning, a 'theological' power (Heath 1977/8, 60), while Dayan muddles his analogies (suture is not a speech but a writing, the etymological root of cinematography). As a result it is unclear whether suture is an ideological operation or the basis of any signification whatever. Suture, he argues, stitches together the imaginary and the symbolic: the fantasy of unified being (ego) and the subject as effect of all systems that produce meaning. Quoting Miller, Heath defines suture as 'the general relation of lack to the structure of which it is an element' (26). Whether logic, language, or the film, any utterance creates both the subject of its address and that subject's absence (because it is signified and therefore excluded from the discourse that represents it).

In the third section, Heath moves on to critique Althusser and his student Pêcheux for their pseudo-Lacanian theory of interpellation. Here ideology is described as the discourse of power, a power which calls out to the subject, and which the subject recognizes and in that moment becomes subjected to. Heath argues that interpellation 'presumes the subject it is supposed to constitute' (71), and that the existing politicization of suture confuses imaginary, symbolic, unconscious, and ideology. In fact, suture is a way of naming the relation between these four elements. He adds that Lacan is his own worst enemy when he claims, on occasion, to be the master of truth: there is no final truth. This is the lesson of suture, and the reason why ideology starts with suture, not with the subject.

This account of the constant fading and emergence, the pulsing or flickering between immersion and withdrawal, matches the flicker of projection, the movement from cut to cut or in the space and duration of a single shot. That made the concept an influential one (e.g. Silverman 1983), not least because it recognized that the specific work done by any particular film was different from that of others. Other structural theories tended to lump all films together, perhaps with exceptions from the avant-garde. This theory was more nuanced. It still emerges from time to time (e.g. Butte 2008). But the declining fashion for psychoanalytic film study has seen suture move from target of mockery to forgotten concept, although Slavoj Žižek's intervention into the debate, in the first section of his book devoted to Krzysztof Kieślowski (Žižek 2001, 13–68), has revived the concept (although has not necessarily dispelled the mockery) and has renamed it 'interface' (*see* INTERFACE).

SEAN CUBITT

## Works cited

Berger, John, and Jean Mohr. 1975. *A Seventh Man*. London: Penguin.

Butte, George. 2008. 'Suture and the Narration of Subjectivity in Film'. *Poetics Today* 29 (2) (Summer): 277–308.

Dayan, Daniel. 1974. 'The Tutor Code of Classical Cinema'. *Film Quarterly* 28 (1) (Autumn): 22–31; reprinted in *Movies and Methods*, vol. 1, edited by Bill Nichols, 438–51. Berkeley: University of California Press, 1976.

Heath, Stephen. 1977/8. 'Notes on Suture'. *Screen* 18 (4) (Winter): 48–76; reprinted in Stephen Heath, *Questions of Cinema*, 76–112. London: Macmillan, 1981.

Miller, Jacques-Alain. 1977/8. 'Suture (Elements of the Logic of the Signifier)'. *Screen* 18 (4) (Winter): 24–34.

Oudart, Jean-Pierre. 1977/8. 'Cinema and Suture'. *Screen* 18 (4) (Winter): 35–47.

Rothman, William. 1976. 'Against "The System of Suture"'. *Film Quarterly* 29 (1): 45–50; reprinted in *Movies and Methods*, vol. 1, edited by Bill Nichols, 451–59. Berkeley: University of California Press, 1976.

Salt, Barry. 1977. 'Film Style and Technology in the Forties'. *Film Quarterly* 31 (1): 46–57.

Silverman, Kaja. 1983. *The Subject of Semiotics*. New York: Oxford University Press.

Žižek, Slavoj. 2001. *The Fright of Real Tears: Krzysztof Kieślowski between Theory and Post-theory*. London: BFI.

## Further reading

Branigan, Edward. 2006. *Projecting a Camera: Language-Games in Film Theory*, 133–45. New York: Routledge.

# SYMBOL AND ANALOGON (MITRY)

In 1963 and 1965 Jean Mitry published the two tomes of *Esthétique et psychologie du cinéma* (*EPC*). The result of years of teaching and writing about the cinema, this massive work is Mitry's foundational theoretical statement, around which most of his other works gravitate.

Two distinct, though closely related, projects drive *EPC*: to offer a description of the conditions of the film experience as meaningful; and to offer principles with which to evaluate that experience aesthetically. Two key concepts ensure the unity of the approach: *symbol* and *analogon*.

## Signs

Both concepts relate to the idea of what a *sign* is. There exist vastly different approaches to signs; semiotics being the 'science' that studies signs, one can say that there exist different semiotic theories. One of the most common definitions, however, comes from Augustine: a sign is something that stands for something else (*aliquid stat pro aliquo*). Though Mitry makes use of this definition of the sign to discuss what he calls the *symbol* (which he also refers to as the *linguistic sign*), he otherwise restricts his use of the word 'sign' to a different conception that is rendered by the German term *Vorstellung*. This word is usually translated into English as 'representation', which is rather confusing since symbols are also often thought of as representations (i.e. as standing for something). The distinction is that in the German tradition *Vorstellung* concerns mental representations: for instance, the mental images of the world that we have in perception, in memories, in imagination. Mitry calls these mental representations *psychological signs* and, as we shall see, distinguishes them from *symbols* or *linguistic signs*.

## Psychological signs and symbols

As mentioned, Mitry's approach to the issue of signification in the cinema has him use the rather uncommon distinction of *psychological* and *linguistic* signs. Whereas, for him, psychological signs concern the mental representations we have of the world through perception, linguistic signs are usually understood as forms (in some cases, concrete things that embody these forms, such as spoken sounds or written words) which come to arbitrarily or conventionally stand for abstract mental constructs such as ideas or concepts. Mitry, however, opts for Husserl's broader characterization of these signs as that for which, 'in the act of signifying, signification is not given to consciousness as an object' (Mitry 1963, 120). This characterization has a usefulness which we will consider in a moment. At the core of it lies the phenomenological concept of *intentionality*.

458

Mitry is especially interested in the psychological sign of perception, given its role in our experience of cinema. Perception, for him, is the process whereby, through the senses, the world appears to us as a *given*. What I see when I look at a chair is the chair *itself*, not something I *see as* a chair. The object of perception, in other words, has no *intentionality*, in the sense that it isn't *about* something else. For Mitry, who here momentarily distances himself from the phenomenological tradition, considers the psychological sign of perception as a *Gestalt*: through it something *directly* represents – or better yet: *shows* – itself (the chair, for instance). We shall return below to the role played by the psychological sign in the experience of cinema. Let us just say for now that Mitry considered it to be an important aspect of film that it offers us an experience akin to that of *unmediated, direct perceptions* devoid of intentionality.

Let us now turn to Mitry's conception of the symbol and to the benefit of adopting Husserl's conception of the linguistic sign to characterize it. The upshot is simple enough: namely, to define it as *intentional*. The linguistic sign 'chair', unlike the real chair and, for Mitry, unlike our perception of the chair, is *about* something: it stands for something other than itself, namely the concept of a chair. The usefulness of this conception rests in the fact that it is broad enough to accommodate both verbal signs and film *symbols*. For if, according to Mitry, the cinema can offer us unmediated perceptions – *showing* us worldly things – it can also do more. It can suggest ideas that aren't literally present on screen and only remotely connected/associated with what is seen. In this capacity – *and in this capacity alone* – film symbols are no different from *intentional* verbal signs, which is why Mitry likens them to linguistic signs. The canonical example of this is Dr Smirnov's dangling pince-nez in Eisenstein's *Battleship Potemkin* (1925): it stands for the doctor 'or, more exactly, signifies his "absence"' (Mitry 1963, 121). Even more so, through a process of association the pince-nez comes to signify 'the bankruptcy of the bourgeois class "thrown overboard"' (121). This is akin to verbal signification, but only insofar as *something comes to stand for something else* – in this case, something which is not perceived or perceivable. Yet, this isn't to say that verbal and filmic signification are alike in all other ways, in fact they are profoundly different. Most importantly, filmic significations, filmic symbols aren't *fixed* or conventional, but develop entirely in context and relationally: the same pince-nez in a different film or in a different sequence would more than likely mean something different.

Symbols such as the pince-nez from *Potemkin*, however, don't exhaust the phenomenon of filmic representation – understood here in the broadest sense of the term. Indeed, for the pince-nez to become a symbol of something else, thanks to a chain of context-dependent association of ideas, one must first account for the representation of the pince-nez itself in the film. This is where the psychological sign comes into play.

Here, verbal and film language part company because of the role played therein by perception. Whereas verbal language expresses ideas via concepts whose source lies in the unmediated objects of perception and whose understanding requires a mediating (though vague) mental image, film, claims Mitry, gives us a direct and concrete image of a thing that can be perceived immediately: the pince-nez may well be a symbol of something in Eisenstein's film, but it is also a pince-nez *offering* itself to my perception. But this isn't the whole picture yet. For it doesn't explain how something that has the status of a non-intentional perceptual object can become an intentional symbol. After all, no actual, singular real-life pince-nez stands for the overthrow of an entire social class! What's missing from this account, therefore, is a conception that mediates between the psychological sign as described so far and the symbol. This conception is the image.

## Image-consciousness and analogon

The objects we see on screen may be experienced like the objects of perception, but they aren't *identical* to them since their support is purely visual (for instance, I can't wear the pince-nez or sit on the chair I see on the screen!); rather, they are *analogous*. Consequently, the fact that objects may appear in black and white, that they may be shown through varying focal lengths, that they are flat, etc., doesn't, explains Mitry, alter their analogous character with regard to the perceptual image, as long, that is, as what we are concerned with is an 'ordinary' ('*quelconque*') and 'impersonal' film image, i.e. one exempt from too many aesthetic 'stylings'. A sounder way of saying this would be to add: as long as we 'separate' (a proper philosophical term here would be 'abstract') in our minds the object we perceive *per se* from the way it *filmically* appears to us. Whence, writes Mitry, if 'I don't seek to mobilize *representation* in the same way I can mobilize the *object represented* [the "real" chair], this image appears to my gaze the same way reality itself does' (Mitry 1963, 109, my italics). But what are we to make of what we have just 'abstracted'? Indeed, and thanks in some measure to the presence of the filmmaker, film offers a *framed* and *composed* object, not the physical world itself. To put it differently: the image *qua* image is already laden with *intentionality*. For a material image – a painting, a photograph, a film frame – is always an image *of* something, though it isn't necessarily a symbol. In this sense, the image is akin to a consciousness, for to be conscious is always to be conscious *of* something. Regardless of any symbolic character, therefore, the film viewer faces a *dual object*: the unmediated object perceived directly *and* the intentional object – framed, composed – of the image. Mitry calls this dual object the *analogon*. And it is the intentional part of this analogon that *mediates* between the direct, non-intentional aspect of the film experience and the intentional symbolic experience of film, the latter understood as a form of *language* and, as we shall see, a form of art. Let's see how this mediation is possible.

Language, for Mitry, is that which expresses and communicates thought (ideas, emotions) and its operations (viz. relations of analogy, consequence, causality, etc.). This is achieved through linguistic signs in verbal language and through their 'equivalent' symbols in the cinema – equivalent only under the terms indicated above. If Mitry can be called a semiotician, it is because he investigates the *conditions* for the expression of thought in film as a basis for film language – a notion he uses literally, not metaphorically as did his predecessors.

The first of these conditions is the *objective* presence of the world on screen: the analogon. For Mitry, as we have seen, the nature of this presence is dual. On the one hand, and in part because of movement and depth, the objects seen on screen are experienced like the objects of real perception. On the other hand, if one considers instead what has impressed each frame of a film, one has a 'mere' image, i.e. under such conditions the thing represented tends to fade in favour of its representation: one perceives an *image*, i.e. an intentional object that *forms, frames, composes*. The relation between what is represented and its representation is now *inverted*: one no longer sees *through* an image (as one would through a window), but the image *of* something. As a result the 'literal' film object has a double nature: as 'object proper' (that which is perceived immediately in a manner analogous to the normal functioning of perception) and image-consciousness (the intentional object *of* the image). In the fist instance, the film image can be said to have recorded (and to show) a particular, existent object. If it shows a pince-nez, it is *this* particular pince-nez (the one that stood in front of Tissé's camera at the time of shooting *Potemkin*) that it gives us. In the second instance, however, the now intentional object is framed, composed, and caught in the force field of a *form* (a frame, a composition, a montage, a narrative, etc.). As such, it becomes a function and stands for something general, for a concept or an *idea*. It isn't this particular pince-nez anymore that is seen, but through it (through the image of it) is expressed the idea (or function) of a pince-nez *in general* (this means *any* pince-nez, including all the ones – real or *in potentia* – that aren't on the screen). In this latter case, the image aspect of the analogon becomes the 'existential manifestation of an idea' (Mitry 1963, 133). Camera angle, camera movement, montage, and especially framing[1] all turn what is otherwise experienced immediately into an *image proper* (phenomenologically speaking: an intentional object), i.e. into aesthetically structured forms or representations, and therefore serve the filmic representation of ideas. Here lies the mediation that paves the way to symbolic meaning.

Thus, unlike verbal representation, Mitry conceives cinematic representation as moving from concrete to abstract stuff. And it is on this basis that film can become a language, more specifically an *aesthetic language*. In structuralist terms (and unlike Barthes or Metz) Mitry would have it that only 'connotation' constitutes the language in film, not 'denotation'. Film, therefore, is not *genetically* a language; it becomes so when it symbolically uses the ideas and concepts that emerge in the representation of objects, i.e. when matters of fact become relations of ideas through aesthetic structuring (122).

It should be obvious by now that, taken together, Mitry's conception of film language and his dual understanding of filmic representation (the analogon) aim at overcoming the formative/realist traditions of classical film theory. In his view, film is both like the world it shows *and* very much unlike it. In classical film theory, moreover, the formative versus realist debate typically seeped into film criticism, often serving to justify aesthetic prescriptions. Likewise, Mitry's integrative theory of filmic representation and his conception of film language serve as a basis for aesthetic evaluation.

## Symbol, analogon, and film aesthetics

For Mitry, a key task for art consists in finding the proper form to express a content, understood that form and content are two sides of a single coin. In the process, the content acquires a meaning, a significance, or a value it would not otherwise be represented as having. This is precisely the *raison d'être* of the symbol in film: through it, the film signifies more than it represents. This implies that film art is coextensive with filmic language: 'every artistic expression', writes Mitry, 'results from a connotation' (Mitry 1965, 378). In short, it is through the symbol's associativity (analogies, metaphors, metonymies), whose skin is composed of the analogon in its dual nature, that the film enters into the realm of art.

For the spectator, of course, what makes a symbol is the imaginative ability to see more in a concrete slice of film than what is actually depicted to the senses. The symbol essentially rests in the *mental images* suggested or triggered by the film's formed imagery. Because symbols don't exist in the sensible world, Mitry's aesthetics eschews calls for absolute realism in the cinema (reality, after all, isn't art). This leads him to critique realist films whose depicted reality is so utterly banal as to be devoid of any profound meaning or significance and hinders the spectator's imagination. However, he also concedes that a film could not be made up entirely of symbols for they only make sense relative to the analogon. This is how, for instance, the symbol deepens the otherwise literal meaning of a narrative. As a result, Mitry considers that film ought to be fully comprehensible regardless of the viewer's ability to interpret the symbol. He rejects as 'uncinematic' films that are overtly symbolic even if they are otherwise noteworthy; examples include Bergman's *The Silence* (1963, in *EPC*), Buñuel's *Un chien andalou* (1929, in Mitry 1973), and several sequences from Eisenstein (in Mitry 1978). In such films, explains Mitry, the filmmaker tries to 'shoot' symbols, i.e. illustrating pre-established concepts or arbitrarily imposing symbols on the depicted reality. Rather, the filmmaker should strive to let the symbols grow in the spectator's mind from the filmic representation, *giving the impression that it is reality itself which is fraught with meaning*. Herein lies the key to Mitry's aesthetic. It isn't an apology for a particular film style, mode, or genre but an argument for a more general aesthetic attitude towards the cinema and its relation to the world it captures and structures.

## Debates

It is fair to say that, in the wake of the revolution wrought by structuralism in France and of the enthusiasm generated by Christian Metz's film semiotics as early as 1964 (*see* SEMIOTICS OF FILM), the work of Mitry – long-winded, philosophical, filled with digressions and discussions of logic, aesthetics, philosophy of language, musicology and the study of rhythm, poetry, the history of theatrical and literary forms, epistemology, and even quantum mechanics – quickly fell into oblivion. Though Mitry sought to overcome the realist/formative debate of 'classical film theory', in the end his work was still steeped in it, as Metz himself was quick to point out (1972a). Criticism of Mitry's work came mostly from two fronts. The Metzian front criticized Mitry for his refusal to admit the relevance of linguistics as a scientific method with which to study film language (Mitry's symbol), and the post-1968 political front (Jean-Louis Comolli especially) criticized him for defending realism (on the basis of the analogon) while avoiding ideological considerations.

It is on the ground of his *grande syntagmatique* (*GS*) that Metz (1972b) disagreed with Mitry for failing to acknowledge the presence of paradigmatic structures in his conception of film language. For Metz, the *GS* systematically regulated the arrangement of shots in various spatio-temporal organizations at the level of filmic denotation, providing meanings such as 'consecutiveness' or 'simultaneity', etc. The idea was that the cinema had developed a set of combinatory rules providing filmmakers with an array of structures to choose from and deploy that approximated a syntax in the way they presided over meaning. Mitry continued to disagree with Metz, however, arguing he had neglected to consider the content of the shots being edited into these structures and that, rather than a syntax, what Metz was in fact describing was a logic of narrative entailment, either associative or comparative. According to Mitry (1987, 141–9), though form gives full meaning to content (leading all the way to the symbol and film language), it is the content one wishes to express that nonetheless imposes form. Consequently, for him, there can be no true *cinematic* paradigm or code regulating film language.

Jean-Louis Comolli (2009) offered a different critique altogether. According to him, Mitry's project is marred by contradiction. On the one hand, claims Comolli, Mitry recognizes the 'constructedness' of the film image and yet, on the other hand, he sides with Bazin on the effects of the long take and even advocates in favour of realism – a style which seeks to conceal 'constructedness'. As a result, Mitry ideologically compromises himself. While it is true that Mitry did not consider realism from the perspective of ideological critique, his endorsement of it is more nuanced than Comolli lets on.

Mitry did not adopt realism wholesale – in *EPC* he comes down hard on the realism of De Sica's *Umberto D* (1952). Moreover, he believed that film art was able to manifest itself in two ways: *realism* and *irrealism* – examples of the latter would include experimental films like his own *Pacific 231* (1949) or expressionist films like *The Last Laugh* (Murnau, 1924; see Mitry 1973, 208–14) which are *formally* irrealistic, and films as diverse as Buñuel's *Exterminating Angel* (1962) and Bresson's *Un condamné à mort s'est échappé* (1956) which he claims are irrealistic in *content*. If Mitry showed a preference for realist films, it is because he saw them as more relevant to the contemporary world. Less overtly formalized, they give the impression of being freer, looser, more 'open', much like reality itself. Unlike irrealist films, they don't appear 'locked' into a formal system or limited by it. In advocating for an open cinema, Mitry supported a dramaturgy that is closer to the novel than to classical drama, whose fixed and 'closed' structures reflect the cosmology of Greek antiquity. An open dramaturgy, on the other hand, corresponds more fully with a contingent world marked by change, movement, and history and whose key forms are temporal rather than spatial, a world best expressed by the art of cinema and its ability to literally and freely show and express – given the proper form – the worldly unfolding of things and events.

MARTIN LEFEBVRE

## Works cited

Comolli, Jean-Louis. 2009. *Cinéma contre spectacle*. Lagrasse: Verdier.

Metz, Christian. 1972a. 'Une étape dans la réflexion sur le cinéma'. In *Essais sur la signification au cinéma*, vol. II, 13–34. Paris: Klincksieck.

——. 1972b. 'Problèmes actuels de théorie du cinéma'. In *Essais sur la signification au cinéma*, vol. II, 35–86. Paris: Klincksieck.

Mitry, Jean. 1963 and 1965. *Esthétique et psychologie du cinéma*, vol. I: *Les structures* and vol. II: *Les formes*. Paris: Éditions universitaires.

——. 1973. *Histoire du cinéma*. Vol. III. Paris: Éditions universitaires.

——. 1978. *Eisenstein*. Paris: Éditions universitaires, Jean-Pierre Delarge.

——. 1987. *La sémiologie en question*. Paris: Cerf.

## Further reading

Andrew, Dudley. 1976. *The Major Film Theories*. Oxford: Oxford University Press.

Lewis, Brian. 1984. *Jean Mitry and the Aesthetics of the Cinema*. Ann Arbor: University of Michigan Research Press.

——. 2009. 'Jean Mitry'. In *The Routledge Companion to Philosophy and Film*, edited by Paisley Livingstone and Carl Plantinga. New York: Routledge.

## Note

1 The dual nature of filmic representation for Mitry means that he considers the contour of the image to be both a *cache* (Bazin) and a *pictorial/compositional frame* (Eisenstein, Arnheim) (*see* CLASSICAL FILM THEORY).

# SYMPTOMATIC READING

## Origins and meaning

Contemporary film theory of the 1970s (*see* CONTEMPORARY FILM THEORY; IDEOLOGY, CINEMA AND) is marked by a significant interest in ideological and psychoanalytical critique. The writings of Louis Althusser and Jacques Lacan were repeatedly employed by film critics writing for the French journal *Cahiers du cinéma* and the British *Screen*. In using these authority figures, critics intended to free criticism from the emphasis on authorial intentions as a valid form of interpretation. The auteur theory of the late 1950s (*see* AUTEUR THEORY) was not a valid hermeneutic tool anymore. Film scholars were busy identifying the ways that mainstream cinema reproduces unconsciously the dominant ideology of capitalism as well as the processes of subject construction taking place throughout the film viewing process.

This type of interpretation aimed at revealing the inherent contradictions within the film's narrative, focusing on absences and exclusions that may reveal what the capitalist and patriarchal ideology intends to repress. Widely known as 'symptomatic reading' or 'reading against the grain', this hermeneutic strategy has its roots in Louis Althusser's coinage of the term. In his discussion of Marx's *Capital*, Althusser explains that Marx analyses a text without treating it as a unified object, but searches for structural absences and omissions in the object:

> Such is Marx's second reading: a reading which might well be called '*symptomatic*' (*symptomale*), insofar as it divulges the undivulged event in the text it reads, and in the same movement relates it to *a different text*, present as a necessary absence in the first. Like his first reading, Marx's second reading presupposes the existence of *two texts*, and the measurement of the first against the second. But what distinguishes this new reading from the old one is the fact that in the new one the *second text* is articulated with the lapses in the first text.
>
> (Althusser 1969, 28; original emphasis)

In light of Althusser's comments, symptomatic film readings aim to reveal the cultural dominant in an object which predominates over others. Depending on the writer's background, this dominant discourse can be the capitalist ideology, patriarchy, or the historical unconscious of a period.

Although symptomatic interpretation became the critical norm during the 1970s, we need to acknowledge that many significant intellectuals conducted symptomatic readings of films much earlier. A prominent example is Siegfried Kracauer's study of Weimar films. Kracauer suggested that German expressionism's interest in the madness that permeates authority, as well as the genre's emphasis on issues of group submission, reflected the collective German soul and the political instability in the years that preceded Hitler's ascension to power. In the introduction of his book, Kracauer explains that he is interested in the popularity of certain 'pictorial and narrative motifs' which 'carry most symptomatic weight when they occur in both popular and unpopular films' (2004, 8). In his renowned discussion of *The Cabinet of Dr Caligari* (1920), Kracauer reads the film's finale as symptomatic of the 'psychological revolution' taking place in German society, which forced the people to 'reconsider their traditional belief in authority' (67). Kracauer's study of Weimar cinema is emblematic of symptomatic criticism's interest in placing film objects in their social and historical context.

Another famous intellectual who conducted symptomatic readings of films was Roland Barthes. Barthes's thinking was very influential on contemporary film theory, mainly because of his rejection of authorial intentions as a valid interpretative activity. In his oft-quoted essay 'The Death of the Author', Barthes suggests that the author is nothing but 'the instance writing' (1977, 145); this essay strengthened the anti-auteurist fashion of the 1970s criticism which strived to 'rewrite' films using theories of Marxism and psychoanalysis so as to reveal their hidden meanings.

Characteristic, from this point of view, is Barthes's review of Elia Kazan's *On the Waterfront* (1954). Barthes re-reads the film and tries to reveal its suppressed conservatism. He explains that it is an object which pretends to be leftist, but railroads the audience into responses that justify the existing social order. For Barthes, Kazan treats labour as a moral rather than a political problem. The story employs mainstream cinema's mainstays of plot based upon the binaries of good and evil; the corrupt union bosses manipulate the workers and take advantage of their labour. Barthes suggests that the dichotomy good versus evil fails to reveal the political problem in capitalist societies, which is the capitalist exploitation of labour. This is evidenced in the film's ending, in which the workers revolt, only to end up reproducing their social position after managing to isolate the corrupt union bosses from the market suppliers. Barthes suggests that the film's ending provides a sense of cathartic victory to the audience, but in actual fact it is 'a return to order' for both the workers and the spectators (Watts 2005, 19). Accordingly, the film treats its subject matter in a conventional way and reduces a broader political problem to a moral one.

## *Cahiers du cinéma*

Barthes's symptomatic reading of Kazan's film is indicative of a critical practice employed by contemporary film theory, that is, the view of mainstream cinema as the product of the dominant political and cultural reality. Then again, critics even in a polemical journal such as *Cahiers du cinéma* undertook symptomatic readings of mainstream films, so as to perform oppositional interpretations. The core of their argument was that a reading which searches for the absences within the film can reveal the inherent contradictions of the bourgeois ideology within which mainstream films operate.

One of the most pre-eminent examples of this hermeneutic practice was the analysis of John Ford's fictionalized biography of the early life of Abraham Lincoln – *Young Mr Lincoln* (1939) – by the editorial board of *Cahiers du cinéma* in 1970. By going back to a classic film, the editors of the journal proposed an 'active' reading which is interested in identifying the fundamental absences within the object. Referencing Walter Benjamin's idea that the task of materialist criticism is to place artworks in the historical context of the productive relations, *Cahiers*'s editors explain that the same approach needs to be taken when it comes to films that do not have a manifest political or critical dimension (Collective text 1972, 7). In looking at films that are not necessarily political, they intend to 'make them say what they have to say within what they leave unsaid, to reveal their constituent lacks' (8). Later on they emphasize that they are particularly interested in moments of sexual and political repression, and the choice of films under discussion is based upon the 'negatory force of their writing' which 'provides enough scope for a reading – because they can be re-written' (8).

By re-writing the object, *Cahiers*'s editors aspire to reveal its ideological contradictions, a gesture which can bring to the surface the subversive aspects of the film. This *modus operandi* hinges upon the Althusserian Marxist axiom that capitalist structures are not empirically visible and Freudian psychology's conception of the unconscious as a locus of concealed desires, fears, and repression. Initially, the writers place the film in its political context so as to identify its ideological obviousness. The film was shot during the 1930s recession and the presidential electoral campaign. Fox studios' decision to make a film for a Republican president who had acquired a mythological status as the unifier of the USA was far from being fortuitous. It was a conscious choice connected with big businesses' opposition to the Democratic president's policies and their backing of the Republican candidate. 'Of all the Republican Presidents, he is not only the most famous, but on the whole the only one capable of attracting mass support, because of his humble origins, his simplicity, his righteousness, his historical role and the legendary aspects of his career and his death' (11). As they explain, this political background can explain the reasons why Fox hastened the film's production and gave unprecedented creative freedom to the director (11–12).

Yet the writers quickly distance themselves from this oversimplistic reading and explain that the film is not simply reducible to the ideological conditions of its production; by treating the film not as a unified text with a determinist meaning but as a text in process, they can shift attention from the obvious key thematic implications to the secondary ones, 'which may in turn become the main determinant in other scenes' (14). Indicative of this practice is their analysis of the film's politics. They affirm that the film represses politics in favour of morality and idealistic values of justice, but in a crucial scene it makes an allusion to slavery. Lincoln explains that he left his state because the large influx of slaves set hurdles for the whites looking for work. The writers contend that this moment is instrumental in understanding the inherent contradictions in the narrative. While the film downplays political questions in favour of moral ones, here the problem is posed in terms of money matters rather than morality; 'the accent is thus put on the economic, i.e. the problem of the whites, not the blacks' (18). This scene has a political significance, because the exclusion of the political dimension of Lincoln's life, and in particular any detailed references to the Civil War, serve the purpose of intensifying the moralizing discourse over the political one. It is a conscious rewriting of history aiming at intensifying values of eternal and pre-existing ethics by discarding the historical roots of the problem. Lincoln is de-historicized; he is portrayed as the eternal holder of truth and justice and not the product of specific historical circumstances. His character acquires a mythological status, as if the values he (and by extension the USA) stood for were pre-existing and everlasting. 'Morality not only rejects politics and surpasses history, it also rewrites them' (19). One cannot though ignore the intrusion of the economic and thus the political dimension in the aforementioned scene, in which the film offers a self-reflexive thinking of the values it claims to reinforce.

The writers here reflect on their own 'conspiracy theory' reading. As such, despite the film's discernible ideological operations, they pinpoint the object's inconsistencies to show that the director distances himself from the idealist morals he propagates. They strongly emphasize the repression of the sexual by the political to show how the film builds an idealized and mythical image of Lincoln. An example that shows this eloquently is a scene in the film in which Lincoln ignores Mary Todd's flirtation. This repression of sexual desire serves the purpose of reinforcing the sanctifying image of the character and his identification with justice and law. The character's 'castration' is directly linked with his portrayal as the father figure of the nation. As the writers say: 'Lincoln does not have the phallus, he is the phallus' (31).

The film clearly suggests this when Lincoln drives the witness of a murder case to confess that he is the killer. After harassing the witness, Lincoln reveals the truth only to be established as 'the possessor of truth' (37). At this point, law and justice are directly linked with violence, something that the writers read as 'the classic harshness of rampant justice, but mainly as the culmination of Lincoln's castrating power' (37). This scene is critical to our understanding of the film's structural absences. The unnecessary and excessive violence practised by the central character is not motivated by the narrative, nor by Lincoln's characterization so far. This is an intentional fissure in Lincoln's depiction which calls into question the film's ideological project as a whole (37).

There is in the film an opposition between the character as an iconic figure embodying the moral values of fairness and righteousness associated with the nation and the character as a violent law enforcer. This antithesis causes tensions between the idealized representations of Lincoln as the justice figure and the film's suppressed standpoint that law and violence are the two sides of the same coin. In effect, the film does not accept unconditionally the dominant ideological trends that it propagates, but creates gaps and contrasts which subvert the moralizing paradigms which are associated with the status quo (44).

## Critiques of symptomatic readings

One of the major strengths of symptomatic hermeneutics is the performing of oppositional readings of films whose politics seem to be very flat and oversimplistic. For example, feminist critics have engaged in symptomatic readings of popular films so as to deny monolithic interpretations of objects, e.g. melodramas, which are normally seen as agents of the current state of affairs (Kuhn 1987, 342). Hence, Stephen Heath has read Steven Spielberg's *Jaws* (1975) as an object which reflects the historical paranoia of the Watergate scandal. Heath also explains how the film's working of the dominant ideology in the film industry brings to light issues linked with the function of the industry in itself and thus produces subversive interpretations (1985, 514).

The question, whether symptomatic hermeneutics' focus on displacements and absences within the objects is still valid, continues to divide scholarship. Brian Henderson was one of the first critics to point out a crucial contradiction, that is, that while symptomatic readings intend to reveal absences and to place emphasis on non-posed questions, one senses that certain readings tend to reduce all contradictions within the films and treat them as 'static' objects (1973, 44). Henderson acknowledges the productive features of symptomatic readings, but his critique targets mainly its Anglo-Saxon usages and in particular Ben

Brewster's response to the *Cahiers* article, which was published in *Screen* in 1972. As he says, Brewster treats ideology critique as one-dimensional and turns it 'into a simple knowledge that the film merely reproduces and conveniently puts on view for all to see' (44). In a way, this reduction commits the very same empirical analysis that symptomatic hermeneutics aims to decry. By treating the film as a mere reproducer of certain ideological trends, Brewster fails to ask questions that can reveal the complexity of ideology and of the text in question. Rather than looking for absences in the text so as to rewrite it, this practice is busy identifying an all-encompassing unifying concept in the object under discussion.

More sceptical are critics with a background in analytical philosophy and cognitive film theory. Noël Carroll, for example, calls this critical view of representation as 'conspiratorial' (1987, 396). Carroll calls into question the symptomatic hermeneutical tradition, which distinguishes between implicit ideological and suppressed meanings within a film. For Carroll, this view eliminates any possibility of agency on the part of the audience. He sets as an example empirical audience studies in which audiences enjoyed certain objects, without sharing their ideological viewpoints (400). Carroll conjectures that the relationship between viewing subject and film is an active communicative one and viewers are not simply 'lulled' by certain effects employed by popular forms of representation (405).

More conciliatory is David Bordwell's critique. Bordwell acknowledges that symptomatic criticism and its emphasis on the political unconscious that permeates certain objects have been beneficial for film studies as a discipline. In particular, Bordwell refers to the Women's movement, which employed symptomatic readings of films aiming not only to 'reveal the weak points in patriarchal ideology but also launch an oppositional filmmaking and film viewing' (Bordwell 1991, 91). On the other hand, Bordwell takes issue with the fact that symptomatic criticism overstressed theory rather than focusing on 'the intrinsic value of cinema or even the strengths of particular interpretations' (97). The result was that scholars focusing on the objects themselves were dismissed as naive empiricists. Furthermore, Bordwell asserts that while symptomatic criticism intended to look more closely at formal issues, it ended up overlooking issues of form in favour of symbolic meanings which contradicted the obvious and explicit ones (99). The master code (Marxism or psychoanalysis) employed to rewrite the object was more important than the film's complexity.

Despite any shortcomings, symptomatic criticism has advanced film studies as a discipline, while it has laid the groundwork for oppositional readings of films which are seemingly conservative. By focusing on the repressed meanings that the objects communicate unintentionally, symptomatic criticism demonstrates that film language, like any other language, is not unequivocal but the outcome of the political/historical/social unconscious which shapes the individuals who operate it.

ANGELOS KOUTSOURAKIS

## Works cited

Althusser, Louis. 1969. *For Marx*. Translated by Ben Brewster. London: Penguin Press.

Barthes, Roland. 1977. 'The Death of the Author'. In *Image, Music, Text*, edited and translated by Stephen Heath, 142–8. London: Fontana Press.

Bordwell, David. 1991. 'Symptomatic Interpretation'. In *Making Meaning: Inference and Rhetoric in the Interpretation of Cinema*, 77–104. Cambridge, MA: Harvard University Press.

Brewster, Ben. 1972. 'Notes on the Text John Ford's *Young Mr Lincoln* by the Editors of *Cahiers du cinéma*'. Screen 14 (3): 29–43.

Carroll, Noël. 1987. 'Conspiracy Theories of Representation'. *Philosophy of the Social Sciences* 17: 395–412.

Collective text by the editors of *Cahiers du cinéma*. 1972 [1970]. 'John Ford's *Young Mr Lincoln*'. *Screen* 13 (3): 5–44.

Heath, Stephen. 1985. 'Jaws, Ideology, and Film Theory'. In *Movies and Methods*, vol. II, edited by Bill Nichols, 509–14. Berkeley: University of California Press.

Henderson, Brian. 1973. 'Critique of Cine-structuralism (Part II)'. *Film Quarterly* 27 (2): 37–46.

Kracauer, Siegfried. 2004. *From Caligari to Hitler: A Psychological History of the German Film*. Edited by Leonardo Quaresima. Princeton, NJ: Princeton University Press.

Kuhn, Annette. 1987. 'Women's Genres: Melodrama, Soap Opera and Theory'. In *Home Is Where the Heart Is: Studies in Melodrama and the Woman's Film*, 235–54. London: BFI.

Watts, Philip. 2005. 'Roland Barthes' Cold War Cinema'. *Substance* 34 (3): 17–32.

## Further reading

Collective text. 1996 [1970]. 'Joseph von Sternberg's Morocco'. In *Cahiers du cinéma: Volume 3 1969–1972. The Politics of Representation*, edited by Nick Browne. London: Routledge.

Kotsopoulos, Aspasia. 2001. 'Reading against the Grain Revisited'. *Jump Cut: A Review of Contemporary Media*: http://www.ejumpcut.org/archive/jc44.2001/aspasia/againstgrain1.html.

Mulvey, Laura. 1975. 'Visual Pleasure and Narrative Cinema'. *Screen* 16 (3): 6–18.

# THIRD WORLD CINEMA

## What is the 'Third World'?

A theorization of 'Third World cinema' must begin with the troubled genealogy of the term 'Third World.' For some, the term lumps together the underdeveloped countries of the world, placing them behind the advanced, market-oriented nation-states (First World) and the centralized communist societies (Second World). For others, it points to a geo-political imagination that congealed at the Bandung Conference of 1956, comprising 'non-aligned' countries claiming their autonomy from the Cold War-era polarization of the NATO alliance and the Communist Bloc. 'Third World' is often invoked pejoratively as the domain of stagnation, as if such a state is its natural condition. Alternatively, it conveys a diagnostic insight about the structural imbalances of the global political economy by pointing to a vast 'periphery' held in a relation of dependence by a few 'core' countries. Before the economic crisis of the mid-1970s, the term registered optimism about the newly independent nation-states emerging from their colonial past into a future of unlimited potentialities; soon after, it conveyed the despair of crushing debt burdens. While con-temporary parlance has shifted from 'underdeveloped' to 'developing' countries, and postcolonial backwardness has been historicized as mainly an outcome of colonial exploi-tation, the entire range of nuances continues to inform the paradigms of Third World cinema.

A project of theorizing Third World cinema must take into account (1) the fact that its object is anything but a stable, singular field, and (2) the criticism that to speak of Third World cinema having its own exclusive theory is also to *exclude* this domain from 'film theory proper'. Nevertheless, there is an interesting history behind this vexing category that cannot be ignored. Invoked from multiple cultural, ideological, and epistemological topoi, it has served a range of purposes over the past six decades. The following account begins with that crucial history; only through such an engagement can we hope to reformulate the overall problematic.

## Third Cinema manifesto

In the 1950s and 1960s, the global trend towards decolonization energized the more affirmative connotations of the term 'Third World'. It was in this heady conjuncture that the earliest and, arguably, most influential conceptualization of Third World cinema found articulation in the manifesto 'Towards a Third Cinema' (Solanas and Getino 1997 [1969]). Penned by the leftist Argentine filmmakers Fernando Solanas and Octavio Getino, and originally published in Spanish in the film journal *Tricontinental*, the manifesto presented a sharply politicized topography of world cinema. 'First Cinema' was defined as the cinema of unbridled commercialism, intent on capturing markets and consolidating the status quo: Hollywood was its global exemplar. Armed with technical wizardry and glamorous packaging, this capitalist cinema of spectacles was said to captivate audiences with fantasies indulging bourgeois desires and values.

A deepening unease tinged this glossy world-view in 'Second Cinema', whose core output came from the various European 'new waves'. But that sense of disquiet never developed into a call for the radical transformation of social structures. For all its sophisticated idioms, including experimentations with space–time configuration and contemplative explorations of modern alienation, Second Cinema remained for Solanas and Getino a domain of effete intellectualism and petty bourgeois angst – dealing 'only … with effect, never with cause' (33). Bearing little resonance for popular struggles, this film festival- and art-house-oriented cinema privileged aesthetic innovation over political rupture, generating an elitist canon.

In contrast, 'Third Cinema' sought to revamp the relationship between aesthetics and politics, turning film cultures into an arena of purposeful activism. This was cinema that recognized the 'anti-imperialist struggle of the peoples of the Third World and of their equivalents inside the imperialist countries' as *'the most gigantic cultural, scientific and artistic manifestation of our time'*; its objective was nothing short of the *'decolonization of the mind'* (37; emphasis in original). As Teshome Gabriel summarizes with remarkable clarity, Third Cinema 'seeks to (a) decolonize minds, (b) contribute to the development of a radical consciousness, (c) lead to a revolutionary transformation of society, (d) develop new film language[s] with which to accomplish these tasks' (Gabriel 1982, 3).

Citing infrastructural advances of the mid-twentieth century, including the availability of cheaper and more mobile cameras and tape recorders, high speed film usable in natural light, automatic light meters, along with a greater dissemination of skills and the establishment of alternative distribution networks (16mm film circuits, underground or semi-public screenings), Solanas and Getino stressed new possibilities for breaking the shackles of capital on cinematic production and expanding the social role of the medium. The alignment of these developments with revolutionary agendas produced a *guerrilla cinema* that used its limited resources tactically, often working on the sly without permits, hoodwinking censorship, and challenging dominant institutions and ideologies.

Three defining features emerge from this articulation of Third Cinema as cultural warfare. First, it seeks to free cinema from an internalized conformity to bourgeois aesthetic standards set by imperialist and art cinemas, standards that are constantly updated according to techno-capitalist advances in filmmaking and that remain out of reach for most of the Third World. Instead of endlessly trying to play catch-up with imported and alienating principles, instead of being inhibited by a 'universal' model of 'the perfect work of art, the fully rounded film', Solanas and Getino (1997, 48) exhort cine-workers to address the contradictions of their own social realities with resources and skills at hand. Eschewing technical sophistication, the focus of Third Cinema shifts to a do-it-yourself mode that turns material constraints into an engine of innovation. Such an attitude is at the heart of Julio García Espinosa's clarion call for an 'Imperfect Cinema' (1969) and Glauber Rocha's passionate affirmation of an 'An Esthetic of Hunger' (1965). Together, these manifestos *potentiate* a cultural field that refuses to be held back by a lack of resources and, instead, embraces its historical mission of liberating culture, of making it a part of everyday struggles.

Second, the rhetoric around Third Cinema is stridently militant, often bordering on machismo: 'The camera is the inexhaustible *expropriator of image-weapons*; the projector, *a gun that can shoot 24 frames per second*' (50; emphasis in original). The new filmmaker is imagined in mythic-futuristic terms, as a revolutionary prepared 'to take chances on the unknown, to leap into space at times, exposing himself to failure as does the guerilla who travels along paths that he himself opens up with machete blows' (48). It is not coincidental that practically all the prominent figures of the various Third Cinema movements of the 1960s and 1970s were men. Cuban filmmaker Sara Gómez, who died all too young, remains the notable exception.

Finally, while grounded in history, Third Cinema is resolutely forward thinking: it is a cinema that takes risks, is exploratory in its approach, and prepares society for revolutionary futures. Its original proponents abstain from strict aesthetic prescriptions: they conceive filmmaking as a series of open-ended experiments. Based on frank dialogue and constantly vigilant about its own modalities, Third Cinema remains capable of resolving problems that are bound to arise on the way to cultural emancipation. This dimension of autocritical integrity has often been lost in subsequent evocations that stress Third Cinema's militancy and seek to advance on its basis a concrete, often rigid programme of ideological resistance.

## Inspirations and intersections

The kindred formations and influences that the 1969 manifesto names include worldwide anti-colonial struggles and students' and workers' movements, the Cuban Revolution, Frantz Fanon, the Vietnamese resistance to US imperialism, May 1968, Italy's *Cinegiornali liberi*, Japan's Zengakuren documentaries, the US Newsreel collective, filmmakers Santiago Alvarez and Chris Marker. Some others – most notably, leftist cultural figures Sergei Eisenstein and Bertolt Brecht, Italian neorealism, and the body of critique known as Dependency Theory – while not explicitly invoked, remain palpable presences across its pages. This last extra-cinematic influence, a line of thinking associated with social scientists Raúl Prebisch, Paul Baran, and Andre Gunder Frank, maintains that chronic Third World poverty is a result of the unequal terms on which peripheral countries are integrated into the world system: their primary role is to serve the interests of the wealthy and dominant states. The manifesto clearly echoes this structuralist-Marxist position (37). Within the field of cinema, political documentaries present one paradigmatic form for Third Cinema (Solanas and Getino's *La hora de los hornos* [*The Hour of the Furnaces*, 1968] being an exemplar of both), while the mode of cinematic production (if not the ideologies and sentiments) of the Italian neorealists offers a working model for Third World filmmakers facing infrastructural constraints.

Fanon and Brecht remain, arguably, the two most significant intellectual influences for Third Cinema. The manifesto opens with an epigram from the Martinique-born revolutionary thinker: 'we must discuss, we must invent' (33). Fanon (2005 [1961]) advocates a level of emancipation that goes well beyond the neocolonial stagnation presided over by domestic elites even after political independence from colonial occupation. His call for discussion and innovation sets the stage for the articulation of a cultural programme seeking a decisive end to the more chronic occupation of the mind:

> Insert the work as an original fact in the process of liberation, place it first at the
> service of life itself, ahead of art; dissolve aesthetics in the life of society: only in

this way, as Fanon said, can decolonisation become possible and culture, cinema, and beauty – at least, what is of greatest importance to us – become our culture, our films, and our sense of beauty.

(Solanas and Getino 1997, 40)

If Fanon delineates the historical conditions for a genuine liberation, it is Brecht's theories of stagecraft (*see* BRECHT AND FILM), supplemented by core tenets of Russian formalism and Soviet revolutionary cinema, that provide a set of principles for politicized figuration on the way to social transformation (*see* MONTAGE THEORY II [SOVIET AVANT-GARDE]). Solanas and Getino's injunction to 'place' the filmic work 'first at the service of life itself, ahead of art', draws on a strand of critical modernism that can be traced to Viktor Shklovsky, Walter Benjamin, and Brecht, among others. In spite of the specific inflections of their arguments, what is common between Shklovsky's art of 'making strange', Benjamin's stress on 'shock and astonishment', and Brecht's techniques of 'defamiliarization' is a desire to counter the seductive spectacles and habitual modes of perception that induce a certain numbness and inaction in modern subjects. At stake is the revivification of sensuous engagement, making art and philosophy matter within the messy materiality of quotidian struggles.

As Rey Chow puts it, Brecht develops this need for engagement into a highly reflexive, 'mediatized' strategy of laying bare the means of signification, of rendering thought '*ex-plicit through staging*' (Chow 2011, 138–9; emphasis and hyphen in original). Such 'laying bare' takes very different forms in films like *Deus e o Diabo na Terra do Sol* (*Black God, White Devil*, 1964), *Memorias del Subdesarrollo* (*Memories of Underdevelopment*, 1968), and *El Otro Francisco* (*The Other Francisco*, 1975), all landmarks of Third Cinema. What remains central in each case is the aspiration to involve audiences, to turn them into active participants in a dialogue about the material conditions and historical contradictions of their lives.

Yet another Brechtian argument coursing through the manifesto has to do with the 'impotence of all reformist concepts' in achieving genuine transformation (Solanas and Getino 1997, 41). Declaring that '[r]eal innovations attack the roots', changing the social function of art, Brecht calls for a radical overhaul of the genre: innovations, not mere renovations, are the order of the day (Brecht 1964, 39–41). For Solanas and Getino, films that restrict themselves to 'the denunciation of the *effects* of neocolonial policy' are 'caught up in a reformist game' that safeguards extant social conditions: this is Second Cinema's crucial limitation. A truly radical approach must involve a laying bare of 'the *causes*', an exploration of 'the ways of organizing and arming for change' (Solanas and Getino 1997, 48).

The Brechtian underpinnings that Third Cinema shares with its contemporaneous Euro-American counter-cinema movements induce a certain conflation of the two in subsequent commentaries (*see* COUNTER-CINEMA). Both formations seek to break with the illusionism of Aristotelian poetics, whose linear and seamless narratives – and, in the case of cinema, mesmeric spectacles – elicit impulsive, often cathartic identification from the audience. Counter-cinema, in particular, thrives on undermining spectatorial pleasures: dispensing with linear, causal narratives featuring psychologically rounded characters, privileging structural arguments over individual motivation, presenting multiple storylines and points of view, refusing pat resolutions, and imploding the illusion of reality by revealing the process of filmmaking. But it also turns this agenda of opposing the modalities of commercial entertainment cinema into a rigid formalist doxa: direct address to camera, jumpcuts, long takes, insertion of intertitles, contrapuntal sound design, open-ended narratives, overt didacticism at the cost of entertainment, and so on (Wollen 1972).

By the late 1960s, countries as far flung as India, Senegal, Turkey, and Hong Kong began to experience their own cinematic 'new waves'. Louis Althusser (1971) published his famous essay 'Ideology and Ideological State Apparatuses' in 1970, providing an analytical frame that proved extremely productive for film theory. Laura Mulvey introduced a feminist critical optic to the interrogation of the cinematic apparatus in her landmark 1975 essay 'Visual Pleasure and Narrative Cinema' (*see* FEMINIST FILM THEORY, HISTORY OF). The period also witnessed significant attempts to forge a Brechtian theory of cinema in the pages of the journal *Screen*. What made the Third Cinema intervention distinctive was its stress on postcolonial cultural contingencies and the racialized underpinnings of Third World predicaments. This is why Fanon and his radical polemic on behalf of the global south remained so integral to the manifesto. This is also why Third Cinema, while avoiding narrow formalist orthodoxies, had to embrace the strategic fiction of an authentic (national) consciousness that would replace a false (colonial) one.

## Critical elaborations

The tension between a strategic essentialism and a supple dialogism is one of a series of binary oppositions – theory/practice, vanguard/popular, cosmopolitan/national – that complicates Third Cinema's agenda. Not surprisingly, the most notable disputes over Third Cinema's legacy are centred on these binaries: the tensions haunt subsequent attempts at theorizing cinemas of the Third World. It is tempting to line up dialogism–theory–vanguardism–cosmopolitanism against essentialism–practice–populism–nationalism. Even as this reductive polarity threatens to commandeer our understanding, scholars of Third (World) Cinema demonstrate how it erases historical complexities.

In his attempts to reconcile the 'Third' of 'Third Cinema' with that of the 'Third World', Teshome Gabriel effectively *performs* these confounding tensions. On the one hand, he seeks to articulate an integral film language that arises out of the common cultural and political exigencies of Third World societies. Structural conditions and historical experiences shape a cine-aesthetic along a trajectory that follows Fanon's 'steps of the genealogy of Third World culture': from the 'unqualified assimilation' of Euro-American norms, to the 'remembrance phase' focusing on the reinvigoration of indigenous forms and practices and the fostering of a national consciousness, and then towards a more internationalist 'combative phase' when a 'cinema of mass participation' engages 'the lives and struggles of Third World peoples' (Gabriel 1989, 31–3). Although Gabriel calls attention to the overlapping nature of these stages, the impression of a linear teleology persists, intensifying the essentialism inherent to his search for a common aesthetic across cultures.

On the other hand, Gabriel wants to unhinge the category 'Third' from ontological moorings to advance an ideological and methodological orientation. In the interest of forging an internationalist coalition, he argues that Third Cinema is characterized by 'the ideology it espouses and the consciousness it displays', rather than by 'where it is made, or even who makes it' (Gabriel 1982, 2). This line of thinking proves to be particularly productive over the next two decades: rising political disenchantment about the promises of nationalism, and the attrition of its ideals and institutions by the forces of global capital, induce a shift towards transnational and diasporic frames. But as Paul Willemen rightly observes, Gabriel's bracketing of 'the national question' – a direct corollary of his 'rehomogenisation of Third Cinema' – is a bit premature, as national interests continue to be of great political significance and cultural efficacy. Indeed, Third Cinema remains 'determinedly "national," even "regional," in its address and aspirations' (Willemen 1989, 17).

Debates at a 1986 conference in Edinburgh focused on the role of the intellectual *vis-à-vis* broad, popular cultural formations, an issue that was particularly charged in the post-colonies because of the complications wrought by their colonial histories (Pines and Willemen 1989). A chasm opened up between the so-called theorists and activists around the nature of participation most conducive to social transformation. The latter claimed that an insistence on theoretical sophistication was at one with the tyranny of technical flair and philosophical abstraction that helped suppress cultural creativity and induce mass apathy. In response, Homi Bhabha forcefully enunciated a 'commitment to theory': effective political action required working through all naive assertions of essence, authenticity, or autonomy. Indeed, to theorize was to act (Bhabha 1989).

## Global connections, historical difference

A central impetus of the Edinburgh conference was to learn from global experiences of anti-imperialist cinemas in order to foster audiovisual cultures of resistance in Thatcher-era Britain. Across the Atlantic, similar creative enterprises of indigenous populations, descendants of slaves, and immigrants had begun to rattle the all-powerful US culture industry. But the material differences between the metropolitan 'centres' of colonialism and the 'peripheral' postcolonies remained significant. Seeking to establish the commonalities among these distinctive movements while mindful of their historical differences, Ella Shohat and Robert Stam proposed a broad paradigm of 'unthinking Eurocentrism' invested in combating the persistent and ubiquitous legacies of colonialism (Shohat and Stam 1994). Inspired by the multiple circuits and folds of Third World cinema, they offered a pragmatic map consisting of four overlapping circles. (1) 'A core circle of "Third Worldist" films produced by and for Third World peoples', irrespective of their actual location, and according to 'the principles of "Third Cinema"'; (2) a wider circle of the cinematic outputs of Third World societies, 'whether or not the films adhere to the principles of Third Cinema' – thus presumably including popular-commercial cinema; (3) a third circle of films 'made by First or Second World people' in solidarity with Third World communities and 'adhering to the principles of Third Cinema'; and (4) a fourth circle, 'somewhat anomalous in status, at once "inside" and "outside," comprising recent diasporic hybrid films ... that both build on and interrogate' Third Cinema conventions (28).

This last circle speaks to a vital strand of millennial art inspired by lives lived between places and along borders, and to a central thrust of post-structuralist theory obsessed with interstitial concepts (e.g. extimacy, which confounds the binary inside/outside, as in a Moebius strip). Beginning with the condition of exile, Hamid Naficy provides one of the most sustained accounts of an interstitial mode of cinematic production in *An Accented Cinema*. Focusing on 'films that postcolonial, Third World filmmakers have made in their Western sojourn' and that key Western filmmakers have produced in exile, Naficy offers the 'accent' as a measure of this cinema's material marginality and rough-hewn quality (Naficy 2001, 3). '[T]he accent emanates not so much from the accented speech of the diegetic characters as from the displacement of the filmmakers and their artisanal production modes' (4). Naficy explores the formal tropes (fragmented, multilingual, reflexive narratives; epistolary form and doubled characters) and stylistic flourishes (synaesthetic gestures, layered sound, meandering camera movements) which allow filmmakers to foreground their experiences in exile.

What Naficy brings to the table is a careful analysis of the interlocked nature of cinematic subjectivity and the material conditions of Third Worldist film production. Moreover, his close attention to the *affective* dimensions of exilic life – loss and nostalgia, presence and absence, phobic spaces and liminal panics – draws out an element that had remained only implicit in Third Cinema polemics. But Naficy appears to extol embodied experiences of liminality for motivating an auteurist vanguardism: the realm of the popular-commercial gets bracketed yet again. While his stress on the accent as a mode of criticism appears to align it with the politicized aesthetics of Third Cinema, his analytical transformation of the marginal into an elitist precarity is more resonant with Second Cinema.

Perhaps Naficy draws away too quickly from the cultural–phenomenological dimensions of the cinematic accent – dimensions that he reduces to 'the accented speech of the diegetic characters' – in his desire to foreground the materiality of displaced filmmakers' lives and working conditions. Film language comprises much more than linguistic speech: cinematic signification involves colour, sound, rhythm, pace, texture, and much more. An expansive conceptualization of the *cinematic accent* has to take into consideration the specificities of local lifeworlds that shape their cinematic idioms. These specificities – flavours, tones, and aesthetic traditions, modulated and reworked into singular cinematic accents – are, arguably, most evident in the realm of the popular. Recent scholarship seeks to historicize the melodramatic excesses of Latin American media cultures, the song and dance sequences of Indian films, and the martial arts stylings of Hong Kong cinema, even as it acknowledges a degree of global standardization (Paranagua 1996; Sarkar 2011; Yau 2001). In these studies, the accents are not turned into cultural essences; nor are they dismissed simply as idiosyncratic exceptions to, or degenerate mutations of, some presumed cinematic benchmark from the US or Europe.

Indeed, the popularity of Bombay or Hong Kong cinemas all over the world, well beyond South Asian or Chinese diasporic markets, demonstrates the cross-cultural mobility of cine-accents and undermines any intrinsic sense of the qualifier 'Third' – or the 'accented' – as crude, backward, or peripheral (Morris *et al.* 2006; Rajagopalan 2009). Such considerations underscore the need for a thorough critique and overhaul of film theory, so that it can accommodate and account for Third World cinemas without relegating them to its margins. In that sense, the project of theorizing 'Third World Cinema' gives way to one of *theorizing cinema as such* in the light of its Third Worldist expressions.

BHASKAR SARKAR

## Works cited

Althusser, Louis. 1971 [1970]. 'Ideology and Ideological State Apparatuses'. In *Lenin and Philosophy, and Other Essays*, translated by Ben Brewster, 127–88. London: New Left Books.
Bhabha, Homi. 1989. 'The Commitment to Theory'. In *Questions of Third Cinema*, edited by Jim Pines and Paul Willemen, 111–32. London: British Film Institute.
Brecht, Bertolt. 1964. 'The Modern Theatre Is the Epic Theatre'. In *Brecht on Theatre: The Development of an Aesthetic*, translated and edited by John Willett, 33–42. New York: Hill and Wang.
Chow, Rey. 2011. 'When Reflexivity Becomes Porn: Mutations of a Modernist Theoretical Practice'. In *Theory after Theory*, edited by Jane Elliott and Derek Attridge, 135–48. London: Routledge.

Espinosa, Julio García. 1997 [1969]. 'For an Imperfect Cinema'. In *New Latin American Cinema*, vol. I, edited by Michael T. Martin, translated by Julianne Burton, 71–82. Detroit, MI: Wayne State University Press.

Fanon, Frantz. 2005 [1961]. *The Wretched of the Earth*. Translated by Richard Philcox. New York: Grove Press.

Gabriel, Teshome. 1982. *Third Cinema in the Third World*. Ann Arbor: University of Michigan Research Press.

——. 1989 [1985]. 'Towards a Critical Theory of Third World Films'. In *Questions of Third Cinema*, edited by Jim Pines and Paul Willemen, 30–52. London: British Film Institute.

Morris, Meaghan, Siu Leung Li, and Stephen Chan Ching-Kiu, eds. 2006. *Hong Kong Connections: Translation Imagination in Action Cinema*. Durham, NC: Duke University Press.

Mulvey, Laura. 1975. 'Visual Pleasure and Narrative Cinema'. *Screen* 16 (3) (Autumn): 6–18.

Naficy, Hamid. 2001. *An Accented Cinema: Exilic and Diasporic Filmmaking*. Princeton, NJ: Princeton University Press.

Paranagua, Paulo Antonio, ed. 1996. *Mexican Cinema*. London: British Film Institute.

Pines, Jim, and Paul Willemen, eds. 1989. *Questions of Third Cinema*. London: British Film Institute.

Rajagopalan, Sudha. 2009. *Indian Films in Soviet Cinemas: The Culture of Movie-Going after Stalin*. Bloomington: Indiana University Press.

Rocha, Glauber. 1997. 'An Esthetic of Hunger'. In *New Latin American Cinema*, vol. I, edited by Michael T. Martin, translated by Randall Johnson and Burnes Hollyman, 59–61. Detroit, MI: Wayne State University Press.

Sarkar, Bhaskar. 2011. 'The Mellifluous Illogics of the "Bollywood Musical".' In *The Sound of Musicals*, edited by Steven Cohan, 41–53. London: British Film Institute.

Shohat, Ella, and Robert Stam. 1994. *Unthinking Eurocentrism*. New York: Routledge.

Solanas, Fernando, and Octavio Getino. 1997 [1969]. 'Towards a Third Cinema: Notes and Experiences for the Development of a Cinema of Liberation in the Third World'. In *New Latin American Cinema*, vol. I, edited by Michael T. Martin, 33–58. Translation from *Cineaste* revised by Julianne Burton and Michael T. Martin. Detroit, MI: Wayne State University Press.

Willemen, Paul. 1989. 'The Third Cinema Question: Notes and Reflections'. In *Questions of Third Cinema*, edited by Jim Pines and Paul Willemen, 1–29. London: British Film Institute.

Wollen, Peter. 1972. 'Godard and Counter-cinema: *Vent d'est*'. *Afterimage* 4 (Autumn): 6–17.

Yau, Esther, ed. 2001. *At Full Speed: Hong Kong Cinema in a Borderless World*. Minneapolis: University of Minnesota Press.

# TIME-IMAGE

*The Time-Image* (1985) is the second of Gilles Deleuze's *Cinema* books, appearing two years after the first, *The Movement-Image* (1983) (*see* MOVEMENT-IMAGE). Where the first book had laid out a taxonomy of image types in the pre-war period, the second deals primarily, though not exclusively, with cinema from the postwar period. In this cinema, which spans European New Wave movements as well as political cinemas from Turkey, North America, and Africa, Deleuze marks a shift from films that are concerned with movement to films that display a greater concern for time.

*The Movement-Image* had mapped out the way in which cinema can constitute its own consciousness: movement on screen, camera movement, and movement via editing, or montage, all reflect a certain way of looking at the world, especially if the camera does not simply follow the figures on screen, but instead seeks to linger on or to move through the spaces and moments 'between' actions. This cinematic consciousness is like human consciousness: it is something that exists in the ever-changing 'whole' or universe and, though never capturing the entirety of life, can through its movements suggest it. In the same way that we cannot see everything, but we can intuit that it is there, so too does movement-image cinema open itself on to the 'whole'. In other words, this 'open' system uses off-screen space to give us an indirect image of what Henri Bergson had termed Duration, or the 'whole'/the universe, and which Deleuze here calls time. This is not necessarily images of clocks and the machines that we use to measure time and to regiment experience, but images of *time* itself, as we experience it as opposed to how we try to calculate it.

If Edward Dimendberg (1988) had accused *The Movement-Image* of neglecting real history for the sake of constructing an ideal cinema of (in Dimendberg's view, almost abstracted) movement, then history does have a far greater role to play in *The Time-Image*. Although there are examples of time-image cinema from before the war, the Second World War marks a particular historical moment in which movement-image cinema – although the prevalent form of cinema then and still, arguably, today – is no longer tolerable for Deleuze. The regimentation of movement and the use of media, including cinema, to create a collective consciousness that could wreak such atrocities as the Holocaust had to be challenged. If, in the 'crisis of the action-image' section that concludes *The Movement-Image*, Deleuze identified that, after Hitchcock, (mainstream) cinema had become a cinema of clichés, in which original thought was not encouraged by showing the world anew but crushed through the repetition of images time and again, then the time-image is an elegy for cinemas that endeavour to break with the clichés of Hollywood and to reinstigate original thought through novelty in cinematic practices.

## Deleuze's philosophy of time and its influences

D.N. Rodowick says that *The Time-Image* can function as a good introduction to the two cinema books as a unit, and to Deleuze's philosophical approach in general (Rodowick 1997, ix–xviii). For, as with *The Movement-Image*, *The Time-Image* is a book of philosophy as much as it is a book of film theory. One of the central preoccupations of the book is not what cinema necessarily *is* (although the book has been described as an ontology of cinema), but what films can *do* in terms of creating concepts that help bring original thoughts into being. As such, the work is not about cinema as an end in itself, although it does seek to expose cinema's ability to induce thought. Rather, *The Time-Image* is as much about how time-images can work towards producing new concepts. Since the book itself seeks to achieve goals similar to those that Deleuze attributes to the time-images that the book describes, *The Time-Image* is perhaps better understood, as per Rodowick above, as a book of philosophy rather than, *sensu strictissimo*, a book of film history or criticism.

Underpinning the book's philosophy, then, is a conception of time that, like *The Movement-Image* before it, is Bergsonian in inspiration. If there is an ever-changing 'whole', which Bergson calls 'duration', then the time-image involves a different relationship with this than the movement-image. If the movement-image uses movement to suggest the whole (hence the notion that a movement-image is an indirect time-image), then the time-image in part begins to look at the intervals between movements, not so much to show that time can be split into increasingly smaller divisions (nanoseconds, for example) but, on the contrary, to show that time is continuous and, to employ a term that is sufficient for the time being but which will need refining later on, indivisible. Rather than seeing separate moments in time – as happens in movement-image cinema – time-image cinema involves seeing time itself. This is not to say that movement disappears from time-image cinema, but it is a cinema that is far less concerned with depicting time that is proper to movement, and more concerned with depicting movement that is proper to time.

Indeed, this reversed relationship between time and movement functions as a good starting point for trying to understand Deleuze's otherwise quite obtuse argument: humans commonly use movement to measure time (the distance that light travels from stars is used to measure their age; 32,768 oscillations of a quartz crystal are used to measure a second), whereas here time does not so much 'measure' movement as emerge as the 'whole' in which movement becomes possible. Time-images show that 'whole', not just the movement within it.

## A crisis of movement and the rise of pure optical and sonic situations

Hopefully a clear link can be established between movement-image cinema and anthropocentrism, in that movement-image cinema is about humans that act within a particular situation in order to change it (the SAS' structure of the large form action-image; see MOVEMENT-IMAGE). In time-image cinema, humans are decentred from the narrative. Combining his sense of history with the philosophical here, Deleuze sees in Roberto Rossellini's neorealist films, for example, a crisis of movement such that the characters are incapable of controlling the situation in which they find themselves and instead enter into purely optical and sonic situations. To continue in Deleuze's terms, there is a break in the sensory-motor schema such that characters in films become pure seers, incapable of action.

This crisis of movement/action is historical because the Second World War, the aftermath of which Rossellini so carefully documented, was precisely a situation in which humans had been overwhelmed; not even the combined will of the people could prevent the atrocities from happening – even though so many of them were perpetrated by humans. In the face of history itself – history here being a process as opposed to an object of study – humans are powerless to change it and begin to see that history is bigger than humans as opposed to being the sum of their work. As such, these films depict moments in which characters can only look on, like Ingrid Bergman before the volcano in *Stromboli* (1950), because the world is bigger than them. Rather than a situation in which action can take place, these are moments 'between' actions, in which there is only sound and image – pure optic and sonic situations as Deleuze terms them.

## Crystals of time and sheets of time

Deleuze continues from his discussion of purely optic and sonic situations by establishing the concept of the crystal-image of time. In order to understand the crystal-image, it might be useful to consider the process of crystallization itself. Crystallization can be understood as a moment in which the potential for a liquid to become a solid takes places, and suddenly a property of that liquid, which previously had been invisible, becomes visible, not least because crystalline. The same, then, applies perhaps to the crystal-image, even if my evocation of 'solidity' in the crystal structure might seem misleading. It might seem misleading because in *The Movement-Image* Deleuze praised the 'gaseous perception' of experimental cinema, as opposed to the 'solidity' of normal perception in cinema, and so, with regard to the time-image, crystallization marks something of a reversal of this gas–good, solid–bad schema. However, this reversal does not necessarily constitute a contradiction. For 'gaseous perception' as it pertains to movement is to decentre movement from cinema, while crystallization as it pertains to time achieves a similar goal in that it does not foreground movement, but in fact it makes visible/'solid' that otherwise invisible 'fluid' in which movement takes place (or, better, which gives form/'solidity' to movement), namely time itself.

In cinematic terms, crystals of time are achieved when the present is seen to coexist with the past. This does not necessarily mean that Deleuze is simply praising flashbacks in cinema, for most flashbacks too clearly signal their status as flashback for Deleuze to consider them. That is, they ground themselves too much in a measured and demarcated time (this is now; that was then). Deleuze instead prefers films that do involve flashbacks, and which we may know and recognize as flashbacks, but which intermingle with the 'present' such that we can no longer be sure which is the 'present' and which the 'past', so that the temporal location of the image is brought into question.

From this, Deleuze constructs his theory of layers, or sheets (*nappes*), of time, which coexist simultaneously with others. That is, Deleuze favours films, like those of Orson Welles, in which different layers or moments of time can be seen not as separate moments in a steady flow of cause and effect, but as coexisting moments that are acting on and reacting to each other. It is not simply the moment before that caused the moment now; the whole of history has an effect on the present, and the present similarly changes the whole of history, such that to prioritize the reality status of one over the other is revealed as simply an anthropocentric conceit. This is how Deleuze understands *Citizen Kane* (1941).

From here, it logically follows that Deleuze then shows an interest in films that fail to differentiate in any clear manner between fantasy and reality and between dream and reality, as well as between past and present. This happens most clearly for Deleuze in the cinema of Buñuel and Fellini. However, perhaps the archetypal time-image film is Alain Resnais's *Last Year in Marienbad* (1961). That film refuses to ground its viewer in any of the conventional space-time coordinates (when is this taking place?; is this taking place at all?), and instead we must rethink, or view anew, our relationship both to space and to time.

## The virtual and the actual and the powers of the false

Given that humans can literally see neither the past nor the future, both to an extent remain *virtual*, while the present that we can recognize is the *actual*. Deleuze sees the time-image, then, as being composed of 'circuits' of the actual and the virtual, with the virtual consisting not just of the past as it 'actually' happened, but the virtual as a state of pure potential, which is pregnant with possibilities but which, to use a Deleuzian term, 'crystallize' in the actual.

Furthermore, *The Time-Image* is also interested in what it terms 'the powers of the false'. Here, again, Welles can serve as a good example: during the famous hall of mirrors sequence from *The Lady of Shanghai* (1947), we see many simultaneous and reflected images of Elsa (Rita Hayworth) and Bannister (Everett Sloane) as they try to shoot each other. Although from the human perspective only one of the images of Elsa and Bannister is the 'real' one, in the scene each image is taken to be equally real and each has an effect on the 'present' moment. As such, the false, like the virtual, can be said to have a strong effect on the real world (and vice versa), such that we cannot truly dismiss it as false. This notion perhaps underpins Deleuze's decision to use cinema (an 'art' that typically is understood as 'fictional') to 'do philosophy' (which is considered to be relevant to/about the 'real' world).

## Back to the body

If *The Movement-Image* has the human body at its centre, and if *The Time-Image* initially seeks to decentre the human body from cinema, then at the last the cinema not only recentres on the body but could be said to have a body of its own – not least because, as discussed in relation to *The Movement-Image*, cinema is deemed by Deleuze to have a consciousness.

Indeed, Deleuze elaborates in the final third of *The Time-Image* an argument concerning the cinema's power to think. With regard to *The Movement-Image*, cinema can show us points of view that pertain only to the camera, such that the cinema has its own 'consciousness' as such. Similarly, a film that involves not the 'rational' cuts of continuity editing, but 'irrational' cuts that link the past, the present, and fantasy and dream (such that the film does not necessarily distinguish between them), also functions akin to a brain that unifies the past, the present, and the imaginary. Read politically, this 'thinking' cinema can articulate the thought of a 'people to come' or a 'minor cinema' (*see* MINOR CINEMA). And philosophically speaking, this cinema of thought gives to the cinema a 'body'. Having a body and a brain in this way, cinema for Deleuze elides the imaginary and the real, such that cinema itself is not so much a representation of the world as a fixed object (which recalls to us Bergson's original 1907 critique of cinema in *Creative Evolution*), but cinema is, like the 'whole' of duration, always changing as the imaginary and the real feed back, or 'fold', into each other. In other words, it is not that cinema represents the world or the universe, but that, for Deleuze, the universe is *cinematic*, since it, too, involves feedback between what actually is and what it might become, or, better, is becoming (the virtual, or the imaginary). As a result, Deleuze ends *The Time-Image* by saying that the ontology of cinema is less important than the work that it does, which translates into the concepts that it creates. Cinema, from this perspective, is a philosophy machine rather than a tool for telling stories – a perspective that lends uniqueness to Deleuze's project, even if this makes it somewhat difficult to follow and/or understand.

## Critiques and uses of the time-image

Jacques Rancière (2006 [2001]) points out that Deleuze can often use the same examples – e.g. from Robert Bresson – to describe both the movement-image, particularly the affection-image, and the time-image. As a result, argues Rancière, it is not so much that the two are truly distinct, but that each is a property, or, in Deleuze's terms, perhaps a *potential*, of the same image. Although neither refers directly to Rancière's critique of Deleuze, this perhaps shares common ground with Patricia Pisters (2003) and David Martin-Jones (2006), who both see, in contemporary science fiction, action, and war films not considered by the Frenchman, images that are a combination of movement- and time-images.

However, while implicitly these scholars argue that there is no hierarchy between the movement-image and the time-image, Deleuze does acknowledge that mainstream cinema has become mediocre and that the violence of the image (i.e. its capacity to induce in us new thoughts) has been replaced by violence in the image. Furthermore, the prevalence of clichés is linked by Deleuze to propaganda and state manipulation, such that the fascist propaganda of Hitler is linked to fascist propaganda in Hollywood.

In other words, while there is evidence to suggest that Deleuze is proposing not simply a clear distinction between, say, classical Hollywood cinema and the modernist cinema of 1950s Europe onwards (not least because Deleuze sees time-images in Vincente Minnelli's Hollywood musicals), it seems as though Deleuze does at times let slip his non-hierarchical taxonomy and imply that, at least in the present day, the movement-image as typified by classical Hollywood cinema is, or perhaps should be, rejected in favour of a more experimental or political cinema.

To take this point further, we might accuse Deleuze of a lack of historical knowledge of the cinema: while it is easy to vaunt the achievements of American cinema in the pre-war period, perhaps Deleuze overlooks (by dint of not having seen) the countless, say, Roy Rogers films that were made in the 1930s and 1940s, even though some B-movie directors find their way into his *Cinema* books, such as Jacques Tourneur and Anthony Mann. In other words, perhaps 'cliché' as Deleuze defines it has long since existed in cinema. Even if Deleuze erroneously sees cliché as only a recent-ish development in the cinema, then, perhaps this would only reinforce the idea that the 'thinking' cinema that Deleuze seems to praise (be it movement- or time-image cinema, or both) is a 'minor' cinema, continually struggling against the mainstream and its supposedly deleterious effects.

Finally, while Deleuze might talk about the effects of cinema and how cinema can inspire thought, he can still be accused of talking about only ideal spectators, as Richard Rushton (2009) has explained. However, Rushton's work does signal a new direction in Deleuzian film scholarship; his work on Deleuzian spectators suggests that we might embrace the 'passive' spectatorship model that Deleuze seems to put forward, and yet which has been so vehemently attacked in other areas of film scholarship, particularly the critiques by cognitivists of psychoanalytic and Marxist film criticism. Films do change us, says Rushton, but we do not so much gaze at them (being conscious *of* films) as become conscious *with* them.

WILLIAM BROWN

## Works cited

Bergson, Henri. 1907. *L'évolution créatrice*. Paris: Presses universitaires de France.

Deleuze, Gilles. 1983. *Cinéma I: L'image-mouvement*. Paris: Les Éditions de Minuit.

——. 1985. *Cinéma II: L'image-temps*. Paris: Les Éditions de Minuit.

Martin-Jones, David. 2006. *Deleuze, Cinema and National Identity: Narrative Time in National Contexts*. Edinburgh: Edinburgh University Press.

Pisters, Patricia. 2003. *The Matrix of Visual Culture: Working with Deleuze in Film Theory*. Stanford, CA: Stanford University Press.

Rancière, Jacques. 2006 [2001]. 'From One Image to Another? Deleuze and the Ages of Cinema'. In *Film Fables*, translated by Emiliano Battista, 107–23. Oxford and New York: Berg.

Rushton, Richard. 2009. 'Deleuzian spectatorship'. *Screen* 50 (1): 45–53.

## Further reading

Bogue, Ronald. 2003. *Deleuze on Cinema*. New York and London: Routledge.

Buchanan, Ian, and Patricia MacCormack, eds. 2008. *Deleuze and the Schizoanalysis of Cinema*. London and New York: Continuum.

Flaxman, Gregory, ed. 2000. *The Brain Is the Screen: Gilles Deleuze and the Philosophy of Cinema*. Minneapolis: University of Minnesota Press.

Powell, Anna. 2006. *Deleuze and Horror Film*. Edinburgh: Edinburgh University Press.

——. 2007. *Deleuze, Altered States, and Film*. Edinburgh: Edinburgh University Press.

Rodowick, D.N., ed. 2010. *Afterimages of Gilles Deleuze's Film Philosophy*. Minneapolis: University of Minnesota Press.

# TRAUMA AND CINEMA

Film theorists in the early twenty-first century, including Thomas Elsaesser, E. Ann Kaplan, and Janet Walker, have used psychological theories of trauma in order to understand the cinema. Studies of trauma and cinema attend to the ways that films represent, or fail to represent, catastrophic events in the past. Such approaches tend to promote documentaries that include experimental aesthetic strategies as the films that best reveal trauma's effects. They also analyse fiction films, particularly melodrama, as vehicles for indirectly dramatizing trauma. Thomas Elsaesser's essay 'Postmodernism as Mourning Work' (2001) discusses how trauma raises new questions about cinema spectatorship and fantasy. Elsaesser also speculates about the widespread interest in trauma as itself a symptom of the ways that modern media have changed our experience of history and memory.

## Trauma

The term 'trauma' derives from the Greek word for 'wound' and it was first used in Western medical discourse to describe a physical injury. Trauma assumed a psychological meaning in the late nineteenth century when it was applied to victims of railway accidents who developed neurological disorders without suffering any injury. The theory of psychological trauma explained the delayed mental effects of disturbing experiences. These experiences are 'forgotten' because the conscious mind cannot make sense of them at the time of their occurrence. Later the memories return in the form of nightmares, phobias, or compulsive behaviours. In the 1890s Sigmund Freud proposed his scandalous 'seduction theory' in which he explained hysteria as caused by premature sexual experiences. He later withdrew from this position, proposing instead that hysteria was the effect of sexual fantasies rather than actual encounters. This change of approach showed that trauma could be understood as the effect of either real or imaginary events.

Confronted by the massive combat trauma suffered in the First World War, Freud (*Beyond the Pleasure Principle* [1990]) elaborated his theory of shock. This explained how consciousness developed a 'protective shield' against the assaults of excessive sensory stimuli. Trauma was the result of an external force that broke through this protective shield. Freud also argued that the traumatic effect was due to the destruction of the individual's sense of self. Again Freud appeared to vacillate between explaining trauma in terms of an external event or an internal psychological process. Freud's theory was adapted by Walter Benjamin (*Writer of Modern Life* [2006]) in his account of modern urban experience. Benjamin argued that the role of mass media such as newspapers, photography, and film was to insulate the individual from the disturbing effects of the metropolitan environment.

This was the first time that trauma was linked to film, although not as a representation of trauma but as a means to block it out. In the post-Second World War period Theodor Adorno proposed that Western culture after Auschwitz suffered a trauma. For Adorno conventional forms of representation were inadequate to show the new realities of techno-logical mass murder. Both Benjamin and Adorno analysed the ways that representations function as a form of psychological defence against external threats to the self.

Adorno's discussion of the Holocaust influenced the later development of trauma studies in the United States. But this more recent research has taken different directions from earlier German theorists. Therapeutic work with soldiers suffering combat trauma who returned from the Vietnam War led to the recognition of post-traumatic stress disorder (PTSD) as a psychological diagnosis. Important research was also carried out with Holocaust survivors. The establishment of Fortunoff Video Archives at Yale University stimulated a new inter-est in Holocaust testimony that was discussed by Shoshana Felman and Dori Laub (*Testimony* [1992]) and Cathy Caruth (*Trauma: Explorations in Memory* [1995]). They argued that hor-rors of war and genocide are the cause of traumatic memories that need to be testified to by survivors and witnessed by others. While these scholars derived their understanding of trauma partly from psychoanalysis, they also drew on conceptions of PTSD which located the origins of psychological distress in specific events. This linking of trauma causally to an event led to a new conception of 'historical trauma' that was oriented away from questions of fantasy and desire that were central concerns of Freudian psychoanalysis. Trauma theory was now concerned with the transmission of catastrophic experiences from survivor to witness.

## 'Postmodernism as Mourning Work'

Elsaesser's essay 'Posmodernism as Mourning Work' appeared in a 'Special Debate' in *Screen* in 2001 entitled 'Trauma and Screen Studies'. For Elsaesser trauma theory raised fundamental questions about the ability of the film image to make reference to the real world. This notion of a 'crisis of referentiality' is strongly linked to arguments about the impossibility of representing the Holocaust. Scepticism about realist representation forms part of a larger cultural shift that is sometimes called postmodernism or postmodernity. Elsaesser understands mourning work in the psychoanalytic sense of 'working through' painful memories and gradually becoming conscious of their larger significance. But if the cinema cannot show reality, then how can it adequately mourn past catastrophes? Post-modernism puts the claims of narrative realism in doubt. Elsaesser proposes that trauma theory explains how history can reappear in indirect forms.

Elsaesser explains how trauma theory promises to move research beyond a number of 'deadlocks' (Elsaesser 2001, 194), such as the orthodox Freudian emphasis on fantasy and the Lacanian focus on desire, which dominated screen theory in the 1970s and 1980s. Trauma theory attends to problems of memory and history that allow us to rethink central problems in film theory. The two concepts that Elsaesser elaborates in more detail are latency and trace. In both cases the psychological meaning has parallels in features of cinematic representation.

## Latency

The concept of latency in psychoanalysis pertains to the delayed effects of certain experi-ences on memory and behaviour. A premature sexual experience may not emerge as a trauma for an individual until adult life. Similarly, historical events such as the Holocaust can have social and cultural effects that are not acknowledged until decades after their occurrence. For this reason one can ask why a film about certain past events arises at a later time. Elsaesser posits an analogy between personal memories and cultural representations that is apparently straightforward at this point in his discussion. He then places this comparison in a broader cultural context. He notes that trauma introduces personal memories, autobiography, testimony, and family history into the public domain of historical narrative. Elsaesser claims that the importance of narrative in integrating forgotten or taboo memories gives the media of film and television a prominent public role. Film, by narrating public events in the contexts of everyday life and emotional melodrama, gives weight to the 'traumatic' perspective on history. But is the repetitive representation of specific events, particularly violent or catastrophic ones, best explained by the subjective experience of traumatic memory or in terms of the mediated experience of history? Elsaesser inclines towards the second possibility. By reconstructing and dramatizing events, film creates a 'prosthetic trauma' (197). The mediated event has an emotional and visceral impact that exceeds rational explanation and conscious understanding. The spectator is traumatized, not so much in a psychological sense as in a culturally mediated one.

Another concept related to latency is Freud's term *Nachträglichkeit* (belatedness), which refers to the relation between the events separated in space and time. A disturbing event can only be explained or made sense of by remembering or positing another absent or forgotten event. The two events can then be joined in a continuous narrative. Through narrative, the individual testimony of trauma can then be publicly witnessed and validated. Film mediates the gaps between private and public memory by producing 'traumatic' narratives and representations so that the spectator 'fantasizes history in the form of trauma' (198). The disruptive nature of the traumatic memory can now be understood in terms of film theory's concern with fantasy. Elsaesser suggests that this mediated history emerges in the spaces left by the declining influence of national, ethnic, or religious narratives of identity.

## The trace

The concept of the trace in trauma theory is derived from conceptions of PTSD that explain traumatic memory as a neurological trace retained in a separate part of the brain from other memories. In Caruth's work this neurological understanding of trauma is combined with methods derived from the deconstruction of literary texts. Deconstruction pursues traces of concepts that emerge in texts and contradict or complicate the author's intended meaning. The combination of these theories allows Caruth to uncover the traumas that may be unconsciously registered in a literary or cinematic text. For Caruth trauma can be indirectly recovered through subtle practices of interpretation.

Elsaesser complicates these conceptions of the trace by discussing the capacity of cinema – further enhanced by digital technologies – to 'fake' or simulate the past. The screen image is thereby dislocated from any authentic or original experience. Elsaesser then proposes the notion of a 'negative performative' (199) as a new kind of historical truth. Trauma becomes the performance of what is authenticated, not according to standards of historical truth but in terms of its immediacy. The uncertainty of cinematic referentiality enhances the 'traumatic' effect. Film makes traumatic memory 'at once "real" and "spectral," "historical" and "virtual"' (200). So for Elsaesser cinema, like trauma, can only recover history through its paradoxical absence.

## Trauma and postmodernism

Elsaesser closes his essay with some speculations on trauma with respect to postmodernity. The claim that postmodernism is characterized by the collapse of grand narratives is echoed in Caruth's formulation of trauma as an 'impossible history' (Elsaesser 2001, 200). Trauma theory both invokes history as authentic experience and undermines conventional narrative realist claims about representation. History is transmitted as testimony or melodrama but is suspended as an ultimately unverifiable experience or unlocatable event. Elsaesser concludes by warning of the dangers of trauma theory as a 'catch-all' (201) that appears to move beyond theoretical impasses. The 'more challenging task' (201) is to pursue the complex demands of interpreting traumatic representations as an indirect recovery of historical truth and referentiality.

## Other positions

In another essay included in the *Screen* debate, E. Ann Kaplan considered melodrama as a film genre in which both private trauma and larger historical changes are acted out. She suggested the possibility of a 'cultural trauma' (Kaplan 2001, 202) based in an overwhelming historical event that has not been socially acknowledged or consciously understood. Such an approach, Kaplan admitted, would demand a somewhat speculative account of films as symptoms of deeper social ruptures and conflicts. Janet Walker's essay from the same dossier looked at the ambiguity that surrounds traumatic memories. She returned to the idea that trauma confounds any hard distinction between fact and fantasy. Walker's understanding of 'trauma cinema' includes films that represent 'world-shattering' (Walker 2001, 214) events in non-realist, non-linear modes. The question remains, however, whether for Walker cinema should be understood as a symptom of a past trauma or as the product of an interpretive frame that makes history 'traumatic'. The answer, in Walker's argument, must be the former. The modes of representation that she identifies with trauma cinema are premised on the unrepresentable nature of traumatic events.

Kaplan's and Walker's essays shared an interest in film's capacity to represent or work through the impact of psychological and cultural trauma. For Kaplan narrative realism can only register trauma indirectly. For Walker trauma is best shown through experimental forms of narrative construction. Their approaches, however, tend to position film either as a symptom of trauma or as employing specific strategies to represent trauma. It remains unclear how film can register the unconscious effects of trauma while at the same time consciously and deliberately investigating those effects. But if film does not manifest trauma as a symptom, then is it 'faking' it? Both Kaplan and Walker appear to understand trauma as an event whose psychological impact demands representation. Elsaesser reverses this assumption by seeing trauma as part of a more general uncertainty surrounding representation.

Addressing these problems in her 2007 essay 'Trauma Theory: Contexts, Politics, Ethics', Susannah Radstone wrote of 'the rise of what is becoming almost a new theoretical orthodoxy' (2007, 10). In the influential formulations of Caruth, trauma is aligned with events whose representation is always indirect and mediated. Radstone argues that this leads us to conceive of all language in terms of a general pathology. This contradicts another claim of trauma theory – derived from neuroscience – that trauma is an extraordinary form of memory (13). The notion of trauma as a dissociated memory explains its origins as an event happening to an autonomous individual subject. If trauma is an event of external origin, then the individual subject is implicitly constituted as an innocent victim, effectively removed from larger ideological formations and socially mediated fantasy. Radstone argues that the stakes of such an understanding became clear after the 'events of September 11'. To the extent that 9/11 was seen as a trauma, it positioned Americans as innocent victims rather than acknowledging America's historical role as a world power. Radstone proposes a return to a psychoanalytic approach that acknowledges that all events are mediated by unconscious desire, anxiety, and ambivalence. Radstone does not, however, explicitly endorse Elsaesser's proposition that trauma also needs to be understood in terms of film's destabilizing of reference. Trauma theory has influenced new ways to interpret films, but it has not resolved ongoing debates about cinematic realism, fantasy, and referentiality.

ALLEN MEEK

## Works cited

Benjamin, Walter. 2006. *The Writer of Modern Life: Essays on Charles Baudelaire*. Translated by Michael W. Jennings, Howard Eiland, and Rodney Livingstone. Cambridge, MA: Belknap Press of Harvard University Press.

Caruth, Cathy, ed. 1995. *Trauma: Explorations in Memory*. Baltimore, MD: Johns Hopkins University Press.

Elsaesser, Thomas. 2001. 'Postmodernism as Mourning Work'. *Screen* 42 (2): 193–201.

Felman, Shoshanna, and Dori Laub. 1992. *Testimony: Crises of Witnessing in Literature, Psychoanalysis, and History*. New York: Routledge.

Freud, Sigmund. 1990. *Beyond the Pleasure Principle*. Translated by James Strachey. London: Norton.

Kaplan, E. Ann. 2001. 'Melodrama, Cinema and Trauma'. *Screen* 42 (2): 201–5.

Radstone, Susannah. 2007. 'Trauma Theory: Contexts, Politics, Ethics'. *Paragraph* 30 (1): 9–29.

Walker, Janet. 2001. 'Trauma Cinema: False Memories and True Experience'. *Screen* 42 (2): 211–16.

## Further reading

Kaplan, E. Ann. 2005. *Trauma Culture: The Politics of Terror and Loss in Media and Literature*. New Brunswick, NJ, and London: Rutgers University Press.

Kaplan, E. Ann, and Ban Wang. 2004. *Trauma and Cinema: Cross-Cultural Explorations*. Hong Kong: Hong Kong University Press.

Meek, Allen. 2010. *Trauma and Media: Theories, Histories and Images*. New York: Routledge.

Walker, Janet. 2005. *Trauma Cinema: Documenting Incest and the Holocaust*. Berkeley, CA: University of California Press.

# VOICE

The publication of Michel Chion's *La voix au cinéma* (1982), later translated as *The Voice in Cinema* (1994), foregrounded a series of concepts clustered around the centrality and dynamics of the 'voice' on the cinema soundtrack. The significance of voice, as a primary feature of the soundtrack, repositions the historical divide between silent and sound film by accenting the centrality of the synchronized voice rather than simply recorded sound. It also specifies a theoretical framework associated with 'vococentrism', the *acousmêtre* (to be discussed below), and the qualities of voice as a Lacanian psychoanalytic object. A wide range of texts have addressed the essential pairing of voice and cinema (see Gorbman 1985), most notably those by Rick Altman (1985, 1986), Mary Ann Doane (1980), and Kaja Silverman (1985, 1988), along with more recent publications that decentre cinema and ally recorded sound with an extended array of technological forms with their own histories that include radio, television, and telephony, and an array of audio recording formats and technologies (see Sterne 2012). Chion's monograph, however, remains central because of its pairing of voice and cinema within a post-structural psychoanalytic framework that has been both contested (in part by Silverman 1988) and further developed (Dolar 2006) in recent years.

Whereas the strict chronological divide between silent and sound film has been dispelled in the recent historical literature (see especially Altman 2004), introducing the voice in 'talking pictures', once specified as integral to a film's narration, still remains pertinent. An emphasis on voice helps us specify qualities integral to classic Hollywood cinema (Bordwell *et al.* 1985), even if it may be asserted that the codification of camerawork, genre, and forms of speech began prior to the advent of talking pictures. In other words, Chion, paraphrasing the French filmmaker Robert Bresson, writes that there was never a mute cinema (as in *cinéma muet*), but a deaf cinema (*cinéma sourd*) that was merely 'voiceless' (Chion 1994, 7). Crucially, the central feature of voice–image relations, Chion explains, is not about 'seeing the person speaking, but *not* seeing the one we hear' (9, emphasis added). This difference between seeing the speaking subject and the quality of presence, visually obscured but aurally present, remains elemental. Vococentrism, as analogous to 'phonocentrism' *pace* Derrida (1997 [1967]), is a means by which Chion introduces the *acousmêtre* (also referred to here as the 'acousmatic') which is the analytic paradigm at the centre of the book. Whereas Derrida had consistently argued against the pre-eminence of the spoken word as rooted in phonemes in favour of the trace and writing as a central feature of deconstruction, Chion's notion of vococentrism features the voice without physical presence. This is the first of a series of significant moves in Chion's text.

The formulation of the *acousmêtre* underscores the various ways in which the speaking subject may not be seen, and it is the lack of visual presence that augments its power to be heard and command others. The manner in which Chion builds this argument relies upon a psychoanalytic understanding of 'lack' or 'absence', which then foregrounds a desire *for* the unseen. In fact, the interplay between the gaze, on the one hand, and voice, on the other, emphasizes the 'drives' as underlying primary psychological forces that help define subjectivity, i.e. the subjectivity and responses of the spectator/auditor of a film. In fact, Silverman (1988) contests Chion's address to the voice as a Lacanian object precisely because he fails to incorporate an understanding of gender and sexuality in his analysis of the concept.

## The 'acousmatic'

Chion's description of the *acousmêtre* begins with a gloss on the term as it first appeared in Pierre Schaeffer's *Traité des objets musicaux* (1966), which was part of an attempt to develop a language for describing sounds in-and-of-themselves. Being that Chion is also a recognized electro-acoustic composer within the *musique concrète* idiom, his intimate familiarity with the work of Schaeffer as one of the founding figures of this style of composition and performance leads us to understand that the object voice is not merely the Lacanian *petit objet a* (Miller 1998 [1973]), but a recorded object primed for manipulation and composition (see also Chion 2009 [1983]). Derived from Greek *akousma*, or visualized listening, Chion describes the 'acousmatic' as sound that is heard without its cause or source being seen. He further explains that it refers to a Greek Pythagorean sect whose followers would listen to their master speak behind a curtain so that the sight of the speaker would not distract them from the message (Chion 1994, 18–19). Once Chion has briefly elaborated upon the religious and historical resonance of its philological heritage in the Western tradition, he returns to uses of the acousmatic. On the one hand, it is an auditory effect associated with placing loudspeakers behind the screen (thus a general effect of the cinematic apparatus) and, on the other, a series of procedures in the plot of a film that enable the veiling and unveiling of an initially unseen, speaking character.

The masking of narrative agents in the classical film is often deployed in telling the story and the establishment of point of view (see Branigan 1984). In order to specify the relationship between the acousmatic and film narration, Chion introduces a process of 'de-acousmatization' by which the unseen speaking subject is finally revealed. In other words, part of the mystery and power of voice associated with the unseen speaking subject is the quality of obscured presence. I would venture to say, for further clarification, that Chion's elaboration of the acousmatic and the process of de-acousmatization bears a striking resemblance to the Panopticon as rooted in eighteenth- and nineteenth-century prison architecture that allowed the prisoner to be seen from a central tower without the benefit of a reciprocal gaze. This lack of reciprocity sets up the theatricalization of power in Michel Foucault's perceptive address to Bentham's Panopticon in *Discipline and Punish* (Foucault 1995 [1975]).

Chion's rendering of the *acousmêtre*, however, accents the representational audiovisual quality of cinema, as opposed to the experience and effects of an architectural environment. In other words, the *acousmêtre* relies upon the veiling and unveiling of a fictional narrative agent in cinema endowed with visual presence and the capacity for recorded speech. By qualifying the relationship between speech and visual presence, the hypnotic quality of the voice emerges as specific to cinema. Chion uses a wide array of examples to demonstrate how this functions in film. *The Testament of Dr. Mabuse* (Fritz Lang, 1933) serves as the most enduring example precisely because Mabuse is named as the unseen figure who appears behind a curtain and gives precise instructions as part of a larger diabolical plan which is only revealed in fragments to his gang of criminal workers.

In order to further specify the *acousmêtre* concept, Chion coins the concept of *anacousmêtre*, which refers to the means by which one subject may serve as a proxy for another's voice. Though Prof. Dr. Baum (Oscar Beregi, Sr.) serves as Dr. Mabuse's psychiatrist, Baum is in fact hypnotized by Mabuse (Rudolf Klein-Rogge) and becomes a vassal for Mabuse's diabolical plans to create chaos. When Baum is obscured from view, his voice and unseen presence is therefore identified as that of Mabuse. Other examples provided by Chion that further extend the concept of the *acousmêtre* include the manner in which the computer HAL in *2001: A Space Odyssey* (Stanley Kubrick, 1968) functions as an 'acousmachine'. Unlike other machines, HAL becomes a machine with a soul that is rendered discarnate. Its death by de-activation summons the legacy of the automate contrived as the object of fetishistic desire embodied by Nathaniel's love letters to Coppelius's automate Clara in E.T.A. Hoffmann's *The Sandman* (1982 [1816]). Hoffmann's short story was also a key text utilized by Freud in crafting the concept of the 'uncanny' (*unheimliche*) (2003 [1919]), which has been influential in theories of film and the other arts (for further discussion see Spadoni 2008; Masschelein 2011).

## Kaja Silverman's critique of Chion

It is precisely when the inanimate becomes sexualized as an animate being that the return to gender becomes significant. It is here that Kaja Silverman's primary critique of Chion's work begins. She writes that 'Chion's sorties into the domain of sexual difference seem motivated primarily by the search for poetic props, and so remain for the most part both uncritical and devoid of self-consciousness'. She further claims that he 'circumscribes discussion of the voice within existing gender demarcations', thus pandering to the 'symptomatic' values of Hollywood cinema (Silverman 1985, 60). Her address to Chion's approach suggests that he fails to critically engage with the objectification of women in classical cinema, in spite of his references to sexual difference and the work of French theorists who have established the category of voice within a psychoanalytic framework. More significant perhaps is that her fleeting discussion of Chion's work foregrounds another significant critical strand, which is the gendered and sexualized nature of the voice in cinema.

Silverman's intervention asserts that it is not merely the primacy of the visual gaze that grounds feminist psychoanalytic approaches to cinema, but the voice is equally significant. She illustrates this point by asserting that the female voice in classical cinema is delegated to an interiorized psychic realm of the film's narration. Furthermore, it demonstrates a form of gendered confinement such that the male voice 'constrains and orchestrates', while the female voice is subsumed by the spectacle of the performing female body (see Silverman 1988). An extensive range of psychoanalytic feminist film scholarship has privileged visual cues in a comprehensive analysis of the coding of classical cinema (see in particular the edited volumes by Doane *et al.* [1984], Rosen [1986], and Penley [1988], alongside the contributions, debates, and themed issues of *Camera Obscura*, *Differences*, *Iris*, *Screen*, and *Wide Angle* from the 1970s to 1990s). However, few feminist theorists of this period, with the exception of Silverman and Doane, have explicitly addressed the role and function of the voice in cinema.

## Mladen Dolar

The return of the voice in more recent scholarship has absorbed and redirected much of this previous work. In particular, Mladen Dolar's *The Voice and Nothing More* (2006) de-emphasizes a direct relationship between voice and image in cinema. Instead, he examines the voice in relation to the way Chion theorizes the *acousmêtre* as the irreconcilable gap between the voice and its source. In order to make this claim, Dolar features an understanding of the voice as 'a non-signifying remainder to signifying operations' (35). In other words, the voice itself has a potentially subversive quality that escapes the stranglehold of words being spoken. Here, Dolar carefully challenges the proposition that there is no voice without a body, and explains the pitfalls of this identification by recasting Chion's conception of the *acousmêtre* against de-acousmatization (which he refers to as 'dis-acousmatization' [70]). He explains that the voice can never be completely pinned down to a source, even when the source is seen, because the voice as a fetish object exceeds its visual representation. Dolar refers to Edvard Munch's famous painting 'The Scream' (1893) as an example of how the iconography of its source renders the scream itself mute and exponentially more powerful. He then counterpoints it to the auditory 'Wilhelm scream', which is a sound mix of vocal effects without individual presence. Dolar explains that Chion's conception of 'de-acousmatization' is impossible because the mystery surrounding the source of the voice can never be resolved. To be clear, this proposition is distinct from asserting that the voice cannot be localized in the body, which is crucial to the work of speech therapists and otolaryngologists. Instead, the voice is part of a foundational narrative and fictional structure beyond recording and reproduction, and it is for this reason that Dolar privileges ventriloquism as an apt descriptive alignment of voice and body (see also Altman 1980). In other words, he shifts the terms of verisimilitude and naturalization from ideological special interests, in spite of their felicitous political intent, to philosophical impossibility.

The difficulty with pinpointing the source of the voice, according to Dolar, is integral to a psychoanalytic approach to the gaze that oversteps the capacity of the eye. In other words, lip-synching is simply a superficial operation of pairing. Instead, he focuses on the significance of the acousmatic under the rubric of the gaze (see Ragland 1995). The voice can never finally be reconciled with the visible, which is why it cannot be neutralized and its mystery is the manner in which the voice reveals an interior space, and remains a 'non-corporeal supplement'. Finally, by claiming that the voice cannot be fully synchronized with its source in the image, we are left with a voice that is a supplement to the body, whose visible source can never be fully disclosed.

PETER J. BLOOM

## Works cited

Altman, Rick. 1980. 'Moving Lips: Cinema as Ventriloquism'. *Yale French Studies* 60: 67–79. (Special Issue: Cinema/Sound.)
——. 1985. 'The Technology of the Voice'. *Iris: A Journal of Theory on Image and Sound* 3 (1): 3–20.
——. 1986. 'The Technology of the Voice Part II'. *Iris: A Journal of Theory on Image and Sound* 4 (1): 107–20.

——. 2004. *Silent Film Sound*. New York: Columbia University Press.

Bordwell, David, Janet Staiger, and Kristin Thompson. 1985. *The Classical Hollywood Cinema: Film Style and Mode of Production to 1960*. New York: Columbia University Press.

Branigan, Edward. 1984. *Point of View in the Cinema: A Theory of Narration and Subjectivity in Classical Film*. Berlin and New York: Mouton.

Chion, Michel. 1982. *La voix au cinéma*. Paris: Cahiers du cinéma/Editions de l'Etoile.

——. 1994. *The Voice in Cinema*. Translated by Claudia Gorbman. New York: Columbia University Press.

——. 2009 [1983]. *Guide to Sound Objects: Pierre Schaeffer and His Musical Research*. Translated by John Dack and Christine North. Leicester: Ears. http://www.ears.dmu.ac.uk/spip.php?page=articleEars&id_article=3597 (accessed 25 December 2012).

Derrida, Jacques. 1997 [1967]. *Of Grammatology*. Translated by Gayatri Chakravorty Spivak. 2nd American edition. Baltimore, MD: Johns Hopkins University Press.

Doane, Mary Ann. 1980. 'The Voice in the Cinema: The Articulation of Body and Space'. *Yale French Studies* 60: 33–50. (Special Issue: Cinema/Sound.)

Doane, Mary Ann, Patricia Mellencamp, and Linda Williams, eds. 1984. *Re-vision: Essays in Feminist Film Criticism*. American Film Institute Monograph Publications. Frederick, MD: University Publications of America.

Dolar, Mladen. 2006. *The Voice and Nothing More*. London: Verso Press.

Foucault, Michel. 1995 [1975]. *Discipline and Punish: The Birth of the Prison*. Translated by Alan Sheridan. 2nd edition. New York: Vintage Books.

Freud, Sigmund. 2003 [1919]. 'The Uncanny'. In *Sigmund Freud: The Uncanny*, translated by David McClintock, 123–59. London: Penguin Books.

Gorbman, Claudia. 1985. 'Annotated Bibliography'. In *Film Sound: Theory and Practice*, edited by Elisabeth Weis and John Belton, 427–45. New York: Columbia University Press.

Hoffmann, E.T.A. 1982 [1816]. 'The Sandman'. In *Tales of Hoffmann*, translated by R.J. Hollingdale, 85–125. New York and London: Penguin Books.

Masschelein, Anneleen. 2011. *The Unconcept: The Freudian Uncanny in Late-Twentieth-Century Theory*. Albany: State University of New York Press.

Miller, Jacques-Alain, ed. 1998 [1973]. 'Of the Gaze as *petit objet a*'. In *The Seminar of Jacques Lacan, Book XI: The Four Fundamental Concepts of Psychoanalysis*, translated by Alan Sheridan, 237–68. New York and London: W.W. Norton & Co.

Penley, Constance, ed. 1988. *Feminism and Film Theory*. New York and London: Routledge, BFI Publishing.

Ragland, Ellie. 1995. 'The Relation between the Voice and the Gaze'. In *Reading Seminar XI: Lacan's Four Fundamental Concepts of Psychoanalysis*, edited by Richard Feldstein, Bruce Fink, and Maire Jaanus, 187–204. Albany: State University of New York Press.

Rosen, Philip, ed. 1986. *Narrative, Apparatus, Ideology: A Film Theory Reader*. New York: Columbia University Press.

Schaeffer, Pierre. 1966. *Traité des objets musicaux, essai interdisciplines*. Paris: Editions du Seuil.

Silverman, Kaja. 1985. 'A Voice to Match: The Female Voice in Classic Cinema'. *Iris: A Journal of Theory on Image and Sound* 3 (1): 57–69.

——. 1988. *The Acoustic Mirror: The Female Voice in Psychoanalysis and Cinema*. Bloomington: Indiana University Press.

Spadoni, Robert. 2008. *Uncanny Bodies: The Coming of Sound Film and Origins of the Horror Genre*. Berkeley: University of California Press.

Sterne, Jonathan, ed. 2012. *The Sound Studies Reader*. Abingdon: Routledge.

# EPILOGUE

## Death in (and of?) theory

*Edward Branigan*

Mrs. Fox (Meryl Streep): 'This story [of our lives] is *too* predictable.'
Mr. Fox (George Clooney): 'Predictable? Really? What happens in the end?'
Mrs. Fox: 'In the end? We all die.'

*Fantastic Mr. Fox* (Wes Anderson, 2009)

The film is not exhibitionist. I watch it, but it doesn't watch me watching it. Nevertheless, it knows that I am watching it. But it doesn't want to know. This fundamental disavowal is what has guided the whole of classical cinema into the paths of 'story,' relentlessly erasing its discursive basis, and making it (at best) a beautiful closed object which must remain unaware of the pleasure it gives us (literally, over its dead body).

Christian Metz (1982, 94)

I must now tell you my thoughts about death (and I leave my skeptical readers free to wonder what this has to do with cinema) ...

It is ... absolutely necessary to die, *because while living we lack meaning*, and the language of our lives (with which we express ourselves and to which we attribute the greatest importance) is untranslatable: a chaos of possibilities, a search for relations among discontinuous meanings. *Death performs a lightning-quick montage on our lives*; that is, it chooses our truly significant moments (no longer changeable by other possible contrary or incoherent moments) and places them in sequence, converting our present, which is infinite, unstable, and uncertain, and thus linguistically indescribable, into a clear, stable, certain, and thus linguistically describable past (precisely in the sphere of a general semiology). *It is thanks to death that our lives become expressive.*

Montage thus accomplishes for the material of film (constituted of fragments, the longest or the shortest, of as many long takes as there are subjectivities) what death accomplishes for life.

Pier Paolo Pasolini (1980, 5–6; original emphasis)

## Life and death

Death and collapse are essential to the work of historians and critics. Crises are found in every moment that is worthy of remark, or rather, it seems, the fact of disquieting change – present always from some point of view – is made dramatic to make remarks worthy.

Among the recently deceased, it has been claimed, are the institutions of cinema, the various enterprises of film theory, and the sensibility for appreciating cinema and theory in the face of ever-new forms of new media (Sontag 1996; Rodowick 2007; Andrew 2009). This Epilogue will survey none of these debates directly, but instead will focus on the manner in which death and loss have been productive metaphors within a range of film theories. The wider, more recent debates will then be approached in an oblique manner.

How has death been figured in the *language and rhetoric* employed by theorists to speculate about the fundamental nature of film? Since mortality is a compelling fact of human life, it is not surprising that some theorists will discover within recorded sound and filmed imagery a profound stasis that recalls the past, and embodies death. Is it possible that the next step will find film theory itself at risk of death, or else left in a prolonged state of senility and sterility?

In what follows I will begin by examining aspects of the theories of André Bazin and Jean-Louis Baudry, which, though quite distinct, nonetheless manage to support a common way of describing the power of movies as being somehow ghostly and dead-alive. A spectator's fascination with the moving shadows of film will be linked to his or her inchoate fear of, even wish for, death. The two theories can be synthesized through a process of successive abstractions of death by assigning metaphorical weight to notions of lightness and darkness, shadows, borderlands, intervals, omissions, and especially absence grown to become the sign of an essential Absence. In this connection I will detail Garrett Stewart's amplification of a series of concepts about everyday experience that are formed into a chain of abstractions leading towards film being seen as the materialization of what is not seen – film becoming itself a sign of fundamental Absence.

Finally, I will examine the idea of absence. I will survey a broad range of types of absences occurring in ordinary life, all of which are implicated in the functioning of film, but which are not associated with death. This analysis will bear on the question of the so-called death of film theory. My suggestion will be that film theory remains vital because it need not seek to determine filmic absolutes and to discover an underlying, final Absence. Instead, by exploring epistemological issues arising in ordinary life, film theory will be oriented towards historicizing interpretive communities. Its task will be to dissect multiple expressions of community values appearing through ever-changing metaphors, concepts, and expressive resources that intercept moving imagery. Film draws its vitality from life and language. Film theory's future is open because it tracks life.

## André Bazin's reincarnation of time

André Bazin begins one of the most famous essays in film theory, 'The Ontology of the Photographic Image', with a conjecture: 'If the plastic arts were put under psychoanalysis, the practice of embalming the dead might turn out to be a fundamental factor in their creation' (1967, 9). Although, strictly, only persons, not objects, can be psychoanalysed, the visual arts may be said to *speak* to human needs, as if in seeing them, we hear them (and they see us; Elkins 1996). Exchanges between object and audience may thus be probed, assuming that an artefact's multiple, implicit, and ambiguous, even contradictory, messages can be correctly heard and interpreted. As we shall discuss below, messages are highly sensitive to context and there are many contexts.

Bazin argues that the visual arts are a type of embalming that derives from a person's 'basic psychological need' to defeat death (Bazin 1967, 9). He traces a lineage beginning with Egyptian mummies ('tanned and petrified in sodium', 9) that extends into the creation of clay statues and other 'magic identity-substitute[s]' (10), then continues onwards through medieval and Renaissance painting and portraiture to the camera obscura and photographic camera, and finally to cinema, which embalms not just an object at an instant but also the object captured within a span of time, as in a long-held shot. Abstracting still further, Bazin asserts that cinema alone among the arts is able to embalm *time itself*, pure duration and movement, as if apart from any object, 'change mummified as it were' (15; *see* LONG TAKE; ONTOLOGY OF THE PHOTOGRAPHIC IMAGE).[1]

Death, too, Bazin defines abstractly: 'for death is but the victory of time' (9). Such a conception of death is a perfect match with Bazin's conclusion that cinema's power lies in embalming/delaying time – 'to snatch … from the flow of time' a person's 'bodily appearance' (9; cf. 14). But, one may ask, aren't there innumerable ways to generalize about the fact of death? Is the importance of death to be understood in isolation from the *meaning* of life (about which there will be many opinions), and is the event of death to be described simply as passively 'passing away', succumbing to – being swept away by, drowning in, failing to be snatched from the 'flow' of – the river of time, as opposed to, say, being victimized by a dramatically appropriate fate (the five *Final Destination* films and Richard Kelly's more artful *Donnie Darko*, 2001, 2004), being victimized by hapless happenstance (Edgar Allan Poe's 'A Predicament'), becoming severely disoriented (Adrian Lyne's *Jacob's Ladder*, 1990), being devoured by daily life and finally left to decay (Peter Greenaway's *A Zed & Two Noughts*, 1986), or being analogized (anodynized?) to a gentle, everyday event like boredom ('bored to death'), sleep ('laid to rest'), or relaxing quietly inside a concealed conceit, as in the allegory of Ang Lee's *Life of Pi* (2012)? To take a more extreme example: both the form and content of Apichatpong Weerasethakul's *Uncle Boonmee Who Can Recall His Past Lives* (2010) present a startlingly different notion of the nature of death than that developed in the Western tradition by Bazin and Baudry, and embedded in Western theories of film.

Furthermore, there are many ways to talk about the nature of time and many perspectives on time other than as a struggle or battle against a 'flow' of some thing or another (Bordwell 1985; Lakoff and Johnson 1999; Doane 2002; Lockwood 2005). The snippet of dialogue from the film *Fantastic Mr. Fox* in the epigraph illustrates one of the ordinary ways we think about time – as a *narrative* progression. Not just our sense of time is being narrativized through a story format, but along with it our personal history, our identity/identities, and who we think we will become (Bruner 2002). This approach to personhood is known as 'narrative identity theory' and includes such writers as Daniel Dennett, Alasdair MacIntyre, Paul Ricoeur, and Oliver Sacks. We tell many stories and try to live or avoid them.

Although narrative is strongly temporal and marked by closure, it does not qualify for Bazin as a proper representation for time and death. In aesthetic matters, Bazin's film theory is generally suspicious of both narrative and editing for their ability to abstract away from reality – away from embalming real objects to be reanimated through film projection – in order to promote symbols and the intangible ideas (no matter how true) of filmmakers and screenwriters (Bazin 1967, 12, 14). Also disfavoured by Bazin for the same reason, one imagines, would be the surrealist-inspired technique known as Exquisite Corpse whereby a narrative or collage structure is constructed by a succession of authors, each continuing the work where it had been suspended by the preceding author. Not far off, perhaps, is a Hollywood script that incorporates the superimposed work of multiple authors fashioning time into plot.

The point here is that the sort of temporal phenomena represented by narrative and montage do not fit Bazin's approach to time and death. Instead his theory tends to favour deep focus shots, actual locales, camera movements, and long-held shots for their ability to embalm time and space – to map the continuity and density of a world passing by and away. It should be noted, however, that Bazin's film theory as a whole is enormously complex and subtle (Andrew 2010, 2011). Hence, for theoretical reasons not discussed in the present essay, Bazin might well have admired the unusual Exquisite Corpse film by Weerasethakul, *Mysterious Object at Noon* (2000), where the succession of stories being told by people in the film reveal their material circumstances and how they came to be, making us hear and see the images in quite new ways as a living testament.

## Photographicity

Finally, one should ask why Bazin has chosen the photographic to be the single type of image that will be made compatible with his notions of time and death in defining what it is to be cinema. Figure 8 lists an array of types of images present in film.

By selecting the photograph as the relevant type of image, Bazin (1967) is able to limit the definition of cinema to certain objective qualities on the screen and in production practice (e.g. to effects produced on screen by 'the impassive [camera] lens', 15). For Bazin the photograph of an object acts as a 'fingerprint' (15) because the chemistry of a film's emulsion responds directly to the physics of reflected light. 'Every image is to be seen as an object and every object as an image' (15–16; cf. 13). As a result cinema has the unique and special ability – if it is to be true to its nature! – to embalm a segment of the flow of time for all time. Bazin declares that cinema, when thus electing to mould impressions taken from life, becomes itself a 'death mask' (12).

One may ask, of course, whether cinema must be true to its nature, rather than, for example, seeking to stretch or transcend its natural or present boundaries in order to explore or develop new qualities. One may also question whether photography must be foundational for the other (below listed) sorts of images seen in – i.e. seen because of – film.

PHOTOGRAPH
FILM FRAME (but note that we do
  not see an individual frame,
  i.e. a film is not a slide show)
VISIBLE IMAGE (framed
  by or on the screen, composed of many film frames)
SHOT (many visible images)
OPTICAL OR SPECIAL EFFECT
PICTURE (which is more general than
  a photograph; it stresses the design
  and qualities of a space; it may
  be painted, drawn, computer-
  generated, etc.)
IMAGINED/FICTIVE IMAGE
  (in a plot on the screen or in mind)
VISUAL IMAGE (in mind from a film)
MEMORY IMAGE (from a film once seen)

AFFECTIVE IMAGE
CULTURAL IMAGE (e.g. an
  image of femininity; an
  image formed by one's
  personality, i.e. a mask;
  an image created by
  advertising; or, a
  familiar emblem)
'OBRAZ'/IMAGE (Sergei
  Eisenstein)
AN IMITATION/SEMBLANCE OF
AN INCARNATION OF
AN IDEA OR CONCEPT OF (e.g.
  one's image of a scene,
  a film's theme, or character;
  or, a mental construction
  of a scene's overall space)
A VIVID FIGURE OF SPEECH (a
  visible rhetorical device)

*Figure 8* Some types of images in film.

What kinds of causal relationships (running in which direction?) may obtain among the many types of images in film? Are some causal relations distant or else of no theoretical importance? Are some significant relationships not causal at all (e.g. supervenient or associational)? Finally, and most importantly, what tasks does one wish to accomplish with a film theory based on photographicity, that is, what does one wish cinema *to do*?

## The structure of Bazin's theory

To summarize, Bazin constructs one of the pillars of his theory, an ontology, by making strategic choices among three sets of possibilities for conceptions of imagery, death, and time. He then devises a set of aesthetic principles for cinema consistent with the three choices. The process is illustrated in Figure 9.

*Figure 9* Bazin's initial choices in constructing an ontology.

## Jean-Louis Baudry's 'letter of condolence'

Jean-Louis Baudry interrogates Bazin's photographicity by asking *whose interests* are being served by presenting photography and other sorts of imagery in film. In a famous essay, 'Ideological Effects of the Basic Cinematographic Apparatus', Baudry details elements of cinema's 'ideological machine' that strive to make effective a false, 'reworked "objective reality"' (Baudry 1986, 293) portrayed in film:

> No doubt the darkened room [of a movie theatre] and the screen bordered with black like a letter of condolence already present privileged conditions of [ideological] effectiveness – no exchange, no circulation, no communication with any outside. Projection [of the film] and reflection [from the screen] take place in a closed space, and those who remain there, whether they know it or not (but they do not), find themselves chained, captured, or captivated ... The paradoxical nature of the cinematic mirror-screen is without doubt that it reflects *images* but not *'reality'*.
>
> (Baudry 1986, 293–4; emphases added by translator)

Who has died and become the recipient/subject of a 'letter of condolence', or, in Bazin's terms, who is being mummified in order to be revived in new form? For Baudry, it is the spectator who has died! His or her subjectivity has been appropriated and remodelled by an apparatus. Cinema – narrowly construed as the film appearing on the screen – is dispatching a letter of condolence to its viewers. The spectator's death has resulted from 'ideological effects' produced by the 'cinematographic apparatus' as an entirety. The apparatus's many elements embrace objective reality, scenario, camera, production technology, montage, exhibition, and spectatorship. Importantly, the apparatus incorporates the spectator as he or she is taking in – introjecting – the material offered by the film as well as giving back – projecting onto the film – a series of his or her non-conscious (pre-, sub-, un-conscious) psychic states, urges, fears, and ambivalences (cf. 291, 295). One of these projected fantasies is of his or her death.

The criss-crossing dynamics and triggered ambivalences of Freudian theory invoked by Baudry can be felt in the following student's reaction to the above-quoted passage:

> The projection and the subject are elements of cinema that help the audience reflect on what they have done or will do in their life, and just like a 'letter of condolence', you are happy to receive it.

Although the words of Christian Metz in the epigraph on page 494 derive from a more theoretically rigorous study than the student's reaction, a similarly complicated, tense weave of forces is revealed to be at play when watching a film: 'fundamental disavowal' results in 'pleasure' premised on a 'dead body'.

For Baudry the darkened theatre, along with the spectator's isolation, amount to a forced regression towards a 'hallucinatory reality' (1986, 289), an infantile state prior to Lacan's mirror stage, occurring at an age of between six and eighteen months. This regression strives to lessen present tensions and recapture a time when one's imaginary unity of self/identity was not yet fully formed. The spectator's movement towards being absorbed in a film is in the direction of a gradual dissipation of energy towards sleep, and towards a return to an inorganic state (as in Freud's 'death instinct').

In addition, Baudry imagines (292) that film's aesthetic techniques heighten a spectator's feeling that his or her body is being dispersed, cut into pieces, dissolving identity and its anxieties:

> And if the [spectator's] eye which moves [inside film] is no longer fettered by a body, by the laws of matter and time, if there are no more assignable limits to its displacement – conditions fulfilled by the possibilities of shooting and of film – the world will be constituted not only by this eye but for it … There is a phantasmatization of objective reality (images, sounds, colors).

Such a disembodied eye is perhaps dramatized quite literally as the view of Oscar, a dead man, gliding through and above the scenes of Gaspar Noé's film *Enter the Void* (2009).

Baudry concludes that the cinematic apparatus works to refashion a spectator's body by acting 'to substitute secondary organs, grafted on to replace [the person's] own defective ones' (295). The new organs supplant, not just supplement, our 'defective ones'. At the cinema, we accede to a loss of control – we are taken over and become other in a state of being dead-alive. This is also the state of the apparatus itself, which, with its many parts and techniques, functions like a succession of authors creating the mechanistic structure of Exquisite Corpse (see APPARATUS THEORY [BAUDRY]; APPARATUS THEORY [PLATO]; FANTASY AND SPECTATORSHIP; SCEPTICISM).

## Garrett Stewart's synthesis of Bazin and Baudry

If Bazin celebrates the on-screen presence of an embalmed past returned to life, then Baudry's belief in a 'screen bordered with black like a letter of condolence' may be said to highlight the presence of a profound void in which a black border frames a luminous, seductive image while concealing in darkness an absent cinematic 'apparatus' whose acts of selective presentation and suppression make possible the psychic journeys of a spectator towards the void, which adjoins birth and death. The two rhetorical positions of Bazin and Baudry may be gracefully intertwined in a language drawn from our everyday notions of death. Garrett Stewart speaks of the 'absentation' (Stewart 1999, xi) of photography, editing, and cinema as follows, where I have italicized words connoting absence and death:

> Photography is *death* in replica; cinema is a *dying away* in progress, hence *death* in serial abeyance. Lined up in rows, pieced out, flicked past, then thrown forward toward the lit screen, the elementing photographs on the film track vibrate before us as the *death* throes of *presence succumbing* to a temporality *not* its own, world time transposed to screen time. This is to say that cinema exists in the interval between two *absences*, the one whose *loss* is marked by any and all photographic images [cf. Bazin] and the one brought on by *tossing away* [i.e. being discarded through montage; cf. Pasolini epigraph] each image in instantaneous turn. The effects are different enough to make for two separate media, two distinct powers of *mortal* mediation. Whereas photography en*graves* the *death* it resembles, cinema *defers* the *death* whose escape it simulates. The isolated photo or photogram is the *still* work of *death*; cinema is *death* always *still* at work.
>
> (Stewart 1999, xi; and see pp. 323–8)

Note that many metaphors other than the above 'tossing away' might have been chosen to describe the (deeper … deepest) action of film editing and juxtaposition, resulting in quite different conceptions of the nature of editing. From a proffered description will follow a set of assertions, a frame for thinking about a thing and fixing the description. Theoretical descriptions and metaphors (e.g. 'tossing away') are never just ornamental and are never neutral. Nor is there anything magical or sacred about a description or concept – whether it is stated literally or metaphorically. As Wittgenstein (2009, § 570) maintains: 'Concepts lead us to make investigations. They are the expression of our interest and direct our interest.'

The basic question is: how does one select a fact and description and then make conceptual use of it? Which interests, values, and assumptions are being (presently) served? In this way, a film theory itself is slowly built into a kind of 'apparatus'.

## From light to dark: the tie that binds

How should we read claims that link cinema with death?[2] Roland Barthes (1974, 92) contends that 'to read is to struggle to name, to subject the sentences of the text to a semantic transformation', and that 'reading is absorbed in a kind of metonymic skid, each synonym adding to its neighbor some new trait, some new departure'. Figure 10 traces one possible logic of a metonymic trajectory using familiar cultural imagery that carries us step by step from a daily experience of sun*light*, and from Garrett Stewart's 'lit screen', into the notion of film as moving shadows appearing out of darkness and void to become a foreshadowing of the shadow of death.

## Which kind of absence?

How should we understand the word 'absence'? Which kind(s) of absence should be chosen as important when constructing a film theory? Is absence inevitably tied to death … then

> sunlight → light source for photography → intrinsic lightness and
> contrasts of lightness within a perceptible colour pattern → contrasts of white
> (light) and black (absence of light) → white on black → black on white →
> dark surround → [Baudry's 'screen bordered with black like a letter of
> condolence'] → the emergence of shapes as defined by contrasting
> shadows → shading/shade (shade-ow) → ghost (= a shade) → spirit-work →
> [Bazin's notion of the reincarnation of time by preserving/embalming the
> spirit of its flow] → film as flowing shadows: spectral, irreal, ethereal →
> film's seeming to move based on intervals between film frames (24 still
> frames per second) → an interval as something in which some thing is
> missing → an interval's essential emptiness and absence → a movement is
> never fully present on screen because broken by unseen intervals between
> frames and shots → parts of a movement are *always* missing → hence
> appearances on screen are never fully present → film is an illusory presence
> → film's true being rests on not being (rests on what's missing, never seen
> [Baudry's apparatus]) → non-being as the result of death-work, death at
> work → film as a grand image of the work of death (a trace of intervals, gaps,
> and what is missing) → film on screen as an absence among absences
> [Stewart] → film as Absence incarnate

*Figure 10* One projection path from cinema's lightness to its darkness and absence.

death to film, and to film theory? Consider the absence of 'having once lived though now dead' – the focus of metaphors in several prominent film theories, including those discussed above – with a few other typical sorts of lack found in films:

- 'I *lost* my [book, way, voice, bet, temper, opportunity, place in line].'
- 'I lost *patience* with the main character.'
- 'I lost *track* of the film's plot.'
- 'While lost in *thought* watching the film I must have been playing with my cell phone *absent*mindedly when it fell.'
- 'I lost *time* while watching the film instead of writing the essay.'
- Relationships among things are always abstract to a degree, neither entirely physical nor entirely mental, i.e. relationships are often evident, though *not-quite-present*. For example, we may see two objects, but do we also see in the same physical way that one of them is 'to the left of' the other? Doesn't this relationship exist invisibly *between* the two objects? And yet, we can't simply move the objects to new positions by thinking about them. All relationships are to various degrees partly conceptual. Since film utilizes and portrays many sorts of relationships, many things in film are not-quite-present.
- What happens when we think about a negative relationship, e.g. '*x* does *not* resemble *y*'? That is, do we first imagine various scenarios of how *x* might resemble *y*, and then *cancel* all of these possibilities, making them absent and validating the negative; or do we somehow just cancel the word 'resemble', as if *not* heard? In watching film we make and unmake many comparisons moment by moment.
- Theoretical concepts about relationships that we think are significant in film, or about our own relationships to film, would seem to have numerous degrees of abstractness (i.e. degrees of being schematic or diagrammatic) by referring to entities that are *unobservable*. What sort of 'fact' is a conceptual abstraction or metaphor? (See my 'Introduction (II)' from pages xxi–xl.)

- What are *sensations*? For example, does a sense of depth exist *on* a two-dimensional film screen or partly in mind? Recall that the image on one's retina is curved, inverted, reversed left-to-right, and also two-dimensional. How and where do we see the third dimension? Further, does this imply that sensations about colour and shape are relatively 'more present', less absent in film than depth and movement? (Recall that only static images exist on celluloid and that a projector's speed is constant while movements on the screen appear at many different speeds.) Actually, colour and sound pose novel and distinct problems with respect to degrees of absence.
- What are *feelings*? 'I have *lost* my mind because my *fear* is that tomorrow it *might* rain.' Where is 'fear' and where is its cause, the 'possibility' of rain? Films often seek to evoke emotions about distant possibilities that somehow are made to seem near. Further, is there a feeling associated with *denying* or misrecognizing a feeling? (Baudry's theory begins to address such issues.)
- What are *meanings*? Where are they? Are they *in* a film or in our head? Or perhaps real meaning is to be found in some special ghostly sense, neither here nor there: in the 'spirit' of a word, sentence, or image? Or in a filmmaker's spirit?
- To what degree may a fictional *Sherlock Holmes* be simultaneously present and absent? Do we combine certain real qualities of persons and attach them to an indefinite sort of person and then *cancel* the real sources for the qualities, leaving a fictionally real persona? (Cf. the levels within Ingmar Bergman's *Persona* [1966].)
- Is a *round square* profoundly absent because its existence is impossible, even fictionally? Do some films refer to things impossible?

## The future of film theory

Which kinds of absence are most important to film and suitable for explication by a theory of film? The preceding illustrates our insistence on recalling variants of what is absent and no longer, or not yet, present. We demand explanations that position us (favourably) in everyday entities, states, and processes not firmly present, though commanding our interest. When the focus falls on the place of film in our lives, a theorist will seek to explain those features involving typical absences in order to build a comprehensive theory by strategic selections, emphasis, and elision. A theoretical argument is designed to carefully calibrate its framing of film by using concepts to address present anxieties, disavowals, and values, which include what has been lost, tarnished, replaced, unseen, or hoped for. The problem is how to weave together the types of absences and the priority to be assigned to each.

I believe that our keenest intuitions about cinema, including those expressed in the abstractions and arguments of a formal theory, derive from an everyday world of the living and the rhetoric that expresses our lives. Film theory should be imagined as an ongoing struggle with ordinary forms of absence when we feel that something important has been lost or not yet obtained. Since film is tangled and implicated in many kinds of absence, it would seem a natural impulse to simplify by asking a highly restrictive, ontological question: what is film itself by itself when not in a place? What is its degree of presence outside of context, absent any context, apart from links to persons or things? A theorist may thus be tempted to inquire what film must be when it is not or when it aims to represent what is not – just as Alice in *Alice's Adventures in Wonderland* (chap. 1) 'tried to fancy what the flame of a candle looks like after the candle is blown out'.

## Notes

1 Seemingly, Gilles Deleuze takes Bazin's mummifying of time one step further. He imagines time at certain moments in a film as no longer invisibly passing, but itself become dead or absent or maybe strangely present – but unable to move, frozen in place as a crystalline substantive (*see* TIME-IMAGE). An interesting linguistic example of this approach might be our use of the expression 'for the "time being"'. But, by making time static and noun-like, have we thereby moved any closer to the essence or true being of time? Or have we been misled by our choice of a grammar and so led into an overgeneralization? Deleuze speaks about 'blocks of movements/duration', but what is thereby hidden within the ontological preposition *of* (Branigan 2009; cf. Lakoff and Johnson 1999)? See my 'Introduction (II)', pages xxi–xl.

2 What is the meaning of the activity 'to read'? One prominent set of theories of reading is rooted in semiotics, which has been applied in a variety of ways to film, notably by Christian Metz. This scheme posits that we live within semiosis – an endless frenzy of mental sign production and consumption – and that we expire in a state of signless-ness. The semiotic enterprise as a whole is bracketed by the inorganic: the material of the signifier eventually returns to material by making a circuit through codes to a referent in the world. In this system, there is no outside of language that is not inert. The mirror held to nature shows only us and our chatter, until silenced.

## Works cited

Andrew, Dudley. 2009. 'The Core and the Flow of Film Studies'. *Critical Inquiry* 35 (4): 879–915. [What should the discipline of film studies strive to be in the context of change?]

——. 2010. *What Cinema Is! Bazin's* Quest *and Its Charge*. Oxford: Wiley-Blackwell.

——. ed. 2011. *Opening Bazin: Postwar Film Theory and Its Afterlife*. Oxford: Oxford University Press. [The index lists 34 different pages on the topic of Bazin and 'death'.]

Barthes, Roland. 1974. *S/Z*. Translated by Richard Miller. New York: Hill and Wang.

Baudry, Jean-Louis. 1986. 'Ideological Effects of the Basic Cinematographic Apparatus'. In *Narrative, Apparatus, Ideology: A Film Theory Reader*, edited by Philip Rosen, 286–98. New York: Columbia University Press.

Bazin, André. 1967. 'The Ontology of the Photographic Image'. In *What Is Cinema?* [vol. I], translated by Hugh Gray, 9–16. Berkeley: University of California Press. [The present essay quotes from this translation. A more precise translation is by Timothy Barnard, in André Bazin, *What Is Cinema?*, 3–12. Montreal: Caboose, 2009.]

Bordwell, David. 1985. 'Narration and Time'. In *Narration in the Fiction Film*, 74–98. Madison: University of Wisconsin Press.

Branigan, Edward. 2009. 'Of Prepositions: Lost and Found'. *The Velvet Light Trap* 64: 95–8.

Bruner, Jerome. 2002. *Making Stories: Law, Literature, Life*. New York: Farrar, Straus and Giroux.

Doane, Mary Ann. 2002. *The Emergence of Cinematic Time: Modernity, Contingency, the Archive*. Cambridge, MA: Harvard University Press.

Elkins, James. 1996. *The Object Stares Back: On the Nature of Seeing*. New York: Simon & Schuster, Inc.

Lakoff, George, and Mark Johnson. 1999. 'Time'. In *Philosophy in the Flesh: The Embodied Mind and Its Challenge to Western Thought*, 137–69. New York: Basic Books.

Lockwood, Michael. 2005. 'The Time of Our Lives'. In *The Labyrinth of Time: Introducing the Universe*, 365–82. Oxford: Oxford University Press.

Metz, Christian. 1982. 'Story/Discourse (A Note on Two Kinds of Voyeurism)'. In *The Imaginary Signifier: Psychoanalysis and the Cinema*, translated by Celia Britton, Annwyl Williams, Ben Brewster, and Alfred Guzzetti, 91–8. Bloomington: Indiana University Press. [See also in this book 'The Imaginary Signifier', e.g. 'Every film shows us the cinema, and is also its death' (35).]

Pasolini, Pier Paolo. 1980. 'Observations on the Long Take'. *October* 13: 3–6.

Rodowick, D.N. 2007. 'An Elegy for Theory'. *October* 122: 91–109.

Sontag, Susan. 1996. 'The Decay of Cinema'. *New York Times*, 25 February.

Stewart, Garrett. 1999. *Between Film and Screen: Modernism's Photo Synthesis*. Chicago, IL: University of Chicago Press. [Stewart continues his exploration in *Framed Time: Toward a Postfilmic Cinema*. Chicago, IL: University of Chicago Press, 2007.]

Wittgenstein, Ludwig. 2009. *Philosophical Investigations*. Translated by G.E.M. Anscombe, P.M.S. Hacker, and Joachim Schulte. Revised 4th edition. Oxford: Wiley-Blackwell.

## Further reading

Bazin, André. 1971. 'In Defense of Rossellini'. In *What Is Cinema?*, vol. II, translated by Hugh Gray, 93–101. Berkeley: University of California Press. ['There is ontological identity between the object and its photographic image' (98).]

——. 2002. 'Death Every Afternoon'. In *Rites of Realism: Essays on Corporal Cinema*, edited by Ivone Margulies, 27–31. Durham, NC: Duke University Press. [Cinema is 'the only one of our possessions that is temporally inalienable: dead without a requiem, the eternal dead-again of the cinema!' (31).]

*Lapham's Quarterly* 6(4). 2013. Special issue on "Death".

Mulvey, Laura. 2006. *Death 24x a Second: Stillness and the Moving Image*. London: Reaktion Books.

Oeler, Karla. 2009. *A Grammar of Murder: Violent Scenes and Film Form*. Chicago, IL: University of Chicago Press.

Smith, Douglas. 2004. '"A World That Accords with Our Desires?": Realism, Desire and Death in André Bazin's Film Criticism'. *Studies in French Cinema* 4 (2): 93–102.

Stewart, Garrett. 1987. 'Photo-gravure: Death, Photography, and Film Narrative'. *Wide Angle* 9 (1): 11–31. [This important essay evaluates several theoretical accounts of photography, film, and death.]

# INDEX

Note that page numbers relating to Notes will have the letter 'n' following the page number. References to Figures will be in *italic* typeface. Names of works or films will mostly be indexed under the appropriate author or director.